Wolfgang Klein
Looking at Language

Trends in Linguistics
Studies and Monographs

Editor
Volker Gast

Editorial Board
Walter Bisang
Hans Henrich Hock
Natalia Levshina
Heiko Narrog
Matthias Schlesewsky
Amir Zeldes
Niina Ning Zhang

Editor responsible for this volume
Volker Gast

Volume 317

Wolfgang Klein
Looking at Language

DE GRUYTER
MOUTON

ISBN 978-3-11-068634-0
e-ISBN (PDF) 978-3-11-054911-9
e-ISBN (EPUB) 978-3-11-054730-6
ISSN 1861-4302

Library of Congress Control Number: 2018934490

Bibliographic information published by the Deutsche Nationalbibliothek
The Deutsche Nationalbibliothek lists this publication in the Deutsche Nationalbibliografie;
detailed bibliographic data are available on the Internet at http://dnb.dnb.de.

© 2019 Walter de Gruyter GmbH, Berlin/Boston
This volume is text- and page-identical with the hardback published in 2018.
Typesetting: Integra Software Services Pvt. Ltd.
Printing and binding: CPI books GmbH, Leck
♾ Printed on acid-free paper
Printed in Germany

www.degruyter.com

For Christoph, Georg, Eva, Antonia, Jonathan, Mira

Contents

Bibliography —— XVI

Introduction —— 1

Concepts of time —— 4
1 Introduction —— 4
2 The variety of time —— 6
3 Three recurrent themes —— 17
3.1 Time and change —— 17
3.2 Time and its units —— 20
3.3 Time and the observer —— 21
4 The time concept of human languages —— 23
4.1 The "basic time structure" —— 24
4.1.1 The ingredients —— 24
4.1.2 A more precise definition —— 26
4.2 Temporal relations —— 28
4.3 Temporal relata —— 29
4.3.1 Deictic relatum —— 29
4.3.2 Anaphoric relatum —— 31
5 Concluding remarks —— 32
 References —— 32

A time-relational analysis of Russian aspect —— 34
1 Introduction —— 34
2 Convential wisdom —— 35
2.1 The morphological facts —— 35
2.2 The semantic characterisation of PERF and IMPERF —— 38
3 Lexical content —— 48
3.1 Properties of situations vs properties of the lexical content —— 48
3.2 0-state, 1-state, 2-state contents —— 50
3.3 Simple verbs, prefix verbs, and secondary imperfectivisation in Russian —— 54
4 A time-relational analysis of aspect —— 56
4.1 Time of utterance, time of situation, time of assertion —— 56
4.2 The meaning of Russian perfective and imperfective aspect —— 60
4.3 PERF, IMPERF, and verb forms —— 61
5 Concluding remarks —— 63
 References —— 66

An analysis of the German Perfekt —— 68
1 The problem —— 68
2 Previous research —— 71
2.1 Formal composition —— 72
2.2 The meaning of the Perfekt I: the tradition —— 73
2.3 The meaning of the Perfekt II: recent analyses —— 74
3 Theoretical background —— 76
3.1 Tense and aspect as temporal relations —— 76
3.2 Temporal properties of the lexical content —— 78
3.2.1 Properties of situations vs properties of the lexical content —— 78
3.2.2 FIN-linkable vs non-FIN-linkable expressions —— 79
3.2.3 The lexical content of verb stems I: problems —— 79
3.2.4 The lexical content of verb stems II: argument-time structure —— 81
4 The meaning of the German Perfekt I: FIN and the sentence base —— 82
5 Some consequences —— 85
5.1 German Perfekt vs English present perfect —— 85
5.2 Perfekt vs Präteritum —— 86
5.3 Posttime infinitives —— 87
5.4 The role of adverbials —— 87
6 The meaning of German Perfekt II: The contribution of participle marking and auxiliary —— 89
6.1 The contribution of the verb stem —— 89
6.2 The meaning contribution of GE- —— 91
6.3 The meaning contribution of the auxiliary —— 95
6.3.1 Copula constructions —— 96
6.3.2 The auxiliary *hab-* —— 98
6.4 The two readings of the Perfekt revisited —— 99
7 Conclusion —— 100
References —— 101

Aspect and assertion in mandarin Chinese —— 103
1 Introduction —— 103
1.1 The perfective aspect markers —— 103
1.2 The imperfective aspect markers —— 105
2 Problems with aspect and aspectual particles —— 108
2.1 Four problems with the classical notion of aspect —— 108
2.1.1 Problem A: the definition is entirely metaphorical —— 109
2.1.2 Problem B: perfectivity does not reflect the 'boundaries' or the 'boundedness' of the situation —— 109
2.1.3 Problem C: boundedness and the redundancy of *le* —— 111

2.1.4	Problem D: 'realization of the situation' and *le* —— 212
2.2	Two formal accounts —— 114
2.2.1	Smith's 'two parameters theory of aspect' —— 114
2.2.2	A compositional analysis of aspectual particles —— 118
3	A time-relational definition of tense and aspect —— 120
3.1	'Time of utterance', 'time of situation' and 'topic time' —— 120
3.2	Tense, aspect, and temporal relations between TT, TU, and T-SIT —— 122
4	Time of situation and inherent temporal features of the lexical content —— 123
4.1	Two sources of confusion —— 123
4.2	Types of lexical contents —— 125
4.3	Two-phase expressions in Chinese —— 127
5	Aspectual systems and the English aspect —— 129
5.1	Two dimensions of variation —— 129
5.2	The case of English —— 129
5.3	Time-relational aspect versus aspect as a particular way of presenting a situation —— 130
6	The Chinese aspectual system —— 131
6.1	Aspect and what is asserted —— 131
6.2	The four particles —— 132
6.3	*le* —— 133
6.4	*guo* —— 137
6.5	*zai* and *zhe* —— 140
6.6	Zero marking —— 143
7	Conclusion —— 145
	References —— 146

On times and arguments —— 148

1	Introduction —— 148
2	Event time and clause-internal temporal structure —— 149
3	AT-Structure and descriptive properties —— 154
3.1	The basic distinction —— 154
3.2	Some examples from English —— 158
3.3	Event time redefined —— 162
4	Morphosyntactic operations on the argument-time structure —— 163
5	Three morphological operations in English —— 165
5.1	V_s-Ø: the "bare infinitive" —— 166
5.2	V_s-ing: the "present participle" —— 166
5.3	V_s-ed: the "past participle" —— 167

6	Three elementary syntactic operations in English —— 168
6.1	Be V_s-ing: the (non-finite) progressive —— 168
6.2	Be V_s-ed: the (non-finite) passive —— 169
6.3	Have V_s-ed: The (non-finite) perfect —— 170
6.4	Have been V_s-ing: the perfect progressive —— 171
7	Finite constructions —— 172
7.1	FIN-marking on the verb —— 172
7.2	Grammatical subject —— 174
8	Perfect, progressive, passive reanalyzed —— 176
9	Conclusion —— 179
	References —— 180

On the "Imperfective paradox" and related problems —— 183

1	Introduction —— 183
2	Aristotle's entailment —— 187
3	The Subinterval entailment —— 188
4	The Imperfective paradox entailment —— 189
5	Inherent temporal features of the lexical content —— 190
	References —— 193

Local deixis in route directions —— 194

1	Components in the use of local deictics —— 194
1.1	Setting up deictic spaces —— 195
1.2	Fixing the basic reference point —— 196
1.3	Co-ordination —— 198
1.4	Delimitation —— 199
1.5	Deictic oppositions —— 199
1.6	Analogical deixis —— 201
2	Using local deictics in route directionss —— 202
2.1	Route communications —— 202
2.2	Planning the description —— 203
2.3	Local deixis —— 208
	References —— 211
	Appendix: Selected Transcriptions —— 212

Some notorious pitfalls in the analysis of spatial expressions —— 216

1	Introduction —— 216
2	The range of problems —— 218
2.1	Structure of space —— 219
2.2	Semantic content —— 221

2.3	Context-dependency —— 221
3	The simple case trap —— 223
3.1	The time parameter argument —— 223
3.2	The change-of-place argument —— 224
3.3	The non-object argument —— 226
4	The "property of place"-analysis of spatial reference —— 227
	References —— 229

Time and again —— 230

1	An ambiguity —— 230
2	Three problems —— 232
2.1	Scope effects beyond the lexical verb —— 232
2.1.1	Indefinite direct object —— 232
2.1.2	Indefinite subject —— 233
2.1.3	Adverbials —— 234
2.1.4	Summing up —— 235
2.2	Similar effects with atelic verbs —— 236
2.2.1	Counterdirectional verbs —— 236
2.2.2	A complication —— 237
2.2.3	Summing up —— 239
3	Order of mention and order of events —— 240
3.1	Atemporal situations —— 240
3.2	Other text types —— 241
4	The meaning contribution of *wieder* —— 243
5	Repetitive and restitutive readings reconsidered —— 244
5.1	Inherent temporal structure, descriptive properties and BECOME —— 244
5.2	Access to one or to two time variables —— 247
6	Concluding remarks —— 249
	References —— 251

On the scope of negation —— 253

1	Introduction —— 253
2	Three problems —— 256
2.1	Topic consistency —— 256
2.2	Difference and mutual exclusion —— 259
2.3	Scope sensitivity —— 262
3	Assertion, secondary assertion and assertion-marking —— 264
4	A first analysis —— 267
5	Some refinements —— 268

5.1	Jespersen's surprise and the "canonical position" of sentence negation —— 268
5.2	In and out of scope —— 270
6	Focus effects —— 275
7	A look at two residual problems —— 278
7.1	Replacive negation —— 278
7.2	Metalinguistic negation —— 279
8	Concluding remarks —— 280
	References —— 280

About the German particles *schon* and *noch* —— 283

1	Introduction —— 283
2	A first inspection —— 284
2.1	*schon* —— 284
2.2	*noch* —— 286
2.3	Summing up —— 289
3	Earlier accounts —— 290
3.1	Löbner's presuppositional analysis —— 290
3.2	Krifka's restriction on focus alternatives —— 297
4	The basic idea —— 299
5	The meaning contribution of *schon* and *noch* —— 304
6	Some examples —— 307
6.1	*schon* —— 308
6.2	*noch* —— 311
7	Four problems —— 314
7.1	Topic time, situation time, and adjacency —— 314
7.2	World level order and presentation level order —— 316
7.3	"Scalar" and other types of properties —— 317
7.4	Context integration and "association with focus" —— 319
8	Concluding remarks —— 321
	References —— 322

The information structure of French —— 324

1	Introduction —— 324
2	Some characteristic features of French grammar —— 326
2.1	Inflection —— 326
2.2	Phrase-initial grammatical elements —— 327
2.3	Word-order —— 327
3	Means to mark information structure —— 329
3.1	Choice of NP type —— 329

3.2	Word order —— 330	
3.3	Constructions —— 330	
3.4	Intonation —— 331	
4	Dislocations —— 333	
5	*C'est ... qui/que* constructions —— 337	
6	A tentative synthesis —— 342	
6.1	The structural core —— 342	
6.2	The information structure of the core —— 344	
6.3	Expanding the core —— 345	
7	Summing up —— 350	
	References —— 352	

Quaestio and L-perspectivation —— 354

1	Choices —— 354
2	Levels in production —— 358
2.1	Intake —— 359
2.2	Update —— 360
2.3	Forming a discourse representation —— 360
2.4	Constructing a linguistic form —— 363
3	The Quaestio —— 364
3.1	Questions and answers —— 364
3.2	Topic component and focus component —— 367
3.3	Domains of reference within an utterance —— 370
3.4	Referential movement —— 371
3.5	Deviating from the quaestio —— 372
4	Other constraints on L-perspectivation —— 373
4.1	The hearer model —— 373
4.2	Linguistic system —— 375
5	Linguistic reflection of perspective management: the case of subordination —— 378
5.1	Substantial topic constraints —— 379
5.2	Structural topic constraints —— 381
6	Conclusions —— 382
	References —— 383

Finiteness, universal grammar and the language faculty —— 385

1	Kantian questions —— 385
2	Finiteness —— 389
2.1	Finiteness as an inflectional category —— 389
2.2	Syntactic properties of finiteness —— 390

2.3	Semantic properties of finiteness —— 392	
2.3.1	Specific and non-specific interpretation of noun phrases —— 392	
2.3.2	Tense —— 394	
2.4	Prosodic properties of finiteness —— 395	
2.5	The topic situation —— 396	
2.6	Finite utterance organisation —— 396	
3	Finiteness and Universal Grammar —— 397	
4	'Universal Grammar' and the human language faculty, or: the properties of the bread are not the properties of the baker —— 399	
5	Conclusions —— 400	
	References —— 402	

The basic variety (or: couldn't natural languages be much simpler?) —— 403
1	Introduction —— 403	
2	Two perspectives on SLA research —— 406	
3	Empirical background —— 409	
4	The structure of the basic variety —— 412	
4.1	The lexical repertoire —— 412	
4.2	Utterance organisation —— 414	
4.3	The expression of temporality —— 421	
4.4	The expression of spatiality —— 424	
4.4.1	Theme, relatum and spatial relation —— 424	
4.4.2	The structure of spatial expressions —— 425	
4.4.3	Spatial relations —— 426	
5	The basic variety in use —— 428	
5.1	Its functioning… —— 428	
5.2	… And where it fails —— 431	
6	Basic variety and the human language capacity —— 433	
6.1	A short summary —— 433	
6.2	Basic variety, theory of grammar and second language acquisition —— 434	
6.3	Language before language —— 440	
6.4	Second language acquisition and second I-language acquisition —— 443	
7	Concluding remarks —— 443	
	References —— 444	

The contribution of second language acquisition research —— 449
1	Introduction —— 449	
2	What can SLA research contribute to the understanding of the human language faculty? —— 451	

2.1	Our status within the linguistic sciences —— 451	
2.2	Two views on SLA research —— 454	
2.3	The "real language hoax", or: Learner varieties are the normal case —— 457	
2.4	Can learner varieties really tell us something about the human language capacity? —— 460	
3	Conclusion —— 463	
	References —— 465	

Why case marking? —— 466

1	Introduction —— 466
2	Learner varieties are the normal case —— 467
3	Two questions —— 469
4	Learner varieties and 'real' languages —— 472
5	Lexical repertoire and rules of composition —— 473
6	What is inflection good for? —— 476
7	Case marking and the 'Argument-Time Structure' of verbs —— 477
7.1	Where the BV fails —— 477
7.2	Case marking and the 'argument-time structure' of German verbs —— 480
8	What is a subject, what is an object? —— 487
9	Conclusion —— 489
	References —— 490

The grammar of varieties —— 491

1	Linguistic variability and its analysis —— 491
2	Variety space, overall grammar and probabilistic weighing —— 492
2	Probabilistic weighing I: phrase structure grammars —— 495
2.1	Probabilities —— 495
2.2	Suppes-type weighing —— 496
2.3	Derivation weighing grammars —— 500
2.4	Context-sensitive grammars —— 501
3	Probabilistic weighing II: transformational grammars —— 501
4	Variety grammars in empirical research —— 503
	References —— 505

Index —— 507

Bibliography

Klein, W. (2009). Concepts of time. In W. Klein and P. Li (eds.). The Expression of Time Berlin: Mouton de Gruyter. 5–38.
Klein, W. (1995). A time-relational analysis of Russian aspect. Language 71(4). 669–695. © 1995 LSA.
Klein, W. (2000). An analysis of the German perfekt. Language 76. 358–382. © 2000 LSA.
Klein, W., Li, P., and Hendriks, H. (2000). Aspect and assertion in Mandarin Chinese. Natural Language & Linguistic Theory 18. 723–770. © 2000 Springer.
Klein, W. (2010). On times and arguments. Linguistics 48. 1221–1253.
Klein, W. (1997). On the "Imperfective paradox" and related problems. In M. Schwarz, C. Dürscheid and K.-H. Ramers (eds.). Sprache im Fokus: Festschrift für Heinz Vater. Tübingen: Niemeyer. 387–397.
Klein, W. (1982). Local deixis in route directions. In R. Jarvella and W. Klein (eds.). Speech, Place, and Action: Studies in Deixis and Related Topics. New York: Wiley. 161–182. © 1982 Wiley.
Klein, W. (1993). Some notorious pitfalls in the analysis of spatial expressions. In F. Beckman and G. Heyer (eds.). Theorie und Praxis des Lexikons. Berlin: de Gruyter. 191–204.
Klein, W. (2001). Time and again. In C. Féry and W. Sternefeld (eds.). Audiatur vox sapientiae: A festschrift for Arnim von Stechow. Berlin: Akademie Verlag. 267–286.
Klein, W. (unpublished). On the scope of negation.
Klein, W. (unpublished). About the German particles *schon* and *noch*.
Klein, W. (2012). The information structure of French. In M. Krifka and R. Musan (eds.). The Expression of Information Structure. Berlin: de Gruyter. 95–126.
Klein, W. and Von Stutterheim, C. (2002). Quaestio and L-perspectivation. In C. F. Graumann and W. Kallmeyer (eds.). Perspective and Perspectivation in Discourse. Amsterdam: Benjamins. 59–88. © 2002 Benjamins.
Klein, W. (2009). Finiteness, universal grammar, and the language faculty. In J. Guo, E. Lieven, N. Budwig, S. Ervin-Tripp, K. Nakamura and S. Ozcaliskan (eds.). Crosslinguistic Approaches to the Psychology of Language: Research in the Tradition of Dan Isaac Slobin. New York: Psychology Press. 333–344. © 2009 Taylor and Francis.
Klein, W. and Perdue, C. (1997). The basic variety (or: Couldn't natural languages be much simpler?). Second Language Research 13. 301–347. © 1999 SAGE publications.
Klein, W. (1998). The contribution of second language acquisition research. Language Learning 48. 527–550. © 1999 Wiley.
Klein, W. (2002). Why case marking? In I. Kaufmann and B. Stiebels (eds.). More than words: Festschrift for Dieter Wunderlich. Berlin: Akademie Verlag. 251–273.
Klein, W. (2005). The grammar of varieties. In U. Ammon, N. Dittmar, K. J. Mattheier and P. Trudgill (eds.). Sociolinguistics: An international handbook of the Science of Language and Society. Berlin: Walter de Gruyter. 1163–1171.

Unless said otherwise, © de Gruyter. The authors thanks the publishers for the permission to re-use the papers in this collection.

Introduction

> Denk nicht, sondern schau!
> Wittgenstein, Phil. Unters. §66

In the fourth scene of Bertolt Brecht's "The Life of Galilei", the astronomer tries to convince the Grand Duke and two accompanying scholars that the planet Jupiter has moons. The two scholars reject that idea since it runs against what Aristotle stated. So, Galilei invites them to look through the telescope such that they could see the moons with their own eyes: "Gentlemen, I beseech you in all humility to trust your eyes." Upon which one of the scholars, a mathematician, answers: "My dear Galileo, old-fashioned though it may sound to you, I am accustomed among other things to read Aristotle, and I can assure you that there I do trust my eyes."

Greek and Roman scholars, Aristotle being one of the first, not only created a theory of the universe but also the notional framework which we still use to describe the structure of human languages: noun and verb, subject and object, case and gender, nominative and accusative, tense and aspect, active and passive. There are a few variations in the labels – some say [+N] and [+V] instead of "noun" and "verb"; there are several refinements, such as the distinction between lexical aspect and grammatical aspect; and there are some genuine additions, such as topic and focus (still using Greek and Latin words). But basically, all descriptive grammars and most work in modern linguistics are, so to speak, "Aristotelian". Now, something that is more than two thousand years old may be rock-solid; Euclidean geometry is. The inherited notions of grammar are no rocks; they suffer from two fundamental problems. First, they are informed by two languages with a rich inflectional morphology, up to the early 19th century the trademark of a reputable language. Second, they are usually fuzzy and often completely misleading. Take the notion of "noun". In his *Ars minor* (around AD 350), Aelius Donatus summed up the antique understanding as follows: '*Quid est nomen? – Nomen est pars orationis cum casu corpus aut rem (proprie communiterve) significans (proprie ut Roma Tiberis, communiter ut urbs flumen)*'; moreover, the student had to learn that in Latin, nouns have several *accidentia*, such as *genus* and *numerus*. Now, it is easy to see that the definition does not apply to, for example, *loss, fault, peace, hatred* or *gulp*, nor does it make sense for languages which lack inflection, such as Chinese. Still, it survived almost two millennia. In the *Cambridge Grammar of the English Language* (2002) – a masterpiece of grammar writing by any standard –, the authors define "noun" as follows (p. 32): "a grammatical distinct category of lexemes of which the morphologically most elementary members characteristically denotes types of physical objects (such as human beings, other biological organisms, and natural or artificial inanimate objects)". They do not say what the grammatically distinct features are, but certainly, these features are quite different in Italian, English and Chinese; so, grammatically, "noun" is not a universal category. Semantically, the definition avoids the problem with *loss, fault, peace, hatred* or *gulp*, but only because it is blurred by "characteristically". For verbs, the defining grammatical features are tense and person, rather than case: *Verbum est pars orationis cum tempore et persona sine casu aut agere aliquid aut pati aut neutrum significans*. But what is "tense"? It indicates, so the tradition, that the situation described by the sentence is before, at or after the speech time: *The pope was ill – the pope is ill – the pope will be ill*. Now, this is true in *The pope died*, but in *The pope was ill*, his being ill need not precede the speech time; the pope may well be ill right now – it is just not asserted; and it is certainly false in *The pope was dead*, unless the pope happened to resurrect. Still, practically all descriptive grammars operate with the classical notion of tense, when they describe the verbal system.

Occasionally, they add a concept that has no direct predecessor in the antique tradition. To Aristotle (Metaphysics 1048b), we owe the distinction of verb types such as *telic* vs. *atelic* and thus the idea of "lexical aspect". But the notion of "viewpoint aspect", as exemplified by the contrast between the progressive and the simple form in English or the imperfective and the perfective aspect in Russian, shares all the problematic properties of classical notions like noun or tense. Its definition varies slightly with authors, but the general idea is always the same: (viewpoint) aspect does not relate the situation to a particular time interval, for example the speech time, but serves to present it, or to view it, as "on-going" or as "completed"; in *John was writing a book*, the action is viewed as on-going, and in *John wrote a book*, it is viewed as completed. But first, one cannot see situations as one can view a tree or a match box; so, the characterization of aspect as different ways of viewing a situation is just a metaphor, good as a starter, but far from the precision we should expect from a scientific notion. And second, it does not make sense to call something completed without relating it to a time span at which it is completed: completed when? After all, whatever is completed at some time was on-going at some earlier time. So, aspect is no less time-relational than tense, although the specific temporal relations and the time spans between which they obtain may differ in both cases.

These and similar problems with our notional heritage are easy to see, even without the help of a telescope. But this heritage still shapes our way to describe the structural properties of human languages. Language teachers use it for the beginners as well as for the advanced. Standard works like the *Cambridge Grammar of the English Language*, quoted above, use it. Typological linguists use it when they compare languages in terms of SOV, SVO, OSV, or VSO; after all, such comparisons make only sense, if V, S or O are the same across languages. Modern structural linguists use it when they talk about noun phrases, verb phrases, X-bar theory or head-driven phrase structure grammar. In each of these cases, there are exceptions; but they never reached the crowd. Why are we still in the clutches of this venerable but flawed tradition?

There are, I believe, two reasons. First, we do not have a better shared language in which we can talk about linguistic structure. Second, our language may be so useful not *although* but *because* it is so fuzzy, "for it is the mark of an educated man to look for precision in each class of things just so far as the nature of the subject admits; it is evidently equally foolish to accept probable reasoning from a mathematician and to demand from a rhetorician scientific proofs." (*Aristotle*, Nic. Eth. 1094b). A missionary who sets out to describe a hitherto undescribed language – and a great deal of the languages of the world were first described by missionaries – needs something coarse. But that stage must be overcome, as soon as we are striving for some deeper understanding of how human languages are structured. I do not believe that this is possible by inventing a new and ingenious theory; such a theory must be the result, not the starting point, of an in-depth analysis that shows us which elementary principles are behind the received notional framework.

The eighteen papers of this book were written and, with two exceptions, published between 1985 and 2010; minor errors were corrected, but no attempt was made to revise them substantially, since I see their potential merit less in the answers they give to the problems than in the way in which these problems are approached. The papers cover a wide range of topics, such as the expression of time and space, the structure of learner languages and their gradual development, the role of finiteness and assertion marking, the functioning of particles such as *not*, *already* or *still*, information packaging and information structure in sentences and whole texts. They are tied together by a particular way to look at the linguistic phenomena: the look of an erudite child who has read Aristotle and many others and now eagerly wants to look through the telescope, a child who has preserved a certain naïve curiosity – the curiosity to see with his own eyes how things are. Within such an approach, the notions which we inherited from our learned ancestors have the role of crutches that one should not throw away too early. But at the end they should become dispensable. Or with Wittgen-stein's famous metaphor from *Tractatus* 6.54: We must throw away the ladder after having climbed up on it. This end is not in sight yet. But maybe these papers lead a step or two further up.

Concepts of time[1]

> Time has always been difficult to understand, but in the twentieth century, our un-understanding has become clearer.
>
> J.R. Lucas (1999: 1)

1 Introduction

The experience of time and the need to adapt our life to it are as old as mankind. The sun rises in the morning and sets in the evening, the moon changes its position at regular intervals, plants and animals and humans come into existence, grow, fade and pass away. We act here and now, but we also remember having acted, and we plan and hope to act in the days ahead of us. Some of these events, such as the coming and going of the seasons, are cyclic, that is, they are repeated at intervals which we consider to be equal. Other events are not assumed to be cyclic, such as our first love, the birth of Jesus, or Grandmother's death. All human cultures and societies of whom we know have reacted in three ways to this temporal nature of experience:

- First, *actions are planned and done* accordingly – there is a time to plant and a time to reap; a time to tear down, and a time to build; a time to mourn, and a time to dance, as the Preacher has it in the Bible.
- Second, methods *to measure time* were invented. This is always done by linking some event – the event whose duration we want to measure – to some other type of events which are supposed to occur at regular intervals, such the sequence of the seasons, the fall and rise of the sun, the swing of a pendulum, the oscillation of a quartz crystal; the result are calendars and clocks (Bruton 1993, Landes 1983, Richards 1998).
- Third, we *speak* about time. All human languages have developed numerous devices to this end, and in some languages, the marking of time is even close to mandatory. In English, as in all Indoeuropean languages, the finite verb regularly expresses "tense" – that is, the sentence not only describes some event, process, or state. It also places this situation into the past, present, or future: we cannot say *John be ill*, thus leaving neutral the time of the state thus described. We must say *John was ill, John is ill, John will be ill*. Other

---

[1] I wish to thanks Leah Roberts who corrected my English.

Note: This article originally appeared as Klein, W. (2009). Concepts of time. In: W. Klein and P. Li (eds.). The Expression of Time Berlin: Mouton de Gruyter. 5–38.

https://doi.org/10.1515/9783110549119-002

languages, such as Chinese, have no mandatory marking of time. But this, of course, does not mean that they cannot express time; they just use other means, such as adverbials like *yesterday, right now*, or *very soon*, and they give their speakers full freedom to indicate what happened when.

So, we all adapt our life to time; we use devices by which time is counted and measured; and, above all, we speak about time. We know what it means when someone says *He will arrive tomorrow at five.*, *The meeting has now lasted for almost eleven hours.*, and *Last february, I intended for the first time to spend more than three hours per week in Pontefract*. So, we do understand what time is. But what is it, then?

At this point it is common to quote St. Augustine, who, in the 11th book of his *Confessions*, says:

> Quid ergo est tempus? Si nemo ex me quaeret, scio. Si quaerenti explicare velim, nescio. [What, then, is time? If nobody asks me, I know. If I should explain it to someone who asks, I don't know].

His own way to overcome this clash between practical and theoretical understanding of time is that time is not in the things themselves but in our soul. God, he says, is beyond time, and we get to know all things created by him because he has endowed our soul with memory, experience, and expectation (see Flasch 2004). In other words, our soul – or our mind, as we would probably say now –, is such that we experience the world as *past, presence*, and *future*.

St. Augustine's theory of time is one of many within a rich stream of thought that began with the first Greek philosophers and has steadily unfolded over the millenia and over many disciplines – philosopy, physics, biology, psychology, anthropology, linguistics, to mention but these. They all deal partly with the same and partly with different aspects of time, the result being a hardly permeable jungle of views, opinions, and theories. In fact, the Augustinean question "Quid ergo est tempus?" has found so many answers that one might as well say that there is no answer at all. Thus, the idea that we could ever grasp "the essence of time" is perhaps futile; is is doubtful that there is much more than a kind of family resemblance between a biologist's, a phycisist's, and a psychologist's concept of time.

The aim of this chapter is not to unveil the "very nature" of time; it is rather to prepare the ground for a basic understanding of how temporality is expressed in natural languages.[2] To this end, it is necessary to gain some idea (a) of the

---

[2] The number of books on time is legion. The best general survey is to my mind Whitrow 1980; it is, however, confined to time in philosophy, physics and biology. Fraser 1987 is an easy and broad introduction by one of the best experts on the study of time.

underlying temporal notions, and thus of what people understand by "time", and (b) of the means by which these notions are encoded in the different languages of the world. The second issue is addressed to the following chapter of this book. The present chapter is devoted to the notional category of time. Section 2 reviews the diversity of meanings with which this category is associated; we will glance at some of the key questions which are dealt with in different fields. Section 3 discusses three perennial issues which come up time and again when people reason about time. In section 4, I will sketch a "basic time structure", which, I believe, can serve as a useful starting point for the study of how time is expressed in language.

The following exposition is strongly biased towards "the Western tradition" of reflection on time. Apart from sheer lack of knowledge on my part, this bias has three reasons. First, it is by far the best studied tradition; there is, of course, research on non-European notions of time; but it is comparatively sparse (see, e.g., Needham 1968, Fraser, Haber and Lawrence 1986). Second, only in that tradition do we find this enormous spread of temporal notions across various disciplines, such as physics, biology, or psychology. Third, different as human languages are – our entire way of thinking about their lexical and structural properties is deeply shaped by the Western tradition of linguistics. In Latin, the word *tempus* means both "time" and "tense", and thus, one is easily led to believe that tense is the most immediate reflection of time in language, in fact, that tense is time. This close connection has misled not only linguists but also philosophers who think about time, and so, it is important to understand its roots.

2 The variety of time

This section is a gaze into a jungle – into the rank growth of notions, ideas, problems which have grown from a few germs laid in the Antiquity. At first glance, it would appear to be hopeless to detect any structure in this jungle; but in fact, there are a few recurrent themes which we will address in the following section. It should be clear that this panorama is anything but exhaustive: it is rather meant to give an impression of the abundance of temporal phenomena.

We will begin with philosophy – the mother of any science and the origin of human thought on time. In fact, any such reasoning reflects a particular perspective on reality and the way in which we are able to recognize it – a perspective on us and on the world around us. In this sense, any reflection on time is inevitably "philosophical". But if we speak of "philosophical" theories of time, in contrast to, for example, physical theories, we normally mean the more or less elaborate views of particular philosophers, from Anaximander[3] to Heidegger and Wittgenstein. There are many such theories; here are three characteristic examples from modern times; they stand for very different perspectives on time (Turetzy 1998 is an excellent survey; Le Poidevin and McBeath 1993 is a characteristic collection of articles on 20th century philosophy of time).

A. In Immanuel Kant's *Critique of pure reason* (1781), time and space are properties of human cognition – in fact, the two most fundamental categories of human cognition. They define the way in which our mind experiences, and thinks about, the world. Time, in particular, is "die innere Form der Anschauung", (the inner form of intuition). It defines the way in which we "intuit" external events and facts, such as the running of a horse or the rotation of the earth, but also internal events, such as the feeling of hunger or grief. We cannot know whether time is "real", that is, a property of the world itself; our cognitive apparatus is such that the outer as well as the inner world inevitably *appear* to us as structured by time.

B. In his influential article *The unreality of time* (1908), the British philospher John McTaggart argued that there are two types of event series, each of which represents time: The "A-series" relates to the "earlier-later"-order, to the mere *succession* of events, states, processes. In this sense, Aristotle lived before St. Augustine, and Kant lived after St. Augustine. The "B-series" relates to the difference between "past – present – future". In contrast to the A-series, it requires a particular vantage point, from which the events are seen; this is the present moment – which, in turn, permanently shifts. Under neither understanding is time "real", argues McTaggart (see, e.g., Turetzky 1998).

Kant's and McTaggart's views on time are among the most-discussed in modern philosophical literature; but they are not really new – they elaborate and extend themes that are already found in the antiquity. As we have seen above, St. Augustine also thought that time is a property of our "soul", and that it divides the world, as we can recognize it, into past, present, and future; he also had a clear notion of succession being a crucial feature of time. This is quite different for the third philosophical theory of time which I will mention here.

---

3 In what is probably the oldest fragment of Greek philosophy we have, Anaximander says that the things, as they come into existence and perish, "pay their debts to each other according to the order of time" ("kata tou chronou taxin") – a sentence of which no element is easily understandable (see Turetzky 1998: 6–8).

C. In Martin Heidegger's book *Sein und Zeit* ("Being and Time"), published in 1927, time is not so very much seen as an objective property of the world around us or a subjective property of our way to know the world in or around us. Rather, it is something that shapes human existence. Human time is not an abstract order, real or imaginary, defined by relations such as "earlier" or "simultaneous". It is the slope which separates us from death, a short stretch filled with our sorrows and efforts and griefs. It is the notion of time which surfaces in expression such as "little time is left", "these were hard times", or, in the words of the Preacher quoted above, "there is a time to plant and a time to reap; a time to mourn, and a time to dance". Such a notion of time is not incompatible with the idea of succession and the division into past, present and future; but properties like these are somehow marginal to what time means for humans.

These are three of the very many ways in which philosophers have looked at time. They may not be mutually exclusive; it is not even clear whether they target the same entity or not. And in a way, we do not expect the opinions of philosophers to converge on some phenomenon. But we do expect this in hard science. So, there should be one notion of time in physics. This is not the case. There are at least three approaches towards this chimera.

D. The first of these is the view which underlies the laws of classical mechanics, as first stated by Isaac Newton. In the introductory "definitions" to the *Principia*, Newton distinguishes two notions of time:

> "Tempus Absolutum, verum, & mathematicum, in se & natura sua absque relatione ad externum quodvis, æquabiliter fluit, alioque nomine dicitur Duratio: Relativum, apparens, & vulgare est sensibilis & externa quævis Durationis per motum mensura (seu accurata seu inæquabilis) qua vulgus vice veri temporis utitur; ut Hora, Dies, Mensis, Annus. (Newton, Principia, Book I, Scholium to the Definitions). [Absolute, true, and mathematical time, in itself, by its very nature and unrelated to anything external, flows equably, and is also named Duration: relative, apparent, and everyday time is some sensory and external (accurate or unequable) measure of duration by motion, and it is commonly used instead of true time; such as hour, day, month, year.]

A number of points are remarkable in this short paragraph:
(a) Time is the same as Duration. It is neither an order, defined by "earlier" or similar notions, nor is it in any way related to past, present, future. This does not mean that Newton had no idea of *succession*; in a somewhat mysterious way, it comes in in the term "aequabiliter fluit". But in its absolute as well as in its relative understanding, Newton equates time with *duration*.
(b) We cannot measure "real" time – whatever it is. Instead, we measure the duration of things to which our senses have access. This duration is "relative

time"; it is measured by motion, and the result are units such as hour, day, month, year, etc.
(c) Real time is always the same; still, it "flows", and it flows equably – whatever that means. Newton does not say whether it flows in one direction, although this would seem the most natural assumption. Real time is, so to speak, unaffected and unaffectable by anything. In fact, it is not even related to anything "external"; in particular, it is not related to any *observer*.

Newton's notion of real time is cryptic, perhaps because it has a strong religious background. As he states in the Scholium Generale of the second edition of the Principia (1713) – an addition which is particular famous for Newton's statement "Hypotheses non fingo [I don't make up hypotheses]" – he argues that time is an emanation of God, and God is in time (a position which is in sharp contrast to St. Augustine's, according to whom God is out of time). It may well be that the tremendous success of Newtonian mechanics is completely independent of his conception of "real" time. What is crucial for the laws of motion is the possibility of measuring the time of observable events by motion. This is not possible for real time. What really matters in Newtonian physics is thus relative time. Absolute time, dear as it may have seemed to Newton, is something that lurks in the background, and is perhaps completely superfluous to the physicist.[4]

E. Classical physics, including its notion of time as duration, sometimes leads to undesirable asymmetries. If, for example, a conductor and a magnet move in relation to each other, then there is a electromagnetic effect. This effect should be the same no matter whether the conductor moves, or the magnet moves. But classical physics gives two completely different accounts of the effect for both cases. The problem disappears if we assume that there is no "distinguished frame of reference", in particular no absolute frame of reference, as seems to be implied by absolute time and space. We can choose the position of the conductor as well as the position of the magnet as frame of reference; the laws of physics operate in the same way, no matter what the frame of reference is; the only factor that remains constant is the velocity of the light. This is the basic idea which Albert Einstein worked out in in 1905 in what was later called "special theory of relativity" and which, among others, led to the notion of "relativistic time". This time has peculiar properties,

---

[4] His great opponent Gottfried Wilhelm Leibniz argued that time and space are purely relational – there is no absolute time and no absolute space. In response to this, Newton's spokesman Samuel Clarke gave an argument as to why we need something like "empty space", independent of the properties of objects that are "in space". But no corresponding argument was ever given for "empty time" (see Westfall 1983).

which are often felt to be paradoxical; thus, it may shrink or extend – an idea which seems very different from a notion of time which flows equally and is unaffected by anything external, and no less different from our everyday notion of time.

Usually, a sharp constrast is made between Newton's absolute time and Einstein's relativistic time. This is misleading, because in actual fact, Newtonian physics does not operate with absolute time, either. Absolute duration (scil. absolute time) exists, but it is not accessible to us; all we can measure is relative time. What Newton did not consider was the possibility that the measurable duration of some event could vary with a frame of reference ("Koordinatensystem", as Einstein says in German); exactly this assumption is made in Einstein "relativistic time". But Newton never spelled out how relative duration differs from absolute duration, except that the former is a familiar phenomenon and can be measured by motion, whereas the latter is the "true" duration.

Relativistic time and Newtonian time (in both variants) have three properties in common:

(a) What is crucial is not so much the "earlier – later" order of observable phenomena – their *succession*; it is their *duration*. The famous and perplexing "time dilation" and "time contraction" effects of the special theory of relativity refer in the first place to changes in the duration of some observable phenomena, when measured from different frames of reference. But indirectly, varying duration also affects observed simultaneity and succession between two events. The reason is that *information* about these events needs some time to reach the observer, and this time takes longer or shorter, depending on the relative distance between the place where the events occur, and the frame of reference.

(b) The laws of physics operate equally "in both directions". They do not go "from earlier to later" or "from later to earlier". This asymmetry, so fundamental to the daily experience of time, plays no role under these two conceptions of time.

(c) Similarly, the observer – the person who experiences time – plays no role. There is no past, present or future, no shifting Ego, in relation to which these notions are defined. In relativistic time, there is always a "frame of reference"; but all that is relativized is duration. Einstein never denied that past, present and future are important ingredients of everyday notions of time; but not so in the world of physics (cf. section 3.3 below).

Since the laws of physics do not conform to an "arrow of time", which invariably flies from earlier to later, they reveal the kind of symmetry which physicists like; the theory of special relativity started as an attempt to overcome an undesirable asymmetry. But has nature really no earlier-later orientation? Is the real world, whose laws the physicists try to find, like that? Questions of this sort have given rise to a different notion of physical time.⁵

F. We can imagine that an egg, once fried, returns to its initial state; we can even have a film run backwards, thus apparently reversing the order of time. But we never observe such a return in reality. There are many physical processes which, it seems, obey the "arrow of time". A well-known type of such unidirectional processes are the changes of entropy (roughly: the amount of disorder) in a closed system, as studied in thermodynamics. In Clausius' formulation from 1851, the second Law of Thermodynamics states that the overall entropy of a closed physical system can remain constant or it can increase; but it cannot decrease, unless such a change is caused by influences from outside the system: inherent state changes of the entire system are unidirectional. This has given rise to a physical concept of irreversible time, a concept which is neither Newtonian nor Einsteinian (see, for example, Prigogine and Stengers 1993). It should be noted, though, that irreversibility is not to be equated with the earlier-later asymmetry, as is often done. Even if the fried egg could be restored, the time at which at which it has its original properties again is *later* than the time at which it was not yet fried: the egg is as it was *before*. We will come back to this problem in section 3.1.

The time of physics, in whichever of the three variants mentioned here, does not integrate some of the features which we normally associate with time. It deals with the temporal structure of dead matter, not of living organisms. There are at least three notions of *biological time* -, the life span of the individual, biological evolution, and biological rhythms in the organism.

G. The life of an indivdual has a beginning: birth (or perhaps conception). It has an end: death. And the processes between birth and death are, as a rule, not reversible: they have a certain duration, and they are fundamentally characterized by the earlier and later of growth and decay. This second fact makes biological time crucially different from physical time in the Newtonian or Einsteinian sense. It makes it also different from the time notion of thermodynamics; there is no organic "growth and decay" in the changes of closed systems, except in a very metaphorical sense.

H. Antique and mediaeval thought did not consider the world as entirely static. There are changes, such as the motion of bodies, the changing seasons, or even the notion of subsequent ages – for example, a "Golden Age" followed by a "Silver Age". But

---

5 Reichenbach (1958) is still a very clear treatment of this problem; see also Horwich (1987) and the contributions in Savitt (1993) for a more recent discussion.

it was not until the late 18th century that the idea of *evolution* gained ground – that is, of a temporally directed and rule-governed process which determines directed changes of whole systems, usually towards an increasing complexification. The earliest detailed treatment I am aware of is by Johann Gottfried Herder (1784, vol. I, p. 3–94). Such systems might be, for example, *languages*; Hermann Paul, one of the leading linguists of the 19th century, even argued that only historical linguistics deserves the name of a science, because only this way of looking at language reveals the principles that underlie it, rather than merely stating facts (Paul 1882: 20). They might be *physical systems*, such as the earth, the solar system, or even the entire universe. But by far the most discussed example is the origin and evolution of *life*, which, as is now generally believed in the educated world, is determined by a few principles such as genetic variation, extinction according to fitness, or drift.

I. There is a third way in which we can speak of biological time. Many processes within a living organism follow a "biological rhythm", for example the circadian rhythm which, as a rule, lasts 24 hours in human beings, though with some variation. These rhythms are essentially determined by a "timer" – maybe several timers – inherent to the organism, but this internal timing interacts with influences from outside the organisms, for example the amount of light or heat. This highly complex and only partly understood interaction regulates order, duration and intensity of physiological processes in the organism (a good survey of the present state of research is given in Foster and Kreiman 2004).

In biological research, these rhythms are usually characterized in terms of chemical processes in various types of organisms, flowers, animals, human beings. But they bring us already somewhat closer to the properties of a person who actually experiences time – a notion completely absent in physical time. We find it, for example, in St. Augustine's notion of time as a property of our soul. His argument is entirely based on a very subtle but completely intuitive self-observation. Modern psychology has led to many insights into how time is perceived, remembered and transformed into human actions.

J. What is the *Now* that separates the past from the future and allows us to define what is present? This notion has vexed philosophers from Aristotle to McTaggart, for at least two reasons. First, it "shifts" permanently: there is not a single now, there are infinitely many nows. But there is always a special now – the now right now, so to speak. So, how is this now defined in contrast to all the other nows? Second, the now is supposed to have no extension, hence no duration (and in the sense of physical time, it is not in time at all: no duration, no time). If this is true, then there can be no present. But if there is no present, it seems to make little sense to speak of past and future. Arguments of this sort have led to the idea that time is "not real", a position indeed taken by philosophers from the antiquity until to McTaggart. Now, rather than worrying about these puzzles, psychologists have tried to determine what the minimal unit of perception is, that is, the shortest time at which our sensory organs can, for example, distinguish a change in vision or audition. For human beings[6], this shortest moment is assumed to be somewhere between 30 and 40 milliseconds (Poeppel 1988). But already William Stern noted in 1897 that this shortest moment may not coincide with what we consider to be "present" (whose duration he calculated as 6–7 seconds). This may not solve the philosophical problems connected to the now; but if the present is defined by what is perceived right now, then we know at least how long the now is.

K. How do we experience duration? The duration of some event or state is "objectively" measured by relating it to repeated occurrences of some other event (for example the heart beat or the rotation of the earth around its axis). As everybody knows, this measured duration of an event often sharply contrasts with the subjective duration someone attributes to it. This variation depends on many factors, for example
- the number of subevents – that is, changes we note within the entire period: if "nothing happens" within one hour, then this hour is subjectively much longer than when it is filled by many subevents;
- the degree to which we like the event: sadly, unwanted events seem to last much longer than events which we enjoy;
- the influence of drugs; some drugs "stretch" the subjective duration of an event.

We do not immediately perceive the relative order of events – succession always involves memory or expectation. This brings us to the second factor, the memory of time.

L. Time is closely connected to remembrance. But how do we remember time? This concerns duration as well as succession. In our recollection, the perceived duration of an event is sometimes reverted: idle hours, which did not seem to end, shrink in memory, events which excited our attention and seemed to pass rapidly, as they happened, tend to be very long in memory. If we try to recollect a complex event that we have experienced in the past – say a car accident -, how do we know that subevent A came before subevent B? And how do we record partial

---

6 The idea of such a shortest time span of perception and the possibility that it might vary across species was first introduced the founding father of embryology, Ernst Baer, in 1864. He also beautifully illustrated the dramatic consequences of this variation for the way in which the world is experienced.

overlaps of subevents? In other words, how do we store the order of events, as we perceived them? In some cases, we might have looked at a watch and thus remember "A was at 10:15, B was at 10:16"; but this is surely the exception. Do we use an inner watch which allows us to stick a sort of "time stamp" on all subevents? Or do we just associate pairs of events by a relation "A before B" or "A simultaneous with B", thus eventually forming a complex temporal web of subevents? (see Kelly 2005 for a discussion and how it relates to various other time puzzles).

M. We not only perceive and remember temporal features of what happens in our environment, we also plan and perform actions. These actions often consist of a complex structure of simultaneous and sequential sub-actions. Thus, they exhibit a complex temporal structure. In some cases, the temporal order in which sub-actions are to be performed are more or less dictated by the intended result ("first the socks, then the shoes!"); in other cases, this must be stored as an independent part of the planning ("first push the red button, then the black button"!). Jean Piaget, in his famous theory of child development (1927), argued that a great deal of this development is characterized by increasing abilities to decompose complex actions in subparts and to process and execute them independently; young children treat complex events holistically, as a unit, older children learn to separate and possibly revert its parts. A particularly interesting aspect of the temporal composition of actions concerns the question of whether our "decision" to do something always precedes the action itself. One such sub-phase of a action concerns the decision to perform it: does this decision always precede the action itself? Benjamin Libet and others have shown that this may not always be the case – a finding which has led to considerable discussion on the notion of a free will (Libet 2004).

Humans are similar in some respects, and they are different in others. To what extent does this influence their notions of time? No one assumes that biological differences between individuals bear on the relative order of events, or the division of time into past, present and future. This is perhaps less true for duration: some people seem to be slow, others are fast, and this could be due to the fact that their inner clock runs at different speed. A good example is language processing; there is a number of verbal tasks in which women are on the average much faster. But this biological variation is minor, when compared to the variation in human cultures. In anthropological research, it is often assumed that different societies have developed quite different concepts of time. In what follows, we briefly discuss four examples which illustrate this variation (a very detailed discussion is found in Wendorff 1980).

N. Life in different cultures always follows certain "natural rhythms", such as the sequence of the seasons or the various ages of a person from birth to death. But the degree to which these rhythms dictate human life and thought varies considerably.

Societies in which these rhythms prevail are often said to prefer a "cyclic concept" of time, in contrast to the "linear time", so familiar to us in modern Western societies.

O. A second, related aspect is the degree to which daily life and work are dictated by the mechanical measurement of time. Until a few centuries ago, precise clocks and calendars were exceptional in any society; nowadays, they characterize the entire daily life of more and more societies (see, for example, Dohrn-van Rossum 1996). Note, however, that "mechanical clock time" is not to be equated with the notion of linear time; after all, clocks are based on cyclic events.

P. What role do history and chronology play in a society? All human cultures we know of have some notion of the forebears which may still be "present" in some sense – dead, but still an active force in daily life. This connection to the past may be structured in different ways. Some old cultures, such as the Chinese, the Japanese or the Egyptian culture, are bound to the remote past by an uninterrupted "chain of generations", for example dynasties or families. Others, such as the Greek or the Indian culture, also have strong ties to a very distant past, but they never have the notion of such a linear chain which connects the present to the origin (see Nakayama 1968).

Q. Cultural variation in timing also surfaces in a number of phenomena which we find in all human societies. The most obvious example is *music*: in all its manifold forms, it is always a way to organize sounds in time – to organize their succession or simultaneity, as well as their duration. Music has its roots in our biological clocks; but the way in which it evolves varies massively across cultures (Jourdain 1999). Many other time-related human activities show the same pattern: there is an essentially universal biological root, and there is massive cultural variation – for example dance, poetry, and, of course, language.[7]

This brings us to our final point. There are at least four ways in which language is crucially connected to time. Languages *change in time*, they are *processed in time*, they exhibit a *linear order*, and they *express time*.

R. In the antiquity and in the middle ages, the idea that languages change was not unknown; but this fact, obvious as it is, did not play a substantial role in the way in which philosophers and linguists thought about language. This changed with the

---

[7] Another interesting case are movies which present a complex event within a certain time frame, say 90 minutes; but the "real" time of the event thus represented is, of course, normally much longer. This can be used for special effects, such as in Buster Keaton's silent movie "Seven chances" in which movie time and depicted time converge, as the movie goes on.

advent of historical comparative linguistics around 1800, and for at least a century, diachronic research reigned in the study of human languages. This research has bestowed a tremendous amount of empirical facts upon us, albeit only for a small number of languages. But in contrast to biological evolution, we are still very far from an idea of the principles that determine how human languages change over time (a good survey of the state of the art is Janda and Joseph 2004).

S. One of the miracles of human language is the speed with which it is processed in everyday communication. This becomes immediately clear as we look at a simple question-answer sequence such as: "Where were you born? – In Heidelberg". The person who answers has to identify the sounds, words and rules of the question in about one second, and it takes about another second to produce the answer. This includes the repeated inspection of something like 50,000 lexical items somewhere stored in the brain, but also the storage of the syntactic pattern of the question, the decision to use this pattern in the answer and to omit those parts which would be identical (the answer means "I was born in Heidelberg", and not just "in Heidelberg"), the innervation of a complex articulation pattern, etc. (Dietrich 2007 gives an excellent survey of this research)

T. There are three major modalities by which human languages are encoded – speaking, writing, gesturing. Each utterance, each text follows a *linear order*, which is fundamentally temporal in nature. Linguists often say that a constituent "is moved to the left" or "to the right"; but in fact, this is only a spatial metaphor for the fact that this constituent is somehow processed at an earlier or later time when pronounced or written, heard or read.

U. Independent of whether a culture has a more or less elaborate theory of time – its members are always able to speak about time. They relate personal experiences, they talk about their future plans, they arrange dates, they describe how to bake a cake – all of this requires temporal notions of duration, succession and simultaneity. For a long time, the study of how temporality is encoded was completely dominated by two grammatical categories, tense and aspect, and a lexical category, called Aktionsart, situation type, or sometimes lexical aspect (Binnick 1990 gives an good survey of this research tradition). But this is only a selection of the means which natural languages use to express time; temporal adverbials are by far the most elaborate means.

This concludes our tour through the notions of time; it is easy to see that it is anything but exhaustive; but it surely suffices to give a picture of the diversity of time. Let us return to the initial question: What, actually, is time? If anything is clear by now, then it should be the fact there that is not a single notion of time.

But it is also clear that the many facets of time are not an arbitrary collection of phenomena. There are a number of discernable threads in this wad, three of which will be addressed in the following section.

3 Three recurrent themes

3.1 Time and change

There is no immediate experience of time itself. What we experience are changes around us and in us. We see that it is getting dark and that it is getting light, we feel cheerful, and we feel sad. This experience is ubiquitous, and people have to adopt their life to it. It were the early Greek philosophers that began to wonder about two things. The first of these is a fundamental ontological problem: what does the pervasive experience of change tell us about the nature of reality:

- Is it steadily changing, as Herakleites is supposed to have thought? Among his cryptic sayings, *panta rhei* [everything is in flow] is probably the most famous.
- Is this impression of steady change fallacious, and reality is eternal and immutable, as Parmenides is reported to have thought?
- Do we have different types, or perhaps degrees, of reality – one of them characterized by change, the other one by non-change, as Plato and many others, notably the neo-platonists, argued?

In this discussion of reality, two issues must be clearly kept apart. The first issue concerns the "reality of time": is time "real", or is it just a fiction of our mind? This question has led to vivid discussions, but mainly among philosophers; it is an interesting but somewhat academic problem. The second issue is the nature of reality itself: is there a reality – maybe the only "real reality" – behind the apparent changes, which our senses tell us? Different views which people have taken on this question had dramatic consequences in the history of mankind; the entire dogma of trans-substantiation, so fundamental to Christian faith, depends on the possibility that "real reality" is independent of apparent change or non-change, and many people have died for the one position or the other; so, it is probably an important issue.

The second problem, about which the Antique philosophers stumbled, is not ontological but epistemological. How is it possible that one and the same entity can have two mutually incompatible properties? How can someone be alive and dead, how can someone be in Athens and in Crete? The answer is that this entity has the same property *at different times*. Someone might be in Athens at an earlier time and at Crete at a later time. A difference in time need not lead to a change; but it makes a change possible – or, in a saying of unknown origin: "Time is nature's way of keeping everything from happening at once". Thus, time and change are closely connected to each other.

Changes can be of different sort, depending on the type of property at stake. There are, in particular
(a) spatial properties, such as being in Crete and in Athens, being here and there, being under the blanket or on the blanket;
(b) qualitative properties, such as being red and green, odd and even, immortal and mortal;
(c) quantitative properties, such as getting a bit drunk or heavily drunk, driving seven miles or 99 miles, weighing one ton or nine tons. These properties are usually somehow derived, since they operate on qualitative or spatial changes and indicate differences in degree – either numerically or in a somewhat fuzzier way.

Accordingly, there a different types of changes – spatial, qualitative, quantitative. Any such change is a combination of times and properties. Motion, for example, is a change of spatial properties. Note that the property itself does not change, nor does the time change, although we often say this. What changes, is the assignment of properties to something, for example a person or an object, or perhaps to a full situation. If someone is alive at some time and dead at a later time, i.e., dies, then the property "be alive" does not change; but it so happens that that person does not have it any longer. Similarly, if someone grows from five feet to six feet, the properties "be five feet tall" and "be six feet tall" do not change; but the person has them at different times. And, of course, the earlier time is not suddenly a later time. In a word: neither times nor properties change; what changes is the assignment of properties to something over time.

The distinction between time and change seems an obvious one. But it has led, and still leads, to substantial confusion. In what follows, I will consider two examples that have played an important role in the discussion of time. The first confusion concerns the notion of *irreversibility*, that is, the "arrow of time" discussed above (section 2, point E). The laws of classical as well as of relativistic physics apply equally from earlier to later and from later to earlier: time is "reversible". Biological time – and similarly the time of our daily experience – is oriented: it runs from birth to death, never from death to birth; it is "irreversible". But this common way to state the difference is misleading. It is not time that is reversible or irreversible but the sequence of changes. Take the simple case of a glass which, once broken, cannot return to the state in which it was not broken (and thus really be a glass, and not a mass of pieces): we can image this, even see it on a film that runs backwards; but it is never observed in reality. But suppose reality would indeed allow this to happen – then, there is still an earlier state, in which the glass is not broken, and a later state, at which it is not broken, interrupted by a state in-between, at which it is broken: there is a temporally ordered sequence "not-broken – broken – not broken", each of which is associated with a different time: there are three different time spans, two of which – the first and the last – are associated with the same qualitative properties. The glass does not "return in time" – it has the same properties again a later time. So, the difference between "reversible" and "irreversible" is only whether we can have the sequence of changes "unbroken to broken" as well as the sequence "broken to unbroken", or only the former. But each of these two sequences goes from earlier to later. Even if the order of changes can go in both directions – time cannot: there is no irreversible time.

The second confusion concerns the notion of a *cyclic time* (in contrast to a *linear time*). From the Greek notion of the "Great year" – a very long period after which everything is destroyed by fire and then reborn – to Friedrich Nietzsche's "ewige Wiederkehr des Gleichen [eternal return of the same]", many share in the view that the world passes through cycles of creation, destruction and recreation (the classical treatment is Eliade 1954). In anthropology, it is often said that some cultures or some schools of thought do not have the western notion of linear time: there are time cycles (Wendorff 1980). In linguistics, Benjamin Lee Whorf became famous because of his claim that the Hopi have a completely different view of time than the one found in "Standard European Languages", a view which does not see time as a linear sequence but as a cycle (see the critical examination in Malotki 1983). But in all of these cases, this does not imply that the *time* is cyclic. It only means that the same *sequence of changes* is repeated and thus cyclic. The experience of such change cycles is very natural, on a short scale, as the sequence or day and night, as well as on a larger scale, as the re-appearance of certain stellar constellations. But this does not mean that the time itself comes and goes. We can count the repetitions. The seventh time, when the sun rises in the east, is not the same time as the twelfth time at which this happens. The twelfth time at which the world is re-created is not the fifteenth time at which it is re-created. What might be identical, are the properties which the world has at these different times.

Aristotle, to whom we owe the first systematic examination of time in general and of its relation to change in particular, states this very clearly in his famous definition of time: time is "a number of motion with respect to before and after" (Physics IV, 219 b 1–2). Aristotle's analysis of time is not easy to follow, and it has given rise to various interpretations (see, e.g., Coope 2005). But he not only makes a clear distinction between time and change; without such a distinction, it would make no sense to say that something happens slowly or fast. He also characterizes time as something that can be *counted*. If the entire world is reborn for the seventh time, then this seventh time is *later* that the sixth time at which it is reborn.

3.2 Time and its units

Is there one time, or are there many times? The common idea is that there is one time which can be subdivided into smaller units. These "smaller times" are called time spans, temporal intervals, sub-times, or just "times". We say that there is a time a which we met our first love, and a time at which we lost her or him, and each of these times is a subinterval of the entire time; these subintervals themselves have subintervals: time is somehow nested. Several things can be said about these time spans:

1. They have a *duration*. We do not know whether the "entire time" has a duration. As we have seen above (section 2, point D) Newton equated absolute time with duration; but as soon as he talks about the measurement of time, only smaller time spans – for example the duration of some event – are at issue.
2. This duration can be measured. This is done by relating the time span, which is to be measured, to the duration of some other time spans; these are given by repeated occurrences of specific events (such as the rotation of the earth). We say that time can be measured. In a way, this is puzzling. When can it be measured? Clearly, time does not stand still during the measurement process – thus, the entity to be measured changes during this process. But there is no real puzzle: we do not really measure time, we measure the duration of events, and we say that this duration is the time during which the event lasts. But one thing is the event, another thing is its time, just as there is a difference between a cup and the space which the cup occupies.
3. Time spans do not stand alone. They are related to each other according to an underlying earlier-later order which is unidirectional. But two time spans can also be simultaneous or overlap. In other words, time is a sort of structure whose units are time spans and whose structure is defined by temporal relations such as *succession, overlap, simultaneity*.
4. Each time span in turn consists of time spans. Does this go on forever – i.e., is there is "shortest time"? This is surely the case for human time experience. It is less clear whether nature has a minimal time span. Traditional as well as modern physicists assumed that *natura non fecit saltus* [nature does not make jumps], i.e., there is continuity). It was only in 1900 that Max Planck showed, quite reluctantly, that physicists are well advised to assume that there is a shortest time, whose duration is 5.4×10^{-43} seconds. We can, of course, *imagine* a shorter time, for example, 10^{-44} seconds; such a product or our mind is just meaningless for the laws of physics – and it would still leave us far away from a continuous time, which has no shortest interval.
5. Is there is a "last time span", i.e., does time have an end? And similarly, is there a "first time span", i.e., does time have a beginning? St. Augustine says

no, Stephen Hawking says yes, Immanuel Kant says that both views lead to paradoxes. The reasonable person has no firm opinion on this issue.

3.3 Time and the observer

Neither physical time nor biological time, in the senses mentioned in section 2, know the distinction between past, present, and future – notions which everybody feels to be fundamental to human time. Einstein, in a conversation with Rudolf Carnap (around 1953), explicitly noted this fact: "Once Einstein said that the problem of the Now worried him seriously. He explained that the experience of the Now means something special for man, something essentially different from the past and the future, but that this important difference does not and cannot occur within physics. That this experience cannot be grasped by science seemed to him a matter of painful but inevitable resignation. I remarked that all that occurs objectively can be described in science; on the one hand the temporal sequence of events is described in physics; and, on the other hand, the peculiarities of man's experiences with respect to time, including his different attitude towards past, present, and future, can be described and (in principle) explained in psychology. But Einstein thought that these scientific descriptions cannot possibly satisfy our human needs; that there is something essential about the Now which is just outside the realm of science." (Carnap 1963: 37–38). This distinction between past, present and future requires an observer; this observer cannot be an instrument which measures time, such as a clock. No chronometer, precise as it may be, distinguishes past from future. To this end, an observer is needed who identifies a time span as "being now". Human beings are able to do that. Maybe other animals are able to do it as well, although this question is not easy to answer.

But what is the "now"? In the long philosophical debate on this question, there has never been an answer on which the experts agree. Essentially, there are two different though interconnected problems. First, there is not just one now but infinitely many – the now right now, the nows that are before that now, and the nows that are ahead of us. In other words, time itself seems to be a series of nows. Acccordingly, there is a past and a future relative to each of these "nows". But what distinguishes the "now" right now from all other nows? It must be a special property which somehow comes from the particular observer who experiences the – inner or outer – world as somehow "present", whereas earlier nows are somehow in memory, and later nows somehow in imagination. But on the other hand, the earlier "nows" are also defined in relation to the experiences of some observer, perhaps the same observer at some earlier time; so, the problem cannot be easily reduced to the difference between memory, experience and expectation in our soul, as St. Augustine does. It appears, therefore, that the distinction between now and not-now is not reducible to any other difference. The second classical problem results from the fact that the now does not seem to have an extension; otherwise, it would consist of several moments, some of which are earlier and hence past, and hence not now. But if the now has no extension, it does not exist, and hence, there is no presence; but if there is no presence, there is neither past nor future. Moreover, it is not possible that the entire time is built up from a series of nows, because if they have no extension, time cannot have an extension, either. These are the type of mind-boggling problems that were extensively discussed from Aristotle (Turetzky 1998: 22–25) to our days (see, for example, Dummett 2000).

In the second half of the 19th century, physiologists and psychologists set out investigate the notion of "present moment" with experimental methods. From film watching, everybody knows that when the number of pictures presented to our visual system exceeds about 20 per second, it cannot keep them apart and perceives them as a continous movement. So, there is a shortest time for (in this case visual) experience. But does this shortest time correspond to the "now" which underlies the distinction between past, present and future? When watching a film, or listenening to a tune, our intuition about what is on-going, rather than gone or only to come, seems much longer. So, there must be something in our brain which integrates shortest perceptual moments into a whole – a "perceptual present"; assumptions go that this perceptual present can last a few seconds.

Still a different issue is the now which underlies the linguistic expression of past, present and future. All languages in the world mark such a distinction by tense marking (*he is here vs he was here vs he will be here*) or by adverbials such as *yesterday, last year, very soon*. How is this now defined? Clearly, it cannot be the meaning of a word such as *now* (or its counterparts in other languages). These words refer to a time span with, as the case may be, considerable extension (*As a child, I was very religious, but now, I am not*). The word *now*, when uttered in a speech situation, refers to a time span which INCLUDES the moment of speech, rather to the moment of speech itself; the boundaries of this time span can vary. It seems to be this moment of speech which serves as an anchoring point, in relation to which present, past and future are defined. In fact, this picture is too simple again because the "moment of speech" is usually not a moment – surely not in the sense of the shortest time our brain can experience. We shall return to this problem in section 4. Two facts should be noted, however. First, this temporal anchoring to whatever the "present moment" is usually considered to be fundamental to the expression of time in natural languages. Second, the temporal anchoring point may differ considerably from what in other disciplines is considered as "now".

4 The time concept of human languages

As we have seen in the preceding two sections, there are many notions of time, such as biological time, Newton's absolute and relative time, time as Kantian "Form der inneren Anschauung" and hence a necessary precondition of all cognition, subjective time, as influenced for example by drugs, and so on. These notions are interrelated in many ways, but they cannot be reduced to one concept: there are many. Is there a concept of time which underlies the expression of temporal relations in NATURAL LANGUAGES? Even this is doubtful. In most modern cultures, metrical calendar time plays an important role, so important that we often take it for self-evident. Our life is largely organized around (or rather along) this time, and hence, there are many expressions which refer to it – like *in the year of 2007* or *two hours and thirty five minutes after noon on May 8, 1998*, and so on. But many cultures do not have such a concept of metrical time, nor the notion of one major event in collective history to which everything can be temporally related. Even in Western culture, the full elaboration of this system is fairly recent. The mere fact that people talk of "hours", "days", "years" and "the birth of Christ" does not mean that they have a concept of metrical time, with the birth of the savior, or some other important event, as point zero. Until a few centuries ago, the concept of "hour", for example, just meant "twelfth part of the day", and if the day was short, like in winter, the hour was short, as well. A "day" is simply the time, when there is light, or the time from when people get up until they go to bed again, no matter how "long" this may be in terms of a mechanical or electronical clock.

Therefore, it seems reasonable to distinguish between various layers of time structure that are used in the encoding of time. There is something like a "basic time structure" on which the expression of temporal relations in natural languages is based. This basic time structure must cover basic relations between time spans, such as succession and simultaneity, but also the notion of a basic vantage point – the "now" of an observer. More differentiated structures, like calendaric metrical time, may be added, as cultures develop. It seems likely, although this is an empirical question, that such additional structuring is only expressed by more or less complex lexical expressions, whereas the basic time structure is most often expressed by grammatical categories and by simple adverbs.[8]

---

[8] The following discussion essentially follows Klein (1984), Chapter 4.

4.1 The "basic time structure"

4.1.1 The ingredients

What, then, is this "basic time structure"? This is not easy to say, because at most 5% of the world's languages are sufficiently well described; for all others, our information is very superficial and often based on bold comparisons with familiar languages such as Greek, Latin or English. Hence, we might simply miss important temporal notions encoded in same or even many languages. But such is the state of our knowledge. An inspection of those languages for which our information is more profound shows that the following six characteristics are indispensable:

A. Segmentability: Time, whatever it is, can be divided into smaller segments – "time spans" or "temporal intervals".

As was discussed in section 3.3, there is a perennial debate among philosophers and physicists on whether this division can be infinitely repeated or whether there is some minimal "time quantum". I do not believe that the mind of the common language user has a standing on this issue, and in fact, I would not know of any criterion to decide whether we need infinite segmentability, if we want to describe the linguistic expression of temporal relations. Let us now turn to these relations between time spans.

B. Inclusion: If s_1 and s_2 are time spans, then s_1 may be included in s_2; this inclusion may be full or partial; in the latter case, we may speak of "overlapping".

C. Succession: If s_1 and s_2 are time spans, which are not (fully or partly) included in each other, then either s_1 precedes s_2 or s_2 precedes s_1.

It is usually said that time is linearly ordered. The way in which we have characterized succession here is somewhat weaker: there is a partial order on time spans: time spans can overlap. Again, it is an open question whether this partial order is based on some full order on "time points", which make up the time spans. We normally assume that there is some temporal progression within a time span, and a strict order on time points allows us to reconstruct this intuition in a straightforward way.

These three features allow a clear definition of the "earlier-later" asymmetry between time spans as well as simultaneity. Simultaneity can be full (two time spans completely coincide) or partial, if they overlap.

D. Duration: Time spans may be long or short in duration.

Duration, as regularly expressed in natural language, is not another name for time, as in Newton's definition. It is a property of time spans. It is typically indicated by adverbials, such as for *two days, rapidly, quite a while*. They do not necessarily describe objectively measured time. If we say *It took Shin quite a while to ...*, then we may refer to very "objective durations", depending on whether we talk about drinking a coffee or finding a spouse.

E. Origo: There is a distinguished time span, which we may call "the time of present experience". Everything before that is accessible to us only by memory, everything later only by expectation.

This origo is the dividing point between past, present and future. As was discussed in sections 2. (points I. and J.), and 3.3, such an origo is not part of all time concepts; it plays no role in physical time or in biological time. But it plays an eminent role in the linguistic encoding of temporal relations. The best-known case is the grammatical category of tense; in its classical understanding, tense situates some event in relation to the "deictic origo", which is given by the moment of speech – the linguistic variant of the time of present experience. But there are also many adverbials which are anchored at the deictic origo, for example *today, three days ago* or, of course, the word *now* itself; thus, *today* means "the day which includes the deictic origo". Remember, however, that the meaning of the word *now* is not to be equated with the deictic origo – it refers to a time span which contains the deictic origo, but can be much longer (cf. section 3.3). We can say, for example *Now, the average temperature is much colder than in the pleistocene*.

F. Proximity: If s_1 and s_2 are time spans, then s_1 may be near to, or far from, s_2.

This feature is much less discussed in the tradition than linear order, duration, or the existence of a "now". But it is regularly encoded in natural languages. Proximity and non-proximity in this (non-metrical) sense is exemplified, for example, by expressions like *soon* or *just*; it also sometimes shows up in tense distinctions, like "near future" vs "far future". Note that this concept of "temporal distance" or "remoteness" does not presuppose a concept of metrical time. Quite the opposite, it is not easy to capture the idea of proximity in this sense by metrical distance: *soon* can mean "in ten minutes", like *the meal will be served soon*; but it can also mean "ten months", like in *they soon got divorced again*.

G. Lack of quality: Time spans have no qualitative properties; they are neither green nor sweet, and they have no wheels and no spines. They are contained in each other or just after each other or more or less close to each other, and they are long or short.

In the tradition, this feature shows up in the discussion about how time and change are related to each other (see section 3.1 above). The latter normally relates to changes in qualitative properties or position, the former to the "pure structure", in relation to which such changes are perceived, imagined, or expressed. When we talk about time, then typically, some descriptive properties are *associated* with certain time spans – for example, we may talk about the time at which some event took place, or some state obtained. But we must carefully distinguish between an event or a state, and the time at which these take place or obtain.

4.1.2 A more precise definition

The usual way to give a precise definition to temporal relations is to interpret time spans as closed (sometimes as open) intervals of the real numbers; the "smaller than"-relation between real numbers is then used in the obvious way to define a partial order on the intervals (if $s = [r_i, r_j]$ and $t = [r_k, r_l]$ are closed intervals, then s is BEFORE t iff $r_j < r_k$). This procedure, whilst straightforward and elegant, is not sufficient, however. It provides us both with too much and too little structure. Under the assumptions made in 4.2, the Basic Time Structure does not include the notion of a metrical distance between time spans; the definition just sketched does not, either; but the underlying relation between "time moments", identified with the real numbers, does. It also makes the assumption that time is dense, i.e., that there is no smallest time span, an assumption which may be too strong. But these problems are perhaps not really harmful. It is much more problematic that some crucial intuitions are not captured, in particular the features "origo", "proximity", and "duration". Hence, we need "more" structure.
(a) The most straightforward way to account for the notion of "origo" is to identify it with the moment of speech; in fact, such a "deictic origo" is found in all human languages we know.
(b) It is less clear how one should capture our intuitive notion of (temporal) nearness. One might think to use the natural topology on the real numbers: the neighborhoods of any real number r are exactly those open intervals to which r belongs. But this gives us by far too much: it gives us all environments, rather than the one which marks the borderline between "close" and "far". Our intuitive notions tell us that each time span has a "region" around itself,

whose borders vary with context. The time of drinking a coffee is usually shorter than the time of finding a spouse, and so are the "regions" around these two time spans. Temporal relations between two time spans s and t do not only differ according to whether s precedes t, follows t, or is (partly or fully) contained in t, but also according to whether it is "in the region of t". This region may be very wide, if t itself is "long"; but it may also be short. It may also happen that the region is lexically or grammatically specified.

(c) There is no such straightforward solution for the related problem of duration. The fuzziness of durational notions like *for a while, shortly, very much later* cannot be accounted for by metrical time, on the one hand, nor by introducing simply a "region" around time spans. In some cases, one can relate the relative duration of a time span, such as the time which some event takes, to the average time of similar events. For example, in *She rapidly drank a beer*, the time of this beer-drinking is related to the average time of beer-drinking and found to be shorter than this average time. But there are cases in which this does not work, like in *He slept for a while* as compared to *He slept for quite a while*. It is no surprise, therefore, that the meaning of these expressions is hardly ever precisely described.

The components of the Basic Time Structure are thus:
- an infinite set of time spans (leaving aside whether these are infinitely divisible)
- an order relation on time spans (BEFORE)
- a topological relation IN between time spans
- for each time span t, a distinguished time span which includes t – the REGION of t
- a distinguished time span, the ORIGO.

We may now define the Basic Time Structure as follows:

(1) The Basic Time Structure (BTS) is a structure [/R, $\{t_i\}$, $\{R_i\}$, BEFORE, IN, 0], where
- |R are the real numbers, with the usual order relation <
- $\{t_i\}$ is the set of closed intervals of |R, the "time spans";
- $\{R_i\}$ is a subset of $\{t_i\}$, such that for each t_i, there is exactly one R_i which properly includes t_i (R_i is the REGION of t_i);
- BEFORE is a partial order on $\{t_i\}$, such that: If s = $[r_i, r_j]$ and t = $[r_k, r_l]$ are in $\{t_i\}$, then s BEFORE t iff $r_j < r_k$;
- IN is a relation on $\{t_i\}$, such that s IN t iff they have at least one element in common
- 0 is a distinguished element of $\{t_i\}$, the ORIGO.

The Basic Time Structure is a sort of scaffold which allows us to define various types of temporal relations such as BEFORE, AFTER, IN. These relations obtain between two time spans, which I will call temporal relata. In *John left yesterday*, for example, one of the relata is the time of John's leaving, the other relatum is the time at which the utterance is made, and the relation is BEFORE. Other, much more complex constellations are possible. In what follows, I will first illustrate some characteristic relations[9] and then discuss the various types of temporal relata.

4.2 Temporal relations

Temporal relations obtain between two time spans: a first time span, which I will call THEME, and some other time span, which I will call RELATUM. In what follows, the theme is marked by ------, the relatum is marked by +++++, and the region around the relatum by ( ); the linear order is represented by left-right arrangement:

   a. BEFORE, i.e., the theme precedes the relatum properly:
      ------- +++++
   b. LONG BEFORE, i.e,, the theme precedes the region of the relatum:
      -------- (+++++)
   c. SHORTLY BEFORE, i.e., the theme precedes the relatum, but it is in the region of the relatum:
      (------- +++++)
   d. JUST BEFORE, i.e., as SHORTLY BEFORE, but the theme abuts the relatum:
      --------+++++

In this case, the theme is automatically in the region of the relatum – more precisely, the final part of the theme; in principle, it is not excluded that the theme begins long before the relatum.

   e. PARTLY BEFORE, i.e., a the first part of the theme precedes and the second part of the theme is IN the relatum (the region is irrelevant):
      ---+-+-+-++
   f. INCL, i.e., the theme is fully included in the relatum:
      ++-+-+-+-+++
   g. AFTER, i.e., the relatum precedes the theme:
      +++++ --------

---

9 In all of these cases, the Basic Time Structure allows us to give precise formal definitions. For present purposes, however, it may be more useful to use diagrams that illustrate the various relations.

Other relations, such as JUST AFTER, SHORTLY AFTER, LONG AFTER can be defined analogously. Note that the relation IN has been split here into PARTLY BEFORE, INCL and PARTLY AFTER; if we want such a notion, it can be defined by the usual Boolean operations.

4.3 Temporal relata

When a temporal relation is expressed in some communicative situation, the two relata normally have a different functional status. One of them, for example the time of some event, is somehow "situated" in time; this is done by relating it to some other time span which is supposed to be given in the communicative situation and then functions as a kind of anchoring point. The former is called here, the theme, and the latter, simply the relatum, respectively. The familiar grammatical category of tense exemplifies this functional asymmetry very well. It indicates, at least in its classical understanding, that some event is in the past, present or future – that is, it precedes, includes, or follows the moment of speech. Thus, in *John left*, when uttered in a particular communicative situation, the time of John's leaving is the theme, and the moment of speech is the relatum. Basically, there are three ways in which such a relatum can be given:
- deictic, that is, it can be derived from the speech situation;
- anaphoric, that is, it is mentioned in the preceding context;
- calendaric, that is, it given by some important event in cultural history

Calendaric relata are of lesser interest here; they only differ in which historical event from the shared knowledge of the interlocutors is chosen as an anchoring point – the foundation of Rome, birth of Christ, the Hegira, the beginning of a dynasty, etc. There is no language in which tense is linked to a calendaric origin. But many languages have a rich system of adverbials with such an anchoring point.

4.3.1 Deictic relatum

The Basic Time Structure, as defined above, includes a distinguished time span, called there the origo, which plays a special role in the expression of time. What is the origo in a given communication? Typically, it is identified with the "moment of speech" or, as is often said, the "time of utterance". The latter expression is preferable, since the "moment of speech" is usually not just a moment. Expressions which use this time of utterance as a relatum are usually called "deictic". The verbal category of tense, which is deeply rooted in the grammatical system of many – though not of all – languages is deictic: *He was singing, he is singing, he will be singing* place the time of some event, before, around, or after the time of utterance. But deictic relata also underlie many adverbials. Thus, *three years ago* (in contrast to *three years before*) means "at a time which is three years before the time of utterance", and *yesterday* means "at the day which precedes the day which includes the time of utterance".

The deictic relatum is fundamental to many temporal expressions. But it also raises a number of problems, three of which I will briefly mention here. First, how long is the "time of utterance"? Does it include the whole interval during which an utterance is spelled out, is it only a part of the latter, or is it even longer? Sometimes, a shorter relatum is needed, for example when someone says:

(2) From *now*, it is precisely four seconds until *now*.

We also have the opposite problem, i.e., cases in which the "time of utterance" seems to go beyond the boundaries of a single sentence. Does a longer text, say a lecture or even a novel, have a single time of utterance or a different one for each single utterance of which it consists? In a sense, a coherent sequence of utterances – a text, be it written or spoken – is a unit, and it should have a single relatum. But then, it would be strange to assume that this relatum is, for example, the time at which the whole text was produced: What is then the utterance time of the Bible, or the first book of Moses? In these cases, the characterization of the deictic relatum as "time of utterance" is clearly insufficient.

Linguistic systems most often evolve in spoken communication, in which speaker and listener are equally present. Then, time of speaking and time of hearing collapse, and hence, there is no need to distinguish between the speaker's and the listener's origo. But in other communicative situations, there are clashes, for example in written language (or even in spoken language, when it is stored in some way). In this case, it is regularly the speaker's origo which counts.

The third problem with the notion "time of utterance" concerns possible shifts – i.e., cases in which it is not the origo (the time of present experience) which counts but rather some other time interval. Two such cases are usually mentioned in the literature. The first is exemplified by "vivid narration", like in the historical present, in which the speaker treats past events as if they were happening now. Somehow, the time of utterance is replaced by the time of actual experience; it is the latter which serves as relatum. The other kind of shift is introduced by verbs of saying and thinking, as in these examples:

(3) I thought: Now, I must change my life.
(4) Yesterday, my friend said: Shouldn't we go to Berlin tomorrow?

In these cases, it is not the origo of the real speaker which counts but the origo of the person whose thinking or speaking is being talked about.

4.3.2 Anaphoric relatum

Anaphoric relata are time spans which are given somewhere in the linguistic context. Their role for tense is disputed. In the literature, a distinction is sometimes made between "absolute" and "relative" tenses; the former are purely deictic, whereas the latter also involve an anaphoric relatum. Some text types, for example narratives, are based on a chain of such anaphoric relata. As with all types of anaphora, there are three subcases:
1. The anaphoric relatum is within the same clause (intraclausal anaphora)

In (5), the initial adverbial introduces a time span, to which another time span in the same utterance is related:

(5) At six o'clock sharp, he switched the light off.

2. The anaphoric relation may go from one clause to another, whilst still being in the same sentence (interclausal anaphora):

(6) When the phone rang, he switched the light off.

In cases of this type, it is often said that "two events" are temporally related to each other. But note that the entire *when*-clause only serves to define a time span, which functions as a relatum. In principle, this is not different from the anaphoric relatum in (5), which is simply specified by a clock-time adverbial.

3. The anaphoric relatum may have been introduced in a preceding utterance.

This type of anaphoric temporal linkage is most import for text organization. It is exemplified by well-known discourse principles such as "the principle of chronological order" which states that, unless marked otherwise, the time span of some situation described is after the time span of the situation mentioned in the preceding utterance.

A time span that functions as an anaphoric relatum for some subsequent time span may in itself be based on a deictic relatum. Compare the following two intraclausal anaphoric relata:

(7) Three weeks ago, he didn't have a penny.
(8) Three weeks before that, he didn't have a penny.

In both cases, the initial adverbial introduces a time span, say t6 and t7, respectively. In the first case, this time span t6 is three months before the time of utterance, in the second, t7 is three months before some other contextually given event. Hence, the time span is deictically given in (7) and anaphorically in (8). But in both cases, the time span functions as an anaphorical relatum of the subsequent time span – the time at which he had no penny. The fact that something is an anaphoric relatum of something else does not preclude that it is in itself deictically introduced. On the other hand, we may often get "anaphoric chains"; an anaphoric relatum is temporally related to a preceding one, which in turn is related to another one, and so on, and so forth.

5 Concluding remarks

The ability to talk about time is a fundamental trait of human communication, and all languages we know of have developed means to express time. But in sections 2 and 3, we have seen that time is not a uniform phenomenon. There are numerous concepts of time; they share some features, but they are also divergent in many respects. Which of these concepts underlies the expression of time in human languages? There is no straightforward answer, for at least two reasons. First, we are not well informed about most languages of the world. Second, those languages we know seem to differ in what they encode and how they do it. One way to approach both problems is to start with a relatively simple "basic time structure", which covers the core notions expressed in same of the better-studied languages. In section 4, such a basic concept is defined. As need arises, it can be refined; it can also be simplified, if the language to be described does not use all of features of this structure. But may serve as a point of departure.

References

Aristotle: Physics. (many editions)
Bruton, Eric (1993): The History of Clocks and Watches. London: Black Cat.
Butterfield, Jeremy, ed. (1999): The arguments of time. Oxford: Oxford University Press.
Carnap, Rudolf (1963): Intellectual Autobiography. In Schilpp, P.A., ed.: The Philosophy of Rudolf Carnap. La Salle, IL: Cambridge University Press.
Coope, Ursula (2005): Time for Aristotle. Oxford: Oxford University Press.
Dohrn-van Rossum, Gerhard (1996): History of the Hour: Clocks and Modern Temporal Orders. Chicago: The University of Chicago Press.
Dummett, Michael (2000): Is Time a Continuum of Instants?. Philosophy 75, 497–515.
Eliade, Mircea (1954): Cosmos and History:The Myth of the Eternal Return. Princeton, NJ: Princeton University Press.

References

Flasch, Kurt (2004): Was ist Zeit?. Augustinus von Hippo. Das XI. Buch der Confessiones. Frankfurt/Main: Klostermann.
Foster, Russell G. and Kreitzman, L. (2004): Rhythms of life: The biological clocks that control the daily lives of every living thing. London: Profile Books.
Fraser, Julius T. ed. (1968): The voices of time. London: Penguin
Fraser, Julius T. (1987): Time – the familiar stranger. Amherst: Univ. of Massachusetts Press.
Fraser, Julius T., Haber, F. C., and Lawrence, N., eds. (1986): Time, Science, and Society in China and the West. Amherst: University of Massachusetts Press.
Heidegger, Martin (1927): Sein und Zeit. Jena: Niemeyer.
Herder, Johann Gottfried (1784): Ideen zu einer Philosophie der Geschichte der Menschheit. Riga: Hartknoch.
Horwich, Paul (1987): Asymmetries in Time. Cambridge, Mass.: The MIT Press.
Janda, Richard D., and Joseph, Brian D., eds. (2004): The Handbook of Historical Linguistics. Oxford: Blackwell.
Jourdain, Robert (1997): Music, the Brain, and Ecstasy: How Music Captures Our Imagination. New York: William Morrow.
Kant, Immanuel (1781): Kritik der reinen Vernunft. Riga: Hartknoch.
Klein, Wolfgang (1994): Time in Language. London: Routledge.
Le Poidevin, Robin, and McBeath, Murray, eds. (1993): The Philosophy of Time. Oxford: Oxford University Press.
Libet, Benjamin (2004): Mind Time. The Temporal Factor in Consciousnes. Cambridge, MA: Harvard University Press.
Lucas, J. R. (1999): A century of time. In Butterfield 1999: 1–20.
Malotki, Ekkehart (1983): Hopi Time. Berlin: de Gruyter.
McTaggert, John E. M. (1908): The Unreality of Time. In Mind 17: 457–474. (reprinted in Le Poidevin and McBearth 1993).
Nakayama, Hajime (1968): Time in Indian and Japanese thought. In Fraser 1968: 77–91.
Newton, Isaac (1972): Isaac Newton's Philosophiae naturalis principia mathematica. The 3rd edition, with variant readings, assembled and edited by Alexandre Koyré and Bernard Cohen. Cambridge, MA: Harvard University Press.
Paul, Hermann (1882): Prinzipien der Sprachgeschichte. 2nd edition . Jena: Niemeyer.
Piaget, Jean (1923): Le développement de la notion de temps chez l'enfant. Paris: Presses Universitaires de France.
Poeppel, Ernst (1988): Mindworks: Time and Conscious Experience. Boston: Harcourt.
Prigogine, Ilya, and Stengers, Isabelle (1993): Paradox Time, Chaos and the Quantum: Towards the Resolution of the Time. New York: Harmony Books.
Reichenbach, Hans (1958): The Direction of Time. Berkeley, CA: University of California Press.
Richards, Edward G. (1998): Mapping Time, the calendar and its history. Oxford: Oxford University Press.
Savitt, Steven, ed. (1995): Time's Arrows Today: Recent Physical and Philosophical Work on the Direction of Time. Cambridge: Cambridge University Press.
Turetzky, Philip (1998): Time. London: Routledge.
Whitrow, Geoffrey J. (1980): The natural philosophy of time. Oxford: Clarendon Press.
Wendorff, Rudolf (1980): Zeit und Kultur. Geschichte des Zeitbewußtseins in Europa. Wiesbaden: Westdeutscher Verlag.
Westfall, Richard Samuel (1983): Never at rest. A biography of Isaac Newton. Cambridge: Cambridge University Press.

A time-relational analysis of Russian aspect[1]

1 Introduction

It is generally assumed that, apart from a few cases of ambiguity, every Russian verb form can be assigned to one of two aspects, usually called perfective (PERF) and imperfective (IMPERF). This fact has been stated in various forms by many authors, for example by Timberlake (1982: 302):

> Verbs in Russian belong to one of two aspect categories, the perfective or the imperfective. Although there is some variation in their morphological expression, these categories can be described as morphologically encoded aspect. They are used to express a number of partially distinct semantic features, such as durativity, iterativity, progressivity, completion, and the like. Each use of a particular aspect to express one of these semantic features defines a contextual variant of this aspect.

If it is true that each verb belongs to either PERF or IMPERF, then this raises the question of what the criteria for this assignment are? How does the speaker know, how does the linguist know that a particular verb form is PERF or IMPERF? Since a grammatical category is always a mapping between particular formal means and particular meanings (or functions), two answers are possible:

A. Each Russian verb form is characterised by some explicit marking – by a suffix, an infix, a prefix, a detachable particle, or some other morphosyntactic device. In this sense, the unity of PERF and IMPERF, respectively, is based on its formal marking (barring occasional ambiguities, observed everywhere in human language). The meaning of each aspect can cover a more or less rich spectrum of variants.

B. Each Russian verb form has one out of two precisely defined semantical components, for example 'action seen in its totality – action not seen in its totality'. Then, the unity of PERF and IMPERF respectively, is based on their meaning. In context, this meaning may vary within limits (as does the meaning of most expressions). But there must be a more or less stable and well-defined 'meaning spectrum' for each of the two aspects – a common semantic feature which eventually distinguishes PERF forms from IMPERF forms.

---

[1] I wish to thank Manfred Bierwisch, Larissa Chiriaeva, Bernard Comrie, Hans Kamp, Barbara Partee, Clive Perdue, Rudolf Ružička, Sabine Stoll, Tolja Strigin and two anonymous reviewers for their help.

Note: This article originally appeared as Klein, W. (1995). A time-relational analysis of Russian aspect. Language 71(4). 669–695.

Ideally, unity of formal marking and of specific semantical components should go together in the definition of a category. This is rarely found in human language.² In the following section, we shall examine what the rich literature on Russian aspect says about the formal and semantical definition of the two aspects. There is largely agreement on the morphological facts. In 2.1, we shall concentrate on these basic facts, only briefly mentioning controversial points. As for the semantic side, opinions are somewhat more at variance; in 2.2, we shall consider the three best-known characterisations.

2 Convential wisdom

2.1 The morphological facts

The picture emerging from the rich literature is not entirely uniform. But some details aside, there is a certain consensus about the basic facts. The following summary is based on Isačenko (1968). We give the essentials in the form of three key rules, with some specified exceptions.³

---

2 In fact, the situation is more complicated. In many languages, for example, a particular case is neither uniform with respect to form nor with respect to meaning. Latin genitive, for example, has no fixed meaning, and its morphological marking is highly variable. We cannot say that it is always marked by a *-i* or by *-is* or *-ae*, nor can we say that it is defined by the fact that it expresses 'possession' (or whatever other semantic feature). What renders the genitive a uniform category, is primarily the fact that it is systematically governed by other forms, such as verbs, adjectives, or prepositions: *uti* requires the genitive, just as *cupidus*, in whatever way this genitive may be marked. In other words, the unit of a category can also be based on a constant grammatical function, such as government. But such a proposal has never explicitly been made for Russian aspect, although the two aspects typically exhibit a somewhat different behaviour within the sentence. In particular, it is usually said that the present tense form of the PERF has a future tense meaning, whereas this is not the case for the present form of the IMPERF. Similarly, the interaction of PERF and IMPERF with particular adverbials is different. Whereas such criteria are in practice often used as an argument to assign a particular verb form to either the one or the other aspect, the aspect definition in itself is never based on these differences. Therefore, we shall not deal with this possibility here.
3 There are some other exceptional cases, for example loan words and verbs based on foreign morphemes. But they do not affect the general picture, and are therefore not discussed here. In general, it should be pointed out that the long research tradition on Russian aspect has accumulated an immense stock of facts and observations which is impossible to deal with in a single paper. This article will focus on what I understand to be the core of the problem, the precise definition of the two aspects, and discuss a representative selection of the main problems, leaving aside many interesting but more peripheral issues.

CWI.   Simplex verbs are IMPERF.

Simplex verbs are verb forms without a prefix.[4] There are two exceptions to this basic rule:

CWIa.   A small number (about 30) of simplex verbs are PERF.
CWIb.   A few simplex verbs are ambiguous between PERF and IMPERF.

In what follows, we shall call the imperfective simplex verbs IMPERF-S, and the few perfective simplex verbs, PERF-S.

CWII.   Adding a verbal prefix to a verb form results in a PERF verb form.

There are about 20 such prefixes. The addition of a prefix does not only render (or sometimes keep) the verb PERF, it also has other semantic effects. Three main cases are to be distinguished:

CWIIa.   The verbal prefix modifies the underlying meaning of the verb to which it is applied in a characteristic way – it makes it inchoative, resultative, delimitative, in brief: It modifies the 'manner of action', or, as is often said, it introduces a particular 'Aktionsart'.[5]

CWIIb.   The verbal prefix is 'empty' – i.e., it leaves the meaning of the underlying verb untouched and only modifies its aspect, as in *sdelat'* 'to make' or *pročitat* 'to read'.

This case is rare, and some authors (such as Isačenko 1968) even argue that these derived forms, too, exhibit some modifications, though perhaps weak ones.[6] In what follows, we shall not distinguish between these two cases; both will be labelled PERF-A.

---

[4] This, as anything said here, should be seen from a synchronic perspective. It may well be that from a diachronic point of view, a 'simplex' is compound. For an account of the historical facts, see Regnell (1944).
[5] Note that, in accordance with the Slavist tradition since Agrell (1909), the term 'Aktionsart' is used to refer to 'secondary modifications of a verb content', rather than to verb classifications according to temporal properties in general, as, for example, the Vendler (1963) classification. These secondary modifications can be expressed by prefixes (this is the case in which we are interested here), but also by other means.
[6] For a critical evaluation of this view, see Forsyth (1970: 38–41).

CWIIc.   The prefixed verb has a lexical meaning in its own right which, in the typical case, cannot be compositionally derived from its components.

We shall call verbs of this subclass PERF-D (for 'perfectives forming a derived verb').[7]

CWIII.   Verbs of type PERF-D have an imperfective counterpart, formed by suffixation.

The most important suffix to serve this function is -iv/yv. We shall call this class IMPERF-D (for 'derived imperfective verbs').

If, minor details aside, this picture is correct, then several types of PERF: IMPERF contrasts must be distinguished:
1. Some forms are ambiguous, such as *velet'* 'to command'. This case is atypical, though, and not of particular interest.
2. There are a few pairs IMPERF-S: PERF-S, such as *brosat': brosit'* 'to throw' or *davat': dat'* 'to give'.
3. Some verb forms have no aspectual counterpart (perfectiva tantum and imperfectiva tantum). This case is quite frequent. In other words, whereas it is true that each Russian verb belongs to one of the two aspects, this does not mean that all verbs can be grouped in aspectual pairs.[8]
4. There is a large group PERF-D: IMPERF-D, such as *dokazat: dokazyvat'* 'to prove'. This, again, is a pure aspectual contrast, based on a systematic

---

[7] An exact delimitation between PERF-A and PERF-D is not easy. When should one speak of a 'new verb', and when of an Aktionsart variant of the underlying verb? Isačenko (1968), who insists on a sharp boundary, is forced to make a number of *ad hoc* assignments that are far from being plausible (see, for example, his highly inconsistent argumentation about verbs with the prefix *do-* in 1968: 396).

[8] Sometimes, the opposition IMPERF-S: PERF-A, that is, between a simplex imperfective and one or several perfectives derived from it by prefixation adding a new Aktionsart', is considered to be an aspectual opposition. Then, however, the two 'aspect partners' also differ by meaning features other than the purely aspectual ones. Moreover, the IMPERF partner then often has many PERF counterparts, each of which corresponds to a different Aktionsart'. This is somewhat against the spirit of the notion of a grammatical category; it is if we assumed a tense contrast between a present tense form and some other tense form which, however, does not only differ in time but also with respect to the inherent semantics of the verb. A comparable case in English would be the opposition between *came: was coming in, was coming on, was coming down*. Therefore, we will not adopt this view. (A clear discussion of this problem is found in Forsyth 1970, chapter 3).

morphological process. But its application is confined to verbs of a particular type whose precise boundaries are not easily drawn (cf. footnote 6).

This means that the 'unity of aspect' has no basis in formal marking. The only reason to assume that there are exceptions from Rule CWI is meaning; from a formal point of view, both IMPERF-S and PERF-S, as well as the ambiguous cases, are simplex verbs. In fact, it seems fairly clear that the difference between Russian PERF and IMPERF is only partly grammaticalised (Isačenko 1968: 352), much in contrast to, for example, the English opposition between 'simple form' and '*be-ing*-form', which, with very few exceptions such as *to know, to need*, affects all lexical verbs.

If PERF and IMPERF can be given a uniform definition at all, it must be based on semantic criteria. Which are these criteria? Why are forms such as *dat'* 'to give', *otrezat'* 'to cut off, *perepisat'* 'to cut' unerringly considered to be PERF, whereas *davat'* 'to give', *rezat'* 'to cut', *perepisyvat'* 'to copy' are considered to be IMPERF?

2.2 The semantic characterisation of PERF and IMPERF

There is no generally accepted semantic definition of the Russian aspects. But there have been many attempts to characterise them semantically[9], three of which are particularly prominent. According to the first, PERF presents the action referred to in its totality, whereas IMPERF lacks this feature. This is probably the most common definition. The second definition states that PERF presents the action as 'completed', and IMPERF presents it as 'not completed'. The third definition operates with the notion of a '(inner) boundary': in some way, PERF implies such a boundary, whereas IMPERF does not. These characterisations are not incompatible with each other. In fact, some authors use sometimes the one, sometimes the other.

For all three characterisations, the precise formulation varies from author to author, and often within the writings of a single author. Moreover, most authors also distinguish between the basic semantic opposition as such and various modifications found in particular contexts. In the following discussion, we

---

[9] For a recent survey and a highly critical evaluation of most theories presented to date, see Durst-Anderson (1992: 29–47).

concentrate on the basic opposition (the full spectrum of usages is discussed in Bondarko 1971).[10]

A. The situation[11] is presented in its totality – not in its totality

This characterisation, which goes back to Černy (1877), is by now the dominant definition found in the literature on Russian aspect, shows up in various formulations. We give three characteristic variants:

> Les langues slaves distinguent régulièrement deux aspects du verbe: le perfectif représente l'action dans sa totalité, comme un point, en dehors de tout devenir; l'imperfectif la montre en train de se faire, et sur la ligne du temps [The Slavic languages regularly distinguish two aspects of the verb: the perfective represents the action in its entirety, like a point, beyond any development; the imperfective shows it as it goes on, and on the time axis].
> (Saussure 1917: 161s).

> Der perfektive Aspekt drückt einen Vorgang als ganzheitliches, zusammengefaßtes Geschehen aus, der imperfektive Aspekt läßt dieses Merkmal unausgedrückt [The perfective aspect expresses a process as a holistic, condensed incident, the imperfective aspect leaves this feature unexpressed].   (Isačenko 1968: 350).

> A perfective verb expresses the action as a total event summed up with reference to a single specific juncture.   (Forsyth 1970: 8).

In all of these cases, the IMPERF aspect is the 'negative counterpart' – it lacks the feature of presenting the situation in its totality. This, however, can be understood in two ways. It is either a neutral form – i.e., IMPERF leaves unmarked whether the situation is 'seen in its totality' or not, or it is supposed to express that the situation does not have this feature. Under the first interpretation, the opposition is in a way not PERF: IMPERF but rather PERF: PERF OR IMPERF (where PERF means 'seen in its totality'). The second interpretation, under which IMPERF cannot also have the PERF reading, is the common one, and we shall adopt it here. But authors are not always very explicit in this respect, and occasionally,

---

10 The most comprehensive treatment of the Slavic aspect in general is Galton (1976). Unfortunately, Galton's own definition of the basic aspectual contrast is very general: 'the Slavic languages ... have created special morphological means for the presentation of the temporal succession, in the perfective aspect (pv.), as well as of its contradictory opposite, a state lasting unchanged while other events change; this is done by the imperfective aspect (ipv.).'
11 Following Comrie (1976), we use the word 'situation' as neutral term for events, processes, activities, states, etc.

their formulations also allow the other interpretation according to which IMPERF 'combines' both perspectives.¹²

The characterisations given so far relate specifically to the two Russian aspects PERF and IMPERF. But the same idea is also used in more general definitions of 'perfective' and 'imperfective'. According to Comrie (1976: 3), 'aspects are different ways of viewing the internal temporal constituency of a situation'. The situation may be presented as a whole, without specific reference to its inner constituency ('perfective aspect'), or it may involve a reference to the inner constituency ('imperfective aspect'). In the latter case, there are various ways of doing so, and accordingly, we have different subtypes of the imperfective.

Much the same idea is found in the entry 'Tense and Aspect' (J. Bybee) in the International Encyclopedia of Linguistics (1992):

> ASPECT is not relational like tense; rather, it designates the internal temporal organization of the situation described by the verb. The most common possibilities are PERFECTIVE, which indicates that the situation is to be viewed as a bounded whole, and IMPERFECTIVE, which in one way or another looks inside the temporal boundaries of the situation. [...] These aspects are usually expressed by inflections, auxiliaries, or particles.

The idea that there is some differentiation within IMPERF is also exploited in the literature on Russian aspect (for example in the sense of contextually bounded variants). What is decisive, however, is the fundamental distinction: 'the situation is seen in its totality – not seen in its totality', which will now be critically examined. This distinction is very suggestive: aspects are different ways to 'view' or to 'present' one and the same situation. But it fails on at least two grounds as a satisfactory definition.

1. The characterisation is purely metaphorical, and thus far from being clear. Characteristically, it is accompagnied by spatial and other circumlocutions, such as 'der ... Prozeß liegt geschlossen im Blickfeld des Sprechers [the process as a whole ... is in the speaker's field of vision]' (Ružička 1952: 4), as if the process were a matchbox or the Eiffel tower. A particularly vivid formulation is due to Isačenko (1968: 348). He compares the action described by the verb to a parade which can be seen either from the perspective of a participant or from the perspective of an external observer on the tribune. The former represents the imperfective aspect in which beginning and end

---

12 As we shall see later, both interpretations make perfect sense, but they apply to different verb classes. For what will be called below '1-state verbs', which are always IMPERF, both the 'totality'-reading and the 'non- totality' reading are available, whereas this is not the case for what will be called '2-state verbs'.

are out of view, and the parade cannot be seen in its entirety, whereas the latter, in which the entire action is in view, represents the perfective aspect. Exactly this idea is also found in more recent characterisations, such as Gospodarov's (1990: 195):

> Thus, the use of the Perf. projects a world view according to which a person assumes the position of an external observer who is not immediately involved in the process he describes in the message ... On the other hand, by choosing Imp., the speaker places himself, as it were, inside the very course of the process. The external boundaries are lost from this perspective.

These visual characterisations are highly intuitive. They also makes clear that IMPERF is not considered to be the neutral case, compatible with both perspectives; it rather marks the 'interior perspective'. But they are surely not what one would expect from a precise definition.

2. Suggestive as the totality metaphor in many cases may be, there are a number of very elementary examples in which it does not make much sense. Consider the following example:[13]

(1) Velikan Rodosa vesil$_i$ sto tonn.
     The colossus of Rhodos weighed 100 tons.

The notion that in this case, the situation is, as it were, presented from the inside, in its course, rather than in its totality, seems odd. It is simply a historical fact which is stated here – and this fact is presented in its totality. Note, incidentally, that in English, the progressive form *was weighing 100 tons* would be strange here.[14] In this example, the situation expressed is a singular fact. The same impression obtains for generic facts:

(2) Tridzat' let nazad stoil$_i$ litr piva pjat' kopeek.
     Thirty years ago, a pint of beer cost 5 p.

It is hard to imagine what it should mean here that the situation is presented from the interior, not as a whole, not in its entirety.

---

[13] In the examples, IMPERF is marked by the subsript 'i' and PERF by the subscript 'p', respectively.
[14] In French, only the imparfait, which is often considered to express imperfective aspect, is possible here: *Le colosse de Rhode pesait cent tonnes.* Both the passé simple and the passé composé are distinctly odd.

In the following two cases, the situation is an activity, rather than a – more or less static – fact:

(3) Prošluju noč', Ivan spal$_i$ v komnate dlja gostej.
    Last night, John slept in the guest room.
(4) Včera Severin rabotala$_i$ s dvuch do pjati.
    Yesterday, Sévérine worked from two to five.

In both cases, the Russian verb is IMPERF. It is clear both in 3 and in 4, that the situation is presented in its totality. It is also clear that the situation is bounded and completed – a fact which falsifies the completedness definition of PERF, to be discussed below. It is even difficult to imagine what definitions like 'the activity is shown in its development, from the interior, with special reference to its inner properties, without taking into account its beginning and its end' could mean here. In 4, the boundaries of the situation are even explicitly indicated. Similarly, it is clear that in 3, John's sleep is not described from its interior, as would probably be the case with the English progressive *John was sleeping*. If one had to choose between one of Isačenko's or Gospodarov's spatial metaphors, it would doubtlessly be the position of the external observer which is relevant here – the one which is supposed to represent PERF.

To sum up, the characterisation of the aspects as 'seen in its totality – not seen in its totality' may often reflect a correct intuition – a fact which somehow must be explained -, but it does not provide us with a satisfactory definition of PERF and IMPERF.

B. The situation is presented as completed – not completed

This characterisation which goes back to the eminent Slavist Miklosich (1883: 274) is most popular in textbooks; but it is also found in recent linguistic treatments, such as Fontaine (1983). It is somewhat less metaphorical than the totality-definition, because there are normally relatively clear criteria to distinguish between situations, when they go on and when they are completed (although there remains a strong metaphorical component in the term 'presented as').[15] Nevertheless, it fails on at least two substantial grounds.

---

[15] There is also the problem as to whether 'completed' only means that the action (in the largest sense of the word) is simply over, or whether it is completed according to some inner logic of the action itself. In English, for example, there is a well-known difference between *Chris finished working* and *Chris stopped working*, where in the former case, Chris somehow completed the

1. As was already noted in connection with examples 3 and 4, there are many common usages of IMPERF in which the situation is clearly completed. This is not due to the fact that the situations are in the past and therefore 'over' (a fact which should not matter, anyway, for aspect); the same point can be made for situations in the future:

(5) Zavtra Severin budet rabotat'$_i$/rabotaet$_i$ c dvuch do pjati.
Tomorrow, Séverine will work/works from two to five.

Here, the beginning and end of the situation are even explicitly indicated by the adverbial. The situation is presented as completed at five.[16] Nevertheless, the imperfective is used – a simple consequence of the fact that the verb in question is a simplex verb, without a PERF counterpart with the same lexical meaning.

2. Completion is always relative to a time span (independent of how this time span is related to the time of utterance). If (5) is true, then the situation referred to is completed, for example, at 6 o'clock, and it is not completed at 4 o'clock. Therefore, a statement such that PERF 'presents an action as completed' only makes sense if it means: 'it is presented as completed at some time T'. A speaker who presents some situation as completed does not want to suggest that it was or is completed at any time: It is completed at some time T, as well as at any time thereafter, and is not completed at any time before T. This 'reference point' T need not be made explicit; in particular, how T is related to the time of utterance need not be expressed. But somehow, T must be implied in the utterance. What is this – possibly implicit – time T, at which

---

work he intended to do, whereas in the latter case, his working is simply over and not necessarily 'completed'. Most authors who talk about 'completion' are not very explicit about this point. There is considerable discussion, however, about the closely related question of 'boundary types' or 'limit types' (see, for example, Bondarko 1991: 64-94), a point to which we shall return in the next subsection. The criticism raised below against the 'completedness characterisation' is essentially independent of this distinction. In particular, example 5 can be understood in the sense of 'by which time she will have completed what she intended to do'.

16 One might argue here that, whilst the situation is apparently presented as completed, this is due to the adverbials, rather than to the verb, and this is in agreement with its imperfectivity, as defined here. But then, imperfectivity cannot mean that the situation is presented as non-completed because this immediately leads to a contradiction in the way in which the situation is presented. Such an analysis is compatible, however, with the notion that IMPERF is not confined to any perspective – it simply leaves open in which way the situation is presented, as completed or not, in its totality or not, with or without an inner boundary (as discussed below). As will become clear in section 5, we indeed believe that in some cases, this impression is correct.

the situation is completed? Without an appropriate definition of this notion, the entire characterisation as 'presented as completed – not completed' is hanging in the air.

There is a third weakness of this definition, occasionally referred to in the literature: It gives too much weight to the endpoint of the situation, without taking into consideration its other components, in particular the beginning (Isačenko 1968, Comrie 1976). This is correct but not easily demonstrated. Therefore, we leave it with the two problems mentioned above, each of which seems sufficient to show the inadequacy of this characterisation. Again, however, it should be stressed that the intuitions behind this characterisation are not accidental, and a satisfactory account of aspect must be able to explain them.

C. Presence – absence of an (internal) boundary

This characterisation goes back to Jakobson (1932) and is now used, in one way or the other, by many authors (for example Vinogradov 1947, Timberlake 1984, 1985, Dahl 1985, Bondarko 1987 – partly translated in Bondarko 1991). The following definitions, which are particularly straightforward, are due to Smith (1991): 'The perfective viewpoint ... presents events with both initial and final endpoints.' (301) and 'The temporal schema of the imperfective viewpoint focusses on part of a situation, excluding its initial and final endpoints.' (302). Again, definitions of this sort capture important insights, but there are at least two reasons which render them unsatisfactory.

1. It is common to distinguish between different verb types according to their lexical temporal properties. The best-known example is Vendler's (1957) typology of time schemata as reflected in particular verbs (or verb phrases); but there are many other, much finer classifications (for a recent survey, see Binnick 1991). In most of these typologies, the presence or non-presence of a boundary which is somehow inherent to the situation also plays a role. Thus, Vendler's accomplishments and achievements involve such a boundary, whereas states and activities do not. Now, if the semantics of aspect is defined in terms of 'inner boundary', as well, then the difference between inherent lexical properties of the verb, on the one hand, and aspect, on the other, is entirely confounded. If PERF somehow involves a boundary, then this boundary must be of a different type that the boundary inherent to the lexical content. In Russian, verb pairs such as *dat'* and *davat'* 'to give' or *perepisat'* and *perepisyvat'* 'to copy' are said to have exactly the same lexical meaning; in Vendler's terms, both would be accomplishments, hence involve

some inner boundary. But they differ in aspect. Hence, PERF should add some other, additional boundary. What is this boundary?

2. Consider again some simple examples of the type mentioned above:

(6) Vesnoj 1994 ja rabotal$_i$ v Pariže.
    In the spring of 1994, I worked in Paris.
(7) Včera ja spal$_i$ do obeda.
    Yesterday, I slept till lunchtime.

In both cases, the situation described is bounded. In the first case, the boundary is not explicitly mentioned, but it is clear that it exists, most likely somewhere before the time of utterance. Nevertheless, Russian requires IMPERF here.[17]

This also applies in the second example, where the final boundary is even explicitly mentioned. Therefore, presence or absence of a boundary to the situation cannot be decisive for the choice of an aspect.

Both problems might be accounted for by distinguishing different types of boundaries, for example 'inherent boundaries' versus 'factual boundaries' (or 'actual boundaries'). But a clear definition of these notions is not easily given. The first may be understood to refer to a boundary which is part of the verb's lexical meaning, such as accomplishments or achievements, as compared to states and activities.[18] Then, this cannot be the type of boundary on which the distinction between PERF and IMPERF is based. Thus, it must be the 'actual boundary' which is responsible for aspect. But in the imperfective examples of 6 and 7, there *is* such an actual boundary, and this actual boundary is also reached within the time intervals considered here – in the spring of 1994 and yesterday, respectively.

---

[17] This holds irrespective of whether the work – or the sleep in the following example – has come to a 'natural end', or whether it was interrupted by something external to the 'event' itself.
[18] Breu (1994) gives 'a classification of verb meanings which is determined exclusively by their boundary characteristics.' (24). This classification ranges from 'totally static verbs' such as *to contain, to weigh* to punctual verbs such as *to find, to explode*. About the former, it is said: 'These states of affairs are inalienably connected with their subjects.' (1994: 25). I am not sure, however, whether it is really true that, if my cup contains coffee, this state of affair is inalienably connected to the cup. Similarly, it is surely not an inalienable property of John to weigh 200 pounds, if he happens to weigh 200 pounds. Therefore, it is not plausible when it is argued: 'The totally static verbs (TSTA) ... can never be conceived as a whole owing to the complete lack of boundaries. It follows, therefore, that the Russian TSTA verbs can never be combined with the perfective aspect. Verbs such as *vesit'* 'weigh' ... are therefore imperfectiva tantum.' (1994: 27s). This also neatly illustrates the problems with aspectual definitions such as 'conceived as a whole'.

An exceptionally clear attempt to define an aspectually relevant notion of boundary such that aspectual distinctions can be based on it is found in Timberlake (1984, 1985).[19] Since his analysis also includes a time-relational component and in that respect resembles the analysis suggested in the present paper, I will discuss it in somewhat more detail. Temporal relations are said to obtain between the 'event time' and what Timberlake calls 'the narrative time', the latter being defined as 'the time from which the speaker evaluates the aspectual character of the event' (1984: 36). Based on these temporal relations, three aspects are distinguished, the 'aorist' – the basic configuration of the perfective – and two types of imperfective, called durative and progressive imperfective. In the aorist, 'narrative time includes both the event time (it is an actual temporal limit) and the inherent limit (it is a limit on the potential realization of the predicate).' (1984:37). The difference between the two imperfectives 'lies in the relationship between the event time and the narrative time. In the progressive the narrative time falls within the event time ... In the durative configuration the narrative time includes the event time.' (1984: 37/8). In terms of temporal relations, therefore, the perfective goes with the durative imperfective (for both, the narrative time includes the event time), whereas the progressive imperfective is characterised by the opposite relation. What discriminates between perfective and durative imperfective, is whether an 'inherent limit' – in contrast to an 'actual limit' – is reached within the narrative time. Limits are defined in terms of functions (called 'predicate functions' or 'histories') which assign states or processes (called 'situations') to time intervals. Suppose such a predicate function assigns situation s_n to time t_n for a given (narrative) world. Then, the pair (s_n, t_n) is an actual limit if s_n is not assigned by the predicate function to any time interval t after tn in that world. It is an inherent limit when there is no possible world such that the predicate function assigns s_n to any time interval t after t_n. In a nutshell, at an actual limit, the situation ends but could go on, and at an inherent limit, it ends and could not go on.

There are two problems with this idea. First, an actual limit, as defined here, would not just mean that some state or process no longer obtains but also that it could not obtain again (since t is any time interval after the limit); this is not very plausible. When John's sleeping comes to an end yesterday at seven o'clock, then it should not be excluded that he sleeps again at some later time (although there

---

19 The two papers slightly differ in terminology (as well as in their general aim), but the approach is essentially the same. Both papers, incidentally, give convincing arguments that an analysis of the Russian tense-aspect system purely in terms of the three Reichenbach-parameters R, S and E does not work.

is surely a last sleep for everybody). Second, if John's copying a letter comes to an end at some time, say yesterday at ten, then the perfective would be appropriate: *Ivan perepisal' pis'mo* 'Ivan copied a/the letter'. But innumerable worlds are imaginable in which he is still busy doing this yesterday at eleven o'clock. It is not logically excluded that he does it after the boundary. But quantification about all possible worlds states exactly this.

Therefore, I believe that this important attempt to give clearer shape to the notion of boundary does not work, as it stands. But it reflects an important insight: It is not the existence of a boundary in the real (or narrated) world which matters but whether the action 'could go on' after this boundary. But this 'could go on/not go on' cannot be simply reconstructed by quantification about possible worlds. It has to do with which meaning components are packed into the lexical content of the expression to which aspectual marking applies. In a way, the content of the verb (or some larger expresssion) must say: at some time yes, and at some later time no. This will be discussed in the following sections.

In conclusion, none of the common semantic characterisations found in the literature is satisfactory.[20] But they cover important intuitions which any attempt to characterise the difference must preserve in one way or the other. In the following sections, we will try to give a definition which meets this requirement. This definition is strictly time-relational: it defines both aspects in terms of temporal relations such as 'before, after, contained in, overlapping', which obtain between particular time spans. It has two essential components, both of which are justifiable on independent grounds. The first is rather a prerequisite of the aspect definition proper. A distinction is made between verb contents (and lexical contents in general) which express one state only, and those which combine two partly opposing states. This evokes the old distinction between 'atelic' and 'telic' event types, but it is given a somewhat different turn here. Second, it is argued that a difference has to be made between the time at which

---

20 There are some approaches in the literature which operate with one of the three common oppositions and complement it by some other factor or factors. Thus, Thelin (1978, 1990) uses a feature [± TOTALITY], which gives the basic aspectual contrast, and an additional feature [± TIME] which relates to the particular temporal embedding of the action in the discourse context: some situations are not related to the time axis at all (and a special case of IMPERF in Russian), and the totality – non-totality distinction applies only to those which are linked to the time axis. A similar idea is found in Leinonen (1982). Her basic opposition between 'Totality' and 'Non-Totality' is complemented by the concept of 'temporal localisation', which is used to subdifferentiate between the various aspects). In the present context, we cannot deal with these differentiations, but it should be clear that the core distinction is subject to the same problems discussed above.

the situation described by an utterance obtains, on the one hand, and the time for which *a particular assertion is made in this very utterance,* on the other. Aspect is a temporal relation between these two time spans. Depending on whether the lexical content used to describe the situation is of 1-state type or of 2-state type, the ensuing result is somewhat different. In what follows, this idea will be worked out.

3 Lexical content

3.1 Properties of situations vs properties of the lexical content

It will be useful to start with a distinction which is in a way trivial, but all too often ignored. We may state it as follows:

(8) One thing is the content of a sentence, another thing is the situation to which this sentence, when uttered, refers and which is selectively described by its content.

Consider a sentence such as 9, uttered on some particular occasion:

(9) Einstein analysed something.

It refers to a particular situation, which is said to have obtained in the past. This situation has numerous properties only some of which are selectively described by 9. It is not indicated what the 'something' is (perhaps a bill). Similarly, the situation has some duration, as well as a place where it occurs (relative as these notions may be in Einstein's world). But nothing is said about these and many other properties of the situation referred to. Thus, we must sharply distinguish between the properties of a situation, to which an utterance refers, on the one hand, and the properties of the content of the sentence which is used to describe this situation, on the other.

In interpreting an utterance such as 9, the listener or reader can draw on two sources of information: On various types of contextual knowledge, such as situation information, information from previous utterances, general world knowledge, on the one hand, and on what is 'in the words', on the other. This latter information I will call 'lexical content'. It results from the lexical meaning of the elementary components and they way in which they are put together.[21] A speaker who sets out to refer to some situation will normally select only some of its properties and make those explicit by an appropriate choice of lexical items and by the way in which they are put together. In other words, the content of a sentence is a selective or partial description of a situation. Thus, the situation itself has many more properties than are made explicit by the sentence content. Some of those can be inferred by the listener due to other knowledge sources, others remain entirely implicit.

I dwell on this quite trivial point, since it demonstrates that 'situation types' – for example, whether they are bounded or not – is one thing, and the inherent temporal features of the lexical content of verbs (or larger constructions) is quite a different thing. When it is said that a lexical content[22] such as <Einstein analyse something> does not involve a boundary – in contrast to, for example, <Einstein discover something> -, then this can only mean that nothing is made explicit about beginning and end of the situation referred to. It cannot mean that the situation is of a type which does not have boundaries. Normally, any situation of this type has boundaries (although only context and world knowledge tell us something about them). If there is need, these boundaries can be made explicit, for example by the addition of appropriate adverbials. The following two utterances can well be used to describe one and the same bounded situation:

(10) Séverine worked.
(11) Séverine worked from two to five.

The difference is only that in 10, the boundaries are left implicit, and in 11, they are spelled out. In the second case, this information is part of the lexical content

---

[21] Note that lexical content, as this term is used here, is not just the meaning of 'lexical items'. It is that part of the meaning of some expression, be this expression simple or complex, which stems from the lexicon and the compositional rules of the language – in contrast to any meaning contribution stemming from other knowledge sources, in particular the context in which this expression is used, and world knowledge of the interlocutors. Thus, the lexical content <next spring> of the expression *next spring* results from the application of the lexical content of *next* to the lexical content of *spring*, and the resulting entire lexical content <next spring> is – roughly speaking – 'in the spring which is contained in the year which follows the year which contains the time of utterance'. Used in a particular context, for example in an utterance made on May 24, 1994, this lexical content serves to refer to some subinterval of spring 1995.
[22] In what follows, I shall note the lexical content of a – simple or compound – expression xxx by putting it (in its infinitival form) in pointed brackets <xxx>.

of the entire sentence, in the first case, it is not. The same point illustrated here for boundaries can equally made for many other properties of a situation.

Verb contents – as an essential part of the entire lexical content of a sentence – never specify such a boundary. Nevertheless, we have the clear intuition that there is somehow a clear difference in this respect between, for example, <sleep> and <fall asleep>, <dormir> and <s'endormir>, <schlafen> and <einschlafen>. This intuitive difference and its reasons will be discussed in the next section.[23]

3.2 0-state, 1-state, 2-state contents

Each of the following two utterances relates to a situation in the past:

(12) It was raining.
(13) Chris was sleeping.

In both cases, world knowledge tells us that the time of situation – abbreviated here as T-SIT – has a beginning and an end, hence is bounded, although the lexical contents <rain> and <Chris sleep> do not say anything about these boundaries. There are also lexical contents which normally exclude the possibility of a beginning and an end of the situation which they describe, such as <seven be a prime number> or <John be the son of a widow>. A situation, described by such a lexical content, either obtains without temporal boundaries or not at all:

(14) Seven is a prime number.
(15) John was the son of a widow.

---

[23] The fact that lexical contents such as <Georg sleep on the guestbed> or <Einstein close the window> by themselves contain no information about duration, frequency, or position on the temporal axis has a number of interesting consequences. Thus, they can be used, for example, to describe a situation where whatever they describe obtains once, sometimes, or even regularly – the frequency is simply not specified. It is wrong to assume that utterances such as *Georg slept on the gues-tbed* or *Einstein closed the window* refer to one such occurrence of sleeping on the guest-bed or closing the window. This is only a special case – perhaps the one we first think of. But they can also be used to refer to a situation whose time contains many of Georg's sleeps on the guest-bed or many closings of the window by the eminent physicist. Nothing in the utterance says anything about the frequency, and whether we give it a single-case reading or not, depends on context.

Therefore, it is useful to distinguish between lexical contents which describe situations which are normally[24] limited in time, and others for which this is not the case. Those of the former type, we will call 1-state contents, and those of the latter type, 0-state contents (or 'atemporal contents').[25] In the examples above, this distinction applies to the content of entire sentences. It may already be found in the content of its parts, in particular in the verb content. Then we shall speak of 1-state verbs or 0-state verbs, respectively. In what follows 0-state contents will not be systematically discussed since they are not directly relevant to the problem of Russian aspect.[26]

A situation described by a 1-state content is, as it were, surrounded by situations in which this state does not obtain – by its negative counterparts. In 12, T-SIT is followed and preceded by a situation describable by <not rain>. Similarly, in 13 T-SIT is followed and preceded by situations describable by <Chris not sleep>. A speaker might now want to speak about a longer interval which includes, first, a situation at which it rains, and then its negative counterpart – the subsequent (or preceding) situation at which it does not rain. This is always possible in the case of 1-state contents, and never in the case of 0-state contents. In doing so, the speaker has normally several options, the simplest of which is to describe each situation by a separate sentence, perhaps with the addition of appropriate adverbials which indicate the intended order:

(16) First, it was raining, and then, it was not raining.
(17) First, Chris was sleeping, and then, he was not sleeping.

The lexical content of 17 has then two parts, <first, Chris sleep> and <then, Chris not sleep>. The first part describes the *source state* (abbreviated SS) of the

---

[24] I say 'normally' because it is often possible to give a somewhat derived interpretation to an 'atemporal' lexical content.

[25] There are also lexical contents which are used to describe situations which are supposed to have a beginning, but no end (or vice versa), such as <Caesar be dead>. If there is need, they can be labelled '1-sided 1-state contents'.

[26] This does not mean that this distinction is irrelevant in general. Thus, the English perfect cannot be applied to 0-state contents. We can say, as in 15, *John was the son of a widow* but not **John has been the son of a widow*. Note, further, that there is a difference between examples like 14 and examples like 15. In the former case, the situation as such exists forever. In the latter case, the situation is in a way restricted to 'John's time', more precisely, by the birth of John. We would not say that the situation expressed by 15 already obtained before he was born. Therefore, it would be more accurate to say, that <be the son of a widow> is a 0-state property of John, but <John be the son of a widow> in itself is not 0-state but 1-state. Again, we shall not follow up this point here since it does not play an important role for Russian aspect.

entire complex situation (consisting of two subsituations), and the second part describes its *target state* (abbreviated TS), and when put together, as in 17, they describe a change of state from to SS to TS.

In these examples, the description of the two states is distributed over two sentences. Most languages also provide their speakers with various possibilities to express both states within a single simple sentence. In this case, the change of state is 'packed' into a smaller expression – not necessarily a single word, though. The degree of 'condensation' or 'integration', the 'package density', may vary, and languages have quite different preferences here. We list some of the most important possibilities:

A. Two clauses. SS and TS are each described by a full clause content. This case, illustrated by 17 and 18, has the weakest 'package density'.
B. Two verbs. The lexical verb is enriched by another lexical verb, each of them representing one of the two states, as in *to set out to work, to stop working, to intend to work, to regret having worked*. The 'higher verb' may relate to either the SS or the TS. Moreover, it may simply express that there is another state, in addition to the one expressed by the 'lower verb', or it may characterise this additional state in a particular way.[27]
C. Verb complements. The English verb *to walk* is a 1-state verb. It is possible, however, to add a description of a target position in form of a complement, for example by *into the room*, as in *John was walking into the room*. Note that the adverbial does not describe the place of the entire action, nor the position of John in general, but his position in the target state (independent of whether he ever reaches this target state or not).
D. Detachable verb particles. Compared to C, this is further step towards higher integration. In English, the 1-state verb *to fall* may be enriched by the particle *down*, and the resulting lexical content <to fall down> includes two states, one of them something like moving towards the center of gravity, and the other characterising the target position. We often observe that a particle 'bleaches'. In *John fell down*, it is clear that John is down in TS (independent of whether he ever reaches this position or not). In *John ate his dinner up*,

---

[27] Language development often leads to a certain bleaching of the particular semantic contribution of the 'higher verb', such that, eventually, it only marks the state before or after. A well-known example is the French construction with *aller*, as in *aller dormir*, lit. 'to go to sleep'. Originally, the SS was characterised by a proper movement (and the construction can still be used in this sense). But now, this particular meaning component is often lost, as in *Nestor allait se lever*, and then, the entire construction expresses something like a 'prospective': At the given time, Nestor was in the source state of getting up.

neither the dinner nor John are supposed to be in a spatial position 'up'. The construction is no longer compositional.

E. Prefixes, suffixes, infixes. This case is particularly frequent in German, with examples such as *blühen, erblühen, verblühen* 'to blossom, flower, wither'. In these examples, the construction is compositional, but there are also cases which are either not compositional or only in some usages. It is this strongly integrated way to bundle two states in one morphologically complex word which plays a primordial role for Russian aspect, and we shall come back to this point shortly.

F. Simple verbs. It also occurs that SS and TS are packed into one simple verb lexeme. An English example is *to die* with the lexical content <SS: to be alive, TS: to be not alive>.[28]

These are not the only possibilities for packing two opposing states into the lexical content of a – single or complex – expression, but they seem to be the most important ones. It has also been noted already that the transition between them is continuous and that within each possibility, several degrees of compositionality can be distinguished.[29]

Verbs, simple or complex, whose lexical content includes two distinct states in this sense, will be called '2-state verbs'. It is important to distinguish carefully between lexical content which express a boundary (or two boundaries) and 2-state expressions. Consider again examples 10 and 11 above. They can be used to describe one and the same situation. In both cases, this situation by itself is bounded. In the first case, the lexical content <Séverine work> expresses no boundary, in the second, the lexical content of the verb <work> does not either, but the entire lexical content <Séverine work from two to five> makes 'the endpoints visible'. Still, it is no 2-state content including a source state and a target state. The lexical content of 11 does not explicitly mark that after the first, bounded state of her working, there is a second state where she does not work. When a situation including a final boundary is described by a 1-state expression, then nothing is explicitly asserted about what is the case after that boundary. In 11, there is a strong pragmatic implicature that after the final boundary, she no longer works –

---

[28] Here, as everywhere in language, we might face some instances of ambiguity, i.e., a verb can have a 1-state reading as well as a 2-state reading (just as it can have a 0-state reading and a 1-state reading). So long as this is the exceptional case, it does no harm.

[29] Languages vary in their preferences for the possibilities A – F. The first is found in all languages, the second in all languages with finite verbs. In French, E is rare, and D is virtually non-existent. In English, E is rare, too, but D is very frequent, in all degrees of lexicalisation. In German, D and E are quite common. In Russian, D does not exist, but E is extremely common.

but it is in no way contradictory to assume that she did. In an appropriate context, the implicature can be cancelled. Suppose that all people who do not work for at least three hours a day are fired. Then, someone could easily say *Well, she worked from two to five, in fact, she even worked until six, and that is more than needed.* Normally, one would not say that she worked from two to five, if in fact she worked from two to six, just as one would not say that she had two beers when in fact, she had eleven. But the reasons are purely pragmatic. A 2-state expression, by contrast, includes, in its lexical content, first a state where she is working, and then a state where she is not working. Nothing is said about the boundary between those states – although at some time, the first state is over, and this is why we have the impression that these expressions somehow have an 'inherent boundary'.

3.3 Simple verbs, prefix verbs, and secondary imperfectivisation in Russian

In Russian, morphological variation of a simple verb is quite common. It is plausible, therefore, to relate this variation to the difference between 1-state contents and 2-state contents. The basic rules of lexical content correspond to the rules CWI – CWIII from section 2.1. We label them SI – SIII, respectively:

SI. Simple verbs express 1-state contents.
SII. Prefixation results in a 2-state content.
SIII. Adding a so-called 'imperfective suffix' to a 2-state verb marks its source state as 'distinguished state' for aspect marking.

These rules require some comments. As was indicated in connection with CWI, Rule SI has a number of exceptions: there are some simple verbs which are 2-state, such as *dat'*$_p$ 'to give', and there are some ambiguous cases. Therefore, a more comprehensive treatment would have to cover these expections, as well.

As for SII, its primary effect is to turn a 1-state verb into a 2-state verb. Moreover, the prefix normally adds other meaning components, ranging from giving a particular 'flavour' to one of the two states to creating a completely new 2-state verb, whose meaning cannot be compositionally derived from the original simplex verb. The additional state can be a source state, as in 'inchoative' *zakričat'*$_p$ with the lexical content <SS: not cry, TS: cry>, whereas the simplex *kričat'*$_i$ simply includes one state <cry>. It can also be a target state, as in *pročitat'*$_p$ with the lexical content <SS: read, TS: not read>.

The case is more complex in examples such as *počitat'*$_p$ whose lexical content can be rendered as <SS: to read for x time, TS: not read>. How long 'for x time' is, can be made explicit by an adverbial or simply left to context. The crucial point here is, that the addition of the prefix does not just add a special 'Aktionsart' – it also adds the component 'and then no longer' to the entire lexical content of the underlying simple verb. There are many possibilities in which prefixation may affect the lexical content of the simplex verb above and beyond turning them into 2-state verbs. This is a matter of individual lexical analysis, which we will not go into here (see, for example, Isačenko 1968: 385-418, and Forsyth 1970: 20-30).[30]

Rule SIII applies to a selected subclass of the prefixed verbs – roughly those which are not just an 'Aktionsart modification' but a new word. As was mentioned in footnote 7 above, the borderline between these two cases is somewhat fuzzy, though. In contrast to SII, SIII does not change the lexical content. It does not 'remove' a state from the entire lexical content, in the way that SII adds one. It simply marks that only the first of the two states, called here 'distinguished state', counts for aspect scope (this will be explained in section 4 below). Thus, *perepisyvat'*$_i$ 'to copy' still includes two states (roughly 'to copy and then not to copy'), just as *davat'*$_i$ 'to give' includes two states; but the second of those states falls not in the scope of the assertion time (in a sense to be made precise below). In this respect, its effect is comparable – though not identical[31] – to the transition from English *to die* to *to be dying*. The former encompasses minimally[32] the lexical content <SS: to be alive, TS: to be dead>. To this lexical content, the morphologically complex formation of the 'progressive form' assigns its first state: *to be dying* means roughly 'to be in the source state of the 2-state verb *to die*'. A still closer analogy – no perfect parallelism, though – is the English series of verb forms *to write – to write up – to be writing up*, on the one hand, and the Russian series *pisat'*$_i$ – *perepisat'*$_p$ – *perepisyvat'*$_i$. The first element is 1-state verb, the second a 2-state form, formed by adding a detachable particle in English and a prefix in Russian (with somewhat different meaning modifications in the two cases), and

---

30 It is also possible that prefixation operates on a 2-state verb, in which case it again modifies the meaning to some extent, the result still being a 2-state content.
31 The comparison between 'secondary imperfectivisation' and 'progressive form' should only illustrate the nature of the former. There are also some clear differences. In particular, the former cannot be applied to 1-state contents, as is the case with the English progressive, for example in *to be sleeping*.
32 We say 'minimally' because it is not excluded that one of these states is to be characterised by aditional semantic properties. Thus, there is good reason to assume that the source state is not sufficiently described by <be alive> but also carries some feature like <being in bad shape, with fading vis vitalis>, or whatever. This, again, is a matter of detailed lexical analysis and not directly relevant to the point made here.

the third element is again a 2-state verb whose target state is not in the scope of aspect.

Rules SI-III describe lexical properties of the verb. These properties are the basis for the aspect distinction – they are not this distinction itself. In particular, they cannot explain the intuitions discussed in section 2.2 – for example the fact that PERF somehow given the impression that the situation is presented in its totality, or as bounded. This is only possible when we look at the precise way in which concrete utterances with a finite verb are related to the situation which their lexical content selectively describes.

4 A time-relational analysis of aspect

4.1 Time of utterance, time of situation, time of assertion

Consider the following three utterances, made on the same occasion:

(18) a. Ivan rabotal$_i$ v Moskve.
Ivan worked in Moscow.
b. Ivan rabotaet$_i$ v Moskve.
Ivan works in Moscow.
c. Ivan budet rabotat'$_i$ v Moskve.
Ivan will work in Moscow.

The situations to which they refer are described by the same lexical content <Ivan work in Moscow>. This does not mean, of course, that the situations as such are identical in every respect. Minimally, they differ by the time at which they obtain – the 'time of situation', henceforth abbreviated T-SIT.

Most grammarians assume that the tense marking of the verb indicates how T-SIT (the 'event time') is related to the time of utterance TU. The standard analysis for Russian tense (in the case of imperfective verbs such as *rabotat'*$_i$) then says:

(19) past tense form T-SIT BEFORE TU
present tense form T-SIT SIMULTANEOUS TO TU (or CONTAINS TU)
future tense form T-SIT AFTER TU

This analysis is found in virtually all grammars. It is easy to see that it is false. Utterance 18a is quite appropriate when Ivan is still working in Moscow, that is, when T-SIT CONTAINS TU, rather than precedes it. But if it precedes it, it cannot contain it, and vice versa. Similarly, 18c is not false when Ivan is already working in Moscow at the time of utterance, hence, when T-SIT CONTAINS TU, rather than follows it – a function which is normally assigned to the present tense form. Therefore, it can be said without any contradiction:

(20) Ivan rabotal$_i$, rabotaet$_i$ i budet rabotat'$_i$ v Moskve.
Ivan worked, works, and will work in Moscow.

If the past tense form indeed expressed that 'the event' precedes the 'moment of speech', or, in our terminology, that T-SIT is before TU, then it cannot contain TU, let alone be simultaneous with it. What is really expressed by the past tense form, is rather, that some *subinterval* of T-SIT is before TU. It is only for this subinterval that the speaker makes a statement. Whether the rest of T-SIT is before TU or not, is simply left open: the speaker makes no assertion whatsoever to this effect. The same is true, in the opposite direction, for the future tense form. Hence, a distinction must be made between the time of the situation, on the one hand, and the time for which an assertion is made, on the other. The latter time we call 'assertion time', abbreviated T-AST.[33] Hence, three time spans play a role for the definition of tense and aspect: TU – the utterance time, T-SIT – the time at which the situation obtains, and T-AST – the time for which the assertion is made (or, as one might say, to which the assertion is confined). T-SIT and T-AST may coincide, of course, but they need not. The speaker may simply not know for how long the situation obtained, or may know it but prefer to make an assertion about some other time related to the situation time.

The distinction between T-SIT and T-AST allows us to give a more appropriate definition of tense:

---

33 If tense is a temporal relation between the time of utterance and the time for which an assertion is made, then there is an apparent problem here, since not all utterances make an assertion. Questions or imperatives, for example, do not. In the former case, this is not so very much of a problem because there is still an assertion 'at issue', which is time-bound, and the assertion itself is only made in the answer. The 'time of assertion' need not necessarily be the time for which the assertion is *made*; in more general terms, it is the time for which an assertion is either made or made an issue. The case is more tricky in imperatives. A complete account will have to replace the notion of 'assertion time' by the more general notion of FIN time in combination with an assertion operator with certain scope properties. Under special conditions, this assertion operator is replaced by some other operator (cf. section 4.3 below). For a discussion of how cases other than assertions should be handled, see Klein (1994, chapter 11). There, the notion "topic time" was used, i.e., the time talked about.

(21) Tense is a temporal relation between TU and T-AST.

This gives us the correct readings for 18a-c, and it explains why 20 is in no way contradictory. But it cannot explain why we normally have the impression that tense somehow relates the situation itself temporally to the deictic center. This is explained by the fact that T-AST and T-SIT, in turn, are temporally related to each other. In the examples 18a and 18c, T-AST is a subinterval of T-SIT: the relation is proper inclusion. But this is not the only possibility. It is also imaginable that T-AST contains T-SIT, that T-AST precedes T-SIT, or that T-AST follows T-SIT. I assume that it is these varying temporal relations between T-AST and T-SIT which are expressed by aspect marking. Thus, aspect is a temporal relation between the time of the situation, as described by the lexical content of an utterance, and the time for which an assertion is made by this utterance, in brief:

(22) Aspect is a temporal relation between T-SIT and T-AST.

Languages vary in the way in which they differentiate between these temporal relations, in particular in the way in which temporal relations are 'bundled' into different forms. Thus, the aspectual differentiation encoded by Russian PERF and IMPERF is one particular way to express two such relationships, related but not identical to the English difference between simple forms and progressive forms.

Defining the temporal relationship between T-AST and T-SIT is simple in the case of 1-state contents: the time for which the assertion is made is contained in, follows, precedes etc. the time of the situation, for example the time of Ivan's working. This is much more complicated in the case of 2- state expressions, where the situation described contains two mutually exclusive subintervals: a subinterval which corresponds to the source state, and another subinterval which corresponds to the target state. We shall call these subintervals T-SS and T-TS, respectively. Which one of these is treated on a par with the single state in the case of 1-state contents? Languages may vary in what they consider to be this 'distinguished state' for aspectual marking. Thus, the distinguished state (abbreviated DS) is (a) the only state of 1-state contents, and (b) either the source state or the target state of 2-state contents, depending on the particular language.

If we assume that English treats the source state as DS, we have a very simple definition of the English aspectual system (T-DS is the time of DS; the POSTTIME of T-DS is simply the time after T-DS):[34]

(23) Perfect form   T-AST AFTER T-DS
     Progressive form   T-AST IN T-DS
     Simple form   T-AST OVL T-DS AND T-AST OVL POSTTIME OF T-DS

In simple prose: the perfect form marks that the time for which an assertion is made is after the single state of a 1-state verb (*John has worked in London*) and after the source state of a 2-state verb (*John has closed the window*). The progressive form marks that the asssertion time is a proper subinterval of either the single state (*John was working in London*) or of the source state of a 2-state expression (*John was closing the window*). The simple form, finally, marks that the time for which the assertion overlaps with the single state and the time thereafter (*John worked in London*) or, in the case of 2- state expressions, the source state and the target state (*John closed the window*). In all of the examples, T-AST itself is before the time of utterance, as indicated by tense. There are a few lexical verbs and normally the copula, in which the simple form additionally assumes the function of the progressive form.

Note that a perfect form, such as *John has worked in London* does not say that T-AST is after the time of John's working but after the time of John's working in London, i.e. the aspectual marking has scope over the entire lexical content <John work in London> and not just over <John work>. The importance of this distinction becomes clear with examples such as **John has been dead* vs. *John has been dead for two weeks*. The first utterance says that John is right now in the time after being dead – which is odd (at least for the small minority of people who do not believe in resurrection), whereas the second utterance says that he is right now in the time after being dead for two weeks, for example in the third week after his death.

---

[34] In what follows, we shall use some abbreviations for temporal relations (all of these can be precisely defined – see, for example, Klein 1994, chapter 4 –, but for present purposes, we only give informal definitions; a and b are time intervals, not points):

    a AFTER b :   a is fully after b
    a IN b :   a is fully included in b
    a OVL b :   a and b overlap, i.e. they have a common subinterval.

As usual, we allow Boolean operations on these, such as 'a AFTER b OR a IN b', which means that a cannot be before b, or 'a NOT OVL b', which means that a and b must be disjoint.

4.2 The meaning of Russian perfective and imperfective aspect

In Russian, the aspects, too, express temporal relations between the time for which an assertion is made, on the one hand, and the time of the situation, on the other. But there are two differences. The first one concerns the definition of the distinguished state. In Russian, DS is (a) the only state for 1-state expressions, and (b) the source state of 2-state expressions, if this is explicitly marked (cf. rule SIII above).[35] Second, PERF and IMPERF bundle the possible temporal relations in a somewhat different way than English. The background is the distribution of 1-state verbs and 2-state verbs, as described by rules SI – SIII above. We then have:

(24) 1. PERF   T-AST OVL T-SS AND T-AST OVL T-TS
      2. IMPERF   T-AST OVL T-DS AND T-AST NOT OVL T-TS

We again give an informal paraphrase. The perfective is characterised by the fact that the time for which an assertion is made has a common subinterval with the source state as well as with the target state.[36] Since this is only possible for 2-state verbs, 1-state verbs are automatically IMPERF.[37] In the imperfective, the assertion time must have a common subinterval with the distinguished state, and it must not have a common subinterval with the target state. The DS is either the single state, or the source state when marked as such by rule SIII. Nothing is said on how precisely T-AST should overlap with T-DS: T-AST can be included T-DS, simultaneous to it, and even contain it – provided, of course, that there is no overlap with a target state. Hence, IMPERF is much wider in its range of applications than, for example, the English progressive form which requires T-AST to

---

[35] Thus, in English, every source state counts as distinguished state, whereas in Russian, this status has to be explicitly marked; there is no difference for 1-state expressions; they always count as distinguished state. Incidentally, another way to look at the English facts would be to say that the morpheme *-ing* is simply a marker of the distinguished state, which applies to 1-state as well as to 2-state verbs (except the copula and some stative expressions). But this is a matter of how the English morphology should be analysed and is beyond our present concern.

[36] Forsyth (1970; 74-76) discusses a number of examples in which perfective verbs function like the English perfect. Such a reading could easily be included in the definition of PERF by omitting the first clause, which requires a common subinterval of assertion time and time of the source state. Thus, the definition of IMPERF would simply be: T-AST NOT OVL T-TS. But since these cases seem atypical, the more restrictive definition given here is perhaps preferable.

[37] This corresponds to an observation made by several authors, namely that states and activities (in the Vendlerian sense) are regularly IMPERF (see, for example, Brecht 1984).

be properly contained in the source state or the single state, respectively. This is in accordance with the traditional view that the Russian IMPERF is somehow a 'neutral', 'unmarked' form.

This explains why it is possible (and even necessary) to say *Velikan Rodosa vesil 100 tonn* with the imperfective form (cf. example 1 in section 1 above), whereas in English, it is odd to say *The colossos of Rhodos was weighing 100 tons* with the progressive form; this would really give an 'interior perspective'. In Russian, 1-state verbs can have an 'interior perspective', but they need not. Therefore, they sometimes correspond to the English progressive, and sometimes, they don't.

4.3 PERF, IMPERF, and verb forms

Aspect is basically a temporal restriction on what is asserted. In a nutshell, the definitions in 24 say this:
- in the PERF aspect, the assertion extends over the source state and the target state;
- in the IMPERF aspect, the assertion only affects the distinguished state, that is, the only state in 1-state expressions, and the source state in 2-state expressions.

In Indo-european languages, an assertion is normally made by a finite (non-subordinate) clause. The non-finite, lexical form of a verb does not involve an assertion. Nevertheless, every Russian speaker 'knows' that a non-finite verb form such as *davat'* 'to give', *čitat'* 'to read', *perepyisyvat'* 'to copy' belong to the IMPERF aspect, whereas *dat'*, *pro itat'*, *perepisat'*, belong to PERF aspect: it is part of his or her *lexical knowledge*. They can only be used to mark either the one or the other assertion scope. The most straightforward way to describe this knowledge is to assume that each lexical entry of a verb has a feature which we will call here [± p]. This feature need not be individually learned. To a large extent, it is predictable from the morphological form of the entry. This is what the rules SI-SIII describe; we can interpret them as lexical redundancy rules. A somewhat more straightforward way to formulate this lexical knowledge is as follows:

(25) 1. Each lexical verb in Russian is either [+p] or [−p], unless it belongs to a limited list of 'ambiguous entries'.
   2. Each lexical verb in Russian is [+p], unless:

(a) it is morphologically simple and does not belong to a limited list of exceptions, or
(b) it is marked by the suffix -*iv/yv* (and perhaps some other affixes, not to be discussed here).

The feature [± p] is simply a property of lexical entries. It is not to be confused with the aspect itself. The aspectual differentiation comes into play as soon as the lexical verb becomes part of a finite construction. Then, the 'temporal scope of assertion' is different, depending on whether the verb form is [+p] or [−p]. The effect of finiteness is to assign a set of 'finiteness times' to the situation described by the utterance. The way in which this is done follows naturally from the definition of the two aspects:

(26) 1. If a finite verb is [+p], then its set of finiteness times P is {t: t OVL T-SS AND t OVL T-TS}.
2. If a finite verb is [−p], then its set of finiteness times I is {t: t OVL T-DS and t NOT OVL T-TS}.

In the case considered here, these finiteness times are the potential assertion times of the utterance[38]. It is important to note that finiteness as such does not fix a particular assertion time; it only determines the type of assertion time in relation to the entire time of the situation. If the language in question also has tense marking, then this again narrows down the possible assertion time, for example to those which precede the time of utterance (in the past tense).

Consider now an utterance such as 27:

(27) Ivan čital₁ knigu.
John read a/the book.

---

[38] If no assertion is made by the utterance, the basic aspectual mechanism is exactly the same, but the finiteness times will have a different interpretation than 'assertion times'. This interpretation depends on the particular type of utterance; in imperatives, it may be the time for which the obligation expressed by the imperative is meant to hold, for example. In subordinate clauses, the function of the finite element – whether it involves an assertion or not – interacts with, and can be overruled by, the function of the complementizer and thus give a special interpretation to the finiteness times. Since this does not directly concern the aspectual distinction as such, we shall not follow it up here, because it would require a detailed discussion of the function of various sentence types; it should only kept in mind that 'time of assertion' is only a special interpretation of 'finiteness time' in general.

The lexical verb *čitat'* is [-p] (it is a simplex verb). Tense (past in this case) and aspect (IMPERF) restrict the potential assertion times to the set of those intervals which (a) precede the utterance time, and (b) overlap the only state. This is all that the finite form *čital* itself tells us, and as a consequence, there are still many potential assertion times. Any further narrowing down of this set requires either additional linguistic means, for example adverbials such as *yesterday from four to five, once, sometimes* and the like, or it is left to contextual interpretation. In the latter case, there are three main possibilities:

(a) A specific assertion time is taken from the preceding context, as is often the case in narrative discourse; this leads to a 'definite reading' of 27.
(b) There is implicit existential quantification, in the sense of 'for some time in the past'; this leads to a 'existential reading' of 27.
(c) There is some other type of implicit quantification, in the sense of 'often, ...; sometimes,...; habitually, ...' etc.; this leads to a frequentative, habitual, ..., reading of 27.

Tense and aspect themselves leave this open; they are neither definite nor indefinite;[39] they only narrow down the set of potential assertion times.

5 Concluding remarks

The analysis of Russian aspect suggested here is strictly time-relational. It only operates with notions that are independently needed, such as time intervals, temporal relations between these intervals like 'before' or 'after', and the notion of assertion, which can be confined to a particular time interval. Thus, it is conceptually very simple, and it does make use of the suggestive but highly metaphorical notions so often found in the literature on aspect. But can it do justice to the impressive body of observations accumulated in this literature? In section 2.2, we examined the three best-known traditional characterisations of PERF and IMPERF – the situation is presented in its totality : not in its totality, as completed : as not completed, with an internal boundary : without an internal boundary. How does the present approach deal handle the problems discussed there? And how does it handle phenomena such as the 'imperfectum de conatu' or the notoriously

---

39 Thus, Partee's (1973) classical example of definite tense is just one of the various possibilities of tense (and aspect) interpretation.

difficult 'fact constatation' use of the IMPERF. In this concluding section, we will address some of these questions.

The present approach makes somewhat different predictions for 1-state contents and 2-state contents. Let us begin with the latter, that is, with aspect pairs such as *dat'$_p$: davat$_i$*' 'to give' or *perepisat'$_p$: perepisyvat'$_i$* 'to copy'. Both 'aspectual partners' involve a source state and a target state. The difference is that in the PERF case, the target state is reached within the time for which a claim is indeed made, whereas this is not true for the IMPERF case: the assertion time must not overlap with the target state. This explains why in the PERF, independent of any boundary, the 'action' is felt to be completed; the missing time T (cf. section 2.2.2) in relation to which the completion is considered is the assertion time. By the same token, it becomes clear why the 'action' is felt to be presented in its totality, rather than in its development: PERF encompasses the entire lexical content, whereas IMPERF places the assertion time, as it were, in the midst of the 'action'. No assertion is made about whether the target state is reached or not, since the target state does not overlap with the assertion time.

This temporal limitation of the assertion naturally explains the so-called conative use of the IMPERF (see, for example, Forsyth 1970:71-76). It is not contradictory – although pragmatically perhaps not very felicitous – to say 28 or 29 (the latter example is from Timberlake 1982:312):

(28)   Ivan mne daval$_i$ knigu a potom ne dal$_p$.
       Ivan gave-IMPERF me a book but then not gave-PERF (it to me).
(29)   Kalif bagdadskij rubil$_i$ emu golovu, a on vse-taki živ.
       Kaliph-of-Bagdad cut-off-IMPERF him head, but he still alive.

The reason is simply that a claim is only made about the source state, and nothing is said about whether the target state – the state at which the speaker has the book, or the victim no head – is ever reached: the time for which an assertion is made ends before the target state. This does not preclude, of course, that the target state is reached, and in fact, this is a common implicature. But it is not asserted. Thus, the possibility of a conative use is predicted by the our analysis of the IMPERF.[40]

---

[40] There is no ideal way to translate these 'conative' usages of IMPERF into English. A 'conative' translation such as *Ivan tried to give me the book but then didn't* or *The Kaliph tried to cut his head off but he is still alive* would be odd and misleading. What is meant, is, that the action was undertaken but that the state to which it normally would lead (book with me, victim without head and hence dead) was not reached. The Russian sentence *Ivan mne daval knigu* has the strong

Let us turn now to 1-state contents, most typically expressed by simplex verbs. They have no target state. Thus, there is no risk that the assertion time ever contains it, be it partly or fully. Hence, it is easily possible to present an entire historical fact such as the colossos of Rhodos weighing 100 tons with an IMPERF form, without giving the impression that this situation is seen from within: it is presented in its totality, and this is fully in accordance with the definition of the IMPERF. This also explains the so-called 'konstatacija fakta' use of IMPERF, a perennial problem in the analysis of Russian aspect. Consider the following example (taken from Forsyth 1970:83):

(30) Vy čitali$_i$ *Vojnu i mir?*   čital$_i$
     You read-PAST   *War and Peace?*   Read-PAST
     Have you read   *War and Peace?*   Yes, I have.

In this context, the answer simply states the fact that the speaker has read *War and Peace*. In a different context, the same form could also mean that at some time in the past, he was involved in this activity, without ever bringing it to an end (in which case the English translation should rather be 'I was reading *War and Peace*'). Both readings follow from the definition of IMPERF for 1-state verbs: the assertion time can include the time of the situation, and this leads to the 'fact constatation'-reading, but it can also be included in it, and this leads to the 'progressive' reading. Which reading is intended and understood, depends on the particular context. For the same reason, the IMPERF can encompass a clearly bounded activity such as Sévérine's working from 2 to 5: the assertion time need not necessarily be included in this time, as would be marked by the English progressive form.

In conclusion, it seems that the intuitions behind the classical aspect characterisations simply follow from the time-relational analysis given here. At the same time, this analysis avoids the problems discussed above in connection with these approaches.

There are a number of problems connected to the Russian aspects and their usage which we have not dealt with here – for example the fact that IMPERF forms seem to be more prone to an iterative reading than PERF forms, the interaction between aspect and negation, or, even more importantly, the different interaction of PERF and IMPERF with tense marking (in the present tense, PERF normally,

---

implicature that I eventually had the book (though this is not asserted, and hence, the implicature can be cancelled). An English sentence such as *Ivan tried to give me the book* has the strong implicature that I eventually did not have the book.

though not necessarily, has a future reading).[41] These facts may be accidental; but they might also be a consequence of the definitions of tense and aspect given here. An answer to these questions would require an in-depth analysis of the various ways in which aspect interacts with tense and with contextual information, a task which is beyond the scope of this paper.

References

Agrell, S. (1909). Aspekt und Aktionsart beim polnischen Zeitworte. Lund: Ohlsson.
Binnick, RJ. (1991). Time and the verb. Oxford: Blackwell.
Bondarko, Alexandr V. (1971). Vid i vremja russkogo glagola. Moscow: Prosveščenie.
Bondarko, Alexandr V. (1987). Principy funcial'noj grammatiki i voprosy aspektologii. St. Petersburg: Nauka.
Bondarko, Alexander V. (1991). Functional Grammar. A Field Approach. Amsterdam: Benjamins.
Brecht, Richard D. (1985). The form and function of aspect in Russian. In: Issues in Russian Morphosyntax. Matthew S. Flier and Alan Timberlake, eds. Columbus, Ohio: Slavica Publishers Inc. 9–34.
Breu, Walter (1994). Interactions between lexical, temporal and aspectual meanings. Studies in Language 18. 23–44.
Comrie, Bernard (1976). Aspect. Cambridge: Cambridge University Press.
Černy, E. (1877). Ob otnošenii vidov russkogo glagola k grečeskim vremenam. St. Petersburg.
Dahl, Östen (1985). Tense and Aspect Systems. Oxford: Blackwell.
Durst-Andersen, Per (1993). Mental Grammar: Russian aspect and related issues. Columbus, Ohio: Slavica.
Fontaine, Jacqueline (1983). Grammaire du texte et aspect du verbe en russe contemporain. Paris: Institut d'Etudes Slaves.
Forsyth, James (1970). A grammar of aspect: usage and meaning in the Russian verb. Cambridge: Cambridge University Press.
Galton, Herbert (1976). The main functions of the Slavic verbal aspect. Skopje: Macedonian Academy of Sciences.
International Encyclopedia of Linguistics (1992). Oxford: Oxford University Press.
Isačenko, Alexander V. (1968). Die russische Sprache der Gegenwart. München: Hueber.

---

[41] Hans Kamp (personal communication) suggested that the tense constraint may have to do with the difference between a short assertion time, which is more or less identical to the utterance time ('actual present') and a long assertion time which only includes the utterance time but is in fact much longer ('generic present, habitual present'). A long assertion time can easily overlap with source state and target state, hence PERF should be possible here, and so it is. A very short assertion time cannot overlap with both source state and target state, hence it is somehow 'prolonged' into the future, and the target state falls into the time after the utterance time. I think this line of reasoning is basically correct, although at this point, it must be left to further investigation.

Jakobson, R. (1932). Zur Struktur des russischen Verbums. In: Charisteria Guilelemo Mathesio quinquagenario a discipulis et Circuli Linguistici Pragiensis. Prague. 74–84. (Reprinted in: Selected writings II, 1971. De Hague: Mouton. 3–15).
Klein, Wolfgang (1994). Time in language. London: Routledge.
Leinonen, Marja (1982). Russian aspect, 'temporalnaja lokalizacija', and definiteness/indefiniteness. Helsinki: University of Helsinki. Dissertation.
Miklosich, Franz (1883). Vergleichende Grammatik der slavischen Sprachen 4, Wien.
Partee, Barbara (1973). Some structural analogies between tenses and pronouns. Journal of Philosophy 70. 601–609.
Regnell, Carl G. (1944). Über den Ursprung des slavischen Verbalaspektes. Lund: Harlan Ohlsons Boktryckeri.
Ružička, Rudolf (1952). Der russische Verbalaspekt. In: Der Russischunterricht 5. 161–169.
Saussure, Ferdinand de (1917). Cours de linguistique generale. Paris: Payot.
Smith, Carlota (1991). The aspect parameter. Dordrecht: Kluwer.
Timberlake, Alan (1982). Invariance and the syntax of Russian aspect. In: P. J. Hopper, ed., Tense- Aspect. Between semantics and pragmatics. Amsterdam: Benjamins. 305–331.
Timberlake, Alan (1984). The temporal schemata of Russian Predicates. In: Michael Flier and Richard D. Brecht, eds. Issues in Russian Morphosyntax. UCLA Slavic Studies 10. Columbus, Ohio: Slavica Publishers, 35–57.
Timberlake, Alan (1985). Reichenbach and Russian Aspect. In: Michael S. Flier and Alan Timberlake,eds. The Scope of Russian Aspect. UCLA Slavic Studies 12. Columbus, Ohio: Slavica Publishers. 153–168.
Thelin, Nils B (1978). Towards a Theory of Aspect, Tense and Actionality in Slavic. Acta Universitatis Upaliensis, Studia Slavica 18. Uppsala: Almqvist and Wiksell.
Thelin, Nils B (1990). On the concept of time: prolegomena to a theory of aspect and tense in narrative discourse. In: Nils Thelin, ed. Verbal aspect in discourse. Amsterdam: Benjamins. 91–129.
Vendler, Zeno (1957). Verbs and times. The Philosophical Review 66, 143–160.
Vinogradov, V.V. (1947). Russkij jazyk. Moscow.

An analysis of the German Perfekt[1]

> Der Alte folgte der Leiche und die Söhne, Albert vermocht's nicht. Man fürchtete für Lottens Leben. Handwerker trugen ihn. Kein Geistlicher hat ihn begleitet.
>
> Goethe, Werthers Leiden

1 The problem

In form and history, the German Perfekt is closely related to the English perfect: *(Peter) hat gelacht* '(Peter) has laughed' consists of a past participle and an auxiliary, *haben* (or, in some cases, *sein*). This auxiliary can be non-finite, as in *gelacht haben* '(to) have laughed'; or it can be finite, in which case it can be marked for present, past, and arguably future. But this parallelism is deceptive. It has often been noticed that the Perfekt has two quite different readings, brought out by the two possible continuations in 1 and 2, respectively:

(1) Ich habe im Garten gearbeitet [und muss zuerst einmal duschen].
I have in the garden worked [and must first have a shower].
(2) Ich habe im Garten gearbeitet [und konnte deshalb die Klingel nicht hören].
I have in the garden worked [and could therefore the bell not hear].

The difference is palpable but not easy to characterize. Intuitively, the speaker in 1 describes a present state which is the result of some earlier situation; in English, a translation by *I have worked/been working in the garden* would be appropriate. This is not possible for 2: it means something like *I worked/was working in the garden [and therefore, I could not hear the bell]*[2]. In this case, the speaker apparently does not describe what he or she is like right now as the result of some action in the past but rather expresses that this action took place at some time in the past. Under both readings, there must be some situation in the past in which

---

[1] I wish to thank (f. l. t. r.) Manfred Bierwisch, Mike Dickey, Rainer Dietrich, Cathrine Fabricius-Hansen, Cornelia Hamann, Renate Musan, Irene Rapp, Arnim von Stechow, Christiane von Stutterheim, Angelika Wittek and the reviewers of *Language* for their help. This does not imply that they agree with everything said here.
[2] German does not distinguish between a simple form and a progressive form; in the English glosses and translations, I will normally use the simple form; but it should be kept in mind that the German form may have the meaning of a progressive.

Note: This article originally appeared as Klein, W. (2000). An analysis of the German perfekt. Language 76. 358–382.

https://doi.org/10.1515/9783110549119-004

the person designated by the subject worked in the garden. What is different is the way in which this situation relates to the present. The translations suggest that the German Perfekt has a reading in which it corresponds to the English present perfect, with its characteristic combination of presentness and pastness, and another one in which it corresponds to the (simple or progressive) past.

Other observations point in the same direction. First, there are many instances where German can use the Perfekt, whereas English requires the past:

(3) a. Der Koloss von Rhodos hat hundert Tonnen gewogen.
 *The colossus of Rhodes has weighed one-hundred tons.
 b. Einstein hat Princeton besucht.
 *Einstein has visited Princeton.
 c. In Atlantis wurde viel getanzt.
 *In Atlantis, there has been much dancing.

Second, the German Perfekt combines freely with adverbials that refer to the past:

(4) a. Gestern um zehn habe ich den Brief abgeschickt.
 *Yesterday at ten have I the letter sent-off.
 b. Ich habe den Brief gestern um zehn abgeschickt.
 *I have the letter yesterday at ten sent-off.

Third, it has often been noted that in some German dialects, the Präteritum (which corresponds historically and structurally to the English simple past) is more or less extinct, and the Perfekt has assumed its function (so-called 'oberdeutscher Präteritumschwund', see Lindgren 1957).[3]

These observations suggest the following picture: in modern Standard German, the Perfekt has essentially assumed the meaning of a past tense; in this function, it competes with the Präteritum. But there are some remnants of genuine 'present perfect usage'. As a consequence, there are contexts in which the Perfekt as well as the Präteritum can be used (A.), and there are contexts in which this is not the case, (B.) and (C.).

A. Präteritum as well as Perfekt are appropriate whenever the speaker wants to talk about some event, state or process, in short, situation, that occurred or obtained in the past (cf. exx. 3, 4 above). In these contexts, both forms

---

[3] Note, however, that this is not true for Standard German, or for speakers of southern dialects when they speak Standard German (for a survey, see Hauser-Suida and Hoppe-Beugel 1972). In my own dialect, for example (southwest Germany), the Präteritum is not used except for the copula *war* 'was' and occasionally a modal. But everyday observation clearly shows that people regularly use the Präteritum when speaking Standard German.

would be translated by the English (simple or progressive) past. This does not mean that the choice between Perfekt and Präteritum is completely arbitrary in these contexts; but it appears to be more a matter of style, register, or even personal preference. Very often, the Präteritum is felt to have a literary flavour, whereas the Perfekt sounds more casual.

B. Whenever a present situation is somehow 'presented as a result of a past situation', the Perfekt but not the Präteritum is possible. This is the case in 1 above, where the speaker relates to his or her present state as the result of working in the garden (such as being dirty and in need of a shower). Note, however, that nothing is really ASSERTED about what is presently the case; the assumption that the speaker is dirty, for example, can easily be cancelled. Or suppose someone is invited to join a meal and turns down this invitation with 5:

(5) Danke, ich habe schon gegessen.
    Thanks, I have already eaten.

Here, the Präteritum variant *Danke, ich aß schon* would be distinctly odd, roughly like 'Thanks, I was already eating'. Again, the intuition is that 5 somehow indicates 'I am not in need of eating something at this time' or 'It would not be appropriate for me to eat something at this time'. Something is invoked about the speaker's situation right now; but nothing is really ASSERTED in this regard. The difference becomes more palpable with verbs whose lexical content characterises the resultant state, for example *umkippen* 'topple over':

(6) a. Schau, der Stuhl ist umgekippt.
       Look, the chair has toppled over.
    b. Kurz darauf ist der Stuhl umgekippt.
       Shortly afterwards, the chair toppled over.

In 6a, the initial 'Schau' invites the reading in which there is a chair that is no longer in upright position. In 6b, it is meant that at some time in the past, the chair toppled over. Only in this second reading is the Präteritum possible, too.

C. In contrast to the English present perfect as well as to the Präteritum, the Perfekt is also possible when the situation itself is not in the past. In particular, it combines with adverbials that refer to the future:

(7) Ich habe in einer halben Stunde geduscht.[4]
    I have in half an hour showered.

---

[4] There is also a kind of 'future Perfekt' in German (*werde eingereicht haben, werde geduscht haben*), which can be used in these contexts; but it is by no means necessary, not even preferred.

The last sentence has a past reading ('Within half an hour, I had a shower') and a future reading ('Within half an hour, I will have had a shower').

Let us briefly sum up at this point. A sentence such as *Er hat die Stadt verlassen* '(lit.) He has the city left' can be used in contexts in which it corresponds to the English present perfect. In addition, there are contexts in which it would have to be translated by the simple past, and there are contexts in which the future perfect should be used. The following examples illustrate this; the intended reading is made clear by the adverbial:

(8) a. Gestern um zehn hat er die Stadt verlassen.
 Yesterday at ten has he the city left.
 b. (Gestern hättest du ihn treffen können.) Aber jetzt hat er die Stadt verlassen.
 (Yesterday you could have met him.) But now has he the city left.
 c. Morgen um zehn hat er die Stadt verlassen.
 Tomorrow at ten has he the city left.

Is there a uniform meaning to the Perfekt which covers this range of uses and explains the intuitive differences between them? And if so, how can this uniform meaning be derived from the meaning of its components? These are the two questions to be addressed in this paper. In the next section, we shall first have a brief look at the formal composition of the German temporal system; then, some earlier analyses of the German Perfekt will be critically examined. Section 3 sketches the theoretical background to the present analysis. This analysis proceeds in two steps which correspond to the complex composition of the Perfekt. In section 4, it will be shown how the meaning of the Perfekt results from the interaction of its 'finite component' and its entire 'non-finite component'. Section 5 will examine how this analysis accounts for the observations mentioned above as well as for some other problems connected with the German Perfekt and the English present perfect. Section 6 presents an analysis of the participle and of the German auxiliaries; it is shown how the meaning of various constructions, in particular the Perfekt, follow from the interaction of these components.

2 Previous research

Most relevant research does not address the Perfekt in particular but the entire tense system of German. Opinions vary considerably on how form and meaning of this system are to be analysed. Thus, estimates about the number of German 'tenses' range between 1 and 18 (see Thieroff 1992 for a survey). I will not join in this discussion here but only sketch some basic facts that are needed in later sections.

2.1 Formal composition

In German, as in all Indoeuropean languages, a distinction is normally drawn between 'finite' and 'non-finite' temporal forms of the verb; thus, *lachte, lachst* are finite, whereas *lachen, gelacht haben, gelacht haben werden* are non-finite. This distinction obliterates the fact that 'finite forms' like *lachte* are compound in themselves: they include a non-finite component, the bare verb stem *lach-*, and a finite component, reflected on the surface by past tense morphology. The same non-finite component *lach-* is part of forms which are traditionally called 'non-finite', such as the participle *gelacht* or in the infinitive *lachen*. It is more perspicuous, therefore, to distinguish between the bare stem (abbreviated here by V_s), and various operators which turn Vs into either a 'finite form' or a 'non-finite form', in particular the infinitive and the past participle. The 'finiteness operator' will be abbreviated here as FIN, the two 'non-finiteness operators' as GE- and -EN, respectively. FIN, when morphologically fused with the verb stem, produces 'finite verb forms'. GE- and -EN produce the past participle and the infinitive, respectively. Hence, we have two types of 'non-finite' expressions:
– bare stems that are not finite but can be made finite by fusing them with some FIN; a (simple or complex) form which can be made finite will be called 'FIN-linkable';
– forms which are explicitly marked as non-finite, i.e., participle and infinitive; these cannot be fused with some FIN; but normally, they can be made FIN-linkable again by combining it with another bare verb stem.

In German, FIN has two values, called here FIN_0 and FIN<. They roughly correspond to 'present tense marking' and to 'past tense marking', respectively. Non-finite forms are more varied; the most important cases in the present context are:
1. The bare stem V_s, for example *lach-, hab-, werd-*.
2. The infinitive, which is normally formed by attaching *en* to the bare stem, as in *lachen, haben, werden*.
3. The 'past participle' or 'participle II' (abbreviated GE-V_s); regular verbs form it by prefixing the stem with *ge* and by suffixing it with *t*, as in *gelacht*; irregular verbs form it in different ways, for example by Ablaut, suppletive forms etc.
4. Syntactically compound forms; the two most important cases are:
   a. The nonfinite component of the Perfekt: GE-V_S combined with the bare stem of an auxiliary, as in *gelacht hab-, gestorben sei-*; the choice of the auxiliary depends on various lexical properties of the verb (see Shannon 1989 for a careful discussion).

b. The nonfinite component of the Passive: GE-V$_s$ and the verb stem *werd-*, as in *geliebt werd-, gefunden werd-*.

Any finite form is a combination of FIN$_0$ or FIN< with a FIN-linkable construction. There are many such forms, in particular the following four:

A. Präsens FIN$_0$ + V$_s$ *liebt, hat, ist*
B. Präteritum FIN< + V$_s$ *liebte, hatte, war*
C. Perfekt FIN$_0$ + AUX$_s$ + GE-V$_s$ *hat geliebt, hat gehabt, ist gewesen*
D. Plusquamperfekt FIN< + AUX$_s$ + GE-V$_s$ *hatte geliebt, hatte gehabt, war gewesen*

We shall now discuss what previous research has said about the meaning of the Perfekt.

2.2 The meaning of the Perfekt I: the tradition

Most grammars assume that the Perfekt as well as the Präteritum express the same time-relational meaning: they both mark that the situation referred to by the utterance precedes the time of utterance. The difference is a matter of style, dialect, 'aspect' (in whichever sense), or perhaps textual function. In *Grundzüge* (1981: 508s), the most comprehensive modern German grammar to date, the relevant passages are: 'Präsens und Präteritum charakterisieren das durch das Verb bezeichnete Geschehen oder Sein unter dem Aspekt des Verlaufs ('durativ'), d.h. eine zeitliche Begrenzung wird nicht angezeigt. ... Perfekt und Plusquamperfekt charakterisieren das durch das Verb bezeichnete Geschehen als vollzogen, abgeschlossen ('perfektiv')'['Praesens and Präteritum characterise what happens or is the case – as designated by the verb – from a process point of view ('durative'), i.e., no temporal boundaries are indicated. ... Perfekt and Pluperfekt characterise what happens – as indicated by the verb – as achieved, completed ('perfective').']. In varying formulations, the distinction between 'process side' and 'completion side' is found in virtually all descriptive grammars of German. This notion may well reflect intuitively correct feelings about the usage of these forms in many cases. But it gives rise to a number of objections. First, it is not particularly clear. Second, there are many instances in which it is implausible; the sentence *Bald darauf starb er* 'soon afterwards, he died' is no more process-like or durative than its Perfekt counterpart *Bald darauf ist er gestorben*. Third, it is distinctly odd in cases such as *Der Koloss von Rhodos hat hundert Tonnen gewogen* vs. *Der Koloss von Rhodos wog hundert Tonnen*; it does not make any sense here to speak of completed vs. process-like. Fourth, it is entirely unclear how it could account for the intuitive difference between exx. 1 and 2. And fifth, no attempt is made to explain how the meaning of the Perfekt results from the meaning of its parts.

Essentially, the same arguments apply to the view that the Perfekt is the form that is commonly used in everyday spoken language, whereas the Präteritum is primarily the tense of narrative fiction (a view most strongly advocated by Hamburger 1968); or for Weinrich's influential distinction between two classes of tense forms – those which, like the Perfekt, 'describe the world', and those which, like the Präteritum, 'narrate the world' (Weinrich 1974). I do not want, however, to belittle these views. They are not accidental, and one of the sigilla veritatis of a convincing analysis is the degree to which extent it can explain these intuitive feelings.

2.3 The meaning of the Perfekt II: recent analyses

Modern research on the Perfekt begins with Wunderlich (1970). He was the first to clearly state the ambiguity exemplified in exx. 1, 2, and he assigned two different temporal, rather than aspectual or textual, meanings to the Perfekt. Others followed him in this regard. Bäuerle (1979), for example, states that the German Perfekt has two semantical analyses: a compositional one, in which it corresponds to the English present perfect, and a non-compositional one in which it is but a morphological variant of the Präteritum; no attempt is made to bring these two meanings together. This ambiguity account is a relatively safe but not a very elegant position; it is surely preferable if some construction can be given a uniform compositional meaning, rather than two (or no compositional meaning at all), and if different readings of this construction can be attributed to other factors, such as general context.

This objection, first raised by Fabricius-Hansen (1986: 104) in her subtle study of the interaction of tense forms and temporal adverbials in German[5], carries over to the first of several types of analysis that operate with Reichenbach's three temporal parameters E, R, and S (or variants thereof). Thus, ten Cate (1989) and, in a slightly different terminology, Helbig and Buscha (1974: 128s) postulate two temporal meanings of the Perfekt which, irrelevant differences aside, correspond to Reichenbach's analysis of the English simple past and present perfect, respectively. This criticism does not apply to three other types of Reichenbachian

---

5 Fabricius-Hansen's own account of the Perfekt is very sophisticated, because it systematically distinguishes between 'definite' and 'indefinite' uses of the Perfekt (and other tense forms). As a consequence, no uniform meaning is assigned to the Perfekt, either, though for different reasons.

analyses that have been proposed over the last years; they all assign a single temporal meaning to the Perfekt:

A. E before R & R not-before S (Thieroff 1992)[6]
B. E before R & R not fixed in relation to S   (Ballweg 1988, Zeller 1994, Grewendorf 1995)[7]
B. E before R & R simultaneous to S, and the second
    part of this meaning is shiftable   (Ehrich and Vater 1989, Ehrich 1992)

Under Thieroff's analysis, the German Perfekt essentially corresponds to the English present perfect, except that R can also be in the future. No attempt is made to derive the other reading of the Perfekt. This leaves the crucial problems unanswered. In the two other types of analysis, R itself can be in the past, either because it is not fixed with respect to S at all, or because it can be shifted under specific conditions (discussed in detail in Ehrich 1992). But then, according to both analyses, E is BEFORE this R in the past, and this is not the case with examples such as *Gestern um zehn habe ich den Antrag eingereicht* or *Der Koloss von Rhodos hat hundert Tonnen gewogen*. In all examples that can have the Präteritum as an alternative, the 'event time' must be SIMULTANEOUS TO, or OVERLAP WITH, the 'reference time'. Consider again ex. 1 *Ich habe im Garten gearbeitet (und konnte deshalb die Klingel nicht hören)* in answer to the question 'Why didn't you come to the door yesterday?'. Here, R is clearly included in E, and not before E, as the analysis would require. In order to express that E precedes R, one would have to use the Plusquamperfekt *Ich hatte im Garten gearbeitet*. Therefore, these analyses fail, as well.

There is a second fundamental problem with these and in fact, with any Reichenbach-type analysis: it is anything but clear what should be understood by E and by R. As already noted in Wunderlich (1970: 123), Reichenbach did not bother to define what is meant by 'point of reference'; he uses it just as 'some other time' (for a critical discussion, see Hamann 1987, Klein 1992); hence, this part of the analysis is simply vacuous, so long as R lacks an appropriate interpretation. The other parameter, E, is given such an interpretation – it is the time of the 'event'. But what is the time of 'the event' in a sentence such as *Hans scheint die Stadt um*

---

[6] Thieroff (1992:86s, 189) says that his notion of 'reference time' is different from Reichenbach's; but no definition whatsoever is given, except that it is different from the moment of speaking and the event time.

[7] Neither Ballweg nor Grewendorf formulate their analysis literally in Reichenbachian terms; therefore, the following remarks do not do justice to their analysis in general. I am picking out here only how it might account for the Perfekt ambiguity. (Zeller explicitly states that there is no solution to the ambiguity problem under his analysis).

vier Uhr zu verlassen geplant zu haben 'John seems to have planned to leave the city by four o'clock'? Is it the time of his planning? the time of his having planned? the time of his leaving the city? the time at which someone has this impression ('seems')? Is this one event, or several? If the entire non-finite part *Hans die Stadt um vier Uhr zu verlassen geplant zu haben schein-* corresponds to the 'event', then this event includes a complex internal temporal structure. In fact, this problem already surfaces in comparatively simple cases such as *Ich habe geduscht* with its non-finite part *Ich geduscht hab-*. What is the event at stake – is it the situation of my having a shower, as described by *Ich dusch-*, or is it the situation after such a situation, as described by *Ich geduscht hab-*? As a rule, there is no single 'event time' but a web of temporal variables, each characterised in a particular way, and an appropriate analysis of temporal forms must somehow look into this web. An analysis in terms of 'the event time' and 'the reference time' is bound to fail.

3 Theoretical background

In what follows I will make use of some ideas that have been worked out in detail elsewhere (Klein 1992, 1994). This framework tries to operate exclusively with notions that are independently needed. These are
(a) temporal intervals,
(b) temporal relations between these, such as BEFORE, OVERLAPPING WITH, etc,
(c) the lexical content of simple or complex expressions,
(d) the usual illocutionary roles, of which only 'assertion' will be considered here.

The traditional notions of 'tense' and 'aspect' are reconstructed in this approach as purely temporal relations between particular types of temporal intervals; this will be very briefly discussed in section 3.1. More important in the present context are inherent temporal features, i.e., that facet of temporality which is traditionally dealt with under labels such as 'Aktionsart' or 'lexical aspect'; this will be discussed in 3.2, and then applied to the analysis of participles in 6.

3.1 Tense and aspect as temporal relations

Traditionally, tense is considered to be a deictic and relational category of the verb whereas aspect rather reflects various ways of viewing a situation, for example as 'completed', 'with or without boundaries', and similar ones. Tense expresses a relation between two temporal intervals; these are normally the time at which some sitatution obtains, and the moment of speech. I will call these TIME OF

SITUATION (abbreviated here T-SIT) and TIME OF UTTERANCE (TU), respectively. Thus, 9 refers to a situation, and the past tense marks that the time of this situation precedes TU:

(9) Eva was cheerful.

It is easy to see that this almost canonical notion of 'tense' is inappropriate. If 9 is true, then this does not at all exclude that Eva is cheerful at TU. Hence, the past tense marking is fully compatible with the temporal constellation 'T-SIT includes TU'. What 9 really says is something else: there is some SUBINTERVAL T of the entire situation, and for this particular subinterval T, it is asserted that it precedes TU. Hence, we must carefully distinguish between the time of the situation and the time for which an assertion is made. This latter time I will call the TOPIC TIME (TT). In the special case of declarative sentences, TT is the time to which the assertion made by the utterance is confined. In other sentences, for example in imperative clauses, it may assume a different function, a possibility that will not be explored here.[8]

It is TT which is temporally related to TU, rather than T-SIT itself. If the listener knows anything about how T-SIT is related to TU, then this is by virtue of the fact that T-SIT in turn is temporally related to TT. In 9, TT is interpreted as a subinterval of T-SIT. Other temporal relations are possible: TT may include T-SIT, it may follow it, precede it, etc. Exactly this is what is expressed by the notional category of ASPECT. In the 'imperfective aspect', for example, TT is fully included in T-SIT. This naturally accounts for intuitions such as that 'the situation is presented from its interior, not as a whole, as being incomplete', as common metaphorical characterisations of the imperfective have it. If, by contrast, the time for which an assertion is made includes the time of the situation, then this situation is, metaphorically speaking, 'shown with its boundaries, as completed, in its entirety, from the outside', etc.

---

8 Imperatives, for example, do not express an assertion but the obligation to perform some action. Their topic time is not the time for which an assertion is made but the time for which the obligation holds. Subordinate clauses do not express an assertion, either (though they may indirectly involve an assertion, as in the case of factives). The interpretation of their topic time depends on the particular kind of complementizer and the lexical properties of the matrix clause. It is also possible to stipulate an invisible complementizer for main clauses as the carrier of assertion (and other illocutionary roles); on the surface, its function is realised on the finite verb. This would allow a more uniform treatment across sentence types, but it raises other problems (for some discussion, see Klein 1994, chapter 8).

Under this view, tense as well as aspect are construed as temporal relations between temporal intervals: TU, TT, and T-SIT:

(10) TENSE IS A TEMPORAL RELATION BETWEEN TU AND TT.
ASPECT IS A TEMPORAL RELATION BETWEEN TT AND T-SIT.

The definition of aspect is a simplification, since it operates with the notion of a single T-SIT; but as was already discussed at the end of section 2.3, more than one temporal interval may be involved in 'the event'; this point will be resumed in section 3.2.

3.2 Temporal properties of the lexical content

3.2.1 Properties of situations vs properties of the lexical content

Temporal intervals have a duration, they can be counted, and, due to the structure of time, they are related to each other. But they have no qualitative properties; they are not green, ambitious, or covered with sweat. They can, however, be characterised by the content of some simple or compound linguistic expression, for example *sleep, leave London, leave London for a couple of days*, or *John leave London for a couple of days*. Exactly this is what happens in a sentence. Consider the situation referred to by 11:

(11) I was working in the garden.

This situation has many properties. It has a place, it has a beginning point, an end point and hence a duration, and many others. Only some of these are described by the lexical content of 11. In other words, the lexical content of a full sentence which refers to a situation is a SELECTIVE DESCRIPTION of this situation. The speaker chooses some features which he or she wants to make explicit, and leaves others aside. In 11, for instance, duration or endpoints are left implicit. But they could be made explicit by enriching the lexical content, for example by adding *from lunchtime till eight o'clock, for several hours*. Obviously, this addition does not change the situation itself. Therefore, it is important to distinguish carefully between properties of a situation and properties of the lexical content which describes this situation. In 11, world knowledge tells us that the time of situation has a beginning and an end, hence is bounded, although the lexical content itself does not say anything about these boundaries. It is misleading, therefore, to say that activity verbs such as *to work* refer to unbounded situations, or express an unbounded situation type.

3.2.2 FIN-linkable vs non-FIN-linkable expressions

In what follows, we are mainly interested in the lexical content of verb stems and morphosyntactical constructions based on these. In contrast to adjectives, nouns or prepositions, verb stems are 'FIN-linkable'. Thus, *green, my friend, in London* cannot be directly fused with FIN, whereas *be green, become my friend, remain in London* and, of course, *sleep, sleep on the floor, slay Abel* etc. are FIN- linkable. Infinitives and participles are not FIN-linkable, due to the application of specific morphosyntactic processes to the underlying verb stems. But the attachment of bare verb stem can make them again FIN-linkable. Repeated application of these operations leads to complex forms such as *geschlossen worden sein* 'to have been closed'.

It is important to distinguish between a full finite declarative sentence, such as *Eva was cheerful*, and its non-finite component [Eva be cheerful]. This non-finite component will be called SENTENCE BASE. A sentence base is an 'assertable construction'; minimally, it consists of the surface subject (which can be lexically empty) and a FIN-linkable part; other elements, for example adverbials, particles and other optional constituents can be added and then contribute to the lexical content of the entire sentence base.

3.2.3 The lexical content of verb stems I: problems

The lexical analysis of verb stems belongs to the most difficult areas in linguistics. In what follows, I will only sketch some baseline assumptions, shared in one way or the other by most theories, and try to make clear which additional distinctions are needed if we are to understand the functioning of the Perfekt. As usual, it is assumed that a lexical item, such as *dusch-*, is a complex of at least three types of information: (a) phonological, (b) categorial (it is a verb and belongs to a particular inflectional class), and (c) semantic. The latter is what is called 'lexical content' here.

What constitutes the lexical content of a verb stem? It has often been said that verbs somehow refer to 'events', whereas nouns refer to 'objects'. This notion, familar from the days of the Stoic grammarians, is at best somewhat sloppy; in fact, it is highly misleading. The lexical content of a verb CONTRIBUTES to the description of a situation. What it contributes is the specification of (qualitative or spatial) properties which some entities have during some temporal intervals. Thus, the verb *sleep* does not refer to an event; it assigns some property to some argument A at some time t_i. I shall say that it assigns a property to a pair $<A, t_i>$. It does not say, of course, what A and t_i are; these are variables which must be filled appropriately. The lexical content of a verb may also provide other types of 'argument slots', for example a world variable, a place variable, and perhaps others; these will not be considered here.

Here, we are specifically interested in the temporal features of verb stems. They come in because the qualitative and spatial properties assigned to the arguments are RELATIVE TO TEMPORAL INTERVALS. The crucial problem is here that more than one argument and more than one temporal interval may be involved. This obvious fact about the inherent temporal properties of verb meanings is only very insufficiently reflected in familar categorisations such as Vendler's four time schemata, and even less so in the common way in which the 'argument structure' of a verb is described. It would be more appropriate to speak of an 'argument-time structure'. Consider 12:

(12)   Cain slew Abel.

It seems uncontroversial that the lexical content of the stem *slay* contributes at least the following bits of information:
1. There is a temporal interval t_1 at which the second argument (specified in 12 by *Abel*) is assigned the property of being alive, and another interval t_2 at which this same argument is assigned the property of being dead.
2. There is an interval t_3 at which the first argument (specified by *Cain*) is somehow active in a particular manner ('hit').
3. The three intervals are temporally related to each other. Clearly, t_2 is after t_1. It is less clear how t_3 is related to these; it must overlap with t_1, but surely, it need not be fully simultaneous to t_1: the lexical content of *slay* does not say that the first argument 'hits' during the entire lifetime of the second argument, and it is not excluded that this activity extends into t_2; sentence 12 is not false when Cain is still hitting when Abel is dead already.
4. They are also interrelated in non-temporal ways; we assume that the activity of Cain is somehow 'causally related' to Abel's death. Similarly, we assume that t_2 is not just after t_1 but that what is the case at t_2 would not be the case if t_1 would not be the case.

In view of these facts, what are the 'boundaries' of a situation described by 12? What is the 'posttime' or the 'poststate'? Is it the temporal interval after Cain's activity, is it the time after Abel's being alive, or even the time after Abel's being dead? In other words, which of the three temporal variables in the meaning of *slay* matters – t_1, t_2 or t_3? In this particular case, t_2 is excluded. There is no time after Abel's being dead at which Abel would not be dead, hence there is no reasonable notion of posttime in this sense. But this is different for otherwise similar verb stems, such as in *Cain opened the window*. In this case, the 'second interval of the second argument' is the window's being open; there may well be an interval afterwards at which the window is not open. It should be clear, therefore, that just talking about 'the time of a situation' or, accordingly, the 'time after the time of some situation' generally is a gross oversimplification. As was pointed out in section 2.2, we normally do not just deal with a single 'event time' but with a cluster of various temporal variables. Therefore, a satisfactory analysis cannot treat the 'event' as a whole and assign it a simple 'event time'; instead, it has to look at the various temporal variables within a construction and even within the lexical content of a simple verb.

3.2.4 The lexical content of verb stems II: argument-time structure

There are numerous proposals of how to decompose the lexical meaning of verb stems. In what follows, I will list five ingredients which I believe are indispensable if such an analysis is to be appropriate.

A. PROPERTIES FOR ARGUMENTS FOR TEMPORAL INTERVALS. The lexical content of a verb stem should be described as a cluster of pairs $<A_i, t_i>$, where A_i is some argument and t_i is some temporal interval, with qualitative or spatial properties provided for each of these pairs.

B. SOURCE STATE – TARGET STATE ASYMMETRY. If two temporal intervals are specified for an argument, I will call these temporal intervals 'source state' and 'target state', respectively, of that argument[9]. The most salient case here is a 'yes-no'-specification, i.a., the argument has some property in the source state and does not have it in the target state (or vice versa). But weaker contrasts are also possible. An interesting borderline case of a '2-state specification' is given when some argument only exists in one state but not in the other; this is the case for 'verbs of creation and annihilation', such as in *John baked a cake* or *John ate a cake* (see von Stechow 1997).

C. DURATIONAL PROPERTIES OF TEMPORAL INTERVALS. The lexical content may also contain information about whether the argument has this property forever (as in for example *be a prime number*), whether there may be a prior but no later time at which it doesn't have it (*be dead*), etc.

D. INHERENT TEMPORAL RELATIONS. If properties are specified for different temporal intervals, then these are temporally related to each other: they may follow each other, overlap, be simultaneous, etc.

E. OTHER RELATIONS. Typically, the lexical content also indicates a 'counterfactual relation' between the various specifications: t_x with properties

---

[9] Note that 'target state' and 'source state' are relative to individual arguments; this is different from many older distinctions found in the literature, e.g., Abraham's (1995: 138-9) 'monophasic' and 'biphasic' verbs, or '1-state' and '2-state' verbs in Klein 1992.

P would not obtain unless t_y with properties Q obtains. In honour of David Hume, who was the first to use counterfactuality in order to characterise the necessary connection between two objects of our cognition, I will say that the two substates are 'H-connected'. In *Cain slew Abel*, the specification of the second argument for the second time (i.e., Abel's being dead) is H-connected to (a) Abel's prior state of being alive (Cain could not have slain Abel if Abel had not been alive before), and (b) to Cain's activity (Abel would not be dead if Cain had not done what he has done). The second of these relations is usually seen as a sort of 'causal relation', whereas the first is more of a general presupposition. The notion of 'H-connection', as defined here, seems sufficiently broad to encompass these various relations.

These ingredients of the lexical content are needed in order to sort out the contribution of past participle and auxiliary, respectively, to the Perfekt meaning. First, however, we will consider their contributions as a whole.

4 The meaning of the German Perfekt I: FIN and the sentence base

A sentence with a finite verb form can be decomposed in the finite component FIN and a non-finite component, the 'sentence base'. We shall illustrate this for four tense forms of *der Stuhl umkipp-* 'the chair topple over':

(13)	Finite sentence	FIN	sentence base
a. Präsens	Der Stuhl kippt um.	FIN_0	[der Stuhl umkipp-]
b. Präteritum	Der Stuhl kippte um.	FIN<	[der Stuhl umkipp-]

(14)	Finite sentence	FIN	sentence base
a. Perfekt	Der Stuhl ist umgekippt.	FIN_0	[der Stuhl umgekippt sei-]
b. Plusquamperfekt	Der Stuhl war umgekippt.	FIN<	[der Stuhl umgekippt sei-]

Semantically, FIN locates TT on the temporal axis. As a rule, FIN< expresses that the TT precedes TU. The interpretation of FIN_0 is more difficult. I shall assume here that FIN_0 indicates that TT either includes TU or follows TU. Hence, it only excludes that the topic time properly precedes the moment of speech; since nothing is said about the boundaries of TT, this definition does not exclude that TT 'extend' into the past. In fact, TT can be 'the entire time', from beginning to end; after all, the entire time also includes TU. Alternative analyses are that FIN_0 only marks the relation 'TU is included in TT', or that it is an unmarked form with respect to the tense relation. For the moment, we shall not consider these alternatives and see later where the present analysis leads us.

The sentence base is a compound construction, and this inevitably raises the question of its syntactic composition. Since I want to keep the following discussion as neutral as possible with respect to the various syntactic theories on the market, it will only be assumed that the sentence base minimally consists of a 'surface subject' (abbreviated SUBJ) and some simple or complex construction PRED which expresses a predication over SUBJ. Hence, the minimal structure of a sentence base is [SUBJ PRED]. This is a gross oversimplification on many grounds. In particular, it does not make explicit the various temporal parameters that go with SUBJ or with PRED. As should be clear from the discussion in 3.2.3, a predication that assigns some properties to an argument is relative to some temporal interval and perhaps a place and a world. Hence, SUBJ should actually be considered a cluster of an argument at a time in a world at a place. Similarly, the predication may involve various argument specifications at various temporal intervals; this will be examined in section 6 below. For the moment, however, the discussion will be confined to the elementary structure [SUBJ PRED]. SUBJ is normally filled by one of the verb's lexical arguments, but it can also be a lexically empty argument or an expletive. PRED is a FIN-linkable expression; it can be a simple verb stem, a more complex VP, a copula construction, and perhaps others. This seems sufficiently general to be in agreement with most, if not all, syntactic theories.

In 13, the sentence base is [der Stuhl umkipp-]. It does not sort out a specific situation but rather characterises all temporal intervals with those properties. The sentence base by itself does not carry any claim that such a temporal interval, or several temporal intervals, with these properties ever existed, or will exist, or often exists, or that some particular time is such a temporal interval. This information is only brought in when FIN and the sentence base are linked. Morphologically, the process of FIN-linking is realised by the inflection on the lexical verb in 13a, b FIN marks that TT overlaps with a T-SIT with the properties described by the sentence base. The only difference stems from FIN: in 13a, TT must not precede TU, whereas in 13b, it must precede TU.

In 14, the base form *umkipp-* is replaced with the compound form *umgekippt sei-*. The morphosyntactic changes are clear: the verb stem is replaced with the participle, and the auxiliary is added. Both operations have semantic effects. I will describe these effects jointly by a temporal operator POST. Its function is to assign posttimes to the interval to which it is applied. If t is some interval, then POST (t) is any interval after t. Note that POST is a purely temporal relation. It does not say anything by itself what is the case at some POST (t). But if the interval t itself is assigned particular properties, then POST (t), too, may have particular properties. This is best explained by applying it to 14a.

The sentence base of 14a is the same as in 13, except that now POST is added. Where is it added? If the sentence base has the form [SUBJ PRED], then POST could be applied either to the entire sentence base, resulting in a new, compound sentence base [POST [SUBJ PRED]]; or it can be applied to just VP; in this case, the resulting sentence base is [SUBJ POST-PRED]. Hence, 14a could be represented as 15 or as 16:

(15) FIN_o + [POST [der Stuhl umkipp-]]
(16) FIN_o + [der Stuhl POST-umkipp-]

Under the first reading, TT is a posttime of some situation which is selectively described [der Stuhl umkipp-], i.e., the sentence *Der Stuhl ist umgekippt* is false iff its TT is not preceded by a situation where the chair toppled over. Under the second reading, TT overlaps with an interval with the properties of [der Stuhl umgekippt sei-], that is, if SUBJ at TT does not have the 'posttime properties' of PRED at TT. If PRED is a verb stem such as *umkipp-*, then at least some of the posttime properties are lexically specified, since *umkipp-* specifies source state as well as target state of its only argument; world knowledge may add others. If, however, the verb only specifies the properties of some argument at a single time, as is the case for *arbeit-*, then all properties of the argument at the ensuing state must be inferred from world knowledge. The person referred to in SUBJ may be tired, for example; but this is implicated rather than asserted.

As for SUBJ, it must make sense to assign the 'posttime properties' of PRED to SUBJ at TT. If, for example, the chair was completely burned three weeks ago, then this chair cannot have the posttime properties of *umkipp-* right now. Therefore, sentence 14a can have the first but not the second reading, if the chair does not exist at TT. It is also possible that SUBJ has no lexical argument and the lexical content of PRED does not include the specification of posttime properties. Impersonal constructions such as *Es hat geschneit* 'It has snowed' or *Hier ist getanzt worden* 'there was dancing here' are examples. They are still felt to have the two readings, although the LEXICAL CONTENT of the two sentence bases gives the same information for both of them. What is left is the intutive feeling that in the first case, the situation described by the sentence base is in the past, whereas in the second case, the situation described by the sentence base is in the present and has the 'posttime properties'. But since these are not lexically specified, they are not asserted but only implicated. If PRED is *schnei-*, then such an implicated posttime property may be the fact that right now, the 'world' is white outside. Imagine someone who wakes up in the morning, looks out of the window and says:

(17)   Schau mal an, es hat geschneit.
       Look at that, it has snowed.

Here, the speaker characterises the present situation, as he or she sees it: the world at TT at this place is characterised as having the (implicated) posttime properties of *schnei-*. But *es hat geschneit* can also be used in contexts in which the entire situation is said to have obtained in the past, for example in a narrative sequence:

(18) When we arrived yesterday, the weather was still fine.
But half an hour later, it *has been snowing.

The difference is more palpable if, as in *Hier ist getanzt worden*, the 'place parameter' of SUBJ is filled by a spatial adverbial. The place referred to by *here* exists in the past (at the time of dancing) as well as right now. But what is understood under the POST-PRED reading is something like that the 'here-right now' has some specific properties, say the various traces of earlier dancing at this place, whereas this is not required under the 'wide scope reading' of POST. This explains why in English, where only the former reading is possible, sentences such as *In Atlantis, there has been much dancing* are as odd as *Einstein has visited Princeton*, whereas the corresponding German sentences are fine.

Under the present analysis, we would expect the same ambiguity for the Plusquamperfekt, as in 14b *Der Stuhl war umgekippt*. Out of context, the most plausible reading is that at TT (which is in the past), the chair has the posttime property; hence, the chair is not in the scope of POST. But it can also mean that the entire situation precedes TT, for example in a narrative: *Der Stuhl war umgefallen, ich hatte ihn wieder aufgestellt, aber er war wieder umgefallen*. Hence, the prediction is indeed borne out.

5 Some consequences

In this section, we will resume some problems from the preceding sections and discuss how the present analysis accounts for them.

5.1 German Perfekt vs English present perfect

In German, POST can operate over PRED alone or over a full sentence base. English only admits the first of these. Therefore, 19a is odd, whereas its German counterpart 19b (= ex. 4) is fine:

(19) a. The colossus of Rhodes has weighed 100 tons.
b. Der Koloss von Rhodos hat hundert Tonnen gewogen.

In English, this would mean that for right now and for the colossus of Rhodes, this latter is claimed to be in the posttime of weighing 100 tons, an assertion which does not make much sense. In German, this reading is possible, too, and it is no less odd than its English counterpart. But there is another reading: the time right now is a time after an interval with properties of [the colossus of Rhodes weigh 100 tons]. And this is perfectly plausible.

For an English sentence with the present perfect to be felicitous, two conditions must be satisfied: (a) it must make sense to talk about 'posttime properties', and (b) the subject must 'exist' within TT, here and right now. If the lexical content specifies a permanent property of some entity (for example the lexical content of *be the son of a priest*), then it is pragmatically odd (though not wrong) to assign a posttime property to this entity. Therefore, 20 is odd:

(20)   Our president has been the son of a priest.

Such a sentence would make sense only if it could be otherwise at TT, that is, if someone's being the son of a priest at some time would not require his being the son of a priest at any later time. Exactly this is meant by 'permanent property of someone'. The corresponding German sentence is odd, as well, for precisely the same reasons.

If the lexical content does not specify a permanent property, then a sentence of this form is still odd in English, if the subject does not exist at TT – and if this is known to the speaker:

(21)   Einstein has visited Princeton.

This sentence is not odd to a speaker who does not know that Einstein has passed away, just like the sentence *The king of France was bold* is not odd to anyone who does not know that there was no king of France at the time for which the assertion is made. Nor is it odd if Einstein does not refer to the physical person who can visit Princeton, but to some entity which, in a way, is still present, as in *Einstein has influenced me more than any other patent office employee*. Having influenced someone is a 'posttime property' which still can be assigned to Einstein, although he is dead.

5.2 Perfekt vs Präteritum

Under the POST-[SUBJ PRED] reading, the Perfekt is normally translated by the simple or progressive past in English. In German, it can be replaced with the Präteritum. But there is still a subtle difference between Perfekt and Präteritum. In both cases, the situation itself is in the past. Thus, a speaker who wants to talk about some situation in the past is free to choose either form. They differ, however, in what is chosen as the time for which an assertion is made. This can be a time at which an interval with the described properties is over (Perfekt), or it can be a time which overlaps such an interval in the past (Präteritum). Thus, the choice is more an issue of how the situation in the past is presented: the Präteritum places the listener, as it were, in the midst of the situation in the past, as 'on-going, process-like'; whereas the Perfekt (under this reading) sees it from after the fact, as 'completed'. Exactly these are the metaphorical characterisations found in descriptive grammars for the these forms (cf. section 2.2 above). But these intuitions do not define the meaning of these forms, they naturally follow from this meaning. By the same token, it becomes plausible why the 'Perfekt' often gives the impression of 'describing the world', whereas the Präteritum gives the impression of 'narrating the world' (Weinrich 1974): the former talks about the 'now' as the result of something that occurred in the past, whereas the latter talks about the past itself and what then occurred.

5.3 Posttime infinitives

Under the present analysis, the two components of a Perfekt, FIN_0 and POST, are given an independent meaning, and the entire meaning results in a well-defined way from their interaction. FIN_0 indicates that TT does not precede TU. The meaning contribution of POST is 'time after the time of full sentence base' or 'posttime properties of a VP'. If no sentence base is involved, as in non-finite forms of the VP alone, then the difference should disappear, and German and English should behave alike. There is indeed no reason to assume that, e.g., *im Garten gearbeitet zu haben* can have two different readings:

(22) a. Im Garten gearbeitet zu haben, ist ein gutes Gefühl.
          In the garden worked to have, is a good feeling.
      b. Er bestreitet lebhaft, gestern um zehn im Garten gearbeitet zu haben.
          He denies vividly yesterday at ten in the garden worked to have.

Note that here, English tolerates an adverbial which refers to the past, whereas this is not possible with the finite form of the present perfect.

5.4 The role of adverbials

Nothing in the form of the Perfekt itself tells us which reading is intended. This is simply a matter of which scope the operator POST has, and as is often the case with operators, this scope is not structurally fixed. But there may be preferences, just as with quantifier scope in sentences such as *every cat loves a dog*. There seems to be such a preference for the 'wide scope' version of POST. In fact, it takes some effort to find convincing examples for the POST-PRED reading. Like all preferences, this one can be overruled by other factors, for example by a particular context, or else by adverbials which are only compatible with the non-preferred reading. An example of such a context is the situation described in connection with ex. 5, where the invitation to join a meal is turned down with *Danke, ich habe schon gegessen*. What is at stake here are the (inferred!) posttime properties of the invitee and speaker who, as a consequence, does not just talk about a situation in the past but about what is the case with him or her ('not being hungry').

Consider now adverbials that specify the position of some interval on the time line, such as *at that time, once, tomorrow at ten, now, then* etc. In a sentence such as *Ich habe im Garten gearbeitet*, there are two temporal intervals that could be specified by a temporal adverbial: a temporal interval at which the speaker is working in the garden, and a temporal interval after such an interval. The latter is TT. Examples 8a-c, repeated here, illustrated this:

(8) a. Gestern um zehn hat er die Stadt verlassen.
 Yesterday at ten has he the city left.
 b. (Gestern hättest du ihn treffen können.) Aber jetzt hat er die Stadt verlassen.
 (Yesterday you could have met him.) But now has he the city left.
 c. Morgen um zehn hat er die Stadt verlassen.
 Tomorrow at ten has he the city left.

In 8a, the past-time adverbial *gestern um zehn* cannot specify TT, since TT must include or be later than TU. Therefore, the adverbial must indicate an interval of the type [er die Stadt verlass-]. Sloppily speaking, it gives the 'event time', not a time at which the 'event' is over (the 'reference time'). No such contradiction arises, if the adverbial indicates a time which includes TU, such as *jetzt*, or which is later than TU, such as *morgen um zehn*. In these cases, the adverbial can easily specify a posttime.[10]

---

10 This analysis naturally accounts for the fact that the adverbial can have a 'reference time reading' in 8b, c but not in 8a. But it does not exclude an 'event time reading' for 8b, c – which these sentences normally do not have. This must have a different reason. Musan 1998 suggests an explanation which I am adopting here. Note that FIN_0 in itself already contains some information about the position of TT on the time line: TT includes or follows TU. Ehrich 1992 has

6 The meaning of German Perfekt II: The contribution of participle marking and auxiliary

In this section, we will try to disentangle the role of the two components of POST – the effect of applying GE- to the verb stem and of adding an auxiliary to the resulting form.

6.1 The contribution of the verb stem

A full description of the lexical content of some Vs must indicate (a) what the spatial or qualitative properties of the various time-argument pairs are, and (b) how the various property assignments are related to each other (cf. 3.2.4). As with all lexical information, this can be done individually for each lexical item, by lexical default rules, or by a combination of both. Since this is not a study on the various types of verb contents, the following discussion will be confined to four examples (*schlaf-* 'sleep', *einschlaf-* 'fall asleep', *hass-* 'hate', *öffn* '(transitive) open'), which represent four core types of lexical contents. There are more complex cases; but I not think that these affect the analysis of the Perfekt. I shall use the abbreviations <A, t_s> for 'first argument at first (and perhaps only) interval', <A, t_t> for 'first argument at second interval', <B, t_s> for 'second argument at first (and perhaps only) interval' and finally <B, t_t> for 'second argument at second interval'.[11] As for the argument variables A and B, it will be only assumed that the verb treats them as asymmetrical; in particular, no assumption is made about 'thematic roles'.[12]

---

noted that 'stative verbs' can hardly have the 'future reading' by themselves; they require an adverbial. Musan argues that the 'result state' (in her terminology) is a state and hence obeys this constraint. In the present framework, this means that if an assertion is made about some time in the future, this has to be marked by an adverbial; therefore, a future time adverbial is regularly interpreted as indicating that TT is after TU. In 8b, there is no adverbial that could shift TT into the future; hence, TT must include TU and follow T-SIT, and consequently, the adverbial *jetzt* cannot modify T-SIT itself. It only higlights that the assertion is made about the 'now'.

11 The subscripts in t_s and t_t are reminiscent of 'source state' and 'target state' respectively. But note that the first interval of the first argument need not be fully simultaneous to the first interval of the second argument; normally, it is only required that they have a common subinterval (cf 3.2.4).

12 It appears to me that notions such as 'thematic role' or 'case role' are only a gross and not very informative categorisation of the properties which the lexical content assigns to particular arguments. The 'theta-criterion' in generative grammar, for example, is simply a consequence of the fact that the verb content assigns spatial or qualitative properties to its arguments.

schlaf-
There is only one property assignment for <A, t_s>: A is assigned the property 'asleep' throughout t_s. In the event of FIN-linking, A becomes SUBJ, or in somewhat different terms: The noun phrase in SUBJ is assigned the properties which the lexical content provides for <A, t_s>.

einschlaf-
Again, there is only one argument variable, A. But distinct properties are assigned to it for two distinct subintervals. Hence, we have an assignment for <A, t_s> AND an assigment for <A, t_t>. In the first state, A is specified as being not asleep; in the second state, A is specified as being asleep. The two states are H-connected: you cannot fall asleep unless you are not asleep to begin with. The lexical content does not say anything about the temporal nature of the transition between source state and target state, although world knowledge may inform us about it. In the case of FIN-linkage, the noun phrase in A is assigned the properties of <A,t_s>.[13]

hass-
There are two argument variables, A and B, each characterised for one interval; hence, we have property assigments to <A, t_s> and <B, t_s>. It is difficult to specify the relevant qualitative properties: As for A, it is somehow strongly emotionally involved ('Hatred is the longer pleasure', Byron); there is hardly any qualitative (or spatial) characterisation of B, except that it is somehow the object of A's feelings. In an intuitive sense, the property which the lexical content assigns to A is 'stronger' than the one which it assigns to B. Again the noun phrase in SUBJ is assigned the properties which the lexical content provides for <A, t_s>.

öffn-
Here, the argument-time structure is <A, t_s>, <B, t_s> and <B, t_t>, where the last pair is H- connected to the two other ones. The property assignment is that at t_s, B is not open, and at t_t, B is open. As for A, it is only specified that there is some activitiy of whatever sort at some interval t_s. If, for example, John opens the garage, then he might turn a handle, push a button, or say 'Open, Sesame!'. If John opens a letter, the nature of his activity is very different. All that matters is that this activity overlaps with the source state of B, and that the two states are

---

13 It is assumed here that even if the verb stem contains two intervals for the argument that is to become SUBJ, only one of those is chosen as TT (the first one), when this verb stem is made finite. But it may well be that the property assignments of <A, t_s> and of <A, t_t> are asserted together, i.e., TT contains t_s and t_t. I believe that this is the case with the English simple form (except for some verbs such as *to know*), whereas it is not, or at least not generally, true in German.

H-connected: For *John opened the garage* to be true, the garage must be open AND it were not open without John's activity AND it were not open if it had already been open before. In the case of FIN-linking, the noun phrase in SUBJ is assigned the <A, t_s> property.

6.2 The meaning contribution of GE-

GE- operates on V_s. Morphosyntactically, it turns V_s into a form, the past participle, that is no longer FIN-linkable. This has two consequences. First, it cannot bear finite verb morphology. Second, it is no longer possible to construct a 'sentence base'. This does not mean, of course, that GE-V_s cannot specify the properties of some argument, for example as a nominal modifier.

It is much more difficult to characterise the semantic effect of GE-, since the past participle occurs in a variety of constructions. The most important of these are (see, e.g., Litvinov and Nedjalkov 1988, Lenz 1993, Rapp 1997, Wunderlich 1998):
A. THE PERFEKT. This is the construction in which we are primarily interested here.
B. THE PASSIVE. This is normally formed by combining the participle with the auxiliary *werd-* (there are some other auxiliary-like verbs in this function, such as *kriegen, bekommen* etc., cf. Leirbukt 1997).
C. PREDICATIVE CONSTRUCTIONS. These are formed by combining the participle of transitive verbs with the copula *sei-*, as in *die Tür war zugesperrt* 'the door was locked' (or some other 'light verbs', such as *wirk-*, *bleib-*, as in *die Tür wirkte zugesperrt* 'the door gave the impression of being locked', *die Tür blieb zugesperrt* 'the door remained locked'). The first construction is often called 'Zustandspassiv' ('stative passive') in German, in contrast to the dynamic 'Vorgangs-Passiv' ('process passive'), which is formed with *werd-*.
D. ATTRIBUTIVE USES. In this function, the participle modifies a noun, as in *eine zugesperrte Tür, der ertrunkene Riese*. In German, this construction is far more elaborate than in English. Essentially, all participles derived from transitive verbs can occur in this function, as well as participles from intransitive verbs, if these are 'telic', i.e., if, in the framework used here, the argument is lexically characterised for two time variables. In both cases, the attributive participle can be extended, as in *eine von mir selbst zugesperrte Tür* 'a by myself locked door' or *der im heimischen Schwimmbad ertrunkene Riese* 'the in the local swimming pool drowned giant'. In some cases, attributive participles are even infelicitious unless they are extended; thus, *ein umgebenes Dorf* 'a surrounded village' is odd, whereas *ein von allen Seiten von Wäldern umgebenes Dorf* 'a from all sides by forests surrounded village' is fine.

Do all of these uses reflect a uniform semantic operation of GE- on the verb stem? Two substantial obstacles render such an analysis difficult. First, there are clear instances of intransitive verbs in which the participle has the feature 'posttime' but not the feature 'passive', as in *der ertrunkene Riese, der entlaufene Hund, der verstorbene Papst*. Second, there seem to be clear cases in which the participle has the feature 'passive' but does not express a posttime property, as in *das Dorf ist von Wäldern umgeben* 'the village is surrounded by forests'.

One solution, tentatively assumed in Bierwisch (1996), is as follows: GE- changes the morphosyntactic properties but is semantically empty; the components 'passive' and 'posttime' ('Perfekt' in Bierwisch's terms) are brought in by the auxiliaries *haben, sein, werden*. This solution is ruled out because essentially the same semantic regularities are found in attributive use where there is no auxiliary: *a drowned giant* is dead already, due to earlier drowning, and *ein von Wäldern umgebenes Dorf* is a village which is surrounded by forests, and not surrounding them.

The safest position, as always, seems the assumption that the contribution of GE-, and hence the participle, do not have a uniform meaning at all. This is surely possible but not very desirable. Morphologically, the participle behaves exactly alike in all uses (except that it is inflected as an attribute, cf. *ein entlaufener Hund* vs. *der Hund ist entlaufen*; but this is generally true for attributive vs predicative constructions, cf. *ein grünes Haus* vs *das Haus ist grün*). Moreover, it does not explain which meaning the participle has under which circumstances.

The line which I will follow here is somewhat different. The idea is this. In the bare verb stem, it is always the property assigment to $<A, t_s>$ which is used for predication and, where possible, modification – that is, the property assignment to the first (and perhaps only) argument at the first (and perhaps only) time span. GE- operates on the lexical content of the verb stem and selects a different property assigment:

(23)   GE- changes the property assignment for modification and predication.

We will illustrate this with the four examples from 6.1. Consider first *schlaf-*; its lexical content contains only one property assignment, i.e., the one for $<A, t_s>$. As a consequence, no other property assignment is possible. Hence, *geschlafen* by itself does not indicate the properties of any argument to which it is syntactically applied. Therefore, constructions such as *ein geschlafener Riese* should not be interpretable. This is indeed the case. In the case of *ein-schlaf-*, by contrast, we have assigments for $<A, t_s>$ as well as for $<A, t_t>$. Rule 23 requires a change, hence the second property assignment must be chosen. Therefore, *ein eingeschlafener Riese* describes a giant which is asleep after having been not asleep before; and this is exactly what it means. If there are two arguments A and B but only one temporal interval for each, then the assigment for <B, t$_s$> is chosen. Therefore, *der gehasste Riese* should be the giant which has the second argument properties of *hass-*. And in fact, it is. Note, though, that in its bare form, this construction is sometimes felt to be a bit odd. It is perfect, however, when the participle is expanded, as in *der von vielen gehasste Riese*. We shall return to this point in a moment. Consider, finally, verb stems such as *öffn-*; their lexical content specifies properties for <A, t$_s$>, for <B, t$_s$> and for <B, t$_t$>. There is a problem here because two 'other' property assignments are available, and it is not clear from 23 which one is to be chosen. If the maximally different property assignment is selected (different argument, different time), then *ein geöffnetes Fenster* 'an opened window' should be a window which has the target state properties of the second argument of *öffn-* (including H-connection): it is open, and it would not be open if it had not been closed before, or without the activity of someone. This is indeed the normal interpretation. Hence, one would have to add to 23 the clause: 'and if there are several property assignments, it takes the maximally different one'.

There is a slightly different way to state the effect of GE-. It maintains the same idea, but is much simpler than 23 in its revised form – at the price of a debatable assumption about lexical contents. If the lexical content assigns two mutually exclusive properties to some argument, then this is only possible if it contains two temporal variables for this very argument. Thus, a window cannot be open and not open at the same time. It may well be, however, that the lexical content assigns identical properties to an argument at different times. At first, this looks somewhat odd: if the lexical properties of argument A are the same at t_i and t_j, why should there be two variables? But there are clear cases of this sort. Consider, for example, the difference between *John was in Spain* and *John remained in Spain*; whereas the former simply says with respect to some temporal interval that John is in Spain at that time, the latter involves two times spans, both characterised by the fact that John is in Spain. This naturally explains why *John was dead* is a normal sentence, whereas *John remained dead* is odd – unless one believes that someone who is dead at interval t_1 could be not dead at some later interval t_2. Another type of examples are sentences such as *Chris kept the door open*, in which the second argument is specified for two temporal intervals with identical properties. Hence, the idea that property assignments could be identical for the same argument at two different temporal intervals makes perfect sense. With this possibility in mind, we may assume the following default rule for the lexical content of verbs with two arguments:

(24) In the default case, the first of two arguments is specified for one interval, and the second is specified for two intervals.[14]

This is much in line with Dowty's idea that the prototypical 'patient' is a change-of-state argument (Dowty 1991, ex. 28) – except that we only assume that the second argument is specified for two temporal variables, with possibly identical property assignments. Note that sameness refers to what the lexical content specifies for the two intervals. This does not preclude choice of the earlier or the later interval invites somewhat different connotations.

Under this assumption, we can replace 24 with the following rule:

(25) GE- selects the property assigment of the second temporal interval.

If there is only one argument and only one time, as in *schlaf-*, there is no appropriate property assigment. This explains why *der geschlafene Riese* is not interpretable. If there is only one argument, but two times, then the specification of the second time is selected. This gives us the correct reading of *der eingeschlafene Riese*. If there are two arguments, the target state property of the second one is selected, and this gives us the correct reading of *der gehasste König* as well as *das geöffnete Fenster*.

This analysis is extremely simple. In particular, it explains, rather than stipulates, why 'atelic verbs' cannot have an attributive participle, whereas 'telic verbs' can. It also explains why the participle is sometimes 'passive': the first argument cannot have a second temporal interval if there are two arguments; hence, <B, t_t> is chosen. It does not explain, though, why the attributive participle is sometimes a bit odd, when B is identically specified for both intervals, as in *gehasst*. There may be two interrelated reasons for this. First, the properties selected in this case are close to nil, and second, they are identical to what is assigned to <B, t_s>. Which properties, for example, does *hass-* assign to its second argument? They are faint, and therefore, *der gehasste Riese* has hardly any additional lexical content and hence hardly any 'contrastive potential', unless it is enriched by some additional information such as *der von seinen eigenen Kindern gehasste Riese* – in which case the construction is fine. We observe the same problem when the difference between the source state properties and the target state properties of a single argument is weak. Thus, *ein erheblich gewachsener Baum* is much better

---

14 Since 24 is a default assumption, there may be deviations, which then must be noted as idiosyncrasies in the lexicon. Candidates are, for example, receptive verbs such as *krieg-, bekomm-* 'to get, to obtain' or verbs such as *kost-* in *zehn Mark kosten* 'to cost ten marks'.

than *ein gewachsener Baum*, in which the contrast is less clear. In general, there is a tendency to 'maximise' the contrast between what is assigned at two different time spans, if the lexical content by itself does not provide such a constrast. Thus, a verb such as *beobacht-* 'observe-' does not specify two states for its second argument. Hence, *ein beobachtetes Haus* should simply be a house which is under observation. Since this assignment is the same for both time spans, it should correspond to the two sentences *Ein Haus, das beobachtet wird* ('process passive'), as well as to *Ein Haus, das beobachtet ist* (so- called 'state-passive'), and this is indeed the case. Nevertheless, there is a intuitive feeling that *ein beobachtetes Haus* has a particular property which 'results' from the fact that it is under observation.

The inclination to add information beyond the straight effect of applying GE- often leads to a certain independence from this operation, that is, the participle becomes more or less 'lexicalised'. This process can take two forms. First, qualititave or spatial properties that are not part of the underlying lexical content of the verb stem but are typically implicated, can be added. This is, for example, the case in *ein gekochtes Ei* 'a boiled egg', where the egg must not just be in the target state of being boiled: it must have a particular consistency. Second, the H-connection may be lost; a typical English example is *a crooked street*, where the adjective is not felt to describe a property that is H-connected to some preceding action by someone (the Lord? the builders?). In both cases, the participle has acquired a more or less independent meaning: essentially, it is has become an independent adjective; in fact, the German counterparts of *crooked* or, similarly, *tired*, are adjectives: *krumm* and *müde*.

The present analysis of GE- leaves, of course, 'einiges, das immer noch zu fragen oder zu bemerken bleibt bei diesem wunderbarsten worte unserer sprache' ['something that remains to be asked or noted about this most wondrous word of our language'] (Grimm's Dictionary, vol. 4, col. 1622, about *ge-*). But in general, it seems to account very well for the attributive usage of the participle above; note that under this analysis, notions such as 'passive function' vs 'perfect function' of the participle disappear; they simply follow from (25).

6.3 The meaning contribution of the auxiliary

Various verb stems combine with the participle in order to build FIN-linkable expressions. The most important of these are *hab-, sei-, werd-, bleib-* 'have, be, become, remain'. Traditionally, *hab-* and *sei-* are called 'auxiliaries', when used to form the Perfekt; *sei-* and *werd-* can be used to form the two 'passives'; *bleib-* is normally not considered to be on a par with the other three. The conventional picture is surely not false, but it misses some important facts. In particular, it ignores that *sei-*, *werd-* and *bleib-* are regularly used in 'copula constructions', such as *grün sei-*, *grün werd-*, *grün bleib-*. This is not the case for *hab-*. Therefore, it would be much more natural to consider all combinations of a participle with *sei-*, *werd-*, *bleib-* as copula constructions; the verb stems should have the same function as in other copula constructions, independent of whether the result is traditionally called a 'passive' or a 'Perfekt'.[15] Only *hab-* requires a special analysis. This is the line which we will follow here.

6.3.1 Copula constructions

What is the function of the copula in sentences such as 26?

(26) a. Der Himmel war blau.
       The sky was blue.
    b. Der Himmel wurde blau.
       The sky became blue.
    c. Der Himmel blieb blau.
       The sky remained blue.

The expression to which they apply, here *blau*, expresses a qualitative property of some argument at some time, i.e., it is of type <A, t_s>. It is not FIN-linkable, but the copula renders it FIN-linkable, and A is to become the grammatical subject. So far, all three copulae behave in the same way; but they differ in their temporal function. The copula *sei-* leaves the temporal characteristics unaffected; it simply assigns this property to A at t_s. The copula *werd-* adds a property assigment for the same argument at an earlier time, <A, t_x>, with t_x before t_s; this assignment is different from what is assigned to <A, t_s>. The copula *bleib-* adds a property assignment to the same argument at a later time, <A, t_y>, with t_y after t_s; in this case, however, the properties assigned to A at t_s and at t_y are the same. In other words, *werd-* as well as *bleib-* add a second temporal interval for the single argument. As a result, both *Der Himmel wurde blau* and *Der Himmel blieb blau* are two-state expressions, but only the former expresses a change of state.

What happens if the expression to which the copula applies is not an adjective but a participle? This depends on the lexical content of the particular participle.

---

[15] Various authors have proposed analysing the 'Zustandspassiv' in this way, see recently Rapp 1998). The idea to treat the 'Vorgangspassiv' on a par with the copula-function of *werd-* was first elaborated in Musan 1996.

In cases such as *geschlafen*, there is no argument-time pair, hence, no copula construction should be possible. This is borne out out by the facts: neither *Hans ist geschlafen* nor *Hans wurde geschlafen* nor *Hans blieb geschlafen* is interpretable. Next, consider *eingeschlafen*, which assigns the posttime properties of *einschlaf-* to its argument. Exactly this is expressed by *Hans ist eingeschlafen* – the Perfekt of *einschlafen*. Similarly, we get the predicted reading when attaching *bleib-*: a sentence such as *Hans blieb eingeschlafen* means that he is still *eingeschlafen*, after some earlier interval at which he already had this property. Normally, it needs a special context in which it makes sense to say this; but the sentence has exactly the reading which is predicted by the copula function of *bleib-*. This, however, is not true for *werd-*: it is not possible to say *Hans wurde eingeschlafen*. I have no convincing explanation of this peculiar behaviour; it seems a total idiosyncrasy.[16]

Let us now first look at the fourth type of participles, such as *geöffnet*. Combination with *sei-* simply indicates that the argument has this property, i.e., *Das Fenster ist geöffnet* means that the window has the <B, t_t> property of *öffn-*. Combination with *bleib-* adds a later interval with the same property assignment. The more interesting case is *geöffnet werd-*; it goes back to an interval before the posttime of the second argument. In contrast to *blau werd-*, the earlier interval is lexically characterised; it is the time at which the window is not open and at which someone is somehow active. In other words, *werd-*, when attached to *geöffnet*, brings us back to a stage with the <A, t_s> property and the <B, t_t> property of *öffn-*. It reverses the effect of GE-, except that now, the second argument is the grammatical subject. The so-called 'process passive' simply results from the meaning assigned to GE- by rule 25, on the one hand, and the application of the copula *werd-*, on the other.

This leaves us with participles of the sort *gehasst*. They behave exactly as *geöffnet*, except that *gehasst ist* and *gehasst wird* assign the same property to their argument. As a result, we have two sentences, such as Der *König wurde gehasst* and Der *König war gehasst*, which mean more or less the same, except that the interval is different; in the first case, it is the interval at which the other argument 'hates', i.e., it is the interval with the property assignment <A, t_s>. Normally, the

---

[16] The point made here is not that 'predicative constructions' and 'passive constructions' with *werd-* are exactly the same but that the meaning contribution of *werd-* is the same in both cases; differences result from the other component. In both cases, there might be additional constraints. Thus, *werd-* cannot be used with spatial properties, i.e., is possible to say *Hans war hier*, *Hans blieb hier*, but not *Hans wurde hier*. It is even odd for some qualitative adjectives, such as *tot*; the sentence *Hans wurde tot* is understandable but surely not what one would normally say. It may be that the formation of these constructions is blocked by the systematical availability of synonymous expressions. Thus, *Hans wurde eingeschlafen* would mean exactly the same as *Hans schlief ein*; similarly, *Hans wurde tot* would mean the same as *Hans starb*.

first of these two sentences is preferred; the second one is not impossible, though; it somehow gives a particular flavour of a 'resulting property'. This is parallel to what has been said above (end of section 6.2) about *das beobachtete Haus:* A sentence such as *Das Haus ist beobachtet* gives much more of an impression of some specific property assigned to the house than does *Das Haus wird beobachtet*.

Summing up, the copula analysis proposed here correctly predicts the relevant properties of the *sein*-Perfekt as well as the two passives. There is one asymmetry, though, not mentioned so far, between the *sein*-Passiv and the *sein*-Perfekt. Compare the following two sentences:

(27)   Der Riese ist eingeschlafen.
(28)   Der Riese ist erschlagen.

Sentence 27 can be used to describe a present property of the giant but also an event in the past. It could be continued by ... *laßt uns jetzt fliehen* 'let us try to escape'. It could also be followed by ... *und hat bald darauf ganz fürchterlich geschnarcht* 'and in a moment, he was snoring terribly'. In short, it can have a [SUBJ POST- PRED] reading, but also a POST [SUBJ PRED] reading (cf. section 5). Ex. 28 can only have the first reading – it describes present properties of the giant; the other reading must be expressed by *Der Riese ist erschlagen worden*. This asymmetry is apparently due to the different status of the argument which is marked as grammatical subject. This will be discussed in section 6.4.

6.3.2 The *auxiliary hab-*

Apart from its function as a main verb and in some modal constructions such as *Hans hat zu kommen* 'Hans has to come', *hab-* can only be combined with participles in order to form a Perfekt, more precisely, with participles of the type *geschlafen, gehasst, geöffnet*. These are exactly those that have no 'posttime specification' for the first argument, either because they provide no second time interval at all, as *schlaf-*, or because they provide such an interval, but only for the second argument, as *hass-* and *öffn-*. But clearly, a Perfekt such as in *Eva hat geschlafen* involves such a later time span. Hence, it is the function of *hab-* to provide a $<A, t_i>$ slot. This means that *geschlafen hab-, gehasst hab-, geöffnet hab-*, but also *eingeschlafen sei-* have $<A, t_s>$ as well as $<A, t_i>$. But whereas in *geschlafen sei-*, the second slot comes from the lexical content of the verb stem, the three other constructions owe it to the addition of *hab-*.

Note that *hab-* does not provide an additional qualititative or spatial properties; it only gives us a later time for A. All we can say about what is the case with A at that later time comes from world knowledge. This corresponds exactly to what was said in section 1 about examples such as *Ich habe geduscht*: it may be that the speaker is clean, but this is not asserted – it is only inferred. In those cases in which the lexical content of the verb stem provides us with a property assignment for <B, $t_{t'}$>, we may, of course, say something about the properties of B at that later stage. Thus, in *Georg hat das Fenster geöffnet*, the lexical content does not allow us to say anything about what is the case with Georg at that later time; but it allows us to say that the window is open. There is a caveat, however: *hab-* provides us with a second interval for A, and *öffn-* provides us with a second interval for B. This means that $t_{t'}$ in <A, $t_{t'}$> and in <B, $t_{t'}$> need not completely coincide. Therefore, *Georg hat das Fenster geöffnet* should have a reading at which, at the later time, the window is closed again. And so it is.

In conclusion, this analysis gets us exactly the semantic properties of *hab-* and *sei-* Perfekts that we expect. There are some borderline cases, though. For example, there are a number of intransitive verbs for which it is not entirely clear whether they specify only one interval for their argument or two, especially motion verbs such as *lauf-, schwimm-, flieg-*. They take *sei-* as well as *hab-*. But they must take *sei-* if it is clear that there is a target interval: thus, **Er hat in den Garten gelaufen* is impossible, whereas *Er hat im Garten gelaufen* is not excluded. Therefore, these verbs do not speak against the present analysis; they just reflect transitory cases of lexical content, surely not an uncommon phenomenon. But they are much in agreement with an analysis that does not speak of 'posttime' in general but of individual 'posttimes' for different arguments.[17]

6.4 The two readings of the Perfekt revisited

The Perfekt ambiguity arises as soon as the non-finite but FIN-linkable constructions *geschlafen hab-, eingeschlafen sei-, gehasst hab-* and *geöffnet sei-* are integrated into a full finite clause. This means, first, that the verb stem undergoes certain morphological changes; second, that TT is marked; and third, that SUBJ is appropriately filled. Consider, for example, *Eva hat geschlafen*. The morphological change goes from *hab-* to *hat*. The time interval of this verb is marked as TT, and since in this case, FIN is FIN_0, the time for which the assertion is made must not precede the moment of speech. This temporal interval is the 'posttime of A'. The NP in SUBJ is *Eva*. Two

---

[17] A real exception are the three copula verbs which, against all odds, form their Perfekt with *sei-* rather than with *hab-*. This seems to be a lexical idiosyncrasy, and in fact, traditional grammars regularly describe it as such.

argument-time slots are contained in *geschlafen hab-*: <A, t_s> and <A, t_t>. This leaves open whether the NP in SUBJ is interpreted with respect to interval t_s or with respect to interval t_t. In the first case, Eva is assigned the property 'asleep', and it is said that TT is a temporal interval after an interval where Eva has this property. This is the 'simple past'-reading of the Perfekt. In the second case, Eva is interpreted at this later interval itself, that is, at TU, which implies, among other things, that Eva must somehow exist at this time; this gives us the 'present perfect' reading of the Perfekt. The situation is exactly the same with *eingeschlafen sei-*, except that here, <A, t_t> stems from the lexical content of *einschlaf- itself*, rather than from the auxiliary.

This becomes clearer when we have a closer look at what, under a more detailed analysis, is involved in SUBJ: It should include a time parameter (the topic time), a place parameter (which is optional), a world parameter, and finally a nominal argument. German, as many other languages, requires a 'grammatical subject' marked by case and perhaps other features, such as position or agreement with the verb. This does not mean, however, that an NP which satisfies these syntactical requirements is also interpreted with respect to the other parameters in SUBJ, in particular with respect to time – if the lexical content provides options. English requires this: if the first argument 'is raised to SUBJ', to use a familiar *façon de parler*, then it must be interpreted with respect to the other parameters there. In German, 'raising to SUBJ' does not imply this. It is this difference which is eventually responsible for the difference between German Perfekt and English present perfect, despite their similarity in origin and in formal composition.

7 Conclusion

The present analysis of the German Perfekt only operates with notions that are needed independently – temporal relations, temporal intervals, the characterisation of these intervals by the lexical content of simple and complex expressions, the distinction between 'finite' and 'non-finite' expressions, and finally the notion of assertion (in the case of declarative clauses). It appears that this notional repertoire suffices to assign a uniform meaning to the Perfekt, which results from the meaning of its parts and which predicts the different readings which the Perfekt is supposed to have. It also neatly explains its difference from the Präteritum, with which it often competes, as well as its difference from the English present perfect. At the same time, this analysis gives us the core properties of the German 'Vorgangspassiv' and 'Zustandspassiv'. Traditional categories such as 'Perfekt' or 'Passiv' are not primitive notions of linguistic theory; they turn out to be nothing but gross ways of clustering semantic and syntactic properties of their components.

In the epigraph to this paper, I quoted the most famous switch from Präteritum to Perfekt in the German literature – the end of Goethe's 'Die Leiden des jungen Werthers'. The most recent English translation (by E. Mayer and L. Brogan, The Modern Library, N. Y. 1993) does not, and cannot, contain such a switch: 'The old man and his sons followed the body to the grave; Albert was unable to; Lotte's life was in danger. Workmen carried the coffin. No clergyman attended.' In the original, the narrative up to Werther's funeral is in the Präteritum, i.e., TT precedes TU and overlaps with T-SIT. But then, the last sentence all of a sudden shifts to the Perfekt. This indicates that the time about which something is asserted switches to the here-and-now, that is, to a perspective from which the event itself is done and over. Exactly this is the intuitive feeling which we have here.

References

Abraham, Werner (1995). Deutsche Syntax im Sprachenvergleich. Tübingen: Narr.
Abraham, Werner, and Janssen, Theo, eds (1989). Tempus – Aspekt – Modus. Die lexikalischen und grammatischen Formen in den germanischen Sprachen. Tübingen: Niemeyer.
Ballweg, Joachim (1988). Die Semantik der deutschen Tempusformen. Düsseldorf: Schwann.
Bäuerle, Rainer (1979). Temporale Deixis, temporale Frage. Zum propositionalen Gehalt deklarativer und interrogativer Sätze. Tübingen: Narr.
Bierwisch, Manfred (1996). The compositionality of Analytic Tenses. Berlin: Humboldt University, ms.
Dowty, David (1979). Word Meaning and Montague Grammar. Dordrecht: Reidel.
Dowty, David (1991). Thematic Proto-Roles and Argument Selection. Language 67. 547–619.
ten Cate, Abraham (1989). Präsentische und präteritale Tempora im deutsch-niederländischen Sprachvergleich. In Abraham und Janssen 1989. 133–154.
Ehrich, Veronika (1992). Hier und Jetzt. Tübingen: Niemeyer.
Ehrich, Veronika, and Vater, Heinz (1989). Das Perfekt im Dänischen und im Deutschen. In Abraham and Jansen 1989. 103–132.
Fabricius-Hansen, Catherine (1986). Tempus fugit. Düsseldorf: Schwann.
Grewendorf, Günther (1995). Präsens und Perfekt im Deutschen. Zeitschrift für Sprachwissenschaft 1995. 72–90.
Grundzüge einer deutschen Grammatik (1981). Berlin: Akademie Verlag.
Hamann, Cornelia (1987). The awesome seeds of reference time. Alfred Schopf, ed, Studies on Tensing in English 1. Tübingen: Niemeyer. 27–69.
Hamburger, Käte (1968). Die Logik der Dichtung. Stuttgart: Metzler.
Hauser-Suida, Ulrike, and Hoppe-Beugel, Gabriele (1972). Die Vergangenheitstempora in der geschriebenen deutschen Sprache der Gegenwart. Düsseldorf: Schwann.
Helbig, Gerhard, and Buscha, Joachim (1974). Deutsche Grammatik. Leipzig: VEB Enzylopädie.
Leirbukt, Oddleif (1997). Das bekommen-Passiv im Deutschen. Tübingen: Narr.
Lenz, Barbara (1993). Probleme der Kategorisierung deutscher Partizipien. Zeitschrift für Sprachwissenschaft 12. 39–76.
Lindgren, Kaj (1957). Über den oberdeutschen Präteritumschwund. Helsinki: AASF.

Litvinov, Viktor, and Nedjalkov, Vladimir (1988). Resultativkonstruktionen im Deutschen. Tübingen: Narr.
Klein, Wolfgang (1992). The present perfect puzzle. Language 68. 525–552.
Klein, Wolfgang (1994). Time in language. London: Routledge.
Musan, Renate (1996). On werden. Berlin: Humboldt University, ms.
Musan, Renate (1998). The core semantics of the present perfect in German. ZAS Arbeitspapiere 10. 113–145.
Rapp, Irene (1997). Partizipien und semantische Struktur. Zu passivischen Konstruktionen mit dem 3. Status. Tübingen: Stauffenberg.
Rapp, Irene (1998). Zustand? Passiv?–Überlegungen zum sogenannten 'Zustandspassiv'. Zeitschrift für Sprachwissenschaft 15. (1996, recte 1998). 231–265.
Shannon, Thomas F. (1989). Perfect auxiliary variation as a function of 'Aktionsart' and transititivity. In: Joseph Emonds et al., eds., Proceedings of the Western Conference on Linguistics 1988. Fresno: California State University. 254–266.
von Stechow, Arnim (1997). Verben des Entstehens und Vergehens. University of Tübingen: Dept. of Linguistics, ms.
Thieroff, Rolf (1992). Das finite Verb im Deutschen. Tübingen: Narr.
Weinrich, Harald (1971). Besprochene und erzählte Welt. Stuttgart: Kohlhammer.
Wunderlich, Dieter (1970). Tempus und Zeitreferenz im Deutschen. München. Hueber.
Wunderlich, Dieter (1998). Participle, Perfect and Passive in German. Düsseldorf: University of Düsseldorf, ms.
Zeller, Joachim (1994). Die Syntax des Tempus. Opladen: Westdeutscher Verlag.

Aspect and assertion in mandarin Chinese

1 Introduction

Aspect, or aspect marking, has received a great deal of interest in Chinese linguistics in the last thirty years.[1] This interest might be due to the fact that markers of aspect are the only kind of morphology-like devices in the language. In Chinese, there is no inflectional morphology to express tense, number, gender, or case. Hence, aspect is a special grammaticalised category in Chinese.

Most analyses of Chinese aspect in the literature focus on four aspect markers: *le, guo, zhe,* and *zai*. In a sentence, the first three markers follow the verb, while the last one precedes the verb. Despite the immense interest and the numerous studies devoted to Chinese aspect, the precise function of each of these markers is still under considerable debate. There is agreement that they do not relate the situation described by the sentence to the time of utterance but express various perspectives on the situation; hence, they express various aspect rather than tense relations, and are often called aspect particles or markers (Li and Thompson 1981). There is also agreement that *zhe* and *zai* somehow characterise the situation as 'imperfective', 'progressive' or 'durative' whereas *le* and *guo* express a 'perfective' (or perhaps 'perfect') aspect. Detailed linguistic analyses of these particles vary considerably from author to author. In this introduction, we first present a standard version of the functions of aspect particles on the basis of standard analyses such as those espoused by Chao (1968) and Li and Thompson (1981). We then point out some problems with such analyses and our plan to proceed with a new analysis.

1.1 The perfective aspect markers

The particle *le* is generally considered a perfective marker: according to traditional analysis, it presents a situation in its entirety, as an event bounded at the beginning and the end, and without reference to its internal structure.[2] *Le* has often been

---

[1] A conservative estimate is that over two hundred articles have been published on the linguistic analyses of aspect markers in Chinese.

[2] There is also a sentence-final *le* whose relation to the verb-final *le* is a matter of dispute in the literature. A clear demarcation of, or even the existence of, the two kinds of *le* has been difficult

---

Note: This article was written in cooperation with Ping Li and Henriette Hendriks and originally appeared as Klein, W., Li, P., and Hendriks, H. (2000). Aspect and assertion in Mandarin Chinese. Natural Language & Linguistic Theory 18. 723–770.

https://doi.org/10.1515/9783110549119-005

characterised as marking completion (see Chao 1968). However, some researchers emphasise its perfectivity and argue that *le* does not by itself indicate a completed event or action (e.g., Li and Thompson 1981): the meaning of completion often comes from the meaning of the verb with which *le* occurs. For example, when the verb encodes a situation with a clear temporal boundary, *le* indicates that the situation comes to its natural endpoint, that is, it is completed, as illustrated in (1). But when the verb encodes a situation with no natural boundary, *le* signals the termination rather than completion of a situation, as in (2) (see Li 1990; Shih 1990; Smith 1991).

(1) Qi-chi zhuang-dao -le fangzi.
    car   hit-break   -LE house
    The car knocked down the house.
(2) Xiao yazi you –le yong.
    duckling swim-LE stroke
    The duckling swam.

The example in (1) contains a so-called 'resultative verb construction' (RVC; see section 4.3) that encodes a telic, resultative endpoint (i.e., the break-down of the house), where the perfective *le* indicates that the end result has been achieved (i.e., the event is completed). In contrast, (2) contains an atelic activity verb *you-yong* 'swim' that encodes no natural endpoint, and *le* indicates that the event took place and terminated at some indefinite point. Finally, in traditional analyses (e.g., Chao 1968; Rohsenow 1976), *le* can also indicate the inception or inchoativity of a situation, for example, as in *Zhangsan pang le* 'Zhangsan became fat'.

Another perfective particle, *guo*, has been generally characterised as an 'experiential marker': it indicates that an event has been experienced at some indefinite time, usually in the past,[3] and that the resultant state no longer obtains at the time of speech. As a perfective marker, it is concerned with the external, rather than the internal structure of the sitation. According to some authors,

---

to prove in the literature (see Thompson 1968; Rohsenow 1976, 1978; Li 1990), especially when we are concerned with examples like *Zhansan pang-le*, in which *le* is both at the end of the sentence and at the end of the verb. Our discussion of the perfective *le* is relevant primarily to the verb-final *le* (including *le* that is both verb-final and sentence-final). Similarly, we ignore some of the complications associated with *zai* because of its function as a locative preposition (see Li 1993).
3 Because *guo* is frequently associated with the past, it has sometimes been considered as having a tense function (cf. Chao 1968). However, it does not by itself indicate pastness: an explicit reference time in the future can be provided and *guo* can be used to indicate that the event will be experienced at some indefinite time in the future.

guo is more of a 'perfect' than a 'perfective' marker, given that it involves two distinct times, reference time and speech time, and its indefiniteness characteristic (Smith, 1991). Examples (3a–b) illustrate the differences between *le* and *guo*.

(3) a. Lisi da-po   –le yi-ge   beizi.
       Lisi hit-break -LE one-CL⁴ cup
       Lisi broke a cup.
   b. Lisi da-po   -guo yi-ge   beizi.
      Lisi hit-break -GUO one-CL cup
      Lisi once broke a cup.

In (3a), the sentence refers to a situation in which the broken pieces of the cup may be still be laying on the ground; *le* indicates a completed action of breaking. In contrast, in (3b), the sentence is appropriate only when referring to an experience that Lisi had – that she has once broken a cup (at some indefinite time in the past), and that the resulting state of breaking no longer holds true at the time of utterance. This last characteristic of *guo* – the resulting state no long obtains – distinguishes *guo* not only from *le*, but also from the English perfect; the English perfect conveys a 'current relevance' meaning whereas *guo* does not (*Mary has broken a cup* is a more appropriate translation for (3a) than for (3b)). This characteristic of *guo* is what Chao (1968) and Smith (1991) called the "discontinuity" meaning of *guo*.

Finally, Li and Thompson (1981, p. 192) stated that *le* and *guo* differ in "definiteness": *le* not only indicates boundedness but also marks a "specific or definite event", whereas for *guo* it suffices that some event of the type described by the sentence has occurred sometime. This point has also been made elsewhere, for example, in Mangione and Li's (1993) compositional analysis of *le* and *guo* (see section 2.2.2): "… *le* marks a specific event time, which is ordered before and closely to its sentences reference time, while *guo* can be taken as providing an existential quantification over times which are earlier than the *guo* sentence's reference time" (1993, p. 68). Thus, this difference, in whichever precise form it is couched, reflects a common intuition about the function of these two particles.

1.2 The imperfective aspect markers

The particle *zai* has had a long historical development, appearing first as a verb, then as a locative preposition, and only recently as an imperfective aspect marker

---

4 CL stands for classifiers.

(see Li 1988, 1993, for discussion).[5] As a preposition, *zai* can occur both preverbally and postverbally, while as an aspect marker it can occur only preverbally (Zhu 1981; Li 1990, 1993). Its main function as an aspect marker is to indicate that an action or event is in progress, hence the title of progressive marker. The particle *zhe* indicates that a situation is viewed as enduring or continuing (i.e., durative), often as a backgrounding information, for example, in V + *zhe* + V constructions (e.g., *xiao-zhe shuo* smile-ZHE speak 'speaking with a smile').

According to traditional analyses, the two imperfective markers differ in the verb types to which they can be applied: *zai* cannot be used with stative verbs that indicate fully homogeneous states, whereas *zhe* can be used with verbs that indicate at least some homogeneous states but normally not 'dynamic' events. For example, if a verb can have either a dynamic or a static reading, then the former is brought out by the use of *zai*, as in (4a), whereas the latter is usually brought out by the use of *zhe*, as in (4b).[6]

(4) a. Lisi zai chuan yi-jian qunzi.
    Lisi ZAI put-on one-CL skirt
    Lisi is putting on a skirt.
  b. Lisi chuan-zhe yi-jian qunzi.
    Lisi wear-ZHE one-CL skirt
    Lisi wears a shirt.

Along this line, Smith (1991) proposed that *zai* has a dynamic meaning, while *zhe* has a static meaning (see section 2.2.1). It would appear, however, that dynamicity or stativity comes from the verb to which the particles apply, rather than from the particles themselves, in sentences (4a–b) as well as in other cases. Such interactions between particles and inherent meanings of verbs also seem to be true with other particles, for example, the interpretation of *le* with different types of verbs (see sections 1.1 and 6.2.1; see also Li and Shirai 2000 for a general discussion of such interactions in Chinese, English, Japanese, and child language).

So far, the most careful and comprehensive exposition of the various uses of Chinese aspect particles is found in Li and Thompson (1981, pp. 185–237):

---

5 Historically, progressive aspect has an intimate relationship with locative expressions in many languages (Comrie 1976, p. 99; Bybee et al. 1994). One can still find historical traces in expressions like English *asleep*, which comes from *at sleep* (cf. Vlach 1981). The Chinese *zai* is a locative verb in origin, and it is therefore not surprising that it could develop into a progressive aspect marker.

6 In the Beijing dialect, *zhe* can be used on both the static and the dynamic meaning of such verbs, especially when the particle *ne* is added to the sentence (see 6.5; Ma 1987).

A. The verbal aspect suffix *le* expresses perfectivity, that is, it indicates that an event is being viewed in its entirety or as a whole. An event is viewed in its entirety if it is bounded temporally, spatially, or concepttually.
B. The aspect suffix *guo* means that an event has been experienced with respect to some reference time. When the reference time is left unspecified, then *guo* signals that the event has been experienced at least once at some indefinite time which is usually in the indefinite past.
C. In Mandarin there are two aspect markers that signal the durative nature of an event: the word *zai* and the suffix *zhe*. The usage of the durative markers in a sentence depends on the meaning of the verb.

In a more recent systematic treatment, Smith (1991) gives the following characterisations (again, these characterisations only cover the basic functions, depending on context and on the particular verb to which the particle applies):

A'. *Le* spans the initial and final points of the situation (p. 344) and perfective *le* presents closed non-stative situations (p. 347).
B'. The second perfective in Mandarin is indicated by the verbal suffix *guo*; the viewpoint presents a closed situation and also conveys that the final state of that situation no longer obtains (p. 348).
C'. Mandarin has two imperfective viewpoints: *zai* and *zhe*. *Zai* is a typical progressive; *zhe* has a static meaning (p. 356).

These and similar characterisations more or less reflect the *opinio communis* on these four particles. We believe that this view is intuitively plausible, but we also think that it suffers from a number of inadequacies. In this paper, we will advance a somewhat different view. This new view uses the general temporal framework of Klein (1994), according to which aspect expresses a temporal relation between the time at which the situation described by the sentence obtains, on the one hand, and the time for which an assertion is made by this sentence, on the other. We will argue that the main function of the particles in Chinese is to impose specific temporal constraints on the assertion made by the particular utterance in which they occur. This new analysis is not incompatible with the previous idea that these particles have a particular aspectual value. In fact, we will show that the basic intuitions in previous studies about the functions of the four particles, as well as a number of other empirical facts, follow naturally from the analysis that we suggest here.

This paper is organised as follows. In section 2, we discuss four substantial problems that previous analyses of Chinese aspectual particles face. Some of these problems have to do with the general definition of aspect, whereas others are specific to the case of Chinese. One of those is the observation, noted by several authors (see sections 2.2 and 6.2.1), that the presence or absence of aspectual particles in Chinese affects the 'assertive status' of the utterance – what is understood to be asserted and what is just inferred from context. This observation, which cannot be accounted for by existing approaches, is the point of departure for our new analysis. This section also includes a discussion of two current formal accounts of Chinese aspectual particles. In section 3, we argue that the proper analysis of tense and aspect requires a distinction between the time at which some situation (process, state, event) obtains, on the one hand, and the time about which something is asserted by the sentence, on the other. The traditional notion of aspect as different ways to 'view' a situation can be reconstructed as a purely temporal relation between these two time intervals. In section 4, we discuss how this time-relational perspective of aspect is related to the inherent temporal properties of the proposition which is used to describe the situation; in particular the distinction between '1-phase contents' and '2-phase contents'. In section 5, we show how the general idea can be spelled out for different languages and illustrate it briefly with English, thus preparing the basis for a comparative analysis of the Chinese aspectual particles *le*, *guo*, *zhe*, *zai*, and zero marking (i.e., no explicit marking). In section 6, we present our analysis for Chinese and, in section 7, we conclude how it accounts for the various problems raised in section 2.

2 Problems with aspect and aspectual particles

Most existing analyses of Chinese aspectual particles are based on what one might call the 'canonical notion' of aspect – the idea that aspect reflects different views on a situation. This notion of aspect can be found in comprehensive descriptive grammars such as Chao (1968) and Li and Thompson (1981) as well as specific treatments of aspectual particles, as Li (1990), Smith (1991), and Yang (1995). In what follows, we shall first discuss this traditional approach and point out a number of serious problems with it (section 2.1). We will then discuss Smith's (1991) attempt to give the classical analysis a more precise shape (section 2.2.1). We will finally examine Mangione and Li's (1993) analysis, a compositional analysis which departs from the classical approach (section 2.2.2).

2.1 Four problems with the classical notion of aspect

An aspectual analysis in traditional terms is well illustrated by Li and Thompson's characterisation of the particle *le* quoted above, according to which it "indicates that an event is being viewed in its entirety or as a whole". This definition is very much in accordance with common characterisations of perfective aspect found in the literature, for example Comrie (1976, p. 3): "Aspects are different ways of viewing the internal temporal constituency of a situation". The situation may be presented as a whole, without specific reference to its inner constituency, in which case we are said to use the perfective aspect, or it may involve a reference to the inner constituency, in which case we are said to use the imperfective aspect. There are also various ways of viewing the inner constituency, and accordingly, we have different subtypes of the imperfective. Much of the same idea, though with a slightly different focus, is found in Smith (1991): "Sentences with a perfective viewpoint present a situation as a single whole. The span of the perfective includes the initial and final endpoints of the situation: it is closed informationally" (p. 103) and "imperfective view-points present part of a situation, with no information about its endpoints. Thus, imperfectives are open informationally" (p. 111).

This definition of aspect, found in varying formulations, is well established. It is very suggestive, and very useful for descriptive as well as pedagogical purposes. But on closer inspection, it raises a number of substantial problems.

2.1.1 Problem A: the definition is entirely metaphorical

If it is said that aspects are different ways of 'viewing' a situation, then it is not at all clear what 'viewing' means here. It cannot have its literal meaning: events, states, processes, in short, situations are not like houses or little dogs which you can 'view' – they are abstract entities which have something to do with time, and you cannot see them at all. Thus, at best we are using the word 'view' only metaphorically. This metaphor of 'viewing something', intuitively appealing as it might be, is in need of explanation. What does it mean that, for example, in the English simple form, the situation is seen, viewed, or presented 'in its entirety', 'as a whole', or 'without reference to inner constituency'? What does it mean that in the progressive, the situation is not seen in its entirety, without boundaries, or with reference to inner constituency? Again, these metaphors may have some intuitive plausibility in cases such as *John read a book* vs. *John was reading a book*, but they are not very suggestive in other cases such as *They hoped for a better future* vs. *They were hoping for a better future* or *He stood on his toes* vs. *He was standing on his toes*.

2.1.2 Problem B: perfectivity does not reflect the 'boundaries' or the 'boundedness' of the situation

A core element in the definition of perfective and imperfective are the notions of 'boundary' and, not identical but related, 'boundedness'. They are found not only in the various definitions discussed above but also in a great deal of the aspect literature (see, for example, Dahl 1985 for a crosslinguistic study along these lines and Binnick 1991 for a comprehensive historical discussion). But this idea is problematic in many ways. The first problem is that it fails to distinguish between the properties of the situation itself and what the sentence makes explicit about this situation. It is often said, but simply not true, that verbs such as *sleep*, *watch* and *walk* typically refer to unbounded situations, whereas *die*, *run a mile*, and *bake a cake* refer to bounded situations. In reality, with very few exceptions, all situations are bounded, or have some temporal boundaries (see more discussion in section 4.1). Hence, it is at best misleading to speak about 'bounded' and 'unbounded' situations as situation types. Now, one could argue that independent of what the situation itself is like, it may be presented, viewed or described, as bounded. But then, we are back to the problem of what 'viewed' or 'presented' means. In particular, what does it mean to present a situation as unbounded if it is bounded, or vice versa? This brings us to the second problem.

It is easy to see that imperfective aspect ('viewed without boundaries') is compatible not only with a situation that has boundaries but also with the explicit specification of these boundaries. In English, for example, it is possible to say *George was living in London for seven years, Chris was working from two to five, I will be teaching from now till lunchtime*, etc. In Russian, these sentences have even to be in the imperfective aspect. In French, one can say *Jean travaillait de cinq à six seulement* 'Jean worked from 5 to 6 only' and *Le bureau était fermé pendant deux heures* 'The office was closed for two hours'. In all of these languages, the imperfective variant of the particular verbal system is entirely appropriate if not better than the perfective, or, as in Russian, even the only one that is possible. In these cases, not only is it true that the situation has boundaries, but they are explicitly indicated. One might argue that aspectual marking concerns only the verb, and has nothing to do with the marking of boundaries by other devices such as adverbials. But it would be clearly odd to say that the aspect presents the situation as unbounded, whereas at the same time, the adverbials explicitly mark it as bounded. This seems a clear contradiction, but there is nothing contradictory or odd in these sentences.

Interestingly, there is also the opposite case: a situation marked as perfective without any clear boundary. In French, there is a clear difference between the 'imperfective' *Il était gros* and the 'perfective' *Il fut gros*. In neither case is there a clear boundary of his being fat. The perfective variant expresses rather a kind of inchoativity of the state. Similarly, the Chinese equivalent of the French perfective sentence, *ta pang-le* 'he fat-LE', indicates neither boundedness nor that the situation is viewed as a whole. The meaning shade that *le* adds is best rendered by 'he got fat', in contrast to 'he was fat' (Li and Thompson 1981).

Our discussion so far has been concerned with the received characterisations of aspect such as 'viewed as a whole', 'with boundaries', 'without reference to the inner constituency of the situation'. These characterisations communicate valuable intuitions, but they are surely not what one could call theoretical terms. Therefore, they should be replaced by precisely defined terms of a linguistic theory that are able to capture these intuitions. Some authors are already aware of this problem. For example, although Smith (1991) regularly used formulations as "makes the endpoint visible", "presents a non-closed situation", she discussed in detail a more precise characterisation of these notions (see discussion of her formalisation in section 2.2). In our analysis, boundedness of an event can he precisely captured by how the time span of assertion falls into or includes the time of situation (see sections 3.1 and 3.2).

We now turn to two specific problems with the aspectual differentiation in Chinese.

2.1.3 Problem C: boundedness and the redundancy of le

In an early study of the function of *le*, Thompson (1968) argued that the central meaning of *le* is to mark an event boundary. Li and Thompson (1981, pp. 185–202) gave a very careful list of factors which make an event (or, more generally, a situation) bounded: a definite object, a measure expression, the fact that the sentence is the first in a series, and others (including, sometimes, merely contextual factors). Only when these factors are available can *le* be added. The function of *le* has been defined as indicating that an event is being viewed in its entirety or as a whole, in other words, bounded (as discussed earlier). But if this is the function of *le*, why should it be added to a sentence if the boundedness of the situation is already indicated in one way or another? Thus, this particle seems to have no independent functional value: it marks a situation as bounded which is already marked as bounded, or presents it with its boundaries when the boundaries are already indicated. This would make sense only under the assumption that we deal here with different types of boundaries which a situation can have.

It would also follow from this analysis that constructions with and without *le* should be functionally equivalent. In fact, this is often felt to be the case for the so-called resultative verb constructions, when used in context (out of context, most sentences without any aspectual particle sound somewhat odd). Thus, the following pair of sentences are often considered to be semantically equivalent:

(5) a. Zhangsan xie-wan zhe-feng xin.
 Zhangsan write-finish this-CL letter
 Zhangsan finished writing the letter.

b. Zhangsan xie-wan-le   zhe-feng xin.
   Zhangsan write-finish-LE this-CL letter
   Zhangsan finished writing the letter.

But there are many other examples where this is not the case, for example:

(6) a. *Zhangsan   si.
       Zhangsan   die
    b. Zhangsan   si-le.
       Zhangsan   die-LE
       Zhangsan   died.

Sentence (6a) will sound odd even with context, whereas (6b) is perfect. Hence, the function of *le* cannot just be to indicate something as bounded.

2.1.4 Problem D: 'realization of the situation' and le

If the function of *le* cannot be adequately described by the established characterisation, then what is its function? It has repeatedly been noted that *le* influences the meaning of the utterance in a way which, at first, seems to have nothing to do with its aspectual function. Thus, in his detailed empirical investigation of the various usages, Spanos (1979, p. 81) noted that *le* is used when people feel that it is "necessary to explicitly state the realization of a given action", especially the realization of a closed (i.e., bounded) situation.

Li and Thompson (1981, pp. 196–197) noted that inherently bounded verbs such as *si* 'die' and *wang* 'forget' generally occur with the perfective aspect marker *le*. But interestingly, these verbs can describe situations in a so-called irrealis mood when combined with modal verbs, such as in *ta yao si-le* (he will die LE): *yao si* (will die) by itself is incompatible with the traditional definition of perfective aspect. Thus, it appears that the crucial point is not whether the event is viewed in its entirety, but whether the event is 'presented as real'. Along this line, some researchers argue that *le* seems to convey a modal, rather than an aspectual meaning; for example, Chu and Chang (1987) suggested that *le* is a marker of 'realis' rather than perfective aspect. This is seen in a sentence like *wo lai-le* 'I come LE', where *le* indicates that the speaker has not yet but is about to come: *le* does not indicate that the situation is viewed in its entirety, but rather that the realisation of the event is imminent.

Yong (1997) made a similar observation concerning the realisation-of-situation meaning of *le*. He argued that without *le*, the sentence often denotes a habitual meaning, such as in *ta (xingqitian) xi yifu* (he (Sunday) wash clothes) 'he washes clothes (on Sundays)'; with *le*, the sentence shows that the situation has actually happened, such as in *ta xi-le yifu* (he wash LE clothes) 'he (has) washed clothes'. Finally, according to Chu (1976), in a sentence like *ni kan zheben shu, wo kan neiben* 'you read this book, I read that', in which there is no *le*, the persons involved "may or may not actually read or attempt to read the books concerned. When they do the actual reading, they may or may not finish reading" (p. 47). If Chu is correct, then this utterance in a way only 'mentions' the possibility that 'you read this book and I read that one', without explicitly asserting that any part of what is expressed, be it the activity or its result, was really achieved.[7]

In marking what was really the case, the particle *le* plays a crucial role: it indicates that the action and/or the goal are actually achieved:

(7) Wo xie-le xin, keshi mei xie-wan.
 I write-LE letter but not write-finish
 I did letter-writing but did not finish the letter.

(8) Ta zi-sha-le san-ci.
 he self-kill-LE three-times
 He tried to kill himself three times.

In both cases, it is marked that the activity as such – the action that leads to a written letter or to be dead, respectively – is 'real'. Thus, with *le*, the action is asserted as having actually occurred. Although it is the standard assumption that the goal is also achieved from the first part of these sentences, this is not asserted, as is shown by the fact that sentence (7) is in no way contradictory. The impression that the event is actualised becomes stronger when a specific resultative component is added to the verb, such as *xie-wan* 'write-finish' in (7).[8] This leads us to the following patterns (adapted from Chu 1976, p. 50):

(9)

		action 'real'	goal 'real'
action	(sha)	open	open
action + LE	(sha-*le*)	yes	open
action + result	(sha-si)	open	open
action + result + LE	(sha-si-*le*)	yes	yes

---

[7] A possible, and in fact very natural, way to interpret this utterance is that it expresses a kind of weak imperative, roughly as in English: (*We must read these two books.*) *You read this one and I read that*. But it is not really asserted that this double action is the case or will be the case; instead, it is interpreted as something which ought to be the case. This interpretation is only inferred from the previous utterance, or context in general, and it is not the only possible interpretation.

[8] According to Chu (1976), even in the RVCs, the meaning of the realisation of result can be cancelled; see the following table. Native speakers seem to disagree on this particular point; for example, Tai (1984) regards such a cancellation as impossible.

What these observations demonstrate is the fact that the addition of the particle *le* somehow indicates that the situation, or part of the situation, is, was, or will be 'real': the particle affects the 'assertion status' of what is expressed by the utterance.[9] A satisfactory account of the function of *le* must explain this fact.

2.2 Two formal accounts

The first two problems discussed above result from conceptual unclarities of the canonical notion of aspect, under which an aspect is a particular way 'to view' or 'to present' a situation. In what follows, we shall examine two accounts which, in different ways, try to overcome these problems. Smith (1991) adopted the traditional notion but attempted to give it a more precise shape, whereas Mangione and Li (1993) approached the problem from a very different perspective.

2.2.1 Smith's 'two parameters theory of aspect'

Fundamental to Smith's comprehensive treatment of universal and language-specific properties of aspect is the distinction between 'view-point aspect', such as Perfective and Imperfective, and 'situation type aspect', such as State, Activity, Accomplishment, Achievement, and Semelfactive (i.e., what is traditionally called 'Aktionsart'). They are defined independently, but are brought together in a full sentence and then give rise to a particular temporal interpretation of this sentence. The interaction between the two types of aspect may be constrained; the English variant of the Imperfective, the progressive, for example, is in general not compatible with the situation type State. Our following discussion will be confined to the two situation types Activity and Accomplishment and their interaction with the two viewpoint aspects Imperfective and Perfective, a constellation which is found in many languages, including English and Chinese.

An activity, such as the one described by *The child walked*, is a situation which involves some internal dynamism (this distinguishes it from stative situations), and it has an 'arbitrary final point', whereas an accomplishment such as *John built a house*, which is process-like, has a 'natural final point'. Thus, both activities and accomplishments have boundaries, but they differ in that activi-

---

9 There are good reasons to assume that similar phenomena can be observed in many other languages (Ikegami 1985); see, for example, the so-called 'conative usage' of the Russian imperfective (Forsyth 1970). In fact, the English progressive, as in *John was building a house* (in contrast to *John built a house*) may be interpreted in this way: the activity is said to be real, but not the 'resultant state'.

ties simply stop at some arbitrary point, whereas accomplishments end because the nature of the event requires this; after their final point, the 'resultant state' begins. This informal characterisation is made more precise by Smith as follows (some notations: I is an interval, which is made up of instants t_i; the situation type S has an initial point S_I and an arbitrary final point $S_{F(A)}$ or a natural final point $S_{F(N)}$):

> *Activity*: Situation S obtains at interval I, with the condition that for some $t_i ... t_n$, included in I, S does not obtain at t_{i-1}, S_I obtains at t_i; and for t_n following t_i $S_{F(A)}$ obtains at t_n and S does not obtain at t_{n+1}.[10]
>
> *Accomplishment*: Situation S obtains at interval I, with the condition that for some $t_i ... t_n$, included in I, S does not obtain at t_{i-1}, S_I obtains at t_i and for t_n following t_i, $S_{F(N)}$ obtains at t_n; Resultant State R obtains, and S does not obtain, at t_{n+1}. (Smith 1991, p. 170)

These definitions indeed avoid Problem B discussed in section 2.1.2: irrespective of viewpoint aspect, the situations by themselves have boundaries, and the question is only whether a particular viewpoint makes these boundaries 'visible' or not. But they raise other problems. Situation types are defined in terms of what obtains at some temporal points within some interval I – the interval at which the situations are located (Smith 1991, p. 170). It is not clear whether this interval I is the time of the situation itself or some time which (properly or improperly) contains the situation. According to the definitions, it should he the latter; but this leads to the undesirable result that if a situation S obtains at some time I, for example, yesterday at four, then this situation also obtains at any interval I' which contains I. This is so because the conditions are naturally met by any superinterval of I, for example, the entire week which contains yesterday at four; in fact, it would entail that if a situation ever obtains, it obtains forever. This is clearly not what is intended. It appears, therefore, that the interval I must be interpreted as the 'time of the situation' and t_{i-1} as well as t_{n+1} cannot be contained in I.

In a sentence, the situation aspect is combined with a particular viewpoint aspect. Its role has been informally characterised, in line with the classical notion of aspect, as "an independent lens on the situation talked about ... makes visible all or part of a situation, without obscuring the conceptual properties of the situation type" (p. 171). Its formalisation starts with the idea that viewpoints are something that is related to particular intervals, and the intervals are specified

---

[10] There seem to be two obvious misprints in the original definition of activities: "and for t_n following t, $S_{F(A)}$ obtains at t_i and ..."; this would mean, however, that the arbitrary final point obtains at the initial point of the interval, instead of at its final point t_n.

independently of situation types. "For each sentence we specify an interval that occurs at a particular time, and a viewpoint located at that time. The viewpoint focuses on the situation as it unfolds in time" (pp. 171–172). How does this viewpoint then relate to the situation; in other words, what does it mean that it focuses on the situation in a particular way, or that it makes visible all or part of the situation? For the two viewpoints Imperfective and Perfective, Smith gives these formal characterisations:

> The viewpoint Imperfective is located at interval I; with the condition that for all times t in I, an interval of the situation S obtains, and there is no time at which the endpoints of S obtain. The viewpoint Perfective is located at interval I; with the condition that the situation S obtains at I, and there are times t^i, t_n included in I at which the endpoints of S obtain; and at times t_{i-1}, t_{n+1} included in I the end points do not obtain. (Smith 1991, pp. 172–173)

Such definitions of perfective and imperfective aspect avoid Problem A discussed earlier: aspect is defined by viewpoints, and viewpoints are located in terms of intervals that obtain at specific times. These definitions also rest crucially on the notion 'interval'. However, it is not clear from these definitions how the 'viewpoint interval I' is related to the 'situation interval I'. It seems that they should not be the same interval, because if they were, the definition for the imperfective viewpoint would become contradictory: I would contain (as in situation I) and not contain (as in viewpoint I) the initial point and the final point. Indeed, it seems that the situation interval I is simply irrelevant when viewpoint aspect is applied to situation aspect, for example, Perfective viewpoint to Activity in English: "Perfective (S) presents a situation at interval I, with the properties of S; and the condition that for t_i, t_n, included in I, S does not obtain at t_i; and for t_n following t_i, $S_{F(A)}$ obtains and does not obtain at t_{n+1}" (Smith 1991; p. 174).

The source of the problem appears to be that viewpoint aspect as well as situation aspect are defined by means of the notion 'S obtains at interval I'. But then the I cannot be the same in both definitions, or the S cannot be the same, or the distinction between the two aspects is irrelevant. The latter two options can be ruled out; hence, a rigid distinction should be made between a 'situation time I_s' and a 'viewpoint time I_V', and it should be explained how these two intervals are related to each other.

In an earlier part of her book, Smith suggests a somewhat different interpretation of what "make part of the situation visible" means: "Only what is asserted is made visible" (Smith 1991, p. 99). This interpretation is not resumed in the formal definitions discussed above, but it is fully compatible with our definition of aspect. In section 3, we will propose an analysis which follows exactly this line. Before we proceed, however, we will highlight Smith's formal analysis of the Chinese aspectual particles *le, zai* and *zhe* (*guo* is not given a formal definition, though informally treated in her analysis).

According to Smith, the perfective *le* differs from the English perfective in that it presents Accomplishments with an arbitrary final point:

> *Accomplishment*: Perfective (S) presents a situation S at interval I, with the properties of S, and with the condition that for some $t_i \ldots t_n$ included in I, S does not obtain at t_{i-1}, S_I obtains at t_i; for t_n following t_i, $S_{F(A)}$ obtains at t_n, S does not obtain at t_{n+1}. (Smith 1991, p. 175)

This characterisation would mean, however, that in Chinese, Accomplishments have an arbitrary, rather than a natural, final point, and thus fall under the definition of Activities; or else the Perfective aspect changes the properties of the situation. But the latter is explicitly excluded, here in the clause "with the properties of S": viewpoints cannot turn Activities into Achievements, or vice versa. In fact, by doing so one would undermine the entire system of the two-aspect theory.

In Smith's analysis, perfective *le* in Chinese is confined to non-stative situations:

> *Le* appears only in dynamic sentences. When stative constellations occur with this morpheme, they have a shifted interpretation. One shift is inchoative: the focus is on the coming about of a situation. (p. 346).

This analysis avoids Problem B (i.e., boundedness of *le*), but for the price that *le* no longer has a uniform function: there are now two verb-final *le* that differ only by the fact that one applies to stative sentences and the other to non-stative sentences (see more discussion in 6.2.1 on 'shifted interpretation').

As for the two Chinese imperfective particles, Smith's definition of *zai* is similar to that of the English progressive; her definition of *zhe* follows the viewpoint schema of the 'resultative imperfective': "The resultative presents a situation S with $S_{F(N)}$ at an interval I. There is no time t in I at which S_I obtains or S_F obtains. For all times t in I, $S_F < t$" (p. 177). These definitions capture the common observation that the two particles differ in the verb types to which they can apply: *zai* does not go with statives, whereas *zhe* is in general compatible with all verb types. The definition of *zhe* emphasizes that the situation in question is in its resultant state at the interval I. However, this definition is problematic for sentences such as (10):

(10) Zhangsan xie-zhe   yi-feng xin.
    Zhangsan write-ZHE   one-CL letter
    Zhangsan is/was writing a letter.

This sentence means that Zhangsan is or was writing a letter, not that the letter-writing situation is or was in its resultant state.

To summarize, Smith's formal analysis avoids Problems A and B discussed in section 2.1, but it suffers from other inherent problems such as the definition of 'interval': crucial to the definition of viewpoint aspect and situation aspect is the notion of 'S obtains at interval I', for which there are two possible I's, but it is not clear how they are related in the two-component aspect theory. Moreover, it does not adequately capture the functions of the Chinese particles, for example, with respect to Problems C and D – the fact that the aspectual particles are not redundant with lexical contents of verbs and that they somehow affect the assertion status. Thus, while Smith's formal account is indeed a substantial step beyond traditional accounts of aspect and Chinese aspectual particles, it runs into considerable conceptual and empirical problems.

2.2.2 A compositional analysis of aspectual particles

Mangione and Li (1993) follow a quite different approach to analyse the Chinese aspectual particles. They analyse aspectual particles as sentence operators (on a par with, for example, negation particles) that take the underlying sentence and add a particular meaning component to it.[11] Hence, they first consider the conditions under which an 'atomic' sentence (i.e., without an aspectual particle) is true, and then, what the addition of the particle changes.

As for the underlying atomic sentences, two verb types, called transitional and non-transitional, are distinguished. Roughly speaking, the semantics of the transitional, but not the non-transitional verbs includes a resultant state. An atomic sentence φ with a non-transitional verb is true if and only if it is true at E, where "E is a contextually or structurally established event time" (p. 80). An atomic sentence φ with a transitional verb is true if and only if (a) it is true at E, (b) E is a subinterval of some contextually or structurally established interval I, (c) E precedes another contextually or structurally established subinterval of I, called RES ('result time'), and (d) there is at least one sentence δ which is necessarily true if φ is true and which is true at all subintervals of RES. In a nutshell, atomic sentences are true at some interval E; in the case of sentences with transitional verbs, it is additionally required that some other sentence (which logically follows from the atomic sentence) is true throughout the 'result time'.

---

11 Mangione and Li's technical treatment of these sentence operators, cast in the spirit of (extensional) truth functional semantics, is quite different from what is normally done in this field. In what follows, we shall not dwell on the formal side of their analysis, but rather explain informally what is intended.

According to this account, the function of the particles *le* and *guo* is to relate the atomic sentences in one way or another to the 'reference time'; more precisely, they relate them to 'a contextually or structurally given reference time containing unit' called REF. The particular effect of *le* is to mark that some 'contextually or structurally established interval' I contains both E and REF, such that E precedes REF. The particular effect of *guo* is to mark that some indefinite time interval T precedes REF, where T is equated with E (for non-transitional sentences) and with I (for transitional sentences). In other words, for a sentence with *guo* to be true, the atomic sentence must be true, and 'its full time', which is either E, or E and result time, must precede the REF (and, consequently, the reference time itself).

Since this analysis does not use notions such as 'seen in its entirety, with or without boundaries', it indeed avoids Problems A–C discussed in section 2.1. But it faces Problem D, namely, it does not capture the 'realisation of situation' aspect of the *le* function. In addition, it has many other problems which are no less substantial. The first of these has to do with the truth conditions of atomic sentences, in particular those with 'transitional' verbs. There is always a sentence δ which is necessarily true if φ is true and which is true throughout the result time, for example the sentence 'two plus two is four'. Hence, this condition, as stated here, is irrelevant, and there is no difference between the transitional and non-transitional sentences. This problem is a notorious one, and it is not easy to overcome. Dowty's (1979) notion of 'inertia worlds' is an elaborate, but still arguable, way to solve it (for a recent discussion and a highly suggestive proposal on how it might be overcome in model theoretical semantics, see von Stechow 1996).

As a consequence, the functions of *le* and *guo*, respectively, are reduced to this:

le: E before REF and E and REF belong to I
guo: T before REF

where E, I and REF are 'contextually or structurally established time units' and T is just some time unit, thus reflecting the 'indefinite' character of *guo*. But as soon as *guo* is applied to the atomic sentence, T is identified with E of this sentence (it is said to be coreferential; Mangione and Li 1993, p. 99 and *passim*). Consequently *guo*-sentences are no less specific with respect to their event time than *le*-sentences. Hence, the specific-existential distinction also disappears, so that the only difference between *le* and *guo* is that for *le*, E and REF must belong to the same specified time unit I. Therefore, Mangione and Li's analysis essentially says the following: (a) Atomic sentences have an event time, but no reference time; (b) Sentences with *le* and *guo* have an event time and a reference time, the former preceding the latter; the difference *le* and *guo* is that for *le*, the event time is closely related to the reference time (they are in the same interval), but for *guo* there is no such condition.

Point (b) does not really cover what is known about the function of these particles (cf. section 2 above and Mangione and Li's informal description in their section 1). Point (a) is no less problematic. What is the reference time? As defined here (Mangione and Li 1993, p. 88 and *passim*), it is a time which is contained in a larger interval of a contextually or structurally specified time unit REF, and furthermore, it is said that there is only one such time in REF. Thus, it cannot directly be equated with Reichenbach's (1947) 'point of reference', which, anyway, is not clearly defined either (e.g., see Hamann 1987). Without further specification, it is difficult to say what REF and reference time are in simple cases like:

(11) a. Zuotian, ta xie-wan-le zhe-feng xin.
    Yesterday, he write-finish-LE this-CL letter
    He finished writing this letter yesterday.
  b. Zuotian, ta si-le.
    Yesterday, he die-LE
    He died yesterday.

Even if the notion of reference time is equated with REF, there is considerable doubt as to whether the difference between the particle-free atomic sentences and those with *le* or *guo* is simply the presence of such a contextually or structurally established temporal interval. This analysis cannot explain, for example, why a sentence such as (5a) (see section 2.1 3) seems fine, whereas (6a) is odd. More important, this analysis does not solve Problem D: the difference with respect to 'event realisation' cannot be explained by the presence *versus* absence of a reference time.

Despite these objections, we believe that there is a number of important insights in Mangione and Li's account. In what follows, we will suggest an analysis which reconciles these insights with more traditional accounts in terms of 'perfective' and 'imperfective' aspect, and with Smith's notion that the 'visibility function' of the viewpoint aspect is linked to what is asserted in a sentence.

3 A time-relational definition of tense and aspect

3.1 'Time of utterance', 'time of situation' and 'topic time'

The characterisation of aspect which we propose here is strictly in terms of temporal relations, such as 'prior to' (>), 'contained in' (≤), or 'posterior to' (<), between temporal intervals. This analysis, in a way, brings aspect on a par with tense. Tense is generally assumed to be a deictic-relational category. Thus, the past tense form in (12) is said to indicate that the time of the situation described by <Eva be cheerful> precedes the time of utterance (TU):

(12) Eva was cheerful.

It is easy to see, however, that this description cannot be correct: the time of the situation may, but need not, precede TU. What is said by uttering (12) is not false, when Eva is still cheerful at TU, that is, when the time of the situation includes TU, rather than precedes it (a constellation which is normally supposed to be expressed by the present tense). What is claimed by (12), is rather that there is some time span, T, which precedes TU, and that this time T falls entirely into the time of the situation described by the utterance. Whether the time of the situation itself precedes TU or includes it, is simply left open: the speaker makes a commitment only to this subinterval T of the entire situation time (for example, the time of the party yesterday night, when (12) is uttered in response to the question 'How was Eva yesterday at the party?').

Hence, we must carefully distinguish between two types of time spans which are relevant to an utterance: (a) the time span at which the situation obtains; we will call this interval 'time of situation' (abbreviated T-SIT), and (b) time span about which something is said; we will call this interval 'topic time' (abbreviated TT).[12]

In the particular sentences that express an assertion, the topic time is the time about which an assertion is made, and we might speak of 'time of assertion' instead of 'topic time'. But there are, of course, other illocutionary roles. For example, questions do not make an assertion, but there is an assertion 'at issue', which is time-bound, and the assertion itself is made in the answer to the question. Thus, the 'time of assertion' can be broadly interpreted to include the time for which an assertion is either made or made an issue. Another example is imperatives, for which 'assertion' needs a more general account such as 'speech act function time' in combination with an assertion operator with certain scope properties (see Klein 1994, for a discussion of how cases other than assertions should be handled). Topic time or, more specically, time of assertion can be represented in many different ways. It can be explicitly specified by an adverbial in the sentence-initial position, as in *Yesterday at five, I finished the book*; it can be the time of some other situation mentioned in the preceding context, as in the first sentence of *I entered the room. He had left*; or it can be specified by a question, as in *What did you notice when you entered the room? – The light was on*.

---

[12] The notion of 'topic time' can be considered to be an interpretation of Mangione and Li's REF (or perhaps the reference time which it contains). Under this interpretation, there is a similarity between our approach and Mangione and Li's, though there remain many differences.

3.2 Tense, aspect, and temporal relations between TT, TU, and T-SIT

Although T-SIT and TT are separate constructs, they may be fully simultaneous, as in sentence (12). In this case, the 'classical definition' of tense comes out correct; but this is only a special case. In general, tense does not express a temporal relation between T-SIT and TU, as in the classical definition; rather, it expresses a temporal relation between TT and TU. If the listener knows anything about how T-SIT is related to the TU, it is by virtue of the fact that T-SIT is temporally related to TT. In (12), for example, TT is understood to be a proper subinterval of T-SIT. Other temporal relations between TT and T-SIT are also possible, for example: TT might be after T-SIT, or (fully or partly) contain T-SIT. It is these relations between TT and T-SIT that aspect is concerned with. Thus, a speaker might want to make an assertion about some time span in the future (e.g., tomorrow at ten), and state that this TT follows T-SIT. English expresses such a constellation by a combination of future tense and perfect aspect:

(13)   Tomorrow at ten, John will have left.

Under this view, both tense and aspect indicate temporal relations between different temporal intervals: (a) Tense indicates a temporal relation between TT and TU; (b) Aspect indicates a temporal relation between TT and T-SIT.

Temporal relations are supposed to obtain between time spans. Let R be the real interval [0,1] with the usual topology and the order relation < between its elements. A time span (or temporal interval) is any subinterval of [0, 1]. Temporal relations between time spans can be defined in the usual way, for example, $[r_1, r_2]$ BEFORE $[r_3, r_4]$ iff $r_2 < r_3$, and so on. In the present context, the following three relations are particularly important (S and T are time spans, e.g., $[r_1, r_2]$ or $[r_3, r_4]$):

    a. S AFTER T: last interval of T precedes first interval of S
    b. S IN T: S is a proper subset of T
    c. S OVL T: S and T have a subinterval in common (i.e., they 'overlap')

A particular aspect in language can then be described as a Boolean combination of temporal relations, for example, 'S AFTER T OR S IN T' or 'S NOT OVL T'. In principle, any Boolean combination of temporal relations is possible, but only some of these possibilities are realised in natural languages. In other words, languages vary in the way in which they choose to grammaticalise the Boolean combinations. For example, one form of aspect marking could indicate that TT is properly included in T-SIT, whereas another form could indicate that this is not the case (i.e., perfective) – in the latter, TT may follow, precede, or contain

T-SIT, except that it cannot be properly included in T-SIT. Another possibility is that it may have an entirely 'neutral' aspect form which is compatible with all temporal relations, and a 'marked' form for the relation T-SIT fully included in TT; this is sometimes claimed to be the case for Russian, where the imperfective is considered to be the unmarked, while the perfective the marked form. Still another possibility is the distinction between (a) imperfective: TT properly included in T-SIT, (b) perfective: T-SIT contained, properly or improperly, in TT, and (c) perfect: TT after T-SIT. There are still other possible ways to cluster temporal relations (including to have one form for everything), but it should be clear that 'perfective aspect' in one language is not necessarily the same as 'perfective aspect' in another language (see Klein 1995, for details). As we shall see, Chinese 'perfective' and English 'perfective' are similar in many ways, but they also differ in some respects. The time-relational analysis of aspect allows a precise definition in each case and a comparison of the 'corresponding' aspect.

In addition to the temporal relations between TT and T-SIT, languages also vary in the way in which they treat different kinds of T-SIT. Because this variation affects the way TT is related to T-SIT, we now take a closer look at it.

4 Time of situation and inherent temporal features of the lexical content

4.1 Two sources of confusion

Ever since Aristotle, it has been assumed that there are different types of situations whose properties are roughly reflected in different types of expressions (see Binnick 1991, chapter 6, for a good survey). Nothing seems more natural than to derive the properties of the latter from those of the former. But this practice has been a permanent source of confusion (see Li 1990, Li and Shirai 2000 for a discussion). Vendler's (1967) well-established categories of "state, activity, accomplishment and achievement", for example, actually target at 'time schemata', but often they have been applied to the meaning of expressions, such as verbs, verb phrases, or full sentences (it seems that even Vendler himself was not entirely sure whether time schemata should refer strictly to the temporal properties of events/situations or to the semantic properties of verbs, or to both). This practice has led to many substantial problems, and Problem B discussed in section 2.1.2 is a case in point.

The confusion between what is part of the lexical content (i.e., semantic properties of lexical expressions) and what is part of the situation is the first confusion we are concerned with. For example, the following sentence refers to a situation which, according to standard assumptions about English tense, obtains in the past:

(14) Adam slept.

This situation has many properties, for example, a location, a beginning, and an end point, hence a duration, among others. But only some of these properties are described by the 'lexical content' of (14) – by the meaning of the individual words contained in (14) and the way in which they are put together. Here we designate the lexical content of a constituent by its infinitival form placed between angled brackets. Thus, the lexical content of (14) is denoted by <Adam sleep, and the lexical content of *slept* by <sleep>. The lexical content of a sentence which refers to some situation is a selective description of this situation: the speaker chooses some features which she wants to make explicit, and leaves out others. In (14), place and endpoints of the situation are left implicit, although the perfective aspect asserts part of the time after the state of sleeping while the content of that time period is not lexically specified (see the perfective definition below). It would be easy to make them explicit by enriching the lexical content, for example, by adding *from two to four, for two hours,* or *in the basement.* In all of these cases, the real-life situation which is described is the very same – but the lexical content is richer, and hence more features of the situation are made explicit. In the process of sentence comprehension, the lexical content of the sentence can also be enriched by all kinds of information available to the listener from other sources – deictical, anaphorical, general world knowledge, and so on.

The second potential confusion concerns the difference between what is asserted and what is implicated with respect to the lexical content of a sentence. For example, all situations, with very few exceptions, have a beginning and an end, and hence are bounded; certainly (14) refers to a bounded event, unless one assumes that Adam sleeps forever. But what is unclear from (14) is where the boundaries are and how they are related to the utterance time. Consider now a lexical content that includes an explicit specification of a boundary, as in:

(15) Adam slept from two to four.

Here, the situation is just as well bounded as in (14), but in contrast to (14), there is an explicit boundary specification. If (15) is true, does this imply that Adam no longer slept after four (or did not sleep before two)? This seems to be a natural assumption, but it need not be the case at all. All that is asserted by (15) is the fact that during that time, Adam slept, and nothing is said about what he did before or after that time. Anything else is only a – perhaps very strong – implicature.

Without any contradiction, (15) could be continued by *in fact, from one to seven*. A contradiction would arise if the lexical content were something like <Adam sleep until four and then not sleep>, in other words, if the lexical content had included first some state or activity and then the opposing state or activity. Such a lexical content is expressed, for example, by *Adam woke up*. Similarly, *Adam fell asleep* contains the two opposing states, but in reverse order, <Adam not sleep and then sleep>. We shall shortly return to the notion of 'two-phase expressions', in contrast to 'one-phase expressions' such as 'sleep' in (14) and (15).[13]

Thus, the two sources of confusion we attempt to identify here involve (a) the confusion between what is included as part of the lexical content and what is not, and (b) that between what is asserted and what is implied by the sentence. To avoid these confusions, we need to understand more clearly the different types of lexical contents, which brings us to the next section.

4.2 Types of lexical contents

The term 'lexical content' applies to all sorts of linguistic expressions (i.e., words, phrases, clauses, and full sentences); in the present context, we are mainly interested in the lexical content of simple and complex verbs. There are verb contents which, when applied to some argument(s) at some time T, are supposed to apply to the argument(s) at any other time T' as well. For instance, a number can be odd or even, but if it is odd at some time, then it is odd at any time. Properties of this type are often called 'atemporal' on 'individual level predicates' (Carlson 1978). For some verb contents this is not the case: if they are true for some argument(s) at some time T, then it is assumed that there is a 'contrasting time T' at which they are not true, as in *to sleep, to be hungry, to work*. We call the latter '1-phase contents', and the former '0-phase contents' (of verbs, phrases, sentences). Situations described by 1-phase contents are always bounded, whereas situations described by 0-phase contents are the only ones that do not have boundaries: if they obtain at all, they obtain without temporal limits.[14]

---

[13] In Smith's (1991) analysis of situation types, this distinction is captured by the difference between 'natural final point' and 'arbitrary final point' (see section 2.2.1). We believe, however, that the distinction concerns less the nature of the final point but the question of whether one phase or two phases belong to the lexical content.

[14] '0-phase contents' and '1-phase contents' were called '0-state contents' and '1-state contents' in our previous studies. The new terminology is adopted here because of the possible confusion that the term 'state' may lead to. In addition, we would like to point out that although our study is concerned particularly with verbs due to the nature of aspect, our discussion of lexical contents

This distinction is straightforward, because it is based on a simple criterion – behaviour with respect to time span at which it can be true (or not true). But for at least three reasons, it is too crude. First, some lexical contents describe situations which, when true at some time Ti, are also true at any time Ti+1, but may not be true at Ti–1, for example, <John be dead and (the sabre tooth tiger be extinct). One might call them one-sided 1-phase contents': they have a pretime Ti–1 at which they are not true, but no 'posttime' Ti+1 at which they are not true. Second, it is often a matter of belief to which category an expression might belong (if you believe in resurrection, then (be dead) does not last forever, and might not be true at Ti+1). Third, phases can be further differentiated, for example, on the basis of whether they are homogeneous or dynamic. Sometimes a verb can even characterise a phase either as homogeneous or as dynamic, such as the English verbs think and love and the Chinese verbs chuan 'put on/wear' and na 'take/hold' (see further discussion in section 6.2.3). These three considerations, however, do not affect our principled distinction which has many consequences in syntax and semantics.[15]

A situation that is (selectively) described by a 1-phase content has a beginning and an end, although nothing may be said about what precisely these boundaries are. The time span during which the situation obtains, T-SIT, is preceded and followed by time spans during which it does not obtain. In contrast to this situation a speaker might also want to talk about a time span, within which such a situation first obtains and then, still within the same time span, does not obtain (or vice versa). In this case, there is a 'change of state' within the same span. Such a change of state is encoded by a '2-phase content' in language. Languages provide their speakers with very different possibilities to express such a change from 'yes' to 'no' (or 'no' to 'yes') within the same time span. Minimally, they collapse these two opposing states in one lexical morpheme, typically a verb stem as *arrive* in *John arrived*. Maximally, they express the two phases by two different adjacent (and temporally ordered) sentences, as in *First, John was* not at target position, and then, he was at target position. Both methods express two subsequent phases and, as in the examples, they are characterised by two different positions of John. Their meaning is quite similar, but obviously they are in different ways accessible to adverbial modification and other syntactic operations. Between these

---

also applies to other parts of speech. For example, in most cases, adjectives are 1-phase expressions – there are arguable cases of some lexicalised participles like *broken* and *closed* that one might want to consider as 2-phase expressions. See discussion on 2-phase expressions below.

15 In what follows, we shall not consider 0-phase contents further since they play no relevant role for the problems at hand. Note, however, that they may play a role for aspectual differentiation. For example, they do not admit the perfect, as in **the book has been in Chinese* (one has to say *the book was in Chinese*).

two extremes of '2-phase' expressions, we find a number of constructional possibilities, for example, verb stem plus prefix, as in German *erstechen* vs. *stechen* ('to kill by stabbing' vs. 'to stab') or *erblühen* vs. *blühen* ('to become flowering' vs. 'to flower'), verb stem plus detachable particle, as in English *to wake up* or in German *hochziehen* ('pull up'), or two consecutive verb stems, as in Chinese *ti-dao* ('kick-fall').

These and many other constructions reflect various ways in which a change of state can be lexicalised – from the most dense 'packaging' into a single morpheme to no lexicalisation at all. At the very least the constructions must somehow express what the two opposing phases are; other meaning components can be included, for example, information about the 'path', the 'manner', the temporal nature of the transition, or factors such as causation or intentionality. Note that if the two phases are packed into one word (as in <to arrive>), then the two phases cannot be expressed independently of each other; they are lexically connected, no matter what other (causal or intentional) relation may obtain between them. This does not exclude, however, that they can be selectively addressed by adverbials and other types of modification. As we shall see in section 6 below, this fact is also important for the use of aspectual particles in Chinese.

In what follows, the first phase in such a change-of-state expression shall be called the source phase, and the second phase, the target phase. A simple or complex expression whose lexical content includes a source phase and a target phase will be called a '2-phase expression'. The crucial factor for this distinction is not whether the situation described by the expression involves boundaries, or whether the situation is bounded (cf. section 4.1). For example, <John be in London from Friday to Monday> does not involve two phases – it is a 1-phase lexical content with explicitly specified initial and final points. But <John be in London and then not> and <John leave London> are 2-phase contents, because they (minimally) include a phase and its opposite. Thus, the utterance *John was in London from Friday to Monday*, if true, does not necessarily imply that he was not in London afterwards (though there may be a strong implicature to this effect), whereas *John left London* necessarily implies a phase where he was not in London after having been there.

4.3 Two-phase expressions in Chinese

Chinese has an extremely transparent system to express source phase and target phase. This system is the so-called 'resultative verb construction' (RVC), in which the two phases are separately described by two consecutive verb stems, such as *xie-wan* 'write finish', *fang-xia* 'put-down', and *ti-dao* 'kick-fall'. This is the most common pattern for expressing change of state: almost any verb can be followed by another verb that marks the target phase. But there are also some simple verbs in which the two phases are projected into one morpheme, for example, *dao* 'to arrive'; in such cases, both phases are simultaneously expressed, in contrast to RVCs whose first component may be used in isolation (i.e., expressing source phase only). Examples (16a–c) show one verb expressing a source phase only, an RVC expressing two phases, and a simple verb expressing two phases, respectively.

(16) a. Zhangsan zai sha yi-tou niu.[16]
 Zhangsan ZAI kill one-CL cow
 Zhangsan is killing a cow.
 b. Zhangsan sha-si-le yi-tou niu.
 Zhangsan kill-die-LE one-CL cow
 Zhangsan killed a cow.
 c. Zhangsan dao jia-le
 Zhangsan arrive home-LE
 Zhangsan arrived home.

The first component in an RVC can include all kinds of information about the source phase, which by itself is a 1-phase content. For example, it may (a) include an agentive component, such as *chi* in *chi-wan* 'eat-up', (b) be goal-oriented, such as *sha* in *sha-si* 'kill-die', and (c) be entirely static, such as *xiang* in *xiang-dao* 'think-get'. But RVCs are usually classified according to the particular meaning of their second component. The three most important types of the second component are: (a) simply to indicate that the target phase is reached (e.g., *wan* 'finish', *cheng* 'complete'), (b) to give some qualitative characterisation of the target phase (e.g., *diao* 'empty', *po* 'broken'), and (c) to give a locative specification – the target place (e.g., *shang* 'up', *xia* 'down'). Although the formal structures of RVCs are more complicated than indicated here, our brief sketch will suffice for the present purposes (for a detailed analysis, see Chao 1968, pp. 435–480; Li and Thompson 1981, pp. 54–68; or more recently, Li 1995, 1999; Yong 1997).

---

16 The Chinese verb *sha* differs from the English translation equivalent *kill* in that it does not include the target phase of being dead as part of its lexical content. Thus, *sha-le ta san-ci* (kill-LE it three-times) in Chinese is fine, but *killed it three times* in English is odd.

5 Aspectual systems and the English aspect

5.1 Two dimensions of variation

Languages vary in the way in which they grammaticalise particular aspects, that is, particular temporal relations between topic time TT and time of situation T-SIT (as discussed in 3.2). Languages also vary in the way in which temporal characteristics of situations are encoded in lexical contents. These two types of variations are well reflected in Smith's (1991) notion of a limited but well-defined 'parametric variation' of aspect. Although our analysis differs from Smith's in many ways, we similarly assume two dimensions of variation in the semantics of aspect, and ask (a) which temporal relations between TT and T-SIT are grammaticalised in a language? and (b) how are the different types of T-SIT described in a language? In the preceding two sections we provided a time-relational account of these two questions; in this section, we examine how the interaction of these two dimensions yield a language-specific aspectual system and illustrate it with English.

For 1-phase expressions, T-SIT involves only one interval. A situation described by a 2-phase expression such as <Adam fall asleep> includes two distinct time intervals: a source phase which can be described by <Adam not be asleep>, and a target phase which can be described by <Adam be asleep>. To which of the two phases is TT related? Languages must select either the source phase or the target phase and treat it on a par with the single phase of a 1-phase expression. This fact is best captured by the notion of distinguished phase. The distinguished phase (DP) is (a) the only phase in the case of 1-phase contents, and (b) either the source phase or the target phase in the case of 2-phase contents. Thus, whether the source phase or the target phase is chosen as DP is the second dimension of cross-linguistic variation of aspect. TT is not related to the different types of T-SIT themselves, but to the time of their distinguished phase. We now illustrate these points with the English aspectual system.

5.2 The case of English

In English, the DP for aspectual marking is: (a) the single phase for 1-phase contents, and (b) the source phase for 2-phase contents. Thus, the temporal relations between TT and T-SIT in English, as grammaticalised in aspect, can be represented by using the notions of T-DP (time of DP) and posttime/pretime of T-DP (the time after/before T-DP), as follows:

(17) Imperfective: TT IN T-DP
      Perfective: TT OVL T-DP and POSTTIME OF T-DP
      Perfect: TT AFTER T-DP

Normally, these three aspectual relations are encoded by the progressive form, the simple form, and the perfect form, respectively; exceptions exist, such as the copula or verbs like *to know, to consider* which do not distinguish 'Imperfective' and 'Perfective' by morphological forms.

According to our time-relational definition of tense and aspect, a sentence such as *John was sleeping*, a 1-phase expression, has a tense component and an aspect component. The tense component indicates that the topic time precedes the time of the utterance. The aspect component expresses that the topic time falls within the time of a situation described by <John sleep>. Nothing is asserted about the boundaries of this situation, or whether the boundaries are related to the time of utterance. By contrast, a sentence such as *John was falling asleep*, a 2-phase expression, includes a source phase <John is not asleep> and a target phase <John is asleep>, about one of which an assertion is to be made. By our above analysis, in English, the distinguished phase to which the topic time is related is the source phase. Thus, the topic time is fully included in this source phase (i.e., TT IN T-DP), and the assertion made is confined to a subinterval of this phase. Nothing is asserted about whether the target phase is actually reached; by default, the listener may be led to assume that John was eventually asleep, but this assumption can be easily cancelled, for example by continuing the sentence with *when he suddenly heard a blast*. Such cancellations are not possible with perfective or perfect forms, as in *John fell asleep* or *John had fallen asleep*; in these cases, TT either overlaps with the posttime of T-DP or is after T-DP, and thus the assertion includes the target phase.

5.3 Time-relational aspect versus aspect as a particular way of presenting a situation

The strictly time-relational definition of aspect proposed here operates exclusively with notions that are independently defined – time intervals and temporal relations, on the one hand, and assertion and situation, on the other. Three time intervals play a particular role: TU, the time at which the utterance is made; TT, the time for which an assertion is made; and T-SIT, the time at which some situation obtains. This definition of aspect does not use intuitively suggestive but entirely metaphorical characterisations such as 'viewed in its entirety, with boundaries, from the inside/outside, with special reference to the inner constituency of the situation', and so on, but at the same time it naturally captures the intuition behind these characterisations. For example, according to this analysis, the English progressive form marks that the TT is fully included in T-DP, i.e., in the first or only state of T-Sit in the case of English. Therefore, we have the feeling that only part of the situation is 'presented' or that the situation 'is seen from the inside' or 'without reference to its boundaries'. Exactly the opposite is the case for the perfective: T-DP and the time afterwards is at least partially included in TT. Hence, we have the feeling that the single phase (in 1-phase expressions) or the source phase (in 2-phase expressions) is presented as 'completed', 'with boundaries', or 'as a whole'. Finally, in the case of perfect, TT is after T-DP, whence the feeling that the single phase or the source phase are 'over' at the time about which something is said; if there is no proper 'time after', the perfect sounds odd, as in *John has been dead*.

6 The Chinese aspectual system

Much of our previous discussion has been on problems associated with traditional analyses of aspect and of aspectual particles in Chinese. We attempted to overcome these problems with a new framework of time-relational definition of aspect. Since this framework is developed not just for English, Russian, or other Indo-European languages, it should apply equally well to Chinese and should help us to explain some of the difficult puzzles in the analysis of Chinese aspect. We have shown above that the new framework solves the general problems with aspectual characterisations, the problems A and B (see sections 2.1.1 and 2.1.2). In this section we shall see how it can overcome problems C and D, the specific problems with the Chinese aspectual particles.

6.1 Aspect and what is asserted

Let us begin with a brief recapitulation. A lexical content such as <Adam sleep>, <Eva fall asleep> or <Cain wake up>, is a selective description of a situation. The lexical content by itself does not specify when, for which time, and how often such a situation obtains. The lexical content does not make a claim, either, about whether such a situation obtains at all. To specify that the situation obtains, all Indo-European languages, for example, choose a form of the finite verb to mark that a particular time span, the topic time TT (a) precedes, follows, or contains the time of utterance, and (b) precedes, follows, includes, or is included in the time of a situation with the properties indicated by the lexical content. In this view, the finite form in (a) corresponds to the tense function, and that in (b) to the aspect function.

Chinese does not have finite verbs. But the 'finiteness function' can be expressed by optional particles; in the case of aspectual particles, they assert that TT precedes, follows, includes, or is included in the time of a situation described by the sentence. The position of TT on the time line (as well as its duration), however, must be marked by adverbials or left to the context; in other words, aspectual particles do not mark tense in Chinese. In contrast to finiteness marking in Indo-European languages, aspectual particles may be omitted, in which case no assertion is marked, and as a consequence, the sentence may sound awkward if not interpreted in an appropriate context. The absence of aspectual markers and its consequence remind us of Problem D (see section 2.1.4, to which we shall shortly return): without a particle, the sentence does not make an assertion about whether the situation, or part of it, is realised (not that it could not be real). Let us now turn to the concrete functioning of the individual particles.

6.2 The four particles

The four aspectual particles in Chinese can be roughly summarised as follows in our time-relational analysis of aspect:

(18) a.   le   TT OVL PRETIME T-DP AND T-DP
     b.   guo   TT AFTER T-DP
     c.   zai   TT IN T-DP
     d.   zhe   TT IN T-DP

In the following, we will see how this framework of analysis accounts for the use of the four particles as described in descriptive grammars and briefly summarized in sections 1 and 2 above. Chinese differs from English in its treatment of the distinguished phase. In English, the DP is (a) the single phase for 1-phase contents, and (b) the source phase for 2-phase contents; in Chinese, the DP is (a) the single phase for 1-phase contents, and (b) the target phase for 2-phase contents. This naturally explains a fact which has often been noted in the literature: English is more 'action-oriented' while Chinese is 'result-oriented' (Chu 1976, Li 1990, Yong 1997). In Chinese, the particular emphasis on result is reflected in the use of a language-specific construction, the RVC (see section 4.3).

6.3 le

The traditional analysis as discussed in sections 1 and 2 states that *le* presents a situation as (a) specific and (b) as viewed in its entirety or as a whole; in some cases, it may also mark the coming-about of a situation. These functions, as well as the assertive role of *le* can be precisely reconstructed by the definition in (18a). This definition states that TT overlaps with the distinguished phase as well as part of the time before the distinguished phase. The definition can be best illustrated with some simple diagrams. In what follows, +++++ indicates the distinguished phase, ----- the source phase of 2-phase expressions, and [ ] the topic time TT. Let us first consider 1-phase expressions, in which the distinguished phase is a single phase. In this case, TT must include some time before this phase, and at least the beginning part of the phase. It is left open where it closes; in particular, it can, but need not, include the end point – therefore, it is not contradictory to say the two clauses in (19), whereas that the English counterpart sounds odd).

(19) Ta   xie-le   xin,   keshi   mei   xie-wan.   [++++++]+++++
      she   write-LE   letter but   not   write-finish
      She wrote a letter, but did not finish writing it.

This definition also explains the 'inchoative flavour' which is often found with *le*, as in (20) – in our definition, an inchoative reading is part of the perfective aspect and comes naturally as a function of the assertion.

(20) Ta pang-le.   [+++++++++++]
      she fat-LE
      She became fat.

In (19), *le* with the verb *xie-xin* (write-letter) asserts that the activity of letter writing took place (and terminated), and the 'scope of assertion', as we might say, closes at a time prior to the end point of the event. In (20), *le* with the verb *pang* (be fat) asserts that the state of being fat has become true, and that the scope of assertion closes at some arbitrary point during this state – hence, we get the reading that she has become fat and is still fat at TT, precisely an inchoative reading (one can draw the diagram in (20) differently, such that the closure is at a different point – in other words, it is unknown when she will stop being fat). This inchoative reading is absent in (19) because the closure of the scope of assertion implies that the letter-writing activity already terminated (although it was not completed). The difference between (19) and (20) seems to suggest that the inchoative reading is a function of the inherent meaning of verbs used in the sentence. Some authors suggest just that: the inherent meanings of the verb might contribute to whether *le* conveys an inchoative meaning. For example, Shih (1990) argued that *le* indicates inchoativity when combined with atelic verbs, but completed-action meaning when combined with telic verbs. Comrie (1976) showed that in many languages the combination of perfective aspect with stative but not process verbs indicates an inchoative meaning. Finally, Smith (1991) suggested that the perfective *le* can be used only with dynamic verbs; when it is used with stative verbs, it has the so-called 'shifted interpretation': inchoative meaning is the result of such a shift (see also discussion in section 2.2.1).

Although the inherent meaning of the verb seems important in this case, it is unlikely to be the only explanation for determining the inchoativity of *le*, since inchoative readings can also arise when *le* is combined with a typical non-stative activity verb in some cases, as in (21):

(21) Zhangsan xiao-le, erqie xiao-de hen kaixin.
Zhangsan laugh-LE and laugh-DE very happily
Zhangsan started to laugh, and he laughed very happily.

Moreover, stative verbs with *le* do not have to be interpreted with an inchoative reading. For example, sentence (22) shows that a quantification after the verb can release the inchoative meaning and give the sentence a normal perfective reading in which TT covers the entire T-DP.[17]

---

[17] Some authors will be tempted to say that there are two kinds of *le* involved here: (22) has a verb-final *le*, and thus it does not convey an inchoative meaning; if the quantification phrase is removed from the sentence, it has a sentence-final *le*, and thus conveys the inchoative meaning. But this is hardly a principled account, given that the differences between (i-a) and (i-b) cannot be explained in this way.

(i) a. Zhangsan zhidao-le.
 Zhangsan know-LE
 Zhangsan knew (about it).
 b. Zhangsan zhidao-le zhe-jian shi.
 Zhangsan know-LE this-CL matter
 Zhangsan knew about this matter.

The verb *zhidao* 'know', in this case, is also a stative verb, but the meaning in these two sentences does not change as a function of whether le ends the sentence: in both cases, the sentence indicates Zhangsan's coming into possession of the knowledge of something ([++++]+++++, diagrammatically).

(22) Zhangsan bing-le liang tian.
    Zhangsan sick-LE two day
    Zhangsan as sick for two days.

In Smith's (1991) analysis, such a quantification triggers another shifted interpretation, in which the focus changes from the initial point to the final point, or changes out of the state (p. 347). Our analysis does not involve such shifts or switches of interpretation. We assume that these differences arise due to the scope differences of TT; for example, the assertion can close at different points during the phase of the event. All the interpretations are within the possible variations of a perfective meaning, as defined by the relations between TT and T-DP.[18]

One significant difference between Chinese and English in aspect marking, according to Smith (1991), is that Chinese separates the notion of completion from that of simple closure. This was somewhat puzzling, since accomplishments in traditional analyses carry a clear endpoint, yet the perfective *le* in Chinese, unlike perfective aspect in English, does not indicate the endpoint (or completion). Smith illustrated this puzzle with example (23):

(23) Zhangshan xue-le Fawen, keshi hai mei xui-hui.
    Zhangshan learn-LE French but still not study-know
    Zhangsan studied French but he never actually learned it.

She showed that it was difficult to translate the same verb *xue* in the two clauses with the same English verb, unless one renders it with an imperfective aspect as 'Zhangsan was learning French'. Thus, *xue-Fawen* 'learn French' is an accomplishment, but its combination with *le* does not lead to a completion meaning.

This puzzle is naturally explained in our analysis, since *xue-Fawen* belongs to 1-phase expressions, just as *xie-xin* 'write-letter' does, whereas *xue-hui* 'study-know' belongs to 2-phase expressions. The difference between *xue* and *xue-hui* in (23), and the aspectual meaning differences therein, is captured by how TT marks the DP, and what the DP is in each case. This brings us now to 2-phase expressions in Chinese.

For 2-phase expressions in Chinese, the target phase is the distinguished phase DP, and as a consequence, the source phase is the pretime of DP. By the definition of (18a), *le* indicates that T-DP as well as its pretime are included within

---

18 We would like to note, however, that our definition does not rule out the role of factors such as finer distinctions of inherent verb meanings (e.g., state *versus* process) in the aspectual interpretations of a sentence. These factors, including contextual information and world knowledge, currently are not part of the core definition in our aspectual analysis.

TT. The most common type of 2-phase expressions are RVCs, as *xue-hui* 'study-know' in (23) or *xie-wan* 'write-finish' in (24).

(24) --------[------+++++++++]
    Zhangsan xie-wan-le xin.   source   target
    Zhangsan write-finish-LE letter   *xie*   *wan*
    Zhangsan finished writing the letter.

In (24), the source phase is the activity of writing a letter, and the target phase is that this activity, during which the letter is written, is over. Both phases overlap with TT and hence are within the scope of assertion as marked by *le*, which is illustrated by the diagram next to the sentence. Therefore, the 'result' cannot be cancelled as in (7) or (19); this is in full agreement with the observations discussed earlier, such as that made by Chu (1976) (see section 2.1.4).

This analysis works in the same way for all types of RVCs (see discussion in section 4.3). That is, the use of *le* marks an assertion for (a) the completion of the event (e.g., *wan* 'finish'), (b) the qualitative characterisation of the target phase (e.g., *si* 'die', *po* 'broken'), or (c) the locative specification, the target place (e.g., *shang* 'up', *xia* 'down'). Without *le*, it is not asserted that any of the target phases is actually realised.

The same analysis also works for monomorphemic 2-phase verbs. For example, (25) asserts that the target phase of being at home is reached; the lexical content of *dao* 'arrive' incorporates both the source phase and the target phase, and the function of *le* is to relate the scope of assertion to the T-DP, the time of the target phase, plus its pretime, part of the source phase.

(25) --------[------+++++++++]
    Zhangsan zhongyu dao-le jia.   source   target
    Zhangsan finally arrive-LE home   not at home   at home
    Zhangsan finally arrived home.

The definition of *le* given here is simple and uniform, and it accounts for most of the empirical observations about the usage of this form. Aspectual particles are 'assertion markers' that indicate for which time span the assertion is made, and this naturally accounts for the problems discussed in sections 2.1.1 to 2.1.4. Note that the role of assertion is not entirely an unfamiliar notion in the discussion of Chinese aspect. Smith (1991, pp. 345–346), for example, indirectly calls for this notion in her analysis of the perfective *le* with RVCs. Discussing examples like (23) and (24), she remarked that a sentence like (24) "cannot be conjoined with an assertion that the situation continues" such as in (7); in other words, what is asserted in (24) is that the letter-writing situation is completed, in contrast to that in (7).

Our time-relational analysis of aspectual particles in Chinese also naturally explains some of the intuitions suggested by traditional metaphorical analyses. For example, Li and Thompson (1981) as well as Smith (1991) state that the function of *le* is to indicate that the event is being viewed with both initial and final boundaries as a single whole (see section 1). Chao (1968), on the other hand, proposed that *le* conveys the meaning of 'completed action'. Chao (1968) and Rohsenow (1976, 1978) also assigned the 'coming about' or inchoative meaning to *le* (and more recently as one of 'shifted interpretations' in Smith's 1991 analysis). All of these characterisations naturally result from the way in which the topic time relates to the time of situation. Since the use of *le* indicates that TT always includes the target phase for 2-phase expressions, and often by default for 1-phase expressions, one gets the sense of a complete boundary of the event. The 'completed action' sense emerges when one considers the 2-phase expressions such as RVCs combined with *le*, in which case the TT marks that target phase has been reached. Finally, one may also get a 'coming about' or inchoative meaning because *le* can mark an assertion for only the initial part of T-SIT, as in 1-phase expressions.

What remains to be explained, though, is the 'definite' or 'specific' flavour that goes with *le* (in contrast to *guo*; see Li and Thompson 1981, Chao 1968, and discussions in sections 1 and 2). This flavour seems to result simply from the fact that T-SIT must overlap with TT in the sense specified in (18). Hence, TT 'fixates' on T-SIT: if there is a specific assertion time, there must also be a specific situation time that matches with it. Note that TT itself is not localised in temporal order by *le*, because aspectual particles do not express tense. Thus, if TT is to be further specified in relation to TU, this information must come from adverbials or from the general context.

6.4 *guo*

According to traditional analyses (Chao l968; Li and Thompson 1981, Smith 1991), *guo* marks that the situation must have obtained at least once, and that its resulting state no longer obtains. In contrast to *le*, it has an 'indefinite' or 'experiential' flavour. How does the definition in (18b) reconstruct these facts?

Our definition of *guo* is very simple: *guo* indicates that the time about which something is asserted falls into the posttime of the distinguished phase. Thus, it is defined in the same way as the English perfect (see (17) in section 5.2), but with one important difference for 2-phase contents: English chooses the source phase whereas Chinese chooses the target phase as the distinguished phase. Therefore, *guo* behaves like the English perfect for 1-phase contents but not for 2-phase contents. In English, the TT of the perfect is after the source phase, and thus it normally falls into the target phase. Since in Chinese the target phase is the distinguished phase, the TT of *guo* is a time at which the 'result' of the target phase is past already.

(26) John has left the country.   ------------- ++++[++++]++++
                                                    source   target

(27) Zhangsan chu-guo   guo.   ------------- ++++++++++++ [ ]
     Zhangsan leave-GUO country   source   target
     Zhangsan has been to other countries.

In both examples, the source phase is <he be in country>, the target phase <he be out of country>. In (26), TT is included in the target phase, but at the same time it includes TU, the time of utterance (as indicated by the present tense form *has*); hence the feeling of 'current relevance'. In (27), the position of TT relative to TU (a function of tense, see section 3.2) is not marked, since there is no tense marking in Chinese. But wherever TT may be relative to TU, the entire T-SIT, including both the source phase and the target phase, precedes TT, giving the impression that the event 'has been experienced at least once at some indefinite time' (Li and Thompson 1981, p. 226). Thus, sentence (27) also indicates that the resulting phase, i.e., Zhangsan being *chu-guo* 'abroad', no longer obtains; this is what Chao and Smith called the 'discontinuity' meaning of *guo*. This partly identical, partly different function of English perfect and Chinese *guo* is a simple consequence of the different choice of 'distinguished phase' in these two languages.

Compare now the following two sentences:

(28) John has died.
(29) *Zhangsan   si guo.
     Zhangsan   die-GUO
     Zhangsan has once died.

Whereas the English sentence is perfectly normal, the Chinese sentence is distinctly odd (Li and Thompson 1981, p. 230; Mangione and Li 1993).[19] This difference immediately follows from the present analysis. The English sentence means: John is now in the time after the source phase of dying, i.e., John is now dead. The

---

19 An anonymous reviewer pointed out, quite correctly, that sentences such as this are fine: *Chun-li si-guo san-ge ren* (village-in die-GUO three-CL person). But to our interpretation, this sentence does not carry the meaning 'in this village, three people have once been dead' (which would indeed be odd) but the meaning 'at some time, the village had the property of having three people who died', a reading that indicates what happened to or what affected the village.

Chinese sentence means: Zhangsan is after the target phase of dying, i.e., after the phase of being dead, and unless you believe in resurrection, this does not make much sense. This analysis naturally explains what is often said of *guo* – that its use requires a situation to be repeatable to guarantee an indefinite reading (cf. Smith 1991, pp. 350–351).

This analysis is further confirmed if we look at sentence (30), in which the same verb *si* does occur with *guo*, because the verb conveys the meaning of 'out of order' rather than 'being dead'.

(30) Zhe   jiqi   si-guo   hao   ji-ci   huo.
     this   machine   die-GUO   very   several-CL   fire
     This machine was out of order several times.

Since the machine can be 'dead' and then 'resurrect' (i.e., be repaired), it is perfectly okay to use *si* with *guo* in this context. In fact, sentence (29), when modified by the adverbial phrase *hao ji-ci* 'several times' (i.e., *Ta si-guo hao ji-ci*), can be used in a novel way to refer to a situation in which a patient is not really dead but fainted several times and almost died each time.

Given this analysis of *guo* and *si*, why is it perfectly okay to say sentence (31), in which the RVC indicates clearly a 2-phase content, but not (29), in which the main verb is the same as the second component of the RVC in (31)?

(31) Zhangsan   da-si-guo   yi-ge   ren.[20]
     Zhangsan   hit-dead-GUO   one-CL   person
     Zhangsan once killed a person.

Although the person involved is dead, and the sentence does not convey any meaning of Zhangsan's resurrection, the use of *guo* in this sentence is perfectly okay. The important difference, however, is that in (29) the main verb applies to the experiencer, Zhangsan, the only argument of the sentence, whereas in (31) the main verb (i.e., the RVC) applies to the agent, Zhangsan; and the experiencer of death, or the patient, is someone else (i.e., *yi-ge ren* 'one person'), the object of the sentence. Thus, it is perfectly possible that Zhangsan, the agent, will *da-si* 'kill' another time, but it is not possible for Zhangsan, the experiencer, to *si* 'die' another time, given the constraint that TT marks the assertion after the entire time of the situation.

---

20 We owe this example to an anonymous reviewer.

Finally, how do we explain the 'indefinite' or 'existential' flavour, a property often assigned to *guo* in the literature in comparison with *le*? Our analysis of *le* was that TT overlaps with and thus fixates on a particular T-SIT. Because TT fixates on T-SIT, if there is a specific assertion time, there must also be a specific situation time that matches with it. This is where the 'definite' or 'specific' flavour of *le* comes from. In contrast, *guo* leaves open the precise position of T-SIT in relation to TT: it only says that T-SIT, or more precisely, T-DP, somehow precedes TT. This condition is satisfied by any situation time, or set of situation times, of the required type before TT.[21] Our comparison of *le* and *guo* is clearly seen in sentences (32a–b), where (32a) indicates that the target phase <Zhangsan be out of country> currently obtains because TT covers the DP, i.e., target phase, while (32b) indicates that the target phase no longer obtains because TT is entirely preceded by the DP. Hence, the definite-indefinite distinction between *le* and *guo* need not be stipulated, but naturally follows from our definitions in (18).

(32)

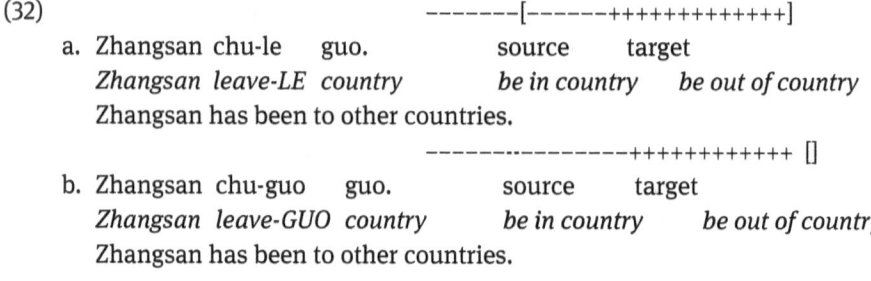

a. Zhangsan chu-le guo.   source   target
   Zhangsan leave-LE country   be in country   be out of country
   Zhangsan has been to other countries.

b. Zhangsan chu-guo guo.   source   target
   Zhangsan leave-GUO country   be in country   be out of country
   Zhangsan has been to other countries.

6.5 *zai* and *zhe*

Both particles are traditionally assigned the function of imperfective markers. Our analysis is consistent with this view. Under the definition in (18c–d), they both indicate that the time to which the assertion is confined is fully included in the distinguished phase. Hence, they express the same imperfective aspect. For example, the same situation is described in (33a) and (33b), in which the main verb *xiang* 'think' is a 1-phase expression.

---

21 This definition does not exclude the possibility of a specific or definite reading of *guo*: as noted by Chao (1968) and Smith (1991), a specific or definite reading of *guo* may be obtained by the use of contextual information or pragmatic knowledge.

(33) a. Zhangsan zai xiang nei-jian shi.   ++++[++++]++++
       Zhangsan ZAI think that-CL matter
       Zhangsan is thinking about the matter.
    b. Zhangsan xiang-zhe nei-jian shi.   ++++[++++]++++
       Zhangsan think-ZHE that-CL matter
       Zhangsan is thinking about the matter.

The exact distribution of *zai* and *zhe* has been under intense debate (see section 1.2). The difference between them is complicated by factors of pragmatics and dialectal variation. For example, the use of *zhe* is much more common in written than in spoken language, whereas *zai* is more common in spoken than in written language. *Zhe*, as compared to *zai*, is frequently used to indicate background events. Finally, the borderline between these two particles has become blurred, especially in northern dialects; in some dialects, *zai* and *zhe* can be combined together even in a single sentence (Chen 1978). This picture can get even more complicated when we consider a third particle, *ne*, which often co-occurs with *zai* and *zhe* in speech. Some authors consider *ne* as an imperfective marker. For example, Chan (1980) mentioned that ne encompasses the functions of both *zai* and *zhe*. Ma (1987) argued that in the Beijing dialect, *ne* is actually the main device for imperfective aspect. In this article we do not discuss *ne* as an imperfective marker, on grounds that it is largely restricted to the Beijing dialect and that its imperfective function is restricted to answers to questions in colloquial dialogues (Liu 1985). All of these levels of complication lead us to believe that our core definition of their aspectual functions should not include their distributional differences.

But there is one perplexing 'distributional' fact for which our analysis does suggest a partial explanation: neither *zai* nor *zhe* can occur with RVCs, the resultative verb constructions. For example, sentences (34a) and (34b), which contain a standard RVC, are ungrammatical with *zai* and *zhe*, respectively:

(34) a. *Zhangsan zai chi-wan nei-dun fan.
        Zhangsan ZAI eat-finish that-CL rice
        Zhangsan is finishing eating that meal.
     b. *Zhangsan chi-wan-zhe nei-dun fan.
        Zhangsan eat-finish-ZHE that-CL rice
        Zhangsan is finishing eating that meal.

In his analysis of verb types in Chinese, Tai (1984) argued that RVCs in Chinese express only the result and not the duration, even though the first component is a durative verb. This lack of durativity of RVCs, according to Tai, is what prevents *zai* from being used. Tai's analysis, however, does not account for the fact that RVCs can occur with adverbials that indicate durativity of the action denoted by RVCs, in sentences like (35).

(35) Zhangsan hua-le liang-ge xiaoshi chi-wan nei-dun fan.
Zhangsan spend-LE two-CL hour eat-finish that-CL rice
Zhangsan spent two hours finishing eating that meal.

Under the present analysis, neither *zai* nor *zhe* can apply to the first component of RVCs, which indicates the source phase, because in Chinese the distinguished phase is the target rather than the source phase. In contrast, a comparable structure in English is perfectly acceptable (e.g., *John is eating up his apple*), because in English the distinguished phase is the source phase and the imperfective marking applies to the source phase. We can similarly explain why *zai* and *zhe* cannot be used with monomorphemic 2-phase expressions like *dao* (as in *dao-jia* 'arrive home') whereas the progressive *-ing* can be used with the English equivalents like *arrive*. For both *dao* and *arrive*, the source phase is (not be home), indicating a stage prior to the target phase of (be home). In English, the imperfective marking of *John is arriving home* applies to the source phase, which can be diagrammatically represented as --[---]--++++. This analysis is compatible with Smith's (1991) view that progressives with achievement verbs indicate preliminary stages of the event rather than the process of the event itself, if we consider 'preliminary stage' on a par with 'source phase'. In Chinese, however, neither **Zhangsan zai dao jia* nor **Zhangsan dao-zhe jia* 'Zhangsan is arriving home' can be interpreted in a similar way, because an imperfective marking on the source phase is unavailable.

Our analysis, in principle, does not exclude the possibility that *zai* and *zhe* could be applied to the target phase in RVCs and monomorphemic 2-phase expressions. So why is it, in practice, that we never use *zai* and *zhe* with RVCs and verbs like *dao* to mark the imperfectivity of the target phase? We do not have a perfect answer to this question, but one speculation is that the nature of the target phase in these 2-phase expressions somehow prevents the imperfective marking by *zai* and *zhe*. The target phases like *wan* (be done), *shang* (be up), and *po* (be broken) in RVCs all seem to indicate states that result from the source-phase actions (i.e., change of state). It might be that explicit imperfective markings are blocked in these cases because the resulting states by themselves are instantaneous (e.g., we cannot talk about the duration of *po* (be broken)), while imperfective marking requires a duration of event.

6.6 Zero marking

In contrast to tense-aspect marking in Indo-European languages, which are realised by finite forms of the verb, aspectual particles are not obligatory in Chinese. There are two consequences to this 'zero marking'. First, the sentence may sound incomplete or odd, especially when uttered in isolation. Second, as we discussed throughout the paper, aspectual particles are temporal assertion markers. Without such particles, the description provided by the sentence is not linked to any particular time about which something is asserted. The illocutionary status of the sentence will depend completely on pragmatic or contextual factors. For example, in a narrative discourse in which one event is reported after another, it is clear that the descriptions indicate events that have occurred. A sentence without a particle can also be interpreted as a kind of imperative, as discussed earlier (section 3.1). Finally, such a sentence can also be used to indicate a habitual meaning. Compare the following two examples from Yong (1997), as discussed in section 2.1.4.

(36) a. Ta   (xingqitian)   xi   yifu.
       he   (Sunday)   wash   clothes
       He washes clothes (on Sundays).
    b. Ta   xi-le   yifu.
       he   wash-LE   clothes
       He (has) washed clothes.

(36a) is easily understood to mean that he regularly or typically washes his clothes on Sundays. No assertion is made with respect to any particular interval, though, as would be the case in (36b) when *le* is added.

We shall not follow up the various contextual factors that invite or even impose a particular interpretation on zero marking sentences. But the optionality of aspectual particles has one interesting consequence on the interpretation of RVCs and related constructions. Compare again the following two sentences:

(37) a. Ta   xi-ganjing   yifu   (jiu   zou-le).
       he   wash-clean   clothes   (then   go-LE)
       He washed clothes clean (and then left).
    b. *Ta   xi   yifu   (jiu   zou-le).
       he   wash   clothes   (then   go-LE)
       He washed clothes (and then left).

Sentence (37a), which has a standard RVC, sounds perfectly normal if followed by the clause in parentheses (or in similar contexts). In contrast, sentence (37b), which lacks the second component of the RVC, is distinctly odd in the same context. In both sentences, *le* modifies the verb in the second clause that serves as the context. Whereas this *le* is sufficient for the specific TT to which the first clause in (37a) can be related, it is not enough in (37b); another *le* has to be added to the first clause in (37b) to make the sentence grammatical: *Ta xi le yifu (jiu zou -le)*. This discrepancy shows that the seeming redundancy of *le* with RVCs, discussed as Problem C in section 2.1.3, stems from the fact that RVCs specify a clear target phase, and the TT of *le*, which marks that a second phase is reached in the second clause, is highly compatible with, and easily accessible to the target phase, as in (37a). When no target phase is incorporated into the lexical content of the expression, as in (37b), then the omission of *le* makes the sentence incomplete with respect to the status of assertion (and the scope of further assertion does not apply to it).

Smith (1991) argued that sentences without aspectual morphemes have a neutral aspect, a default value of aspect that allows for more than one interpretation depending on the context and world knowledge. Our above analysis is compatible with the notion of neutral aspect, but differs from it in one crucial way. Neutral aspect assigns an overly flexible interpretation to a given sentence, and assumes that both perfective and imperfective interpretations can arise with the same sentence. Our analysis assumes that it is rarely the case that the same sentence can have both a perfective and an imperfective reading: discourse or situational contexts almost always disambiguate the two interpretations. In many cases, it is even obligatory to use the aspectual particles to make the assertion status clear, as in (37b). In fact, Smith's Chinese example of neutral aspect (Smith 1991, p. 121) is problematic:

(38) Zhangsan dao jia de shihou, Mali xie gongzuo baogao.
    Zhangsan arrive home DE time,   Mali write work   report

Smith interpreted this sentence as indicating both a closed (perfective) reading (Mali began writing the report when Zhangsan arrived) and an open (imperfective) reading (Mali was writing when Zhangsan arrived). However, the main clause of the sentence cannot stand as it is in (38): an aspect marker, *le* or *zai/zhe*, has to be present on the verb to achieve the supposed perfective or imperfective reading. What is most interesting about this example is that the zero marking in the subordinate clause carries a perfective reading, which asserts that Zhangsan arrived home (i.e., *dao jia* equal to *dao-le jia*). This is because the backgrounding event *dao jia* 'arrive home' is a 2-phase expression, and the conjunctive phrase *de shihou* 'the time' indicates a time at which the target phase is reached. When the backgrounding event is a 1-phase expression, however, *de shihou* 'the time' will result in an imperfective reading, as in (39) where the order of the two clauses in (38) is reversed.

(39) Mali xie gongzuo baogao de shihou, Zhangsan dao jia-le.
Mali write work report DE time Zhangsan arrive home-LE.
When Mary was writing the work report, Zhangsan arrived home.

In this case, *le* is obligatory for the main clause, given that the backgrounding clause provides a different aspect. The subordinate clause does not have any aspectual particles, as the main clause in Smith's original sentence, but it is confined to an imperfective reading. In any case, these examples show that the range of neutral aspect in Chinese is severely limited, and the aspectual vagueness due to the omission of particles can be compensated by other linguistic devices or by discourse factors.

7 Conclusion

The characterisation of Chinese aspectual particles has been notoriously difficult for several decades in Chinese linguistic research. These particles have been studied in many different perspectives, and have been assigned many different functions. Our purpose in this article is not to give an exhaustive account of all the functions of these particles. Instead, we attempt to provide a simple but precise picture of the particles in an alternative framework of analysis. We reviewed several existing influential accounts of aspectual particles in Chinese, in particular, Li and Thompson (1981), Mangione and Li (1993), and Smith (1991). We discussed four problems, some general, some specific, associated with these accounts. We argued in particular that all these characterisations are intuitively plausible, but none of them is precise.

The analysis of Chinese aspectual marking we proposed here operates exclusively with notions that are independently defined – time intervals and temporal relations, on the one hand, and assertion and situation, on the other. This time-relational analysis does not use intuitively suggestive but entirely metaphorical characterisations in traditional definitions of aspect, but it captures the intuition behind their characterisations. In the imperfective aspect the assertion is a confined time span which is fully included in the time of the situation, and thus we often have the impression that only part of the situation is presented, or that the situation 'is seen from the inside' or 'without reference to its boundaries'. Thus, this analysis reconstructs these informal characterisations in terms of simple temporal relations between temporal intervals. Our analysis presents a simple and precise account of the functions of the Chinese particles *le, guo, zai* and *zhe* in terms of which part of the sentence's descriptive content is asserted.

References

Binnick, Robert I. (1991). Time and the Verb: A Guide to Tense and Aspect. New York and Oxford: Oxford University Press.
Bybee, Joan L., Perkins, Revere, and Pagliuca, William (1994). The Evolution of Grammar: Tense, Aspect, and Modality in the Languages of the World. Chicago: University of Chicago.
Carlson, Greg (1978). Reference to Kinds in English, unpublished Ph.D. dissertation. Amherst: University of Massachusetts.
Chan, Marjorie (1980). Temporal Reference in Mandarin Chinese: An Analytical Semantic Approach to the Study of the Morphemes, Journal of the Chinese Language Teachers Association 15, 33–79.
Chao, Yuan R. (1968). A Grammar of Spoken Chinese. Berkeley: University of California Press.
Chu, Chauncey C. (1976). Some Semantic Aspects of Action Verbs. Lingua 40, 43–54.
Chu, Chauncey C. and Chang, W. Vincent (1987). The Discourse Function of the Verbal Suffix -le in Mandarin. Journal of Chinese Linguistics 15, 309–334.
Chen, Cheng Y. (1978). Aspectual Features of the Verb and the Relative Position of the Locatives. Journal of Chinese Linguistics 6, 76–103.
Comrie, Bernard (1976). Aspect: An Introduction to the Study of Verbal Aspect and Related Problems. Cambridge: Cambridge University Press.
Dahl, Östen (1985). Tense and Aspect Systems. Oxford: Basil Blackwell.
Dowty, David R. (1979). Word Meaning and Montague Grammar. Dordrecht: D. Reidel.
Forsyth, James (1970). A Grammar of Aspect. Cambridge: Cambridge University Press.
Hamann, Cornelia (1987). The Awesome Seeds of Reference Time. In A. Schopf (ed.). Studies on Tensing in English 1, Tübingen: Niemeyer. 27–69.
Ikegami, Yoshihiko (1985). Activity-accomplishment-achievement – A Language that Can't Say I burned it but it did not burn and One that Can. In A. Makkai and A. K. Melby (eds.). Amsterdam Studies in the Theory and History of Linguistics. Amsterdam: John Benjamins. 265–304.
Klein, Wolfgang (1994). Time in Language. London: Routledge.
Klein, Wolfgang (1995). A Time-relational Analysis of Russian Aspect. Language 71, 669–695.
Klein, Wolfgang (In press). An Analysis of the German Perfekt, Language.
Li, Charles N. and Thompson, Sandra A. (1981). Mandarin Chinese: A Functional Reference Grammar. Berkeley: University of California Press.
Li, Ping (1988). Acquisition of Spatial Reference in Chinese. In Peter Jordens and Josine Lalleman (eds.). Language Development. Dordrecht: Foris. 83–99.
Li, Ping (1990). Aspect and Aktionsart in Child Mandarin, unpublished Ph.D. dissertation. Leiden: University of Leiden, NL.

Li, Ping (1993). The Acquisition of the zai and ba Constructions in Mandarin Chinese. In J. C. P. Liang and R. P. E. Sybesma (eds.). From Classical Fü to 'Three Inches High': Studies on Chinese in Honor of Erik Zürcher. Leuven/Apeldoorn: Garant Publishers. 103–120.

Li, Ping and Shirai, Yasuhiro (2000). The Acquisition of Lexical and Grammatical Aspect. Berlin and New York: Mouton de Gruyter.

Li, Yafei (1995). The Thematic Hierarchy and Causativity. Natural Language and Linguistic Theory 13, 255–282.

Li, Yafei (1999). Cross-componential Causativity. Natural Language and Linguistic Theory 17, 445–497.

Liu, Ning S. (1985). Lun -zhe jiqi xiangguan -de liang-ge dongtai fanchou' (On -zhe and its two related verbal categories). Yuyan Yanjiu (Language Research) 9. 117–127.

Ma, Xiwen (1987). Beijing fangyan-li -de -zhe (-Zhe in the Beijing dialect). Fangyan (Dialectology) 1, 17–22.

Mangione, L. and Li, Dingxuan (1993). A Compositional Analysis of -guo and –le. Journal of Chinese Linguistics 21, 65–122.

Reichenbach, Hans (1947). Elements of Symbolic Logic. London: MacMilllan.

Rohsenow, John (1976). A Unified Treatment of Lexical, Verbal, and Sentential Aspect in Mandarin Chinese. In Salikoko Mufwene, Carol Walker, and Sanford Steever (eds.). Papers from the 12th Regional Meeting of the Chicago Linguistic Society. 523–532.

Rohsenow, John (1978). Syntax and Semantics of the Perfect in Mandarin Chinese, unpublished Ph.D. dissertation. Ann Arbor: University of Michigan.

Shih, Ziqiang (1990). Decomposition of Perfectivity and Inchoativity and the Meaning of the Particle le in Mandarin Chinese, Journal of Chinese Linguistics 18, 95–123.

Smith, Carlota (1991). The Parameter of Aspect. Dordrecht: Kluwer.

Spanos, George (1979). Contemporary Chinese Use of -le: A Survey and a Pragmatic Proposal. Journal of Chinese Language Teachers Association 14(1). 36–70; 14(2), 47–102.

von Stechow, Arnim (1996). Target States, paper presented at the Colloquium 'On Time', 3 February 1996, Nijmegen.

Tai, James (1984). Verbs and Times in Chinese: Vendler's Four Categories. In David Testen, Veena Mishra, and Joseph Drogo (eds.). Papers from the Parasession on Lexical Semantics of the Chicago Linguistic Society. 289–296.

Thompson, J. (1968). Aspects of the Chinese Verb. Linguistics 38, 70–76.

Vendler, Zeno (1967). Linguistics in Philosophy. Ithaca, New York: Cornell University Press.

Vlach, F. (1981). The Semantics of the Progressive. In P. Tedeschi and A. Zaenen (eds.), Syntax and Semantics 14: Tense and Aspect. New York: Academic Press. 271–292.

Yang, Shu-Ying (1995). The Aspect System of Chinese, unpublished Ph.D. dissertation. Victoria, Canada: University of Victoria.

Yong, Shin (1997). The Grammatical Functions of Verb Complements in Mandarin Chinese. Linguistics 35, 1–24.

Zhu, De-Xi (1981). "Zai heiban-shang xie zi" ji xiangguan jushi ['To write characters on the blackboard' and its related sentence patterns]. Yuyan Jiaoxue yu Yanjiu [Language Teaching and Research] 1, 4–18.

On times and arguments[1]

1 Introduction

Ever since its beginnings, research on the expression of temporality in natural languages has centered around three notions, all of which are closely related to the verb – tense, aspect, and Aktionsart.[2] This research has pleased us with many remarkable findings. But it is perhaps fair to state that opinions still vary considerably on how these notions are to be defined and how they work in particular languages. There is no generally accepted analysis of temporal constructions such as the English progressive, the German *Perfekt*, or the Russian aspect, although the literature on each of these constructions is legion. Moreover, there are hardly any attempts to show how the meaning of these constructions follows from the way in which they are built up from their components. In what follows, I will suggest a way to look at time in language, which deviates considerably from this tradition while trying to preserve the intuitions which guided it. Two assumptions are basic to this approach:

(i) As a rule, the notion of simple "event time" should be replaced by the more general notion of a "clause-internal temporal structure".
(ii) The arguments of the verb (and other verbal constructions) are temporally parameterized.

The lexical content of a verb assigns descriptive properties to certain arguments at certain times. These times are connected to each other by temporal and possibly other relations. Compound constructions, up to the level of the clause, result from morphological and syntactic operations on this "argument-time structure". Under this approach, traditional notions such as tense, aspect and Aktionsart, but also perfect, progressive or passive, turn out to be special cases of how time spans and temporal relations between them are clustered. These ideas will be

---

1 I wish to thank Manfred Bierwisch, Claudia Maienborn and the reviewers for helpful comments. Correspondence address: Max Planck Institute for Psycholinguistics, P. O. Box 310, 6500 AH Nijmegen, The Netherlands. E-mail: wolfgang.klein@mpi.nl.
2 Binnick 1991 gives a comprehensive survey; see also Binnick's impressive – and somewhat discouraging – online bibliography www.scar.utoronto.ca/~binnick/TENSE/index.html. Dahl (2000) and Ebert and Zúñiga (2001) give a good impression of the state of the art for European and Non-European languages, respectively.

Note: This article originally appeared as Klein, W. (2010). On times and arguments. Linguistics 48. 1221–1253.

https://doi.org/10.1515/9783110549119-006

unfolded in Sections 2–3 and illustrated for some elementary morphosyntactic operations in English in Sections 4–7.

The aim of this paper is, of course, not to give answers to the many problems that were so intensively discussed in almost two millennia of research on temporality; any such idea would be more than presumptuous. The idea is rather to sketch a new and simple way to approach these problems, a way which systematically derives the meaning of classical temporal categories, such as past participle, perfect, passive or progressive from the manner in which the corresponding expressions are built up. I have therefore focused on the key ideas of this approach; thus, many issues are only sketched, and many details are completely ignored. In a way, the following considerations should primarily be seen as an invitation to follow a certain way which I believe to be promising.

2 Event time and clause-internal temporal structure

Under its traditional definition, tense is deictic and relational: broadly speaking, it relates the time of the event to the time at which the sentence is uttered. Usually, three possible temporal relations are distinguished: time of event before time of utterance, time of event simultaneous to time of utterance, time of event after time of utterance, thus giving rise to the basic distinction between past, present and future, respectively. This idea is already found in Aristotle and the Stoic philosophers. It is easy to see that it is by far too simple even in the case of Classical Greek, for which it was invented. If there are more than three tense forms, then three deictic-temporal relations are not enough; other factors must be taken into consideration. One possible solution is the introduction of a "third temporal interval", an idea which apparently originated in the late 18th century (Seuren 1998: 73–74) and is then found in the writings of many grammarians, most explicitly Hermann Paul in his analysis of the Indo-European tense system (Paul 1886: 228–229; see the discussion in Ehrich 1992: 65). Modern linguists often ascribe it to the philosopher Hans Reichenbach, who operated with three temporal parameters E, S, and R, which he called "point of event", "point of speech" and "point of reference", respectively (Reichenbach 1947). Analyses based on these three parameters have become almost classical over the last fifty years; they have even made their way into pedagogical grammars. But it is easy to show that each of them faces problems that go beyond the concrete difficulties to analyze a particular linguistic system, such as the tense system of English, German, or Russian.

In this paper, I will not address S and R (for a discussion, see, e.g., Kratzer 1978; Hamann 1987; or Klein 1994) but only the "event time". What is this event time? Reichenbach treated it as a point. Most authors nowadays say that it is time span of undefined length – the time at which the "event" takes place, or could take place. Thus, in a simple sentence such as *Caxton left*, it is the time at which the "leaving event" took place. How is this in (1):

(1) Caxton seemed to have planned to leave at five.

What is the "event" of (2), and more specifically, what it is the corresponding event time? This is not immediately apparent. Is it the time at which something seems to be the case, is it the time of Caxton's intended leaving, the time at which he planned to do something, the time at which he had planned to do something, the time at which he seemed do do something? What we have here is rather a whole array of time spans, each of which is characterized by one or several descriptive properties. We do not have a single "event time", described by a simple verb, but a complex temporal structure which is described by several components of the clause, in particular various verbal elements. This clause-internal temporal structure consists of several interrelated temporal intervals, one of which (the time at which something seems to be the case) is related to some time span beyond the clause – maybe S or R, or some time span provided by a matrix clause. In what follows, I shall simply speak of a "clause-external time", abbreviated as tex, thus leaving aside for the moment what precisely this temporal anchor is.

In (1), minimally five time spans play a role in this clause-internal temporal structure:

(2) (external) Caxton   seemed   to have   planned   to leave   at five
     t_{ex} t_1 t_2 t_3 t_4 t_5

There is a time at which something seems to be the case, there is a time at which someone apparently planned something, there is a time at which possible planning is over, there is a time at which someone apparently had planned to leave, and there is a time specified by "before five". Between these altogether six time spans, there are certain temporal relations:

(a) t_{ex} is after t_1
(b) t_1 overlaps with t_2
(c) t_2 is after t_3
(d) t_3 is before t_4
(e) t_5 is most likely identical with t_4; but other readings are possible, especially if *at five* is de-stressed
(f) t_1 overlaps with t_2, and t_2 in turn overlaps with t_4

Thus, there is not a simple E – there is a complex temporal structure which any analysis of temporality must account for. In particular, the following four questions must be answered:

(3) (i) Which intervals constitute the internal temporal structure of the clause?
(ii) How are these intervals related to each other? This problem resembles the familiar issue of argument control, except that the relation between the entities that fill the variables is not just "identical" but may also be "before, after, overlapping, simultaneous" etc – in short, all sorts of temporal relations that can obtain between two time spans.
(iii) Which temporal properties go with the various intervals? By that, I mean properties such as duration, frequency, or position on the time line. Typically, these properties are specified by various types of adverbials, such as *for an hour, often, or yesterday at five*. They can be inserted at various places, and thus may relate to various time slots in the temporal structure.
(iv) Which descriptive properties go with the temporal intervals? In other words, how are these temporal intervals characterized other than being before or after other time spans, or being short or long? In (2) there is a time at which something seems to be the case, a time at which someone apparently plans to do something, etc. This information is primarily provided by the descriptive content of the various verbal elements; it can also stem from other sources, such as world knowledge or situational information – in short, by the context.

Note that a clear distinction is made here between bare "time structure" itself (the temporal intervals and the temporal relations between them), on the one hand, and the "descriptive information" that goes with these intervals, on the other. In (4), for example, the bare time structure would be exactly the same, but the descriptive properties that go with the various intervals are different:

(4) Caxton believed to have promised to call before noon.

Thus, the clause-internal temporal structure has two different ingredients – a distinction which is crucial for the approach that will be proposed here, and which is normally not made in traditional research on temporality.

In (1) and (2) the clause-internal temporal structure is provided by a complex verbal construction, and, somehow, it corresponds to the structural makeup of this construction. How is this, if there is only a simple verb, as in (5)?

(5) Wynkyn felled a tree.

Morphologically, the form *felled* is compound: it merges a finite and a non-finite component. The former will be discussed in Section 7. The latter is the "lexical part", also found in the infinitive *to fell*, in the participle *felling* or in the finite form *fells*; this part I will call Vs (for "verb stem"). Does the lexical content of a bare and simple Vs such as *fell* include a complex temporal structure as well? For the situation described by (5) to be true, at least the following conditions must be met. (The descriptive characterizations given below, such as "be upright", are only illustrative; they are not meant to be an exhaustive and satisfactory meaning description):

(6) (i) There must be a time t_1 at which Wynkyn does something, for example swinging an ax or maneuvering a chain saw, or utter a magic spell; I will simply say he must somehow "be active".
(ii) There must be a time t_2, at which the tree is "upright".
(iii) There must be a time t_3, at which the tree is "on the ground".
(iv) Various temporal relations obtain between these times. Thus, t_3 must be after t_2. The time t_1, the time at which Wynkyn is active, must somehow overlap with t_2, i.e., the time at which the tree is upright; it may reach into t_3, but this is irrelevant for Example (5) to be true.

These four conditions do not cover the full lexical content of *fell*. In particular, there is also a causal, and not just a temporal, connection between the acting of Wynkyn and the fact that eventually, the tree is "on the ground". Following David Hume's famous analysis of causality (Lewis 1973), we can state this connection as a counterfactual condition: "If the first argument were not be active at t_1, the second argument would not be on the ground at t_3." Such a nontemporal relation, often referred to by some operator CAUSE, is an indispensable component of the lexical content of many verbs. But it is not directly relevant to our present concern, and so, I will not discuss it here but focus on the temporal side.

It appears, therefore, that not only compound expressions, such as *seem to have planned to come*, but also bare V_s, such as *fell*, can already provide a rich temporal structure. This brings us to the core assumption of the present approach:

(7) The lexical content of a verb (or a larger verbal expression) assigns descriptive properties to certain arguments at certain times. These times are connected to each other by temporal and possibly other – for example causal or modal – relations. The lexical content of the verb itself does not specify the arguments

nor the time spans; it only provides argument-time variables, which must be filled appropriately in order to obtain an interpretable utterance.

Under this assumption, arguments are *temporally parameterized*: it may well be that a single verb assigns mutually exclusive properties to one and the same argument. This is no contradiction because the assignment is relative to different times. Thus, the direct object, for example, may have a "first time" at which it is assigned property A, and a "second time", at which it is property B, whereas the subject, for example, has only one time, at which is assigned property C by the lexical verb.

Let me state this somewhat more systematically. As any lexical entry, Vs is a cluster of (at least) three types of features – those which constitute its form ("phonological" or "graphematical"), those which constitute its meaning ("semantic") and those which constitute its combinatorial properties ("categorial"). The semantic features of a verb include a *structural component* and a *descriptive component*. The structural component is the "Argument-Time-Structure" (AT-structure) of the verb. It consists of various AT-pairs together with a specification of temporal and non-temporal relations between them; it is a pure scaffold, so to speak. The descriptive component consists of the various descriptive properties that are assigned to these AT-pairs. These two components can be coupled in different ways. They may be conflated into a single morpheme, as is the case with *fell*. In predicative constructions, such as *be alive*, the descriptive property is contributed by *alive*, whereas the copula verb *be* in itself does not specify a descriptive property; it only has an AT-structure, and it can be made finite (in contrast to the other component *alive*). Many other cases are possible, but I will not go into these here. I should point out, however, that much the same point can be made for some other lexical items, such as nouns or adjectives. The adjective *green* assigns a property to some argument at some time, the noun *water* assigns a property to some argument at some time; at some other time, the same argument may have the property of being ice or steam or a supermarket tomato.[3] The difference between nouns and adjectives, on the one hand, and verbs, on the other, lies primarily in their categorial features. Nouns and adjectives cannot directly be made finite, but they admit other morphosyntactic operations; for example, they can be combined with a copula, yielding a construction which then in turn

---

3 In "stage level predicates", the time of the adjective is a subinterval of the time of the noun, in "individual level predicates", the two times are identical. The temporal parameterization of adjectives and nouns along these lines also suggests a straightforward analysis of seemingly paradoxical constructions such as *the melted ice*, which, of course, is no ice when melted (on temporality in noun phrases, see Enç [1986]; Musan [1997]).

can be made finite. I shall say that verbs are FIN-LINKABLE, whereas nouns and adjectives are not (or rather: only indirectly) FIN-LINKABLE.

A V_s, as a lexical item, is the starting point for a whole series of morphological and syntactic operations, which bring forth various types of compound expressions up to the level of the finite sentence. These operations enrich or modify the underlying AT-structure and its descriptive counterparts in various ways. They may select, for example, a subinterval of some interval given in the AT-structure, as I believe is the case with the English suffix -*ing*, or they may add a "pretime" or a "posttime". They may provide these additional times with some descriptive properties or not, they may also "fill" an argument slot or a time slot, for example *Wynkyn* in Example 5 or *at five* in Example 2, respectively. We shall examine a number of these operations in Sections 5–7.

3 AT-Structure and descriptive properties

3.1 The basic distinction

The idea that the lexical content of a verb has a rich internal structure is not new. It is found in traditional lexical semantics (see, for instance, Lyons 1977; Cruse 1989) as well as in a number of more formal approaches (e.g., Dowty 1976; Jackendoff 1991; Pustejowsky 1995; Wunderlich 1997, to mention but a few). Representations such as "x CAUSE (BECOME (y be dead))", where x and y refer to the argument variables, are typical of these latter approaches. The present approach differs from these in two respects. First, it is assumed that arguments are temporally parameterized, i.e., there is not just an x but "x at t_1", "x at t_2" etc. Second, a sharp distinction is made between the AT-structure – the structural skeleton, so to speak – and the descriptive properties which go with the various AT-pairs of this structure. In particular, it is assumed that a morphosyntactic operation can add a new temporal interval without providing some descriptive properties that would go with this additional interval. The English construction *having slept*, for example, relates to a time after a more or less extended sleeping interval; but nothing in the lexical content of *having slept* tells us what the case is at that "posttime": it is a just a time after a sleeping time.[4] Whatever we assume to be the case

---

[4] If t is a temporal interval, a "posttime" of t is any time which is immediately after t, i.e., t can have different posttimes, which differ by the time at which they end; analogously for "pretimes" of t (for a more detailed discussed of the various notions of time and on the temporal structure, as it

at the *having-slept* time is due to contextual and world knowledge, on the one hand, and to the usual pragmatic principles of communication.

How do we decide what the argument-time structure of some V_s is? The answer is relatively simple (but surely not trivial) for the first part – what are the arguments?, and I shall not go into this issue here. But how many times go with a given argument? As with any kind of lexical analysis, there are two ways to proceed when answering that question: we can ask our semantic intuitions, and we can look how the item in question interacts with other expressions. Both ways have their inherent problems, as is well illustrated in the familiar attempts to determine various types of "Aktionsarten"; their definition is either based on intuitions with respect to properties such as "homogeneity", "duration", and similar ones, or they are based on tests such as the interaction with certain adverbials such as *for two hours* vs. *in two hours* (see Klein 2009b for an extensive discussion). As regards the AT-structure of a verb, we typically have some intuition whether they involve a "change" with respect to some argument or not. Thus, in *The cup stood on the table*, we do not assume a change of the (single) argument *the cup*, whereas in *The cup fell onto the table* or *The cup broke*, there is such a change, for example a change in position. But this intuition is often vague, and more importantly, it relates to the descriptive properties, rather than to the bare temporal properties itself. Crucial to the AT-structure is not the intuition of whether the content of the verb includes many more or less different subintervals but the fact that some subinterval is accessible to morphological or syntactic operations in the particular language. Just as the argument variable, the time variable which goes with it is a foothold for potential structural processes.

Consider the following sentence:

(8) Froben studied Russian for two years.

Clearly, studying Russian includes many different phases – Froben must learn case endings, syntactic patterns, memorize vocabulary items, and so on and so forth; thus, these two years encompass many activities all of which belong to his

---

is reflected in natural languages, see Klein [2009a]). Note that a posttime/pretime of t can have the same descriptive properties as t itself. After a sleeping interval, for example, there can be another sleeping interval. This is, for example, important for the analysis of expressions such as *still sleeping*, which adds a sleeping interval to a sleeping interval; we will come back to this in a moment. Terminologically, one could perhaps differentiate between the bare "posttime", on the one hand, and the "poststage", in which time and particular descriptive properties are combined, on the other. I shall not do this here, since both terms are often used interchangeably in the literature. Note that the familiar BECOME-operator does not separate between the function of a mere temporal shift and a change in descriptive properties: the argument must always become "something different".

studying Russian. So, learning Russian has a number of subintervals, characterized by particular properties. But none of these subintervals seems accessible to a morphosyntactic operation in English, just as the various entities involved. Neither the times during which he has learned vocabulary items nor these vocabulary items themselves are accessible to such operations – although they are clearly involved in the meaning of *study Russian*. This expression does not have an argument variable for "vocabulary items", and similarly, the adverbial *for two years* in (8) cannot not pick out a specific, descriptively well-characterized subintervals. When some other adverbial, such as *many years ago, in Chasan, with mixed feelings* etc, is added, it does not specifically address one of these subintervals. In other words, we must carefully keep apart the descriptive content, one the one hand, and the temporal variables with which this content goes, on the others: the fact that there are subintervals does not mean that they can be addressed by some morphological or syntactical operation.

Suppose a V_s provides two times for an argument. This "two-times argument" can be the only argument, as in *die*, or one of several arguments, as in *kill*. Then, the descriptive properties associated with this argument at the first time and at the second time can differ to varying degrees:

A. They can be mutually exclusive

This case is illustrated by the only argument of *die* and by the second argument of *kill*: these verbs say that the relevant argument is alive at the first time and dead at the second time.[5]

B. They may differ in degree

Typical examples are V_s such as *rise, raise, fall, melt*. Their descriptive properties are relational with respect to the two times. If the temperature rose, then this means that there is an accessible interval at which the temperature is higher than at an earlier accessible interval.[6] In some cases, it is assumed that the extreme is reached at one

---

5 Note that, of course, these verbs themselves don't say anything about whether these states ever obtain, let alone whether the second state is ever reached. This is only possible in relation to some externally rooted time, for which such a claim can be made (see Section 7).

6 I believe that the higher-lower asymmetry of the same argument at two times is crucial for the meaning of these verbs; but it surely does not exhaust their descriptive content. In particular, the two AT-intervals may have subphases with internal rises and falls, depending on the particular entity which is falling or rising. When the shares fell yesterday by 11%, then this fall is probably not monotonous, whereas when a tree fell, it is unlikely that there were some small rises

of these times; thus, *the fallen temperature* normally means a temperature which is lower than at the first time, whereas *the fallen leaves*, without any further qualification, is understood to mean leaves which are not only lower than at the first time but are "on the ground". Otherwise, the difference must be specified: *the leaves had fallen by two meters*. I do not think, however, that these preferences in interpretation should be seen as a part of the lexical meaning of *fall*; they are an issue of world knowledge. Otherwise, one would have to assign many meaning shades to the lexical meaning of this verb, depending on which argument it is applied to.

C. They may be identical

Examples are *stay, remain*, or *keep, as* in *The door remained open* or *Winter kept us warm*. This case sounds perplexing at first; why should a verb involve two intervals with the same descriptive content? But remember that the criterion for assuming an AT-pair is the accessibility to some operation rather than our intuitions about homogeneity or heterogeneity. Sentences such as (9a)–(9c) show that it is possible to access a second subinterval only (note that in these examples, descriptive properties and AT-structure are distributed over several words):

(9) Gutenberg was forbidden to stay in Strasbourg.
     Gutenberg did not stay in Strasbourg.
     Gutenberg had almost stayed in Strasbourg.

The lexical content of *stay in Strasbourg* provides a first time with descriptive properties "be in Strasbourg" and a later time with the same descriptive properties "be in Strasbourg". The interdiction *was forbidden* in (9a) only relates to this later time, rather than to the entire time of his being in Strasbourg. In (9b), it is not negated that he was in Strasbourg at some time but that he was not there at some later time, at which he could have been there, too; this applies analogously for the counterfactuality in (9b): *almost* "weakly negates" his being in Strasbourg only for the later time.[7]

---

in-between. In any event, these potential subintervals are not accessible to morphosyntactic operations, hence they are not relevant to the AT-structure.

7 Both sentences can (at least marginally) have a reading in which both times are affected. This is a characteristic scope ambiguity, if some operation applies to a monomorphemic expression with several AT-pairs: it cannot easily select between the possibility to apply to both or to just one of the intervals enshrined in this single morpheme.

As any lexical analysis, the precise determination of the AT-structure which some verb (or larger verbal construction) is a very difficult issue, which I cannot pursue here.[8] But I hope the general idea is sufficiently clear from this brief discussion. Let me conclude it with two remarks. First, I believe that the missing separation of these two components has been the source of numerous problems with the familiar event type classifications. Thus, verbs of the *die* type are traditionally considered to be "telic". But what about verbs which involve a gradual change, such as *rise* of *fall*? Are they "telic" or "atelic" (as in Garey's [1957] terminology), are they "accomplishments" or "activities" (as in Vendler [1957])? In a way, they behave like activities, as is illustrated by the fact that they can take a durational adverbial: *the shares rose for two days*. But as was first noted by Fabricius-Hansen (1980), sentences such as *Then, the shares fell again* show the repetitive-restitutive ambiguity of *again* which is characteristic of telic verbs. Thus, it is possible to modify only the second time – the time at which the shares were "higher than before" – by an adverbial. Hence, they behave like accomplishments. Under the present analysis, this behavior is predicted.

The second point is methodological and not specific to the present approach. Ideally, lexical items as well as morphosyntactical operations should always make the same meaning contribution. But natural languages are not like that. They are products of historical development. Expressions, be they simple or compound, can be *ambiguous*, they can be *idiomatized*, and they can exhibit *idiosyncratic properties*. A verb such as *to open* can have a one-argument structure as well as a two-arguments structure. Similarly, we may expect that there is a one-time reading for an argument as well as a two-times reading. On the morphosyntactical level, one might hope that the attachment of, for example, *be* to another word has always the same effect. But we must be prepared that there are exceptions. All we can hope is that our analysis reduces the number of ambiguities, idiomatic cases, and idiosyncrasies as much as possible.

3.2 Some examples from English

In this section, I will illustrate the general idea with some examples from English.[9] Let us begin with the "skeleton", that is, the bare AT-structure, and only

---

[8] More detailed considerations including a discussion what the AT-structure implies for case marking in German are found in Klein (2002).

[9] I have chosen English here and in the following sections, first because any reader of this paper is easily able to verify the claims made here, and second because its temporal features are more

then turn to descriptive properties which go with this structure. Theoretically, there is no limit to the number of arguments or of temporal intervals coupled with an argument. In actual fact, however, languages seem to impose severe restrictions on their verbs. I was not able to find cases which convincingly show that a single argument can be accessed at more than two times, although nothing excludes this in principle, just as nothing seems to exclude verbs with ten or twelve arguments. Since this exposition is only illustrative anyway, I will assume here that English has only "one-time arguments" and "two-times arguments". In the latter case, these two times will be called "source time" and "target time". Note, however, that the difference is only temporal: the source time is just earlier than the target time. Nothing is said about whether the two times are adjacent.

How many arguments can a Vs have? Again, this is difficult to answer; in English, one or two are the most common cases; three is not infrequent; four is almost excluded. In what follows, I will confine the discussion to the most common cases, that is, verbs with one or two arguments. In English, we seem to have the following four patterns:

(10) **Common AT-structures of English**
Type A. One argument at one time: typical examples are *sleep, dance, vibrate, be*.
Type B. One argument with source time and target time: typical examples are *die,* (intransitive) *drown, rise, remain*.
Type C. Two arguments at the same time: typical examples are *cost, weigh* with a measure phrase.
Type D. Two arguments – one at one time, one with source and target time: in this case, the time of the one-time argument overlaps the source time of the other argument. Typical examples are *leave, close, slay,* (transitive) *drown, observe*.

Many other patterns are imaginable. For instance, we could have a variant of type C, in which the two time variables are not identical. We might have a pattern with two arguments and two times for each of them. Finally, we might have variants of type D with quite different temporal relations; for example, it could be that only time of the first argument should precede the source time of the other, or overlaps the target time, rather than its source time. I was not able to find such a verb, when going through various morphosyntactic operations that can apply

---

extensively investigated than those of any other language; see, for example, Declerck (2006) for a recent and very comprehensive analysis.

to verb stems. So, I will assume for the moment that English distinguishes only these four AT-structures. This is sufficient for present purposes.

By and large, types A and C correspond to the traditional notion of atelic verbs, whereas types B and D are telic. Note, however, that the distinction made here is exclusively based on the inherent AT-structure, whereas the traditional distinction merges temporal and descriptive properties. Many English verb stems, such as *melt, close, drown* are ambiguous between type C and type D: they must have a two-times argument, and they can, but need not, have a one-time argument. In the latter case, the single-time argument most often goes with the descriptive property "be active". Therefore, the two-times argument is prototypically a "change-of-state argument", whereas the one-time argument is prototypically an "agent" (cf. Dowty 1991).

Let us now turn to the descriptive properties that can go with these structures. Now, a satisfactory analysis of lexical meaning is perhaps the most difficult task in linguistics. The main reason is the lack of an appropriate descriptive language for lexical meaning. How should we describe the target time properties of the second argument of *leave* in *He left the room, he left many traces, he left his children*, if not by the past participle *left*? Therefore, no attempt will be made here to give a satisfactory analysis of the full lexical content of English verbs. I will confine the discussion to two general comments.

The first of these concerns the difference between "homogeneous" and "heterogeneous" intervals. It was argued above that the situation described by *Froben studied Russian for two years* is in many ways heterogeneous; it contains numerous subphases with different descriptive properties. None of these, however, is accessible to a morphosyntactic operation.[10] But independent of what is needed for the AT-structure, we might wish to differentiate between intuitively homogeneous intervals from intuitively heterogeneous intervals. Such distinctions play an important role in traditional Aktionsart classifications, as reflected in the opposition between "states" and "activities". It is not clear whether such a distinction has a reflex in morphosyntax. It has often been argued that "statives" in English cannot take the progressive form; in fact, this is one of the standard Vendler tests. But this argument is shaky, since many intuitively stative V_s can be in the progressive (*It was hanging on the wall, the cup was containing water, we were hoping for a better future*). I believe,

---

[10] As will be argued below, the construction *(to) be studying* yields a subinterval of *(to) study*; but this subinterval does is not characterized by specific properties; it is not, for example, the interval at which the subject learns the Russian aspect or rehearses the instrumental. In fact, this subinterval can be as unspecified with respect to these properties as the entire interval.

therefore, that this restriction, confined to a verb such as *know, understand* and a few others, is essentially a remnant of historical development (König 1980; Denison 1993: 371–410). This, however, is not to deny in general, that the difference between intervals for which each subinterval exhibits the same descriptive properties, and those for which this need not be the case, may play a role in grammar.

The second comment relates to the descriptive property "be active". This feature is apparently never associated with a target time, be it of the first or of the second argument; but it is very frequently associated with a first AT-pair. This may be due to the fact that the actor's being active initiates the entire event (I owe this idea to Dieter Wunderlich p.c.). Whenever the feature "be active" is present, other descriptive features may be present, too. Thus, not any kind of activity on Wynkyn's part would qualify in (5). But these additional qualifications are hard to pin down. We often hear that Louis XIV *built* Versailles. In fact, he did not lift a single stone. We say that an architect *built* a house, or that a mason *built* a house. But all they share is that they are somehow active, and that without this activity, this house would not have come into existence. This fuzziness of the "be active" feature may have consequences for more complex constructions. Consider, for example, a sentence as (11).

(11) We are leaving Riva tomorrow.

Under the traditional analysis, (11) seems contradictory: the present tense marks the "event" as being right now, whereas the adverbial marks it as being tomorrow. Under the present analysis, *leave* involves three time spans – a time at which the first argument is somehow "active", and two times for the second argument (a time at which Riva is not left by us, and a time, at which it is). How is "active" to be understood? Does it necessarily involve some movement? Or is it enough to have taken the first preparatory steps, perhaps even to have made the appropriate plans? I think the latter is the case, and intuitively, this is the impression suggested by (11) (see Williams [2002], who discusses numerous examples of this sort). If this is correct, there is no contradiction whatsoever: (11) simply means that the moment of speech (or whatever the external time is) is included in the first and only time of the first argument of *leave*, AND tomorrow must include subintervals in which we are "active" AND we are first in Riva and then out of Riva.[11]

---

11 And, of course, that the latter would not be the case if we were not "active" – if we include the "cause relation".

3.3 Event time redefined

Example (11) has brought us back to the issue of "event time", discussed in Section 2. All verb stems have a temporal structure that is hooked up to some external time, when the verb is made finite. This temporal structure may consist of a single interval, if there is only one AT-pair, as in *sleep* or *laugh*. Then, the temporal structure coincides with the classical notion of "event time". But we can extend the notion of event time to more complex cases, such as *leave*, if we consider a larger interval which includes subinterval of all components of *leave*:

(12) The event time associated with a verb V is a temporal interval which includes subintervals of all temporal intervals provided by V.

Thus, the event time of *Wynkyn felled a tree* is an interval which includes three subintervals: some "be-active time" of Wynkyn, some time at which the tree was upright, and some time at which it was on the ground. Thus, each accessible stage of the whole "event" is represented in this event time. This definition also captures, as a special case, verbal expressions like *sleep*, which provide only one AT-pair; the event time of sleep is a time span which includes a sleeping interval of its only argument. The notion of event time, as defined here, is "duration indefinite", i.e., it can be longer or shorter, provided it contains the required subintervals. Assumptions on its duration in a given utterance depend on context. If the temporal structure is not simple, then there is often a tendency to consider the shortest interval with the required properties as event time. This leads to the impression that verbs such as *to find*, are "punctual", since the minimal interval which includes subintervals of all relevant intervals is very short. But this is wrong; it may easily take someone a whole afternoon to find a kilo of mushrooms. And it should be noted that the "time of finding" is not the – perhaps very short – time at which the last mushroom is found. This would be the time of finding the last mushroom, not the time of finding a kilo of mushrooms. In other words, to find is not "punctual", because finding something has no temporal extension. It is punctual, because the minimal interval which includes subintervals of all intervals provided by its lexical content can be extremely short.

The definition in (11) can be extended to still more complex temporal structures, such as the one of *seem to have planned to come at five*, which does not describe a single clearly shaped event but a aggregation of events. Such a broad notion, however, seems not very useful. More sensible are perhaps intermediate notions of event time. Thus, we may say that *Wynkyn was felling a tree* has, as its event time, the subinterval in which Wynkyn was active with his axe – no matter whether the tree eventually fell or not. It is a practical question whether such a notion of event time, on whatever level of complexity, is needed. I believe that it could be useful for the simple verb, for example in the analysis of the "perfect" (cf. Section 6); but at present, I see no use for other, more complex notions of event time.

4 Morphosyntactic operations on the argument-time structure

Let me begin with some standard assumptions. Lexical entries such as *leave, fall* or *sleep* are clusters of three types of features – phonological features, semantic features, and categorial features (such as "is a noun", "belongs to inflectional paradigm 17", etc). These feature sets are the starting point for various operations which turn a lexical entry into a more complex expression. Operations can be morphological, i.e., within word boundaries, and they can be syntactic, i.e., go beyond the boundaries of a word. They change or maintain the three types of features in a characteristic way; they may also serve to integrate the complex expression into the context.

All operations take some expression and turn it into a new expression by changing some of its phonological, categorial and semantic features. Under the present approach, essentially two types of operations come into play here. Firstly, there are operations that fill the argument variables and the temporal variables, e.g., by an NP in the former case or by a temporal adverbial in the latter. Secondly, there are operations which do not fill some existing variables but somehow modify the descriptive properties, the AT-structure, or both. In the present context, we are primarily interested in this second type of operations (but see Section 7 on the grammatical subject).[12]

Consider a verb stem such as *sleep*, which has only one AT-pair, abbreviated here as $<A, t_i>$, where A is the argument variable and t_i the variable for the time at which the property of being asleep is assigned to A. Operations can change

---

[12] I assume that a substantial part of argument realization can be described by a small number of default operations. In Germanic languages, a single argument is normally realized as the grammatical subject (and marked by nominative); this argument can be a one-time or two-times argument. If there is a one-time argument and a two-times argument, the former is normally realized as the grammatical subject and the latter as the direct object. As a consequence, the subject of an intransitive verb can be like the subject of a transitive verb or like the object of a transitive verb. This may underlie the familiar "unergative-unaccusative" distinction of verbs.

this elementary AT-structure. Let us first examine the temporal side. Since t_i is a temporal interval, there are, due to the very nature of time, also intervals before t_i, there are intervals within t_i, and there are intervals after t_i; we may call these *pretimes* of t_i, *subtimes* of t_i, and *posttimes* of t_i, respectively (see Note 3). Operations on *sleep* can assign one of these intervals to t_i, which is then accessible to further operations. I shall simply say that they add a subtime, a pretime, or a posttime. It is also imaginable that such an operation adds a somewhat more complex interval, for example an interval which overlaps t_i and the time after t_i. The crucial point is always that an additional temporal interval is henceforth available for further morphological or syntactic operations.

Whenever the existing AT-structure is enriched in this way, descriptive properties can but need not be added, as well. Thus, German *los-*, as in *losrennen* "to start running", adds a pretime, about which nothing is said except that it is not yet a running time, and English *-ing*, as in *sleeping*, adds a subtime, which preserves the descriptive information of t_i. There are also syntactic operations which serve this function, for example phase verbs such as *to begin to;* whereas *John slept* involves one time, *John began two sleep* involves two times – a time at which John indeed was asleep, and an earlier time about which nothing is said except that it is not a sleeping time (of John). The addition of *plan to*, as in *to plan to sleep*, not only adds an accessible "pretime" but also characterizes this pretime as a "planning time".

Turning now to the argument side of operations on the AT-structure, the simplest case is surely that the argument variable is maintained. Thus, *losrennen* has the same argument variable as *rennen* "to run"; *to be going to sleep* or *to plan to sleep* have the same argument variable as the underlying V_s *sleep*. There are other possibilities, as in *to seem to sleep*, as has been extensively studied in work on argument control; I shall not go into these here. There is an important consequence of adding such a pretime for the same argument: the argument is then interpretable at several times – for example at the sleeping time itself as well as at some pretime of the sleeping time. In other words, we have what was called above "temporally parameterized arguments". In this case, the parameterization is not part of the V_s but results from the morphological operation. Since the argument variable is usually filled only once, for example by the grammatical subject, this raises the question at which time this grammatical subject is interpreted – is it interpreted at the "topmost time", i.e., by the one added by the operation, or at some embedded time? This becomes important as soon as the entire temporal structure of the clause is related to some clause-external time, for example the moment of speech. We shall come back to this question in Section 7.

A verb stem like *sleep* provides only one AT-pair. What happens, if some operation is applied to a V_s with several AT-pairs, such as *fell*? Then, either one of them must be selected, or else the operation works simultaneously on several of them. This varies from operation to operation and has to be marked specifically in the definition of this operation. A common case, for example, is that the first argument at its first (and perhaps only) time is targeted. Thus, the operation which turns bare *fell* into *felling* provides a subinterval of the time at which the first argument "is active" – whatever precisely this activity may consist of. This time overlaps with the source time of the second argument, but it need not overlap with the target time of the second argument (see (6iv) above).

The net effect of AT-operations is to provide an additional AT-pair, with or without additional descriptive content. This means that the new pair is now available for further morphosyntactic operations. This process can be repeated, up to the construction of a finite clause and – as in subordinate clauses – even beyond. Example (2) *Caxton seemed to have planned to leave at five* illustrates such a chain of operations, which leads from the V_s *leave* to the finiteness marking by *-ed* on *seem*. Since the formation of such a chain is stepwise, it seems natural to assume that each operation applies to the AT-pair brought about by the immediately preceding operation. This last-added pair – the topmost pair in a complex construction – I shall call the "accessible pair".[13] In principle, however, it is not excluded, that other, "enshrined" AT-pairs are still accessible. This may vary from operation to operation; it may also be different for argument variables and for time variables.

5 Three morphological operations in English

We shall now illustrate this with some examples from English. The starting point is the bare verb stem V_s. In principle, all operations discussed in the following affect phonological, categorial and semantic features. But in the present context, we are mainly interested in their effect on the AT-structure and the accompanying descriptive properties. Therefore, the phonological and the categorial side will only be briefly dealt with; in fact, most changes are straightforward. It should be clear that the discussion in this section cannot claim to cover all problems connected to form and function of these constructions; the idea is rather to illustrate how the idea of an argument-time structure and various operations on this structure yield a new and, in the event, surprisingly simple picture of what is traditionally described under labels such as, for example, past participle.

---

[13] This term should not be given too much theoretical weight. It is just an easy way to refer to the argument-time pair which, at a given point, is subject to an operation.

5.1 V$_s$-Ø: the "bare infinitive"

In English, the bare infinitive is phonologically (and orthographically) identical with V$_s$ (in contrast, for example, to Dutch or German, where -*en* is attached to V$_s$). As to the categorical features, the main change is that the resulting structure is no longer FIN-LINKABLE. There is no reason to assume that this operation changes the AT-structure or the descriptive properties.

5.2 V$_s$-ing: the "present participle"

This form is usually assigned several functions, sometimes kept apart by labels such as "present participle" v$_s$. "gerund". I assume that this distinction, if really needed, only concerns categorial features, in which we are not primarily interested here; the main change in this regard is again, that V$_s$-*ing* is no longer FIN-LINKABLE. As to the phonological features, the effect is simple: -*ing* is attached.

How does the attachment of -*ing* affect the AT-structure? This is best seen in cases, in which no other operation interferes. In the finite progressive *John was working*, for example, not only the -*ing*-marking, but also *be* and the finiteness marking on it contribute to the entire meaning; it is not easy to tell these contributions apart. In attributive constructions such as *the sleeping dog* or *the falling snow*, we observe the effect of bare -*ing*. Intuitively, these constructions give the impression that the argument, to which the present participle is attached, is somehow "in the midst of the event". We can capture this intuition by assuming that -*ing* adds, as an accessible interval, a subtime of the first (and possibly only) time of V$_s$. In the case of *sleep*, there is only one such interval (type A in 10); hence, *sleeping* relates to a proper subinterval of a sleeping interval; in terms of descriptive properties, this subinterval is also a sleeping interval. In the case of intransitive *drown* – type B in (10) –, the form *drowning* gives us a subtime of the source time of the only argument – roughly characterized by properties "not yet dead, under water". When derived from transitive *drown* (type D in (10)), the form *drowning* gives us a subtime of the first argument – a subtime of the time at which the subject "is accessible"; this time overlaps with the time at which the other argument has its first-time properties, i.e., roughly "not yet dead, under water". In both cases, *drowning* does not imply that the event is completed in the sense that the subject (in the intransitive case) or the object (in the transitive case) is dead.

We can sum up the effect of this operation as follows. Phonologically, it adds -*ing* to V$_s$. Categorially, the resulting expression cannot directly be made finite. Semantically, it adds a new AT-pair, such that

(a) the argument is the first (and possibly only) argument of V_s, and
(b) the time is a subtime of the first (and possibly only) time of that argument.

In other words, the English -*ing*-construction places the argument to which the present participle is applied somewhere "in the midst of the event" – and exactly this is our intuition.

5.3 V_s-ed: the "past participle"

English has two suffixes -*ed*, one of which results in a finite form (simple past of regular verbs) and the other one in what is traditionally called the past participle. Here, we are interested in the operation which leads to the latter (for the former, see Section 7). Its consequences for the phonological features vary; in the simplest case, the suffix -*ed* is attached to the stem; but there are, of course, many irregular forms, not to be discussed here. There are changes in the categorial features; in particular, the resulting form is no longer FIN-LINKABLE.

As the contrast between *the falling snow* and *the fallen snow* shows, -*ed* relates the argument *the snow* to the second, rather than to the first, time of the only argument of *fall*. This is also the case in *the killed soldier*, except that *kill* has two argument slots – it belongs to type D from (10). Only one of these arguments has two times; thus, *killed* describes what is the case with the two-times argument at its second time: roughly, being dead after being alive, and this due to some activity of the other argument.

What happens if V_s does not provide such a second time, as in *sleep* or *laugh*? These verbs have only one argument at one time. Then, the attachment of -*ed* should not lead to a construction that is able to assign properties to an argument. This is indeed the case – we cannot say *the slept dog* or *the laughed waiter*. This presupposes that -*ed* itself does not add a new argument slot at some later time: it only adds a new time variable, which must be the second time of an argument – a target time.[14]

The effect of this operation can thus be summed up as follows. Phonologically, it adds -*ed* to V_s (barring a number of irregular forms). Categorially, the resulting expression cannot directly be made finite. Semantically, it does not add a new argument variable, but it adds a new time – the target time of the first or second argument.

---

14 This is surely not the only restriction on the use of the past participles in attributive constructions. Thus, we can say *the drowned giant*, but not *the died giant*. Some of these restrictions seem quite idiosyncratic; but there may also be more systematical constraints, an issue not to be discussed here.

In this section, we have examined three simple morphological operations on V_s. On the phonological level, their effect is to add Ø, *-ing* and *-ed* (with some irregular variants), respectively. On the categorial level, their main effect is to turn a FIN-LINKABLE expression into a non-FIN-LINKABLE expression. On the semantic level, they all change the AT-structure, but not the descriptive properties. Ø adds nothing; *-ing* adds a subtime to the time of the first (and possibly only) AT-pair; *-ed* provides no argument variable; but if V_s provides a target time for some argument, then this target time is the new accessible time. In other words, these operations are essentially calculations on temporal structures – they do not add any new descriptive content. But they may apply the descriptive content provided by the verb stem at different times than before.

This is a very simple analysis. It does not stipulate semantic ambiguities, it is in agreement with the empirical facts; it explains why attributive constructions with intransitive V_s such as *slept* are impossible, whereas attributive constructions derived from intransitive V_s, such as *fallen* or (intransitive) *drowned*, are possible – barring other restrictions. The resulting constructions are accessible to several other operations, which act on the new accessible AT-pair. We shall now have a look at three of these operations.

6 Three elementary syntactic operations in English

The operations discussed in this section lead to the constructions which are traditionally called (non-finite) "progressive", "perfect", and "passive", respectively. As we shall see, most properties of these constructions follow naturally from some simple assumptions about AT-structure.

On the phonological level and on the categorial level, the three operations are very similar: some element is juxtaposed before V_s-*ing* or V_s-*ed*, and the resulting construction is made FIN-linkable. In what follows, I shall therefore focus on the semantic side.

6.1 Be V$_s$-ing: the (non-finite) progressive

Semantically, this operation simply maintains the accessible AT-pair; the effect is merely on the categorial level: *be closing* assigns descriptive properties of the first subtime of *close* – the "activity time", so to speak – to some argument (which, when the construction is made finite, can be filled by the grammatical subject).

In other words, the effect of this operation is exactly the same which turns *green* into *be green*, and *a teacher* into *be a teacher*.

6.2 Be V$_s$-ed: the (non-finite) passive

The simplest assumption is, that here, too, *be* functions like a normal copula: it maintains the accessible AT-pair. Differences only result from the fact that the accessible pair of V$_s$-*ed* is different from the accessible pair of V$_s$-*ing*. A past participle such as *closed* assigns target time properties to its argument – if there is an argument slot at all, i.e., if the underlying V$_s$ has a two-times argument (see Section 5.3). This is the case for transitive *close*, and therefore, *be closed* assigns target time properties to an argument, when this argument is syntactically realized. It is not the case for verbs such as *sleep*. Therefore, *The dog is slept* should not be possible, and it isn't.

This analysis naturally explains the static but not the dynamic reading of the English *be*-passive: for *The egg was boiled,* it says that at some time in the past, the egg had the target-time properties of *boil*-. But this sentence can also mean that within a time in the past, the egg had first the source time properties of the second argument of *boil*- (somehow exposed to water, but raw) and then the target time properties of *boil*- (i.e., be boiled). In this regard, the dynamic *be*-passive in English deviates from all other *be*-constructions – *be green, be a teacher, be in Riva, be sleeping*. It also deviates from other West-Germanic languages such as Dutch or German, in which the static reading is expressed by the immediate counterpart of *be*, and the dynamic reading by a "change-of-state copula" (*worden* in Dutch, *werden* in German). Such a copula also existed in Old English; but it was abandoned and replaced by *become* or, to some extent, by *get* in predicative constructions. In the "passive", i.e., in combination with a past participle, it was replaced by *be* or by *get*.[15] This historical development has led to a system with an apparent ambiguity, and this renders a coherent analysis of the meaning contribution of *be* difficult: we have the usual static *be* for all types of uses and a dynamic *be*, that is only found in the dynamic reading of the "passive".

In the present framework, the static and the dynamic reading of *be* V$_s$-*ed* differ in that the static reading just picks out the time of the accessible AT-pair, whereas the dynamic *be* V$_s$-*ed* picks out this time and a pretime of it. Thus, *be*

---

15 Old English had a *beon/wesan*-passive as well as a *weordan*-passive; opinions disagree to some extent on whether the former was confined to static passive or whether it already had both readings (see the survey in Denison [1993: 413–445, especially 417–419]).

adds an AT-pair which has the same argument as the accessible pair and a new time which is (a) the time of the accessible pair OR (b) the time of the accessible pair and a pretime of it. In the latter case, it includes the transition from pretime to accessible time, and this yields the dynamic reading. Now, *be green, be a teacher, be sleeping* cannot have a dynamic reading, whereas *be boiled* can. The dynamic reading is only possible, if the pretime is a source time – that is, the first time of a two-times argument; *green, a teacher, sleeping* do not provide a source time, whereas *boil* does.

We can now describe the effect of attaching *be* in all usages as follows. Phonologically, it is juxtaposed to the left of the expression to which it applies. Syntactically, it makes the resulting expression FIN-LINKABLE. Semantically, it adds a new AT-pair such that
- the new accessible argument is the same as the old accessible argument,
- the new accessible time is the old accessible time OR optionally the old accessible time and its pretime, if this pretime is a source time.

This is less elegant than to say that *be* only makes the expression FIN-LINKABLE, and thus changes its morphosyntactical properties; but just as historical development often leads to and wipes out certain irregularities, it also may lead to and wipe out ambiguities.

This immediately brings us to the second problem, also connected to historical development. Under the present analysis, it should be regularly possible to have constructions such as *The snow is fallen, the pope is died*, because the underlying intransitive V_s, and thus the resulting participle, provides an appropriate AT-pair. In the static reading, these constructions were common in Old English, but in contrast to other West-Germanic languages (Shannon 1989), they are marginal in modern English (see Elsness 1997: 237–272 for a detailed account of this development). The dynamic reading never evolved. In both cases, this may be due to a competition. In the static reading, there was a competition with *the snow has fallen, the pope has died*, which, as we shall see below, yields virtually the same meaning. In the dynamic reading, a construction such as *the snow is fallen, the pope is died* would mean the same as the *snow fell, the pope died*, and therefore, it never evolved.

6.3 Have V_s-ed: The (non-finite) perfect

There has been considerable discussion on the semantics of the English perfect (see, for example, Comrie 1976: 56–61; McCoard 1978; Fenn 1987; Elsness 1997; Iatriou et al. 2001; Katz 2003). Note, however, that we are talking here about the non-finite perfect, that is, forms such as *have slept, have fallen, have left*. For these expressions, an analysis in terms of an "extended now" or of "current relevance", as often advocated in the literature, does not make much sense: there is no moment of speech, nor any other clause-external time, to which they are linked. Intuitively, all of these expressions relate to a time after a time with the descriptive properties provided by V_s *sleep, fall, leave*, respectively. In other words, they add a posttime, and they do not say anything about the descriptive properties which are assigned to any argument at this posttime.

We can thus describe the effect of *have* as follows. Phonologically, it is juxtaposed to the left of the expression to which it applies. Syntactically, it makes the resulting expression FIN-LINKABLE. Semantically, it adds a new AT-pair such that

- the new accessible argument is the first (and possibly only) argument of V_s,
- the new accessible time is a time after a time which overlaps with all subintervals provided by V_s

In *have slept*, the new time is a time after some interval at which someone has the properties *sleep*, and the new argument is the same as the old argument (but it need not have the "sleep properties" at that later time!). In *have fallen*, the posttime is after some interval in which the relevant argument was first higher, then lower. In *have left*, the posttime must be after an interval which includes (a) the time of some activity of the first argument, which is taken over into the new AT-pair, and (b) the source time as well as the target time of some other argument. In neither case does the operation itself say anything about the descriptive properties of the argument of *have* at the posttime. If the temperature is assigned the property *to have fallen*, then it must have gone from "higher" to "lower". But it is not excluded that it has risen again. The only exception are verbs whose target time is considered to last forever – such as in *have died*.

We conclude this section with a brief look at combined operations with *be* and *have*.

6.4 Have been V_s-ing: the perfect progressive

Consider sentence (13):

(13) Fust had been cooking a pea soup (when the stove exploded).

It means that at some time in the past, Fust was in the posttime of some x-interval. This x-interval is a "*be-cooking* time"; it is the time at which Fust is somehow accessible, putting the pot on the stove, pouring water and peas into it, or whatever else might belong to this activity. It need not, but can, overlap the time at which the soup is ready, of course. In this particular example the "non-completed" reading is more likely: we assume that he is still in the midst of his soup making, when he is so unpleasantly interrupted.

What is the meaning contribution of *have been cooking* to (13)? Let us look at the various steps that bring forth this expression:
- V_s *cook*: it is a verb of type D, includes three AT-pairs, one for the first argument ("Fust") and two for the second argument ("pea soup")
- *-ing* added: selects a subtime of the first AT-pair (Fust's activity)
- *be* added: *keeps* the AT-structure, makes the expression FIN-linkable
- *-ed* added: adds a posttime (but no argument slot) to the accessible AT-pair, i.e., it creates a time after a "be-active with cooking" time
- *have* added: adds an AT-pair with an argument of *be cooking* and a time after *be cooking*-interval; makes the expression FIN-LINKABLE.

In other words, the meaning of the (non-finite) perfect progressive follows step by step from the various morphological and syntactic operations we have assumed so far.

7 Finite constructions

The constructions we have derived so far are all non-finite but FIN-LINKABLE, that is, they can directly be made finite. This requires a morphological as well as a syntactical operation:
- the topmost FIN-LINKABLE ELEMENT must be marked as finite, and
- one of the arguments must be filled appropriately by a (possibly phonologically empty) NP, the grammatical subject.

In what follows, I will discuss these two operations in turn (for a more detailed discussion of finiteness, see Klein [2006]).

7.1 FIN-marking on the verb

FIN-marking, too, is an operation on phonological, categorial and semantic features of the element to which it is applied; this is the topmost verbal element of the entire non-finite expression. Here, we shall only deal with the semantic side. In that regard, FIN-marking has three effects:

1. It adds a new interval, let us call it t_{fin} for the moment,
2. it relates t_{fin} to the external time – it "anchors the sentence in time", so to speak, and
3. it somehow characterizes t_{fin}.

The fact that FIN-marking adds a new accessible time t_{fin} is best illustrated by examples like (14):

(14) Why did Göschen not come to the meeting yesterday? – He was ill.

The assertion made by *He was ill* does not target the full time span provided by *be ill*. Göschen could still be ill at the moment of speech; in *He was dead*, this is almost certainly the case. For (14) to be true, it is only required that there is some time which (a) is in the past and (b) includes some time at which he is ill: it is this time about which the assertion is made. This is the "finiteness time" t_{fin}. Note that t_{fin} can be a subinterval of his being ill, but also a superinterval of his being ill: in both cases, t_{fin} includes a subinterval at which he is ill.

We can naturally extend this idea to verbal expressions with more than one AT-pair:

(15) FIN-marking on some FIN-LINKABLE V adds a new time t_{fin} which includes subtimes of all the time spans provided by V.

FIN-marking always applies to the topmost V of some construction. The temporal relationship between t_{fin} and other time spans within the entire verbal construction depends on the way in which this construction is built up. When, for example, the construction *be cooking* is made finite, as in *Unger was cooking*, then a subtime of the FIRST interval of *cook* is selected as t_{fin} – the "be active"-time of the first argument. This results from the various operations discussed in Sections 5 and 6. Under this analysis, the bare verb stem *cook* (type D) includes three time variables, one for the first and two for the second argument.

The present participle *cooking* selects a subinterval of the only time of the first argument, *be cooking* maintains this time and the argument and makes the construction FIN-LINKABLE. When *cook* is directly made finite, then an interval which contains subintervals of all intervals provided by *cook* is selected as t_{fin}. This leads to the impression that *Unger was cooking a pea soup* is already true when he was putting the peas into the water etc.: Unger is "in the midst of the action", the event is presented as ongoing, as the traditional terminology has it. In *Unger cooked a pea soup*, however, there must be a time in the past within which (a) he did that, and (b) there was first no pea soup and then, due to his efforts, there was a pea soup. In other words, all subintervals must be (partly) included in t_{fin} – in the time about which the assertion is made: the "event is presented as completed". In other words, our analysis naturally leads to the perfective-imperfective difference between the English simple form and the progressive form.

The resulting t_{fin} is then related to the clause-external time, for example the moment of speech, or the time of some higher verb (cf. Section 2). English provides three possibilities here:

(16) (a) The external time is a subtime of t_{fin} (= present tense).
    (b) The external time is a posttime of t_{fin} (= past tense).
    (c) The external time is a pretime of t_{fin} (= future tense).

So far, t_{fin} is just another time span. Which descriptive content, if any, goes with it?[16] In Examples (14) and (16), it is the time to which the assertion made by the utterance is confined. This characterization does not work for sentences which do not make an assertion. But we can naturally extend it to clauses which have a different function. Generally speaking, t_{fin} goes with the functional properties of the clause whose topmost internal time it is. Thus, if this clause is declarative, such as *Göschen was ill*, then t_{fin} is indeed the time to which the assertion is confined. If this clause is an imperative, such as *Close this window!*, then t_{fin} is the time, at which the obligation is meant to hold. If it is a subordinate clause, then the interpretation of t_{fin} varies with the type of this clause; in temporal clauses, for example, it may be just the time during, before or after which something is the case (*while/before/after Koberger had been sleeping*). Hence, the interpretation depends on the sentence type, and perhaps other factors. As an overarching expression, which is not directly bound to the language-specific device of finiteness marking, I shall use the term "topic time" introduced in Klein 1994.

7.2 Grammatical subject

Non-finite expressions, such as *leave, have left, have been leaving*, include a more or less complex AT-structure with several time variables and several argument

---

[16] Precisely this is the main problem with Reichenbach's R – is it just another time span, or does it have certain descriptive properties? If not, the distinction between the various tenses in a Reichenbach framework breaks down, because there is always "another time span", which overlaps with S or E.

variables. In particular, one and the same argument variable may be coupled with different times: arguments are temporally parameterized. When such an expression is turned into a finite clause, one of its arguments is realized as the grammatical subject, i.e., by a noun phrase with particular categorial and phonological features, such as position or nominative case. From which AT-pair is the relevant argument chosen? The first part of the answer is simple:

(17) The first (and possibly only) argument of the topmost verbal element is realized as grammatical subject.

But since arguments are temporally parameterized, this very argument may be coupled with different times within a complex construction. The most natural assumption is surely that the grammatical subject always goes with the first me of the topmost verbal element. In *Wynkyn has felled a tree*, Wynkyn is said to have right now (*has!*) the *have-felled-a-tree*-properties. Thus, the argument realized as grammatical subject is interpreted at the topmost time.

I assume that this is always the case in English. Other languages, however, may go for different options. In German, for instance, the grammatical subject is chosen in the same way; but there is reason to assume that it can also be interpreted at an embedded position: it need not be interpreted at the topmost time. Compare (18a) and (18b), uttered on May 8, 1998:

(18) (a) Gutenberg has left Strasbourg.
     (b) Gutenberg hat Straßburg verlassen.

In English as well as in German, the topmost AT-pair comes from the auxiliary *has/hat*. It provides the topic time, which includes the moment of speech (according to 16a), and the argument slot is filled by *Gutenberg*. In English, this argument necessarily acquires the posttime properties of *leave Strasbourg*: as a consequence, Gutenberg is said to be in the posttime of leaving Strasbourg at the utterance time. This does not make much sense if Gutenberg is dead at the utterance time (and if the interlocutors know this); therefore, (18a) should be odd, and so it is.[17] In German, this odd reading is possible, as well. But there is a second reading, under which Gutenberg, when referred to by the grammatical subject, is assigned the properties of *leave Strasbourg*, rather than of *have left Strasbourg*. Then, the sentence means something like: "the moment of speech falls into a time after a time

---

[17] It does make sense, though, if we talk about Gutenberg as someone who, in a way, still exists, as in *Gutenberg has changed our world more than any other goldsmith*. Then, the sentence is not odd (or not for that reason).

at which Gutenberg leaves Strasbourg". This reading is practically identical to the simple past. Therefore, the German perfect can have a "present perfect reading" and a "simple past reading", and this is what is generally assumed in the literature on the German perfect (see, e.g., Wunderlich 1970; Fabricius-Hansen 1986; Thieroff 1992; von Stechow 1999; Klein 2000; Musan 2002).

Thus, the English perfect and the German perfect have the same composition; the difference results from the fact that in German, the "grammatical subject" need not be interpreted at the "topmost level", i.e., at the topic time. This difference is not specific to the interpretation of the subject. A temporal adverbial in initial position in German need not be interpreted as specifying the topic time. Thus, the sentence *1448 hatte er Straßburg verlassen* can mean that his leaving occurred in 1448, but also that in 1448, he was no longer in Strasbourg. The corresponding English sentence *In 1448 he had left Strasbourg* normally has only the latter reading, that is, the reading in which the adverbial specifies the topic time rather than the "event time.

8 Perfect, progressive, passive reanalyzed

In this section, we shall illustrate how the present analysis accounts for various finite English forms, in particular the finite perfect, the finite progressive and the finite passive. The first group of examples is based on V_s with one AT-pair only:

(19) (a) Grüninger slept.
 (b) Grüninger was sleeping.
 (c) Grüninger has slept.
 (d) Grüninger had slept.
 (e) Grüninger had been sleeping.

In (19a) the topic time is before the external time, and it (properly or improperly) includes some of Grüninger's *sleep*-time. In (19b), the topic time is before the external time, too, but the topmost time – the *be-sleeping*-time – is explicitly marked as a subtime of *sleep*. This is an impression of being in the midst of sleeping.[18] In (19c), the topic time includes the external time, whereas in (19d),

---

18 Under this analysis, the simple form of a Vs with just one temporal interval can have an "imperfective" reading: the sleeping time can be properly or improperly contained in the topic time. This primarily depends on how long topic time and the sleeping time are understood to be in the

the topic time precedes the external time. At this topic time, Grüninger is assigned the posttime properties of sleeping. There is no lexical specification of what these properties are: the lexical content of *sleep* gives no information on what is the case with someone after a sleeping interval. He may sing or dance or work, he may be dizzy, it may even be still asleep. This last reading is not very suggestive in this case. It is more likely in (19e), where the time about which an assertion is made is only a subtime of a sleeping interval. Therefore, a sequence such as (19f) is quite natural:

(19) (f) Grüninger had been sleeping, when the phone rang.

Let us now turn to a V_s with more than one AT-pair:

(20) (a) Plantin printed a bible.
 (b) Plantin was printing a bible.
 (c) Plantin has printed a bible.
 (d) Plantin had printed a bible.
 (e) Plantin had been printing a bible.
 (f) The bible was printed.

In (20a) as well as in (20b), the topic time is in the past; the difference is only whether this topic time must include subintervals of both arguments (i.e., his activity as well as the unprinted and printed stage of the bible) or only needs to include some subinterval of his activity stage. The former leads to a "perfective" reading, the latter to an "imperfective" reading. In (20c), the topic time includes the external time, and for that time, the sentence assigns to Plantin the posttime properties of *print a bible*. Just as with (18a), this should be odd if Plantin does not exist at the external time, at least for speakers who know that he does not exist right now, and so it is. No such effect is observed for (20d): Plantin's time is coupled with some time in the past, and this should be fine. In (20c) as well as in (20d), the book must be printed at the topic time, and this is the intuitive feeling we have. In (20e), the topic time is in the past, it is after a subtime of

---

relevant context: a short topic time in relation to a long sleeping time naturally leads to an "inside perspective", and vice versa. Moreover, the fact that there is a competing form – the progressive – which explicitly targets a subtime of the time provided by *sleep* invites a "perfective" reading of the simple form. This analysis seems to fit the intuitions best, or at least the intuitions of those I have asked. If such an imperfective reading is to be excluded, one would have to add "properly" to (15). If the verb involves more than one time span, such as with *come* or *cook*, it is automatically excluded, because subintervals of all their times must be included in the topic time.

Plantin's activity (*been printing*); but it is not asserted that the bible was ever printed. Example (20f), finally, has two readings: the underlying *be printed*, to which fin-marking is applied, must overlap with the time at which the book is ready ("static passive"); it can also include a time at which the book is not yet ready and someone is active with whatever is necessary to print it ("dynamic passive").

Let us conclude this tour through various English forms with two examples in which present tense is coupled with the future adverbial *tomorrow*. The first of them was already discussed above (Example 11):

(21) (a) We are leaving Riva tomorrow.
 (b) The train leaves Riva tomorrow at five.

In (21a), the crucial question is what the descriptive properties of the "source time" of *leave* – the time of which *be leaving* selects a subinterval – are. They describe "our being active". If we assume that this being active does not require some actual moving, but also involves the planning stage, maybe packing and other preparatory activities of leaving a place, then this sentence should be fine, even if we assume that *tomorrow* specifies the entire "event time" (in the sense of (12), i.e., a time which includes subtimes of all intervals provided by Vs). It may well be, therefore, that a part of the source time of the first argument as well as parts of the two times of the second argument are included in the time described by *tomorrow*. At the same time, the source time of the first argument may overlap with the utterance time. Hence, under the present account, there is not only no contradiction between the present tense and the future time adverbial *tomorrow* – the account also predicts the particular flavour of this sentence: right now, we are somehow in the preparatory stage of leaving.

Such an explanation is not possible for (21b), an utterance with a very different flavour: rather than giving the impression that the train is in some initial stage of leaving, it has the flavour of a "scheduled time": it is somehow fixed when the train leaves (cf. Williams 2002). Under the present analysis, FIN-marking only requires the topic time to include the external time; it says nothing about the duration of the time to which the assertion made by (21b) is confined. The topic time can be a very short interval, it can also be a very long interval, which reaches into the future and into the past. If this time is indeed very long, the assertion is temporally less confined, and the statement has a more principled character. Such a long topic time can also fully include the "event time", even if this event time is in the future (as indicated here by *tomorrow at five*). This explains why (21b) is possible without contradiction and why it has its "scheduled character".

9 Conclusion

In Section 2, it was argued that the classical notions of event time should be replaced by the more general notion of a clause-internal temporal structure which is closely connected to argument structure. An argument-time structure consists of a number of argument-time variable pairs; the temporal variables are related to each other by relations such as "overlapping, before, included in" and other ones. There are also other relations between AT-pairs, for example causal or modal relations; these were not considered here. The AT-pairs of a verb stem are connected to descriptive properties: as soon as the argument variables are filled, the verb stem assigns descriptive properties to these arguments at the matching times. AT-structure and the associated descriptive properties form the semantic features of the verb stem. In principle, there could be very many types of AT-structures. In actual fact, their number in English seems restricted to a few patterns – but this is an issue which requires further investigation.

More complex expressions are brought forth by a number of morphosyntactic operations which selectively change the phonological, morphological and semantic features of the expression to which they are applied. A few of these operations were considered here. They allow a very simple compositional analysis of traditional categories such as the (present and past) perfect, static and dynamic passives and the progressive. They predict many special effects of these constructions, for example the impression that the progressive somehow "looks into the interior" of the situation described. They also naturally explain why constructions such as *the slept dog* or *the dog is slept* are not interpretable.

There is hardly any violation of the principle "one form – one meaning". The only major exception is the ambiguity of *-ed* as a marker of past tense and past participle. There are, of course, a number of idiosyncrasies on each level, such as irregular forms of the past participle or the restriction, that some forms on *-ing* cannot be combined with *be*, as in *(to) be knowing*. Essentially, they are historical residues, as often found in natural language.

What becomes under this approach of the classical notions Aktionsart, tense and aspect? Most Aktionsarten can systematically be reconstructed in terms of AT-structure and accompanying descriptive features (see the discussion in Section 2.2). Tense is reconstructed as the relation between the clause-internal temporal structure and some clause-external time, for example the time of utterance. The crucial link is the topmost time of the internal structure – the topic time. In the simplest case, the three tenses past, present and future are defined as temporal relations between the time of utterance and the topic time: the time of utterance may be before, included in, or after the topic time. There are several complications, for example when the topic time is not related to the deictically given time of utterance, but to the time of a higher *verbum dicendi vel sentiendi*, as in *Froben thought that Sweynheym was a lousy printer*.

Let us turn now to the notion of aspect, the way in which some event described by the utterance is "seen" or "presented", as traditional metaphorical characterizations of this notion have it. In simple cases, such as *Elzevier left, Elzevier had left, Elzevier was leaving*, aspect is the temporal relation between the highest temporal interval in the construction (the topic time), and the intervals which the topic time includes. In *Elzevier left*, these are subtimes of the three intervals provided by *leave*. Since the topic time includes parts of all intervals, it gives the impression that the event as a whole is shown within the time about which a claim is made: the event is shown in its totality, the verb form is "perfective". In *Elzevier has left*, the topic time only includes a time after a complete interval described by *leave*, whence the "perfect" – which is a combination of "after" and "completed". In *Elzevier was leaving*, the time to which the assertion is restricted is a proper subinterval of the source time of *leave*; it is completely open whether the second state is ever reached. That is possible, but it is not asserted; whence the feeling that only the interior of the event is shown: it is "imperfective".

In more complex cases, such as Example (2) *Caxton seemed to have planned to come at five*, the notion of aspect becomes somewhat fuzzy. If there is need, however, it can easily be defined, for example for the relation between the topic time and the temporal structure of *seem*. But such a definition does not include the "event proper", Caxton's potential leaving at five. If we want to include this part of the sentence as well, we have to include further temporal relationships – *to come* is a "prospective", as seen from the time of his planning, and his planning in turn is a "perfect" as seen from the time at which something seems to be the case. All of this is possible, but perhaps of little use.

References

Alexiadou, Artemis, Rathert, Monika & von Stechow, Arnim (eds.) (1993). Perfect explorations. Berlin & New York: Mouton de Gruyter.
Binnick, Robert (1991). Time and the Verb. Oxford: Oxford University Press.
Comrie, Bernard (1976). Aspect. Cambridge: Cambridge University Press.
Cruse, D. A. (1989). Lexical semantics. Cambridge: Cambridge University Press.
Dahl, Östen (ed.) (2000). Tense and aspect in the languages of Europe. Berlin & New York: Mouton de Gruyter.
Declerck, Renaat (in collaboration with Susan Reed & Bert Cappelle) (2006). The Grammar of the English verb phrase 1: The grammar of the English tense system. Berlin & New York: Mouton de Gruyter.
Denison, David (1993). English historical syntax. London & New York: Longman.

Dowty, David (1976). Montague grammar and word meaning. Dordrecht: Reidel.
Dowty, David (1991). Thematic proto-roles and argument selection. Language 67. 547–619.
Ebert, Karen & Zúñiga, Fernando (eds.) (2001). Aktionsart and aspectotemporality in Non-European languages. Zürich: ASAS.
Ehrich, Veronika (1992). Hier und Jetzt: Studien zur lokalen und temporalen Deixis im Deutschen. Tübingen: Niemeyer.
Elsness, Johan (1997). The perfect and the preterite in contemporary and earlier English. Berlin & New York: Mouton de Gruyter.
Enç, Murvet (1986). Towards a referential analysis of temporal expressions. Linguistics and Philosophy 9. 405–426.
Fabricius-Hansen, Cathrine (1980). Lexikalische Dekomposition, Bedeutungspostulate und *wieder*: Ein Beitrag zu einer Montague-Grammatik des Deutschen. In Dieter Kastovsky (ed.). Perspektiven der Lexikalischen Semantik. Bonn: Bouvier. 26–40.
Fabricius-Hansen, Cathrine (1986). Tempus fugit. Düsseldorf: Schwann.
Fenn, Peter (1987). A semantic and pragmatic examination of the English perfect. Tübingen: Narr.
Garey, Howard B. (1957). Verbal aspects in French. Language 33. 91–110.
Hamann, Cornelia (1987). The awesome seed of reference time. In Alfred Schopf (ed.), Essays on Tensing in English 1. Tübingen: Niemeyer. 26–40.
Iatridou, Sabine, Anagnostopoulou, Elena & Izvorski, Roumyana (2001). Observations about the form and meaning of the perfect. In Michael Kenstowicz (ed.), Ken Hale: A life in language. Cambridge, MA: MIT Press. 189–238.
Jackendoff, Ray (1991). Semantic Structures. Cambridge, MA: MIT Press.
Katz, Graham (2003). On the stativity of the English perfect. In Artemis, Rathert & von Stechow. 205–234.
Klein, Wolfgang (1994). Time in Language. London: Routledge.
Klein, Wolfgang (2000). An analysis of the German perfekt. *Language*, 76, 358–382.
Klein, Wolfgang (2002). The argument-time structure of recipient constructions in German. In Werner Abraham & Jan-Wouter Zwart (eds.). Issues in formal German(ic) typological studies on West Germanic. Amsterdam & Philadelphia: John Benjamins. 141–178.
Klein, Wolfgang (2006). On Finiteness. In Veerle van Geenhoven (ed.). Semantics in acquisition. Dordrecht: Springer. 245–272.
Klein, Wolfgang (2009a). Concepts of time. In Wolfgang Klein & Ping Li (eds.). The expression of time. Berlin & New York: Mouton de Gruyter. 5–38.
Klein, Wolfgang (2009b). How time is encoded. In Wolfgang Klein & Ping Li (eds.). The expression of time. Berlin & New York: Mouton de Gruyter. 39–82.
König, Ekkehard (1980). On the context dependence of the progressive in English. In Christian Rohrer (ed.). Time, tense, and quantifiers. Tübingen: Niemeyer. 269–291.
Kratzer, Angelika (1978). Semantik der Rede. Kronberg: Scriptor.
Lewis, David (1973). Counterfactuals. Cambridge, MA: Harvard University Press.
Lyons, John (1977). Semantics. Cambridge: Cambridge University Press.
McCoard, Robert (1978). The English Perfect: Tense choice and pragmatic inferences. Amsterdam: North Holland.
Musan, Renate (1997). On the temporal interpretation of noun phrases. New York: Garland.
Musan, Renate (2002). The German perfect. Dordrecht: Kluwer.
Portner, Paul (2003). The (temporal) semantics and the (modal) pragmatics of the English Perfect. Linguistics and Philosophy 26. 459–510.
Paul, Hermann (1886). Principien der Sprachgeschichte, 2nd edn. Jena: Niemeyer.

Pustejovsky, James (1991). The generative lexicon. Cambridge, MA: MIT Press.
Reichenbach, Hans (1947). Elements of symbolic logic. New York: Macmillan.
Schlüter, Norbert (2002). Present perfect: Eine korpuslinguistische Analyse des englischen Perfekts mit Vermittlungsvorschlägen für den Sprachunterricht. Tübingen: Narr.
Seuren, Peter (1998). Western linguistics. Oxford: Blackwell.
Shannon, Thomas (1989). Perfect auxiliary variation as a function of "Aktionsart" and transitivity. In Joseph Emonds, P. J. Mistry, Vida Samiian & Linda Thornburg (eds.). Proceedings of the Western Conference on Linguistics (Fresno, October 14–16, 1988). Fresno, CA: California State University. 254–266.
von Stechow, Arnim (1999). Eine erweiterte Extended Now-Theorie für Perfekt und Futur. Zeitschrift für Literaturwissenschaft und Linguistik 113. 86–118.
von Stechow, Arnim (2002). Binding by verbs. Unpublished ms. University of Tübingen: Seminar für Sprachwissenschaft.
Thieroff, Rolf (1992). Das finite Verb im Deutschen: Modus–Tempus–Distanz. Tübingen: Narr.
Vendler, Zeno (1957). Verbs and time. The Philosophical Review 66(2). 143–160.
Williams, Christopher (2002). Non-progressive and progressive aspect in English. Bari: Schena.
Wunderlich, Dieter (1970). Tempus und Zeitreferenz im Deutschen. Munich: Hueber.
Wunderlich, Dieter (1997). CAUSE and the structure of verbs. Linguistic Inquiry 28. 27–68.

On the "Imperfective paradox" and related problems

1 Introduction

In English, as in most languages, a sentence can appear in various tense and aspect forms, such as

(1) John was sleeping.
(2) John slept.
(3) John has slept.
(4) John had slept.
(5) John will sleep.

On some level, the meaning of these sentences, when uttered on some occasion, is the same; very roughly speaking, they have the same lexical content, which we may describe as [John sleep]. On some other level, it is not the same. Their truth values are different, although not completely different. There may be entailment relations between them. For example, we would say that in a situation where (1) is true, (2) cannot be false. Similarly, if someone claimed (4), then he is also committed to (3). On the other hand, there is no such relation from (2) to (5), or from (5) to (1).

Entailment relations of this kind depend on the various aspect and tense markers in the sentences. But they also depend on the particular lexical meaning of the words, notably the verb.[1] For example, while we would say that someone who was sleeping also slept, this does not hold for a verb such as *to leave*. 6a does not entail 6b:

(6) a. John was leaving.
    b. John left.

It may well be that eventually he managed to leave, and this may even be the most natural course of events; but it is also possible that he changed his mind and

---

[1] Throughout this paper, I do not systematically distinguish between verbs, copula constructions and verb phrases. This is not to mean that these (and other) distinctions are negligible in general for the description of aspect, tense and inherent temporal features, quite to the opposite. But they are not relevant to our present concern. Therefore, I will mostly speak of "verbs".

Note: This article originally appeared as Klein, W. (1997). On the "Imperfective paradox" and related problems. In M. Schwarz, C. Dürscheid and K.-H. Ramers (eds.). Sprache im Fokus: Festschrift für Heinz Vater. Tübingen: Niemeyer. 387–397.

https://doi.org/10.1515/9783110549119-007

stayed. In other words, the existence of a particular entailment relation not only depends on tense and aspect but also on the particular "temporal character" of the verb, its "Aktionsart", or whatever the terms are. In fact, such entailment relations have been used as an important criterion in the analysis of verb types from Aristotle to most recent classifications.

I think all attempts in this direction are on shaky ground, and in this paper, I will try to show this for three such entailment relations which have played, and still play, a major role in the rich literature on temporality. These are the following ones; apart from the labels, the presentation essentially follows Dowty (1979, p. 55–60 and 133–134), whose exposition is particularly clear; x is some subject, V some verb or verb phrase:

A. Aristotle's entailment
x is Ving recte x has Ved

Aristotle's entailment discriminates between "atelic" and "telic" verbs (Garey's 1957 terminology) or between "activities" and "accomplishments" (Vendler 1967; in what follows, I shall often use Vendlers terms, because they are probably best-known). Compare again:

(7) a. John is sleeping.
    b. John has slept.
(8) a. John is leaving.
    b. John has left.

7a entails 7b, but 8a does not entail 8b.

B. The Subinterval entailment
x Ved for y time recte x Ved for any subinterval of y

This entailment, so the assumption goes, discriminates between states and activities, on the one hand, and accomplishments and achievements, on the other.[2] Thus, if on some occasion, John slept for seven hours, then he slept for any

---

[2] Since states and achievements normally do not tolerate the progressive, Aristotle's entailment (as well as the following one) cannot, or often not, used for discriminative purposes, although the distinction is in a way quite parallel.

subinterval of those seven hours. But if he left London, and it took him two hours to do so, then he did not leave London at any subinterval of those two hours.

C. The Imperfective paradox entailment
x was Ving entails x Ved

Note that here, the "event"[3] referred to by V is in both cases in the past, whereas Aristotle's entailment goes from an on-going "event" to some "event" in the past (albeit perhaps with a special relation to the present, as expressed by the present perfect).

As in the preceding cases, activities and accomplishments exhibit a different behaviour. If, on some occasion, John was sleeping, then we can truthfully say that the slept. But if he was leaving the kitchen, then we can't necessarily say that he left it. The non-entailment becomes particularly clear for verb phrases with an "effected object", such as *to build a house*. Clearly, if John was building a house, this does not entail that he ever built it.

Before turning to these entailments in more detail, a word about the notion of entailment is in order. The general idea is clear: a entails b, if b can't be wrong when a is true. There are several problems, though, two of which I will mention. First, should we consider a and b to be sentences, or utterances, or still something else? This is a difficult question, but no one which need to bother us here. In what follows, I shall always assume that the a and b are sentences uttered on some particular occasion by the same speaker.

Second, the interpretation of such an utterance not only depends on what is explicitly said but also on a number of contextual factors. These must be kept constant. For example, it does not make much sense to speak of a possible entailment between *He was sleeping* and *He slept* unless we assume that *he* refers to the same person. Unfortunately enough, the situation is not always so straightforward. Contextual factors are often implicit. Under the assumption that water freezes below zero degrees, is it then correct to say, that

(9) a. The temperature was below zero.

entails

(9) b. The water was freezing.

---

[3] The term "event" is used here in a very global sense, such as to comprise events proper, processes, states, etc.

We would surely say "yes", and we would not like to accept an argument such as "Yeah, but I meant the temperature outdoor, and the water on the hot stove". Similarly, no reasonable person would be inclined to accept that 10a

(10) a. It is winter.

entails 10b:

(10) b. It is summer.

although this is clearly correct under the common notions of summer and winter, if different hemispheres are meant in both utterances. We may call this the problem of "hidden parameters", and any discussion on whether there is an entailment or not makes only sense if these "hidden parameters" are made explicit, or tacitly kept constant. Nothing forbids us, of course, to define the notion of "entailment" such that it includes inferences across hidden parameters, such that the entailment from 10a to 10b is valid. But I see no point in such a definition.

There may be other hidden parameters than place. Consider, for example:

(11) a. John died.

We would not want to say that 11a entails

(11) b. John did not die.

although if there is a time at which John died, there must be a time at which he is alive, and a time at which he is dead (this, I think, is the meaning of "to die"). Hence, there is also a time (actually, many times) in the past at which 11b is true.[4]

There are more hidden parameters, but the point should be clear. My main argument in what follows is that A – B are fallacious in that they most often ignore hidden parameters.

---

[4] This is not correct if the negation in (11b) has wide scope. Examples such as *Yesterday morning, he was hit by a car and seriously hurt. But he did not die. He died, however, seven hours later from a heart attack.* show that the negation in sentences such as *He did not die* need not have wide scope. Note, incidentally, that a definite analysis of the simple past avoids the false entailment for the simple reason that it automatically keeps the "hidden time parameter" constant.

2 Aristotle's entailment

Aristotle distinguished two types of verbs, verbs of **kinesis** and verbs of **energeia** (see Potts 1965, Taylor 1965). The first group, exemplified by *to watch, to think* is not goal-oriented, the second group, exemplified by *to learn (something), to become healthy,* is goal-oriented. And he says about them (Metaphysics 1048b):

> Thus, you are watching and thereby have watched already, you are thinking and thereby have thought already; by contrast, you are learning (something) and have not learned (it) already, and you are becoming healthy and have not yet become healthy. At the same time, we are living well and have lived well, we are happy and have been happy. Otherwise, the process should have ended at some time, like the process of becoming meagre. But it has not come to an end at the present moment: we are living, and have lived.

Numerous authors drew on this distinction, either directly or indirectly. A famous example is Garey's distinction between "atelic" and "telic" verbs, the former being those "which do not have to wait for a goal for their realization, but are realized as soon as they begin"(Garey 1957, p. 106). Even better known is Vendler's distinction between four "time schemata" which are more or less well reflected in four verb types. Two of them, state verbs and achievement verbs, do normally not assume the progressive, hence the entailment as stated above does not directly apply to them. But the logic behind the distinction among those is quite the same. State expressions are "atelic", achievement expressions are "telic". Thus, from *He is in London*, it follows *He has been in London*. This is the case with which I will begin here.

If you are in London, then you have been in London. But the time of your being in London and the time of your having been in London are not the same. The latter is a proper subinterval of the former. This becomes immediately clear, if the time intervals are made explicit by some time adverbial, for example by *all week* or *for three days*. If you are in London all week, you haven't been in London all week. And if you are in London for three days, then this does not entail that you have been in London for three days. In fact, if it is true that you are (right now) in London for three days, then this even excludes that (on this occasion) you have been there for three days. The same argument can be made for activities in progressive aspect. Thus, if John is sleeping for two hours, this does not entail that he has slept for two hours (although it is true that he has slept for some indeterminate subinterval of those two hours).

In both cases, Aristotle's entailment is only correct if an implicit parameter, the duration of the "event" denoted, here your being in London or John's sleeping, is not kept constant. Note that the "event" always has such a duration, no matter whether it is lexically specified by some adverbial or not. The addition of an adverbial such as *for two hours* or *all week* makes this duration explicit, it does not change the nature of the "event" in question. Sleeping always lasts for a certain time, and so does being in London, although it may not be explicitly said how long.

3 The Subinterval entailment

Although the idea that some verb types have the "subinterval property" is much older, Bennett and Partee (1972, p. 14) were the first to couch it in this form:

> Subinterval verb phrases have the property that if they are the main verb phrase of a sentence which is true at some interval of time I, then the sentence is true at any subinterval of I including every moment of time in I.

By now, the subinterval property is generally considered to be the major criterion to distinguish between state/activity-like verbs and accomplishment/achievement-like verbs. There two problems with this notion, a minor one and a serious one. The less serious problem is that one would like to be able to ignore "minor interruptions". Consider, for example:

(12) John slept for more than ten hours.

Then, we would not like to say that this is wrong because he woke up for a moment and went to the bathroom. So, there are "irrelevant" interruptions which, under a "literal" interpretation of the Subinterval entailment, would violate it. I think exceptions of this type can be booked under the global fuzziness of natural language, just as we would not say that *He left at four* is wrong, because he left a minute past four.

The second problem is much more serious. Whenever you sleep, you sleep somewhere – in the guestroom, on the floor, next to the elevator, wherever. This place need not be specified, but it can, and there is little reason to assume that the nature of the activity is changed by rendering its place explicit. Consider now:

(13) For three months, John slept on the floor.

In this case, we would not be inclined to assume that John slept during each subinterval of those three months. John could be a normal adult, and then we would assume that, if (13) is true, there were some 90 intervals of about eight hours each, during which he slept (on the floor!), and some different 90 intervals of about 16 hours, during which he did not sleep at all. John could also be a two-weeks-old baby, with a somewhat different distribution of pertinent subintervals. And John could be a hibernating bear, in which case we would indeed assume that this sleep is not interrupted by a (relevant) subinterval, during which he did not sleep.

Nothing forbids us to call the first two possibilities "iterative" or "frequentative", and the last one "semelfactive". Then, we could save the Subinterval entailment by saying that it only applies under a semelfactive reading. But "semelfactive" means in this case only that his sleeping is not interrupted. Then, the Subinterval entailment boils down to "*x Ved for y time* entails *x Ved at any time during y,* **unless there is some interruption in his Ving**". Which is trivially true.

The crucial hidden parameter in this case is the "frequency" of the "event". We are inclined to assume that there is regularly an implicit "semel" (i.e., one time); but as examples like (13) show – and it is not difficult to find others -, this is only a special case. If *sleep* is the main verb phrase of a sentence true at some interval of time I, then it depends on how long I is, on the one hand, and on world knowledge, on the other, whether we assume this sentence to be true at any subinterval of I. The subinterval property, as defined here, is not part of the lexical content of *sleep*.

4 The Imperfective paradox entailment

Although other authors had noticed the problem before, Dowty (1979, p. 133/4) was the first to recognize its importance for the analysis of English aspect, notably English progressive. If, upon some occasion, John was building a house, then this does not entail that he built a house. But if John was pushing a cart, then this entails that he pushed a cart.

I think the point is well-taken for accomplishments (and achievement verbs to the extent to which they tolerate the progressive). The point is less well-taken, in fact wrong, for activity verbs, and the reason is, that the time for which the relevant claim is correctly made is not kept constant. This becomes clear, if the relevant time is explicitly marked. Suppose a witness is asked at court:

(14)   What did John do yesterday between ten and eleven p.m.?

Then, the time for which the witness has to give testimony is precisely fixed: It is yesterday between ten and eleven. An appropriate answer might be:

(15)   He was sleeping.

This answer is truthful if John slept all night. But would it have been an appropriate answer to say *He slept*? Surely not.

The same point is more suggestive if the relevant time, for which he is claimed to sleep, is very short, as in (16) – given in answer to the question *How is the baby*?

(16)   I just looked into his room. He was sleeping.

Then, (16) does not entail at all that he slept at the time at which the speaker looked into the room.

Summing up, there is no Imperfective paradox entailment for accomplishments. But there is no such entailment for activities, either – if the relevant parameters are kept constant. The crucial parameter in this case is the time for which the claim is made. If this time is say 10 o'clock, then it may well be that x was Ving at ten o'clock without that x Ved at ten o'clock. So, the Imperfective paradox entailment is much the same as the inference from *John was dead* to *John was alive*: If there was a time at which John was dead, there was also a time at which John was alive – albeit not the same time.

5 Inherent temporal features of the lexical content

Do these observations mean that there are no temporal differences between various verb types, such as state verbs, activity verbs, etc, or whatever the classification may be? Surely not. It should be clear, however, that these differences concern the lexical content of the various expressions, not the "events" they refer to. By lexical content, I mean that part of the meaning of some simple or compound expression which stems from the lexical meanings of the words the way in which the words are put together. In that sense, it contrasts with contextual information, on the one hand, and reference, on the other. The lexical content of a verb such as *sleep* or of a compound expression such as *John sleep* does not occupy a place in time. It is neither long nor short, nor before or after the time of speaking. The "event" to which such a lexical content contributes to refer in an utterance does occupy some interval on the time axis. Therefore, it inevitably has a number of properties which are typical of time spans. Their exact nature depends on the kind of time structure which one assumes to underlie natural language. This is a matter of dispute, but let us assume that time spans

- have a position relative to other time spans, notably the time utterance
- have boundaries and, as a consequence, a duration (i.e., a multiple or fraction of some regular event)
- can be counted

Thus, if the utterance *John slept* is true, then the event of his sleeping has a position on the time axis (in this case, it is before the time of utterance), and it has a duration, although nothing is said about this duration. In fact, the utterance *John slept* need not necessarily refer to just one such event; as example like *For two days, Napoleon slept very well* or utterance (13) above illustrate, the exact number is left to the world knowledge of the listener.

None of those properties of the event(s) belongs to the lexical content *[John sleep]*. This particular lexical content by itself does not tell us anything about the position of the event on the time line, nor about its duration or its frequency. But this information can be added, if there is need. Usually, this is done by appropriate adverbs. Thus, the speaker could specify a position by adding *yesterday at lunchtime*, a duration by *for two hours*, and a frequency by *twice*. In all of these cases, the lexical specification can be definite or indefinite. I shall say, that a lexical content which includes a (lexical) specification of a definite position is "p-definite"; similarly for definite duration (d-definite) and definite frequency (q-definite). For example, the lexical content *[John sleep twice]* is d-definite, and *John sleep* or *John sleep sometimes* is not. Note that the addition of such an adverb does not change the nature of the "event". It only makes properties of the "event" explicit which are left implicit otherwise.

It seems that simple verbs (or adjectives + copula) are never p-definite, d-definite or q- definite in this sense. It is this fact which leads to the "hidden parameters" discussed above: If neither duration, nor position, nor frequency are lexically fixed, then it easily escapes our attention that they are different in both utterances. Consider again Aristotle's entailment in which duration is the relevant "hidden parameter". In

(17) a. John is sleeping.
 b. John has slept.

the duration of John's sleeping is not d-definite. But in both cases, the event – if the utterance is true – has a fixed duration, and this duration must be different. In the Subinterval entailment, the crucial parameter is frequency. An expression such as *John slept on the floor* is not q-definite; but the entailment is only correct if only one "sleeping on the floor" is meant. And the Imperfective paradox entailment works for activity verbs only if the position of the relevant time span is shifted – which is possible, since it is not fixed by the lexical content of the utterance.

This does not mean that the lexical content of verbs does not contain any information about the intervals to which they can be linked (or more precisely, about the intervals of the "event(s)" to which they can refer). In particular, they can require that any such interval includes two opposing sub-intervals. Such is the case for a verb like *die* which requires a first sub-interval in which the argument, say John, is alive, and a second sub- interval, in which this very argument has the opposing property of being dead. Nothing is said about whether this transition is smooth or abrupt: It is only required that there are these two sub-interval in this order. Verbs (and lexical contents in general) of this type might be called "two-state verbs" (or "two-state contents"). Note that neither the two sub-states are d-definite nor the entire lexical content. The verb *die* does not say anything about how long the being alive should be, nor, about how long the being dead should be, and it is meaningless to specify the entire duration of someone's being alive and being dead. Therefore, one can't say – to use a familiar example – *John opened the window for two hours*, unless only one of the states (the state of the window's being open) is meant.

The fact that "two-state verbs" involve two mutually exclusive states, such as being not open and being open, or being alive and being dead, has another important consequence. If there is an interval which includes the transition from one state to the opposing one, i.e., if it is true at some interval that John opened the window, it must contain a subinterval at which the window is not open, and a later sub-interval at which it is open. Hence, the whole interval must be of necessity "interrupted". This is not so for *John slept for three days*, which does not, by its lexical content, include two distinct subintervals. Hence, the interval at which it is true can be interrupted, but it need not. Note, further, that, if *John was opening the window* is true at some interval T, then T is homogeneous: It only includes the first of the two states, i.e., that state at which John is somehow active in getting the window open, but not the state at which it is open. Hence, *John was opening the window* normally – although not necessarily – has the subinterval property. If John was opening the window at some interval T, he also did so at any subinterval of T (with the qualifications mentioned above).

There are also lexical contents which require that they either apply to an argument forever or not at all. This is the case for "atemporal properties", such as a door's being steel in contrast to a door's being open. If we call the former "0-state" and the latter "one-state", we get a simple classification of verbs (and adjectives) according to the inherent temporal properties of their lexical content.

When combined with other expressions, these lexical contents can be enriched in various ways, such as to specify the duration, the position, the frequency of the intervals of the events, which they can refer to in an utterance. We shall not follow this up here; the general point should be clear, however.

References

Bennett, M., and Partee, B. (1972). Toward the logic of tense and aspect in English. Santa Monica, California: System Development Corporation. (Reproduced by Indiana University Linguistic Club, Feb. 1978; this version is quoted).

Dowty, D. (1979). Word meaning and Montague Grammar. Dordrecht: Reidel.

Garey, H.B. (1957). Verbal aspect in French. Language 33. 91–110.

Potts, T. (1965). States, activities, and performances I. Proceedings of the Aristotelian Society 39. 65–84.

Taylor, C.C.W. (1965). States, activities, and performances II. Proceedings of the Aristotelian Society 39. 85–102.

Vendler, Z. (1967). Verbs and times. In: Id., Linguistics and Philosophy, Ithaca: Cornell University Press. 97–121.

Local deixis in route directions[1]

> Here comes the night
> *Van Morrison*

This study deals with the semantics of local deictics like *here, there, left, right*, i.e. with expressions that are used mainly to refer to localities and whose reference depends in a systematic way on contextual factors like position of speaker, direction of gaze, and others. There are numerous contributions to a theory of context dependency (see, for example, Kratzer & von Stechow, 1976), and there are some instructive studies of local deixis in particular (e.g. Bühler 1934; Fillmore 1971; Atkinson & Griffiths 1973; Miller & Johnson-Laird 1976, Chap. 6.1; Clark 1977), but it is surely no over-statement to say that we are still far from an understanding how deixis – and local deixis in particular – really works in actual communication. It is obvious that what *here* means in an utterance is largely determined by the context of that utterance. Sentences like *Here are the tigers* or *Come here!* seem to have an open slot that is filled by contextual information when they are uttered; this contextual information may be given by prior verbal expressions, by succeeding verbal expressions, by common perception in the speech situation, by gestures, etc. Not very much is known about this process, about its components and how they interact. In this paper I try to contribute to an understanding of this mechanism in two ways – one more theoretical, the other more empirical. In the first section, several problems are outlined which, in my view, are basic to the use of deictic expressions and of local deictics in particular. In Section 2, some results from an empirical study about the use of local deictics in route directions are reported. The first part makes no claim to be a theory of deixis; rather, it forms a heuristic frame of analysis, and perhaps a starting point for such a theory.

1 Components in the use of local deictics

The following considerations focus upon *here* and *there*; but it should be clear that there are a number of other local deictics which are not dealt with here. A

---

[1] I wish to thank V. Ehrich, R. Jarvella, A. Kratzer, W. Levelt, M. Miller, E. Schegloff, M. Silverstein, J. Weissenborn, and D. Wunderlich for helpful comments and criticism on earlier versions. Special thanks go to Elena Lieven, who has made numerous stylistic corrections: if my English is understandable, it is mainly to her merit.

Note: This article originally appeared as Klein, W. (1982). Local deixis in route directions. In R. Jarvella and W. Klein (eds.). Speech, Place, and Action: Studies in Deixis and Related Topics. New York: Wiley. 161–182.

https://doi.org/10.1515/9783110549119-008

speaker who uses expressions like *here*, etc., in some speech situation refers to certain denotata. By saying *It's pretty cold here*, he may refer by *here* to a room, to a corner of a room or to Siberia, depending on the particular context. A listener who wants to understand this utterance has to identify the specifically intended denotatum of *there*, just as he has to identify the denotata of proper names, of adjectives, or of verbs. But the identification problem is different in at least one respect: *Siberia* in general denotes Siberia, but *here* doesn't denote here. Solving the identification problem in deictic reference involves the solution of a whole series of sub-problems and at least the following ones: a common deictic space must be set up; a basic reference point ('origo') must be set up; speaker and listener must coordinate their perspectives; what *there* and *there* refer to must be delimited; the deictic oppositions of the language must be utilized; analogical deictic spaces must be established. The comments I shall make now on these problems treat them mainly as research problems, not as problems a speaker and listener have to solve together, though this is exactly what they do have to do in order to achieve successful communication.

1.1 Setting up deictic spaces

In general, the possible denotata of local deictics are localities, such as rooms, apartments, streets, cities, countries: they can be considered as subspaces of 'deictic spaces', such as the space of visual perception, or the space constituted by our geographical knowledge. But the denotata of local deictics need not be localities. When somebody says, *Two problems should be kept apart here*, he surely doesn't refer to a locality in the literal sense of the word, but to a very abstract 'place' in a train of thoughts. And if we read, *In 1806, Shelley wrote his 'Elegy'; here, the spirit of English romanticism found its...*, no locality is denoted, unless the denotatum of *in this poem* is regarded as such. Uses of that type might be called metaphorical; this is perhaps accurate, but it doesn't say very much: it is just a terminological immunization of the problem. What we have to account for is the fact that there may be very different deictic spaces; some of these uses may be primary in a diachronic or in an ontogenetic sense; others might be derived from the primary ones; but this doesn't obviate the fact that they all are at the disposal of a normal speaker, and that, in a specific communication situation, it should be clear which deictic space is being referred to. For instance, is it the space of visual perception, as in *Here is my home*, or the space that is constituted in our memory by our geographical knowledge, as in long-distance calls, when somebody says *It's raining here*, or even a much more abstract space, as in *I can't go into detail here?*, the deictic space of speakers and listeners need not be identical for a successful communication, but they must be sufficiently similar, and to make them so might well be a part of the communication; this is the case, for example, in route directions.

In its most general sense, a deictic space is nothing but a set of elements provided with some structure (an order or a topology); its subsets, or some of them, arc the possible denotata. Deictic spaces may differ in
(a) what is considered to be their elements, such as minimally discriminable units of perception, words (as in the Shelley example?), etc.;
(b) subsets which are possible denotata, such as visual objects, poems, etc.;
(c) kind of structure characterizing the deictic space;
(d) number of dimensions: the space of visual perception is generally thought to be three-dimensional, a map that often serves as an analogical deictic space (cf. Section 1.7 below) is two-dimensional, a 'train of thought' might be considered as one-dimensional (it often is), etc.;
(e) kind of metric – if there is any: for most deictic spaces, we seem to have a concept of distance, but it is often doubtful whether it really fulfils the criteria of a metric. The concept of deictic space raises a number of problems for empirical research:

What then, are the deictic spaces used in actual communication, since the notions 'space of visual perception', 'geographical space', 'space of trains of thought', are somewhat fuzzy labels generated from specific examples? How do speaker and listener make sure that they are referring to the same, or a sufficiently similar, deictic space in a given situation? How are these different concepts of space interrelated, and. in particular, which structural properties are conserved in the transition from basic deictic spaces (visual perception, for instance) to more abstract ones?

Agreement upon the deictic space by speaker and listener is the first prerequisite for successful deictic reference: the intended subspace – locality or whatever – is now to be localized within this deictic space. This is done by a series of techniques, the first of which is to fix the basic reference point.

1.2 Fixing the basic reference point

Given a deictic space, one of its elements must be fixed as the basic reference point, in relation to which the denotata can be determined. In the unmarked case, this 'origo' (a term used by Bühler 1934) is given by the position of the speaker: every participant of a speech situation brings his perspective with him, and it is that of the speaker that is crucial for the identification of denotata: *here* denotes a space around the origo: *there* denotes a space that does not contain the origo. This presupposes of course that the speaker (or his body, or perhaps his eyes) can be interpreted as an element of the deictic space in question, as, for example, in the space of visual perception. If this is not the case, some reference unit must be set up in the corresponding deictic space. This is often done in anaphorical uses of *here*, as in sentences like *The reader is referred to Morton (1976); here, the problem of recursive reference is treated in full detail.*[2] On the other hand, an origo given by the speaker may be shifted. This is often done by pointing gestures: *The picture here originally hung there* (pointing with a finger to some place), or in the case of analogical deixis (cf. Section 1.7 below): *If the church is here* (pointing to some spot on the table), *our home is just here* (pointing to another spot). The origo proper is not lost, it is just suspended in favour of another 'secondary origo', and it is always possible to go back to it without making this explicit.

Fixing the origo raises again a number of empirical problems. How is the (primary) origo precisely characterized – is it the speaker's body, his trunk, his eyes, his reach? How are secondary origins introduced, e.g. by pointing gestures with fingers, chin, eyes, by verbal means? How do children acquire the technique of origo shift?

Explicit origo shifting should not be confused with change of origo due to the speaker changing location during his utterance. If somebody moves through a room saying: *From here, it's precisely one, two, three, four, five metres to here*, the denotatum of *here* changes within one speech act, and the origo is shifted, too, within that speech act. But it is still the basic type of origo implicitly given by the speaker's position. This constitutes a clear argument against the assumption that the origo is bound to the speech act. This seems to be the position held in Wunderlich (1971). If a speech act (or the speech situation that exactly corresponds to a speech act) is restricted to utterances of just one speaker whose position is unchanged, it doesn't matter, because both assumptions (origo bound to speech act; origo bound to position of speaker) coincide. But as soon as examples where this is not the case are taken into consideration, it becomes apparent that the speaker's position is crucial. Moreover, this view can easily be linked to the extended research on children's egocentrism and to adults' orientation: we learn to shift, but basically, we see, grasp, feel, structure, our surroundings from where we are.

---

[2] I don't see any substantial difference between deictic and anaphoric use of *there* (and. in a similar way. of 'he', 'that', etc.) Anaphorical (and in the same way cataphorical) use is just that special case of deictic reference where the reference unit *is verbally* introduced into the context, whereas in other cases it is there by gestures, by shared perception, or by shared knowledge.

1.3 Co-ordination

In the following, I shall only consider unmarked cases, i.e. cases where the origo is implicitly given by the speaker's (stable) position. The listener must take over this orientation; he must project it onto his own system of orientation, which is not at issue as long as he is listening. As soon as he starts speaking, roles are changed, and *his* orientation becomes central; the projection task becomes his. In many cases, the problem of co-ordinating two systems of orientation is trivial. The denotatum of *there* often encloses both speaker and listener, and any difference in their position and hence in their orientation is irrelevant – though it exists. But there are many cases where the different position becomes important. A particularly clear example is telephone calls: 'The weather is wonderful here' – 'Oh, here it's raining'. Of course this is not restricted to telephone calls, but also happens in face-to-face interaction. If somebody outside a house is speaking to somebody leaning out of the window, he may say 'It's cool here', and the other speaker may respond: 'Oh, you should feel it in here!' In cases like this, the denotatum of *there* centres so narrowly around the respective origo that it doesn't include the position of the respective listener. This point becomes move obvious, if not only the position of the speaker, but also his direction of gaze is important, as with the local deictics 'left' and 'right'. If speaker and listener are facing each other, one's 'left' is the other's 'right'. In this case, the co-ordination is very simple;[3] it is more complicated if there is an angle of 90° between the two directions of gaze, because then, the speaker's *left* is the listener's *right*, if the listener is to the speaker's left and the locality referred to is between them; if it is not between them, it is to the left of both listener and speaker. Things are much more unclear with *there* and *there*, in cases when a non-trivial co-ordination is necessary: the speaker's *there* is often the listener's *there*, one of the speaker's *there*'s is the listener's *there*, the speaker's and the listener's *there* may overlap without coinciding totally, etc. These mappings are very complex, and they become still more complex if shifted origins are considered. This leads to research problems such as: How do these mappings work in the unmarked case where speakers change position? How do they work in the case of shifted origo?

---

[3] This may lead to some confusion with people who professionally take over the listener's orientation, such as opticians and ophthalmologists. The usual method of co-ordinating perspectives then leads to wrong results. On the other hand, it seems that in imperatives, it is generally the listener's perspective that is decisive: 'turn right!' always means 'tum right from your perspective!' This is true at least in route directions.

1.4 Delimitation

Fixing the origo of a given deictic space and mapping the two systems of orientation doesn't guarantee that the subspaces – the denotata – can be identified. The denotatum of *here* is indeed not the origo itself, but some space enclosing the origo. Saying *it's cold here* means *it's cold within some area around the speaker*, and neither the origo nor the word *here* indicate how far this area reaches. The boundaries are fixed by the context of the utterance. This delimitation follows certain principles. *here* may refer to the chair on which I am sitting, to the room where I am. to the house where I am, to the street, the city, etc., in widening circles around the speaker which may or may not include the listener.[4] But it is very unlikely that a particular *here* will be used to refer to a chair (with speaker) and the surrounding space at an exact distance of 69.3 cm or to the room and two adjacent rooms – unless they form a cognitive unit in some sense, such as the reach of the speaker, or in the second example, an apartment. In many cases, the delimitation is immediately supported by some verbal means, e.g. *here in this tiny cabin, he spent half a year*, or *here in Heaven, they sing too much*; but this does not have to be the case. We often reconstruct the borders of *there* (and other local deictics) by our knowledge of the world. If somebody says *I'm sitting very comfortably her*, our general knowledge tells us that *there* does not refer to the Earth, whereas in *there is no justice her'*, it doesn't refer to a chair.

Obviously, the delimitation is not always very sharp; the borders are often diffuse. But fuzziness of denotata is not a specific problem of local deixis. The central empirical problems raised by the necessity of delimitation are: What are the possible borders within a given deictical space (a room might be a denotatum, but not a room and half of the next)? How is the delimitation established in a given speech situation – by verbal context, by components of our factual knowledge, by gestures?

1.5 Deictic oppositions

Deictic space, origo, co-ordination, and delimitation make it possible to identify the denotatum of *here* in a given context – it is a subspace of the deictic

---

[4] It is precisely this idea that makes the assumption of deictic spaces being provided with a topological structure so tempting. When a structure is defined, the possible denotata can be identified with the neighbourhoods or rather a subset of the neighbourhoods. If it is some distinguished element of the topological space, the possible denotata of *there* could be subsets of all those neighbourhoods that contain x as an element. But suggestive as this idea may be – it does not give us the topology.

space including the origo within certain boundaries. But *here* is not the only local deictic expression. It belongs to a certain system that, according to the language, may have two (*here-there*), three (*hier-da-dort* or *aquí-allí -allá*), or even more components. And there are, of course, other groupings of deictical expressions, like *left-right* which form their own system. Several proposals have been made to characterize the oppositions of such deictic systems in different languages, such as 'proximal' versus 'non- proximal' for English (e.g. Clark 1977), or 'proximal-middle-distal' for Bella Coola (Davis & Saunders 1975). or the traditional 'near the speaker-near the listener-near the third one' in Latin grammar for *hic-istic-illic*.

But even in the comparatively simple *here-there* system of English, things are sometimes rather complicated, because what 'proximal' and 'non-proximal' mean again depends on the context. It is apparently possible to say *here comes my mother*, when she is at a distance of KM) metres, but one can also say *there is my mother*, when she is at a distance of 10 metres; *there* can be used if the denotatum is closer to the speaker than to the listener (but 'distant' from both), but it can also be used precisely in the sense of the opposition 'speaker-here' versus 'listener-there' (e.g. *You can't see it from there, only from here*) The system seems to work roughly as follows: in a given situation, a *there* always denotes a subspace of a deictic space around an origo (shifted or unshifted); the rest of the deictic space is – in that situation – open for possible denotata of *there*: *there* denotes some subspace of the complement of a *here*. Precisely what it denotes is then marked by three characteristics:

(a) negatively by the respective denotatum of *there* – if no *here*' is used in that particular situation, the whole deictic space is open for *there*, except that it must not include the origo;[5]
(b) by some additional information concerning the location within the space, e.g. some pointing gesture, some verbal expression – as in the case of anaphoric or cataphoric *there* – by shared perception, etc.;
(c) by some additional information concerning the delimitation (as in the case of *there*).

If the opposition is understood in this way, the proximal-non-proximal distinction is just a special case. The situation is much more complex with three-step systems, as *hier-da-dort* in German, where *da* – apart from its other meanings –

---

[5] This is somewhat simplified, since there cannot be applied to places with objects which the speaker is touching. I cannot say *the book there* when touching it. Touching turns everything into here.

competes both with *there* and *there*: *Ich bleibe ein paar Minuten da* versus *das Buch muß irgendwo da* (pointing with the finger) *gelegen haben*. These systems differ from language to language, and the analysis of their constitutive oppositions is one of the research problems raised by them. The other one is by what means a speaker makes clear in a given speech situation where his *there* is located and what its borders are (cf. (b) and (c) above).

Basically, we now have all the components that usually interact to determine what is referred to by *there* or *there*. This mechanism of deictic reference with shared deictic space, origo fixing, co-ordination, delimitation of subspaces, and deictic oppositions looks rather complex, but I don't see what could be omitted from it. On the contrary, the system becomes even more complicated if we take into account some other everyday uses, namely those that involve analogical deictic spaces.

1.6 Analogical deixis

If somebody points to a red spot on a map and says: *Here is my home*, he wants to say *At the place that in reality corresponds to this spot*, and he is normally understood that way. In this case, we have two deictic spaces involved: the map, and the geographic space represented by the map. The map functions as an analogue, and by pointing to an element of the map. I am referring to the analogous place in the real space. The mapping is here (!) clearly given by the projection. But analogical deixis is also possible when the mapping is not given by some geometrically defined relation, but by some – perhaps vague – resemblance. If somebody points to his own shoulder and says: *The bullet hit him here*, he refers to the corresponding part of the body of some other person. In the same way, it is possible to refer to 'generic places'. If a professor of medicine says in a lecture: *The needle must be inserted precisely here*, pointing on some part of his own hand, he doesn't actually refer to the part of his hand he is pointing to – he would be astonished if the students all wanted to inject him there – nor to the corresponding part of some other specific person, but to the part of the 'generic hand', of which he used his own as an instance.

The central empirical problem of analogical deixis is the kind of mapping between the deictic spaces involved. It is apparently possible to say *The bullet hit Charlie here* (pointing on one's shoulder), even if Charlie is not a human being, but a grizzly bear; it's impossible, however, if Charlie is a snake. This seems the right point to close these comments on the mechanism of local deictic reference. Perhaps they raise more problems than they clarify, but they may serve as a basic framework for further analysis. In the following, some results concerning the use of deictics in route directions are outlined. Though there will often be no explicit reference to the conception, the whole study should be seen in the context of this framework.

2 Using local deictics in route directions

2.1 Route communications

In English, there seems to be no standard term for the complex co-operative verbal action that consists of asking for route directions and giving them – as for instance *Wegauskunft* in German; in the following. I will call this action 'route communication'. It is a very common type of complex verbal action. By complex verbal action, I understand activities like giving a talk, recounting a narrative, explaining a game, describing an apartment, arguing together, etc. In general, several participants – at least two – are engaged in such an action, but their role might be different. According to that, I classify them as basically monological or basically non-monological (giving a talk is basically monological, arguing together is basically non-monological); a complex verbal action might indeed be composed of several passages, some of them being monological, some not. A second subdivision follows the type of information to be presented or elaborated: it may prestructure the verbal planning to a high or a low degree. Narratives are strongly prestructured by the temporal order of events, explaining games weakly structured; that's why most people soon get confused when they try to explain a complex game. In the weakly prestructured case, people typically try to introduce some temporal ordering, e.g. by following the running of the game, by imaging a tour through an apartment (Labov & Linde 1975), etc. Route communication shows a clearly asymmetric role of its participants that is reflected in the verbal tasks they have to carry out: the person who asks for directions (henceforth F) wants to know something, and he tries to get this information from somebody he takes to be competent and willing to give it (= A). F's initial tasks are: (a) getting into contact with A: (b) making clear what he wants: (c) succeeding in getting A to take over the task of giving him directions. If he succeeds, it is up to A to make clear to F how to reach his destination: he has the task of (d) describing the way (route directions proper), and (e) making sure that F understands. It is then up to F. who set the task, to take it back and to conclude the interaction. F then has the task of (f) attesting to A that his job is done; (g) acknowledging A's help; (h) ending the contact. As a rule, these three groups of tasks correspond to a clear interactional scheme of successful route communication. In the first part ('introduction'), F is dominant from an interactive point of view: (a)-(c) are carried out. In the second part ('central sequence'), A takes over and becomes dominant: (d) and (e) are solved. In the third part ('conclusion'), F is dominant again: (f)-(h) are carried out. There may be deviations. If F is successful with (a), but not with (b), everything drops until (h). There may also be overlaps or repetitions, but typically a route communication follows this scheme.

Route communications are interesting from an interactive, a cognitive, and a linguistic point of view. They are all closely linked, of course; but in the following, I shall concentrate on the third aspect, with some remarks on the second one, where necessary; almost nothing will be said about the interactive aspect. Only point (d), the route directions proper, is dealt with here, because it is the most yielding in the present context (for a more comprehensive analysis of route communications, see Klein 1979).

The study is based on 40 route communications in natural context. They were gathered in May 1977 in the inner city of Frankfurt/Main by students (see Figure 1). At the upper Zeil (a), the main shopping street, or at the Hauptwache (b) (a small historical building from the early eighteenth century) people were asked either for the Alte Oper or the Goethehaus, both well-known landmarks in Frankfurt. The whole action was covertly recorded using a Nagra SNN audio tape recorder. Approximately 100 route communications were recorded, some of them very noisy because of the traffic. The first 20 for each destination (Alte Oper, Goethehaus), if fully understandable, were selected and transcribed for further analysis; they are labelled as O1 – O20 and G1 – G20; a selection is given in the appendix. The transcription is in standard orthography, with some slight touches of dialectal pronunciation for some speakers. Pauses and parallel speaking were transcribed as accurately as possible. Sometimes, more than one person answered; in this case, indices are used: A1, A2, etc.

2.2 Planning the description

In order to describe how to go from the starting point to the destination, A must have some cognitive representation of the area in question. In general, he owes his knowledge to his own previous experiences, e.g. he remembers what he has seen and heard and how he moved, or how the streetcar moved, and this remembrance must be structured into a cognitive map, e.g. he knows that at a certain place there is such and such a building where he can turn left, that he can't cross the street there, etc. Two people may have different favourite routes, and their attention may be focused on different objects. There are likely to be objects which

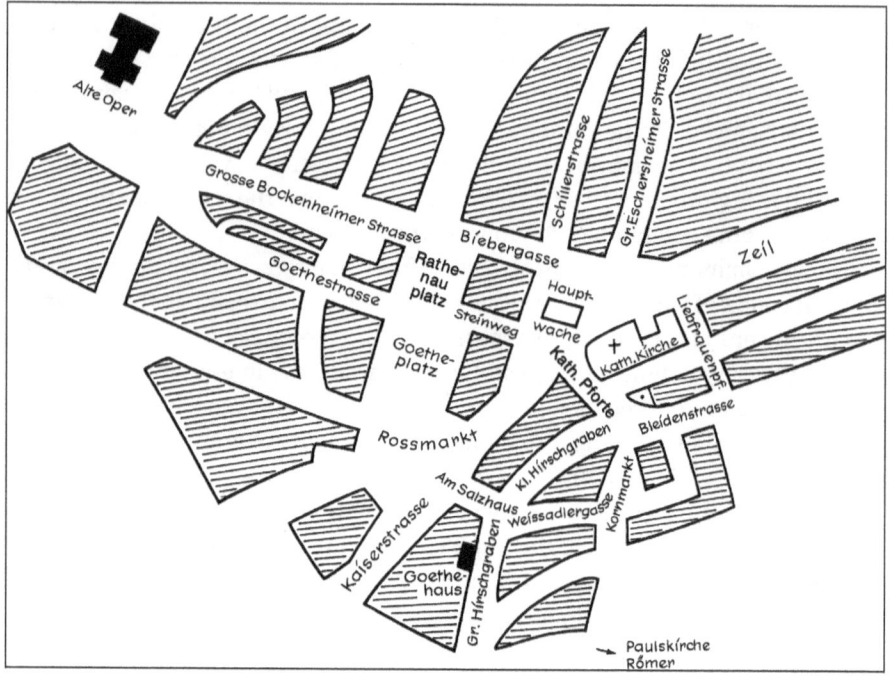

Figure 1: Simplified picture from Frankfurt/inner city.

are salient landmarks for nearly everybody (cf. Lynch 1960), but whether the image somebody has of an area is marked by book stores or fashion shops will differ between individuals. Thus, cognitive maps may be differently structured to a large extent. Moreover, they can be vague, incomplete, or even wrong in some respects (see, for a recent discussion of this concept, Downs & Stea 1973, 1977). This can, but need not be, relevant for route directions.

A's cognitive map is activated, at least to some extent, by F's initial request. What A has to do then is localize the starting point and destination on his map. Such a segment of a cognitive map with starting point and destination localized will be called the 'primary plan' of the route direction. Localizing the destination is sometimes not easy, and it might involve complex strategies (cf. text O3, G2, or the fantastically complex G1). The starting point in general raises no problems because it is in the domain of visual perception, whereas a great deal of what else is represented in the primary plan – for instance, the destination in most cases – is not in the domain of visual perception; indeed. A sometimes looked or even turned around to find out where he was – to localize his position. Building up the primary plan may be done in advance, or step by step. Consider G11:

(G11) F Entschuldigung, können Sie mir bitte sagen, wo's zum Goethehaus geht?
          Excuse me: could you tell me how to get to the Goethehaus?

       A Ja
          Yes
          [3 seconds] Goethehaus? ja, gehen Se da rauf, immer geradeaus.
                      Goethehaus? yes, go up that way, always straight on.
          erste Straße links, erste Straße rechts
          first street to the left, first street to the right

       F erste links, erste rechts. dankeschön.
          first left, first right.   thank you.

       A ja
          yes

A makes a planning pause after the question: then he reaffirms himself that he has correctly understood the question, indicating that he is able and willing to answer; and then, he carries out his description in one stroke. When speaking, he apparently has a sufficiently clear primary plan; he is an 'advance planner': His counterpart may be called 'stepwise planner'. A clear example is in G15:

(G15) A Ja ; [10 seconds] hier die Zeil runter, auf der andern Seite,
          Yes;   here down the Zeil, on the other side,
       F ja
          yes
       A [14 seconds] praktisch gehen Se jetzt hieran [13 seconds] eh [3 seconds]
                       in fact   you go along here now   er

          Sie müssen wohl von hinten rüber,   weil da ne Ampel ist,   ja:
          you probably have to cross over from there , because lights are there, yah:

          da hinter der Kirche lang;   dann gehn Se
          there along behind the church; there you go

          rechts die Straße wieder grad runter und dann müssen Se
          down that street to the right again   and there you have to

          bis zur [2 seconds] wie heiß'n das?   auf der linken Ecke [4 seconds]
          go to the   what's it called again? The left corner

          bis die ne Rolltreppe kommt,   da is Möbel Mann,   diese Straße
          till you reach the an escalator, there's Möbel Mann, that street

          müssen Sie links rein;   und die erste wieder rechts;
          you have to go in to the left; and the first one again to the right;

F   gut. dankeschön.
    okay. thank you.
A   also, auf der einen Seite ist,   eh
    well, on the one side, there is, er

Neckermann, Reisebüro,   und auf der andern Straßenecke ist Möbel Mann;
Neckermann, a travel agency, and on the other street corner there is Möbel Mann;

die Straße links rein und dann die erste rechts.
that street you go in to the left, and then, it's the first right.

Though reflecting at the beginning, A has no clear plan when he starts speaking. He soon comes to a point that is problematic; he then reflects on the situation – he tries to elaborate his primary plan there – restarts at the beginning, arrives again at the point of confusion, reflects again, and then advances a little bit further, until the next unclear position is reached; he tries to picture the situation there to himself, and then is able to continue to the end. After that, he has no difficulty in recapitulating a part of his description; the plan being there, he is able to repeat, vary, or extend his description. He doesn't work out a complete plan in advance, but starts speaking as soon as he has got the first bit ready, and he then goes on step by step. Planning in advance and planning stepwise are complementary techniques, and it is an open question whether they represent individual styles or whether their use simply depends on the particular task. Having a gap in the conversation – and a long planning pause is such a gap – is awkward, and it may well be that A in G15 starts simply because he doesn't like the prospect of a gap.

The primary plan, whether built up in advance or stepwise, is a first condition for a successful description. But less than the whole primary plan is reported, of course; this would contain a lot of information that is superfluous for the purpose of the required route directions. The speaker must select from it and arrange those pieces of information he thinks to be relevant for the listener. He has to form a 'secondary plan' which will immediately underlie the linearized sequence of verbal expressions, with which he describes the route. The organizing principle of this secondary plan is that of an 'imaginary journey' through the primary plan from starting point to destination. During this journey, certain points of the primary plan are selected and marked; this series of 'fixed points' forms the skeleton of his description. His directions have three components: fixed points are introduced, directions relative to the fixed points are marked, and actions (or events) are indicated. Consider the following passage from 04:

(04)   F   ja
           yes
       A   Ja, [5 seconds] jetzt gehn Sie vor, bis ganz vorn hin
           Yes,   you go on here,   until right before
       F   ja
           yes
       A   bis Sie an den Kaufhof stoßen, dann gehen Sie links rein,
           till you run into the Kaufhof,   then you go there to the left
       F   ja
           yes
       A   die Bibergasse, nun die gehen Sie entlang und dann halten Sie sich
           the Biebergasse, well you go on here and then you stick

           dann ganz links, dann kommt erst die Schillerstraße.
           to the left,   then you come first to the Schillerstraße
       F   mhm
           mhm
       A   die überqueren Sie   da is vorn an der Ecke is ein Herrenboutique.
           there you cross over there is on the corner there is a men's shop.

           da gehn Sie dran vorbei.
           there you go right past.

The first fixed point after the starting position is the Kaufhof (a big department store); here, the walker has several possibilities, one of which is marked: *links rein*. In other cases, possible alternatives are explicitly excluded. This is not done in the present example; here, only the right direction is indicated as such, in fact, given twice: once by the deictic statement *links rein*, and then by the additional information *die Biebergasse*; A has incorporated a unit of his primary plan that is not absolutely necessary but which provides additional help. Then, the route is repeated until a new fixed point is reached: Schillerstraße. In this way, point after point is selected, verbally introduced, and this skeleton is completed by commentary or additional information that helps to make sure that F gets the message. And he has got it if he has succeeded in building up a rudimentary image of the area, one that essentially consists of a series of selected points, and if he knows what he has to do at these points.

This information is given by three types of descriptive expressions[6] that the speaker uses: expressions that introduce fixed points, deictic expressions that

---

6 The expressions used in the route directions may be subdivided into three classes, according to their function: descriptive expressions, commenting expressions, and interactive expressions. The speaker may comment upon what he says, or on the difficulty of the task or route; typical are expressions like 'oh, that's quite near', 'well, it's complicated', etc. with interactive expressions.

link certain fixed points, and expressions for what F has to do there or what happens there: in a sequence like: ... *until you get to a small house with green shutters; there, turn left*, a fixed point ('a small house with green shutters') is introduced: the local deictic *there* refers to that fixed point, or rather to a locality close to that fixed point, and then the listener is told what has to be done at the denotatum of *there*.

2.3 Local deixis

After these general considerations on planning, let me turn to the specific problem of deictic reference in route directions. It is characterized by two specific features:
(a) Speaker and listener do not share a deictic space at the beginning. They share a perceptual space, but this is not enough. The listener at first doesn't have available the deictic space represented by the speaker's cognitive map of the area in question. Hence, A has to provide F with the idea of such a deictic space, or the indispensable elements of it; and this is what is achieved by introducing fixed points and giving additional information.
(b) The origo is given by the location of the speaker which, in this case, doesn't differ crucially from that of the listener. But then, the location of the speaker and listener – of the imaginary walker – is constantly shifted, or rather thought of as shifting during the imaginary walk.

In general, there is no problem of co-ordination: the orientation of A and F in the imaginary walk is thought to be identical, and at the starting point, it either differs in a trivial way that doesn't affect the use of deictics or A changes his position or his direction of gaze (or causes F to do so) to this effect. The delimitation is generally based on factual knowledge; it is rarely explicitly specified. The deictic oppositions are as usual, and analogical deixis is rarely used. In the following, I shall concentrate on the two points mentioned above: building up a rudimentary deictic space that mainly consists of a series of fixed points, and the moving origo and its function for the identification of denotata. The fixed points used are streets, places, buildings, etc. There are essentially four ways for a listener to recognize what the speaker intended as a fixed point:

A checks whether F got the message or simply whether F is still following his explanations, and F signals that he is still receiving and that A can and should continue; a standard technique is 'mhm' with question intonation on A's side and with affirmative intonation on F's side (for some details see Klein 1979, pp. 33-37).

(a) On the basis of his previous knowledge, the speaker expects that the listener simply will know some landmarks, or he can check this by questions like: *Do you know where ... is?- Yes – Okay, there it's.*
(b) On the basis of visual introduction, mainly by pointing gestures, e.g. in G17, where A says: *Sehen Sie dieses Schild Bill-Binding da oben ja?-* F: *Ja, ja –* A: *Okay, und dann da geradeaus.* This is only possible for the space of visual perception, of course.
(c) On the basis of (non-deictic) descriptions, such as in G6: *bis Sie an den Platz kommen, wo eh son'n großes Brunnen rausspringt, da gehn Se links runter,* or G16: *Un wenn Se e Stück drin sin, wo die Leute da sitze, dann...*
(d) On the basis of indications relative to a previous fixed point; this is often done with expressions like 'the first ... after', 'the next ...'. etc., e.g. in G16: *da gleich bis zur nächste Ampel.* This strategy is very frequent, and some speakers, as A in G11, use it exclusively: the first reference point is that starting point, and all other indications of fixed points are related to this first one.

Typically, these possibilities are used in combination with each other. In the following, one example (from G10) is considered in some detail. F's reactions are omitted; the fixed points are underlined:

(G10) A Am beste is, Sie gehn jetzt *auf die anner Seit: un hinner der Kirch* überqueren Sie *die Straß*, ja? Dann gehn Se *an de Kaiserstraß* e Stück erunter, bis Se an *de nächst Ampel* komme; da gehn Se links erein un dann sind Se gleich *dort:* da links, gell, da links erein. e Stück, un *da geht links e Straß un rechts;* die rechte Straß, das is der *Große Hirschgraben;* da kommt gleich 's *Goethehaus.*
[You best go to *the other side* now: and behind the church, you cross *the street,* okay? There you go a bit down the Kaiserstraße, till you get to the next light; there you turn left and then you are almost *there;* there to the left, all right, there to the *left,* a bit. and there *to the left* and *to the right* is a cross street; the street on the right, that's the *Große Hirschgraben;* shortly after that is the *Goethehaus.*]

Die anner Seit (= the other side) is a type 4 expression, combined – as often happens – with non-deictic information; it refers back to the original location: that side which is not here.[7] The next fixed point *hinter der Kirch* (= behind the church) is visual with a deictic component: 'behind'. What is meant is 'behind the

---

[7] It is precisely the deictic character of the word 'other' that is used in the famous riddle about the village of liars, the village of truth-tellers, and the cross-roads where somebody from one of the villages – it is not known which one – is sitting. If one has to find out with a single yes/no question whether the village of the truth-tellers is to the left or to the right, one must ask: *Would*

church that is before our eyes'. The next one is *die Straß* (= Katharinenpfad); it is again a type 4 expression: *die Straß* here means: that street that you will reach if you go on behind the church. The next fixed point, *an de Kaiserstraß*, has a peculiarity: an expression may be used this way only if the denotatum can be assumed to be known to the listener, i.e. the way in which the fixed point is introduced corresponds to type 1. But A can't assume that F knows the Kaiserstraße; either he assumes it nevertheless, or he assumes that F is able to read a street sign, i.e. that he is able to acquire the necessary knowledge. There follows again a fixed point of type 4, *die nächst Ampel*. The next point, *dort*, is clearly deictic, but it doesn't fit the general pattern: it is the first marking of the final destination; it means *there, where you want to go*, rather than *at the traffic lights*. (Incidentally, this is one of the rare cases where the strictly serial order of the fixed points is given up.) The lights are taken up by the deictic expression *da links, gell, da erein*, which, however, doesn't introduce a new fixed point. Again, this is done by an expression of type 3: that place, where there is a street to the left and a street to the right. This expression also contains a deictic component, and it could be argued that it is a combination of types 3 and 4. With its aid, the next and – apart from the destination itself – last fixed point is introduced: *der große Hirschgraben*. All that remains is the final marking.

Such a series of fixed points, together with some additional information perhaps, forms a rudimentary picture of a deictic space; the picture is completed if the imaginary traveller becomes a real one, and it is sufficient to set up – by means of local deictics – a lot of localities where certain actions are to be performed.[8] This is done by the deictics *hier, da, and dort. There* is usually used to refer to a space around the initial location whose borders are not specified – because there is no need to do so. The denotatum of *dort* and *da* (in local sense) is *not* the fixed point with which it is used: *bis Se an de nächst Ampel komme; da gehn Se links rein. Da* refers to the space around the imaginary position of the speaker at the fixed point in question. No delimitation is used; it is expected that F will draw the borders from his factual knowledge.

How this mechanism works is perhaps more clearly to be seen with the deictics *left* and *right*, whose denotatum not only depends on the – real or imaginary – position of the speaker, but also on his – real or imaginary – direction of gaze. There is one case in the data where the same street, the Biebergasse or its

---

somebody from the other village send me left for the village of the truth-tellers. The reference of *somebody from the other village* is different depending on the person sitting there.

8 A similar result can be obtained by using temporal deictics; they are determined by the sequence of actions: *dann* means 'at the moment after you have done what 1 previously said'. I don't consider these uses here.

continuation, the Freßgasse, is described in relation to the same fixed point one time as to the left (O1),

(O1) A Hier vor bis zum Kaufhof [...] und da halten Sie sich rechts, geradeaus durch die Freßgasse

the other time as to the right (O4).

(O4) A Jetzt gehen Sie vor, bis ganz vorn hin, bis an den Kaufhof stoßen, dann gehen Sie links rein, die Biebergasse

This is simply due to differences of position and their consequences. In O1, the original position is in the *Zeil* (see Figure 1); speaker and listener gaze in the direction of the Hauptwache. If F is thought to move in this direction and if – and this seems most natural – he maintains his direction of gaze, the Freßgasse (or the Biebergasse) will be to his right, as soon as he arrives at the fixed point Kaufhof. In O4, the original position is south-east of the *Hauptwache:* speaker and listener gaze towards the Kaufhof, and at this fixed point, the Kaufhof, the Biebergasse is to the left. What *links* and *rechts* – and analogously *dort, da, hier* – mean is determined by the origo and by the direction of gaze. In route directions, both position and direction underlie a constant imaginary change. In this case, the determinants of local deixis are set up by the explicitly fixed points, on the one hand, and by the normal and expected course of events – of walking and looking in an imaginary space.

References

Atkinson, M. & Griffiths, P.D. (1973). Here's here's , there's , here an d there. Edinburgh Working Papers in Linguistics 3 (mimeo).
Bühler, K. (1934). Sprachtheorie. Jena: Fischer.
Clark, E. (1977). From gesture to word: on the natural history of deixis in language acquisition. In J.S. Bruner & A. Garton. Eds. Human growth and development. Wolfson College lectures 1976. Oxford: Oxford University Press. 85–120.
Davis, P. W. & Saunders, R. (1975). Bella Cool a nominal deixis. Language 51. 845–858.
Downs, R. & Stea, D. (eds) (1973). Image and environment. Chicago: Aldine.
Downs, R. & Stea, D. (1977). Maps in minds. New York: Harper & Row.
Fillmore, C. (1975). Santa Cruz lectures on deixis, 1971. Bloomington, Ind.: Indiana University Linguistics Club.
Klein, W. (1979). Wegauskünfte. Zeitschrift für Literaturwissenschaft und Linguistik 33. 9–57.
Klein, W. & Levelt, W.J.M. (1978). Sprache und Kontext. Die Naturwissenschaften 65. 328–335.
Kratzer, A. & von Stechow, A. (1976). Äußerungen und Bedeutung. Zeitschrift für Literaturwissenschaft und Linguistik 23/24. 97–130.

Labov, W. & Linde, C. (1975). Spatial network s as a site for the study of language and thought. Language 51. 924–939.
Lynch, K. (1960). The image of a city. Cambridge, Mass.: MIT Press.
Miller, G.A. & Johnson-Laird, P.N. (1976). Language and perception. Cambridge, Mass.: Harvard University Press.
Wunderlich, D. (1976). Studien zur Sprechakttheorie. Frankfurt/Main: Suhrkamp.

Appendix: Selected Transcriptions

(O2)   F   Zum alten Opernhaus
To the old Opera House

        A   Ja?   jaaa [10 seconds] da gehen Sie jetzt bis zur Zeil
Yes? yahhh   you go now as far as the Zeil

        F   ja
yes

        A   oben drüber, ja
above there, yes

             oben drüber, nicht unten durch
above there, not below

             oben drüber, gehen durch die Goethestraße durch, und dann kommen
above there, you go through the Goethestraße,   and shortly you will
Sie direkt an die alte Oper
be at the old Opera

        F   dankeschön
thank you

        A   bitte, Wiedersehen.
you're welcome, see you.

(O17)   F   Entschuldigen Sie, können Sie mir sagen, wie man zur alter Oper kommt?
Excuse me, could you tell me how to get to the old Opera?

        A   na. oh ja doch [2 seconds] Sie können [2 seconds] hier rauf [2 seconds] bis
well, oh yes,   you can   here that way   till

        F   jaha
yah uhhuh

        A   [6 seconds] ehm, ich muß auch erst überlegen weil's von bissel
ehm, let me think first myself   'cause it's been

        F   ja
yes

        A   verbaut wurde :   [4 seconds] Sie gehen jetzt hier eh zur Ecke dann
changed a bit here   now YOU go here to the corner   then
links oben über den Platz, dann gehn Sie geradeaus, das ist die
to the left up above across the square, then straight on, that's the

	F	ja
		yes
	A	Goethestraße, also nicht diese, sondern die nächste dann rauf, und dann
		Goethestraße, that is not this one but the next one, up it then, and then
	F	mhm
		mhm
	A	stoßen Sie direkt das ist dann auf der rechten Seite ist dann die alte Oper
		you run mmediately into that is on the right side then is the old Opera
	F	mhm
		mhm
	A	das sehen Sie schon;
		you'll see it then
	F	gutt, dankeschön
		okay, thank you
	A	bitte
		you're welcome.
(G2)	F	Können Sie mir sagen, wie man zum Goethehaus kommt?
		Could you tell me, how to get to the Goethe House?
	A	Goethehaus ?
		Goethe House?
		nee. Großer Hirschgraben war das. glaub ich
		no. it was Großer Hirschgraben. I think
		keine Adresse?
		no address?
	F	bitte?
		sorry?
	A	Großer Hirschgraben, die Straße [5 seconds] Wissen Se nicht.
		Großer Hirschgraben, the street You don't know.
		fragen wir nochmal.
		we'll ask somebody else.
(G4)	F	Können Sie mir sagen, wie man zum Goethehaus kommt?
		Could you tell us how to get to the Goethe House?
	A	Zum wie?
		To the what?
	F	Goethehaus
		Goethe House
	A	Güterhaus?
		Goods House?
	F	Goethe
		Goethe

	A	hm, das ist hier etwa. Goethe,
		hm, that's here somewhere, Goethe,

        Goethe, Goetheplatz, Goetheplatz und Goethehaus, he.
        Goethe, Goethe place, Goethe Place and Goethe House, hey,

	F	ja, ja, ja.
		oh yes, sure,
	A	ich glaube da is da, oder? ganz in der Nähe davon
		I think it's there, or? around here somewhere

        wenn Sie hierher, also wenn Sie jetzt über die Straße gehen.
        if you here, well, if you cross the street now.

	F	ja
		yes
	A	ja und dann gehn Sie gerade, ich glaube da wo ist die Kirche
		okay, and then go straight on, I think there where is the church

        da muß sie[!] irgendwo sein
        there she must he somewhere

	F	ja, danke
		yes, thanks
	A	bitte.
		you're welcome.
	F	okay.
		okay.
(G17)	F	Entschuldigung, können Sie mir sagen, wie man hier zum
		Excuse me, could you tell me, how to get to the

        Goethehaus kommt?
        Goethe House here?

	A	ja, Moment [2 seconds] okay [1 second]
		yes, just a moment okay
	F	ja
		yes
	A	du mußt hier durch, ja? und [4 seconds] okay.
		you have to go through here, alright? and okay.

        wie am besten, ja, hier durch, ja?   is auch eine Straße: sehn Sie
        what's the best, yes; through here, okay? there is another street: do you see

        dieses Schild Bill-Binding Bier da oben , ja?
        this sign Bill-Binding Beer up there, yeh?

F ja, ja
   yes, sure

A okay, und dann da geradeaus
   okay, and then straight on

F mhm
   mhm

A und jetzt is es entweder, es gibt eh zwei kleine Gasse.
   and now it's either,   there are er two small side streets,

   ja, eh immer geradeaus, und dann kurz vor Berliner Straße,
   yes, ah, you keep going straight, and then shortly before the Berliner Straße,

   eh eh, irgendwo in dieser Richtung, das weiß ich auch nicht so weit
   ah ah, somewhere in that direction; I'm not quite sure, either so far

F is gut, danke
   that's fine, thanks

A fünf Minuten, ja? auf der rechten Seite
   in five minutes, okay? on the right side

F ja, is gut, vielen Dank
   yes, that's fine, thanks a lot

A eh aber zuerst hier runter
   but first down here

F okay.
   okay.

Some notorious pitfalls in the analysis of spatial expressions[1]

1 Introduction

Space and time are two equally fundamental categories of human cognition, and it would be very surprising, indeed, if they had not found rich expression in human language. All natural languages we know of show elaborate means to express temporal and spatial relations. These means include, for both categories, the inherent lexical content of words, inflectional marking, adverbials, prepositions, various complex syntactic constructions, and principles of text organisation (such as, for example, the "principle of natural order": Temporal order of mention corresponds to temporal order of events). What is different for time and space, though, is the extent with which the linguistic tradition has dealt with them. Whereas the expression of temporality has been continuously and systematically investigated from the Greek over Priscian and the Junggrammarians to Montague, there is much less comparable work on "spatial reference", as I shall say here as a shorthand term for all types of spatial expression. This asymmetry is probably due to the fact that at least in Indoeuropean languages, temporality is regularly grammaticalised in verb morphology. Every finite verb carries tense, and hence, reference to time is obligatory (and not very functional since often redundant) in all sentences with a finite verb. This is not the case for spatiality. Even where the expression of space is to some extent grammaticalised, for example by case marking, it is hardly ever obligatory.[2] This relative neglect of spatiality does not mean, of course, that studies on space and its reflection in

---

[1] Some of the ideas outlined here were presented at a conference organised by IBM Germany in Dresden, June 1992. I wish to thank Helmut Schnelle for a very instructive discussion after the talk. I am also grateful to my collegues from the project "The expression of time and space" at the MPI für Psycholinguistik, Nijmegen, notably Manfred Bierwisch, Melissa Bowerman, and Veronika Ehrich, for many helpful discussion. Many thanks, too, to Steve Levinson and Dieter Wunderlich. None of them should be held responsible for my views.
[2] It is possible, though, that spatiality is deeper rooted in the structure of sentences than would seem at first glance, an assumption which give rise to so-called "localist theories". There is, for example, the old notion that all cases are derived from locatives (see, for example, Wundt 1904, chapter 6, section II). Even if this were true, it would not mean that any case marking now serves

Note: This article originally appeared as Klein, W. (1993). Some notorious pitfalls in the analysis of spatial expressions. In F. Beckman and G. Heyer (eds.). Theorie und Praxis des Lexikons. Berlin: de Gruyter. 191–204.

https://doi.org/10.1515/9783110549119-009

human language were absent in the linguistic tradition. But it is only some twenty years ago that it started to excite more than casual interest, and it is quite telling that this increasing interest is found less among structural linguists but among researchers who are more concerned with the interrelation of language and other aspects of human cognition – in psycholinguistics, cognitive anthropology, artificial intelligence. Despite the considerable progress which has been made especially in the course of the last ten years,[3] it is probably fair to say that research on spatial reference is still in the cradle, especially when compared to what has been done on temporality. This applies to very specific problems, such as the semantic analysis of spatial terms within a particular language – what do words such as *on, at, by* mean, when compared, for example, to German *an, auf, bei*? – as well as to issues of a more general kind – what are the organising principles behind the expression of spatiality, how do spatial expressions fit into the compositional structure of sentences, etc?

None of these questions will be directly addressed, let alone answered, in this paper.[4] Its aim is a more modest one. In the next section, I will give a necessarily very general survey or the wealth of problems involved in the analysis of spatial reference. There are so many interacting components that it seems hopeless to attack the problem in its entirety; the most reasonable procedure to deal with these problems is to start with very simple cases. In doing so, there is however a number of potential pitfalls which are often stepped in – surely not by everybody, but sufficiently often to deserve some discussion, to which I will turn in section 4. They concern (a) the non-separation of object and place of object, (b) the role of so-called directionals, and (c) the relative neglect of spatial expressions without objects being involved. Finally, it is argued that these problems can be avoided by what may be called the property-of-place analysis of spatial reference. This analysis is briefly sketched in the last section of this paper.

---

to express space, and hence the expression of space would be an obligatory category. For a recent discussion of localist theories, see Wunderlich and Herweg (1992), section 5.

3 See Wunderlich and Herweg (1992) for a good survey on the linguistic research; Hermann (1990) is representative for recent work in experimental psychology: Levinson (1992) for cognitive anthropology. There is a whole series of edited volumes, such as Jarvella and Klein (1982), in which spatiality is discussed from various points of view; Weissenborn and Klein (1982) gives some idea of crosslinguistic variation; the state of the art is perhaps best represented by the contributions to Habel et al., eds. (1989).

4 More details on my own views are to be found in Klein (1990, 1991). For a critical assessment, see Wunderlich (1990).

2 The range of problems

Traditional wisdom as well as most recent research regularly distinguishes between two basic types of spatial reference, mostly termed "static" vs. "dynamic" (terminology varies, but the basic distinction is the same). Typical examples are (1) and (2), respectively:

(1) The cup was on the table.
(2) The cup fell onto the table.

The first sentence describes some spatial arrangement which is claimed to apply throughout the time for which this claim is made – here some unspecified time in the past. This does not exclude that the cup was moved there, nor that it will leave this position again. But for the time at issue, no such claim is made: the arrangement is static for that time. The second sentence makes an explicit claim about such a movement. This is not only reflected in the verb, here *walked* in contrast to *was*, but also in the choice of a particular preposition, here *onto* vs. *on*. The object, here the cup, follows some trajectory, a path, as is most often said, which ends up on the table, and this path is expressed by the verb of movement (or of motion) together with the directional preposition *onto*. Most researchers assume that expressions like (1) are in a way more basic in their semantic structure, because everything needed for the description of (1) is also needed for the description of (2), but not vice versa: the latter also requires some notion of path and/or direction. This is not unchallenged, but we shall follow the general line here and ask, what is indispensable for the semantic analysis of (1), and what then has to be added for dynamic cases such as (2).

If (1) is uttered upon some occasion, then three conditions must be fulfilled, if the listener is to understand it:
A. Referential domain: Speaker and listener must have the same, or at least a sufficiently similar, representation of the domain of reference, i.e., of space.
B. Linguistic meaning proper: Speaker and listener must know the language-specific meaning of the various spatial expressions used.
C. Contextual integration: Speaker and listener must be able to integrate "linguistic meaning proper" and contextual information of various types.

None of these conditions is trivial, neither for speaker and listener nor for the researcher who wants to analysis their functioning. Linguistic research tends to focus on the second task, the analysis of linguistic meaning proper, and to neglect the two others. In what follows, I shall briefly comment upon these conditions and try to show why no sensible analysis of spatial reference is possible without considering all of them.

2.1 Structure of space

The notion of space[5] which underlies (1) and (2) is what one might call "normal perceptual space" – that kind of space which underlies our everyday perception and action, when we see this and that, hear this and that, move from here to there. Such a space is assumed to consist of smaller entities ("places"), for which a twofold structure is defined: There are three dimensions (vertical, horizontal, transversal, or up-down, left-right, front-back), and there are topological relations, i.e., a place can be (partly) contained in some other place or in the neighborhood of some place.[6] It is this structure which is reflected in the meaning of spatial terms such as *on* vs. *under, beneath above, in* vs. *out, near, around, left* vs. *right*, etc. But it is easy to see that not all usages of spatial terms operate with this type of space. I give some simple examples:

(3) a. Sparta is in Greece.
 b. Sparta is on the Peloponnes.
 c. Sparta is not on the map.
 d. I can't get this idea out of my head.
 e. I can't get this idea out of my mind.
 f. I can't get this girl out of my head.

Would we say that Sparta is in the same way contained in Greece as, say, the coffee is contained in the cup? In other words, does geographical space have the same structure as immediate perceptual space? Probably not: We would not assume that Greece is in the same way a three-dimensional entity as, for example, a cup. Why do we say then that Sparta is on the Peloponnes – surely no less and no more a three-dimensional entity than Greece? Or are these different notions of Sparta, a two-dimensional and a three-dimensional one? Such a possibility is supported by usages like in (3c): Here, we are talking about a two-dimensional representation of Sparta on a two-dimensional map. Hence, the underlying space is somehow a conceptual reduction of "real" three-dimensional space. But if this is true, why does one then say *on*, as in (1)? Is the *idea* in (3d) a three-dimensional

---

5 In contrast to the linguistic analysis of space and its expression, the philosophical tradition is long and rich. The most comprehensive survey is Gosztonyi (1976). It is interesting, though, that in this long tradition, all sorts of arguments show up, physical, psychological, anthropological, even theological. But philosophers seemed hardly ever interested in the ways in which people speak about space in everyday language.
6 All of these notions can be made more precise, see, for example, Wunderlich (1982) or Klein (1991).

entity, contained in another three-dimensional entity *head*? This seems possible for the head, less so for the *idea*? Ideas are generally not assumed to have a dimension, let alone three. But how is this in (3e), where neither idea nor mind are usually considered to have dimensions? But even if the entities at issue are normally understood to be three-dimensional, like girls, spatial relations can be stated between them which show that we often do not mean them to have three-dimensions, as is illustrated by (3f).[7] In other words, "normal perceptual space" is surely an important type of space, maybe even the most important one for spatial reference. But it is no less sure that it is not the only one which underlies the use of in fact quite normal and simple types of spatial reference.

The existence of various types of space is not the only problem. Imagine you are flying from Egypt to Germany, and just above Greece, a friendly pilot explains the scenery:

(4) Greece is just beneath us. The big island beneath Greece, slighty to the right, is Crete, and the little white spot behind Crete is another island called Karpathos.

Clearly, *beneath* in the first and in the second sentence mean something very different, because beneath Greece in the first sense, there is only the Hades. Somehow, the definition of the dimensions has changed, and so it has from the second to the third sentence. In other words, we not only have different concepts of space but can also easily **switch** from one to the other within a coherent piece of discourse.

These few observations leave the linguist with two basic questions: (a) How should one characterise the various concepts of space which underlie the meaning of spatial terms, and (b) How are they related to each other? Most work on spatial expressions so far is concerned with very basic arrangements in "normal perceptual space", and the two tasks have hardly been tackled. In a way, this is understandable, because the analysis of spatial representation in the human mind seems beyond the realm of linguistic research in the usual sense of the word. But without such an analysis it would seem hopeless to specify the meaning of spatial terms and their use in concrete utterances. I think a realistic

---

[7] I should point out here that it is no answer to say that this usage is "metaphorical". This may be correct or not, but even if it is correct, it does not say anything: It encapsulates a mystery by a word, like an intruder in a bee hive. This is a strategy we often find in science, for example in the medical sciences where unexplainable observations are sometimes covered by the expression "placebo effect", thereby hiding the fact that these observations are simply a mystery.

solution to both problems must indeed start with some notion of "basic space" and then study various transformations of this basic space: It can be reduced by dropping one or two dimensions, it can be enriched by metrical structure (not found in all cultures), etc. I also think that the most reasonable candidate for this "basic space" is indeed the notion of space which underlies examples such as (1) or (2), hence simple spatial constellations between three-dimensional objects. But in proceeding so, one is easily trapped, a point to be returned to shortly.

2.2 Semantic content

The second problem is the language-specific meaning of spatial expressions. This problem naturally divides into two sub-tasks. First, we must specify the lexical meaning of elementary expressions, for example as prepositions like *in, on, under, beneath, behind, between, past, near,* adverbs such as *here, there, to the left, anywhere, yonder,* of motion verbs, sometimes of case marking, etc. Second, we must somehow describe how these elementary terms are integrated into larger constructions, such as in *The second book on the upper shelf to your left comes from Japan.* It is these two tasks linguists normally focus on. But it would be an exaggeration to say that the problems are solved. I will mention but one, the seemingly infinite polysemy (or perhaps homonymy) of spatial prepositions such as *in* or *on*. Examples such as (1), (3b) and (3c) illustrate the point, here for *on,* and rather than quoting other examples, I refer the reader to what is said about *on, in, at, under* in (!) any comprehensive dictionary of the English language – an illuminating and sometimes discouraging experience.

A linguist, in contrast to a dictionary maker, cannot be satisfied with listing the various usages and give illustrative. Somehow, they have to be related to each other in a systematical way. I think the only method of doing so is to start with something like a 'core meaning' and to study the various cognitive operations which lead to many particular usages. And again, it seems intuitively most plausible to take simple arrangements such as (1) or (2) to represent of the core meaning, here of *on* – with all the risks this may have.

2.3 Context-dependency

It has often been noted that many spatial terms are context-dependent, for example *here* vs. *there, left* vs. *right* or *front* vs. *back*. Their meaning is systematically related to the position of the speaker or addressee, or to the position of some other entity mentioned in context. Thus, *here* means something like 'place which includes the position of the speaker', and *there* means something like 'place which excludes position of the speaker'; *left, right, front, back* not only depend of the position of the speaker but also on his direction of gaze. Not all languages make use of this type of structural context-dependency for spatial reference. Many languages lack terms for *left* and *right*. This does not mean, though, that their speakers have a different representation of space. They had probably died out for long if they did not distinguish between whether the tiger is to the left or to the right. They just do not use their body orientation to describe these sub-spaces. Where use is made of spatial deixis and of spatial anaphoricity, its exact functioning can be very complex, and has been the subject of much research (see, for example, the papers in Klein and Weissenborn 1982, Ehrich 1992).

There is a second, more global type of context-dependency which plays a substantial role for spatial reference. The interlocutor's understanding of *here* in a concrete utterance not only depends on his ability to identify the position of the speaker but also on his general world knowledge. This is best illustrated by familiar examples such as *I cannot see you from here* vs. *Computers are much more expensive here than in the US*, where the boundaries of what is referred to by *here* are very different.

This "global context-depencendy" also solves part of the apparent polysemy in prepositions such as *under*. Compare, for example:

(5) a. The old couple was sitting under an oak tree.
    b. The mole was living under an oak tree.

Clearly, the old couple is not in the same spatial relation to the tree as the mole, although this relation is in both cases labelled *under*. It is not the lexical meaning of this word but our knowledge of old couples, on the one hand, and of moles, on the other, which tells us what exactly the spatial configuration is.

Hence, what the linguist should do is to sort out what the "lexical meaning proper" of such a term is and what comes from context. Again, it would not suffice to say that contextual information plays a role – this is correct but trivial – but show what the principles are according to which linguistic information proper and contextual information interact in a given utterance to yield a consistent and meaningful interpretation.

In this brief *tour d'horizon* of the various components involved in spatial reference, we could only touch upon the major factors which play a role in its functioning. All of them are important, and the examples given above are surely not far-fetched. Now, it would seem hopeless to deal with all of these problems at once, and just as in other domains of scientific investigation, I think it is on the one hand important to be aware of the entire complexity of the problem at hand, and on the other to start with what one might consider the most elementary and "prototypical" cases. As many other researcher, I would assume that the best starting point are indeed simple configurations such as described by (1), and then extend the analysis systematically to other, more complex cases. But this procedure, reasonable as it is, has its pitfalls, some of which will be discussed in the following section.

3 The simple case trap

Consider again a simple static spatial description such as (1), repeated here:

(1) The cup was on the table.

The analysis which suggests itself is this: In such a locative description, reference is made to an object, here a cup, and it is said that this cup is in a particular spatial relation to another object, the table; this spatial relation is expressed by the word *on*, in contrast to, for example, spatial relations as expressed by *under, behind, above* etc. Languages differ with respect to the spatial relations which they encode, and also in the way in which these spatial relations are encoded.

I think this picture has the seductive charm of all simple accounts; but it is a strong and in fact misleading oversimplification. Its first pitfall is the fact that it does not sharply distingish between objects and the place of objects in local expressions. There are (at least) three arguments which necessitate such a distinction:

3.1 The time parameter argument

Consider a sentence like (6):

(6) Peter is sitting exactly where Mary was sitting yesterday.

Such a sentence is entirely unundersandable unless we assume that there is some entity different from Peter and Mary – a certain place, say place L. What (6) says, is simply, that at some time, namely right now, L is occupied by Peter, and at some other time, namely yesterday, L was occupied by some other entitiy, Mary.

It is L which remains constant, whereas the objects (here: persons) which are at this place change. A somewhat more circumlocutional way to state (6) would be:

(6)' The place where Peter is sitting now is identical to the place where Mary was sitting yesterday.

The question whether there is a space, and hence individual places, independent of objects being there is an old and higly controversial philosophical issue, which we surely do not want to comment upon here. But it appears that the way in which people talk about space requires a clear distinction between places and objects. I simply see no way how else the meaning of (6) could be described: We must assume that there is some constant entity, a place, irrespective of the objects which temporarily occupy it.

3.2 The change-of-place argument

In (6), the place is kept constant, and it is successively occupied by two different entities: first Peter, then Mary. The exact counterpart is a situation in which the object is kept constant in an utterance and two places are involved. In fact, utterances of this type are extremely common: it is all those which involve a change-of-place expression or, to use the more common term, a movement expression, as in (2) or in the following two examples:

(7) John came from Alabama.
(8) John went to Lousiana.

In (7), the place where John first is is "in Alabama", and the place where he is thereafter is not specified in the utterance; it is only clear that it is not in Alabama. The same is true for (8), except that here, only the second place is specified (IN-Lousiana) and the first place is left open (NOT-IN Lousiana). We may conveniently call the first place and the second place in these change-of-state expressions, "source place" and "target place", respectively. Then, the meaning of (7) and (8) can be made more explicit by the following rough paraphrases (details aside):

(7)' The source place of John is IN-Alabama, and the target place of John is NOT-IN Alabama.
(8)' The source place of John is NOT-IN Lousiana, and the target place of John is IN-Lousiana.

I do not want to say that these paraphrases are communicatively appropriate; they only render the semantic structure more explicit.[8]

Three additional remarks on this point:
1. Under this analyis, change-of-place expressions are just a special case of change-of- state expressions in general, such as, for example, *to close a window or to die*. A verb such as *to die* involves a first state in which the argument, say John, is not dead, and a second state, in which he is dead. Here, some "qualitative properties" of John is at issue, whereas in *to come* and *to go*, the two distinct states are characterised by two different places.
2. An utterance with a target state (in particular, target place) need not say that this target state/place is in fact reached – either at all, or within the interval considered. Thus,

(9) John was walking to the station.

does not imply does that he ever reached the target place (AT-station); still, AT-station is the target place. The situation is exactly as in non-spatial utterances like (10):

(10) John was baking a cake.

Clearly, the "target state" involves that there be a cake, due to John's efforts. But (10) does not imply that this target state is ever reached within the interval about which (10) makes a claim. It is simply left open.

3. So-called "directionals" such as *into, onto* vs. *in, on* or German *in* + Acc. vs. *in* + Dat. never denote a direction. They simply mark a place to be a target place (or, less frequently, to be a source place, such as *from*, or even rarer, to be an "interim place", such as *via* or German *über*). Nor do they denote a 'path' or a 'trajectory'. Consider again (7): Depending on where John

---

8 No one would normally speak this way, and hence, the paraphrases are no communicatively appropriate versions of the original examples. They only render the semantic structure more explicit. Since this point was occasionally cast into doubt, it might be helpful to illustrate it by a more familiar example. No one would deny that in
  (i) The old man shaved himself.
  the word *himself* refers to the same person as the expression the old man. Hence, the semantic structure of (i) is something like
  (i)' That person who is the only old man in the given context shaved that person who is the only *old man* in the given context.
  But it is not very likely that anybody except a linguist understand (i)' in the sense of (i).

was before (i.e., depending on his source place, not made explicit in this utterance), the 'direction, path, trajectory' is very different, and (7) does not say anything about them: It only says that his target place is IN-Lousiana. This is not to deny that it is possible to express directions or trajectories or pathes. But that is not the function of what is commonly called 'directionals'.[9]

3.3 The non-object argument

As Wittgenstein once put it: Our reasoning often suffers from an unbalanced diet of examples. I think that linguistic reasoning on spatial reference is a good example: they are strongly biased by some properties of the "prototypical" constellation, i.e. by utterances which involve three-dimensional objects localised in three-dimensional space. In fact, spatial expressions need not localise objects at a particular place. Consider the following simple examples:

(11)   Kant is famous in Spain.
(12)   The final will be played at the Meazza stadion.
(13)   It is too hot under the roof.

These examples are perfectly normal spatial expressions, definitely no exotic cases. But we cannot say that they localise an object (or person) at some particular place. Kant is (or was) perhaps an object, and he is referred to in (11).[10] But he was never in Spain, nor is this said by (11). What (11) says, is rather that the place, or perhaps one of the places, where Kant is famous is such-and-such a place. This is even clearer for (12). Only under a very liberal interpretation of the notion 'object', we might say that a final is an object. Even under this assumption, (12) does not say that this highly abstract object is localised at the Meazza stadion. It rather says that the place where the final will be played is a place of a certain kind. And finally in (13), there is no object at all, that would be localised, or would stand in a spatial relation to the roof. Or should we assume

---

9 This idea is very much at variance with what is commonly assumed about dynamic spatial reference, in which notions such as 'path', 'directionality' etc. play an important role. The only exception I know of is Kaufmann (1989).
10 I say 'perhaps' because it is not clear in (11) whether Kant as an physical entity is at issue here or rather something like his achievements, his ideas, his philosophy, which one would not so very much consider to be an object (in the sense in which a cup is an object).

that by (13), some event, the too-hotness, is said to be lower than the roof? What (13) means is something like that a particular place, an UNDER-the-roof-place, has a certain property, namely that it is quite hot there. Or compare examples such as (14) and (15):

(14) In München, there is a Hofbräuhaus.
(15) In München, it was really chilly.

It makes some sense to say that the Hofbräuhaus is located in the interior space of München. But in (15), the spatial relation seems, if anything, to be rather the opposite: München is spatially included in the chill (or chilly area), rather than the chill in München (this point was first made in von Stutterheim 1991).

What is the lesson to be drawn from the discussion in this section? We said that is reasonable to start the analysis of spatial reference by studying simple cases such as (1) – the localisation of objects in physical space. But the suggestive notion that utterances of this type simply refer to two objects and specify the spatial relation, here *on*, between them is very misleading. The semantic form of spatial reference must be somewhat more abstract, if it is supposed to cover the various facts mentioned in this section. What can this general semantic form be? In the concluding section, I will briefly address this question.

4 The "property of place"-analysis of spatial reference

Consider once more (1). Under the assumption, justified above, that what we are dealing with is not just the cup but the place where the cup is at some time, (1) can be paraphrased as follows:

(1)' The/a place where the cup was (at some time in the past) was (at the same time) an ON-place of the table.

What an ON-place of the table is, depends on how exactly the lexical meaning of English *on* is analysed; we can assume, for present purposes, that ON-places of the table are all those places which are higher than and in contact with the place where the table is. This analysis easily extends to the other cases discussed above. Consider, for example, (11) – (13). In these cases, the defining property of the places at issue is not the fact, that an object is there, but the fact, that, for example, Kant is famous there:

(11)' The/a place where Kant is famous is IN-Spain.
(12)' The/a place where the final will be played is AT-Meazza stadion.
(13)' The/a place where it is too hot is UNDER-roof

In all of these examples, only one place is at issue, which is then further characterised as a place of a particular type. How about so-called directionals, as in (2), repeated here:

(2)　The cup fell onto the table.

As was said above in connection with examples (7) and (8), I do not think that *onto* expresses any direction, nor does it involve a 'path', as is often assumed in the literature. Utterance (2) simply says firstly that the place at issue is an ON-place of the cup, and secondly, that it is a target place (in the sense explained above). In this particular case, there is indeed some directionality involved. But this directionality stems from the lexical meaning of *to fall*: it involves movement according to gravity. But consider (8), where the movement verb is *to go*. All it says is that the target state of John's activity is an IN-place of Louisiana. No path, no direction whatsoever are described. Many paths lead to Louisiana, all of them compatible with (8). This applies accordingly to (7), except that here, it is the source place, rather than the target place, which is at issue.

Under the present analysis, the prototypical spatial arrangement of two three-dimensional objects, such as exemplified by (1), is just a special case of spatial expressions: What is at issue, is not the/a place where, for example, Kant is famous at some time, or where it was too hot, or where John is striving for to be, but the place where, for example, a cup is at some time, and it is said that this place is a such-and-such place – for example a place which is higher than and in contact with the place where some table is at that time. This is not to deny that in (1), REFERENCE is made to the cup, and not, at least not directly, to the place where the cup is at that time. But the PREDICATION does not specify properties of the cup as such, like its being made of China, or yellow, or half-broken, or ugly, but of the place which it occupies at some time.

The general scheme of a spatial expression sketched here does not solve all the problems mentioned in section 2. What it allows us, however, is to start indeed with very simply cases, such as (1) or (2), to determine the role of the various components – representation of space, meaning of simple and complex expressions, integration of contextual information – and then to extend this analysis successively to other, more complex or simply more abstract ways in which spatial information can be expressed in natural language.

References

Gosztonyi, Alexander (1976). Der Raum. Geschichte seiner Probleme in Philosophie und Wissenschaften. Freiburg: Alber.
Habel, Christopher, Herweg, Michael, and Rehkämper, Klaus (eds.) (1989). Raumkonzepte in Verstehensprozessen. Tübingen: Niemeyer.
Herrmann, Theo (1990). Vor, hinter, rechts und links: das 6H-Modell. Psychologische Studien zum sprachlichen Lokalisieren. In Zeitschrift für Literaturwissenschaft und Linguistik 78. 117–140.
Jarvella, Robert, and Klein, Wolfgang (eds.) (1982). Speech, Place, and Action. Chichester: Wiley.
Kaufmann, I. (1989). Direktionale Präpositionen. In Habel, Herweg, Rehkämper (1989). 128–149.
Klein, Wolfgang (1990). Überall und nirgendwo. Subjektive und objektive Momente in der Raumreferenz. In Zeitschrift für Literaturwissenschaft und Linguistik 78. 9–42.
Klein, Wolfgang (1991). Raumausdrücke. In Linguistische Berichte 132. 77–114.
von Stutterheim, Christiane (1990). Einige Probleme bei der Beschreibung von Lokalisationen. In Zeitschrift für Literaturwissenschaft und Linguistik 78. 98–112.
Weissenborn, Jürgen, and Klein, Wolfgang (eds.) (1982). Here and there. Crosslinguistic studies in deixis and demonstration. Amsterdam: Benjamins.
Wunderlich, Dieter (1982). Sprache und Raum. In Studium Linguistik 12. 1–19.
Wunderlich, Dieter (1990). Ort und Ortswechsel. In Zeitschrift für Literaturwissenschaft und Linguistik 78. 43–58.
Wunderlich, Dieter, and Herweg, Michael (1992). Lokale und Direktionale. In: Arnim von Stechow and Dieter Wunderlich (eds.). Semantik. Ein internationales Handbuch der zeitgenössischen Forschung. Berlin, New York: de Gruyter. 758–785.
Wundt, Wilhelm (1904). Die Sprache. Leipzig: Engelmann. 2nd. ed.

Time and again[1]

> Immer wieder kehrst du Melancholie.
> *Trakl*

1 An ambiguity

Like its English counterpart *again*, the German adverb *wieder* yields two different readings when combined with a telic verb:

(1) Er   hatte ihren Namen wieder vergessen.
     He   had   her   name   again   forgotten.

This can mean that it was not the first time that he had forgotten her name, or it can mean that he had learned her name and then forgotten it. In the first case, the entire process that is partly described by <to forget her name> is repeated. In the second case, it may well have been the first time that he forgot it: but an earlier state – a state in which her name was not present to him – is restituted. Thus, sentence 1 has a 'repetitive reading' and a 'restitutive reading'. This terminology, which we owe to Harweg (1969), is very suggestive but also somewhat misleading. In the restitutive reading, something is repeated, as well: it is just not the entire process but the state in which it results. Thus, the difference is only in WHAT is repeated. This difference is very often brought out by intonation, a fact which has found no explanation whatsoever in the rich literature on *wieder*. If the main stress is on *vergessen*, then only the resulting state is said to obtain again, whereas main stress on *wieder* indicates that the entire action did not happen for the first time.

As any other ambiguity, this one may have lexical or structural reasons. If it is lexical, then there must be two (or more) lexical entries *wieder* with the same phonological but different categorial or semantical information. This assumption has one point in favour: in many languages, the two readings are served by different morphemes. In French, for example, and similarly in other Romance

---

[1] This paper was written for my friend Arnim von Stechow. I wish to thank a number of more or less anonymous people who helped me with comments on an earlier version of this paper. They should not be held responsible for most remaining errors.

Note: This article originally appeared as Klein, W. (2001). Time and again. In C. Féry and W. Sternefeld (eds.). Audiatur vox sapientiae: A festschrift for Arnim von Stechow. Berlin: Akademie Verlag. 267–286.

https://doi.org/10.1515/9783110549119-010

languages, the restitutive reading is often expressed by a prefix *re-* attached to the verb stem, whereas the repetitive reading is expressed by an adverbial such as *de nouveau*. But this argument is not particularly forceful; we would not assume that English *only* or German *nur* are lexically ambiguous just because their French counterpart varies between *seul, seulement* and *ne...que*, depending on what it is applied to. Two points, however, speak strongly against the notion that there are two lexical entries *wieder*. First, it is not a very desirable assumption in general; lexical ambiguities should be seen as the *ultima ratio* (see also Kamp and Rossdeutscher 1994: 197). Second, the contribution which *wieder* makes to the entire meaning of the sentence seems exactly the same under both readings: AND THIS NOT FOR THE FIRST TIME. The difference is only in what the 'this' relates to. If it can be shown that the two readings only result from what *wieder* is applied to in the sentence in which it occurs, then such a solution is clearly preferable.

The main problem with a purely structural solution is simply that, barring intonation, there is no obvious structural difference between the two readings of example 1. Hence, we must assume that there is a more abstract level of representation in which the underlying sentence *Er hat ihren Namen ... vergessen* has two different structures. This level may belong to syntax or to semantics. Since the difference between the two readings lies in what does or does not obtain for the first time – the entire process as described by the verb or its resultant state –, this level must be sufficiently differentiated such as to give selective access to various components of the verb's meaning. Therefore, this meaning must somehow be 'decomposed'. Various proposals to achieve this are found in the literature; they may, but need not, be combined with a lexical ambiguity. The best-known treatments for English *again* are McCawley (1973) and Dowty (1979, chapter 5). German *wieder* has been most systematically investigated by Cathrine Fabricius-Hansen (1980, 1983 and 1995) and, more recently, by Arnim von Stechow (1995, 1996).

In what follows, I shall assume some familiarity with these proposals, and I shall not try to examine their merits and shortcomings. In spirit, the analysis presented here resembles von Stechow (1996); but there is also a number of substantial differences which will become clear as we go along. My starting assumption is that *wieder* indeed makes a constant meaning contribution in all of its use. This meaning contribution is 'and this not for the first time'. The expression 'this' has variable reference, and thus, we must clarify how it is fixed in a given sentence; furthermore, we must clarify what 'not for the first time' means. This will be done in three steps. First, I will discuss a number of problems connected to *wieder* which go beyond the simple repetitive-restitutive ambiguity; some of these are familiar from the literature, whereas others are new; this discussion will highlight the fact that this ambiguity is just a special case of a much wider scope ambiguity. Then, I will show that a difference must be made between the temporal order of events and the temporal order in which the events are presented in discourse. This distinction is fundamental to an understanding of what 'not for the first time' means. It is also fundamental to an understanding of a fact which is regularly mentioned in earlier research but is hardly ever addressed and has never found a satisfactory solution – the intonational difference between various readings of *wieder*. Finally, I will show that the traditional repetitive-restitutive ambiguity is easily accounted for if we assume that the verb content may contain one or two time variables.

2 Three problems

> Wieder so ein Abend, wieder so ein endloser Abend beim Griechen.
> *Hubert Selby*, Last exit to Brooklyn

2.1 Scope effects beyond the lexical verb

In sentence 1, the ambiguity is closely related to the meaning of the lexical verb *vergess-*: it is either the entire process or only its resultant state to which 'and this not for the first time' applies. As was first noted in Fabricius-Hansen (1983: 99–103), this picture is by far too simple; the varying effects of *wieder* may also involve other parts of the sentence.

2.1.1 Indefinite direct object

The following two sentences only differ by the position of *wieder* in relation to the direct object:

(2) a. Arnim hat wieder einen Gipfel bestiegen.
    Arnim has again a mountain top climbed.
  b. Arnim hat einen Gipfel wieder bestiegen.
    Arnim has a mountain top again climbed.

In 2b, it must be the same mountain top which he has reached for the second time (or, more precisely, not for the first time), whereas this is open in the case of 2a. It appears that not only the verb meaning but also the indefinite object is sensitive to the scope of *wieder*: in 2a, the "repeated part" is described by <einen Gipfel besteigen>, whereas in 2b, the repeated part is described by <besteigen>.

Three facts are remarkable in connection with this observation. First, we have the same difference when the lexical verb *besteig-* and hence the lexical information expressed by it PRECEDES the adverb *wieder*, as in 3:

(3) a. Arnim bestieg wieder einen Gipfel.
    Arnim climbed again a mountain top.
  b. Arnim bestieg einen Gipfel wieder.
    Arnim climbed a mountain top again.

Therefore, we cannot simply say that the scope of *wieder* goes to the right – at least not on the surface. This is only possible under the assumption that, on some other level of representation, the lexical part of the verb, as expressed by the lexical verb, follows *wieder*.

Second, the neat difference between 'repetitive' and 'restitutive' seems somehow blurred. Both sentences have a repetitive reading, the difference being in what is repeated. It is much less clear whether one of them, or even both, can also have a restitutive reading. In 1, such a reading is suggested when the lexical verb, rather than *wieder*, is stressed. If this is done in 2a, b or 3a, b it is still hard to image that only an earlier state of Arnim's being on a mountain top is restituted, even if we believe that he is born there; but it is perhaps not excluded.

Third, the behaviour of *wieder* in 2 and 3 matches the scope properties of other adverbials, such as *zweimal* (cf. Klein 1994, chapter 8):

(4) a. Arnim hat zweimal einen Gipfel erstiegen.
    Arnim has twice   a mountain top climbed.
  b. Arnim hat einen Gipfel zweimal erstiegen.
    Arnim has a mountain top twice climbed.

Here, too, it must be the same mountain top in 4b, whereas this need not be the case in 4a. Whatever makes *einen Gipfel* specific – this effect is blocked by the adverbial. Or to put it the other way around: SPECIFICITY IS RELATIVE TO THE ACTION WHICH IS SELECTIVELY DESCRIBED BY THE LEXICAL VERB, and if there are two such actions, then each one has a 'specific mountain top'.

2.1.2 Indefinite subject

The observations just stated are not confined to the direct object. They have also been noted for the subject, whose position is relatively free in German and hence may be before or after *wieder;* again, it was Fabricius-Hansen (1983: 100), who first pointed out this fact:

(5) a. Bald darauf ist wieder jemand gestorben.
Soon afterwards has again someone died.
b. Bald darauf ist jemand wieder gestorben.
Soon afterwards has someone again died.

In 5a, the repeated part is described by <someone die>, whereas in 5b, it is <die>, and this dying is applied to the same person. Therefore, 5b is distinctly odd, when *wieder* is stressed. Interestingly enough, it is marginally possible when *gestorben* is stressed, thus giving rise to a restitutive reading. Such a reading is much more plausible when the subject is definite:

(5) c. Bald darauf ist er wieder gestorben.
Soon afterwards has he again died.

This makes a perfect continuation to a preceding sentence such as: *Im folgenden Jahr wurde ihnen ein Junge geboren.* This points to the fact that restitutivity must somehow be related to 'maintenance of information' from an immediately preceding sentence, a point to which we will return shortly.

2.1.3 Adverbials

The contribution which the lexical verb makes to the meaning of the entire sentence can be further specified by adverbials. If the lexical verb describes an action, then an adverbial may describe the position of this action on the time line, its duration, or if it was done deliberately or not. Is this additional information in the scope of *wieder* or not – i.e., does it belong to the 'something' which is said not to obtain or occur for the first time? In contrast to English (cf. von Stechow 1995, section 10), this is very flexible in German:

(6) a. Frau Rubi hatte das Lädchen wieder für drei Tage geöffnet.
Missis Rubi had the shop again for three days opened.
b. Frau Rubi hatte das Lädchen für drei Tage wieder geöffnet.
Missis Rubi had the shop for three days again opened.

In both cases, the adverbial indicates the duration of the resultant state, not of the action. In 6b, nothing is said about the duration of an earlier state at which the shop was open, whereas in 6a, the preferred understanding is that this earlier state lasted three days, as well; it MUST have this reading if *wieder* carries main stress.

(7) a. Arnim hatte das Axalphorn wieder am letzten Donnerstag bestiegen.
    Arnim had the Axalphorn again   last Thursday   climbed-on.
   b. Arnim hatte das Axalphorn am letzten Donnerstag wieder bestiegen.
    Arnim had the Axalphorn last Thursday   again climbed-on.

In 7b, it is completely open when Arnim had climbed on the Axalphorn before; the positional adverbial only indicates the time at which he had achieved it again. Sentence 7a, by contrast, sounds somewhat odd, unless *am letzten Donnerstag* does not refer to a fixed day (a 'p-definite day' in the terminology of Klein 1994), for example if it is meant to refer to the last Thursday in the month. Hence, it appears that in 7a, the contribution of the adverbial belongs to the repeated part.

All adverbials considered so far provide temporal information. But we observe the same effect for non-temporal adverbials:

(8) a. Arnim hat Frau Rubi wieder ungern verlassen.
    Arnim has Missis Rubi again (?)   left.
   b. Arnim hat Frau Rubi ungern wieder verlassen.
    Arnim has Missis Rubi (?)   again left.

In 8a, he must have left her at least once before, and furthermore, it is said that he didn't like to do this in either case. Sentence 8b, by contrast, can have a repetitive and a restitutive reading, where the latter one is a bit marginal. In both cases, the adverbial *ungern* only applies to his present leaving her – hence, it is not in the scope of *wieder*.

2.1.4 Summing up

Most of these observations are not new. But it seems worthwhile to explicitly note four conclusions to be drawn from them.
A. If the repetitive-restitutive ambiguity is due to differences in the scope of *wieder*, then it is only a borderline phenomenon of the scope variation which this adverbial has.
B. As a rule, elements which follow *wieder* are in its scope, and elements which precede it are not. But there are exceptions; if, for example, the lexical verb is

amalgamated with the finite part of the verb and, as a consequence, precedes *wieder*, then the contribution of this verb is in the scope of *wieder*.
C. Somehow, the availability of a restitutive reading seems to be connected to (a) which information is maintained from the preceding utterance, and (b) to the amount of lexical material found in the scope of *wieder*.
D. Some of the scopal properties of *wieder* are also found in other adverbials.

We shall return to these four conclusions below.

2.2 Similar effects with atelic verbs

Initially, the repetitive-restitutive ambiguity was only stated for verbs whose lexical meaning expresses a change of state. Such verbs are often called "transformative", "resultative", or "telic" – this being the term chosen above. In Vendler's familiar classification, the ambiguity applies to achievements and accomplishments. It was again Fabricius-Hansen (1983, 1995) who pointed out a number of related effects for other verb types.

2.2.1 Counterdirectional verbs

The first case noted by Fabricius-Hansen concerns verbs such as *to fall-to rise, to come-to go*, and similar ones, which, in a way, express opposing directions (in what follows, intonational prominence is marked by boldface):

(9) a. Die Aktien sind **wieder** gefallen.
       The shares have again fallen.
    b. Die Aktien sind wieder **gefallen**.
       The shares have again fallen.

In 9a, the shares must have fallen before. This may have happened a while ago; but the most natural reading is that they continued their fall, for example if they first fell from 5600 to 5400 and then from 5400 to 3754. Other than with telic verbs, there is no lexically defined resultant state; the 'repetition' simply goes into the same direction. In 9b, by contrast, no earlier movement into this direction is required; it is appropriate when the shares first rose up to a certain level and then fell: the direction is reverted, whence the term counterdirectional. This does not preclude, of course, that at some earlier time, the shares may have fallen; but nothing to this effect is required.

A second, even more perplexing case are static expressions. Consider the following examples:

(10) a. Im folgenden Herbst waren sie wieder auf der **Axalp**.
   In the next   fall   were they again on the Axalp.
 b. Im folgenden Herbst waren sie **wieder** auf der Axalp.
   In the next   fall   were they again on the Axalp.

In both cases, it is required that they were on the Axalp before. But 10a, in contrast to 10b, requires a change from not being on the Axalp in the preceding fall to being on the Axalp in the next fall. In a way, therefore, the contrast between 10a and 10b corresponds to the difference between restitutive and repetitive readings in example 1 *Er hatte ihren Namen wieder vergessen*, where either only the state of not-knowing is repeated, or the change from knowing to not-knowing. Fabricius-Hansen (1983: 100) concludes that the difference cannot be only due to the semantical complexity of the predicate.

2.2.2 A complication

But the case is more complex than has been assumed in the literature. Sentence 10b is distinctly odd, when their stay on the Axalp is NOT preceded by an interval at which they are NOT on the Axalp. If this were the case, a different adverbial has to be chosen, such as *noch* or *immer noch*:

(10) c. Im nächsten Herbst waren sie **immer** noch auf der Axalp.
   In the next   fall   were they still   on the Axalp.

The constellations described by 10a-c are as follows (t <YXZ> is a time span t at which XYZ obtains, t_i immediately precedes t_j):

(10)'	a.	t_i <they not	be on the Axalp>
		t_j <they	be on the Axalp>
	b.	t_i <they not	be on the Axalp>
		t_j <they	be on the Axalp>
	c.	t_i <they	be on the Axalp>
		t_j <they	be on the Axalp>

In other words, 'not for the first time' appears to exclude mere continuation of a situation; it must, obviously, be possible to talk about a first time, a second time, and so on. The problem is the fact that 10b no less than 10a requires a transition from not-being on the Axalp to being on the Axalp. But if 10a as well as 10b require that there be some interval earlier than tj at which they are on the Axalp – what, then, is the difference between 10a and 10b?

The crucial difference is whether they also were on the Axalp in the preceding fall – or, more generally speaking, AT THE TIME TALKED ABOUT BEFORE. What is at issue, is not the interval which immediately precedes the event time, but the preceding 'topic time', as I shall say. This preceding topic time is not explicitly specified in the utterance itself; it is given in context, usually in the immediately preceding utterance, and it contrasts to the time about which 10 itself says something – *im folgenden Herbst*. If the initial adverbial in 10 were *im Jahre 1982*, then the topic time of the preceding utterance might be, for example, *im Jahre 1979*. Let us call the topic time of the utterance itself TT_a, and the topic time of the preceding utterance TT_{a-1}, respectively. Then, we can describe the difference between 10a and 10b as follows. In 10a, they must not have been on the Axalp at TT_{a-1}, whereas in 10b, they must have been on the Axalp at TT_{a-1}, as well. In both cases, they must be on the Axalp at TT_a itself, and moreover, there must be a time TT_x earlier than TT_a, at which they are at the Axalp, as well. It is open, however, whether TT_x is identical to T_{a-1} or not.

All of this becomes clearer as soon as the topic time of the preceding utterance is made explicit, as in 11:

(11) a. Im Herbst 1980 waren sie in Riva Faraldi. Im folgenden Herbst waren sie wieder auf der **Axalp.**
In the fall of 1980 were they in Riva Faraldi. In the next fall were they again on the Axalp.
b. Im Herbst 1980 waren sie auf der Axalp. Im folgenden Herbst waren sie **wieder** auf der Axalp.
In the fall of 1980 were they on the Axalp. In the next fall were they again on the Axalp.

At this point, we begin to suspect the reason for the difference in intonation: it must have to do with what is maintained from the preceding sentence. We will postpone this point, however, for a moment and briefly look at another example:

(12) a. Die nächste Tagung war wieder in **Rom.**
The next workshop was again in Rom.

b. Die nächste Tagung war **wieder** in Rom.
   The next workshop was again in Rom.

The difference is much the same as in 10, except that in 12, the topic time is not explicitly indicated by an adverbial in initial position. In both cases, there must have been a meeting in Rome before. But this, of course, is not the meeting to which the subject of 12a, b refers: *die nächste Tagung*. It is not plausible to assume that the next meeting already had taken place once before. What must have taken place is an earlier meeting in a series of meetings, and *die nächste Tagung* relates to the last meeting in this series which was mentioned immediately before. Again, this is best made clear by embedding it into context:

(13) a. Die dritte Tagung war in München. Die nächste Tagung war wieder in **Rom.**
   The third workshop was in München. The following workshop was again in Rom.
   b. Die dritte Tagung war in Rom. Die nächste Tagung war **wieder** in Rom.
   The third workshop was in Rom. The following workshop was again in Rom.

In 11 as well as in 13, we have a 'topic shift'. But whereas in 11, this shift only involves the time talked about, it also involves the subject in 13. Part of the lexical information of *die nächste Tagung* is maintained from the preceding utterance: *die ... Tagung*, whereas another part is shifted: *nächste*; it is this latter part which carries contrastive accent. There is also a shift in the topic time; but unlike in 11, this shift is not made explicit. So far, 13a and 13b are identical. They differ in what else is shifted or maintained. In 13a, the reference to the spatial predicate <in Rom> is shifted, whereas in 13b, it is maintained from the preceding utterance. Therefore, it is destressed in 13b but not in 13a. We shall come back to this point below, but first draw a short intermediate conclusion.

2.2.3 Summing up

Two major conclusions can be drawn from these observations:
A. There are two – not mutually exclusive – reasons why in a part of sentence with *wieder,* something is felt to be 'repeated': It can be maintained from the previous utterance, and is thus indicated as 'not for the first time', or this repetition is brought in by the meaning contribution of *wieder*, this contribution being 'and not for the first time'. This is immediately reflected in

intonation, because maintained information is (normally) destressed. Note that both reasons may apply at the same time: something which is in the scope of *wieder* may be maintained from the preceding utterance (and then it is destressed, thus giving prominence to *wieder* itself).

B. What matters, is not so much the temporal relation between events themselves but the order in which these events are described in the unfolding discourse.

In the next section, we will first address point B; it will naturally lead us to point A.

3 Order of mention and order of events

> Wieder mal ist es so weit ...
> Degenhardt

3.1 Atemporal situations

The complications discussed so far do not affect a general point made in the first section: the meaning contribution of *wieder* is always 'and this not for the first time'. But what if it does not make sense to speak of a first and a second time because the situation at issue obtains forever? Being a prime number is a permanent property. If something is a prime number at some time t, then it is also a prime number at any other time. Hence, the three facts *Seven is a prime number. Thirty one is a prime number. Ninety one is a prime number* are not temporally ordered. They all apply at the same time – namely forever. There may be a temporal order, however, in the way in which these facts are STATED in ongoing discourse. Suppose that some student has to determine which natural number is a prime number. Then, it might be perfectly natural to say:

(14) a. Neunzehn ist wieder eine **Primzahl**.
      Nineteen is again a prime number.
  b. Neunzehn ist **wieder** eine Primzahl.
      Nineteen is again a prime number.

Sentence 14a is natural in a sequence such as ... *Siebzehn ist eine Primzahl, achtzehn ist keine Primzahl, neunzehn ist wieder eine Primzahl.* In such a context, 14b, i.a. with stress on *wieder*, would be distinctly odd. But it is perfectly natural when the list under consideration is different. Suppose the poor pupil is given the list in the following order: 14, 99, 11, 13, 16, 23, 19. This list gives the **topics** he has to say something about, and it fixes the **order** in which he has to say it. As a consequence, it also defines the topic shifts. In this case, the sequence of utterances which answers the underlying question would be *Vierzehn ist keine Primzahl,..., sechzehn ist keine Primzahl, dreiundzwanzig ist eine Primzahl, neunzehn ist wieder eine Primzahl.* In this case, *wieder* can be stressed. The reason is that there is a shift in the topic talked about, but not in the property assigned to this topic. What can be stressed is therefore not this property *be a prime number* BUT THE FACT THAT THIS IS NOT THE FIRST CASE MENTIONED SO FAR WITH THIS PROPERTY (thirteen also had (!) it); therefore, the word *wieder* carries main stress, rather than *be a prime number*.

In the case of prime numbers and other atemporal properties, there is no temporal sequence on the 'fact level' – a number is either a prime number or not, and this at any time. But these atemporal facts may be ASSERTED in varying order. There is a temporal sequence on the discourse level, and it is this order which is relevant here. In particular, such an assertion may maintain parts of a 'preceding' assertion, and this is immediately reflected in intonation.

3.2 Other text types

In the preceding section, I had chosen examples which do not allow for a temporal order of events because the event itself is atemporal. One might consider this case to be exceptional; but there are many texts that do not lend themselves to a temporal order, although the facts described are not atemporal. Take, for example, the description of a completely static scenery, say on a picture. In such a text, it is easily possible to say:

(15) Gleich daneben steht wieder eine Eiche.
      Right next to it stands again an oak.

Depending on the preceding utterance, different stress patterns are possible. An oak's standing on a particular place is usually a long-term property, but it is not atemporal, such as being a prime number. Still, 15 does not mean that this is not the first time that an oak – or this oak – is standing there. It means that it is not the first time during the construction of the entire text that a situation is characterised as having the properties <an oak stand at some place>.

Whenever a speaker sets out so solve a complex verbal task – for example in answer to questions such as *What happened yesterday to you? What is on the picture? How do I get from here to Frau Rubi? Which number on the following list is a prime number* –, then he (or she) has to perform a whole series of subtasks.

In particular, he must decide which bits of information from his underlying knowledge base are to be transformed into a sentence ('selection'), and since not everything can be said at the same time, the speaker has do decide in which order to arrange the resulting sentences ('linearization'). The task of linearization is considerably simplified if the underlying knowledge base involves an inherent temporal order. This is, for example, the case of a narrative, in which the information bits are 'subevents' of a complex event, or in the case of a baking recipe, in which case the information bits are actions to be performed in a certain order. Then, linearization regularly follows a principle which is sometimes called 'principle of chronological order' (PCO); in ancient rhetoric, it was referred to as the interdiction of a *hysteron proteron*:

(16) PCO: Unless marked otherwise, order of mention corresponds to order of events.

This means that the individual situations are 'mentioned' in the order in which they occurred, or should be performed.

The speaker's task is much more complicated if there is no such inherent temporal sequence in the knowledge base. One solution is to impose such a temporal order. In route directions, for example, the underlying knowledge base is spatially, rather than temporally, structured. But the speaker presents this information in form of an imaginary wandering through this space, that is, in form of a sequence of actions. These actions, in turn, have a temporal order which then underlies the speaker's order of mention in constructing the entire text. In picture descriptions, very often a 'gaze tour' serves this function. The bits of information presented in the individual sentences are spatial (*Daneben steht wieder eine Eiche*); but they are presented in the order in which the speaker scans the picture.

There is no such natural 'temporal projection' of underlying knowledge, if the question to be answered is, for example *Why is the Axalphorn more dangerous to climb on than the Rothorn?*, Then, it is much less obvious how the speaker should solve the linearisation problem. In the case of the prime numbers, as in example 14 discussed above, the speaker might work through a list, and if no such list is externally given, he might follow the 'natural order' 1, 2, 3,.... This order in itself is not temporal, but it provides a bases for the (temporal!) order in which the individual sentences of the entire text follow each other.

In all of these cases, *wieder* can be used in a sentence, when an earlier sentence describes a situation with properties that are similar in relevant aspects. It does not matter whether these situations themselves exhibit a temporal order or not. If, as is typically the case in narratives, the order of mention reflects the order of events, then there is also a temporal precedence of the situation itself, which is said to not occur for the first time. But this is just a special case that, for whichever reason, enjoys a special preference among linguists.

4 The meaning contribution of *wieder*

> Das Feuchte wird trocken, das Trockene wieder feucht.
> *Herakleitos*

In section 1, we assumed that *wieder* regularly makes one meaning contribution to the entire meaning of the sentence in which it occurs: *and this not for the first time*. The discussion of sections 2 and 3 has not falsified this idea; but it has to be made more precise in at least three respects.

(a) The feature 'not for the first time' does not relate to the 'fact level' but to the 'discourse level', i.e., to the temporal order in which the facts are asserted in ongoing discourse. There need not be a real temporal precedence of a situation to some other situation, although this is not excluded, of course; very often, both types of order coincide.

(b) Second, the 'this' is normally not the full situation described by the sentence in which *wieder* occurs (the 'topic situation'). It must be a related situation which shares some properties with the topic situation – the properties which are in the scope of *wieder*. In the default case, these are the properties described by that part of the sentence that follows *wieder*.

(c) Another important factor of text construction may intervene – the mechanism of 'referential movement' (Klein and von Stutterheim 1987), i.e., the way in which information is freshly introduced in the *wieder*-sentence or maintained from a previous sentence. The details of this mechanism are complicated. In straightforward cases, however – and only these are considered here -, maintained information is destressed, whereas non-maintained information is not. As a consequence, information in the *wieder*-sentence may be 'not for the first time' because it is in the scope of *wieder*, and is thus marked to be not for the first time, or because it is maintained from a previous sentence, or both.

A simple illustration will help. Suppose a sentence has the form X-*wieder*-Y, where X is the part which precedes *wieder*, and Y is the part which follows *wieder*. Then, an earlier sentence must describe a situation which also has the properties described by Y. This, and only this, is the meaning constritution of *wieder*. It may now be that the immediately preceding sentence provides this information. Then, the Y-properties are maintained and, as a consequence, destressed, as in the sequence *X1 auf der Axalp. X2* **wieder** *auf der Axalp*. But it may also be that there is a shift with respect to Y, and then, Y is stressed, as in *X1 in Riva Faraldi. X2 wieder auf der **Axalp***. The X-part, by contrast, is not in the scope of wieder. But it also takes part in referential movement, i.e., it may be maintained or shifted. In the sequence *Im Jahre 1979 waren sie auf der Axalp. Im nächsten Herbst waren sie wieder auf der Axalp.*, the 'topic time' is shifted, and everything else is maintained. Complications arise when X (and similarly Y) is composed such that parts of are maintained whereas other parts are new; these complications may lead to very complex patterns of referential movement. But they have nothing to do with the functioning of *wieder* in particular.

5 Repetitive and restitutive readings reconsidered

fan ferd ich dich fiedersehn
Jandl

Under the analysis of *wieder* just discussed, its scope is highly variable. It must include the information provided by the lexical verb (even if, due to some morphosyntactical operation, this verb stem happens to precede *wieder*). It may also include many other components of the sentence (see the examples in section 2.1). Can this variability also go into the other direction, i.e., can the scope of *wieder* also be narrowed down to only parts of the information provided by the lexical verb? We shall address this question first from a more general point of view and then turn to the specific issue of the repetitive-restitutive distinction.

5.1 Inherent temporal structure, descriptive properties and BECOME

Do morphosyntactial operations always treat lexical units as impermeable entities, or do they have access, albeit limited perhaps, to their inner structure? The lexical entities at issue here are verbs (including copula constructions). The notion that a verb can be lexically decomposed is very old. It underlies all attempts in traditional and structural word semantics (see, e.g., Lyons 1977). This does not mean, however, that these components, or at least some of them, might be 'visible' to morphosyntactical operations. This idea came first up in Generative Semantics, where the tree representing a sentence such as *Cain killed Abel* not only contained lexical items and syntactic categories but also abstract predicates such as CAUSE, BECOME and similar ones, which would allow us to give to this sentence as structure such as [Cain CAUSE [Abel [BECOME be dead]]]. The idea was violently attacked from various sides, but resumed and elaborated by various semanticists, such as Dowty (1979) or Jackendoff (1991). We shall not follow up this discussion here but only consider the role of 'lexical decomposition' for the analysis of *wieder*.

In its original form, the repetitive-restitutive ambiguity was confined to those verbs which are called 'telic', 'resultative', 'transformative', or verbs of 'achievement' and 'accomplishment'. The crucial feature of these verbs is the fact that they somehow involve a distinct change-of-state, and in the repetitive reading of *wieder*, the entire change must be repeated, whereas in the restitutive reading, only the resultant state is said to be restored. In lexical decomposition, it is assumed that the lexical content of the verb stem contains an operator, mostly called BECOME or CHANGE, which accounts for this change-of-state. As a rule, more such operators are found in lexical decomposition, for example CAUSE, DO or ACT; but since this is of secondary importance to our present concern, I will only consider the change-operator. The presence of such an operator offers a straightforward way to account for the repetitive-restitutive ambiguity of *wieder* (with respect to telic verbs): *wieder* may have the change-operator in its scope, and then, the 'entire event' is repeated; or *wieder* has scope over only the part after the change-operator, and then, only the resultant state is repeated, i.e., restituted. This idea was first suggested by McCawley (1973) and then elaborated and considerably refined by authors such as Dowty (1979) for *again* and by von Stechow (1995, 1996) for *wieder*. But independent of the varying forms in which it was implemented, this type of decomposition faces two major problems.

The first of these problems is straightforward: the analysis does not work if there is no change-operator in the verb and hence no scope variation relative to it. Therefore, it may function in the case of telic verbs; but it is hard to see how it can account for the other cases discussed in sections 2 and 3, in particular for static predicates. The second problem has to do with the notion of a change-operator itself. It stems from the fact that this notion confounds two interrelated but in principle independent features of verb meaning. These are its TEMPORAL STRUCTURE, i.e., intervals and subintervals and the temporal relations between them, and its DESCRIPTIVE PROPERTIES, such as being open or being on the Axalp. Compare, for example, the two sentences *Arnim slept* and *Arnim woke up*. In the first case, a descriptive property ('asleep') is assigned to Arnim at some time t_i; morphological marking indicates that this time t_i is (normally) in the past. In the second case, two distinct properties are assigned to Arnim; first, say at t_j, he must be asleep, and then, say at t_k, he is not asleep; again (!), morphological marking indicates that both times are (normally) in the past. Hence, the lexical content of the verb *to wake up* comprises two temporal variables, t_j and t_k, which are sequentially ordered and which are associated with different descriptive properties. In this case, the properties 'asleep' and 'not asleep' are mutually exclusive, a constellation which is perfectly well covered by the notion of a change-operator, such as BECOME.

But it is also imaginable that a verb stem comprises two time variables with less divergent descriptive properties. Take, for example, *The shares fell* and *The shares rose*. For the first sentence to be true, it is necessary that at some interval t_k, the shares are 'lower' on some scale than at some earlier interval t_j. For the second sentence to be true, the shares must be 'lower' at the first interval t_j than at the second interval t_k. Verbs of this sort (Fabricius-Hansen's counterdirectionals, cf. section 2.2.1) are not 'telic' or 'resultative'. The familiar Vendler tests identify them as activities, rather than as accomplishments or achievements. I am not sure whether they should be described by a change-operator; surely, such an operator would be different from the conventional BECOME.

Is it possible that the lexical content of a verb provides two time variables with identical descriptive properties? At first, this idea sounds odd. But compare the two sentences *Arnim was on the Axalp* and *Arnim remained on the Axalp*. They both assign a 'static' spatial property to Arnim; but somehow, the second sentence gives the impression that Arnim was there at some time tj and then, at some later time t_k, he could have gone but hasn't. The difference is brought out more clearly if we add a modal verb, such as in *Arnim was allowed to be on the Axalp* and *Arnim was allowed to remain on the Axalp*. In the first case, the permission concerns his entire stay, whereas in the second case, it only concerns the second subinterval. If we replace *allowed* with *inclined*, the first construction *Arnim was inclined to be on the Axalp* becomes odd, whereas *Arnim was inclined to stay on the Axalp* is perfect. In order to describe the semantic effect of these morphosyntactical operations appropriately, we must assume that they have selective access to the verb content – to a subinterval which is descriptively not different from the first interval. The addition of constructions such as *be allowed* or *be inclined* is just one of several morphosyntactical processes which demonstrate this fact. Another, simpler case is negation. In *Arnim was not in Riva*, his entire stay there is denied; in *Arnim did not stay in Riva*, it is only denied that he was there at a second subinterval during which he could have been there.

The conclusion is therefore, that we must carefully distinguish whether a verb content has one, two or even more temporal variables, on the one hand, and the descriptive properties which characterise these subintervals, on the other. An operator such as BECOME conflates these notions. There is no change in verbs such as *to remain* or *to stay*, and similarly in German *bleiben*; still, there are two subintervals which are selectively accessible to morphosyntactical operations. There are also exceptions in the opposite direction. The situation described by *Arnim worked at his house* includes many quite heterogenous subintervals, hence many 'changes'. None of these subintervals, however, is selectively accessible to any morphosyntactical operation, such as negation, adverbial modification or addition of another verb stem. The linguist's decision whether a lexical verb involves one or more temporal variables can therefore not be based on mere semantic intuition; it must explore how the content of this verb stem can be modified by all sorts of morphosyntactical operations. With this in mind, let us now come back to the problem of the repetitive-restitutive ambiguity.

5.2 Access to one or to two time variables

In what follows, I will assume that 'telic' verbs as well as 'counterdirectionals' have two temporal variables, t_s and t_t. They only differ with respect to the properties assigned to t_i and t_j. What happens if *wieder* is applied to such a verb – does it affect both variables and the properties assigned to them, or can it selectively address one of them? I assume that the following principle applies:

(17) The particle *wieder* affects the time variable of a lexical verb in its scope. If there are two such variables, rather than one, *wieder* MUST affect the second one, and it CAN additionally affect the first one.

'Affect' means that the descriptive properties associated with the relevant time variable contribute to the 'this' in 'and this not for the first time'. This will become clear in a moment. Principle (17) immediately gives us the restitutive and the repetitive reading, respectively. Consider again example 1 from section 1, now in its two intonational variants:

(1) a. Er hatte ihren Namen **wieder** vergessen.
    He had her name again forgotten.
   b. Er hatte ihren Namen wieder **vergessen**.
    He had her name again forgotten.

Suppose the verb stem *vergess-* has two subintervals t_s and t_t with properties <x present in mind of y> and <x not present in mind of y>, respectively; the variable x relates to the object, y to the subject, t_s precedes t_t; I do not claim that this is an exhaustive analysis of the lexical content of *vergess-*; but it will suffice for present purposes. Then, either the sequence <x present in mind of y> and then <x not present in mind of y> is repeated, or only the subpart <x not present in mind of y>

is repeated. Other parts of the sentence, such as *er* or *ihren Namen* can still be maintained information; this, however, is not due to the effect of *wieder* but to the anaphorical character of these elements. As was argued above in section 2, the difference in intonation reflects maintenance or contrast of the verb itself. Why does this lead to a repetitive vs restitutive reading? In 18, the two constellations are made more explicit:

(18) a. Er hatte ihren Namen vergessen.   Dann hatte er ihn wieder vergessen.
        t_s<present> t_t<not present>   wieder [t_s<present> t_t<not present>]
    b. Er hatte ihren Namen gehört.   Dann hat er ihn wieder vergessen.
        t_s<not present> t_t<present> t_s<present> wieder [t_t<not present>]

In 18a, the first situation ends up with <not present in mind>, i.e., the target state of *vergess-* already obtains; it cannot be restored by what is described in the sequel; mere continuation would have to be expressed by *(immer) noch* rather than by *wieder*. The only interpretation which makes sense in this context is a complete repetition of the lexical verb, here in its participle form *vergessen*. Since it is completely repeated from the preceding utterance, it is destressed; as a consequence, the immediately preceding element *wieder* appears to be stressed in the 'repetitive' reading.

Consider now 18b. Here, the preceding situation ends with <present in mind>; here, it does not make sense to repeat the entire cycle from <present in mind> to <not present in mind>. All that can be repeated is the target state <not present in mind>, i.e., an earlier state is 'restituted'. The lexical verb *vergessen* is not maintained from the preceding utterance: there is a shift from *gehört* to *vergessen*. Hence, in the 'restitutive' reading, the verb itself is stressed. This explains the intonational mystery of the repetitive-restitutive ambiguity.

We have exactly the same constellation when the descriptive properties are gradually different, such as example 19:

(19) a. Die Aktien sind **wieder** gefallen.
        The shares have again fallen.
    b. Die Aktien sind wieder **gefallen**.
        The shares have again fallen.

Here, the asymmetry between the two intervals is best captured by assigning properties such as <lower> or <higher> to t_s or to t_t, where the comparative predicates <lower> and <higher> always relate to the other subinterval in the lexical content of the same verb. Hence, we have:

(19')   a. Gestern sind die Aktien gefallen.   Heute sind sie **wieder** gefallen.
              t_s<higher> t_t<lower>   wieder [t_s'<higher> $t_{t'}$<lower>]
        b. Gestern sind die Aktien gestiegen.   Heute sind sie wieder **gefallen**.
              t_s<lower> t_t<higher> t_s' <higher> wieder [$t_{t'}$<lower>]

Consider first 19a. At the end of the preceding day, the shares had reached a certain level. It is not said what their value is, but for the sentence to be true, this value must be lower than at t_s. Suppose the value is 220 at t_s and 200 at t_t. Under the non-trivial but normal assumption that the second sentence continues the description of the first sentence, the value at t_s' is 200, and therefore, the shares must be lower at t_t ', for example 180. Hence, the entire sequence from higher to lower is repeated. Consider now 19b. Here, the two verbs, *steig-* and *fall-*, are non-maintained information, they are in contrast (and hence marked by contrastive stress). Therefore, the value at t_s was lower than at t_t, say 170 vs 200. At t_s ' the value is 200, and at t_t ', it must be lower than that, say 170, 180 or 190. The precise value is not fixed, but in any event, it must be lower than at t_s' and thus lower than at t_t; as a consequence, the 'lower value' which obtained before is restituted. The intonational fact in both readings follow again from what is maintained from the preceding utterance and from what is shifted. In 19a – the 'repetitive' reading – the lexical verb is maintained and hence destressed. In 19b, it is shifted and hence not destressed.

6 Concluding remarks

> All das ist wieder nicht richtig ausgearbeitet.
> von Stechow

Under the analysis of *wieder* proposed here, this word is not ambiguous. The contribution which it makes to the meaning of the entire sentence is always the same: AND THIS NOT FOR THE FIRST TIME. What 'this' relates to, is provided by the sentence in which *wieder* occurs. The term 'not for first time' does not primarily relate to the temporal order of the situations themselves but to the order in which these situations are stated on ongoing discourse. In special text types, for example narrative texts, 'order of events' and 'order of mention' may be closely interconnected, and then, 'first time' relates to the order of events.

Variability in meaning does not come in because *wieder* is lexically ambiguous but because it can be inserted at different places in the sentence. As a consequence, the elements that are in its scope vary. As a rule, the scope of *wieder* includes all elements to its right. There are exceptions; thus, the lexical part of a verb may be fused with its finite part and then precede *wieder* but still be in its scope. A special situation may arise when only the lexical verb is in the scope of *wieder*. Then, its precise effect depends on whether the lexical content of this verb stem involves one or two time variables; the last one of these and the descriptive properties coupled with it must in any case be in the scope of *wieder*; another time variable may, but need not, be included. This is the source of the repetitive-restitutive ambiguity.

The particle *wieder* interacts with the mechanism of 'referential movement', i.e., the way in which information is freshly introduced or maintained from previous utterances in a text. Such an interaction is in no way specific to *wieder*. But it has the peculiar consequence that, if some information is marked as 'not for the first time', then this may be due to the fact that it is in the scope of *wieder*, or it may be due to the fact that it is 'maintained' from the preceding utterance; both possibilities may go together. This is clearly reflected in intonation: maintained information is (normally) de-accentuated. Under a repetitive reading, the entire verb is maintained from the preceding utterance and hence de-accentuated, leaving main stress on *wieder*. Under a restitutive reading, the verb is normally new with respect to the preceding utterance, and therefore, it is not de-accentuated.

While I believe that the analysis of *wieder* suggested here is correct, it is also clear that it needs refinement in several respects. This is most clear for the mechanism of referential movement and its consequences for intonation. As is well known from the literature, this mechanism is much more complex than what has been said above. It is easy to see, for example, that 'maintained information' need not necessarily be destressed; after all, it is possible to place contrastive stress on an anaphorical element, which by definition expresses maintained information. Or consider a question-answer sequence such as *Was the oak tree on the left or was it on the right? – It was on the right*. Then, *on the right* is no less maintained from the previous utterance than *was* or *it*; still, it must carry stress. In some cases, maintenance does not relate to the immediately preceding sentence but to an earlier one, especially if the text is partitioned into foreground sentences and background sentences; then, maintenance may jump over a background sentence (cf. Klein and von Stutterheim 1987). These problems are complex, and they may affect the interaction with *wieder*. But they also show up when no *wieder* is involved.

A second refinement concerns scope. It is likely that scope assignment is more complex than the simple rule 'scope of *wieder* goes to the right'; we already mentioned the fusion of finite and non-finite component of the verb, which places the finite verb into the 'wrong' position. Other exceptions in both directions are possible, as is the case with many other scope-bearing elements.

A third refinement has to do with the 'order of events'. As was argued in section 3, the notion 'not for the first time' is in the first place related to the temporal structure of discourse, rather than to the temporal order of the situations, that are described by the sentences which form the discourse. But often, there is also an 'earlier' and 'later' with respect to the reality which is depicted. According to the traditional principle stated in (16), order of events and order of mention are simply mapped onto each other ('principle of chronological order'). Normally, however, a sentence – even a simple sentence – involves not just one temporal variable, which is interpreted as 'the event time' but a whole structure of temporal intervals, including what has been called above the 'topic time'. The precise nature of this temporal structure is a vast field, and a simple rule such as 'order of mention corresponds to order of events' is therefore a gross simplification. A last point, somehow related to this one, concerns the inherent temporal structure of lexical entries. In section 4, it was said that a lexical item may contain two such intervals. Again, I think this is an oversimplification. As I have argued elsewhere (Klein 2000), there are good reasons to assume that these intervals are relative to the individual arguments of the verb. Hence, it would be more appropriate to speak of 'Argument-Time pairs'; the lexical content of a verb may provide several 'AT-variables'. If this is correct, it also has consequences for what precisely is in the scope of *wieder*, just as it has consequences for the scope properties of other adverbials.

All of these refinements are important, and they are anything but easy to achieve. But they are not specific to the functioning of *wieder*. They existed in the same way, if we didn't have this wondrous word in our language.

References

Dowty, David (1979). Word meaning and Montague Grammar. Dordrecht: Reidel.
Fabricius-Hansen, Cathrine (1980). Lexikalische Dekomposition, Bedeutungspostulate und wieder. Ein Beitrag zu einer Montague-Grammatik des Deutschen. In Dieter Kastovsky (ed.). Perspektiven der Lexikalischen Semantik. Bonn: Bouvier. 26–40.
Fabricius-Hansen, Cathrine (1983). Wieder ein *wieder*? Zur Semantik von *wieder*. Rainer Bäuerle, Christoph Schwarze und Arnim von Stechow (eds.). Meaning, Use and Interpretation. Berlin: de Gruyter. 97–120.
Fabricius-Hansen, Cathrine (1995). Wiedersehen mit *wieder*. Unpublished lecture notes.
Jackendoff, Ray (1991). Semantic Structures. Cambridge, Mass: MIT Press.
Harweg, Roland (1969). Zum textologischen Status von *wieder*. Orbis 18. 13–45.
Kamp, Hans and Rossdeutscher, Antje (1994). DRS-construction and lexically driven inference. Theoretical Linguistics 20. 166–235.
Klein, Wolfgang (1994). Time in Language. London: Routledge.

Klein, Wolfgang (2000). An Analysis of the German Perfekt. Language 76. 358–382.
Klein, Wolfgang and von Stutterheim, Christiane (1987). Quaestio und referentielle Bewegung in Erzählungen. Linguistische Berichte 109. 163–185.
Lyons, John (1977). Semantics. Cambridge: Cambridge University Press.
McCawley, James D (1973). Syntactic and logical arguments for semantic structure. In Osamu Farujimura (ed.). Three dimensions in linguistic theory. Tokyo: TEC Corporation. 259–376.
von Stechow, Arnim (1995). Lexical decomposition in syntax. In Urs Egli et al. (eds.). The lexicon in the organisation of language. Amsterdam: Benjamins. 81–118.
von Stechow, Arnim (1996). The Different Readings of *Wieder* 'Again': A Structural Account. Journal of Semantics 13. 87–138.

On the scope of negation[1]

> I shall henceforth not use the word *not*.
> Bertrand Russell

1 Introduction

All languages provide their speakers with the possibility to negate a sentence, for example by adding an affix to the verb, as in Japanese, by using a negative verb, as in Finnish, or by special particles such as *bu* or *mei* in Chinese, *not* in English, *ne...pas* in French or *nicht* in German; very often, a language combines several of these means (see Dahl 1979, Payne 1985, Bernini and Ramat 1996, Miestamo 2005, for typological comparisons). The most common device is particles. Their form and functioning vary considerably across languages and within a language; but four features are commonly held to be characteristic. First, they are syntactically optional, i.e., the sentence without the particle would also be syntactically complete. Second, they preserve the illocutionary role of the sentences, i.e., they do not turn an assertion into a question, or a question into a command. Third, they can be inserted at various places and under varying forms in the sentence.[2] German, the language under investigation here, is particularly flexible in that regard:

(1) a. Isa ist gestern zum ersten Mal nicht gekommen.
    Isa has yesterday for the first time not come.
 b. Isa ist gestern nicht zum ersten Mal gekommen.
    Isa has yesterday not for the first time come.

---

[1] This paper was originally written in 2006 and is first published here after substantial revision. Over the years, it was presented to a number of various audiences; I wish to thank the participants for useful discussions. I am also very grateful to Manfred Bierwisch, Christine Dimroth, Cathrine Fabricius-Hansen, Arnim von Stechow, Rosemary Tracy and Heide Wegener for helpful comments. They all should not be held responsible for my errors.

[2] There is, of course, a difference between (a) a *sentence* – i.e., an abstract object with a particular linguistic structure, (b) the *propositional content* (or *proposition*) expressed by such a sentence, – and (c) an *utterance* –, i.e., the event of uttering or understanding such a sentence on some occasion. In what follows, I shall often ignore this distinction, and simply speak of "sentences", as long as there is no major risk of misunderstanding.

https://doi.org/10.1515/9783110549119-011

c. Isa ist nicht gestern zum ersten Mal gekommen.
   Isa has not yesterday for the first time come.
d. Nicht Isa ist gestern zum ersten Mal gekommen.
   Not Isa has yesterday for the first time come.

There are some restrictions; thus, *nicht* cannot be placed immediately before the finite part of the verb, as in *Isa nicht ist ...*, and it cannot be placed after the non-finite part of the verb, as in *... gekommen nicht*. The particle *nicht* is often replaced with some other form, if the immediately following constituent is indefinite; the most common case is (inflected) *kein*, as in *Er hat keine zwei Bier getrunken* "He has not drunk two beers" instead of *Er hat nicht zwei Bier getrunken* (which is also possible); others include *niemand* for *nicht jemand* and *nichts* for *nicht etwas*.[3] Similar variations are observed in other languages with negative particles. In what follows, I shall often use the abbreviation NEG for the negation particle in its various variants.

The fourth common feature concerns their meaning. Ever since Aristotle, it has been assumed that the core function of NEG is to reverse the truth value of a (declarative) sentence:

> [Sentence] Negation in language is classically identified with the truth-functional operator ~, which switches the truth value 'true' into 'false' and vice versa. (Payne 1992, 75).

Thus, if 2a is true, 2b is false, and vice versa:

(2) a. Eva was at home.
    b. Eva was not at home.

This idea seems so obvious that it is hard to imagine how it could be wrong. Still, the vast literature on this issue has identified numerous problems which demonstrate that the 'truth reversal account' does not do full justice to the function of (sentential) negation in natural languages (Horn 2001 is the standard exposition; see also Jacobs 1991 for a careful discussion with particular reference to German).

---

[3] The exact conditions under which *nicht* is replaced by some other form are difficult to determine and not a subject of this paper. One important factor is surely that in a merged form, such as *kein*, the two components cannot be separately focused, as is possible in *Er hat NICHT ein Bier getrunken* vs. *Er hat nicht EIN Bier getrunken*. But there are other factors, as well. I should add that I do not believe that these forms are "negative quantifiers", in the sense that they only "negate" the quantified NP to which they belong syntactically.

In this paper, I will examine some substantial problems which, I believe, have not yet found sufficient attention, if any, and I will then propose a new analysis of NEG in German. This analysis is very simple and it solves a great deal of these problems, as well as some others discussed in the literature. It brings negation by *nicht* and its morphological counterparts in line with the functioning of so-called focus particles (König 1991), i.e., words such as *auch* 'also', *nur* 'only', *sogar* 'even' and similar ones, with which *nicht* shares many syntactic and semantic properties. The discussion is confined to German because the position of NEG in German is very flexible, because there is a comparatively transparent relation between this position and the semantical properties of NEG, and, of course, because it is the language I know best. The general idea and many of the specific observations transfer to other languages, for example English; but they are also non-trivial differences, some of which will be briefly touched upon.[4] For ease of exposition, I will sometimes use English examples, if they do not differ from German in crucial respects.

I have tried to keep the presentation as short and transparent as possible; this naturally means that many issues which are relevant in one way or the other are only briefly hinted at, or are not even referred to at all. I also avoided to couch the analysis in terms of one of the various specific syntactic or semantic frameworks that are now on the marked; this is not to belittle the merits of a such frameworks, but I wanted to state the analysis in such a way that it is accessible to any linguist who is interested in negation, independent of his or her theoretical orientation. Under this analysis the meaning contribution of NEG is the same in all its usages, and it is very simple. Many observations on the apparently complex behavior of NEG result from the way in which its meaning interacts with properties of (in this case) German sentence structure; but this is not the place to dig into the mysteries of German syntax. Similar considerations apply to the interaction of NEG with information structure, in particular with focus. In sections 5 and 6, I have tried to sketch my views on the interaction with syntactic structure and with focus. But obviously, this discussion does not exhaust the intricacies of this interaction.

---

4 English is much less flexible in the way in which the particle can be inserted into the clause. Moreover, this insertion often requires to separate finite and non-finite components of the verb: the former has to be realized by a special construction (*do*-support). I do not think, however, that this is crucial to the function of negation as such (see also footnote 7). See Welte (1978) for a useful discussion of differences between German and English negation.

2 Three problems

2.1 Topic consistency

In simple cases such as 2a, b, the truth reversal function of the negative particle seems beyond doubt.[5] But this impression is deceptive. In fact, truth value reversal only holds under specific additional assumptions, which are often not made explicit. In 2a, b, for instance, it must be assumed that THE TIME TALKED ABOUT, or the 'topic time', as I shall say, is the same. The tense marking *was* only says that the topic time is some interval in the past. Nothing in the linguistic structure of two sentences themselves ensures that this time is the same in 2a and 2b: it is just a tacit assumption, which may be reasonable on not, depending on the particular discourse context.

It must furthermore be ascertained that the object or person talked about is the same. This becomes apparent when the name *Eva* in 2a, b is replaced by an indefinite pronoun:

(3) a. Someone was at home.
    b. Someone was not at home.

Clearly, 3a and 3b do not exclude each other, even if the topic time is the same. In fact, it is almost certainly true that, if someone was at home at a certain time, it is also true that someone was not at home at that time. Truth reversal only applies when the "topic entity" – i.e., the object or person talked about – is the same in both cases.[6] Again, the linguistic structure in itself does not guarantee this in 3a, b. There are, of course, sentences which are incompatible with 3a, for example *Nobody was at home* or *No one was at home*. In these sentences, the negative element is inserted at a different position than in in 3b. The "incompatible counterpart" may also require other changes, as in German *Jemand war nicht zu Hause* vs. *Niemand war zu Hause*. It is an interesting issue to explain why this position of the negation or the use of a different form lead to exclusion. But this is not the primary task when we want to understand the function of negation. The linguist's task is not to find an incompatible sentence but to explain the effect which a negation has when inserted at a particular place in a particular structure.

---

[5] I do not share, though, in Noam Chomsky's view on some exceptions: "[...], everything has to be singular or plural, but not everything has to be a chair or not a chair." (Chomsky 2002, 111).
[6] Note that this also applies when a proper name such as *Eva* is used: after all, there are many Evas on the world; so, it must be assumed that positive and negative sentence are about the same Eva.

A third parameter that has to be kept constant may be the place talked about. Thus, 4a and 4b can well be true at the same time, when 4a relates to Riva and 4b to Bergen:

(4) a. It was raining.
    b. It was not raining.

We may push this to the extreme, when the two places which are understood but not made explicit are on different hemispheres. If 5a relates to Heidelberg and 5b to Sidney, then the positive sentence is TRUE if and only if the negative sentence is true:

(5) a. It was summer.
    b. It was not summer.[7]

A fourth topic parameter is the world talked about. Thus, Alexander can be a hero in a novel and a monster in real history. If the world talked about in 6a is the world of a novel, and the world talked about in 6b is reality, then 6a and 6b are mutually compatible:

(6) a. Alexander was admirable.
    b. Alexander was not admirable.

Assertions in natural language are always relative to situations talked about or, as I shall say, "topic situations".[8] Such a topic situation can be characterized by a number of parameters – a time, a place, a protagonist, a world, and maybe others. These parameters together with the context define restrictions on the assertion – the claim made only relates to this situation (or situations, if more than one are talked about). By asserting something, the speaker marks that, in his or her mind, a certain descriptive content, for example being at home or being admirable, applies to such a topic situation. The truth reversal function of negation operations within these constraints: positive and negative sentence must

---

[7] Here is a real-life example which illustrates the same point. At the end of the most popular sports program on German TV, the invited guest is usually asked to shoot at a small fake soccer goal. Six shots are allowed, but in more than thirty years, no one ever scored six times; three hits is a good result. Suppose someone says about yesterday's show: *Three times, Tulse scored*. Then, this sentence is true exactly *Three times, Tulse did not score.* is true.
[8] I use the word *situation* as an overall label for all sorts of events, processes, actions, states, etc.

apply to the same topic situation. I will call this requirement TOPIC CONSISTENCY. In many cases, topic consistency is tacitly assumed to be the case. But as the example above illustrate, it is by no means trivial.

The need to keep the topic situation constant has some interesting consequences when the sentence "speaks about itself", i.e., if the speaker assigns particular properties to the very sentence by which the assertion is made. These properties can relate to the form side of the sentence. Consider, for example, 7:

(7) a. The number of words in this sentence is not ten.

Sentence 7a is false. Thus, the non-negated sentence should be true:

(7) b. The number of words in this sentence is ten.

But again, this sentence is false. The reason is not paradoxical but straightforward: "this sentence" does not refer to the same sentence in both cases: there is no topic consistency. In 1a, "this sentence" refers to 1a, and in 1b, "this sentence" refers to 1b. Now, 1a and 1b differ in the number of words, and hence, it is possible that both of them are false. Exactly the same point can be made for 2a, b:

(8) a. This sentence contains no negation. [false]
    b. This sentence contains a negation.   [false]

Containing or not containing a negation belongs to the form properties of a sentence; but in contrast to a property such as the number of words, it has semantic repercussions; so, in a way it relates to a form property as well as to a meaning property of a sentence. This becomes clearer when the term "negation" is not used to refer to a lexical item but to the "assertion status" of the sentence:

(9) a. This sentence is no negation. [false]
    b. This sentence is a negation.   [false]

In all of these examples, the expression *this sentence* refers to different sentences in a and b, respectively. Therefore, the law of contradiction is not violated.
Consider now 10:

(10) a. This sentence is not true.
     b. This sentence is true.

Unlike in exx. 7 – 9, it is not easily visible whether 10a/b are true or false.[9] Let us assume that 10a is true. What follows from this for 10b? Nothing – just as from *This cup is not old*, nothing follows for *This cup is old*, if *this cup* does not refer to the same cup in both sentences. Clearly, the expression *this sentence* in 10a refers to a different sentence than the expression *this sentence* in 10b. What 10a says is "Sentence 10a is not true", and 10b says "Sentence 10b is true". This applies analogously if we do not talk about sentences but about the propositions which they express. In 10a, the proposition to which the sentence refers is [this proposition be not true]. In 10b, the proposition which the speaker marks as correct is [this proposition be true]. And no one can argue that these are the same.

This leads to an important observation: somehow, a declarative sentence with a negation expresses two assertions, rather than one: it says that according to the speaker, something is true, and that something is not true. But this "something" is not the same: what the speaker marks as true is the content of the entire sentence INCLUDING the negation, and what he marks as false is the sentence WITHOUT the negation. This is no problem as long as both sentences speak about the same entity, as in *Eva was cheerful* and *Eva was not cheerful* (under the assumption that Eva is the same person in both cases, and that the time talked about is the same, etc). But it becomes a problem when the negative sentence is "self-referential" – a quite misleading term. In this case, the two sentences – the sentence with the negation and the sentence without the negation – are made an issue, and these sentences are clearly different. Hence, there is no topic consistency.

2.2 Difference and mutual exclusion

How does NEG affect the meaning of an expression to which it is attached? Simple expressions such as the word *cheerful* as well as compound expressions such as the construction *have left Riva for the first time in three years* indicate certain descriptive properties, which stem from the conventional meaning of the lexical items, certain rules of composition, and also from contextual sources (as in the case of deictic or anaphoric expressions). If such an expression is preceded by *not*,

---

[9] Normally, the meaning of a sentence specifies the conditions under which it is true. But already for the positive sentence *This sentence is true.*, I would not know the conditions under which it is true, or not true. This is not a problem of so-called self-referential sentences in general; it is easy to see that *The number of words in this sentence is nine.* is true. Nor does it apply to more general forms of the "lyer", such as *I am always lying*. This sentence is false if at least one case can be found in which the speaker is not lying, and true otherwise.

then the resulting larger expression also expresses certain properties, for example the properties associated with *not cheerful* or the more complex properties associated with *not have left Riva for the first time in three years*. Intuitively, not much is said what these "*not*-properties" are: it is only said that they must be DIFFERENT from *cheerful*, or that they must be DIFFERENT from *have left Riva for the first time in three years*.[10] In the first case, it could be [green], [sad] or [at home], whatever [not cheerful] can be and whatever makes sense in the context. In the second case, the difference can relate to any part of the compound expression. Thus, it could be the property (the different part is marked by small capitals) [have SEEN Riva for the first time in three years] as well as [have left PONTEFRACT for the first time in three years], [have left Riva for the SECOND time in three years] or [have left Riva for the first time in FOUR years], to mention but a few of the possibilities.

Apparently, there is a close connection between a negation by *not* (or similar negative particles) and the notion of "different". So, one might conclude that the meaning contribution of NEG is just to create a "different property" – different from the one expressed by the construction to which NEG is applied; the more complex this construction, the more possibilities are there in which way the expression can differ in meaning.[11] Now, something may of course have some property P and a property which is "different from P". Thus, Eva can at the same time (and in the same world etc) be cheerful and at home.[12] We must therefore clearly distinguish between two different semantic features of NEG, which I will call "difference feature" and "exclusion feature", respectively.[13] The difference

---

10 This difference relates to a shift in meaning, the syntactic status is preserved. I do not mention this in the following.

11 Opinions may vary on what counts as "different". First, difference may be a matter of degree or quantity, as in *It was not warm, it was hot.* or *He did not eat an apple, he ate apples.* Second, it may be that a speaker, in a particular situation, considers, e.g., *to be cheerful* and *to be happy* or *to be Paris* and *to be the capital of France* as different, whereas other speakers do not, for whatever reason. Third, the difference may relate to the descriptive content but not to the entity referred to, as in *It was not the evening star, it was the morning star.* In many cases, peculiar usages of this type give rise to "metalinguistic negation" (cf section 7.3).

12 Under the present approach, the crucial entity is the "topic situation" – the situation about which something is said. Just as in the case of difference between properties (see preceding footnote), opinions may vary as to whether a particular situation can have a certain property together with some other properties. Thus, some people may say *Alexander was a hero and a mass murderer*, others may say *Alexander was not a hero, but a mass murderer* – depending on whether you think that one and the same person (at the same time, in the same world) may have both properties or not.

13 In many languages, including older German (Jäger 2005) and some German dialects, the negation is "distributed" over two forms, a phenomenon which is normally treated under the more

feature accounts for the effect of attaching NEG to a simple or complex expression and turning into an expression whose meaning is different; nothing is said about what exactly the difference is. The scope of NEG may vary: it can affect a whole proposition, but also a smaller part of it. The exclusion feature concerns the relation between two whole propositions and says that they are mutually exclusive under topic consistency, i.e., when asserted about the same situation. The exclusion feature is not scope-sensitive.

Before going on, it will be useful to introduce a few terminological conventions. A *sentence* is a linguistic structure, an *utterance* is the realization of such a structure on some occasion. The descriptive content of a sentence is called its *propositional content* or briefly *proposition*; each of these notions deserves detailed discussion, which I will spare here. The descriptive content of some expression xyz will be noted as [xyz], in the case of a sentence in its non-finite form and with the verb in final position. Thus, the proposition expressed by 10a is [this sentence not true be], and the proposition expressed by 10b is [this sentence true be]. The descriptive content of the expression *Eva Charlotte* is [Eva Charlotte], which is the property to be named Eva Charlotte. Note that different positions of the negation express different propositions. Thus, the counterparts of exx. 1a-d are:

(12) a. [Isa gestern zum ersten Mal nicht gekommen sein]
 b. [Isa gestern nicht zum ersten Mal gekommen sein]
 c. [Isa nicht gestern zum ersten Mal gekommen sein]
 d. [Nicht Isa gestern zum ersten Mal gekommen sein]

In all of these cases, the negation splits the whole proposition into two parts, which I will label α and ω, respectively. So, a proposition with a negation has the form $\alpha \text{NEG} \omega$. If NEG is omitted, we also have a proposition, $\alpha\omega$, which has four "negative counterparts", all of which are incompatible with $\alpha\omega$. But they do not mean the same, because the scope of the negation varies. For a native speaker, these differences are palpable; but they are not easy to pin down. In the next section, we will have a closer look to these differences.

Note that an utterance such as *Isa ist gestern zum ersten Mal nicht gekommen* (= 1a) in a way involves two propositions, $\alpha \text{NEG} \omega$ and $\alpha\omega$. But only the former is directly asserted when the sentence is uttered: the verb is made finite, it shows up

---

general phenomenon of "negative concord" (Zeijlstra 2004). It would be interesting to examine whether one of the elements is used to express the exclusion feature, whereas the other mark those elements whose meaning must be different.

in second position, there is a final intonational fall. Similarly, the sentence, when uttered, carries certain markers on how it is embedded in the flow of discourse. Thus, it may be that some part is de-stressed, because it is expresses maintained information; then, the last part which is not de-stressed is perceived as focus. We will come back to these point in sections 3 and 6.

2.3 Scope sensitivity

Compare 13a and 13b:

(13) a. Gestern ist Isa zum ersten Mal nicht gekommen.
  [gestern Isa zum ersten Mal nicht gekommen sein]
  Yesterday has Isa for the first time not come.
(13) a. Gestern ist Isa zum ersten Mal nicht gekommen.
  [gestern Isa zum ersten Mal nicht gekommen sein]
  Yesterday has Isa not for the first time come.

Both are false, if she has not come yesterday for the first time. But what is the intuitive difference between them? A speaker who utters 13a is committed to the claim that
(a) Isa has not come yesterday, and
(b) the situation talked about is the first in a series at which Isa could have come but did not.

The following simple diagram illustrates what must be the case for 13a to be true; $s_1, s_2, ..., s_{gestern}$ is a series of potential occasions at which she could have come:

$$\begin{array}{lllll} & s_1 & s_2 & .... & s_{gestern} \\ \text{13a:} & \text{come} & \text{come} & \text{come} & \text{not come} \end{array}$$

If Isa came yesterday, then 13a is false, and if she came yesterday, but also on s_1 or s_2 or ..., then 13a is false, as well.

The claims to which the speaker is committed when asserting 13b are very different. It may well be that she indeed has come yesterday – but not for the first time. For, for many speakers, this is the first reading that comes to mind. Consider the following constellations:

$$\begin{array}{lllll} & s_1 & s_2 & .... & s_{gestern} \\ \text{13b}_1\text{:} & \text{come} & \text{not come} & \text{come} & \text{come} \end{array}$$

	come	come	come	come
13b₂:	come	come	come	come
13b₃:	come	come	not come	come

In all of them, Isa has come yesterday, but not for the first time: only that constituent is negated. But 13b is also compatible with constellations in which she has not come at all yesterday, for example:

	S_1	S_2	....	$S_{gestern}$
13b₄:	not come	not come	not come	not come
13b₅:	not come	come	not come	not come

These readings are less obvious, and not all speakers of German like them at first sight.[14] But take, for instance, a discourse in which someone claimed *Gestern ist Isa zum ersten Mal gekommen*. Then, someone may object: *Falsch, gestern ist sie nicht zum ersten Mal gekommen. Sie war noch nie hier, weder gestern noch sonst wann.* 'Wrong, she did not come yesterday for the first time. She has never been here, neither yesterday not at any other time' or *Falsch, gestern ist sie nicht zum ersten Mal gekommen. Sie war zwar letzte Woche hier, aber definitiv nicht gestern, sondern heute morgen.* 'Wrong, she did not come yesterday for the first time. She was here last week, but definitely not yesterday but this morning'.

In 13b, ω is *zum ersten Mal gekommen*; in readings 13₁₋₃, the difference created by NEG concerns *zum ersten Mal* 'for the first time' – i.e., the initial part of ω. In the less intuitive readings 13b₄₋₅, the difference concerns *gekommen*, i.e., the last part of ω. Apparently, speakers do not like it when the difference concerns a later, rather than the initial, part of the expression in the scope of NEG. But as readings 13₄,₅ show, this preference is not a structural constraint – it is rather a kind of maxim: "Don't make the scope larger than necessary!"[15]

---

[14] When I mentioned these readings in talks, hardly anyboldy agreed; but with few exceptions, all agreed after some discussion.

[15] The preference is only observed if *nicht* COULD be placed later, as is the case here ("..., *zum ersten Mal nicht gekommen*"). There are also expressions in which the negation cannot be placed between two constituents, for example combinations of modal and lexical verbs, as in ... *kommen nicht musste* 'come not had-to', which is distinctly odd; instead, NEG must be preposed, as in ... *nicht kommen musste*. In this case the difference can equally well concern the lexical verb *kommen* and the modal verb *musste*. This strong tie between modal verb and lexical verb also prevents the insertion of elements other than NEG, for example temporal or spatial adverbials. But this is one of many arcana of German syntax, and it has nothing to do with negation in particular (the interaction between modal verbs and negation is extensively discussed in Ehrich 2001, Penka and von Stechow 2001).

The position of NEG partitions the proposition in different ways; we can illustrate this as in 14 (omitting the tense marking in α):

(14)   α   NEG   ω:
   13a: gestern, Isa, zum ersten Mal   nicht   gekommen
   13b: gestern, Isa   nicht   zum ersten Mal gekommen

How does the different partitioning explain the intuitive differences discussed above? Before turning to this question, a few words about the notion of "assertion" are in order.

3 Assertion, secondary assertion and assertion-marking

Every human language allows its speakers to assert that a proposition expressed by a sentence is true. Sentences are selective descriptions of situations. Since one and the same descriptive content can relate to different situations, it must also be clear which situation is talked about. So, the speaker must indicate that some situation talked about has certain descriptive properties. Typically, there is a canonical way to achieve this. In Indo-european languages, the proposition is normally provided by some 'assertable construction', which consists minimally of a verb and an appropriate filling of its arguments; various optional elements, for example temporal adverbials or modal particles, can be added; the "assertion-marking" results from the interaction between the position of finiteness, which is regularly encoded by a verbal element,[16] and intonation. Consider, for example, the content described by [a unicorn in the garden be]. When the corresponding finite form, such as *was*, is placed in initial position, the resulting English construction *Was a unicorn in the garden* does not indicate an assertion: finiteness must be expressed in second position. But this does not suffice: if the utterance does not end with an intonational fall, it does not mark assertion, either.[17]

---

[16] In English, finiteness can be entirely separated from the lexical content of the verb by "*do*-support". Auxiliaries play a similar function. It is not accidental that in many languages, finiteness bears a particular relation to negation; *do*-support illustrates this (see also Dahl 1979 for other examples); but we shall not try to explore this connection here; see, however, Klein 2006 on the interaction between finiteness and assertion.
[17] There are a number of additional factors which may come into play here, for example, in a subordinate clause, the type of subordination or whether the matrix verb is factive. These conditions are complicated and not an issue of this paper.

As was discussed in section 2.1, it must also be clear which situation – or situations – the descriptive properties are meant to apply to. No one can answer the question *Was it raining?* without knowing what this topic situation is. The necessary information comes from context; but part of it can be provided by elements of the sentence itself; in that case, they must be marked as "topic information". Languages differ in the way in which they indicate what in a sentence belongs to its topic part and what not. Position, for example, is an important means to this end; but there may be others, for example special particles and intonation.[18]

Truth-functional semantics does not deal with assertions, in the sense in which this notion is used here: assertions indicate the conviction of a speaker, be it weak or strong, true or false. Truth-functional semantics deals with the conditions under which some proposition, as expressed by a particular construction, is true. Thus, the proposition of the sentence *1492 is a prime number* is false, independent of whether someone asserts this or not. We may, of course, ask the question of whether a speaker is RIGHT when indicating that he or she takes a particular proposition to be true. But this is not a question of truth-functional semantics. We can also expect, or at least hope, that speakers are consistent in their statements, that is, do not mark a sentence and its negative counterpart as true (under topic consistency). But again, this is a pragmatic requirement on reasonable communication.

In English or German, finiteness placement and intonation are not the only devices to indicate the speaker's opinion that something is true. For instance, if a speaker adds the particle *wieder* 'again' to a sentence, then he marks that, in his view, some earlier situation meets some of the descriptive properties of this sentence, as well; what exactly these descriptive properties are, depends primarily on the position of this particle. In *Hans hat wieder ein Fenster aufgemacht* 'Hans has again a window opened', the relevant properties are described by *ein Fenster aufmachen*, and these properties are assigned to an earlier (non-adjacent) situation. In *Hans hat ein Fenster wieder aufgemacht*, the relevant properties are only *aufmachen*, and these – or even only a part of those, namely the resultant state of *aufmachen*[19] – are assigned to an earlier situation. Similarly, if a speaker adds *nur* 'only' to a sentence, then she marks her conviction that no other (contextually

---

18 Opinions vary on what is considered to be the topic component of a German sentence. Often, the position before the finite part (Vorfeld) is considered to be a topic position. Other authors assume that also parts after the Finitum can serve, or even preferredly serve, this function (Frey 2004). These are complicated issues, and they do not matter for the central argument of this paper.
19 This leads to various readings of *wieder*, often discussed in the literature; see, for example, Fabricius-Hansen 1995, von Stechow 1996, Klein 2001.

relevant) descriptive properties apply to the same topic situation; again, what these descriptive properties are depends on where *nur* is inserted. In *In Prag hat nur Mick gesungen* 'In Prag has only Mick sung', the topic situation is some situation "in Prag at some time in the past", and the crucial property is Mick's singing; the particle *nur* indicates that, according to the speaker, this topic situation has no other contextually relevant property. In *In Prag hat Mick nur gesungen* 'In Prag has Mick only sung', the topic situation also involves Mick (as an agent), and the crucial property is just singing; here, the addition of *nur* indicates that this situation has no other contextually relevant property, such as, for example, playing guitar.[20]

Such particles as well as NEG function as 'secondary assertion' markers. They assert the truth of some "other" but related proposition. In principle, the functioning is independent of the 'canonical marking' by finiteness and intonation; *wieder* or *nur* serve the same purpose, no matter whether the construction in which they are included is an assertion itself. This independence, however, does not preclude close interactions between the two types of assertion marking.

The notion of secondary assertion marking is closely related to the familiar notion of "presupposition". There are various reasons why I avoid this notion here. First, it is now used in so many senses that it has lost almost any clarity (see, for example, the discussion in Seuren 1993, Beaver 1997, or Atlas 2004). Second, it seems very natural to assume that languages provide their speakers with devices to indicate that the proposition expressed in some sentence is true, as well as with devices to indicate that some other but related proposition is true. Third, the notion of a secondary assertion allows a uniform treatment of *nicht* and other particles such as *wieder, nur, auch* and similar ones. It may well be possible to develop an analysis under which *wieder, nur* or *auch* trigger certain presuppositions, which vary with the position of these particles (see, for example, Kamp and Rossdeutscher 1994). But I fail to see that the particle *nicht* triggers presuppositions in any comparable way. In particular, it is not obvious how the differences between 13a, b, as described in the previous section, could be accounted for by different presuppositions.

Thus, I believe that negative particles such as *not, (ne) ... pas* or *nicht* function very much like "focus particles": they indicate a secondary assertion. In the next section, this idea will be spelled out. In sections 5 and 6, we shall consider some complications.

---

[20] Note that English is much more restricted in the way in which such a particle can be inserted in the initial structure.

4 A first analysis

Compare the following three sentences, uttered on some occasion:

(15) a. Isa ist gestern gekommen.
 b. Gestern ist Isa gekommen.
 c. Ist Isa gestern gekommen?

They express the same the same proposition [Isa gestern gekommen sein]. 13a, b show the marks of a "primary" assertion (here in written form). They indicate the speaker's conviction that some situation has those descriptive properties. What is that topic situation? This information may come from context, but it may also be that part of the descriptive content is used to identify the topic situation. As said above (cf footnote 18), it is not clear how this works in German. For the sake of this exposition, I will assume that word order alone is responsible and that only the part before the finite verb serves that function; I will also ignore the role of tense marking. So, 13a says that according to the speaker, some situation with Isa as an agent has properties [gestern gekommen sein] and thus altogether properties [Isa gestern gekommen sein]; 13b says that some situation which was yesterday has properties [Isa gekommen sein] and thus altogether properties [Isa gestern gekommen sein]. 13c does not carry the marks of an assertion, it only raises the issue whether some situation has properties [Isa gestern gekommen sein]. I will not discuss the question of whether topic marking is similar here, since it immediately leads us into a jungle and it is not relevant for our present purpose.[21] Here, the point is only that in 13c, there is no primary assertion.

What happens now when NEG is inserted at some place, as in 16:

(16) a. Isa ist gestern nicht gekommen.
 b. Gestern ist Isa nicht gekommen.
 c. Ist Isa gestern nicht gekommen?

Here, the proposition is [Isa gestern nicht gekommen sein] and this is what is asserted with the usual marks for an *Isa*-situation in 16 and a *gestern*-situation in

---

[21] A question always defines the topic situation of the answer. But there is good reason to assume the question itself may have varying topic situations. Thus, *Ist Isa gestern gekommen?* and *Ist gestern Isa gekommen?* are clearly different. The former is normally answered by *Ja, Isa ist gestern gekommen;* an answer like *Ja, gestern ist Isa gekommen.* is also possible, but has the flavor of a sort of "re-topicalisation". A jungle.

16b. Then, the scope part ω of NEG, here [gekommen sein] is changed to some different property than [gekommen sein]. In what follows, I will designate any property different from ω by ω*. This is the difference function of NEG. Moreover, it is asserted that according to the speaker, αω and αω* are mutually exclusive. This is the "secondary assertion", which corresponds to the exclusion feature of NEG. In 16b, there is exactly the same secondary assertion – but there is no primary assertion. So, we may sum up the effect of NEG in German as follows:

(17) Meaning contribution of NEG:
1. NEG partitions the proposition in a scope part ω and a non-scope part α.
2. NEG modifies ω to ω*, where ω* is some property that is different from ω.
3. It asserts that αω and αω* are mutually exclusive.[22]

So, informally, NEG says that if the situation talked about has a property different from what it is in the scope of NEG, then this is incompatible with its having the property in its scope. It does not say whether the topic situation has any of those properties, unless the utterance itself marks it.

This analysis of NEG accounts both for the traditional function of NEG, i.e., truth reversal, as well as for the scope effects connected to the particular place at which the NEG is inserted. As to the latter point, we have assumed so far that the scope of NEG goes "strictly to the right", i.e., ω is simply the part which follows NEG; moreover, we have assumed that it always goes "until the end of the sentence". Both assumptions, made here for expository purposes, are too simple. I believe, though, that they indeed represent the default case in German, and that exceptions follow from some general properties of German syntax, for example by what is often described as "subject raising". We now turn to two important refinements.

5 Some refinements

5.1 Jespersen's surprise and the "canonical position" of sentence negation

In his seminal study *Negation in English and other languages* (1917: 86ss), Otto Jespersen stated that the position of the "negative" (element) in languages such

---

[22] "Incompatible", as used here, does not mean "logically incompatible"; it expresses the opinion of the speaker on whether the situation described by α in fact can have the property ω as well as the property ω*.

as German or English is often "wrong". If the entire sentence is negated, it should appear in front of the entire sentence. Now, this argument makes only sense under the additional assumption that a linguistic element only affects linguistic material which follows it. This assumption need not be true. In fact, examples such as 1–4 above show that the exclusion function is completely independent of the position of the negation. This is even true if the particle is inserted within a noun phrase, for example in 18a:

(18) a. Eva hat einen nicht sehr langen Brief gelesen.
          Eva has a not very long letter read.

Here, the element *nicht* within the noun phrase *einen nicht sehr langen Brief* also excludes that the sentence without the particle, i.e., *Eva hat einen sehr langen Brief gelesen*, is true (under topic consistency!): the truth reversal effect has nothing to do with the scope of the particle.[23] And on the other hand, there are good reasons why a negation can show up in different positions: it enables the speaker not only to mark that the sentence without the particle is wrong, but also to mark which particular other statements are true. Thus, these "illogical" languages are perfectly reasonable.

These considerations also suggest two other conclusions. First, there is little reason to assume that in languages like German, NEG has a "canonical position", as is either explicitly stated or tacitly assumed in most literature on the issue. This assumption may be justified in languages whose word order is more rigid. But in German (or, for example, in Dutch), it can show up in many places, in each of which it indicates that the sentence without the particle is false, and each of which has a different scope.[24] Second, the familiar difference between "sentence negation" and "constituent negation" (or "phrasal negation") is replaced by a more flexible notion of varying negation scopes. In a way, *nicht* is always sentential, because it always reverses the truth value of the entire sentence. But this

---

23 The truth reversal effect even applies to so-called lexical negation, as expressed by English *a-* or German *un-*. The assertion *It was an atypical comment* excludes that *It was a typical comment* be true.
24 The negative element can show up in many but surely not in all positions. The exact constraints are not easily determined. Some of very clear; thus, NEG cannot appear after the nonfinite verb, as in **Hans ist gekommen nicht*. But in other cases, the constraint requires special features of the element which follows NEG; thus, a pronoun immediately after NEG sounds awkward unless it is stressed, as in *Hans hat nicht IHN angerufen*. This is often seen as a constraint on NEG; as such, it would be very idiosyncratic. It would be much more tempting to derive this and similar constraints as restrictions on what can be marked as "different".

concerns only one of its two functions, and it does not preclude that NEG affects selected parts of the sentence in different ways.

5.2 In and out of scope

The difference feature of NEG varies with scope. In the exposition so far, it was assumed that this part, ω, is simply defined by order: it is the part of the entire constituent structure which follows NEG, the remainder being the non-scope part α. This was a simplification. I take it to be the default; but there are many complications, which are related to the morphosyntactic properties of German. Ideally, these exceptions should follow from general rules of German syntax, rather than be idiosyncratic properties of negation. In what follows, we shall briefly discuss four complications of this type.

The first is exemplified by 17a above: intuitively, the ω-part is confined to *sehr langen*, rather than to extend to the end of the sentence: *sehr langen Brief gelesen*. This is nicely illustrated by the fact that this part can be marked as parenthetical, as in 18b, but not as in 18c:

(19) b. Eva hat einen – nicht sehr langen – Brief gelesen.
    c. *Eva hat einen – nicht sehr langen Brief – gelesen.

So, what 18a marks is that she read a letter, and that this letter was either long, but then not very long, or it was not long at all: the properties are either different with respect to *sehr*, or they are different with respect to *lang*, or they are different with respect to both. In other words, α has two components, interrupted by ω: (*Er hat einen*)$_{α1}$ NEG (*sehr langen*)$_ω$ (*Brief gelesen*)$_{α2}$. The end of the NP is a sort of right barrier to the scope of NEG. This is in line with the general fact that other NP-internal elements do not look beyond the NP, either; so, the restriction is not specific to negation. But this only concerns NPs. Is there a general way to derive ω from the structure of the sentence and the position of NEG?

There is no straightforward answer. An easy way out would be to refer to familiar syntactic notions such as c-command.[25] The scope of *not* is then identified with the c-commanded domain of *not*. The problem with this and similar tree-geometrical definitions is that they heavily depend on the structural assumptions which underlie the construction of the tree: it is not god-given that a particular

---

[25] A node X c-commands a node Y exactly if the first branching node which dominates X also dominates Y. There are variants, but they do not affect the argument.

node dominates another node. The tree must be constructed such that, next to other criteria, it reflects the scope of certain elements. Thus, we would be forced to stipulate a whole series of potential *not*-nodes just in order to cover its various scopes as reflected in examples 1-4 from section1, let alone cases such as 18a.

The second problem is illustrated by the following slight variants of 13a, b, in which the German perfect is replaced by the (almost synonymous) preterite. The perfect consists of a finite component, *ist*, which is in second position, and a non-finite, lexical component, *gekommen*, which is in final position. In the preterite, finite and non-finite component of the verb are merged into one form, which takes the position of the finite, rather than of the lexical, component. This has nothing to do with negation in particular; it is a standard feature of German morphosyntax. As a result, both components of the verb precede NEG:

(20) a. Gestern kam sie zum ersten Mal nicht.
Yesterday came she for the first time not.
b. Gestern kam sie nicht zum ersten Mal.
Yesterday came she not for the first time.

This fact does not affect the status of the lexical content of *komm-*; it still belongs to ω: 20a functions exactly as 13a, and 20b functions exactly as 13b. In other words, the difference between ω and ω* may concern *komm-* or *zum ersten Mal* or both, although the EXPRESSION of [komm-] precedes the negation. There are various ways to describe this morphosyntactic operation; we may stipulate, for example, that the finite and non-finite component of the verb are merged "in final position" and then "raised" from this position into the second position while leaving a trace which is in the scope of NEG; or that the phonological features of the verb are moved, whereas the semantic features are left behind. These are highly theory-specific issues of implementation within a particular framework. The crucial point is that there are morphosynactic rules which do not affect the scope situation, and this type of "verb movement" is an example for such a rule.

The third example also relates to a syntactic property of German which is often described in terms of a movement rule. It concerns the position in front of the finite element in declarative clauses. This position ("Vorfeld") is to be filled by just one major constituent; this can be the subject, as in 1–4, but also an adverbial, as in 19 or 20, or an object, a case not exemplified here. It is often assumed that this Vorfeld constituent is moved there from a position behind the finite element (here, too, the term "move" should not be overrated). This is a general property of German syntax, which has nothing to do with NEG in particular. But it has dramatic consequences for NEG. Consider the following example, in which the Vorfeld is filled by a quantified subject:

(21) a. Alle Kinder waren nicht in der Schule.
     All children were not at school.

This sentence has two readings which can be paraphrased as follows:

(21) b. For all children, it was true that they were not at school.
     c. Not for all children, it was true that they were at school.

In contrast to the corresponding English sentence, 21b is the preferred reading in German. This preference can be reversed by a particular intonation: with a rise in the second syllable in *alle* and no fall until *nicht*, reading 21c is strongly preferred. Thus, this "intonational topicalisation" (Jacobs 1982, 1997) invites a "scope reversal": it means what is normally expressed in German by 21d:

(21) d. Nicht alle Kinder waren in der Schule.
     Not all children were at school.

One way to analyze this ambiguity is to assume that 21a has two semantic representations, for example on some level of "logical form". In one of those, NEG is "moved" from its surface position to the position in front of the quantified noun phrase. Such an analysis is not desirable, since it destroys the idea that a negation in a particular position has a fixed scope; this renders a satisfactory account of scope properties extremely difficult. We are forced to assume that there is a clash between "syntactic scope" and "semantic scope", a clash which must be remedied, for example, by the assumption of movements that are specific to negation and not needed for independent reasons.

It seems much more natural to assume that the ambiguity results from a constraint that is needed for independent reasons, such as the familiar constraint that there is precisely one major constituent in the Vorfeld. This constituent is "moved" there from a position which is either before or after NEG, and thus in or out of its scope. Compare the following sentences, in which the Vorfeld is filled by expletive *es*; this is possible in both cases, although 22a is perhaps not a paragon of an elegant sentence:[26]

(22) a. Es waren alle Kinder nicht in der Schule.
     b. Es waren nicht alle Kinder in der Schule.

---

[26] German is much less restricted in this regard than English. In many cases, it even tolerates definite noun phrases after expletive *es*, where this would be clearly excluded with English *there*: *Es war endlich der Frühling gekommen* ("there has finally come the spring").

In these cases, the topic component of 22a, b is only referred to by lexically empty *es* and characterised by the topic time encoded in the tense marking of the finite element. The two cases differ by the position of the subject *alle Kinder* in relation to NEG. In 22a, α is *es waren alle Kinder*, and ω is *in der Schule sein*. Thus, the assertion is about a situation with properties "about all children, at some time in the past", and NEG indicates the speaker's conviction that this topic situation has a property different from "be at school" (and, of course, this is incompatible with the possibility that it has the properties "be at school"). Hence, we should have only one reading, and so we do.

In 22b, the subject follows NEG and thus belongs to the ω-part of the sentence. Therefore, the topic situation is only vaguely narrowed down by the tense marking – it must be some time in the past, and any further identification is left to contextual information. In this case, it is not said of all children that they have the property "different from be at school". The difference required by *nicht* can relate to any element of ω, i.e., *alle Kinder in der Schule (sein)*, preferredly the first constitutent *alle Kinder*. Exactly this is the meaning of 22b.

As any other major constituent, the subject *alle Kinder* can be "raised" to the Vorfeld, resulting in a 21a (possibly supported by intonational marking ("I-topicalisation").[27] This movement can operate from 22a (ignoring the expletive *es*), where *alle Kinder* is not in the scope of NEG, as well as from 22b, where it is in the scope of NEG. The natural result are two readings of 22a. This operation is "scope-preserving", i.e., if the topicalised constituent did not belong to ω before, it does not belong to ω afterwards, and if it did belong to ω before, it does so afterwards.[28]

This syntactic operation is no idiosyncrasy of NEG: it is just the way in which German "fills" the Vorfeld, or more generally speaking, how a proposition is turned into a concrete finite sentence uttered in a particular context with

---

[27] It is an interesting issue why movement from within NEG seems to require this intonational support; if the Vorfeld is ambiguous with respect to topic status, as I am inclined to assume, then a particular intonation might be a device to resolve the ambiguity. But this leads us into the very general problem of how topic-hood is marked in German, an issue by far to difficult to be pursued here.

[28] Note, incidentally, that we also get the correct reading of *Nicht alle Kinder waren in der Schule* under the assumption that in 22b, *nicht alle Kinder* (rather than only *alle Kinder*) can be moved into initial position. This sentence is true when at least one child was not in school. One might wonder why in some cases, only *alle Kinder* is moved in initial position and sometimes *nicht alle Kinder*. Again, this is not an issue of NEG in particular but of the way in which the topic-comment structure of an utterance is marked in German.

reference to a specific situation. The scope ambiguity of 19a follows automatically; it has nothing to do with NEG in particular. We should expect a similar ambiguity for constituents other than the subject in this position and other than quantified expressions. This is indeed the case. Thus, 23a can have reading of 23b and of 23c:

(23) a. Deshalb hat Hans nicht angerufen.
Therefore has Hans not called.
b. Hans hat deshalb nicht angerufen.
c. Hans hat nicht deshalb angerufen.

As in 23a, the latter interpretation usually requires additional intonational topic marking (rise in the second syllable of *deshalb*, fall in *nicht*). Under the first reading, 23a means "This is the reason, why he has not called". Under the second reading, it means as: "He has called, but not for that reason."

Let me conclude this section on what is in and what is out of the scope of negation with a fourth phenomenon. It concerns a perplexing ambiguity, which has often been discussed in the literature (see, e.g., Partee 1993 and the literature quoted there). The following sentence has a natural and a "stupid" reading:

(23) a. Olga geht nicht in die Kirche, weil sie fromm ist.
Olga does not go to church, because she is pious.

It can mean that her being pious is the reason for not going to church, and it can mean that it is not the reason for her going to church. Consider now sentences 22b, c, which correspond to these two readings, but in which the reason is indicated by an adverbial, rather than by a clause:

(24) b. Olga geht nicht aus Frömmigkeit zur Kirche.
Olga goes not   for piety   to church.
c. Olga geht aus Frömmigkeit nicht zur Kirche.
Olga goes for piety not to church.

We naturally get the two readings of 24a under the assumption that the causal clause is "moved to the right" either from within NEG or from without NEG. Again, such a movement has nothing to do with negation in particular; it is also found when the sentence contains no negation at all. But precisely this general property of German syntax automatically accounts for this otherwise perplexing ambiguity.

6 Focus effects

It has often been noted that the semantic contribution of NEG not only varies with its position but also with the intonation of the sentence to which it belongs. In particular, its function seems to be closely connected to the (prosodic) focus, that is, the element which is particularly highlighted (see, for example, Hajičova 1973, Koktova 1987, and specifically for German Jacobs 1982). Some examples illustrate this (the focus is marked by small caps):

(25) a. Gestern ist Isa nicht ZUM ERSTEN MAL gekommen.
     b. Gestern ist Isa nicht zum ersten Mal GEKOMMEN.

Depending on which elements are focused, different parts seem to be "negated". In 25a, we get the impression that the speaker wants so say something like "Yesterday, Isa has come, and this was not for the first time." In 25b, the speaker rather wants to say: "Isa has done something for the first time yesterday, but it was not coming." This suggests that it is this focused constituent which is the "true scope" of NEG. This and similar observations have given rise to the "association with focus" analysis first proposed by Jacobs for focus particles and for negation, and then elaborated by a number of authors (see Lang 2002, section 6.4, for a survey). This analysis has led to a number of important observations and insights; but it also raises a few problems.

First, what is the difference between "intonational scope" and "positional scope", as illustrated by the contrast between neutral 13a and 23b, repeated here for ease of comparison?

(26) a. Gestern ist Isa zum ersten Mal nicht gekommen.
     b. Gestern ist Isa nicht zum ersten Mal GEKOMMEN.

In 26a, *gekommen* is singled out by the position of NEG; in 26b, *gekommen* is singled out by intonational marking. Now, these two sentences do not mean the same. For instance, 26b is easily compatible with the idea that she was absent on earlier occasions as well, whereas this is excluded in 26a (cf. the analysis of this sentence in section 2.3). Hence, we would have two "NEG scopes" in the same simple sentence.

Second, an association with focus is problematic when the negation itself carries main stress. This is possible, for instance, when *Gestern ist sie zum ersten Mal gekommen* was asserted before and is now denied:

(27) a. Gestern ist sie zum ersten Mal NICHT gekommen.
     b. Gestern ist sie NICHT zum ersten Mal gekommen.

It does not make much sense to say that the "negated part" is only the negation itself. Note that the meanings of 27a and 27b are distinctly different, although the negation is "focused" in either case – and this difference is exactly the one described for 13a, b above.

Third, the main accent can also be on a constituent which is not, or need not be, in the syntactic scope of NEG. Consider the following intonational variants of the scope contrast:

(28) a. GESTERN ist sie zum ersten Mal nicht gekommen.
 b. GESTERN ist sie nicht zum ersten Mal gekommen.
 c. Sie ist GESTERN zum ersten Mal nicht gekommen.
 d. Sie ist GESTERN nicht zum ersten Mal gekommen.

In none of these sentences do we get the impression that *gestern* is somehow "negated". So, the constituent which carries the main accent may somehow interact with the negation, but it need not. It would not help to stipulate that the focused constituent must be "in the scope of NEG", because the scope effects noted in connection with 13a, b (see section 2.3) surface in much the same way if there is no focused constituent in the scope of NEG, as in 28a–d.

It will be useful to compare the various focus variants of a sentence, in which the negation is in the same position. Sentences 27a, 28a, 13a, repeated here for ease of comparison, all require that she did not come yesterday and that yesterday is the first time at which this was not the case:

(30) a. Gestern ist sie zum ersten Mal NICHT gekommen.
 b. GESTERN ist sie zum ersten Mal nicht gekommen.
 c. Gestern ist sie zum ersten Mal nicht gekommen.

These sentences only differ in the way in which they are integrated into the flow of discourse. Thus, 30a requires an assumption according to which *Gestern ist sie zum ersten Mal gekommen* is taken to be true, and 30a contradicts or corrects this assumption. In the most obvious case, this assumption was explicitly stated before; but it may also be "somewhere in the air". In any case, the speaker must see some reason to correct this explicit or implicit claim. Consider now 30b. Here, the "discourse state" is different: it has already been settled that she had not come for the first time, i.e., *ist sie zum ersten Mal nicht gekommen* is considered to be maintained information. All that remains to be decided is the precise time at which it was the case, and this time is specified by *gestern*. Sentence 30c, finally, is neutral in that regard: no information, in whatever part of the sentence, is marked as maintained by de-stressing.

Let us now look at sentences 25b, 26b and 14b, repeated here, in which *zum ersten Mal* is in the scope of NEG:

(31) a. Gestern ist sie NICHT zum ersten Mal gekommen.
 b. GESTERN ist sie nicht zum ersten Mal gekommen.
 c. Gestern ist sie nicht zum ersten Mal gekommen.

Here, the topic situation is described as being yesterday. But it need not be a "first time situation", as in 30a–c. In all three cases, ω^* is "different from *zum ersten Mal gekommen*"; this difference may be with respect to *zum ersten Mal*, with respect to *gekommen* (not preferred), or with respect to both. So far, the three sentences in 31 do not differ. They vary, however, in the way in which the sentence is integrated into the flow of discourse, and this variation is exactly parallel to the one described for 30 above.

These observations suggest that intonational focus has nothing to do with the negation and how it works. It only reflects the way in which information is "updated" in discourse, i.e., maintained or revised. In this update, negative statements play a particular role insofar as they often deny something that is tacitly assumed or even explicitly stated in preceding discourse (Geurts 1998). But the way in which the update is organized is a mechanism in its own right; it is in principle completely independent of the way in which negation works. The particle *auch* 'also' functions in much the same way, except that it does not rule out something; it rather marks that the sentence which contains it is compatible with some other contextually relevant claim. This and similar particles, including NEG, relate the proposition which contains them to some other proposition. This other proposition can be, and often is, something that has been said in the preceding discourse. It can also be something that is considered to be some contextually relevant element of shared knowledge.

Not all sentences contain such particles, and languages provide their speakers with many other means to integrate a sentence into the flow of discourse – devices which operate in the same way for sentences with and without such particles. For example, it is possible to mark which part of the sentence contains material that is assumed to be given. One way to do this is to de-stress this material, with the result that the last element that is not de-stressed is prosodically highlighted and therefore it is perceived as focused. This has nothing to do with negation in particular – it is just a common way to mark information as marked as maintained or not. If some non-given information falls into the ω-component of a negative sentence, then this part is perceived as the element of ω which is "up for revision" from the preceding state of knowledge, and thus that part of ω which is responsible for the "difference feature" of negation. In other words, some information may be "different" (a) because it is not maintained and therefore not de-stressed, or (b) because it is in the scope of NEG. These two sources of difference marking must not be confused.

Let us consider a final set of examples, in which ω is [zum ersten Mal gekommen sein] and in which the intonational focus varies:

(32) a. Gestern ist sie nicht ZUM ERSTEN MAL gekommen.
 b. Gestern ist sie nicht zum ersten Mal GEKOMMEN.
 c. GESTERN ist sie nicht zum ersten Mal gekommen.

In one way or the other, ω* must differ from ω = [zum ersten Mal gekommen sein]; but it is not said in which one. In 32a, *zum ersten Mal* is highlighted and *gekommen* is de-stressed, and thus the sentence is set against a discourse background characterized by "different from *the first time*". In 32b, *gekommen*, is highlighted, and thus, the assertion made 32b is set against a background characterized by "different from *gekommen*". In 32c, *nicht zum ersten Mal gekommen*, i.e., NEGω*, is maintained and thus de-stressed, and only *gestern* is "new" and perceived as focused. In all of these cases, the role of *nicht* is exactly the same: the meaning of *zum ersten Mal gekommen* is turned into a different meaning, and due to the exclusion feature, αω is false.

Thus, it is the normal integration of a sentence into discourse by highlighting and de-stressing certain elements which leads in this special case to the idea that just the highlighted element is "negated". There is no reason to assume that the meaning contribution of NEG depends on focus: it is always the same, regardless of the information structure of the sentence.

7 A look at two residual problems

The rich literature on negation in general and in German in particular has brought numerous problems to the fore (see Lang 2002 for a good survey). In what follows, I will very briefly address two problems which have played an important role in this research and, by way of illustration, sketch how they fare under the present approach.

7.1 Replacive negation

It has often been assumed that there is a special case of negation that licenses or even requires a special kind of continuation (see Jacobs 1991, Lang 2002, section 5.1, Horn 2001).

(33) a. Nicht Isa hat gestern zum ersten Mal gesungen.
    Not Isa has yesterday for the first time sung.
  b. Isa hat gestern zum ersten Mal nicht gesu/ngen, ... [with a final rise].
    Isa has yesterday for the first time not sung.

In these and similar cases, German strongly invites a continuation with the conjunction *sondern*, as in 34a, b:

(34) a. ..., sondern Hans (hat gestern zum ersten Mal gesungen).
  b. ..., sondern (zum ersten Mal) getanzt.

(The part in brackets can be elided). But there is no structural necessity to add such a continuation, which would result from a special type of negation.[29] Thus, 33a can easily be continued by *Das hatte ich zwar auch gedacht. Aber es war falsch. Es war Hans, der gestern zum ersten Mal gesungen hat* 'That's what I thought myself. But it was wrong. It was Hans who sang for the first time yesterday'. In 33b, it is not the NEG placement but the missing final fall which invites a continuation. In other words, there is no structurally defined "replacive negation" in German. But sometimes, there is strong pragmatic pressure to specify what exactly the difference between ω and ω* is, rather than just saying that they differ. This is typically the case when the sentence with NEG is used to correct some earlier assumption (or explicit statement), and it says that this assumption is false because ω is different is some particular respect, as specified in the continuation; note that here the phonological highlighting is not caused by a final de-stressing. This, I believe, is the most important pragmatic source of so-called "replacive negation" in German. But there may well be other conditions under which such a pragmatic pressure arises.

7.2 Metalinguistic negation

Negative particles are sometimes used in cases in which, in a way, not the content of something is marked as false but the way in which this content is put into words: the negation is "metalinguistic" (Horn 1985). A good example is Lt. Calley's famous statement at court about the people he had killed (quoted after Lang 2002, section 5.2):

---

[29] Whereas the use of *sondern* requires that it is preceded by a negation: *sondern* is not mandatory; but if it is used, it must be licensed in this way.

(35) a. They weren't people, Sir, they were the enemy.

Under the present analysis, *not* marks that, in the eyes of Lt. Calley, they had a property different from *be people*, here *be the enemy*, and that having that latter property is not compatible with their being people. Not everybody may share in the opinion that being the enemy and being people exclude each other, not even temporarily – but this is not an issue of how NEG functions. In German as in many other languages, metalinguistic negation is neither structurally nor lexically a special kind of negation – it rather concerns the reasons why someone considers two properties as mutually exclusive and thus feels entitled to express a negation.

8 Concluding remarks

The analysis of negation that is proposed here is based on two core ideas:
(a) Assertions are relative to the situation talked about ("topic situation"), and truth reversal only works under topic consistency, i.e., an assertion and its negative counterpart must have the same topic situation;
(b) NEG has two features in its meaning, a "difference feature", which is scope-sensitive, and an "exclusion feature", which is not scope-sensitive.

This analysis is very simple, it gives a uniform meaning to the particle NEG, and it solves several problems with the traditional idea of "truth reversal". It certainly does not solve all problems of negation. First, there are other linguistic means to negate something than particles such as *not, no, nicht,* or *ne...que*; about these means, nothing is said here. Second, NEG always makes the same meaning contribution to a sentence; but it also interacts in many ways with other linguistic devices of this sentence, for example its syntactical structure or the way in which the sentence, when uttered, is integrated into the flow of discourse. This interplay leads to many complications, some of which were briefly addressed in sections 6 and 7; there are certainly others. I do not believe, however, that such complications affect the analysis of NEG itself.

References

Atlas, Jay (2004). Presupposition. In Laurence R. Horn and Gregory Ward. Eds. The Handbook of Pragmatics. Oxford: Blackwell. 29–52.
Beaver, David (1997). Presupposition. In Jeremy van Benthem and Alice ter Meulen. Eds. Handbook of Logic and Language. Amsterdam: Elsevier. 939–1008.

Bernini, Giulio, and Ramat, Paolo (1992). Negative sentences in the languages of Europe. Berlin, New York: de Gruyter.
Brandtler, Johan (2006): On Aristotle and Baldness – Topic, Reference, Presupposition of Existence, and Negation. Working Papers in Skandinavian Syntax 77. 177–204.
Chomsky, Noam (2002). On nature and language. Cambridge: Cambridge University Press.
Dahl, Östen (1979). Typology of Sentence Negation. Linguistics 17. 79–106.
Ehrich, Veronika (2001). Was nicht müssen und nicht können (nicht) bedeuten können: Zum Skopus der Negation bei den Modalverben des Deutschen. In Reimar Müller and Marga Reis. Eds. Modalität und Modalverben im Deutschen. Hamburg: Buske. 149–176.
Fabricius-Hansen, Cathrine (1983). Wieder ein *wieder*? Zur Semantik von *wieder*. In Rainer Bäuerle, Christoph Schwarze and Arnim von Stechow. Eds. Meaning, Use and Interpretation. Berlin: de Gruyter. 97–120.
Frey, Werner (2004). A medial topic position for German. Linguistische Berichte 198. 153–190.
Geurts, Bart (1998). The Mechanisms of denial. Language 74. 274–307.
Hajicova, Eva (1973). Negation and Topic vs. Comment. Philologia Pragensia 16. 81–93.
Horn, Lawrence R. (1985). Metalinguistic negation and pragmatic ambiguity. Language 61. 121–174.
Horn, Lawrence R. (2001). A natural history of negation. 2nd ed. Chicago: Chicago University Press.
Jacobs, Joachim (1982). Syntax und Semantik der Negation im Deutschen. München: Fink.
Jacobs, Joachim (1991). Negation. In A. v. Stechow, D. Wunderlich . Eds. Semantik. Berlin, New York: de Gruyter. 560–596.
Jacobs, Joachim (1997). I-Topikalisierung. Linguistische Berichte 198. 91–133.
Jäger, Agnes (2005). Negation in Old High German. Zeitschrift für Sprachwissenschaft 24. 227–262.
Jespersen, Otto (1917). Negation in English and other languages. Kopenhagen. (also in Otto Jespersen. Selected Writings. London: Allen and Unwin. 3–151).
Kamp, Hans, and Rossdeutscher, Antje (1994). DRS-construction and lexically driven inference. Theoretical Linguistics 20. 166–235.
Klein, Wolfgang (2001). Time and again. In Caroline Féry, & Wolfgang Sternefeld Eds. Audiatur vox sapientiae: A festschrift for Arnim von Stechow , 267–286. Berlin: Akademie Verlag.
Klein, Wolfgang (2006). On Finiteness. In Veerle van Geenhoven. Ed. Semantics in Acquisition. Dordrecht: Springer. 245–272.
Koktova, E. (1987). On the Scoping Properties of Negation, Focusing Particles and Sentence Adverbials. Theoretical Linguistics 14. 173–226.
Kroch, Anthony (1979). The semantics of scope in English. New York: Garland.
Lang, Ewald (2002). Syntax und Semantik der Negation. Lecture notes. Berlin: Humboldt-University.
Miestamo, Matti (2005). Standard Negation: The Negation of Declarative Verbal Main Clauses in a Typological Perspective. Berlin: de Gruyter.
Payne, John R. (1985). Negation. In: T. Shopen. Ed. Language typology and syntactic description 1. Cambridge. Cambridge University Press. 197–242.
Partee, Barbara (1993): On the "Scope of Negation" and Polarity Sensitivity. In Eva Hajicova. Ed. Functional Approaches to Language Description (Sgall Festschrift). Prague. 179–196.
Payne, John R. (1992). Negation. In Timothy Shopen. Ed. Language typology and syntactic description 3. Cambridge: Cambridge University Press. 197–242.
Penka, Doris, and von Stechow, Arnim (2001). Modalität und Modalverben im Deutschen. in Reimar Müller and Marga Reis. Eds. Modalität und Modalverben im Deutschen. Hamburg: Buske. 263–286.

Seuren, P. (1992). Präsuppositionen. In Dieter Wunderlich and Arnim von Stechow. Eds. Handbuch Semantik. Berlin: de Gruyter. 286–318.
von Stechow, Arnim (1996). The Different Readings of *Wieder* 'Again': A Structural Account. Journal of Semantics 13. 87–138.
Welte, Werner (1978). Negationslinguistik. München. Fink.
Zeijlstra, Hedde (2004). Sentential Negation and Negative Concord. PhD dissertation. Amsterdam: University of Amsterdam.

About the German particles *schon* and *noch*[1]

1 Introduction

It is remarkable how little agreement has been reached about the function of some linguistic devices that are found in most languages, that are most common in each of these languages, and that are mastered by children at a relatively early age. To this class of puzzling items we may also count particles such as German *schon* (roughly 'already')[2] and *noch* (roughly 'still'), just as their counterparts in other languages. There are a number of analyses in lexicography, in which the various usages of these items are carefully documented and classified, and there are a number of attempts to discover the general principles behind these usages. But agreement is at best partial, and in fact, several crucial properties have not yet been addressed at all. In this paper, I will suggest a new way to approach this problem. The discussion is confined to German; but I believe that many of the following considerations in principle transfer to other languages, although there is considerable variation in detail.

Schon and *noch* belong to a wider class of lexical items which are sometimes called "focus particles" (König 1991, Dimroth and Klein 1996). These include, for example, words such as *nur* 'only', *auch* 'also', *sogar* 'even'. They share a number of properties, three of which are of particular importance. First, they are optional, i.e., the sentences in which they occur are syntactically complete without the particle. Second, they show up in various positions in a sentence, and accordingly, they modify the meaning of the sentence in different ways: they have "scope". Third, they interact with the "information structure", in particular with the focus, of the sentence. To these properties, we may add a fourth one of a different kind: they all seem to be heavily multifunctional. This also applies to the two particles which are the subject of this paper. In the next section, I will briefly go through their main usages.[3]

---

[1] This paper, originally written in 2007, is first published here; but earlier versions were presented on several occasions; I am grateful to the audiences and to Manfred Bierwisch for critical comments and helpful suggestions.
[2] All English glosses throughout this paper are approximations; they are meant to give the reader a first idea, and should not be seen as accurate translations. Where necessary, the particular flavour is described in the text.
[3] The following discussion is primarily based on an inspection of various comprehensive German dictionaries, in particular DWB, WDG and *Duden*, and on König 1991. I also looked through numerous examples from "Digitales Wörterbuch der Deutschen Sprache" (www.dwds.de).

https://doi.org/10.1515/9783110549119-012

2 A first inspection

2.1 *schon*

The particle *schon* has two main functions, usually called TEMPORAL and MODAL (see, e.g., König 1977, 1991, 1993, Abraham 1980, Ormelius 1992). The temporal function is illustrated in 1a-g.

(1) a. Johannes hat schon sieben Bier getrunken.
 'Johannes has already seven beers drunk.'
 b. Maria war schon mit Johannes verlobt.
 'Maria was already with Johannes engaged.'
 c. Maria war mit Johannes schon verlobt.
 'Maria was with Johannes already engaged.'
 d. Der Papst war schon tot.
 'The pope was already dead.'
 e. ?Schon der Papst war tot.
 '?Already was the pope dead.'
 f. Schon war der Papst tot.
 'Already was the pope dead.'
 g. Mach das Licht aus, wenn es nicht schon aus ist.
 'Switch the light off, if it not already off is.'

In 1a, the particle is found in what is often assumed to be its "standard position" – just after the finite element. But many other positions are possible; they go hand in hand with varying scope properties. The difference in meaning between 1b (standard position) and 1c is palpable though not easy to pin down. Thus, 1b can, for example, be used to cast doubt on the assumption that Maria will marry Josef, with whom she is engaged – she has been engaged with some other man, Johannes, before, and hasn't married him. It can also mean that at the time talked about, she was engaged with Johannes, and therefore could not become engaged with Josef. In each of these cases, 1c would be inappropriate. But 1c can be used to indicate that at the time talked about, Maria was in the "engagement stage" with Johannes, and that next, she will be in the "marriage stage"; so, it could be continued by, *und die Hochzeit war für kommende Woche geplant* 'and the wedding was scheduled for coming week'. Note that "A mit B verlobt sein" and "A mit B verheiratet sein" follow a certain temporal order: being engaged precedes being married.

The difference between 1d and 1e is more salient: 1e is distinctly odd, whereas 1d is not. As 1f shows, the reason cannot be that *schon* is excluded in this position.

Hence, *schon* cannot only show up in various positions; its syntactic status is also somewhat ambivalent.⁴ Example 1g illustrates another fact. It has often been assumed (Abraham 1980, Löbner 1989, 1999; see also van der Auwera 1993, Mittwoch 1993, Michaelis 1996) that the regular negation of *schon* is not *nicht schon* but *noch nicht*. But 1h shows that this is not always the case; especially in conditionals, *nicht schon* is perfectly normal.⁵

In all of these cases, *schon* does not change the truth value of the sentence in which it occurs (this applies similarly to *noch*). Nor does it change the illocutionary role – questions remain questions, declaratives remain declaratives, and so on. But what DOES change when *schon* is added? The first impression in all of these examples is that *schon* somehow highlights the fact that the proposition holds for the time talked about, when compared to a proposition – perhaps even the same proposition – made about some later time: it highlights a TEMPORAL CONTRAST to a later time. The time talked about can be in the present, in the past or in the future, and the time to which it is contrasted is later, perhaps immediately afterwards. We nicely observe this effect when *schon* is isolated, for example in a short dialogue such as 2:

(2) Wir müssen gehen. – Schon?
    'We must go? Already?'

The elliptic *schon*, short for *Wir müssen schon gehen?*, does not deny the earlier assertion "we must leave", but it asks whether this could not be later than at the time talked about. Note, incidentially, that it is hardly possible to highlight *schon*

---

4 A fundamental principle of German syntax states that in declaratives, there is exactly one major constituent before the finite element. This need not be the subject but can also be a different argument or an adverbial. The fact that words such as *schon* (and similarly *noch*) can fill this position alone but also in combination with some other major constituent forces us to assume either that the principle is false (Scylla) or that *schon* is sometimes a major constituent, sometimes not (Charybdis). The situation is made even more complicated by the fact that under specific intonational conditions, also constructions such as *Goethe schon trug keinen Zopf mehr* are possible (similarly with *noch*), at least to my judgment (speakers tend to disagree here). I will not follow up these cases.

5 I think that *noch nicht* should not be seen as a special, non-compositional item – the negative variant of *schon* – but the application of normal *noch* to a negated property. In *Lukas war noch nicht gesund* 'Lukas was not yet healthy', for example, it is said that Lukas' not-being-healthy endures, just as in *Noch war Hans nicht gesund* or in *Hans war noch gestern nicht gesund*. In many cases, this is tantamount to *Lukas war schon gesund* being false, whence to *Lukas war nicht schon gesund*. This fact results from the normal meaning contribution of *noch/schon*, on the one hand, and the negation by *nicht*, on the other. It is a different issue why *noch nicht* is often preferred over *nicht schon*.

in the full sentence: *Wir müssen gehen? – Wir müssen SCHON gehen?* sounds distinctly odd. I have no explanation for this fact.

So far about the temporal use of *schon*. The modal use is illustrated in 3a-c:

(3) a. Du hast schon recht.
 'You are right already.'
 b. Hättest du nicht anrufen können. – Schon. Aber es war mir nicht danach.
 'Couldn't you have called? – Already. But I did not feel like that.'

This modal use is quite common. English *already*, the closest temporal counterpart of *schon*, does not have it. In fact, there is no direct counterpart to modal *schon*. In 3b, the effect is perhaps best be rendered by "Sure, I could. But I didn't feel like that". In 3a, the particular meaning shade could perhaps be conveyed by "You are right, fine – but ...". In neither case does it deny the truth of the underlying assertion, but it adds something like "that's not the whole story".

Temporal and modal *schon* also differ in two other respects. First, modal *schon* can be stressed, whereas temporal *schon* can't, unless used in isolation (as noted above). Second, modal *schon* is confined to declaratives, whereas temporal *schon* also shows up in questions and commands. I see no obvious way to subsume temporal and modal use under one meaning. Unpleasant as this is – they are best treated as two different words.[6] In what follows, only the temporal *schon* will be examined.

2.2 *noch*

The particle *noch* is more complex. At least three uses are commonly distinguished – temporal, additive, and comparative.[7] The temporal function is illustrated in 4a–h.

(4) a. Johannes schläft noch.
 'Johannes sleeps still.'

---

[6] The diachronic evidence is not very helpful, either. A potential starting point of such a unifom analysis could be that the "that's not the full story" connotation which modal *schon* evokes. In a way, this leads the listener to expect an assertion which is still to come and which provides additional information: "it is true what has been said, but wait for this: ...".

[7] German has also a word *noch* which corresponds to English *nor*, as in *weder – noch* 'neither – nor'. Its syntactic and semantic properties are very different, and it has a different historical background, so, it is best considered as a completely different word.

b. Er hat den Antrag noch eingereicht.
   'He has the application still submitted.'
c. Er duschte noch.
   'He showered still.'
d. Ich muß noch packen.
   'I must still pack.'

In 4a, the first intuition is that the action, here Johannes' being asleep, continues, i.e., it is said that he is asleep at the moment of speech and this was also the case at the left-adjacent time. Thus, *noch* has a "continuative reading". It also creates the impression that his sleeping could be over by now, or that his sleeping at this time runs against expectation. Note, however, that this cannot be the proper meaning of temporal *noch* (as is assumed, for example, in Hoepelman and Rohrer 1981). It is easily possible to say 4e (see Klein 1994, 116):

(4) e. Erwartungsgemäß schlief Eva zu dieser Zeit noch.
       'As expected slept Eva at that time still.'

Here, Eva's still being asleep exactly confirms the expectation.

The continuative function is particularly salient when *noch* is isolated, as in the following mini-dialogue:

(4) f. Markus ist der beste deutsche Tennisspieler. – Noch.
       'Markus is the best German tennis player. – Still.'

In 4f, it is not denied that Markus is the best German tennis player right now; but attention is drawn to the fact that this might soon no longer be the case. It invites the idea that the proposition is true in the past and right now, but not in the future: THE TIME FOR WHICH THE ASSERTION IS MADE IS THE LAST TIME, FOR WHICH THIS ASSERTION IS TO BE MADE.

But the continuative reading is not the only one that is possible. This is illustrated in 4b; here, *noch* does not indicate that he continues the submission of the proposal but rather that this submission follows some earlier action (for example conceiving or writing the proposal). It also may invite some "contrast to the right", for EXAMPLE THE ONE EXPRESSED BY *BUT THEN, HE FELL SERIOUSLY ILL*. IN A WAY, THEREFORE, 4B ALSO SUGGESTS A CONTINUATION, but this continuation does not concern the predicate in the scope of *noch*, i.e., *einreichen*. Let me call this the "further-to" reading. Sentence 4c is ambiguous between continuative and further-to reading. It can mean that right now, he is under the shower, and so he was at the immediately preceding time. It can also mean that, further to some earlier activity, he has taken a shower, for example in a sequence such as *Johannes ist vor ein paar Minuten eingetroffen. Er duscht noch. Dann kommt er zu uns.* lit. 'Johannes has a few minutes ago arrived. He showers still. Then comes he to us'.[8] Sentence 4d shows the same ambituity as 4c. But there is an additional complication because it is unclear whether the obligation expressed by *muss*, the action of packing, or both continue.[9]

All of these readings are temporal, although the "further-to"-reading has some additive flavour. It leads us to the so-called additive use of *noch*. Consider the following examples:

(5) a. Ich kenne noch eine interessante Geschichte über deinen jetzigen Freund.
   'I know still an interesting story about your present friend.'
   b. Johannes hat noch sieben Bier getrunken.
   'Johannes has still seven beers drunk.'
   c. Rechts davon steht noch ein Haus.
   'To the right of it stands still a house.'
   d. Noch schätzte Goethe den Blankvers.
   'Still appreciated Goethe the blank verse.'
   e. Noch Goethe schätzte den Blankvers.
   'Still Goethe appreciated the blank verse.'

In principle, 5a can also have a temporal reading – I still know it, but soon, I will have forgotten it. But the more natural understanding is: I know an interesting story about your present friend on top of another interesting story I know (about him or about someone else). It can also mean "On top of something else I know". In other words, something is added, but it need not be of the same type, and therefore, it is not a continuation in the sense of 4a. This is not possible when *noch* is highlighted, as in 5b. In b, the addition is *sieben Bier trinken*, on top of having drunken seven beers.[10]

---

[8] A nice example of this type is the following sentence from the German translation of Elisabeth George's novel "Missing Joseph" (chapter 16). A bishop is just in his fitness room, and his secretary says to inspector Lynley: "He has another appointment in an hour, and he'll need an opportunity to shower before that." In German, this is elegantly translated as: "Er hat in einer Stunde den nächsten Termin, und er muss vorher noch duschen."

[9] Note that English *still* has the continuative reading, whereas it is less clear where and when it can have the "further-to"-reading. In 4c, is at least marginally possible, especially when used in a higher clause. So, an appropriate translation might be: *He still managed to submit the application*. This is not possible in 4c, d, where the particular connotation is probably best rendered by "first" (*First, he will have a shower* or *But first, I must pack*).

[10] It is arguable, though, whether the number must be identical, i.e., 5b could also said when the seven beers are added to, say, nine beers or four beers which he already had.

Example 5b also has a temporal ingredient – the beers added are also "later beers", they are added to the beers Johannes had drunk before. This is not the case in 5c – it only expresses that this house is standing there in addition to some other house (with *ein Haus* being de-stressed) or something else than a house. Note, however, that there is a different type of temporal order, which does not reflect the facts of the world but the order in which these facts are presented by the speaker and understood by the listener. Thus, 5c could be used in a picture description, in which the speaker first said: *In der Mitte steht ein Haus. Rechts davon steht noch ein Haus.* 'In the middle stands a house. Right of it stands still a house.' Sentences 5d, e are perfectly possible, but only under a temporal interpretation. This restriction is without exception, if the particle alone fills the initial position, as in 5d.

The "comparative use" is different from but somehow related to the further-to use:

(6) a. Johannes ist alt, Fritz ist älter, und Otto ist noch älter.
  'Johannes is old, Fritz is older, and Otto is still older.'
 b. Die Geburtenrate liegt noch unter der japanischen.
  'The birth rate lies still under the japanese (birth rate).'

In 6a, *noch* indicates that the age of Otto goes beyond a degree described before, which in turn is higher than some level of comparison given in context. In principle, this also applies to 6b, although no direct comparative is used: it is assumed that the birth rate of Japan is already low, but the birth rate talked about goes further down. Somehow, this use is related to the "further-to"-reading in the sense of 5c.

2.3 Summing up

The particles *schon* and *noch* share a number of properties, in particular:

(7) 1. They are syntactially optional.
 2. When added, they do not change the truth value and the illocutionary role of the sentence to which they are added.
 3. They can show up in various positions, and this variation leads to changes in meaning: the particles have scope-properties.
 4. They seem to interact with the focus structure of the sentence, as reflected in the prosodic properties of the sentence.
 5. Each particle has a wide range of uses. But in all cases, except perhaps modal schon, they somehow relate the content of sentence in which they occur to some other sentence content – something that is, or could be, true at a later or earlier time.

It is not obvious how the various readings of *schon* and *noch* can be subsumed under one meaning. In fact, most of the traditional lexicographical literature simply lists the uses, and most of the linguistic treatments are confined to temporal readings. In what follows, I will start with these cases but then try to include the others.

The remainder of this paper is organised as follows. In the next section, I we will have a look at two earlier analyses, Löbner (1989, 1990, 1999)[11] and Krifka 2000. Other relevant work, not explicitly discussed here but important in the research tradition, includes Abraham 1980, Hoepelman and Rohrer 1981, König 1991, 139–162,[12] van der Auwera 1993; regrettably, a more comprehensive discussion is beyond the scope of this paper. In sections 4 and 5, a new analysis is proposed and exemplified. Section 6 is devoted to a few complications.

3 Earlier accounts

3.1 Löbner's presuppositional analysis

Löbner considers *schon* and *noch* as focus-sensitive particles, a view shared by many other authors. More crucial to Löbner's analysis is the idea that the role of *schon* and *noch* is to trigger a special presupposition. A second important aspect is their participation in a wider set of phenomena subsumed under the notion of "phase quantification", an aspect in which we are less interested in the present context.

Four types of temporal *noch/schon* (non-temporal uses are not dealt with) are distinguished; in all cases, the particles are considered to be associated with the focus:

(8) "type S : (association with the sentence focus in an imperfective sentence)
das Licht ist schon/noch an
the light is already/still on." (p 48)

---

[11] Löbner's three publications differ in a number of interesting details, partly inspired by earlier criticism of van der Auwera 1993, Michaelis 1996. The following discussion is based on the most recent version, Löbner 1999.
[12] König says (p. 140) that his analysis essentially follows Löbner 1989; his coverage of the phenomena, though, is much broader.

In this case, called the basic use, the focus associated with the particle is "the natural focus of the sentence" (p. 48). In all other cases, the focus is narrowed down (marked by small capitals):

(9) a. "type F: (association with a narrow focus in an imperfect sentence)
Sie haben schon/erst drei seiten gelesen [...]
you have read already 3 pages/only three pages so far" (p. 49)
b. "type Tpf: (association with a time adverbial in focus in a perfective sentence)
sie kommt schon/erst morgen an
she is arriving as early as/as late as tomorrow" (p. 50)
c. "type Tipf: (association with a time adverbial in focus in an imperfective sentence)
ich war schon/erst gestern da
I already was there yesterday/I was there only yesterday" (p 50)

Thus, *schon* only appears in imperfective sentences except when a time adverbial is in focus. This does not seem to be correct. First, perfective sentences are easily possible when something else than a time adverbial is in focus, such as in 10:

(10) a. a. Er hat gestern schon einen NEUEN Antrag gestellt.
'He has yesterday already a new proposal submitted.'
b. Er hat schon gestern einen NEUEN Antrag gestellt.
'He has already yesterday a new proposal submitted.'

So, focality of the time adverbial is perhaps not crucial.
Second, consider sentences such as 11a-d, which are of type S (i.e., no adverbial, sentence focus):

(11) a. Der Ballon war schon/noch geplatzt.
'The balloon has already/still burst.'
b. Er hatte den Beweis schon/noch gefunden.
'He had the proof already/still found.'
c. Er fand noch einen weiteren Beweis.
'He found still a further proof.'
d. Das bewies schon Gödel.
'That$_{acc}$ proved already Gödel.'

Verbs such as *platzen, finden, beweisen* are generally assumed to be punctual, and it is difficult, if not impossible, to use them in the imperfective aspect (in the sense of Comrie 1976, to which Löbner refers). Sentences 11a, b do not mean that at some time in the past, the ballon was already/still in the situation of bursting, or he was in the situation of finding the proof. One might perhaps argue that the German pluperfect is imperfective. But this would not apply to sentences 11c, d. So, it appears that both particles also occur in sentences which are not imperfective. I am not sure whether this problem is really serious, since the analysis could perhaps be reformulated such as to include perfective sentences, as well. In any event, Löbner only considers "stative propositions" P, whose truth is evaluated against an "evaluation time" t_e.

The analysis of the basic use is very simple. Essentially, the particles, when inserted into a sentence, trigger a presupposition which the sentence does not have otherwise. This is stated in the following truth conditions of *schon* and *noch*, respectively (the omissions marked by [...] in the following quotes relate to the expressions *noch nicht* and *nicht mehr*, not considered here):

(12) "Truth conditions for type S schon (te, P) [...]:
   a. Both schon and [...] trigger the presupposition that there is a phase of not-P starting before te and that up to te at most one change between not-P and P has occurred.
   b. Schon (te, P) is true [...], iff the presupposition in (a) is fulfilled and P(te) is true." (p. 53s)

(13) "Truth conditions for type S noch (te, P) [...]:
   a. Both noch and [...] trigger the presupposition that there is a phase of P starting before te and that up to te at most one change between not-P and P has occurred.
   b. Noch (te, P) is true [...], iff the presupposition in (a) is fulfilled and P(te) is true." (p. 54).

In a nutshell, when *schon/noch* is added to *Das Licht war an*, then this adds an earlier "presupposition phase", at which the light was not on in the case of *schon*, and at which was on in the case of *noch*.

This analysis is embedded in the overall idea of what Löbner calls 'phase quantification'. Phases are subsequent intervals on the time which differ by their polarity, roughly, they either have a certain property or they don't. If a sentence contains a particle such as *noch* or *schon*, then not only the "truth interval" which contains the evaluation time is considered but also the preceding "presupposition interval". The truth interval is P. The presupposition interval is not-P in the case of *schon* and P in the case of *noch*. This is exactly what the presuppositions in 12 and 13 should capture.

In the present context, we are not concerned with the general issue of phase quantification but with the more specific question of what *schon* and *noch* contribute to the meaning of a sentence, and this is stated in 12 and 13 for the basic use. The other types differ from the basic use in two ways: (a) the focus is narrow, and thus, the focus alternatives are smaller units; (b) the focus alternatives are ordered on a scale, for example *zwei Seiten, drei Seiten, vier Seiten, fünf Seiten* (type F) or *vorgestern, gestern, heute, morgen, übermorgen* (type T in its two variants).

Löbner's analysis is very compelling, because it is so simple: the particles only add a presupposition. But it also raises a number of problems, three of which I will discuss here.

A. Presupposition added

The net effect of adding *schon/noch* is the triggering of a presupposition (summed up here from the quotes in 12 and 13):

(14) The particle triggers the presupposition that there is a phase of not-P (in the case of *schon*), or P (in the case of *noch*) starting before t_e and that up to t_e at most one change between not-P and P has occurred.

As it stands, the second clause is a bit cryptic. The presupposition can hardly be that there has never been more than one change from not-P to P before t_e. Neither *Das Licht war schon an* nor *Das Licht war noch an* preclude that there are many earlier phases at which the light was on or not on. So, one should probably add "within some contextually relevant interval". As Löbner's informal explanations indicate, the idea is apparently that the "presupposition phases" must be left-adjacent to the "truth phase". With respect to *schon*, he writes (p. 53): "Obviously, the overall interval considered must not contain more than one change from not-P to P." And the corresponding statement on *noch* is: "Both *noch noch* (t_e, P) and [...] presuppose that P was true at some time before t_e. On this background, *noch* (t_e, P) expresses the fact that P has been true since that time and is true at t_e." (p. 54). If the presupposition phase is not left-adjacent to t_e, the word *wieder* 'again' must be used.

So, the presupposition phase must be left-adjacent to the truth phase. Thus, we can restate the effect of the two particles as follows:

(15) a. *schon*: there is a not-P phase left-adjacent to t_e.
     b. *noch*: there is a P phase left-adjacent t_e.

Is this really what the addition of the particles *schon* and *noch* achieves? Consider a normal case such as 16:

(16) Mozart war schon tot, Haydn lebte noch.
  'Mozart was already dead, Haydn lived still.'

The sentence itself does not say when the evaluation time t_e is, except it must be somewhere in the past. Let us suppose the context makes clear that it is the year when Schubert was born, 1797. In such a context, 16 is appropriate and even correct. But *schon* does not add the presupposition that Mozart was not dead up to 1797. Nor do I think that *noch* adds the presupposition that Haydn was alive up to 1797. If that were a presupposition, it should also follow from the corresponding negative sentence, i.e., 'Haydn lebte nicht mehr'. But this sentence could well be true, if Haydn had died in 1780. There is a net conclusion: Whatever the function of *schon* and *noch* in the basic use is – it must be something else than what is stated in 14 or 15.

There is a second, perhaps less important, problem with *schon* in particular. The presupposition, as required by 15a, is excluded by predicates which, due to their inherent meaning, apply right from the beginning or not at all, such as being new.[13] In this case, the presupposition cannot be fulfilled, and therefore, *schon* should be impossible (Löbner 1999: 51s). This is indeed the case:

(17) *Der Wagen ist schon neu.

But note that we also have the opposite case, i.e., predicates which, when they apply to some entity at some time, apply to that entity at any time later. In fact, they are odd:

(18) *Goethe war noch tot.

Now, 15b does not say anything about later times; it only requires P to be true at some time earlier than t_e. Still, we have the same effect. Hence, the impossibility to have such a presupposition cannot be the reason for the oddity of 18, and since 17 and 18 seem parallel, it is unlikely that it is the reason for the oddity of 17, either.

---

13 As a rule, these expressions also have a derived meaning under which there are not forever in the one or the other direction (for example *dead* in the sense of "very exhausted"). These meanings are not at issue here.

There is also a problem with *noch* in particular. If *noch* is added, this may indicate that P is assumed to have obtained before t_e, but it need not: the continuative reading is just one possibility. Let me repeat one of the examples (cf. 4c):

(19)   Er duschte noch.

This can mean that at the time talked about, he was still under the shower (continuative reading, the only one which goes with English *still*). Or it means that further to something else said about him, he did something, namely having a shower, just before doing something else, for example having dinner. This reading is found in contexts such as "he came home, but before joining his family for dinner, *er duschte noch*." Although under this reading of 19, the predication P does not apply to the earlier time, there is still a sort of continuation: before we turn to something new, the earlier "sequence of actions" is concluded by something else, namely having a shower; this is what we have called the "further-to"-reading in section 2. In other words, *noch* can be used when the predication P obtained before, but also when it did not. There is no presupposition in the sense of 15b.

The following two problems do not concern the core idea but the range of phenomena that is covered by the presuppositional analysis.

B. Narrow and broad focus

In Type S use, the particles have sentence focus. Consider now examples such as in 20 (small capitals indicate intonational focus):

(20)   a.   Sven hatte schon das LINKE Auge verloren.
             'Sven had already the left eye lost.'
         b.   Johannes hatte schon ein Bier BESTELLT/ein Bier bestellt.
             'Johannes had already a beer ordered.'
         c.   Der VORDERE Kotflügel war schon repariert.
             'The front fender was already repaired.'
         d.   Von HINTEN sah der Wagen noch ganz gut aus.
             'From behind looked the car still quite good.'

Clearly, narrow focus is possible here, as well. Note that these examples do not involve a scale.

We also have the opposite problem: in type F and type T, the focus need not be on the temporal adverb or the other scalar element:

(21) a. Peter hatte schon drei Bier GETRUNKEN.
'Peter had already three beers drunk.'
b. Peter hatte vorsorglich schon gestern die ROLLÄDEN heruntergelassen.
'Peter had as a precaution already yesterday the roll shutters let down.'
c. Der Kanzler hatte schon drei CHINESISCHE Studenten zugelassen.
'The provost had already three Chinese students admitted.'
d. Der Kanzler hatte schon drei chinesische Studenten zugelassen. (with "natural focus", rather than focus on *drei*).

In other words, the question of what is focused is independent of the fact of whether the predicate has scalar alternatives or not. This does not falsify the presuppositional analysis from 12 and 13, in fact, it makes it more general; but it forces us to look in a different way at the role of focus and scales.

C. Scopal differences

The particles *noch* and *schon* can show up in different positions, and this variation leads to different interpretations. In section 2, a number of examples were given. Here are two other examples of varying scope, in which the differences are particularly palpable:

(22) a. Beethoven schrieb schon an einer zehnten Symphonie.
'Beethoven wrote already at a tenth symphony.'
b. Schon schrieb Beethoven an einer zehnten Symphonie.
'Already wrote Beethoven at a tenth symphony.'
c. Schon Beethoven schrieb an einer zehnten Symphonie.
'Already Beethoven wrote at a tenth symphony.'

(23) a. Goethe trug noch einen Zopf.
'Goethe wore still a pigtail.'
b. Noch trug Goethe einen Zopf.
'Still wore Goethe a pigtail.'
c. Noch Goethe trug einen Zopf.
'Still Goethe wore a pigtail.'

All of these are perfectly correct in German. But the effect of the scope differences is dramatic. In 22b, for example, we have the impression that Beethoven hardly waited to begin with his 10th symphony, whereas in 22c, we get the impression that someone else was not the first who wrote at a 10th symphony. These effects of scope differences must be explained.

Löbner's account is a milestone in the analysis of these particles; but I do not think that it covers their particular meaning contribution appropriately. Some other problems were pointed out in Krifka 2000, who suggests a different analysis.

3.2 Krifka's restriction on focus alternatives

Krifka, too, relates these particles (called by him, following König 1991, aspectual particles[14]) to the focus and, more specifically, to focus alternatives. But the core idea is quite different. It is couched in the framework of "alternative semantics", as developed by Jacobs 1983, Rooth 1985, von Stechow 1990, and others; see also Krifka 2006. In this framework, the meaning of a sentence is determined with reference to various alternatives which the focus of the sentence has. The focus may in principle be any constituent. Krifka sums up his analysis of *noch* and *schon* as follows (Krifka 2000, p. 4):[15]

> First, all uses of aspectual particles are focus-sensitive [...]. Second, they impose a restriction on the alternatives on the focus that are to be considered [...]. Third, this restriction is based on an intrinsic ordering of the alternatives, which I will call $\leq_A$. And finally, this ordered set is aligned to the ordering of times or to a related ordering.

The restriction which accounts for the effect of *schon* and *noch* is very simple and elegant:

> The basic idea is that *already* indicates that the valid alternatives are ranked lower than the focus, on the relevant ordering of alternatives, whereas *still* indicates that the alternatives are ranked higher (p. 4)

In other words, the addition of *noch* excludes all alternatives lower than the actual focus value from consideration, and *schon* excludes all higher alternatives from consideration. If we imagine the alternatives to be ordered from left to right, then *schon* only "looks to the left" and *noch* only "looks to the right". Consider 24:

(24) a. Lydia ist schon drei$_F$ Monate alt.
b. Lydia ist noch drei$_F$ Monate alt.

The focus value in 24a, b is *drei*. Focus alternatives are *einen, zwei, drei, vier, fünf, sechs, ...* The addition of *schon* excludes *fünf, sechs, ...* from the set of alternatives

---

[14] Actually, König says that *schon* and *noch* can be used as focus particles as well as aspectual particles; the latter shows up in interaction with particular aspects.
[15] Krifka deals with German *schon* and *noch* as well as with their primary English counterparts *already* and *still*. There are some differences, but these do not matter here.

considered, whereas the addition of *noch* excludes the "earlier" alternatives *eins, zwei* from consideration.

This analysis is very suggestive: Something is asserted to be true, and *schon* contrasts this assertion to "lower" alternatives – that is, that Lydia is younger than three months at the time talked about; whereas *noch* contrasts it to "higher" alternatives, that is, to the possibility that Lydia is older than three months at the time talked about. Examples like 24b reflect Löbner's type T, in which a temporal adverbial is focused.[16] The analysis naturally extends to type F, in which some other measure that gives rise to a scale is in focus, as in *Lydia hatte schon [drei]$_F$ Seiten gelesen* 'Lydia had already three pages read'. It is less clear, though, how it can be generalised to particles of Löbner's type S, the "basic use", as in *Lydia schlief schon/noch*. Krifka says (p. 7):

> They can be treated as focus-sensitive if we assume that the focus is over the whole sentence, leading to an empty background [...]. Also, the alternative in this case is the negation of the proposition in question.[17]

But as pointed out in section 3.1B, exx 20 and 21, this use is also compatible with narrow focus, just as the two other types are compatible with a broader focus.[18] Similarly, the problems noted under 3.1C extend to Krifka's analysis: it does not account for the scope differences illustrated in 22 and 23.

Now, this only concerns some phenomena that are not covered by the analysis. How does the analysis fit the basic intuitions about what *schon* and *noch* add when inserted into a simple sentence such as *es regnete* 'it rained/was raining'?

(25) a. Es regnete noch.
   b. Es regnete schon.

Under Krifka's analysis, 25a is constrained to constellations in which only the temporal sequence of focus alternatives {first *es regnete nicht*, then *es regnete*}

---

[16] Actually, Löbner assumes that the entire adverbial, here [*drei Monate*]$_F$ is in focus, whereas Krifka confines it to [*drei*]$_F$. It appears to me that this very narrow focus introduces an additional contrastive component that is not really intended; 4b sounds like a correction of an earlier assertion, such as *Lydia ist zwei Monate alt*. I do not think, however, that this point is crucial to the argument.

[17] Note that for this idea to work, the propositions must be temporally parameterized: a situation described by *Es regnete* is both preceded and followed by a situation described by *Es regnete nicht*. So, there is a "later not-rain" and an "earlier not-rain".

[18] As an aside, an empty background typically leads to "thetic sentences"; but this may but need not be the case for Löbner's "normal use".

is considered. In 25b, the sequence of alternatives is the opposite, i.e., {first *es regnete*, then *es regnete nicht*}. In each case, the focus value (i.e., the alternative that is asserted) is *Es regnete*. (see Krifka's ex. 29, p. 7).

The most straightforward understanding of 25a is surely the continuative reading: it is raining after some earlier raining. But under Krifka's analysis, earlier states are not under consideration at all. The same reasoning applies to the "further-to"-reading, which also indicates some continuity, albeit no maintenance of the predication itself. As to 25b, its core reading is something like "It could have rained later, but in actual fact, it was raining 'already' at the time talked about". Again, I do not see how this is covered by the restriction of the focus alternatives to the sequence "rain, not rain" (and selecting the former).

In what follows, I shall suggest a somewhat different analysis, which preserves some fundamental insights of earlier work while avoiding the problems noted above.

4 The basic idea

Let me begin with some preparatory remarks. As usual, a distinction is made here between (a) a sentence, i.e., a linguistic object of a particular form, (b) the proposition expressed by such a sentence, and (c) an utterance, i.e., the instantiation of a sentence in a particular communicative situation. The form of a sentence not only depends on the proposition which it expresses, but also on (a) its illocutionary role, and (b) its information structure, i.e., the way in which it is embedded into the flow of information. The former shows up, for example, in particular markers; thus, in order to mark his conviction that the proposition is true, the speaker must place, for example, the finite verb in particular position and end the sentence with an intonational fall. These are the standard "assertion markers" in English, Dutch or German. Opinions on how information structure – both its function and its encoding – are considerably at variance, and I will not dare to enter this terminological and conceptual jungle here (see, for example, Lambrecht 1994, Büring 2003, or Molnár and Winkler 2006). But I will briefly explain how I use the notions of "topic" and expecially "topic situation", which are needed in what follows. This is best done by looking a simple example, such as 25c, the sentence which underlies 25a, b:

(25) c. Es regnete.
       It rained/was raining.

Is this sentence, uttered here and now by me, true or false? Even for someone who knows what the whole world is like, it is impossible to answer this question, unless it is clear WHICH SITUATION IS TALKED ABOUT. If it happens to be the

situation characterised by "August 12, 2006, Boltenhagen", the answer would have to be "yes". If it happens to be "Sept. 28, 2006, Nijmegen", the answer would have to be "no". In other words, assertions (as well as other types of sentences) are relative to "topic situations", as I shall say. Such a topic situation is characterised by various features, for example a "topic time" (this is the time talked about), a "topic place", a "topic person or object" (often encoded as the grammatical subject), possibly a "topic world" (e.g., fictitious vs real), and perhaps others. The information which allows the listener to identify the topic situation comes from several sources. It can be provided:
(a) by an explicit question, which includes the necessary information, for example 'How was the weather on Sept. 28, 2006, in Nijmegen?';
(b) by contextual information, for example if the sentence is part of a longer text;
(c) by information which is included in the sentence itself.

In 25, there is not very much topic information in the sentence itself. The tense marking on the verb makes clear that the "topic time" is somewhere in the past. It could be made more precise by an adverbial, such as in "on September 28, 2006, it rained". Similarly, information about the topic place, the topic entity and other features of the topic situation can be added. This could even include the specification that the situation talked about is a "first time"-situation, as in "for the first time, it rained". It is important to distinguish here between three notions:
1. The "topic situation", that is, the situation itself with its various features that can be described.
2. The "topic information" which describes some of these features; this information can come from the context, but it can also be contained in the sentence.
3. The "topic marking" in a sentence, that is, the way in which it is made clear which part of the sen-tence serves to describe certain elements of the topic situation; this can, for example, be the position, a special particle, or prosodic features.

In what follows, the terms "topic" and "comment" will be used in the second sense, i.e., the "topic" of a sentence is that part which serves to characterise specific features of the topic situation; the comment is that part which includes other information. Note that the "topic" need not be a single constituent; it can, for example, include information about topic time, topic place as well as topic entity. I will not say anything here on how this topic status and comment status of some information in the sentence is marked in German or English; these are very complicated issues, and in many cases, there is no clear and consistent marking at all. In the present context, the most important notion is the "topic time". It is regularly encoded by the finite verb, but it can also be made more explicit by temporal adverbials. We will come back to this notion in more detail in section 6.

After this glance into Pandora's box, let us come to our issue proper, the particles *schon* and *noch*. The analysis which I will suggest brings their functioning in line with a series of other particles, such as *auch, nur, sogar, wieder* oder *doch*, and the negation by a particle such as *nicht*. They can be inserted in a sentence at a number of places; the exact constraints are complex, and no attempt will be made here to determine them.[19] But whenever inserted in a sentence, such a particle partitions the sentence into two parts, called here α and ω; ω is the scope of the particle, and α is that part which is not in the scope of P. In the simplest case, ω follows the particle, and α precedes it:

(26) a. Deshalb hat er gestern schon angerufen. 'Therefore has he yesterday
      α   P   ω
already called'
b. Deshalb hat er schon gestern angerufen. 'Therefore has he already
      α   P   ω
yesterday called.'

Scope assignment is not always that simple. In particular, there are two well-known syntactic complications in German. The first of these concerns the position before the finite element; it is commonly assumed that in declarative clauses, one major constituent is "moved" into this position.[20] If its "original position" is after P, this constituent still behaves as if it were in the scope of P; the "movement" is scope-conservative. Second, if the finite and the non-finite component of a verb are merged in one form (as in *schlief*, in contrast to *hat geschlafen*), then

---

[19] The first systematic investigation is found in Jacobs 1983. In this and much later work, e.g., von Stechow 1991, Büring and Hartmann 2001, the position of "focus particles" is crucially linked to the position of the focus. For reasons which are briefly discussed in section 6.4, I believe that particles such as *schon* and *noch* (and at least some other focus particles) operate in principle independent of focus structure. If this is correct, constraints which result from information structure and constraints which can be formulated in terms of phrase structure should be clearly separated. This would involve many other issues than mere positional properties, for example the mysterious fact that many focus particles themselves can be focused, whereas this is not possible for others (such as temporal *schon*).

[20] The exact way in which this operation is spelled out is highly theory-specific. I do not want to defend any particular creed in this respect, and therefore, the term "moved" should not be over-interpreted; "movement from A to B" simply means here that some constituent, though it shows up in position B, behaves in certain respects as if it were in position A.

this verb form is regularly placed in second position in declarative clauses; but its lexical content belongs to ω, since its "original position" is after P. Thus, in 26c, the verb meaning "angerufen haben" belongs to ω, rather than to α, although most of its expression precedes the particle *schon*:

(26) c. Deshalb rief er gestern schon an.

In what follows, I shall ignore these complications and work with the idealized assumption that the scope of P is the part which follows P, and the non-scope is the part which precedes P. This is only for ease of exposition; I trust the reader will make the necessary adjustments where needed.[21]

The basic idea is now that focus particles such as *noch*, *schon* and others function as a "secondary assertion marker". They do not mark the proposition of the sentence in which they contained as asserted but an "other" related proposition. This "other proposition" may be explicitly expressed by some other sentence in context. But it may also be not made explicit at all but just "somewhere in the air" in the broader communicative context. In what follows, I shall use the label ALIUD for the "other proposition", whether it is made explicit or not.

This means that three propositions come into play: the proposition with the particle, the proposition without the particle, and the "other proposition". The first of these is made explicit by an actual utterance and carries the usual markers of the illocutionary role (assertion in our examples) and of topic-hood; the others are derived, and the particle and its position fulfil this role of markers:[22]

(27) (a) αPω: this is the proposition with the particle P; α is the non-scope part of P, ω is the scope part of P. This is the proposition expressed by the actual utterance.
(b) αω: this is the proposition without the particle.
(c) α'ω': this is the "other proposition" ALIUD. It is assumed to consist of two parts, which are defined in relation to α and ω; we will come back to that in a moment.

---

[21] There may, of course, be other syntactic complications. But I do believe that the scope in German regularly goes to the right of *schon* or *noch*, and that deviations from the default are not specific to these particles but follow from general principles of German syntax.

[22] As said above, the derived propositions, or parts of it, may show up in the linguistic context. In particular, the particle sentence may take up material from the immediately preceding sentence, in which case this material may be marked as maintained by de-stressing. This leads to a particular intonation structure, which in turn is the source for focus effects; we shall discuss this in section 7.4.

When integrated into a sentence, the particle splits it into two parts and adds a secondary assertion: it says that to the mind of the speaker, the topic situation characterised by α' has properties ω'. The exact way in which this works varies from particle to particle. It may be, for example, that α' = α, i.e., the topic situation of ALIUD is exactly the one identified by α; but it may also be α' and α only differ with respect to the topic time, for example, if a claim is made about the same subject at different times. Similarly, the properties assigned to such a topic situation in ALIUD may be exactly those provided by ω; but it may also be that it is required that they are different, or partly different.

Let me illustrate this idea with examples with the focus particle *nur* 'only'. In this case, α' must be identical with α, and ω' must be some property which is different from ω; the secondary assertion is that ANY SUCH ALIUD IS INCOMPATIBLE WITH αω:

(28) a. Matthäus hat Maria nur besucht.
'Matthäus has Maria only visited.'
α   P   ω
Matthäus hat Maria ausgeführt. (= ALIUD)
'Matthäus has Maria taken out.'
α'   ω'

b. Matthäus hat nur Maria besucht.
'Matthäus has only Maria visited.'
α   P   ω
Matthäus hat Petra besucht. (= ALIUD)
α'   ω'

The topic situation of ALIUD is the same as defined by α; in 28a, this topic situation must involve Matthäus and the topic time (here only indicated by the tense marking on the finite verb); in 28b, the topic situation involves Matthäus, Maria and the topic time. In both cases, ω' must somehow be different from ω. In 28a, the only possibility for such a difference concerns the lexical verb *besucht*; ω' could, for example, by *ausgeführt*; in 28b, it can also concern *Maria*, as in the example *Petra besucht*, and it can concern *ausgeführt*, and it can concern *Maria* as well as *besucht*, as in *Petra ausgeführt*. The particle *nur* always says that αω and any such ALIUD are incompatible; what ALIUD is varies with the position of the particle.

In principle, the particles *schon* and *noch* function in much the same way. The difference lies in the relation between α and α' and the relation between ω and ω'. In a nutshell, *noch* adds an assertion about α at an earlier topic time, and *schon* adds a potential assertion about α at a later topic time. In other words, the topic situations of αω and ALIUD are the same except for their time component. The ω'-part can be different from but also identical to ω. Accordingly, we get somewhat different readings. In other words, whereas a simple sentence asserts (or asks, or commands) something about a particular situation, a sentence with *noch* or *schon* preserves this assertion and relates it to the "same"[23] topic situation at some earlier or later time. In the next section, we shall elaborate this general idea.

5 The meaning contribution of *schon* and *noch*

As sections 1 and 2 have illustrated, the concrete effect of inserting *schon* or *noch* into a sentence is not easy to capture. This is somewhat at variance with the fact that children seem to have no problems with these words at a very early age (see, e.g., Nederstigt 2003). I will start with the assumption that the meaning contribution of the two words is simple and constant in all cases (except the modal usage of *schon*). The apparent complexities, which render a satisfactory account so difficult, must have different reasons.

Let us begin with a very simple case:

(29) a. Es war acht Uhr. Die Kinder waren schon im Bett.
 'It was eight o'clock. The children were already in bed.'
 b. Es war acht Uhr. Die Kinder waren noch im Bett.
 'It was eight o'clock. The children were still in bed.'

In a way, both *schon* and *noch* make the sentence "look to the left and to the right", i.e., they relate the situation talked about to some earlier situation and to some later situation:

(30) 1. An assertion with *schon*
 (a) says that something ("the children" in this example) has a particular property ("be in bed") at the time talked about ("eight o'clock"), compared to the possibility that this something has a particular property at a later time, and

---

[23] Since the topic time is actually a factor which determines the topic situation, it is strictly speaking not correct to say "the same topic situation at an earlier/later time"; what is really meant is "a topic situation which is the same except for its topic time, which is earlier/later".

(b) invites the idea that this something did not have the relevant property at some earlier time.

2. An assertion with *noch*
   (a) says that something has a particular property at the time talked about, and that this is in continuation of, or in addition to, something which applied to the same something at some earlier time.
   (b) invites the idea that this something does not have the relevant property at some later time

The (b)-property is particularly salient, when *noch* is isolated, as in example 4f from section 2.2: *Er ist der beste Tennisspieler des Landes. – Noch.* Here, the isolated *noch* suggests he will soon no longer be the best tennisplayer. But this impression can easily be cancelled. In 29b, for example, it is not excluded that the children are in bed at 8:30 or at 10:00.

In conclusion, the (b)-feature is a pragmatic implicature. The reasoning which underlies this implicature is this. An utterance like *Die Kinder waren schon/noch im Bett* (with proposition αPω) does not just assert that the proposition „the children be in bed" (= proposition αω) holds at some time in the past but it also relates it to a proposition asserted about some earlier time (*noch*), or some later time (*schon*). Thus, the particle introduces a series of (minimally) two temporally ordered assertions.[24] If is made explicit that some assertion is about the first/last time in a series, then this invites the idea that this time is the first/last time ABOUT WHICH THIS ASSERTION CAN BE MADE in a given context. In other words, the beginning/end of the series is also the first/last time of which the interlocutor is led to believe that something has the relevant property. In 29a, the interlocutor is led to believe that the children were not in bed before eight. Essentially, the same effect is also observed in assertions such as *He had seven beers* when, in fact, he had twelve beers, or *He has to correct three term papers*, when he has to correct 200 term papers. In each case, the statement is interpreted as "no more/less in the list".[25]

This accounts for the typical implicature of *schon* and *noch*. What now is their meaning contribution proper? These are the (a)-features, i.e., the fact that *schon*

---

[24] If such a mini-series is introduced, it is not necessarily but often perceived as a part of a longer series.
[25] I assume, and my friend Steve Levinson says, that the underlying principle is Grice's second maxim of quantity: "Do not make your contribution to the conversation more informative than necessary."

explicitly relates the sentence in which it occurs to some assertion about a later time, and *noch* relates it to an assertion about some earlier time. We may sum this up as follows:

(31) a. α *schon* ω is true if (a) αω is true and (b) α'ω' is contextually relevant and possibly true.
b. α *noch* ω is true if (a) αω is true and (b) α'ω' is contextually relevant and true.

ω is the scope part of the particle, α is the non-scope part of the particle (in simple cases, they follow/precede the particle); α' is identical with α except for the topic time, which is right-adjacent/left-adjacent to the topic time of α'; ω' may but need not be identical with ω. In principle, ω' can thus be any imaginable property that is contextually relevant.

Note that under this analysis, *schon* and *noch* are largely symmetrical, but there is one crucial difference. In the case of *noch*, the speaker is committed to the assertion that ALIUD is true, whereas this is not the case for *schon*: ALIUD is just a possibility which is made explicit. In both cases, the two topic times must be adjacent within the order of topic times; this requirement may be too strong, a point to which we shall return in section 7.1.

As to the relation between ω and ω', it is only assumed that the property expressed by ω' are contextually relevant, and, due to the difference between α and α', it must be a later or earlier property of the "same" topic situation. It can be different from the one in αω, it can also be the same. In other words, "later property" of x does not mean "different property" of x – it can be the same descriptive property at a later time. The choice made here leads to different readings. If it is the same property in the case of *noch*, then we have a "continuation" (*Es regnete noch*). If it is not the same, we have an "addition", whose precise nature depends on what is different. Thus, in *Er hat noch geduscht*, showering is added to some earlier activity or activities, and it is suggested that this is indeed the last activity of a series, whereas in actual fact, it is only the last one about which something is asserted. In the case of *schon*, it is not asserted that that the "later" α'ω' is indeed true: αω is only contextually related to α'ω'. If ω and ω' are identical, then the property in question is typically the beginning of a longer period in which this property applies. If it is different, we have varying possibilities; in particular, ω may belong to a naturally ordered sequence of properties, for example drinking one, two, three, ... beers, or being obliged to correct 10, 9, 8, ... term papers, or to be in love, engaged, married, divorced, re-married.

Very informally, we may say that *schon/noch* add the information: "and now compare this to α at a later/earlier time!". This looks like a weak contribution, it just relates the assertion that is actually made by the sentence to something else which the listener should consider. But the effect can still be very strong – not with respect to αω, but with respect to α'ω'. In *Schon Beethoven schrieb an einer 10. Symphonie* (= 22c), for example, nothing is claimed to be the case at some later time. But the addition of *schon* to *Beethoven schrieb an einer 10. Symphonie.* makes clear that SOMEONE ELSE WAS NOT THE FIRST TO WRITE AT A 10. SYMPHONY. And in *Es regnete schon*, the word *schon* makes clear that some other (contextually relevant!) time was not the first time at which it was raining. Such an addition, of course, makes sense only in a context, in which there was reason to assume that it only rained at the later time, and this explains the feeling that something "runs against expectation".

The effect varies sharply with the position of the particle, more precisely, with its scope and thus the nature of ALIUD, as well as with the type of property in its scope. It is this fact which renders a satisfactory analysis of these particles so complicated. This will be illustrated in the next section.

6 Some examples

The following examples are based on four "sentence bases", i.e., non-finite sentence contents into which the particle can be inserted at positions x and y:

(32) x Bruckner y einen Zähltick haben.
      'Bruckner have a number tic.'
(33) x Bruckner y krank sein.
      'Bruckner be ill.'
(34) x Bruckner y tot sein.
      'Bruckner be dead.'
(35) x Bruckner y blaue Augen haben.
      'Bruckner have blue eyes.'

They differ by the type of property, in particular by its temporal characteristics: *einen Zähltick haben* as well as *krank sein* are more or less static temporal properties; they can apply to someone at a time, and not apply at some other time to the very person. The property *tot sein* is different – it has no "contrast to the right". When someone has that property, there is an earlier time at which he was not dead, but there is no later time at which he is not dead (resurrection aside). Finally, *blaue Augen haben* is an "individual level property", i.e., something has it or does not have it – but if it has it, it has it at any time (again, there are reinterpretations, which are not considered here).

These sentence contents provide the descriptive base of a finite sentence. They can be turned into an assertion by making the verb finite and placing this finite component into second position; moreover, there must be an intonational fall at the end. At the same time, it encodes the topic-comment structure of the sentence. In the present context, we are not interested in the details of this complex process but in the effect of insertion *schon* or *noch*.

6.1 *schon*

The resulting structures are:

(36) a. Schon Bruckner hatte einen Zähltick.
     b. Bruckner hatte schon einen Zähltick.
(37) a. ?Schon Bruckner war krank.
     b. Bruckner war schon krank.
(38) a. ?Schon Bruckner war tot.
     b. Bruckner war schon tot.
(39) a. Schon Bruckner hatte blaue Augen.
     b. ?Bruckner hatte schon blaue Augen.

Note that some of these (marked by ?) are odd, and among others, we will try to answer the question why this is the case. The (a) and (b) variants differ in the scope of the particles. We will now compare these in turn.

In 36a, the intuitive impression is that, first, Bruckner is said to have had a number tic, and second, it is also said that he had this property before someone else, for example Mahler or Schönberg, had it (it is not asserted that Bruckner was the first to have a number tic!). How does this intuition follow from the present analysis? In 36a, *schon* has scope over the entire sentence content, i.e., ω = *schon Bruckner einen Zähltick haben*. Thus, α is empty except for the topic time,[26] and ω' can in principle be any property that is contextually relevant. If the main accent is on *Bruckner*, and this seems the most normal prosodic pattern in 36a, then the most likely contextual alternative is something like *Mahler hatte einen Zähltick*.

---

[26] Note that the topic time of $\alpha P\omega$ is only marked by the tense of the verb. It must be, of course, a time at which Bruckner can have a number tic, and thus, there is some indirect information about the topic time. The precise relation between the "α-time" and the "ω-time" is a highly complex issue, especially when they are sequential (as in the case of the pluperfect).

This ALIUD may have been explicitly asserted in the preceding context, or it may just be somehow "in the air". The *schon* in 36a indicates that Bruckner's having had a number tic is earlier. This is exactly the intuition we have. Now, 36a can also have a different intonation, with stress on both *Bruckner* and *Zähltick*. In this case, the ALIUD is something that differs with respect to *Bruckner* as well as to *einen Zähltick haben* – while still being contextually relevant. Such an ω' could, for example, be *Mahler schwer neurotisch sein* 'Mahler be very neurotic', with ALIUD being expressed by *Mahler war schwer neurotisch*. Again, 36a leaves such an ALIUD untouched, but says that Bruckner's having a number tic is earlier.

Consider now 36b. Here, Bruckner is not in the scope of *schon*. It belongs to α; therefore, the "other proposition" is about situations which include Bruckner at a time later than the one of 36b, and ω' must somehow be contextually related to *einen Zähltick haben*. Therefore, ALIUD is constrained to properties that can be reasonably assigned to Bruckner, and if the relevant property is such that he can have it only during his life time (such as having a number tic, in contrast to being born in St. Pölten), then ω' must be a stage-level property of Bruckner. The particle *schon* relates Bruckner's having a number tic at a certain time to a statement about Bruckner at a later time, at which he has either a number tic (ω = ω'), or some other property that might be relevant in this context, for example *Wahnvorstellungen haben* 'have hallucinations'. Both readings are possible. In the first case, it is only indicated that he had the number tic somewhat earlier than expected – the "later time" is not the first time at which he has a number tic. In the second case, it is indicated that his having a number tic precedes some other, perhaps more serious mental problem.

Note that 36b has a second reading. It is less obvious, but becomes clear when *Bruckner* is intonationally highlighted. Then, all of a sudden 36b intuitively corresponds to 36a – the particle has apparently scope over the entire content, although it is placed after Bruckner. This reading is predicted by standard assumptions about German syntax, according to which there is exactly one constituent before the finite verb in declaratives, and any constituent can be "moved" in this position (cf. footnote 20). Thus, the structure which underlies 36b can be *Bruckner schon einen Zähltick haben*, but also *schon Bruckner einen Zähltick haben*. In the second case, the speaker is free "to topicalise" either *schon Bruckner* or only *Bruckner* (or only *schon*, a case not considered so far). This, and the particular intonation which goes with this choice, depends on the way in which the speaker wants to embed αPω into the flow of discourse. The net result is that structures such as 36b are ambiguous as regards the scope of the particle, an ambiguity which immediately follows from our analysis and standard assumptions about German syntax.

Let us now turn to 37a, b. In principle, they should function exactly as 36a, b; but here, the "full scope variant" 37a is odd. This, too, follows naturally from the present analysis: whereas there are many contexts in which it makes sense to say that someone else than Bruckner was not the first to have a number tic, it is more difficult to imagine a context in which it would make sense to draw attention to the fact that someone else than Bruckner was not the first person to be sick. But it indeed possible, for example when Bruckner, Hinz and Kunz are the only three candidates for performing an organ concerto, and it turns out that Hinz is sick. In such a context, 37a – with main stress on Bruckner – is not odd at all. There is no such problem with 37b (except, of course, under the 37a-reading).

The reason that 38a is odd is the same as for 37a, except that it is perhaps even more difficult to imagine a reasonable context (I award 5 Euros for a really good example). Being dead is neither a clear case of a stage level property nor a clear case of an individual level property – it is somewhere in-between: it has a beginning but no end with respect to its subject. As 38a, b show, such an in-between property functions exactly like a stage-level predicate with respect to *schon*. Is this different for a clear individual-level property such as *blaue Augen haben*?

It is. The "wide scope variant" is fine, and the narrow-scope variant is odd. Again, this is predicted by the present analysis. In 39a, the addition of *schon* marks that according to the speaker, someone else is not the first to have blue eyes. This is a reasonable statement in some contexts, and hence, 39a is fine. In 39b, the possible situations are life-time situations of Bruckner, and the addition of *schon* marks that some later "Bruckner-time" is not the first time at which he had blue eyes. But if having blue eyes is a life-time property, then such an additional assertion does not make any sense, and hence, 39b is odd. It is fine, though, if this assumption is given up, for example if *blaue Augen haben* does not refer to the colour of the iris but to Bruckner's make-up for a halloween party.

All properties considered so far, be they simple or complex, are of the atelic type. Let us conclude this tour with a telic predicate, as in 40:

(40) a. Schon der Kreiselsatz wurde von Emmy Noether bewiesen.
‚Already the gyro theorem was by Emmy Noether proven'
b. Der Kreiselsatz wurde schon von Emmy Noether bewiesen.
‚The gyro theorem was already by Emmy Noether proven'

The usual reading of 40a, with *wurde schon von Emmy Noether bewiesen* being destressed, is: something else was not the first thing proven by Emmy Noether, and this follows from our analysis. In 40b, ω is only *von Emmy Noether bewiesen werden*, and ω' must be a property for which it is assumed that it is later, for example *von Gödel bewiesen werden*. Note that αω and ALIUD, i.e., *Der Kreiselsatz wurde von Emmy Noether bewiesen* and *Der Kreiselsatz wurde von Gödel bewiesen* are not incompatible: it could be that they both proved it. The secondary assertion introduced by *schon* is only that the former is earlier than the latter.

6.2 *noch*

In section 1, it was shown that *noch* has at least three readings, called there continuative, further-to, and comparative. Under the present analysis, all of these result from a constant meaning contribution, which is essentially temporal: *noch* relates the sentence in which it occurs to an assertion about some earlier time. The various readings must come from other factors which interact with this constant meaning contribution. We will examine this for the *noch*-counterparts of 34–37.

(41) a. Noch Bruckner hatte einen Zähltick.
　　 b. Bruckner hatte noch einen Zähltick.
(42) a. ?Noch Bruckner war krank.
　　 b. Bruckner war noch krank.
(43) a. ?Noch Bruckner war tot.
　　 b. ?Bruckner war noch tot.
(44) a. Noch Bruckner hatte blaue Augen.
　　 b. ?Bruckner hatte noch blaue Augen.

In 41a, the intuitive impression is that the sad series of people with a number tic has come to an end with Bruckner. But this is only an implicature: there is no contradiction, if the sentence is continued with: "and he was definitely not the last one". What cannot be cancelled is the relation to some ALIUD, according to which something must have been the case before. The most natural candidate, if Bruckner carries main stress, is that someone else had a number tic at some earlier time. This is in complete agreement with 30b. Note that 41a combines temporal and further-to reading: ALIUD – for example *Grillparzer einen Zähltick haben* – is earlier, and that is added to αω, i.e., the assertion that Bruckner had a number-tic. In the 'narrow-scope' reading of 41b (i.e., the reading based on *Bruckner noch einen Zähltick haben*), the potential topic situations must be 'Bruckner-time'-situations, and ω' is some contextually relevant counterpart to *einen Zähltick haben*. This property must apply earlier than ω; in its descriptive content, it may be identical to ω or different from it. It is this difference which leads to the temporal or to the additive reading, respectively. If ω and ω are identical, then this means that his having a number tic is continued. If they are different (e.g., *Halluzinationen haben*), then having a number tic is added.

Turning now to 42, we note some oddness when the particle has scope over the entire sentence. The particle *noch* invites the implicature that Bruckner is the last person in a series about which such a claim can be made, and there are not many contexts in which this is very telling. It would make sense, though, in a world in which, due to the progress of medicine or to divine intervention, sickness has become extinct, and then, 42a (and 42b in its wide scope-reading) would not be odd anymore. In its narrow-scope reading, 42b is like 41b; it can also have both readings, although the additive version sounds less plausible.

In 43, both versions are odd. In 43a and in the wide-scope version of 43b, the reason is the same as in 42a. The explanation is trickier, if Bruckner is not in the scope of *noch*. Under the continuative reading, 43b means that Bruckner was dead at the time talked about, and that this was not the first time at which he was dead. This is odd: if he was dead at some earlier time, he is dead forever, and hence, the addition of *noch* is not felicitous. But this does not exclude the "further-to reading", roughly: in addition to what I have said about Bruckner before, I now say that he was dead. But it is very difficult to imagine a context in which such a assertion makes sense – perhaps after a question like "What else is to be said about Bruckner?".

In 44, the wide-scope variants are fine, because it is said that Bruckner was not the first person – but maybe the last one – which had blue eyes, and for the narrow-scope variant to be pragmatically felicitous, it must be possible that Bruckner first had blue eyes and then not.

Let me now turn to some other cases that oscillate between a continuative and a "further-to" interpretation:

(45) Bruckner hat noch drei Bier getrunken.
      'Bruckner has still three beers drunk'.

This can mean that at the time talked about, he is still busy drinking three beers. This continuative reading – the usual one in *Bruckner war noch krank* – is not excluded in 45, but highly unlikely.[27] The normal understanding is that ω' describes "an independent earlier event", which has the same, partly the same or no descriptive properties of *drei Bier trinken*. If ALIUD happens to be provided by the immediately preceding sentence, then we may have the following sequences:

---

[27] The reason, I assume, is that drinking three beers has a clear end – defined by the last sip –, and thus, it is assumed that the action expressed by ALIUD has reached that final boundary. Therefore, αω is assumed to describe a new event of drinking three beers.

(46) a. Bruckner hat drei Bier getrunken. Dann hat er noch drei Bier getrunken.
'Bruckner has three beers drunk. Then has he still three beers drunk.'
b. Bruckner hat zuerst einen Obstler getrunken. Dann hat er noch drei Bier getrunken.
'Bruckner has first a brandy drunk. Then has he still three beers drunk.'
c. Bruckner hat zuerst einen Germknödel gegessen. Dann hat er noch drei Bier getrunken.
'Bruckner has first a yeast dumpling eaten. Then has he still three beers drunk.'
d. Bruckner hat drei Bier ausgegossen. Dann hat er noch drei Bier getrunken.
'Bruckner has three beers poured out. Then has he still three beers drunk.'

They vary in intonation, and as a consequence, different parts of the second sentence are highlighted. In 46a, for example, *drei Bier getrunken* encodes maintained information and is de-stressed; the last element which is not de-stressed is *noch*, and therefore, it is perceived as "focused". In 46d, the only new element is *getrunken*, and therefore, this element is intonationally highlighted and thus assumed to be the "focus". All of this results from the way in which information is maintained and introduced. It has nothing directly to do with the functioning of *noch*. But it matters for the particular reading of *noch*, because it tells the interlocutor – at least in many cases – how ω is related to ω'. In all constellations of 46, something is "added", but what is added varies with what is said before. In all constellations, there is also a temporal sequence: ω is assigned later than ω'.

The net conclusion is that *noch* is always "temporal" as well as "additive". The addition can be a mere continuation of the same action – in which case only a "later interval of the same situation" is added, because otherwise, it were no continuation but a second action with the same descriptive properties. It can also be a different, or partly different, situation. This depends on what ALIUD is, and this in turn depends on how αPω is integrated into the flow of discourse.[28]

---

[28] These considerations naturally extend to the "comparative usage", as in *Lukas war noch dümmer als sein Bruder* 'Lukas was still [= even] sillier than his brother', if we assume that the temporal order is provided by the way in which the various assertions are introduced into the discourse. In this case, ω is *dümmer als sein Bruder*, and there must be an earlier assertion, explicit or implicit, which says that his brother was silly.

7 Four problems

7.1 Topic time, situation time, and adjacency

The particles *noch* and *schon* relate the proposition of the sentence into which they are inserted to a proposition about an earlier or later topic time. What does this mean for the order between the situations – states, processes, events? Topic time and situation time may coincide, but this need not be the case. The difference became particularly clear in the pluperfect. Consider 47a, b:

(47) a. At ten, Luke had left.
 b. Luke had left at ten.

In 47a, the time about which a claim is made is 10 o'clock. The time of the event itself, Luke's leaving, is left open – but it must be before the topic time. In 47b, the event time is fixed at 10 o'clock, and the topic time is open, except that it must be in the past (as marked by the form *had*).[29] In both cases, the topic situation is a "post-situation" of the event itself, Luke's leaving, and this is marked by the perfect morphology.

The topic time may also overlap the situation time. Consider 47c:

(47) c. At ten, Luke was sleeping.

Here, Luke's sleeping may extend over many hours – but the assertion, as made by the speaker, is confined to a short subinterval of this situation time. This creates the feeling that we are "somehow in the middle of the situation" or that "we see it from inside" – in other words, it leads to an imperfective interpretation. Consider now 47d, uttered after 47c:

(47) d. At eleven, Luke was still sleeping.

In this case, the normal understanding is that there is one and the same event, shown at two topic times (for example the two times at which someone checked whether Luke finally got out of bed). Sentence 47d corresponds to the continua-

---

[29] Sentence 47c can also have the other reading, especially if the final adverbial is a bit set off by a pause. In other words: in this position, it is open whether the adverbials specifies the topic time or the situation time. For a general discussion on the relation between "topic time" and "situation time", see Klein 1994.

tive reading of German *noch*, as in its counterpart *Um elf schlief Lukas noch*. Note that the two topic times are not adjacent: there is a lot of time between ten and eleven about which a similar claim could be made. But it does not make much sense, either, to say that there are two adjacent sleeping situations – it is one long situation two subintervals of which are "shown".

When defining the meaning contribution of *noch* and *schon* in 30, we had left open whether "earlier" and "later" should be sharpened to "left-adjacent" and "right-adjacent". The short discussion above shows that the particles themselves do not require adjacency. The temporal constituency of the underlying situation or situations depends on many factors. If ω does not explicitly specify a boundary, as in *be sleeping* or *be ill*, then αω and ALIUD are normally interpreted as referring to the same situation. This can but need not be different, if ω explicitly specifies a boundary. Consider 48a, b:

(48) a. Lukas schlief noch bis um 12.
 'Lukas slept/was sleeping still until 12.'
 b. Lukas trank noch ein Bier.
 'Lukas drank still a beer' (i.e., drank another beer)
 c. Lukas zerschlug noch ein Glas.
 'Lukas broke still a glass.' (i.e., broke another glass)

In 48a, the (right) boundary is specified by an adverbial. The sentence has two readings: the most common understanding is surely that there is just one underlying situation in which Lukas continues to sleep until 12; note that ω and ω' are different, though: ω is *sleep until 12*, whereas ω' is just *sleep*. But 48a can also mean that he did something on top of something else he had done before. In 48b, the boundary is signalled by the fact that there is a "last sip". This sentences shows the same ambiguity – except that the preference is exactly the opposite; the normal reading is additive. In 48c, finally, no boundary is specified but it has a defined end-state (glass is broken). Here, a continuative reading is practically impossible.

The exact conditions which yield a particular reading are hard to define. They do not only depend on the type of ω (with boundary, with defined end-state, etc), but also on the aspect, as becomes immediately clear when we compare English progressive, (plu-)perfect and simple form. Another factor is the availability of particles such as *wieder* 'again', which adds the information "something not for the first time": Thus, it also involves two propositions, the one in which the particle is included, and an earlier one which is partly identical. But in contrast to *noch*, these two propositions must refer to two non-adjacent situations. This gives the speaker a choice, and if he or she uses *noch*, then this supports the idea that there is no such temporal gap.

It would be impossible here to sort out the complex interplay of factors which yield a particular reading. The crucial point is that we should not include something like an adjacency condition in 30.

7.2 World level order and presentation level order

The terms "earlier" and "later" with respect to topic times relate to a certain temporal order. What is this order? The immediate idea is, of course, that the order of topic times is given by the corresponding situations times – the order reflects is the temporal relation between events or situations in the real or in a fictitious world. But the terms "earlier" and "later" can also relate to the order in which the two situations are presented in discourse. Hence, the temporal order might be on the "world level" or on the "presentation level", as I shall say.

Order on the world level makes only sense when the situations that are described are such that they exhibit such an order. This is typically the case for all sorts of narratives, the preferred playing ground for linguistic theorizing on temporality. It is also found in instructions, for example in recipes, in which it may be crucial to first break the eggs and then scramble them rather than the other way around. But there are many text types which cannot be based on such a world order, for example picture descriptions, logical arguments, legal texts, or linguistic papers. In these cases, a different order source must be found, for example by introducing a "dynamic perspective". A typical case are apartment descriptions (Linde and Labov 74), route directions (Klein 1979), or room descriptions (Ullmer-Ehrich 1982). In all of these cases, there is a natural way to order the various pieces of information: they are defined by an "imaginary tour" or by a "gaze tour", which allows the speaker to translate static spatial arrangements into a temporal sequence of (imaginary) actions. Many uses of *noch* and *schon* are based on this linearization strategy. Take, for example, sentences such as 50 (Abraham 1980, Ehrich 1992):

(50) a. Kranenburg liegt noch in Deutschland, Berg en Dal liegt schon in Holland.
 'Kranenburg still lies in Germany, Berg en Dal already lies in Holland.'
 b. Kranenburg liegt schon in Deutschland, Berg en Dal liegt noch in Holland.
 'Kranenburg lies already in Germany, Berg en Dal lies still in Holland.'

In both cases, the "earlier" property and the "later" property do not relate to the world level but to the order defined by some travel, which goes from Germany to

Holland in 50a, and from Holland to Germany in 50b. There are more complex variants of such a linearization strategy, for example in instructions in which various things overlap temporally (such as in recipes).

Another type of presentation order is the order in which the utterances of some stretch of discourse are spoken, written, heard or read – the "order of mention", as it is sometimes called. One of the most important features of a well-structured discourse is the "principle of chronological order", an idea which, under the label of (forbidden) "hysteron proteron", goes back to ancient rhetoric:

(51) Unless marked otherwise, the order of mention corresponds to the order of events

It is this principle which renders sequences such as "He fell asleep and switched the light off" sound somewhat strange (see Clark 1970, Labov and Waletzky 1967). Many temporal expressions, for example *then, again*, are often, if not primarily, used in relation to the order of mention.

Summing up, he "earlier" and "later" which underlies the function of *schon* and *noch* can be based on the "world level order", but also on any of various possible "presentation level orders". Which one of these is preferred, depends on the particular text type and the particular communicative context.

7.3 "Scalar" and other types of properties

When αschonω or αnochω are uttered in a particular context, then a reasonable ALIUD with its two parts α'ω' must be available in this context, or it must somehow be accommodated. The particle only says that the topic situation of ALIUD is at a later/earlier time than the one of αω. Contextual information, including world knowledge of the interlocutor, suggest possible ω's and thus possible ALIUDs. This information interacts, of course, with the particular type of ω. If, for example, ω is *im Bett sein*, said about the children, then it is hard to imagine a context in which it would make sense to relate this "stage" of the children to a later/earlier stage described by *gern bei ihrer Oma sein* 'to like to be with their grandmother', whereas it makes a lot of sense to relate it to an earlier/later stage described by *herumtoben* 'to run around' or *müde sein* 'to be tired'.

Consider now a property such as *mit Josef verlobt sein* 'to be engaged with Josef', said of Mary with respect to some topic time. World knowledge makes it plausible that this stage is related to an earlier stage *in Josef verliebt sein* 'to be in love with Josef' and to later stages *mit Josef verheiratet sein*, 'to be married with Josef', *von Josef geschieden sein* 'to be divorced from Josef'. Therefore, 51 naturally invites the idea that ALIUD is at some later state at which Maria was married with Josef:

(52)   Maria war schon mit Josef verlobt.

In 52, ω does not explicitly refer to some temporal order: it is world knowledge which comes into play here. But ω may also contain an explicit reference to some temporal order, as in 52:

(53)   Die Kinder waren schon um sieben Uhr im Bett.
       The children were already at seven o'clock in bed.'

In this case, there is a world order of properties *um sechs Uhr im Bett sein, um sieben Uhr im Bett sein, um acht Uhr im Bett sein* etc. which is seen as crucial for ALIUD: ALIUD must be later than αω, and thus, ω' cannot be *um sechs Uhr im Bett sein*; it must be something like *um acht Uhr im Bett sein, um neun Uhr im Bett sein* etc.[30] The function of *schon* in 53, when compared to bare *Die Kinder waren um sieben Uhr im Bett*, is therefore to indicate that this was not only at eight or nine but "already at seven".

Some ω's do not contain an explicit temporal reference but some component which easily links them to a temporal sequence. This can but need not be relevant for ALIUD. Consider 54:

(54)   Johannes hat schon sieben Bier getrunken.
       'Johannes has already seven beers drunk.'

The bare assertion of αω is that Johannes is in the post-time of drinking seven beers. The addition of *schon* can, and does, evoke two different meaning shades, depending on what is assumed to be ω'. If ω' is identical to ω, then 53 suggests that he does not have this property at a later time but already now. But 53 may also be used in contrast to some later time at which he has then drunken more beers. Thus, there is a "scale" in the amounts of beers to which *schon* is linked. But I do not think that this gives rise to a particular "scalar use" of *schon* – it is the normal temporal usage which gives rise to a particular effect in this context. It should be kept in mind, however, that temporal orders need not relate to the world order. In *Links stehen schon drei Bäume*, the presentation order, rather than the world order, is crucial for ALIUD.

---

30 This, I believe, is the origin of Krifka's analysis discussed in section 3.2

There are different ways in which a scale inherent to some ω and a temporal order between ω and ω' can be mapped onto each other. In 52, is clear that someone cannot have drunken eight beers before having drunken seven beers. But consider 53:

(55)   Das Thermometer zeigte schon 41 Grad.
       'The thermometer showed already 41 degrees.'

The temperature can fall or rise, and depending on what the background of the sentence is, this scale is matched in different ways to the world order. Thus, 54 may evoke the idea: "and later, it may be 42", but also the idea "and later, it may be 40".

There are many other ways in which the particular ω, in connection with a particular communicative context, leads to specific meaning shades. But the basic point should be clear: *schon* and *noch* always make the same meaning contribution. The particular readings result from the way in which this relation interacts with other types of information, in particular the descriptive content of ω and various types of contextual knowledge.

7.4 Context integration and "association with focus"

In earlier work on *schon* and *noch*, these particles are brought in close connection to the focus structure of the sentence in which they occur (see section 3). Under the present analysis, their meaning contribution is entirely independent of the information structure of αPω. But whenever a sentence with a particle is uttered, it is, of course, embedded in the flow of discourse and carries the usual marks of this embedding. This has consequences not only on what is assumed to be focused but also on how the precise relation between αω and ALIUD is understood.

I will illustrate this with two examples. The first one is 52 from section 7.3, repeated here:

(52)   Maria war schon mit Josef verlobt.
       'Maria was already with Josef engaged.'

A potential ω' is *mit Josef verheiratet sein*. Then, the situation described by 54 is naturally perceived as one in a series *Maria in Josef verliebt sein, Maria mit Josef verlobt sein, Maria mit Josef verheiratet sein*. The addition of *schon* to bare *Maria war mit Josef verlobt* contrasts this assertion to the possibility that such a state could only have obtained at a later time than the one talked about. A natural continuation would then be, for example: *Die Hochzeit war für den kommenden Herbst geplant. Aber dann hat sie Johannes kennengelernt.* 'The wedding was scheduled for next fall. But then, she got to know Johannes.'

But according to the definition given in 30, ω' need not be descriptively identical with ω; it could also, for example, be *mit Johannes verlobt sein*. This is particularly plausible if in the preceding discourse, someone has said that Maria is now engaged with Johannes, as in 55:

(55) Maria ist mit Johannes verlobt und wahrscheinlich bald unter der Haube. – Naja. Maria war schon mit Josef verlobt. Den hat sie dann auch nicht geheiratet.'Maria is with Johannes engaged and probably soon under the hood [= married]. – Well, well. Maria was already with Josef engaged. Him has she then also not married.'

In this case, ALIUD is given in the preceding context (and thus naturally contextually relevant), and ω is partly different (*Johannes* vs *Josef*) and partly maintained (*verlobt sein*) from the preceding sentence – not because this sentence is ALIUD but because it is preceding. Following normal rules of intonation, the maintained part is de-stressed, and the new, contrasting part is therefore perceived to be "focused".[31] But this has nothing directly to do with the functioning of the particle: it is exactly the same as in the 51-context described above, in which Josef is not focused.

In 55, there is a clash between "world order" and "presentation order": the former is first *Maria mit Josef verlobt sein* (content of αω) and then *Maria mit Johannes verlobt verlobt sein* (content of ALIUD), whereas the presentation order is the opposite. This is a somewhat uncommon, but possible, constellation: *schon* calls for a "later ALIUD", and therefore, it can only precede αω under violation of the principle of chronological order stated in 51 ("world order corresponds to presentation order"). This is different for *noch*, which calls for an "earlier ALIUD", with the same or a different ω'. Compare 56a, b:

(56) a. Johannes hat NOCH ein Bier getrunken.
            'Johannes has STILL a beer drunk.'
       b. Johannes hat noch ein BIER getrunken.
       c. Johannes hat noch ein Bier getrunken. (with "normal" intonation)

---

31 Obviously, this is a radically simplified picture of how the intonation contour in a sentence is determined. But it will suffice to illustrate the relevant point.

In 56a, *noch* is highlighted. This intonation is appropriate in a context in which it was said before that Johannes had drunken a beer. Then, *ein Bier getrunken* is de-stressed, and *noch* is perceived as highlighted. Moreover, the utterance has an "additive reading" – it states that Johannes drank a beer on top of some other beers which he had drunken before. In 56b, *Bier* is strongly highlighted, and *getrunken* is de-stressed. This is appropriate in a context in which he had drunken something else before; in a way, a new "action" is added, which is partly identical with what is said by this ALIUD. In 56c, nothing is particularly highlighted. Then, the particle relates *Johannes hat ein Bier getrunken* to some earlier action of Johannes, whatever that action is, for example finishing a grant application, and drinking a beer is "added" to that small list of actions. The action could even be drinking a beer, and then, we get a continuative reading. In this case, there is no preceding sentence in which it is asserted that he drank a beer, and therefore, there is no de-stressing. The exact interplay between specific contextual embeddings of αω and the relation between αPω and ALIUD is an issue of considerable complexity, and the few remarks above only give a first idea of what this regularities of this interplay are.[32] The crucial point here is that *schon* and *noch* make their meaning contribution completely independent of the focus structure: these particles are no focus particles. Information structure as well as particles such as *schon* and *noch* link the sentence to other propositions which are somewhere found in the context, but they do this in very different ways.

8 Concluding remarks

In the introduction, I expressed some surprise that particles such as *schon*, *noch* and similar ones are so resistent to a clear and straightforward linguistic analysis, although they are so ubiquitous in human languages and are, as a rule, already mastered by small children. The reason is that the meaning contribution of *schon* and *noch* as such is very simple. Basically, they add the information "and compare this to a later/earlier proposition". The complexities and also the many readings of sentences with these particles result from other factors. These are (a) the way

---

[32] I do not understand, for example, why the temporal usage of *schon* is impossible, when the entire ω is de-stressed and thus *schon* is highlighted. Nor do I understand why *Die Kinder waren NOCH im Bett* is odd (except in metalinguistic use) and has to be replaced by *Die Kinder waren IMMER noch im Bett*. Note, incidentally, that in French, the usual word for "still", *encore*, has to be replaced by *toujours* 'always' in these cases.

in which the particle is integrated into the sentence, i.e., the varying scope, (c) the varying "order sources" for what is earlier and what is later, i.e., world order and presentation order, and (c) the way in which the sentence is integrated into the flow of discourse, i.e., what is perceived as "focused". As long as sentences with these particles exhibit a very simple structure, without much variation in the position of the particles, and as long the contexts in which they are used are limited, as in the communication of children, there should not be many problems, and there aren't.

References

Abraham, Werner. 1980. The synchronic and diacronic semantics of German temporal noch and schon, with aspects of English still, yet, and already. Studies in Language 4, 3–24.

Büring, Daniel. 2003. "Intonation, Semantics and Information Structure". To appear in: Gillian Ramchand and Charles Reiss. Eds. Interfaces. (available under http://www.linguistic.ucla.edu/people/buring/)

Büring, Daniel, and Hartmann, Katharina. 2001. The Syntax and Semantics of Focus-Sensitive Particles in German. Natural Language and Linguistic Theory 19. 229–281.

Clark, Eve V. 1970. How children describe events in time. G. Fores d'Arcais and W.J.M. Levelt, Eds. Advances in Psycholinguistics. Amsterdam: North Holland Publishing Company. 275–284.

Dimroth, Christine, and Klein, Wolfgang. 1996. Fokuspartikeln in Lernervarietäten. Ein Analyserahmen und einige Beispiele. Zeitschrift für Literaturwissenschaft und Linguistik 104, 73–114.

Duden. 2000. Großes Wörterbuch der Deutschen Sprache. Mannheim: Bibliographisches Institut.

DWB. 1854ss. Deutsches Wörterbuch. Leipzig: Hirzel.

Ehrich, Veronika. 1992. Hier und Jetzt. Studien zur lokalen und temporalen Deixis im Deutschen. Tübingen: Niemeyer.

Hoepelman, Jan, and Rohrer, Christian. 1981. Remarks on noch and schon in German. In P-J. Tedeschi and A. Zaenen, eds., Tense and Aspect. Syntax and Semantics 14. New York: Academic Press.

Jacobs, Joachim. 1983. Focus und Scalen. Zur Syntax und Semantik der Gradpartikeln im Deutschen. Tübingen: Niemeyer.

Klein, Wolfgang. 1979. Wegauskünfte. Zeitschrift für Literaturwissenschaft und Linguistik 33, 9–57.

Klein, Wolfgang. 1994. Time in language. London: Routledge.

Klein, Wolfgang. 2006. On Finiteness. Veerle van Geenhoven. Semantics in Acquisition. Dordrecht: Springer. 245–272.

König, Ekkehard. 1977. Temporal and non-temporal uses of schon and noch in German. Linguistics and Philosophy 1, 173–198.

König, Ekkehard. 1991. The meaning of focus particles. London: Routledge.

König, Ekkehard. 1993. Focus Particles. J. Jacobs, A. von Stechow, W. Sternefeld, T. Vennemann. eds. Syntax: Ein internationales Handbuch. Berlin: de Gruyter.

Krifka, Manfred. 2000. Alternatives for aspectual particles. Berkeley Linguistic Society Meeting, Feb. 2000. (available under http://amor.rz.hu-berlin.de/~h2816i3x/lehrstuhl.html).

Krifka, Manfred. 2006. Association with Focus Phrases. Valéria Molnár and Susanne Winkler, eds. The Architecture of Focus. Studies in generative grammar 82. Berlin: de Gruyter. 105–136.

Labov, William, and Waletzky, J. 1967. Narrative analysis. J. Helm, Ed. Essays on the verbal and visual arts. Seattle: University of Washington Press.

Linde, Charlotte, and Labov, William. 1974. Spatial networks as a site for the study of language and thought. Language 51, 924–939.

Löbner, Sebastian. 1989. German schon – erst – noch. An integrated analysis. Linguistics and Philosophy 12, 167–212.

Löbner, Sebastian. 1990. Wahr neben falsch. Duale Operatoren als die Quantoren natürlicher Sprache. Tübingen: Niemeyer.

Löbner, Sebastian. 1999. Why German schon and noch are still duals: a reply to Johan van der Auwera. Linguistics and Philosophy 22, 45–107.

Max, Ingolf, and Malink, Marko. 2001. Zur dreidimensionalen Modellierung der Phasenpartikeln um schon. In: Ereignisstrukturen. J. Dölling and T. Zybatow, eds. Linguistische Arbeitsberichte 76, 89–119.

Michaelis, Laura. 1996. On the use and meaning of 'already'. Linguistics and Philosophy 19, 477–502.

Mittwoch, Anita. 1993. The relationship between schon/already and noch/still: A reply to Löbner. Natural Language Semantics 2, 71–82.

Molnár, Valéria, and Winkler, Susanne. Eds. 2006. The Architecture of Focus. Berlin: de Gruyter.

Nederstigt, Ulrike. 2003. Auch and noch in child and adult language. Berlin: de Gruyter.

Ormelius, Elisabeth. 1993. Die Modalpartikel schon. I. Rosengren, ed. Satz und Illokution. Tübingen: Niemeyer. 151–191.

Rooth, Mats. 1992. A theory of focus interpretation. Natural Language Semantics 1, 45–116.

Ullmer-Ehrich, Veronika. 1982. The structure of living space descriptions. In Robert Jarvella and Wolfgang Klein, eds. Speech, Place, and Action. Chichester: Wiley. 219–250.

von Stechow, Arnim. 1990. Focusing and backgrounding operators. In Werner Abraham, Ed. Discourse particles. Amsterdam: John Benjamins. 37–84

von Stechow, Arnim. 1991. Current Issues in the Theory of Focus. von Stechow, Arnim, and Wunderlich, Dieter, Eds. Semantics – An International Handbook of Contemporary Research. Berlin: de Gruyter. 804–825

van der Auwera, Johan. 1993. Already and still: Beyond duality. Linguistics and Philosophy 16, 613–653.

The information structure of French[1]

> La violence, si tu te tais, elle te tue.[2]
> *Metro sign*

1 Introduction

French, the native language of about 80 million speakers and a medium of daily communication for another 200 million speakers, belongs with Portuguese, Spanish and Italian to the Western group of Romance languages. Three centuries of erudite research on its grammatical and lexical rules, a rigid educational policy which does not appreciate deviations from these rules, and a limited tolerance on the part of those who have managed to master them towards those who are less fortunate in that regard have made it one of the most extensively studied and best-codified languages of the world. In spite of that fact, it is not easy to outline the principles of French information structure for at least three reasons:

(a) Like that well-known small village of indomitable Gauls which once held out against the rigid Roman rule, a growing number of people on the street have managed to escape the rigid rules of grammarians and speak versions of French that are not found in the books. As a result, there are now at least two major versions of French, for which no generally accepted labels exist; some simply call them 'French' and 'bad French'; the most common terms, however, are 'Français standard' and 'Français parlé'. Français standard is what is taught in school – to French kids as well as to foreigners learning French as a second language. It is the language of literature, newspapers, and scholarly works – basically of whatever is written. But it is not just a written language – it is also the spoken language of the educated in formal contexts. So, the opposing term 'Français parlé (spoken French)' is a misnomer: It is the kind of French that people on the street speak in informal contexts, not spoken French in general. The precise conditions of use are difficult to determine and not relevant here. As for the

---

[1] I wish to thank Christine Dimroth, Renate Musan, Daniel Véronique and Jürgen Weissenborn for most helpful comments. As this might not be apparent in the text, since my views are somewhat different, I should also point out here how much I owe to the work of Lambrecht (1994) and de Cat (2007).
[2] Violence kills you, if you remain silent, lit: the violence, if you you be-silent, it you kills.

Note: This article originally appeared as Klein, W. (2012). The information structure of French. In M. Krifka and R. Musan (eds.). The Expression of Information Structure. Berlin: de Gruyter. 95–126.

https://doi.org/10.1515/9783110549119-013

structural differences, they are difficult to determine, too, partly because there is still little systematic work on the properties of Français parlé,[3] and partly because Français parlé is not so much a stable and uniform linguistic system as it is a group of varieties with a number of typical features. In what follows, I shall sum up these variants of French under the label 'français avancé (FA)' (literally: advanced French) and contrast it to 'français traditionel (FT)' (traditional French) – the French you learn in the classroom, read in books, and hear in formal contexts. These terms are not meant to express an evaluation – they just relate to the historical development, may it be seen as decay or as progress.

(b) The established analysis of FT is strongly based on the model of Latin, the language from which it evolved. Considerable weight is given to the inflection of irregular verbs in their written form or to the idiosyncratic conditions under which the subjunctive is used in subordinate clauses. But there is, for example, hardly anything on the way in which information structure is marked by word order or intonation. In the authoritative grammar of Grevisse (15th ed.), just four out of about 1600 pages are devoted to this issue under the label 'la mise en relief' (highlighting).

(c) While the description of FT is based on the model of Latin, the description of FA in turn is usually based on the model of FT. Thus, FA is more or less perceived as a deviation from good French, rather than as something with its own inherent systematicities. Such a perspective, while perfectly understandable for historical reasons, is not favourable to a real understanding of how, for example, the flow of information is organized in everyday interaction.

In view of these problems, on the one hand, and the notorious conceptual problems with information structure that make it very difficult to integrate the findings and accounts of different researchers, on the other, any attempt at giving a consistent picture of French information structure would be presumptuous. In the following, I will therefore not try to be comprehensive but rather concentrate on a few central findings and observations and ignore many details and exceptions. This also applies to what is said about French grammar in general, which, as mentioned above, lies in the shadows of a long, impressive, but also biased and thus misguiding tradition. Here, I will not simply recapitulate the received picture, but try to look at French as it might be represented in the head of an intelligent six-year old that has not yet been under the influence of the written language as taught in the classroom.

---

[3] See, for example, Gadet (1989), Andersen and Hansen (2000), Blanche-Benveniste (2005), Detey et al. (2009). The University of Leuven hosts a large corpus of spoken French (http://bach.arts.kuleuven.be/elicop).

2 Some characteristic features of French grammar

Among all Romance languages, French is probably the one that is most remote from their common ancestor Latin, a language with a sumptuous inflectional morphology and a very free word order. This distance is largely due to massive sound changes, and the very different phonological shape of the words resulting from them. But there have also been substantial developments in morphosyntax, some of which will be illustrated now.

2.1 Inflection

In Latin, nouns, adjectives and verbs are abundantly inflected for case, number, gender, tense, mood, and person. In French, inflectional morphology is radically reduced. The amount of this reduction is often hidden by the conservative orthography of French, which preserves many traits of older developmental stages. We will briefly illustrate this for the regular forms of verbs, nouns and adjectives in written French and spoken French:[4]

'I love'	amo	j(e)'aime	[ʒɛm]
'you love'	amas	tu aimes	[ty ɛm]
'he loves'	amat	il aime	[il ɛm]
'we love'	amamus	nous aimons	[nuz ɛmõ] (FA: [õn ɛm])
'you love'	amatis	vous aimez	[vuz ɛme]
'they love'	amant	ils aiment	[ilz ɛm]

Whereas in English, all forms except for the third person singular are identical, spoken French uses the same forms except for the second person plural in FA and the first and second person plural in spoken FT. In other verb paradigms, this reduction is somewhat less strong, but still much stronger than in Spanish, Portuguese, or Italian. We note a similar reduction in the nominal paradigms, here illustrated for the word 'father':

NOM. SG.	pater	le père	[lə pɛr]
GEN. SG.	patris	du père	[dy pɛr]

---

[4] About 90 % of French verbs, including all new ones, follow the pattern of *aimer*, as illustrated above. There is a second class (type *saisir*), which is also considered to be regular, but it is much more limited and no longer productive, and there are about 500 irregular verbs.

DAT. SG.	*patri*	*au père*	[o pɛr]
ACC. SG.	*patrem*	*le père*	[lə pɛr]
NOM. PL.	*patres*	*les pères*	[le pɛr]
GEN. PL.	*patrum*	*des pères*	[de pɛr]
DAT. PL.	*patribus*	*aux pères*	[o pɛr]
ACC. PL.	*patres*	*les pères*	[le pɛr]

Turning finally to adjectives, the only category which is regularly marked by inflection is number, and this only in the written language: *rouge – rouges* ('red'). There are, however, a number of irregular adjectives which preserve gender marking in the written as well as in the spoken form: *grand – grande* ('big').

In other words, there is hardly any inflectional case marking nor – a few exceptions aside – inflectional number or gender marking in spoken French; the orthography, though, preserves remnants of this marking. This reduction is balanced by another development, also visible in the examples above.

2.2 Phrase-initial grammatical elements

In French, grammatical functions tend to be marked at the beginning of a phrase. Latin has neither obligatory subject pronouns nor obligatory determiners. French has developed them and uses them very systematically. One might even argue that elements such as *je, tu, il, on, le, les*, etc are not really pronouns but a sort of word-initial or phrase-initial prefixes. This view may be an exaggeration (see de Cat 2007: 9–26, for a useful discussion of the arguments in the verbal domain), but the development has clearly been moving in this direction. We may sum this up in a simple maxim:

(1) French is moving from head-final to phrase-initial marking of grammatical functions.

This development is neither complete nor exceptionless; but it goes much beyond what traditional orthography suggests.

2.3 Word-order

Latin is generally known for its relatively free word order; moreover, grammatical relations are often non-local: Adjectives, genitive attributes or several parts of verb complexes can easily be detached from the elements to which they belong.

Aside from the complex inflection of Latin, it is these two features which we hated so much in school. French is generally assumed to have a much more rigid word order, and non-local relations are avoided – two core ingredients of what is referred to as 'la clarté de la langue française' (the clarity of the French language). If you have learned French in school, and you want to say that Jean likes apples, and you remember that the generic use is often expressed with a definite article in French, then you would probably say (here and in what follows, I tried to make the glosses as simple as possible; for reasons of space, they are sometimes placed after rather than under the French sentence):

(2) *Jean aime les pommes.*   'John likes (the) apples.'

But as Trévise (1986: 187/188) puts it: 'this canonical ordering is in fact rarely found in everyday spoken French (and indeed looks like an example made up by a linguist).' Instead, people would use one of the following constructions (adapted from Trévise):

(3) *Jean il aime les pommes.* 'John he likes (the) apples.'
(4) *Il aime les pommes Jean.* 'He likes (the) apples John.'
(5) *Jean il les aime les pommes.* 'John he them likes (the) apples.'
(6) *Jean les pommes il les aime.* 'John (the) apples he them likes.'
(7) *Jean les pommes il aime.* 'John (the) apples he likes.'
(8) *Jean les pommes il aime ça.* 'John (the) apples he likes that.'
(9) *Jean il aime ça les pommes.* 'John he likes that (the) apples.'
(10) *Il les aime les pommes Jean.* 'He them likes (the) apples John.'
(11) *Il aime ça les pommes Jean.* 'He likes that (the) apples John.'
(12) *Il aime ça Jean les pommes.* 'He likes that John (the) apples.'
(13) *Il les aime Jean les pommes.* 'He them likes John (the) apples.'
(14) *Les pommes il les aime Jean.* '(The) apples he them likes John.'
(15) *Les pommes il aime ça Jean.* '(The) apples he likes that John.'
(16) *Les pommes il aime ça Jean les pommes.* '(The apples) he likes that John the apples.'
(17) *Les pommes ça il aime Jean.* '(The) apples that he likes John.'
(18) *Les pommes il aime ça les pommes Jean.* '(The) apples he likes that the apples John.'
(19) *Les pommes il les aime Jean les pommes.* '(The) apples he them likes John the apples.'
(20) *Les pommes Jean il aime ça.* '(The) apples John he likes that.'
(21) *Les pommes Jean il les aime.* '(The) apples John he them likes.'
(22) *Les pommes ça Jean il aime.* '(The apples) that John he likes.'

(23) *Les pommes ça Jean il les aime.* '(The) apples that John he them likes.'
(24) *Les pommes Jean il aime.* '(The) apples John he likes.'
(25) *Ya Jean il aime les pommes.* 'There-is John he likes (the) apples.'
(26) *Ya Jean il les aime les pommes.* 'There-is John he them likes (the) apples.'
(27) *Ya Jean les pommes il les aime.* 'There-is John (the) apples he likes them.'
(28) *Ya Jean il aime ça les pommes.* 'There-is John he likes that (the) apples.'
(29) *Ya Jean les pommes ça il aime.* 'There-is John (the apples) that he likes.'
(30) *Ya Jean les pommes il aime ça.* 'There-is John (the) apples he likes that.'

And so on. Out of context, some of these constructions sound odd at first. None of them but (2) would be tolerated in FT. But all of them – except perhaps (2) – are regularly found in everyday interaction at the market or in the métro – and not in the sense of a repair or a correction. In other words, an unbiased look at FA suggests a very different picture of how sentences are structured in French.

This variability of word order does not seem to apply to FT. But note that even in FT, it is not clear whether the 'basic word order' is Subject-Verb-Object or Subject-Object-Verb. This depends on whether the direct object is a lexical noun (including names) or a personal pronoun:

(31) a. *Jean aime ses enfants.* 'John loves his children.'
     b. *Jean les aime.* 'John them loves'.

This remarkable flexibility and its interaction with a few other devices is crucial to the way in which the flow of information is organized in French.

3 Means to mark information structure

The marking of information structure is usually based on a complex interplay of a few devices, four of which are of particular importance and found in many languages; French is no exception.

3.1 Choice of NP type

In French, as in all languages, one and the same entity can be described by different types of noun phrases, such as *une femme – la femme – Marie – celle-ci – elle – 0* 'a woman – the woman – Marie – that one – she – 0'. The choice between these NP types is often connected to the distinction between 'given' (or 'maintained') vs. 'new' information. This is not false but it misses a crucial point: in the

first place, these items differ in the amount of descriptive information which they carry.[5] Thus, they provide the speaker with different possibilities to adapt the utterance to the context. If some entity is available in the context and is salient, not much descriptive information is needed to make it identifiable. French is quite similar to English in this regard, with two noteworthy exceptions:
(a) There is a systematic difference between 'weak' and 'strong' personal pronouns: *je – moi*, 'I', *il – lui* 'he', etc. Only the latter allow for a contrastive usage and can be stressed.
(b) There are differences in the marking of definite and indefinite NPs. With the exception of names, it is normally not possible to use a bare NP in French: **(La) vie est dure – Life is hard, On a mangé *(des) pommes de terre – we had potatoes*.

This latter difference is a repercussion of Maxim (1) stated above: French shows a preference for phrase-initial grammatical marking.

3.2 Word order

As was already shown in Section 2.3, word order in FT has always been considered to be relatively fixed, whereas we find substantial variation in word order in FA. This discussion shall not be repeated here, but I will simply add one important point. The relative freedom of word order in FA does not include 'weak elements', in particular personal pronouns and a few particles, such as *y, en, ne*, which must be placed in front of the verb, and this in a fixed order. This will be crucial for the analysis suggested in Sections 6 and 7 below.

3.3 Constructions

Many languages use special constructions in order to indicate a particular information status. Such constructions are very frequent in FA and, albeit to a lesser extent, also in FT. The main types are (for additional possibilities, see examples (2)–(30)):

(a) Left and right dislocations, such as

---

[5] Note that this is also true for proper names: the descriptive content of *Marie* is the property to be called *Marie*.

(32) a. *La pomme, elle est rouge.*   'The apple, it is red.'
      b. *La pomme, je l'ai mangée.*   'The apple, I it have eaten.'
(33) a. *Elle est rouge, la pomme.*   'It is red, the apple.'
      b. *Je l'ai mangée, la pomme.*   'I it have eaten, the apple.'

(b) Cleft constructions, such as:

(34) a. *C'est la pomme qui est rouge.*   'It is the apple that is red.'
      b. *C'est la pomme que j'ai mangée.*   'It is the apple that I have eaten.'

(c) Presentationals, which come in two variants – with *il y a* or with *avoir*:

(35) a. *Il y a une jeune fille qui m'a téléfoné.*   'A GIRL called me.'
      b. *J'ai ma voiture qui est en panne.*   'My CAR is broken'.

In FA, the first of these often shows up in a form, in which the historical *il y a* is reduced to a sort of particle *ya* and the original relative pronoun *qui* (or *que*) does not appear any more (cf. (25) – (30) in section 2).

3.4 Intonation

In many languages, intonation is the main tool to indicate a particular information structure – as long as this language is spoken.[6] As Hermann Paul first illustrated, the answers to the following four questions differ saliently in their intonation, whereas the segmental structure is the same:

(36) a. *Wer fährt morgen nach Berlin? – PETER fährt morgen nach Berlin.*
         'Who goes tomorrow to Berlin? – Peter goes tomorrow to Berlin.'
    b. *Wann fährt Peter nach Berlin? – Peter fährt MORGEN nach Berlin.*
         'When goes Peter to Berlin? – Peter goes tomorrow to Berlin.'
    c. *Wohin fährt Peter morgen? – Peter fährt morgen nach BERLIN.*
         'Where goes Peter tomorrow? – Peter goes tomorrow to Berlin.'

---

6 It is a non-trivial question whether one should also assume that written utterances carry intonation. Surely, it is normally not noted down, except occasionally by bold type or similar means. But this does not preclude that the reader mentally reconstructs an intonational pattern, just as a reader is able to reconstruct vowels in a writing system which does not note vowels (see also Müller et al 2006).

d. *Was macht Peter morgen? – Peter* FÄHRT MORGEN NACH BERLIN.
'What does Peter tomorrow? – Peter goes tomorrow to Berlin.'

Roughly speaking, elements which are already found in the question are de-stressed, and elements which correspond to the wh-word are felt to be highlighted (roughly indicated by capital letters). In actual fact, the situation is much more complicated; it is arguable, for example, whether the word *morgen* in 36d is de-stressed or, as indicated above, highlighted. But the general idea is clear: the element which corresponds to the wh-element forms the 'focus' of the answer and is marked by a pitch-accent.

In French, opinions are at variance as to whether there is such a pitch-accent that would suffice to mark focus status. Lambrecht (1994: 22, see also 230), for example, states: 'In spoken French, a canonical sentence such as *Ma voiture est en panne*, with the accented NP in preverbal position, would be unacceptable, because [it is] prosodically ill-formed.' The relevant constituent may well be highlighted, but this does not suffice: Another construction must be used in addition, typically a cleft:

(37) a. *Qui va a Berlin demain? – ?Jean va a Berlin demain.*
b. *Qui va a Berlin demain? – C'est Jean qui va a Berlin demain.*

On the other hand, Fery (2004) showed in a set of experiments, that in simple question-answer settings, French speakers indeed use intonational highlighting to indicate the 'focused' constituent; this is not done by using bare pitch accents, however, but by using a combination of various prosodic parameters. It is also beyond doubt that the question in (37) could be answered with the NP *Jean* alone; but it does not make much sense to say that an isolated constituent bears a pitch accent. There has not been much comparable work on this issue thus far, so, it remains unsettled.[7] Most research on the role of prosody for information structure in French does not explicitly address this issue but rather investigates the prosodic properties of particular constructions, for example dislocations or clefts. In what follows, the intonation shall therefore not be examined in isolation but it is embedded within the discussion of these constructions.

---

[7] It is interesting, though, that French does not seem to have an intonational highlighting of the carrier of finiteness, as in English *John* HAS *arrived* or German *Hans* IST *angekommen*. In order to highlight the assertive function, encoded by this element, French would have to use other means, for example a particle such as *Jean est bien arrivé*, with an accent on that particle (see Turco et al. (submitted), for a careful investigation).

We shall now have a closer look at these four types of devices, taking two salient constructions as a starting point – dislocations, which are considered to be the main device that indicates topic status, and cleft constructions, which are considered to be the main device that indicates focus status.[8]

4 Dislocations

Dislocations are constructions which occur at the left or at the right periphery of a clause and which are somehow felt to be detached from its core part. In spoken FA, they are very common. Examples were already given in (2) – (30) above; here are a few others which illustrate the range (examples are given in standard orthography; the comma is used to indicate the detachment):

(38) a. *Jean, il est malade.*
'Jean, he is ill.'
b. *Il est malade, Jean.*
'He is ill, Jean.'

(39) a. *Paul, je le déteste.*
'Paul, I him hate.'
b. *Je le déteste, Paul.*
'I him hate, Paul.'

(40) a. *A Paul, je lui ai donné le livre.*
'To Paul, I him have given the book.'
b. *Je lui ai donné le livre, a Paul.*
'I to-him have given the book, to Paul.'

(41) a. *Marie, Jean, elle l'aime.*
'Marie, Jean, she him loves.'
b. *Elle l'aime, Marie, Jean.*
'She him loves, Marie, Jean.'

(42) a. *A Aix, j'y était tres heureux.*
'At Aix, I there was very happy.'
b. *J'y étais tres heureux, a Aix.*
'I there was very happy, at Aix.'

(43) a. *De sa divorce, il en parle.*
'Of his divorce, he of-it speaks often.'
b. *Il en parle souvent, de sa souvent divorce.*
'He of-it speaks, often, of his divorce.'

(44) a. *Boire, c'est pas la bonne solution.*
'To drink, that is not the right solution.'
b. *C'est pas la bonne solution, boire.*
'That is not the right solution, to drink.'

---

8 Much to my regret, presentationals, like (25–30 or 35a, b) – which are actually quite frequent in FA –, had to be sacrificed for reasons of space. See, for example, Giacomi and Véronique (1982), Morel (1992), Lambrecht (1994: 143–146), Gast and Haas (2011) offer a comparative analysis, which also includes FT.

In FT, these constructions are exceptions. In FA, they abound. This may be due to the fact that FA has developed further structurally or to the fact that FT is normally investigated in its written form, and that the information flow is different in spoken interaction. I am not aware of any systematic work on the grammatical peculiarities of spoken FT, in contrast to written FT, which would allow us to decide on this. In the following, the main formal and functional properties of dislocations will be outlined.

A. Formal properties

(a) Dislocations are syntactically optional: when omitted, the remainder – the 'core' of the clause, as I shall call it – is still a grammatical sentence. So, their use reflects a free decision on the part of the speaker as to how much information is provided about the NP referent or whatever else is described by the dislocation.
(b) A dislocation is matched by a weak element in its core; this may be a clitic pronoun such as *je, il, le*, a clitic demonstrative, *ce* or *ça*, or a clitic particle such as *y* ('there, at-it') or *en* ('of it, from it, from there'). Such a weak element provides no or only minimal descriptive content and relates to the same entity as does the matching dislocation.
(c) They are perceived to be 'detached' in some way from the core. This need not be due to a pause; normally, intonation marks a break, a point to which I will come below.
(d) Various types of constituents can be used as dislocations. In the most common cases, these are lexical noun phrases, names, prepositional phrases, or stressed personal pronouns. As shown in (44a), other constituents – here an infinitive – are also possible; in these cases, the matching clitic is normally the demonstrative *ce* or *ça*.
(e) A dislocation must be definite, if the clitic is definite. Thus, (45a) is not possible, whereas (45b) is:

(45) a. *Un homme, il était dans la chambre.*
    b. *Des pommes, j'en prends.*

Note, however, that 'generic indefinites' can be dislocated, as in examples such as *Les pommes, Jean les aime* or *Jean les aime, les pommes*. In fact, it is arguable whether these are definite or indefinite, because what is meant here is 'the class of apples'.

So far, no difference has been made between left dislocations and right dislocations. These differ when it comes to intonation.

(f) Left as well as right dislocations have different intonation patterns. There are several studies (Rossi 1999, Beyssade et al 2004, de Cat 2007, Meertens 2008), which diverge in their underlying frame of analysis, but largely converge on the facts which they have uncovered. Left dislocations show a salient pitch rise towards the end of the constituent. As a rule, the peak of this rise has the highest pitch of the entire sentence. The core then begins low; it is probably this onset which is primarily responsible for the impression of detachment which comes with the dislocation. Right dislocations show a much less salient intonation pattern. Normally, they echo the last part of the core, i.e., they show a weak rise if the whole sentence happens to be a question (with an intonation rise on the core), or a diminished fall, if the sentence is an assertion. Often, the contour as a whole is almost completely flat. It is much less clear what creates the impression of detachment in right dislocations. Sometimes, there is a pause, but this need not be the case.

B. Functional properties
Authors agree that dislocated constituents have topic status. This sounds clear, but there are two problems. The first problem is the notion of topic itself. Views on what constitutes a topic vary, and therefore, analyses are less uniform than they may appear to be. As for French in particular, there are essentially two – not necessarily incompatible – theoretical lines of analysis. In his ground-breaking work on the information structure of spoken French, Knud Lambrecht (1981, 1986, 1994) adopts an 'aboutness definition' of topic-hood.[9] He carefully distinguishes between the pragmatic category 'topic' and the grammatical category 'topic expression', which are defined as follows (Lambrecht 1994: 131):

> Topic: A referent is interpreted as the topic of a proposition if in a given situation the proposition is construed as being about this referent, i.e., as expressing information which is relevant to and which increases the addressee's knowledge of this referent.

---

[9] Note that in Lambrecht's approach, 'topic' does not form a pair with 'focus' or 'comment'. The notion of comment plays no role in his framework. Focus is defined as follows: 'The semantic component of a pragmatically structured proposition whereby the assertion differs from the presupposition.' (Lambrecht 1994: 213, see also 51–56). It is that part which leads to an update in the addressee's knowledge or convictions.

> Topic expression: A constituent is a topic expression if the proposition expressed by the clause with which it is associated is pragmatically construed as being about the referent of this constituent.

More recent analyses, in particular de Cat (2007) and Delais-Roussarie et al (2004) have been conducted in the spirit of alternative semantics. Under this approach, the topical parts of a clause provide background information, which identifies, or helps to identify, a number of alternatives, one of which is then specified by the focal part of the sentence.

Here, I will essentially follow this second view, mainly because all aboutness analyses, while intuitively very appealing, run into an elementary problem. Consider the following the sentences:

(46) a. *Cain slew Abel.*
　　b. *Abel was slain by Cain.*

There is wide agreement that in (46a), Cain is the topic, whereas in (46b), Abel is the topic. But in both cases, the proposition also provides information that is about the other referent and that increases the addressee's knowledge of this referent. So, aboutness applies to 'topical referents' as well as to 'non-topical referents'.[10] I do not think, incidentally, that an aboutness definition of topic-hood is meaningless; but it is very difficult to make it so precise that it discriminates between what one feels is the topic and between other elements of a sentence.

The second problem is the fact that there are many similarities between left dislocations and right dislocations, but also some salient differences. We already noted different intonation patterns. These are not accidental but coincide with differences in functional potential. Thus, left dislocations can be used contrastively:

(47) *Jean, il est parti de bonne heure,　et MaRIE, elle est restée.*
　　 'Jean, he has left early,　　　　　and Marie, she has stayed.'

Right dislocations usually do not allow such a contrastive usage; (48) is distinctly odd:

(48) *Il est parti de bonne heure, Jean,　*et elle est restée, MaRIE.*
　　 'He has left early, Jean,　　　　　and she has stayed, Marie.'

---

[10] As an aside, an analogous objection applies to alternative semantics: there are alternatives to an expression that is focussed, but there are also alternatives to an expression that is not focussed. The crucial difference is whether the alternatives are 'up for discussion' or not (see Klein and von Stutterheim 1987).

Right dislocations rather give the impression that something is already established, and that for one reason or the other, a bit more information about it is being added. They do not serve to introduce something as a topic, be it in contrast to some other topic or without such a contrast.

A correlate to this difference is the fact that left dislocations can be paraphrased by a *quant à*-construction ('*as for*-construction'), whereas this is not possible for right dislocations:

(49) a. *Quant à Jean, il est parti de bonne heure.*
b. **Il est parti de bonne heure, quant à Jean.*

Like *as for* in English, *quant à* is often used in FT to introduce a topic; such topics always have a contrastive flavour, although this contrast need not be as immediate as in (47), where the two opposing topics are in adjacent sentences.

So, assigning topic status to left dislocations as well as to right dislocations is perhaps not false; but this topic status is not the same in both cases. In a way, right dislocations give the impression that they go beyond notions such as topic, focus and the like. They do not mark anything as topic, nor do they mark anything as focus: they just provide additional information about something that has already been said – information that the speaker feels to be useful for the listener and for communicative success. I will come back to this important point in Section 6.2.

5 *C'est ... qui/que* constructions

In contrast to dislocations, constructions of this sort are regularly found in all varieties of French. Historically, they were derived from relative clauses (see Dufter 2008 for a careful study of their historical development):

(50) *C'est mon oncle qui a perdu le match.*
'This-is my uncle who has lost the match.'

Note that this structure can still function as a sentence with a normal relative clause. Thus, (50) has two readings, indicated by slightly different intonations, which can be paraphrased as follows:

(50)' a. *The person/entity that has lost the match is my uncle.*
b. *This person/entity is my uncle that has lost the match.*

In the second reading, the weak element *c'* (= *ce*) picks up some entity that is contextually given, either because it was explicitly mentioned, or because it is somehow salient for other reasons. In the first reading, it is much less clear what *c'* refers to. In fact, one wonders whether a speaker of French, who is not influenced by the orthographical tradition, would decompose *c'est* into two separate parts at all. An intelligent six-year old, who has normally mastered this construction perfectly well, may well interpret it as a particle [sɛ], which is matched by another particle [ki] or [kə].

Let us now take a closer look at the formal and functional properties of this construction.

A. Formal properties

(a) The general form is *c'est X qui/que Y*, where
 - X is an NP, a PP (including strong pronouns), an adverb, or even a full subordinate clause
 - X can be definite or indefinite
 - X can be an argument of the verb in the following clause (this is the most common case) or an adjunct of that clause
 - *qui/que Y is* a subordinate clause, where *qui* is used if it is the subject of this clause, and *que* otherwise.
 - Y is a clause of which X is an argument or an adjunct.

(b) Unlike in the case of dislocations, there is no matching element for X in the following clause, unless *qui/que* is considered as such. Note that this element does not always behave like a relative pronoun:

(51) a. *C'est vers midi qu'on est parti.*   'That-is around noon that we left.'
 b. *C'est à toi qu'on veut donner le prix.*   'That-is to you that we want to give the award.'

(c) Although *est* ('is') is historically a finite verb, it is normally neither inflected for number nor for tense. In FT, there are occasional remnants of inflection:

(52) *C'était le Sire de Coussy qui a dit ça.*
 'That-was the Sire de Coussy who has said that.'

This gives some substance to the idea that an intelligent six-year old might just see *c'est* as a sort of particle which can precede an NP or a PP in initial position,

before a very conventional writing system makes him believe that it is a construction with a finite verb.
(d) Unlike left dislocations, the *c'est...que/qui* construction does not have a defined intonational pattern. But there are some typical prosodic features which it exhibits: There is a rise, followed by a fall within the cleft, if the whole sentence is an assertion; the subordinate clause is more or less flat. If the entire sentence is a question, then there is no such fall in the cleft; the pitch remains more or less high until the end. Note, however, that there are many variants of this pattern (see Delais-Roussarie et al 2004, Rossi 1999):

(53) Jean est bien difficile, sans doute.   Mais c'est à lui que je dois mon job.
     'Jean is quite difficult, surely.   But it is he to whom I owe my job.'

Here, there may be a fall (after rise) in *à lui* with the remainder being flat. Otherwise, this assertive fall is only in *mon job*. This has different functional consequences, to which we will turn in a moment.

B. Functional properties
(a) Traditionally, *c'est X qui/que* is seen as a highlighting device ('mise-en-relief'). It indicates that something holds for X, in contrast to the possibility that it holds for something else. Thus, it seems to mark X as the focus of the utterance, in the sense of alternative semantics. This is in line with the fact that, when used in an answer to a wh-question, it corresponds to the wh-part:

(54) *Qui a obtenu le Prix Goncourt en 1913? – C'est Proust qui l'a obtenu en 1913.*
     'Who got the Prix Goncourt in 1913?' – 'Marcel Proust got it in 1913.'
(55) *Qu'est ce que Proust a obtenu en 1913? – C'est le Prix Goncourt qu'il a obtenu en 1913.*
     'What did Proust get in 1913?' – 'He got the Prix Goncourt in 1913.'
(56) *Quand a Proust obtenu le Prix Goncourt? – C'est en 1913 qu'il l'a obtenu*
     'When did Proust get the Prix Goncourt?' – 'He got it in 1913.'.

In all of these cases, English, too, would allow a cleft construction ('It was Proust who ...'); but it would somehow sound marked; in French, the situation is rather the opposite – the cleft construction is quite normal, if not the unmarked case. Note, furthermore, that in all of these cases, the subordinate clause can be entirely omitted.

The idea that *c'est X qui/que* serves to isolate a constituent and to mark it as a focus is not without problems, though. I will come back to this in a moment, but let us first have a look at a different though related functional property.

(b) *C'est X qui/que* indicates that the entity, or entities, referred to by X is the only one which – within a given context – has the property assigned to it by the subordinate clause: X has this property, and no (contextually relevant) alternative to X has it. This is compatible with, but not required by, the notion of focus in alternative semantics: one element is selected from a set of alternatives, but this does not necessarily exclude the possibility that other elements from this set have the same property. The utterance *I want a beer* in answer to the question *Who wants a beer?* does not preclude that other people want a beer, as well (whereas the answer *It is me who wants a beer.* seems to suggest this). So, the *c'est X qui/que* construction does not just indicate focus but a 'contrastive focus' – the relevant property applies to X and to nothing else (within a given context).

Note, however, that in many languages, including French, there are at least two other devices which indicate uniqueness. These are restrictive focus particles like *only*, on the one hand, and definiteness marking, (at least under a uniqueness analysis of definiteness, such as Russell's), on the other. For ease of exposition, I use English examples; French is the same in that regard:

(57) a. *The queen came in.*
 b. *Only the queen came in.*
 c. *It was the queen who came in.*

Whereas (57a) does not really compete, since the uniqueness condition is within the NP (the only entity which, in this context, has the property of being a queen), both (57b) and (57c) are unique with respect to the NP-external property, i.e., the property of coming in on that occasion. Hence, double uniqueness should be redundant. But the addition of *only* is perfectly functional, for example in order to correct an earlier assumption according to which the queen and her beloved spouse came in:

(58) *It was only the queen who came in.*

Note, moreover, that if the relevant property is such that only one entity can have it, we get a clear contrast:

(59) a. *It was the queen who died first.*
　　b. **Only the queen died first.*
　　c. **It was only the queen who died first.*

If *c'est X qui/que Y* indeed meant 'X, and nothing else but X, has property Y', as is assumed in the literature, then (59a) should be as odd as (59b) and (59c); but it is not. So, if there is a uniqueness effect beyond the bare focus function, it must be of a different sort. There has been no satisfactory analysis of this problem so far.

Let us now come to a problem which is not related to uniqueness but to the focus status of the *c'est X qui/que* construction. It occurs with the varying prosodic patterns in sentences like (53), repeated here:

(53) *Jean est bien difficile, sans doute.　Mais c'est à lui que je dois mon job.*
　　 'Jean is quite difficult, surely.　　　But it is to him that I owe my job.'

As was said above, there can be a fall (after an initial rise) at the end of the cleft, with the remainder being more or less flat, or this fall can be deferred to the end of the entire sentence, i.e., in *mon job*. In both cases, the focus should be *à lui*. But how should one then analyze the remainder – does it provide mere background? This may be tenable with the first intonational pattern, in which *que je dois mon job* is low and flat. But note that even with this pattern, it need not express background information: The addressee might not know at all that the speaker has a job. And this analysis is completely implausible for the second intonational pattern, in which the final fall is in *mon job*; this looks suspiciously like typical focus marking with a pitch accent, whereas the rise in or towards *à lui* rather seems to indicate a contrastive topic marking. If this is true, the entire idea of *c'est X qui/que* being a focus marker completely breaks down. So, one must either give up that idea, or one must give up the usual mapping between the intonational marking of contrastive topic and intonational marking of (contrastive or non-contrastive) focus. I do not see how this problem can be solved within current frameworks of information structure.

This concludes our survey of the most characteristic information structural constructions in French and their main properties. In the next section, an attempt is made to integrate these observations into an incipient picture of French information structure. I shall also include the speaker's options to encode varying amounts of descriptive information by choosing a particular type of NP.

6 A tentative synthesis

The following picture deviates in some respects from the received way of looking at French grammar. I will first sketch what I believe to be the 'core version' of a French clause, and then look at various elaborations, which reflect different ways of how the flow of information is organized.[11]

6.1 The structural core

In general, a full sentence requires that the argument slots provided by the lexical verb (or the verb cluster) must be filled appropriately. In French, as in most languages, it is also necessary that the verb be made finite; this aspect will not be examined here.[12] French – unlike Latin, for instance – does not like phonologically empty arguments in finite clauses. Hence, the minimal pattern of a structurally complete French sentence is something like this:[13]

(60) a. *J'y travaille.*
'I here work.'
b. *Tu les as aimées.*
'You them have loved.'
c. *Elle le lui a donné.*
'She it to-him/her has given.'
d. *J'en parle.*
'I about-it speak.'
e. *Ça me plaît.*
'That to-me pleases.'

In other words, a minimal sentence in French consists of

---

11 The distinction between a structural core and various lexical expansions, as made in the following, is a barely structural one; it is not meant to reflect the time course of language production (let alone language comprehension). I am not aware of any psycholinguistic work in that respect.
12 As I have argued elsewhere (Klein 2006, 2010), I believe that finiteness is not just an inflectional category of the verb but in many ways fundamental to the syntactic and the semantic organization of sentences; but a discussion of these aspects would lead us too far away here.
13 In the interest of clarity, a number of minor complications are ignored in the following. I also do not discuss the possibility of phonologically empty material, in particular ellipsis, which allows further reduction of what is made explicit in a sentence.

(a) A string of weak elements. These are elements which carry minimal descriptive content and which cannot be used contrastively (two points which are closely related);[14] the order of these elements is rigidly fixed.
(b) A finite verb. The finite and lexical components of the verb can be split (as in *a donné*), in which case the finite element comes first. In this case, too, the lexical component belongs to the core, because it is that component which defines the argument slots.

The string of weak elements precedes the finite part of the verb (there are some exceptions, if the non-finite part is compound, again not to be discussed here). Such a sequence of weak elements and the finite verb will be called here a 'core sentence' or briefly a 'core'. It contains everything that is structurally necessary; but its descriptive information is highly restricted; essentially, only the verb carries more than bare grammatical information. The core can be now enriched in various ways:
A. The verb can be expanded into a more complex verb cluster, an aspect which is not considered here.
B. Non-clitic NPs or PPs can be used, thus providing more descriptive content.
C. Adverbials and various particles can be added. In FT, one of these, the negation particle *ne*, can intrude into the weak string; it is quite characteristic of the overall structural development of French that this has been given up in its 'advanced' versions.[15]

Since the information flow in discourse is systematically based on the interplay of information which comes from the context, on the one hand, and information which is explicitly expressed by the sentence, on the other, these possibilities to enrich the structural core by adding more lexical information are crucial to information structure. So, if we want to understand how French works in that regard, two questions must be addressed:
– What is the information structure of the core?
– How do elements with more descriptive information go beyond this structure?

These questions will now be discussed in turn.

---

14 In general, expressions can only be intonationally contrasted if they express some content that can be related to some other content (except in metalinguistic usage, where everything can be contrasted and in which, as it were, the form is the content).
15 In FT, the usual negation of (60b) is: *Je ne les ai pas aimées*. Thus, the finite part of the verb is 'framed' by two negative elements. In FA, only the second of these survived. In other word, the 'weak string' is now completely opaque for other elements. It is still possible to insert elements into the core; these, however, cannot precede the finite element. So, the weak string and the finiteness marking form a unit that is structurally locked.

6.2 The information structure of the core

This issue has never been investigated, so, we must be a bit speculative here. Two things are clear in a core such as, for example, (60c):
(a) It makes an assertion, and
(b) the situation about which something is asserted must be clear from the context.

The first point is indicated by the form of the sentence. The second point is less obvious; but it becomes immediately clear if one is supposed to say whether *Elle le lui a donné*, uttered by someone here and now, is true or false. This question cannot be answered unless one knows *what situation the claim is about*. This information is often provided by the (verbal or non-verbal) context, as in (61):

(61) *Est-ce que Marie a donné l'ordinateur a son père? – Elle le lui a donné.*
 'Is-it that Marie has given the computer to her father? – She it to-him has given.'

What is the topic and what is the focus in *Elle le lui a donné*? To my mind, there is no single constituent which could figure as a topic, in the sense that the sentence is specifically 'about this entity', or that this, and only this, constituent provides background information. What the sentence is about, is equally described by *elle*, *le*, and *lui*: It is about a situation which involves three arguments of this sort in the roles of subject, direct object and indirect object, respectively; it is also said by the temporal marking on the verb that this situation, and thus the time talked about ('the topic time'), is in the past. The only open issue is whether this situation has the property described by *donner* or rather the property described by *pas donner*.[16] And the answer asserts that it is the former – the situation specified by the question has the property *donner* in relation to the various arguments in the weak string. Hence, the information structure of the core has two components:

---

[16] The lexical content of the compound expression *pas donner* is very general – it is the property 'being different from *donner*'. Note that one could vary (61) to: *Est-ce Marie a donné ou est-ce qu'elle a prêté l'ordinateur a son père?* ('Has Marie given or has she lent the computer to her father?'). In this case, a more restricted alternative to *donner* is specified as to be settled by the answer.

(62) a. It picks up a situation with a particular configuration between the referents of the 'weak string'.
b. It asserts that the property specified by the verb applies to this situation.

This is, so to speak, the root of French information structure: There is a component which picks up the situation talked about, and there is a component which adds a descriptive property to the already identified situation. The first of these components deviates from established notions of 'topic'. It does not provide background information, nor does it relate to a distinguished referent, for example the grammatical subject; rather it helps to identify the situation talked about – the 'topic situation', as one may call it.[17] The second component, on the other hand, does indeed come very close to the notion of focus in alternative semantics, but also comes close to the notion of focus in the sense in which Lambrecht uses it: it reflects a choice between various alternatives which are up for decision, and it corresponds to the part of the sentence which is relevant for the update of the addressee's knowledge.

6.3 Expanding the core

The core is structurally complete, and often, it suffices for communicative purposes. But it requires a rich context, in which the situation talked about and the protagonists which play a role in it are sufficiently clear. Often, however, the speaker feels the need to provide more lexical information. This then leads to what has traditionally been seen as a 'typical' sentence – a sentence with full lexical NPs and perhaps other elements with descriptive content. Such expansions beyond structural necessity raise two questions:

(63) a. What are the reasons for going beyond what is structurally necessary?
b. How are the expansions integrated into the core – are they added at the beginning, at the end, or within (thus somehow breaking up the core), and does such an expansion affect the core elements themselves, for example by modifying or replacing them?

---

[17] The situation talked about can also be compound of several sub-situations, for example in answer to questions like *Who met whom on which occasion?*. These complications are not discussed here.

As for the possible reasons why speakers choose to expand the core, there are at least four, which will be considered in turn.
A. The speaker believes that in a given context, the sparse information of the core is not enough for the listener to understand which entity is intended as a subject, an object, a place, etc. So, if the communication is to be successful, he or she must provide more explicit information.
B. The speaker wants to give an additional description of the same entity, although this entity is already identifiable by the listener. This, I believe, is the source of many right dislocations, as in (64):

(64) a. *Il l'a fait, cet idiot.*
'He it has done, this idiot.'
b. *J'en parle souvent, de mon enfance.*
'I of-it speak often, of my childhood.'

In (64a), the relevant entity must be given in the preceding context, it is then picked up by *l[e]* and by *en* in the role of subject and prepositional object, respectively, without providing more descriptive information. The additional description in the right dislocation provides more information, which was initially not felt to be necessary for the identification of the entity. This additional information may reflect the speaker's view about the referent, as in (64a), or it may reflect some change in the speaker's opinion about whether the referent is indeed identifiable for the listener ('afterthought'), as in (64b). In this case, the additional description may even be contrastive – which is at odds with the common view on right dislocations (see Section 3):

(65) *Tu dois la prendre, celle à DROITE.*
'You must it take, the-one to the RIGHT.'

Such a subsidiary description can, of course, also be used when the first description in the sentence is already a lexical NP rather than a weak element:

(66) a. *Jean, il l'a fait, cet idiot.*
'Jean, he it has done, this idiot.'
b. *Marie, elle a épousé Jean, son premier ami.*
'Marie, she has married Jean, her first friend.'

All of this explains the somewhat ambivalent nature of certain right dislocations, as discussed in section 3 (see examples (47) – (49)). They do not serve to identify the situation talked about, nor do they select an alternative; in this sense, they are neither topic nor focus. But they may enrich the addressee's knowledge about one of the referents.

C. An expansion allows the speaker to set the relevant entity off against other entities that one might consider in the given context. Weak elements, such as *il, le, y, en, lui* (as indirect object) do not allow this, since they are practically void of lexical content: they only indicate a grammatical function. One might argue that, for example, a particle like *y* indeed carries some descriptive content – it relates to a location. But the only lexical contrast would be between 'location – no location', not between a location in contrast to some other location, making this a contrast which hardly ever it is rather a role difference than a difference between various people that could be referred to by *je*. If such a contrast is to be made, other pronominal elements must be used; in these cases, however, additional contextual information must be available to render identification possible.

D. An expansion may contribute to identify the situation talked about, for example by saying: the situation involves my uncle as an agent, or: it is a situation which is situated in London. Note that this is not the same function which an expansion has when it serves to identify an entity itself: the issue is not to identify my uncle or London, but to indicate that these entities characterize the situation about which something is said; the latter function presupposes the former.

Reason D may therefore go together with Reasons A or C, but not with Reason B. With a type D expansion, the speaker indicates: I am going to make a claim about (or ask a question about) a situation which involves Jean as a subject,[18] perhaps in contrast to a situation which involves Pierre as a subject. In such a case, the speaker also says something 'about Peter' – but this is not crucial. What is crucial is rather that the speaker says something about Jean as an agent in the topic situation. Consider (67):

(67) *Hier, Jean a tué son chien.*
'Yesterday, Jean has killed his dog.'

In such a sentence, something is said 'about Jean', but something is said 'about the dog', as well (in fact, the addressee probably learns more about the dog than

---

[18] I shall leave open here whether this role should be seen as a grammatical role (such as subject), a semantical role (such as agent), or a combination of both. This is not a trivial issue, and it would require considerable discussion.

about Jean by hearing the sentence). The true 'topic' is, however, the SITUATION TALKED ABOUT, which is situated in time by *hier* and characterized as a 'Jean-be-agent situation.' One might say here that the temporal characterization is something external to the situation, a sort of 'frame', whereas the characterization 'Jean-be-agent' is a sort of internal property. Indeed, some authors make a distinction between an 'individual topic' and a 'stage topic' (see, for example, Lahousse 2011). But this is just due to the nature of these properties, times versus agents; in terms of what they do for information structure, they serve the same function.

This concludes our discussion of why a speaker may want or feel the need to go beyond the bare structural core. Let us turn now to the question of how this additional material can be integrated into the core. Essentially, there are three possibilities, depending on whether the weak element is preserved or not and on where the expansion is placed:

A. *Addition*: The weak element is preserved, which automatically means that the expansion must be in a different position that the weak element.
B. *Replacement, type A*: The weak element disappears, the expansion takes its position.
C. *Replacement, type B*: The weak element disappears, the expansion shows up in a different position.

Languages may have different preferences here. In French, one notes a considerable variation between FT and FA. I will now briefly illustrate some possibilities, with *Elle le lui a donné* (= 60c) as a core.

(68) a. *Marie, elle le lui a donné.*
b. *Le livre, elle le lui a donné.*
c. *Marie, le livre, elle le lui a donné.*

All three expansions are additions before the core. If there is more than one such addition, as in (68c), the order of the corresponding weak elements is matched. These additions are 'situation-identifying'; they say, for example, that the situation talked about is a situation with Marie as a subject/agent, or that it is a situation with Marie as a subject/agent and the book as a direct object/theme. In all three cases, the situation talked about involves a third person, only identifiable by contextual information, as an indirect object.

(69) a. *Elle le lui a donné, Marie.*
b. *Elle le lui a donné, le livre.*

Here, we have additions at the right periphery; they do not contribute to the identification of the situation talked about but just provide descriptive material about one of the arguments involved in that situation.

In the following expansions, the weak element is replaced rather than maintained, but the position of the replacement varies (remember, the core is *Elle le lui a donné*):

(70) a. *Marie, elle le lui a donné.*
b. *Elle lui a donné le livre.*
c. *Marie lui a donné le livre.*

These sentences correspond to what children and second language learners normally are taught in school, that is, to FT. But in FA, sentences (70a) and (70c) are quite unusual. In other words, FA prefers additions over replacements: It tends to maintain the grammatical core as an intact unit.

A case of replacements that is found in FT as well as in FA is that of clefts:

(71) a. *C'est Marie qui le lui a donné.*
b. *C'est à son oncle qu'elle l'a donné.*
c. *C'est un livre qu'elle lui a donné.*

They replace one, and only one, weak element,[19] and they are always in initial position; if the first element of the weak string is replaced, the position is maintained, and it is not maintained otherwise. The new lexical material is only provided by X, the constituent that is framed by *c'est ... qui/que*. This frame indicates that this constituent is not situation-identifying but belongs to the updating part of the sentence. Compare the following four sentences:

(72) a. *Il est venu.*
b. *Jean, il est venu.*
c. *C'est Jean qui est venu.*
d. *C'est un de mes amis qui est venu.*

(72a) is the bare core. In order to decide whether or not it is true, when uttered on some occasion, it must be clear what the situation talked about is; the bare core

---

[19] Alternatively, one might say that they are added, and the weak element is replaced by *qui/que*. I see no major difference in these two ways to look at it, except that the latter is a bit more in the spirit of a traditional analysis, in which the lexical NP is picked up by a relative pronoun.

only expresses that this situation involves some (male) person as a subject/agent (and that it is in the past, a point not examined here). The addressee may still be able to decide whether it is true or not, if there is sufficient information from the context. But the speaker may also be so kind as to provide additional information about whom this subject/agent is, if there is reason to assume that the listener does not know this yet. This is what happens in (72b). In FT, this would lead to a replacement of the weak element; in FA, an addition is used instead. This is the traditional 'topic status' of left dislocations.

If the additional lexical material is framed by *c'est ... qui/que*, then the framed constituent, which provides this material, is meant to identify the situation talked about: This situation is assumed to be entirely given in the context, and to be about this situation; it is then assigned the property of having X as – in this example – a subject/agent. It is also indicated that X is the only entity which has this function in this situation (but see the discussion of (57) – (59)). There is no reason to assume that X was already mentioned in that context at all, nor is it excluded that other issues are to be decided with respect to that situation. This entirely depends on how rich the contextual information is. Thus, after a question like *Qui est venu?*, the only issue to be decided is who indeed takes the subject-role in that situation. After a question like *Qui est venu et qui est parti?* 'Who did what?', the situation about which something has to be said in the answer is only weakly specified, apart from more general contextual knowledge: It must be a compound situation in the past, which involves two subsituations, each of which with a person as an agent. The answer then decides on who these two persons are. In both cases, (72c) or (72d) would be appropriate; but they would differ in intonation: In the first case, the assertive fall (after the initial rise) is already in the cleft, whereas this fall is deferred to *venu* in the second case.

7 Summing up

> Que pensez-vous de l'amour? – L'amour? Je le fais souvent, mais je n'en parle jamais.[20]
> Marcel Proust (1954: 178)

As was argued in Section 1, a clear and consistent outline of information structure in French is at present out of reach. In what precedes, I first outlined some essential observations, and then tried to integrate them into a coherent view. In

---

20 'What think-you of the love? – The love? I it make often, but I not about-it never talk.'

both respects, the picture is painted with a broad brush. Many facts are disputable, there are numerous exceptions, numerous riddles, and the synthesis can only give an incipient picture. As any attempt to give such a picture, this one has to fight with the notorious unclarity of even the most elementary notions in information structure. I tried to avoid theoretical deliberations in that direction and to adopt, wherever possible, the frameworks used in the literature on French information structure. But as was shown in Sections 3 and 4, neither an account in which the 'topic' provides background information, nor an account in which it is the referent 'about' which something is said do justice to the observations. So, I made some use of two slightly different ideas, each of which is very simple.

The first of these two ideas concerns the 'topic status'. It is assumed that the 'topic', about which something is said is THE WHOLE SITUATION relative to which the proposition expressed by the sentence is true or false (in more complex cases, it can also be a compound situation, comprised of several sub-situations, a case only marginally mentioned here). This situation has somehow to be identifiable; otherwise, one cannot judge whether an assertion is true or not. This can be done by contextual information, for example by a preceding question. But it is also possible to use material from the crucial sentence itself in order to identify the 'topic situation'. Other material in the sentence serves to say that the situation thus identified has a certain property, about which a decision is taken. And it might also be that the speaker adds material which does not serve any such function.

The second idea that was exploited here concerns the varying richness of descriptive information which a certain expression provides. There are elements which are very poor in that regard and, in a way, only give a bit of structural information, such as clitic elements. And there are expressions which are very rich in that regard. An economical speaker tries to work as much as possible with the former – he or she would operate with a bare structural core. This is possible, when the context is rich enough. If not, the speaker has to add descriptive information, and this leads to various kinds of elaborate structures and thus to a different information flow.

From its Latin origin, French grammar differs by a very reduced inflection, by the tendency to mark grammatical relations at the beginning of a phrase, and the increasing preference for a quite rigid structural sentence core. This core consists of a string of weak elements which correspond primarily to the argument slots provided by the lexical verb, on the one hand, and of this verb, on the other. The order of these elements is fixed. But the need and the possibility to expand the core by all sorts of lexically richer material leads to rich variety of syntactic patterns. The structural difference between traditional French and advanced French is much less in these three developments but in the way in which the core is expanded. The citation from Proust at the beginning of this section illustrates the classical language, examples such as (2) – (30) in section 1 illustrate the advanced way. In fact, all three developmental trends are observed in traditional French, be in its written or in its spoken form, as well as in advanced French, which, as a rule, is only spoken. But since the traditional grammatical analysis of French in all forms, including spoken French, is mostly based on written material, and this in a most conservative orthography, the amount of these developments is often underrated. This blurs the picture of French grammar. Only if we overcame this tradition, we may proceed to a correct idea which role information structure plays in this grammar.

References

Ambrose, Jeanne (1996). Bibliographie des études sur le français parlé. Paris: Didier.
Andersen, Hanne Leth and Hansen, Anita Berit (eds.) (2000). Le français parlé. Corpus et résultats. Copenhagen: Museum Tusculanum.
Beyssade, Claire, Delais-Roussarie, Elisabeth, Doetjes, Jenny, Marandin, Jean-Marie and Rialland, Annie (2004). Prosodic, syntactic and pragmatic aspects of information structure – an introduction. In Francis Corblin and Henriëtte de Swart (eds.). Handbook of French Semantics. Stanford: CSLI Publications. 455–475.
Beyssade, Claire, Delais-Roussarie, Elisabeth, Doetjes, Jenny, Marandin, Jean-Marie and Rialland, Annie (2004). Prosody and information in French. In Francis Corblin and Henriëtte de Swart (eds.). Handbook of French Semantics. Stanford: CSLI Publications. 477–499.
Blanche-Benveniste, Claire (1990) Le Français parlé. Études grammaticales. Paris: Éditions CNRS.
Corblin, Francis and de Swart, Henriëtte (eds.) (2004). Handbook of French Semantics. Stanford: CSLI Publications.
de Cat, Cécile (2007). French Dislocation. Syntax, Interpretation, Acquisition. Oxford: Oxford University Press.
Delais-Roussarie, Elisabeth, Doetjes and Sleeman, Petra (2004). Dislocation. In Francis Corblin and Henriëtte de Swart (eds.). Handbook of French Semantics. Stanford: CSLI Publications. 501–528.
Detey, Sylvain, Durand, Jacques, Laks, Bernard and Lyche, Chantal (eds.) (2011). Les variétés du français parlé dans l'espace francophone: ressources pour l'enseignement. Paris: Ophrys.
Doetjes, Jenny, Rebuschi, Georges and Rialland, Annie (2004). Cleft sentences. In Francis Corblin and Henriëtte de Swart (eds.). Handbook of French Semantics. Stanford: CSLI Publications. 529–552.
Dufter, Andreas (2008). On explaining the rise of c'est-clefts in French. In Ulrich Detges and Richard Waltereit (eds.). The Paradox of Grammatical Change: Perspectives from Romance. Amsterdam: Benjamins. 31–56.
Féry, Caroline (2001). Focus and phrasing in French. In Caroline Féry and Wolfgang Sternefeld (eds.). Audiatur Vox Sapientiae. A Festschrift for Arnim von Stechow. Berlin: Akademie Verlag. 153–181.
Gadet, Françoise (1989). Le français ordinaire. Paris: Armand Colin.
Gast, Volker and Haas, Florian (2011). On the distribution of subject properties in formulaic presentationals of Germanic and Romance: A diachronic-typological approach. In Andrej

Malchukov and Anna Siewierska (eds.). Impersonal Constructions: A cross-linguistic perspective. Amsterdam: Benjamins. 127–166.
Giacomi, Alain and Véronique, Daniel (1982). A propos de 'il y a...'/ 'il y en a...'. Le français moderne 3. 237–242.
Grevisse, Maurice (2011). Le bon usage. Bruxelles: Duculot. (15th edition).
Klein, Wolfgang (2006). On finiteness. In Veerle van Geenhoven (ed.). Semantics in Acquisition. Dordrecht: Springer. 245–272.
Klein, Wolfgang (2010). On times and arguments. Linguistics 48. 1221–1253.
Klein, Wolfgang and von Stutterheim Christiane (1987). Quaestio und referentielle Bewegung in Erzählungen. Linguistische Berichte, 109, 163–183.
Lambrecht, Knud (1981). Topic, antitopic, and verb agreement in non-standard French. Amsterdam: John Benjamins.
Lambrecht, Knud (1986). The grammar of spoken French. Ph.D. dissertation, Austin: University of Texas.
Lambrecht, Knud (1994). Information Structure and Sentence Form. Cambridge: Cambridge University Press.
Lahousse, Karen (2011). Quand passent les cigognes. Le sujet nominal postverbal en français moderne. Paris: Presses Universitaires de Vincennes.
Mertens, Piet (2008). Syntaxe, prosodie et structure informationnelle: une approche prédictive pour l'analyse de l'intonation dans le discours. Travaux de Linguistique 56. 87–124.
Morel, Mary-Annick (1992). Les présentatifs en français. In Mary-Annick Morel and Laurent Danon-Boileau (eds.). La deixis. Paris: Presses Universitaires de France. 507–516.
Müller, Anja, Höhle, Barbara, Schmitz, Michaela and Weissenborn, Jürgen (2006). Focus-to-stress alignment in 4 to 5-year-old German-learning children. In Adriana Belletti, Cristiano Chesi and Elisa Di Domenico (eds.). Language Acquisition and Development. Cambridge: Cambrige University Press. 379–392.
Proust, Marcel (1954). A la recherche du temps perdu, Vol. II. Paris: Gallimard.
Rossi, Mario (1999). L'intonation. Le systeme du français. Paris: Ophrys.
Turco, Giusy, Dimroth, Christine and Braun, Bettina (to appear). Focusing on function words: intonational means to mark. Verum Focus in German and in French. Language and Speech.
Trévise, Anne (1986). Topicalisation, is it transferable? In Mike Sharwood Smith and Eric Kellerman (eds.). Crosslinguistic Influence in Second Language Acquisition. Oxford: Pergamon Press. 186–206.
Weil, Henri (1844). De l'ordre des mots dans les langues anciennes comparées aux langues modernes. Paris: Vieweg.

Quaestio and L-perspectivation

1 Choices

Whatever a language allows its speakers to express – it usually provides them with more than one way to express it. Thus, one and the same historical fact may be stated in an active and a passive variant:

(1) a. In 1453, the Turks conquered Constantinople.
    b. In 1453, Constantinople was conquered by the Turks.

The fact reported by these two sentences is the same; still, there is a difference in the way in which it is 'presented'. Another familiar variation concerns word order:

(2) a. In 1453, the Turks conquered Constantinople.
    b. The Turks conquered Constantinople in 1453.

Again, the historical fact is the same. But it seems that these two sentences answer two different questions; whereas (2a) is perfectly appropriate in answer to 'What happened in 1453?', this is not the case for (2b); it is not fully excluded, but somewhat odd, whereas it makes a perfect answer to 'When did the Turks conquer Constantinople?'. Somehow, the adverbial *in 1453* plays a different role in these alternative sentences: in (2a) it is somehow presupposed, and the real answer to the question is the remainder of the clause, the action of the Turks. In (2b), it is the direct answer to the question – what was asked for is the date; it is more 'in focus' than in (2a). Another pair of variants is this:

(3) a. In 1453, the Turks conquered Constantinople.
    b. In 1453, the Turks were conquering Constantinople.

In this case, the formal difference is not so very much in syntax but in morphology, and this variation, again, is accompanied by a slightly different way in which the same event is presented: in (3b), we are somehow placed within this event – they are just doing it –, whereas in (3a), it is presented more as a completed fact.

In all of these cases, the expression is a finite clause. English also offers possibilities to express the very fact in an entirely different construction, as in (4):

Note: This article was written in cooperation with Christiane von Stutterheim and originally appeared as Klein, W. and Von Stutterheim, C. (2002). Quaestio and L-perspectivation. In C. F. Graumann and W. Kallmeyer (eds.). Perspective and Perspectivation in Discourse. Amsterdam: Benjamins. 59–88.

https://doi.org/10.1515/9783110549119-014

(4) a. Constantinople's conquest by the Turks in 1453
    b. The Turks' conquest of Constantinople in 1453
    c. Constantinople, which was conquered by the Turks in 1453

In these three cases, the construction is no longer a full sentence but rather a complex noun phrase. It is hard to tell what precisely the difference between them is – but there is clearly a difference.

It is easy to come up with many other variants in which the same historical event can be put into words. But the point to be made here should be clear: in one and the same situation, and with respect to one and the same fact, there are numerous ways of expressing it. These variants are in a way equivalent; but they are not entirely equivalent; there are sometimes subtle, sometimes substantial differences, and it is at the speaker's discretion to choose between them.

In all examples discussed so far, the speaker's choice is between various STRUCTURAL options. There are also LEXICAL options: depending on the lexical wealth of the language, the speaker may select between various words when describing the same fact; he may replace *Turks* by *Osmans*, or *Constantinople* by *former Byzantium* or by *Istanbul*, or *conquered* by more prosaic *took*. Again, these options are equivalent in one way, but not in another, and it is left to the speaker to opt for the one or the other.

Lexical choice and structural choice reflect elementary properties of natural language. Whatever precise form a language may have, it inevitably has a repertoire of elementary meaning-bearing expressions (words or morphemes), on the one hand, and rules which allow the construction of complex expressions from elementary ones, on the other: a language consists of a lexicon and a morphosyntax. There is a third type of choice which is perhaps less obvious but no less deeply rooted in the nature of human language. In general, the interpretation of an utterance is fed by two sources of information – by linguistic information proper, or 'expression information', and by contextual information. The former stems from what is in the words and in the way in which these are combined. The latter may be of various types. It may come from what has been said before, it may stem from the perceptual situation, or it may be part of the interlocutor's world knowledge. All of this is familiar, and the reason why it is mentioned here is that this permanent interplay between expression information and context information provides the speaker, when talking about something, with a third choice: he must decide what is made explicit by his expression and what is left to contextual information. In all sentences above, for example, the temporal adverbial *in 1453* may be replaced with *then, at that time, soon afterwards, four hundred and forty-seven years ago* and other phrases, which together with context provide the same information. Hence, we have a third type of choice, to be labelled here CONTEXTUAL CHOICE.

Very often, these three forms of choice are not independent. Often, a particular form of contextual choice must be expressed by a particular word; deictical and anaphorical constructions illustrate the point. Similarly, the selection of a particular lexical item may constrain the syntactic constructions between which a speaker may choose; some verbs, for example, have a passive, whereas others do not; some pronouns ('clitic elements') are restricted to particular positions and hence exclude certain word order patterns, etc. But this regular interaction does not affect the general point to be made here. Whenever a speaker wants to produce an utterance in a particular language, he has to decide between various options with which this language provides him. In particular, he has a lexical choice, a structural choice, and a contextual choice. In each of these, the alternatives between which he has to choose are equivalent in one way, but not equivalent in another way. His eventual decision, therefore, reflects a particular way of presenting what he wants to say – it reflects a particular 'perspective' on the facts stated. If we want to understand the phenomenon of 'perspective taking' in language, we must analyse how these three types of choice function in language production.

This is perhaps not the most common way to approach the problem of perspective and perspectivation in language – the "L-perspectivation". We have chosen it here for three closely interrelated reasons. First, there are a number of fields in which the notion of perspective has a relatively clear definition, for example in mathematics, in visual perception, and maybe in the history of art. In its application to language, however, it has a strong metaphorical character, with all advantages and disadvantages of metaphorical extension: it deals with an important phenomenon, it captures crucial insights, but it is not clearly defined, and it misses what is specific to language. Take, for example, a core notion such as 'viewpoint'. In visual perception, this notion is comparatively well-defined – it is the spatial position at which the observer is, or imagines to be. In language, this notion of viewpoint also plays a role, for example in the use of deictic terms such as *left, right, here,* etc. This, however, is only a special case. It is much less clear what 'viewpoint' means, for example, in the comparatively well-studied case of (grammaticalised) aspect. Verbal aspect is a category found in many, if not most, languages. The difference between simple form and expanded form, as in *The Turks conquered Constantinople* vs *The Turks were conquering Constantinople* (cf. example 3 above) illustrates this category. Linguists normally characterise different aspects, as 'various ways of viewing the situation' and similar characterisations (Comrie 1976). In fact, the linguistic term 'aspect' is a translation of Russian *vid'* 'view'. But clearly, this notion of viewpoint cannot mean two different concrete places from which something is seen. In the case of 'viewpoint aspect', the concrete position of speaker, listener, or any other person, plays no role at all, nor is anything 'seen' differently, if this word is understood in its literal sense. In example 3a, b nothing is seen at all. Even more problematic are cases in which the difference between the use of active and passive, or varying subjective evaluations of what is expressed, are accounted for in terms of 'viewpoint'. This is a very suggestive and intuitively appealing way to give the 'flavour' of the difference; but it can only be a starting point for an explanation proper of what is going on in these cases. Such an explanation must be specific to the particular cognitive domain in which the phenomenon of perspective and perspective taking is observed. It would be more appropriate, therefore, to talk about 'V-perspective' and 'V-perspectivation' (V for 'visual'), on the one hand, and 'L-perspective' and 'L- perspectivation' (L for language), on the other. It is the latter we are dealing with here. This does not preclude that there are many similarities; but simply talking about 'perspective' obliterates the differences – and these are not minor. This already has brought us to the second point, discussed below.

The principles of perspective-taking are in many ways different when language comes into play. Someone may see a tree from various perspectives, he may draw a tree from various perspectives, and he may describe a tree from various perspectives. In the two former cases, the difference in perspective is essentially determined by the nature of our perception. In the latter case, it is determined by highly abstract cognitive principles which determine the choice of words and constructions against the background of shared assumptions among the interlocutors. Now, this example is relatively simple because the common element, the tree, is a physical object. But perspective-taking in language goes far beyond this case. In examples 1-4 above, the common element which is presented from various perspectives is a historical event; hence, it is a much more abstract entity than, for example, a tree which can indeed be seen, drawn, and described from different angles. And there are still more abstract cases in which the intuitive notion of perspective-taking in language makes sense, for example arguments or instructions. In all of these cases, however, the principles of perspective-taking are much the same; they are constraints on choices, in particular the ones mentioned above.

Third, L-perspectivation is a highly complex, active process which involves a series of interrelated decisions on many levels. This is already obvious for the elementary constructions 1-4 above. But in actual fact, the production of such a sentence is normally part of a longer communicative task, in which the speaker transforms selected elements of his knowledge into concrete sound waves. In each phase of this process, the speaker is permanently faced with a multitude of choices. In our example, we have assumed that it is already clear what 'the fact' to be talked about is – here the conquest of Constantinople in the year of 1453. But the decision to talk about something specific is, or at least maybe, one of the many choices which the speaker has to take. This becomes clearer if we look at typical communicative situations in which a speaker is challenged to produce a specific text. Suppose, for example, someone is asked by a passer-by: *How do I get from here to the station?* If the interlocutor takes on this task and sets out to fulfil it by verbal means, then he may be able to do so by producing a single sentence. But as a rule, he will produce an ensemble of well-organised sentences, that is, a text. An essential part of this process is the decision about which information is to be selected for verbalisation, and which part of this selected information is to be packed into a single sentence. Only then does it make sense to ask what structural form this sentence should have and which lexical items it is to contain. Hence, the question of perspectivation crops up on very different levels, and on each of these levels, it takes a slightly different form. What is constant, though, is the idea that there is always a set of alternatives, which are equivalent in one way and not equivalent in another. The question which we will address in the main part of this chapter is now: Are there overarching principles which determine, or at least influence, the speaker's choice and hence the particular perspective which he takes in his production?

The fact that the choice, on whichever level, is always a task of the speaker does not mean that the listener has no role in this process. In fact, he may even 'set the stage' by posing a particular question, which the speaker then has to answer. The example of the route directions question above illustrates the point. Even if there is no explicit question of this sort, the speaker may behave as if there were such a question and a particular listener, or group of listeners, who asks it. As we shall see later, the particular – implicit or explicit – question which the speaker sets out to answer is a core constraint on possible perspectives. It should be clear, however, that it is still left to the speaker how he deals with such a question.

He may not accept it at all, he may accept it but ignore some of the constraints which it imposes on his production, and even if he accepts it in its entirety, the question still leaves him with many degrees of freedom as regards the various choices he has to make. This will be discussed in sections 3–6 of this chapter. It will be useful to begin, however, with a brief look at the various stages of the production process and the way in which the speaker can go the one or the other way.

2 Levels in production

There is considerable theoretical and empirical work on human language production. In this section, we shall not try to review this work (see, for example, Levelt 1989 and Herrmann and Grabowski 1994), but briefly discuss some elementary facts which every theory must deal with. It will be helpful to use a simple example. Suppose someone was involved in a traffic accident and is then asked on some occasion to speak about what happened during this accident. Then, at least the following four cognitive levels may play a role in L-perspectivation.

2.1 Intake

The underlying event itself, the traffic accident in this example, is a complex agglomeration of individual facts and incidents, of persons and objects involved, of temporal, spatial and causal relations. Only some of these are perceived and stored by the individual participants. The process which leads from the 'objective situation' to the particular mental representation which an individual forms of this situation is in many ways 'perspective-driven'. The most obvious source of selection is given by the fact that the perceiver has only restricted sensory access to this situation; he has a particular 'viewpoint' in the literal sense of the word:

> In correspondance of the bodily nature of the perceiving and acting subject, the objects of experience are only present in those aspects that are seen from the spatiotemporal point of view taken by the subject. To be present in *aspects* with respect to a given viewpoint is the basic meaning of *perspective*. (Graumann 1989: 96)

But there are many other factors which govern the way in which a mental representation is built up. They range from very general principles that determine the cognitive processing of visual and other sensory input to highly subjective preferences for one or the other aspect of the situation. Some features of a situation are perceptually more salient than others and hence more likely to be noticed and stored. There are social conventions on what is more and what is less relevant in such a situation. These conventions may be culture-specific, they may be specific to a particular speech community or social group. And finally, there are subjective preferences which depend on the individual's personal history, her interests, his momentary emotional disposition, etc.

The perspectival nature of the intake is not necessarily related to how this situation is later presented in a verbal account. At that point, language plays a role only insofar as particular properties of a language may influence the oberver's attention. Thus, a deictic system which does not discriminate between 'left' and 'right', 'front' and 'back' may lead the observer to ignore certain aspects of the spatial arrangement, or to give them less weight than a system of spatial reference which depends on the position of the speaker (see Levinson 1997). But the existence and the weight of such factors is arguable, and to the extent to which they exist, they are surely weak. In general, the intake is not an active process based on linguistic knowledge; it should rather be seen as a language-independent filter which rules out certain features of the situation and lets others pass. But obviously, this particular filtering has strong consequences for what can later be selected in text generation. It creates the knowledge basis on which the speaker can draw. The clearest case is surely the 'initial vantage point' with which it provides the participant: a time and a position, which then later may surface in the participant's account of this situation, for example in form of a particular 'topic time' (see section 4.3 below).

2.2 Update

Normally, some time elapes between intake and text generation. In the course of this time, the original representation is in many ways transformed in the observer's memory. Certain features are dropped, others are added, some features may change their relative weight, they might gain or lose certain emotional connotations, moral evaluations are added that were absent from the original representation, certain observations may be re-interpreted in the light of later experiences, or due to what other parties say about the situation etc. This steady transformation is not arbitrary. It depends on a wealth of factors, ranging from very general properties of human memory to highly specific and subjective preferences of the individual. Hence, this permanent update may also be considered to be 'perspective-driven'. But then, the original, non-metaphorical meaning of this notion is largely lost and replaced with an understanding of perspective, that is highly suggestive but much less well-defined; we might speak here of 'M-perspectivation' (M for memory), in contrast to I-perspectivation (I for intake) and L-perspectivation. Again, there is no reason to assume that language plays a substantial role in this updating. But its eventual result restricts the available knowledge on which the speaker can base his text generation.

2.3 Forming a discourse representation

In a specific communicative situation, the speaker sets out to verbalise part of what he has stored in memory. This is the point where language, and hence L-perspectivation, comes in. Very often, text generation is initiated by a particular question which the speaker is supposed to answer, for example: 'What did you see?' or 'What did the truck that came from the left side look like?' or 'What did you do yourself?' or 'Have you ever been in danger of life?'. There need not be such an explicit question; the speaker may simply want to speak, for one reason or another, about what he experienced some time ago; in a way, he is posing such a question to himself. In each case, however, there is a particular communicative goal that causes the speaker to activate his updated mental representation and to create a new, temporary conceptual structure, a *discourse representation* (other labels are *conceptual structure*, *preverbal message*, and similar ones). It is this discourse representation which underlies the concrete text to be produced by the speaker. The discourse representation differs in four crucial respects from the final representation in memory:

Selection. The discourse representation contains only selected parts of the entire representation. This selection is determined, or at least constrained, by the particular communicative goal. Selection not only concerns which bits and pieces of the original representation are chosen for verbalisation at all but also at which level of 'granularity' these are to be put into words. Thus, the speaker may decide to give only a very global account of some subevents but go into much more detail for other subevents, or to begin with a global account and then refine it, etc.

Addition. Typically, the material contained in the discourse representation includes bits and pieces of information which stem from other sources than from what the speaker has stored about the original situation. He may add comparisons, try to give explanations, relate the particular subevents or participants to other events or persons, include moral and other evaluations, etc.

Linearisation. Somehow, the various conceptual units which belong to the discourse representation must be sequentially ordered. In some cases, this is comparatively easy; narratives often reflect a simple temporal order of subevents. But as a rule, linearisation is much more problematic. Already in the case of a car accident, subevents may overlap or be completely simultaneous, and then, the speaker has to make a choice of what to represent first. It may also be that the level of granularity is not kept constant, for example if the speaker chooses to give first a rough account and then go into more detail with some of the subevents. In this case, there is is still a temporal ordering, which provides a natural base for linearisation. Other cognitive representations do not involve such a linear order, for example in the case of a picture description or a logical argument. In these cases, the speakers may choose very different 'perspectives', under which the entire information to be verbalised is put into sequential order (see, e.g., Levelt 1982).

Function assignment. There is good reason to assume that already before the decision on the final language-specific form is taken, various bits of information are marked for special linguistic features. This includes, for example, the decision whether a certain entity – person or object – should be encoded as the subject or as the object, whether an active or passive way of presentation is chosen, what belongs to the topic component and what belongs to the focus component of the final utterance, etc. Form and amount of this marking are much at dispute, and in order to keep it different from the eventual language-specific marking of, for example, the grammatical subject or the passive form of the verb, we called it here 'function assignment'.

All four properties are the result of continuous 'perspectival' choices. This is obvious for both aspects of *selection*: the speaker weighs the various elements from his stored knowledge representation and decides which ones to include and on which level of granularity. Note, however, that this decision does not reflect what has been called 'contextual choice' in section 1. Contextual choice is the speaker's decision about *what is explicitly stated and what is left implicit because the speaker assumes that the listener can infer it from context*. Hence, it presupposes that the speaker wants that the listener eventually has this information. *Selection* concerns the speaker's decision which information in which detail the listener should have due to his, the speaker's, efforts. It is an adaptation to the listener – but not in the sense that the speaker plans his text such that it fits the listener's contextual knowledge.

Analoguous considerations apply for *addition*. The extent to which the speaker wants to provide the listener with subjective comments and evaluations on the event, for example, is surely a matter of his 'subjective perspective' on this event. They may be very different, for example, if he is the victim of the traffic accident, a policeman or simply a bystander, they may be different if he is a passionate bike-driver, if he has a driving-license or not, if he had a car accident himself before, etc etc. But all of this has nothing directly to do with L-perspectivation.

The speaker may also choose different linearisation strategies; he may prefer, in the case of the traffic accident, to follow a strictly temporal order wherever this is possible. But he may also choose to tell the events backwards, as seen from the result, and then explain how this result came about. Similarly, he is free to choose where to plug in additional information, such as comments or background statements. Again, one may call this choice perspectival, but it should be clear that this, again, is a different notion of perspective.

The situation is much more difficult with respect to *function assignment*, because the speaker's decision here immediately affects the choice of what to express in which concrete way. The decision, for example, to present a particular participant of the situation as an agent, rather than as a patient, is a 'structural choice', in the sense of section 1. Similarly, the decision to assign certain subparts of the information to the topic component and other subparts to the focus component of the utterance immediately affects the structure of this utterance. Another decision taken at this point is the fixation of a particular 'origo', i.e., vantage point to which times and spaces are related and which is then reflected in the utterance by the choice of particular words, such as the deictic terms *left, right, here* etc. or by particular tense forms. The problem is here that, whatever the speaker's decisions are, they can be implemented in various ways in the final utterance. The speaker may be able, for example, to transform the same – or essentially the same – discourse representation into an English, a German or a French sentence. Or if he chooses his own position as the spatial origo, he is still free to say *here* or *where I was* or *at my position*.This has already brought us to the last level of text generation – the level in which eventual perspectival decisions are transposed to linguistic form.

2.4 Constructing a linguistic form

Whatever the discourse represention is – any language provides its speakers with very specific possibilities to implement it. The discourse representation may fix that a certain element belongs to the topic information; still, there are various ways in which this is marked – by intonation, by word order, by the choice of a particular particle which indicates the information status of some element. Similarly the discourse representation may have fixed that some subevent is presented as on-going, rather than as completed. Metaphorically speaking, the speaker puts himself, and wants to put the listener, 'into the situation', rather than seeing it from the outside. Then, he has still an option between, for example, a particular verbal aspect, an adverbial, or a combination of these verbal means. As was already said in the preceding section, it is very difficult to say to which extent the decision about the eventual form are determined by the formation of the discourse representation itself or by its translation in a concrete linguistic form, and opinions vary considerably on this point. Bierwisch and Schreuder (1992), for example, assume that the discourse representation – their 'conceptual structure' – is neutral with respect to the final linguistic form; as a consequence, it is the same no matter in which language the speaker wants to express it. Under such an assumption, there is no 'function assigment' in the discourse representation, as has been assumed here. We shall not discuss this point in detail (see von Stutterheim 1997, chapter 9). It seems clear, however, that there are intermediate stages between a language-neutral cognitive representation of what is to be expressed, on the one hand, and the final linguistic form, on the other. The precise number and nature of these interim stages is a matter of dispute. So, production may be much more flexible, depending on the nature of the particular communicative task and maybe even the speaker's competence. We shall not try to sort this out here. The crucial point in the present context is this: It is exactly this passage within the entire text generation at which L- perspectivising comes in.

So far, we have given numerous examples which illustrate structural choice, lexical choice and contextual choice; others can easily added. In fact, a great deal of the literature on perspective-taking in language consists of very striking examples and anecdotical evidence for this. But are there any *principles* which determine this part of the process – in other words, are there any general constraints that which are characteristic of L- perspectivation? This is the question which we will address in the next section.

3 The Quaestio

3.1 Questions and answers

What causes a speaker to activate parts of this stored knowledge, build a discourse representation and transform it into sound waves? In the easiest case, this is done by an explicit question on the part of some interlocutor. In the case of a traffic accident, such a question might be, for example 'Which car came from the left?' This question defines, within limits, the communicative task to be solved. The speaker may choose to answer it simply with a single sentence or even a part of such a sentence, for example

(5) A BMW 730 came from the left.
(6) A BMW 730.

What he is asked for by the question, is the specification of some entity. The question raises a set of alternatives – all those x's that could have come from the left on that occasion, and the speaker is challenged to select one of those – the one which really came from the left on that occasion. In other words, the question defines a choice, and it is up to the speaker to deal with this choice. In doing so, he is left with a certain amount of freedom. It is this freedom which allows the speaker, if he takes on the task at all, to set a particular perspective: the question imposes constraints on a possible answer – but it does not determine the answer, of course. In particular, the speaker may choose to go into more detail with respect to the predicates he is asked to specify, and may answer the question by a whole series of interconnected utterances – i.e., with a text:

(7) From my position, I could not see it very well. Everything blue. One of my neighbours had such a car. I guess it must be very expensive, one of these old-fashioned fossils...

Not all utterances in such a sequence are directly 'to the point', which is, here, to contribute to the specification of the object. The first utterance in 7, for example, highlights the role of the speaker's position in the intake phase and thus explicitly introduces a perspectival component. At the same time, it qualifies the reliability of the description: it has not only a spatial but also a modalising component. Clearly, such information can be relevant and important; but it does not directly serve to answer the question. We shall call those utterances which directly contribute to answering the question, its 'main structure', and those which give additional – and communicately often important – material, its 'side structures'. Side structures can be of various type – comments, evaluations, background information, etc. Thus, they are a rich source of perspectivation in one sense of the word (cf. Sandig 1996). For the speaker, they may even be more important than main structure utterances, because they allow him to express his own subjective attitude. But note that this is one way in which the text reflects a particular perspective. What counts as main structure and what as side structure, directly depends on the specific question which the text as a whole intends to answer. In the example, the speaker is asked to specify a particular object. Had the question been 'What happened next with the car that came from the left?', then the categorization as main or side structure would have been the reverse. In that case, the speaker's task would have been to specify a sequence of small events, which in its entirety constitutes a subpart of the entire traffic accident; and this sequence of subevents would then comprise the main structure of the text, its 'foreground'. Any other material – for example a more detailed description of a car, or of some other vehicle involved in the events – would belong to the side structures, or 'background', of the text. The concepts 'foreground' and 'background', are normally not introduces in this way but rather in terms of whether or not they are a 'narrative sequence'. It should be clear, however, that the background-foreground partitioning in narration is only a special case of a much more general phenomenon: they reflect various reactions to the underlying question.

There is a second important feature of 'textual answers' to a question. If the entire information is distributed over a series of several utterances, then certain meaning components within each utterance are maintained from the preceding utterance (or utterances), while other meaning components are freshly introduced. In this example, there is only one crucial entity referred to, the car; it is introduced in the question itself and then merely maintained in the subsequent utterances of the main structure. Had there been more than one vehicle, the related question, 'Where did the cars come from?' would have forced the speaker into a much more complicated pattern of referent introduction and maintenance.

Objects and persons, in brief, the referents of noun phrases, are not the only meaning elements that must be introduced or maintained across utterances. Temporal intervals and subspaces are others. Again, this crucially depends on the nature of the initial question. A question such as *What did the car look like?* leaves time and space constant across the text – more precisely, across the main structure utterances of the text. A question such as *What did you observe?*, by contrast, normally invites regular switches in the spatial and temporal domain. Such a question provides the speaker with more degrees of freedom how to organise his discourse representation and how to put it into words.

Thus, a coherent text that is produced as an answer to a question involves a 'referential movement' within various semantic domains (or, as we shall say here, 'referential domains'), such as persons, place, time, and others. This referential movement is reflected in the use of specific linguistic means – it immediately influences the speaker's lexical, structural and contextual choice.

Summing up, the structure of a text is systematically constrained by the nature of the question which the text in its entirety is produced to answer. These constraints include:
a. the partitioning of the text into main structure and side structures;
b. the assignment of specific meaning elements to the topic component or to the focus of a main structure utterance;
c. the 'filling' of various possible domains of reference within each main structure utterance;
d. the referential movement within the domains from one main structure utterance to the next.

They narrow down the choices of the speaker, if he takes on the communicative task – but they leave him certain degrees of freedom, and thus various ways to 'present his case'. It is this fact which allows the speaker to impose an L-perspective on what he sets out to say. We shall explain this in some more detail in sections 3.2–3.4 below.

Not all texts are solicited by an explicit question. People sometimes take the liberty to speak without being asked, or, to put it alternatively, they define their own questions. In other words, the question which underlies the production of an utterance or a longer text may be explicitly asked, or it may be implicitly given – either by the speaker himself, or just because the situation is such that it suggests a particular question to be answered. We shall use the term QUAESTIO for both cases – a real question in a real dialogue, or an implicit question with a similar function. This idea is not new; in fact, it is already found in ancient rhetoric, although its structural consequences on the concrete form of texts and individual utterances have hardly ever been a concrete object of investigation in the rhetorical tradition (for a discussion, see von Stutterheim1997, chapter two).

As was said above, the quaestio imposes certain constraints on the speaker's answer, providing him at the same time with a limited set of options among which he can choose. In no case is the speaker bound to obey these constraints. If he does not, then this either leads to side structures – for the entire text – or to particular rhetorical effects. In what follows, we shall discuss constraints b. – d. in some more detail (the constraint which leads to a partitioning in 'foreground' and 'background' was already discussed above).

3.2 Topic component and focus component

In general, an utterance can be used to answer very different questions. Consider, for example 8, which could be part of an account of the traffic accident:

(8)   The bike came from the left.

Such an utterance could be made in answer to:

(9)   What came from the left?
(10) Where did the bike come from?
(11) What happened?
(12) What happened next?

In each of these cases, sentence 8 settles an open alternative raised by the question – it specifies one out of a set of candidates at issue. In 9, the alternative to be settled includes those entities – vehicles, as the context suggests – that could have come from the left at that time; and the one is selected among the various possible candidates is 'the bike'. In 10, the possibilities include all the places where the bike could have come from, and what is selected is the particular place described by *from the left*. In 11, the choice is between all those events that could have happened, and what is selected is the particular event of the bike coming from the left. In 12, the alternative raised is very similar to 11, but the time is explicitly restricted: what is asked for are the events that could have happened at some time after the time of a previous event, and one of those is selected and specified in the answer.

In all of these cases, we have an alternative set by the question, and an element from this alternative that is specified in the answer. Such an alternative at issue will be called the 'topic' of the utterance, and the element from that alternative which is chosen and specified, the 'focus' of the utterance. Topic and focus, as these terms are used here, are components of the 'meaning' of an utterance – a person, an action, a time span. They are not the verbal means – a word or an entire construction – which express this meaning. When talking about a speaker's choice in the production process, we must carefully distinguish between the choice of, for example, a person he wants to talk about, and the choice between various ways to do this. Both decisions may reflect a particular form of 'perpectivation'; but only the latter is what is understood here to be L-perspectivation, i.e., the combination of contextual, structural and lexical choice.

It is also important to distinguish between the expression of a topic or focus, on the one hand, and the marking that that entity IS topic or focus, on the other. In 8, when said in answer to 9, the focus is the bike, and this focus is referred to by the expression *the bike*. With a different contextual choice, it could also have been expressed by *that bike* or by *it*. Its focal status is marked by intonation. Intonation is not the only device available to make clear what the focus (or the topic) is; word order or specific particles serve also as devices for this, at least in some languages. Very often, however, it is not explicitly marked at all, or is ambiguous.

Note, finally, that the distinction between topic and focus must not be confused with the distinction between 'given' or 'maintained' information, on the one hand, and 'new' or 'introduced' information, on the other, although these dichotomies may often coincide. Consider, for example, a sequence of utterances such as the following:

(13) There came a car from the left and a car from the right. Which car hit the bike? – The one from the left.

The alternative raised by the question is between the two cars, and the focus of the answer is 'the one from the left'. But obviously, this car has already been introduced, just as everything else in the answer: it is 'maintained information'. This is clearly reflected in the form in which it is referred to in the utterance. The rest of the answer is a repetition of the expression of the topic.

The quaestio answered by an individual utterance may also be derived from the 'higher' quaestio of a whole text, to which the utterance belongs and which the text in its entirety is intended to answer. In this case, there may be global constraints what belongs to the topic component and to the focus component of the individual utterances. Take a question such as 'What happened to you last week?' which elicits a narrative text. It asks for the specification of some complex event, which the speaker may subdivide into a series of sub-events, each of them happening during some time interval ti within the time of the total event. Thus, the quaestio of the whole text can be broken down into a temporal sequence of quaestiones answered by all of those utterances which specify one of the subevents, roughly

1: What happened to you at t_1?
2: What happened to you at t_2?
3: What happened to you at t_3?
...
n: What happened to you at t_n?

For each individual utterance, we have a time span which belongs to the topic component of this utterance. These time spans need not be individually specified, they follow from a general principle – the 'topic condition' of narrative texts. This condition gives us the 'backbone' of the narrative, its main structure. It may be interrupted at any point by utterances which do not answer the general quaestio but rather subquaestiones such as *What did you think of this?*, *What's the point?*, *Would you do this yourself? Are you sure?*, etc., which all lead to side structures of different type. The specification of a particular side structure may also extend over several utterances. For example, a narrative sequence can be interrupted by a descriptive sequence, or vice versa.

Suppose now you happen to be the victim of the traffic accident, and the quaestio is *What happened to you after you saw the car?* It specifies a time span, which is after the time span of the previously mentioned event. It also specifies a person, the addressee in this case ('to you'), and moreover it indicates that what is asked for is an event, not a state, as would be the case with the question 'What was the situation at that time?' Hence, the quaestio narrows down the focus of the answer to include only those events which could have happened to the addressee during the intervening time since the event reported before. The answer which settles the alternative *can* repeat the topic (fully or in part); it can also elaborate on it. But it MUST contain a part which expresses the focus, that is, which specifies an event that meets the conditions mentioned above. This has many consequences for the structure of the utterance. If, for instance, the topic time – the temporal interval about which something is said – is expressed by an adverbial, the protagonist by a noun phrase, and the event in the narrower sense by a verb, and if furthermore the language in question has a rule 'topic expression before focus expression', then a word order such as 'noun phrase – verb – adverbial': the verb must be last. This may conflict with purely syntactic constraints on word order, such as 'the verb is in second position', and different languages have found different ways to solve competing requirements of this type. Intonation, special particles, cleft constructions, passives, etc., or by simply not requiring consistent marking of what is focus and what is topic in these cases. Thus, the speaker's structural choice is narrowed down by two factors: first, by the structural potential of the language, and second, by the quaestio. In section 4.3, we shall come back to this point.

3.3 Domains of reference within an utterance

Any proposition – that is, the content of a full sentence – is a web of meaning components or 'referents', as we shall say here. These are of various kinds – spatial, temporal, personal, modal etc. Ever since the days of the Greek philosophers, there have been innumerable proposals to categorize various domains of referents. It is useful to distinguish at least the following five:

a. time spans
b. places
c. persons and objects
d. states, events, properties
e. modalities, such as the 'possible', 'real', 'necessary', 'fictitious', etc.; this should also include other characterisations by which the speaker indicates a particular subjective attitude to what he expresses.

An utterance selects referents from these domains and integrates them into a whole, the proposition. This is not done arbitrarily; it follows certain principles. Most typically, an element from the domain 'persons and objects' is combined with an element from the domain 'states, events, properties' to form the 'inner core' of the proposition; this inner core is then located in time and space. The resulting combination of referents is then provided with a modality which, in one way or the other, fixes its reality status. This simple picture can be complicated in various ways. Not all domains of reference must be represented; it does not make much sense to associate a proposition such as the one *seventeen is a prime number* with a place. On the other hand, a particular domain of reference may be repeatedly represented (for example, there may be several protagonists of the action; similarly, a sentence may involve more than a single time span and a single place). Therefore, the result may be a very complex structure of referents from these five domains, brought about by the speaker's contextual, structural and lexical choice. What the quaestio does, is to impose constraints on these choices, and thus, on L-perspectivation. It defines, for example, a time frame, about which the speaker is asked to say something; but it is up to the speaker to deal with this time frame: he may choose to speak about the entire time frame, he may split into subintervals, he can leave these implicit or mark them by tense or adverbials, etc. Very often, the quaestio also introduces a vantage point in relation to which the speaker is supposed to describe the various referents. Take, for example, a 'court question', such as *What did you observe from where you were?*. It defines the speaker, sets a temporal frame and a place (time and position of the speaker during the intake phase). Moreover, it also imposes a certain modality on what the speaker is to express. In this example, he is supposed to make assertive statements. But the modality is not 'real with respect to the event' – it is 'real with respect to the speaker's visual perception of the event during the intake'. This would be different, if the quaestio were *What happened at that time?*. Here, the constraints on the speaker's possible choices are much weaker; it would be up to him to indicate crucial features of his perspective. He might say, for example: *From where I stood, I had the impression that...*, thus defining himself his place and the subjective commitment on the reality status of what is described.

3.4 Referential movement

Referential movement is the way in which information from the five domains of reference shifts from one utterance to the next. Suppose that there are two subsequent utterances A and B, in which the proposition consists of just one referent from each of the five domains. This gives the following picture of possible referential movements.

(14)   A: MOD_a $TIME_a$ $SPACE_a$ $PERSON_a$ $PREDICATE_a$
       B: MOD_b $TIME_b$ $SPACE_b$ $PERSON_b$ $PREDICATE_b$

In principle, each referent in B can be maintained from A or freshly introduced in B. In reality, the possibilites are much finer; but in the present context, we will only illustrate the way in which the quaestio constrains referential movement (for a detailed discussion, see von Stutterheim 1997; Kohlmann 1997). If the quaestio is *What happened at that time?*, then MOD in general is defined as 'real'; it remains constant throughout the text – unless the speaker explicitly chooses to deviate from it (see below section 3.5). As for TIME, the quaestio sets a temporal frame which the speaker is expected to deal with. Typically, he would subdivide this time frame into smaller time spans, which are sequentially ordered. Hence, $TIME_b$ is *after* $TIME_a$. This is automatically given by the 'topic condition' on narratives mentioned above. Again, the speaker may deviate from this condition, thus giving raise to side structures or to special rhetorical effects. But if he remains within the frame defined by the quaestio, he is still free to choose the structural and lexical means by which to express this temporal shift. The quaestio does not impose any constraint on what the protagonists are. Hence, the speaker is free with respect to all three types of choice. He can introduce what he wants to, he can maintain what he wants to, in whichever form he wants to. SPACE is again not explicitly fixed by the quaestio: Note however, that in this case, a spatial frame may be implicitly included: the speaker is not supposed to speak about anything that might have happened at that time, but about what happened at that time at some particular place, and his freedom in introducing and maintaining spatial referents is limited to that place. As for the final domain PREDICATE, all that is predetermined by the quaestio, is that it must be 'happenings', rather than, for example, visual properties or states. Otherwise, the speaker is completely free in what he chooses to introduce and to maintain in a particular utterance.

3.5 Deviating from the quaestio

In section 1, we introduced the idea that L-perspectivising can be described in terms of various choices which the special has to make in a given communicative situation – structural choice, lexical choice, contextual choice. In this section, it was discussed how the quaestio limits these choices and hence narrows down the ways in which the speaker can say what he intends to say. Hence, the quaestio is principled constraint on possible perspectives; it is not the only one, and others will be discussed in section 4. It is up to the speaker to which extent he accepts the constraints defined by the quaestio. He may, to begin with, reject the entire communicative task, at the risk of more or less severe social consequences. He may also take on the task but redefine it in his own sense, for example by telling a long-winded story instead of giving an argument, when an argument was asked for. These are radical deviations from the quaestio. What is more interesting are 'local deviations'; they occur when the speaker accepts the quaestio and its constraints in principle, but violates them from time to time. There are two such cases. First, the speaker might include a full utterance, or even a sequence of utterances, which is not an answer to the quaestio. This leads to what has been called 'side-structures'. From a communicative point of view, they may be no less important than the main-structure utterances. In particular, they allow the speaker to express his personal views on what is told in answer to the question, and in this sense, they are important for L-perspectivation. The other case are small deviations within a main-structure utterance. The speaker may, for example, initially accept the position imposed on him by the question, but they present the entire story from a different vantage point. Normally, such changes must be explicitly marked. Suppose, for example, the question was: *What did you observe from your position?* Then, the speaker is actually bound to a particular position, to a particular time and to a particular type of information he is allowed to report: the incidents he has observed. He then may start with a series of utterances which do exactly this, and then switch to something he has heard, or something he has observed later, or he may say something that he has not observed but simply inferred. Deviations of this sort give a particular flavour to the way in which the task is solved; they are, in other words, one of the speaker's means to indicate a particular perspective. This does not devalue the constraints as imposed by the quaestio: It is precisely the violation of these constraints which leads to the specific effect.

4 Other constraints on L-perspectivation

L-perspectivation is analysed here in terms of constraints on lexical, structural and contextual choices. Many of these constraints stem from the quaestio. But these are not the only ones. In the following we will discuss the potential sources for L-perspectivation which interact with the constraints set up by the quaestio. These are (a) the hearer model, and (b) the linguistic system used.

4.1 The hearer model

In planning the amount and flow of information provided as an answer to a particular question, the speaker has to construct a mental model of the hearer (Graumann and Herrmann 1989, Herrmann 1989, Herrmann and Grabowski 1994, Levelt 1989). This model encompasses information and assumptions about the hearer's knowledge base with respect to the subject matter, his factual viewing point, his subjective perspective and expectations concerning the potential communicative content. The hearer model effects crucially influences the way in which the speaker constructs his text, with perspectivation coming into play at different levels. In the construction of a discourse representation, it crucially influences the two types of *selection*; it furthermore is largely responsible for the right balance between what is explicitly said and what is left to contextual information.

The most obvious reflection of the hearer model is the choice of a particular temporal or spatial referential frame. All languages have specific constructions which relate the information expressed to the time of speaking or hearing (*now*, specific tense forms), to the participants of the speech situation (*I, you, he*), and to the position of these participants within the speech situation (*here, there*, or, in a more complex way, *left, right, front, back*). It is the speaker who defines what, in a given situation, should count as the vantage point, the origo in Bühler's (1934) famous analysis of deixis. In the most elementary case, the speaker takes himself as the origo – in particular, his present position and the moment of his own speaking: he defines the perspective. But there are many complications. First, in written communication, it is not at all clear what should count as the moment of speech, or the position of the speaker. These two vantage points must therefore often be explicitly introduced (say by giving date and place at the beginning of a letter). Second, even in spoken communication, the speaker is free, for example, to choose the position of the hearer as the spatial vantage point. This is often observed in instructions, where terms such as *turn left* or *put it on the blue block behind the red block* are normally seen from the hearer's, rather than the speaker's, viewpoint. And finally, the speaker may choose an entirely different 'origo' – for example, some time in the past and the position where he *was*, or where some other person was, at that time. Such a frame can be set by the quaestio. If the quaestio is *What did you observe next?*, then *left* and *right do not* relate to the present position of speaker or hearer but to the position of the speaker at that time in the past. It is a 'Deixis am Phantasma', in Bühler's terms, and this quaestio which introduces it. Other quaestiones are even more complicated in this regard, for example *How do I get from here to the station?* In answer to this familiar question, virtually all speakers choose the perspective of an 'imaginery wanderer', i.e., deictic terms in the route directions relate to the permanently changing fictitious position of a person who moves through the streets (cf. Klein 1982). In other cases, the quaestio itself fixes no origo at all ('Are physical exercises healthy?'), and even if it does, the speaker may occasionally deviate from it. The flexible choice of vantage point is one of the crucial factors in L-perspectivation.

A second relevant factor in contextual choice is given by the assumed amount of shared knowledge. Here again, we can look back at a rather comprehensive research tradition (see the survey in Stutterheim and Kohlmann 1998). Studies on communication between interlocutors with different states of knowledge, such as experts and novices or adults and children, have shown that speakers construct different texts depending on what they take to be shared knowledge. Knowing more or knowing less about a particular subject matter means that the potential maximal amount of knowledge is only presented in parts. As we have argued above, selective knowledge representation is always based on processes of perspectivation. An adaptation to the hearer's perspective in this respect surfaces in different forms. It can be the determining factor for what is taken as the global level of granularity in a text. Usually, the quaestio does not predetermine at what level of specificity a speaker should provide information. In order to produce a consistent globally structured text the speaker HAS to take a choice with respect to the degree of granularity. One factor that governs this choice is the adaptation to the hearer. The scaffolding force of this globally established perspective can be seen in cases where the speaker deviates intentionally from this perspective. He is then led to use specific linguistic devices to mark the local nature of this change. Further evidence comes from cases where changes are required in the course of text production. If, for instance, the hearer requires a change of this parameter, the speaker cannot easily restructure his text without loosing track altogether (cf. von Stutterheim and Kohlmann 1998).

A third domain in which perspectivation is determined by the hearer model are constellations in which the quaestio leaves certain options unspecified, and the choice is led by what, in the speaker's mind, could make understanding easier for the hearer. Consider, for example, a quaestio which asks for the description of some highly complex configuration of entities. One of the speaker's tasks is then to find an appropriate linearisation strategy. The speaker has different options how to connect the entities involved spatially: he can introduce an imaginary person, who walks from entity to entity or he can anchor the entities within some abstract referential frame by means of deictic or intrinsic relations. Which option a speaker will choose is – besides other factors such as the nature of the configuration described – dependent on the hearer model.

So far we have only looked at the role of the hearer model for one component of L-perspectivation – contextual choice. There are also effects on lexical choice which can be traced back to this factor. The speakers may select a particular lexical item among equivalent ones, because they want to impress the hearer, but also because they feel that it is particularly appropriate for the hearer: they base their lexical choice not only on their own lexical repertoire but also on the alleged lexical repertoire of the hearer (E. Clark 1997). A particularly striking case is the adaptation to non-native hearers. Similar adaptations are possible but less often observed for structural choice – except again in communication with non-native interlocutors.

Summarizing we can say that the factor HEARER MODEL implies perspectivation along different dimensions some of which operate at one level with the globally established quest-constraints, some specifying options opened by the quaestio, some concerning local decisions such as lexical choice.

4.2 Linguistic system

When confronted with a particular subject matter and quaestio, speakers of different languages show different preferences for perspectivation of the communicative content (Carroll 1993, Slobin 1991, Talmy 1988). This is not surprising given that languages encode perspective at all levels of the linguistic system. Some of the linguistic means which require perspectivation for their use have been mentioned already. There are phonological means such as stress and intonation patterns which are applied on the basis of processes of perspectivation; morphological devices which encode perspectivity in relation to temporal, spatial and modal categories. Then there are syntactic structures which require perspectivation for their use such as word order in some languages, subordination or phrasal structures (prepositional phrases versus adverbials with respect to the explicitness of the reference object). Languages differ in what type of perspective is frozen in the system and how it is distributed across the range of the different devices. For processes of conceptualisation a relevant distinction is given by the fact that some of these devices are obligatory in nature (e.g. verbal morphology, word order) others can be chosen depending on the specific communicative intention.

This leads us to the following question: is it the case that the respective linguistic system induces specific perspectives on the informational structure to be communicated? In order to answer this question we have to look at texts which have been produced by speakers of different languages under conditions which otherwise remain constant. Studies of this type have been carried out for several languages. We will focus on the language pair English – German, the domain of interest lying on the differences between the two verbal systems.

A crucial contrast between the English and the German verb is related to the notion of aspect. English requires obligatory marking of aspect whereas German has no such device. In English, this goes along with a rich repertoire of phasal verbs, such as *to start, to keep on, to get to*, which are extensively used. German has forms of this type in its lexicon, but the field is less differentiated, and phase markers are not high in frequency. Generally one can say that English provides a rich and structurally diverse repertoire for expressing the phasal structure of events. German, on the other hand, has no obligatory grammatical devices for this semantic category nor is the lexicon in this domain as rich as in English.

Let us now look at complex language productions by English and German speakers with respect to the temporal perspective under which events are presented and the function of the respective devices in context. The texts used as data base are film retellings elicited by a very general quaestio: *Please tell me what happened in the film?* As regards the level and type of event segmentation there are no constraints set by the quaestio. The speaker has to decide which event to select for verbalisation and how to present this event. Here we are only interested in temporal perspectivation. In order to describe temporal structures in texts we will draw upon the notion of TOPIC TIME (1994). Topic time is defined as the time interval for which an assertion is made. Whereas the event time, that is the time for which an event holds, is objectively fixed, the topic time selected in a given utterance is a matter of choice. We can therefore say that one central type of temporal perspectivation lies in the selection of a specific relation between topic time and event time.[1]

This relation has always to be decided upon by the speaker which means that this type of perspectivation is part of what has been described as obligatory choices in constructing a complex informational structure. Given that a particular event is selected for verbalisation, what are the temporal perspectives under which the speaker can present it? He can either look at an event holistically with the topic time including the time of the event: *dann gräbt er ein Loch (e1) und da fällt er hinein (e2)* ('then he digs a hole and there he falls into'). In e1 the topic time interval is given as the post time of some preceding event, marked by the temporal shifter *dann*, the event time lies completely within this time interval, the same pattern shows in the second utterance. Here the topic time is implicitly given as post time of e1 and the time of e2 lies completely within this interval. Typically this temporal perspective goes along with a certain aspect of completeness with respect to the event described. As in the example given above, both events are specified for a point of completion, in this case in the spatial domain. Another possibility for referring to completion of an event lies in referring to effected objects as in *er malt ein Haus*.

This holistic view of a situation can be contrasted with a view which segments events into phases. Under this perspective the topic time established overlaps with parts of the event time. The speaker can choose an inchoative aspect expressed in utterances such as *he starts to dig a hole* or *he starts digging a hole* with a further subtle distinction in perspective concerning the degree of overlap between topic time and event time. Another option lies in an imperfective per-specitivation: *he is digging in the sand*. Here the topic time lies within the time of the situation. Note that the choice of this temporal perspective often goes along with presenting the event without a point of completion – in contrast to what has been said about a holistic perspective above. The last systematic option is given by the perfective aspect which places the topic time after the time of situation: *he has dug a hole*.

When we now look at how English and German speakers proceed in perspectivising events we find a systematic contrast. In the English texts an overall perspective is chosen which establishes a temporal viewing point as a deictic origo to which events are related in a very differentiated manner. Speakers present events

---

[1] Another possibility for establishing a temporal perspective lies in the choice of an origo for anchoring the referential frame. In the unmarked case this is given by the deictic origo, the time of utterance, but as already described in Bühler (1934) the origo can be shifted along different dimensions.

segmented in their temporal phases each one hooked up to the origo rather than related intrinsically to each other. German speakers in contrast follow exactly the latter pattern by linking topic times to event times in the flow of the event chain, as demonstrated above. This implies a holistic or perfective view on the events since temporal boundaries of the event times are needed in order to function as a boundary for the topic time of the following event. This contrast in temporal perspective implies a number of further differences in conceptualising the content to be verbalised such as the explicit presentation of components such as spatial reference or effected objects versus their suppression in overt text.

Speakers of German and English clearly prefer one over the other pattern in the way outlined above. How can these differences be accounted for? Obviously there is an interrelation between the linguistic devices available for the speakers, in that the German speaker cannot draw upon an aspectual verbal system. On the other hand the interrelation between linguistic structure and information organisation in text cannot be that simple. German provides means to express phasal structures of events, only not morphological means but lexical forms. The interesting fact, however, is that speakers hardly makes use of these forms because the global perspective chosen does not induce phasal segmentation! One possible explanation for this intricate interrelation between linguistic structure and perspectivation could lie in the eminent role of obligatory linguistic categories for conceptualisation. Whereas the attention of a learner of English is drawn to aspectual properties of events (cf. Berman/Slobin 1994) this not a prominent category for the German learning child. This in turn could lead to preferences in perspectivising situations for linguistic representation: the patterns we have observed for the adult speakers. These patterns at the level of conceptualisation can again induce language change in that those forms which are used very frequently, e.g. the phasal verbs in English, might in the end turn into new morphological markers.

5 Linguistic reflection of perspective management: the case of subordination

In this section, we will illustrate for one type of constructional device how the principles outlined above are operating in actual text production. This device is subordination. Since paratactic and hypotactic forms can be referentially equivalent, motivation to use a subordinated construction cannot come from the 'substance' encoded, but reflects particular perspectival choices. Based on the results of comprehensive empirical studies (Carroll 1997, von Stutterheim 1997) it will be shown that subordination serves one very general function: it is the most prominent means to maintain a globally established perspective by excluding information which deviates from this perspective from the main body of the text.

Semantically, subordination is a constructive device to exclude a proposition from assertion. This is also reflected in formal properties of hypotactic constructions which in many languages are reduced forms of main sentences as regards finiteness, subject realisation, etc. With respect to its function within textual structure one can say that subordinated information is – metaphorically spoken – backstaged a classical domain of perspectivation. What is behind this metaphor will be shown for one central domain of perspectivation: the topic – focus structure as it is predetermined by the quaestio and specified by further globally functioning factors.

The constraints set up for topic-focus partitioning of a text can basically be of two different types. On the one hand, they concern the determination of particular referential domains as parts of the topic or focus component including cases in which specific references are established as topic elements (*substantial topic constraints*). On the other hand, they determine specific structural properties of the text, here we speak about *topic conditions*. In what follows we will give examples for both types of constraints and their relevance for selecting subordination as an expressive device (cf. von Stutterheim 1997).

5.1 Substantial topic constraints

One of the perspectives to be chosen in a narrative concerns the viewing point from which the events are presented. A well known choice is the one between narrator's and protagonist's perspective. Given that a story involves several important acting characters the speaker may select one as the protagonist or introduce several characters as being potential candidates for that role. Looking at film renarrations in which exactly this choice is opened up we find a very systematic pattern. If the speaker chooses a perspective which is anchored in relation to one protagonist, he will refer to events in which other characters take the role of the agent by means of subordination, as in 15:

(15) er beobachtet eine Frau, die gerade erwischt wird, weil sie ein Brot geklaut hat
he observes a woman who is being caught because she has stolen a (piece of) bread

und sagt zu der Polizei, *die sie geschnappt hat...*
and says to the police man, who has caught her...

This example shows that subordination is not only a backgrounding device in the sense of Hopper (1979), but it is also used for foregrounded events in order to keep the hearer's attention with the global topic candidate of the text.

Let us look at another case. Instructions answering a question of the type *how has x to be done?* show a very clear global topic/focus distribution. In our particular case speakers have to instruct a hearer how to put building blocks together to get a particular object configuration. Here we can say that the objects to be manipulated belong to the topic domain, what has to be specified is the location of these objects. Spatial references therefore form the focus component of the text. A typical utterance in these texts would have the following form:

(16)　du steckst den lila Ring auf die grüne Schraube
　　　you put the purple ring onto the green screw

Besides the information about the actions the speaker might have to specify the objects involved in certain cases. This can be required for the object to be manipulated as well as for the object functioning as reference object in the locational phrase. As regards the linguistic packaging we get a very systematic picture. Information specifying the affected object is more often paratactically integrated, whereas information specifying the reference object is *always* subordinated by a relative clause, e.g.:

(17)　du steckst die grüne Schraube durch den roten Würfel, *der über dem gelben sitzt...*
　　　you put the green screw through the red die, which is located above the yellow one

We explain this absolutely regular pattern in language use across a large number of speakers again as resulting from global perspectivation. The speaker wants to maintain what has been established as focus component in the text. If he made the object reference expressed in this component topic element in its own rights by referring to it in subject position in a main clause, he would change the globally established perspective. The use of a hypotactic construction in this case signals the hearer that this shift of perspective is only a local one without implications for the following text.

A parallel phenomenon can be observed in route directions and descriptions of spatial configurations. Here we get a mirror image of topic/focus distribution and consequently also a mirror image of what is presented in paratactic versus hypotactic form.

(18) a. route direction
    dann gehst du auf die Kirche zu, *die am Ende der Straße zu sehen ist...*
    then you approach the church, which can be seen at the end of the street
  b. description
    wenn man weiter runtergeht da steht rechts in der Mitte eine Kirche...
    if you walk down further there is a church to the right in the middle

Depending on the constraints set up by the quaestio the speaker has to provide different types of information in main structure utterances. The route direction requires information on paths with spatial reference forming the focus component. Further specification of objects introduced as reference objects implies – just as in the case of the instructions outlined above – changing the topic-focus pattern established globally. Descriptions, on the other hand, require information on relative object positions. If the speaker chooses to draw upon an imaginary wanderer then this introduces a dynamic perspective which forms a contrast to the global perspective established by the quaestio.

The use of hypotactic forms reflects exactly this difference between the two text types. In the route directions, object specification in the form of relative clauses is systematically subordinated, in descriptions reference to the motion events is almost exceptionless subordinated. Again, we see the function of this syntactic device in maintaining the global perspective by excluding information constructed from a different perspective from the chain of asserted propositions.

5.2 Structural topic constraints

As has been explained above, the linearisation principle underlying the sequential ordering of information in text production can be interpreted as global topic condition. This, in turn, implies a particular perspective under which the single components of the overall referential structure are related to each other.

Looking again at empirical data, we find that subordination serves the function to integrate information which violates this global constraint. Taking texts which follow a spatial linearisation principle, e.g. descriptions, subordination is used where the speaker locally deviates from this pattern. If, for instance, he switches to an object-oriented linearisation strategy – often linked to a change of the level of granularity – then this is expressed by use of hypotactic forms.

(19) daneben ist ein Cafe, *das über einem Schuhladen ist und dicke rote Vorhänge hat...*
    next to it is a cafe, which is above a shoe shop and has thick red curtains

A parallel pattern can be observed in temporally linearised texts, which follow a chronological order. Violation of the principle of temporal sequencing is also frequently 'put aside' by means of subordination.

Another structural aspect which is subject to perspectivation is the level of granularity chosen at text level. Here the same pattern emerges across different text types. Speaker insert subordinate information which imply a local change of the level of granularity. Again we cannot say that information of this kind is part of background information, but it is backstaged for reasons of perspective – continuity.

To summarise what has been found about the functional motivation of subordination we come to the following conclusions. In order to construct a consistent information structure as an answer to a quaestio the speaker has to establish and maintain certain parameters which allow him to locally proceed in selecting and contouring the single informational units. As has been argued, taking perspectives is one crucial component in this planning process. It has also been made clear that these globally set perspectives function as default values, which means that the speaker is free to deviate from them. In order to meet both demands – maintenance of global perspectives and integration of alternative perspectives – the speaker can draw upon means which openly mark something like a hierarchy of perspectives. Subordination is one of these devices. It prevents the hearer from being led to global changes in perspective where only a local detour is intended. This function is further supported by the fact that information which completely leaves the referential frame of the text usually is not presented in subordinated form (e.g. comments, explanations). Here there is in a way no competition between the newly introduced perspective and the globally established one. Only if the grounds are set to possibly take another point of view on the subject matter the speaker has to make explicit which line he intends to follow by using the respective devices.

6 Conclusions

Not many concepts in the social sciences are so appropriate for metaphorical extension than 'perspective'. We do not want to belittle the heuristic, and even the explanatory, value of such extensions from visual perception to, for example, the way in which certain facts are evaluated by people of varying social background ('from the perspective of a street worker', 'from the perspective of an unemployed widow in Calcutta'). Quite to the opposite: it is not accidental that we feel these extensions of the term to be so suggestive.

But at one point, it must be made clear, what is specific to 'perspective' and 'perspectivation' in a particular field. In the paper, we have tried to do this for L-perspectivation – for the way in which natural language allows its speakers to express a certain perspective. It was argued that this is essentially a matter of three choices which the speaker must permanently make in the course of his production process: lexical choice, structural choice, contextual choice. All three choices, and hence the speaker's L-perspectivation, are constrained by a number of interacting factors. The most important of these is the quaestio which the speaker sets out to answer. Others include adaptation to the hearer and the specific possibilities of the language in question. This list is surely not exhaustive. We only looked in passing at the role of the speaker's subjective attitude, because it may lead to 'side-structures' in his text. But subjective attitudes also influence the lexical choice independent of the particular quaestio, and it may well be that this influence follows certain principles. But their investigation is primarily a matter of social and emotional psychology, rather than of linguistics. It is the linguistic constraints on L-perspectivation that were discussed here; these constraints are often strong; but they do not determine the speaker's choice.

References

Bierwisch, M. & Schreuder, R. (1992). From concepts to lexical items. Cognition 42. 23–60.
Bühler, K. (1934). Sprachtheorie. Die Darstellungsfunktion der Sprache. Jena: Fischer.
Canesius, P. (Ed.) (1987). Perspektivität in Sprache und Text. Bochum: Brockmeyer.
Comrie, B. (1976). Aspect. Cambridge: Cambridge University Press.
Carroll, M. (1993). Deictic and intrinsic orientation in spatial descriptions: A comparison between English and German. In J. Altarriba (Ed.). Cognition and Culture: A Cross-Cultural Approach to Cognitive Psychology. Amsterdam: Elsevier. 23–44.
Carroll, M. (1997). Information organisation and direction of attention when structuring space in English and German. In J. Nuyts & E. Pederson (Eds.). Language and conceptualisation. Cambridge: Cambridge University Press. 137–161.
Clark, E.V. (1997).Conceptual perspective and lexical choice in acquisition. Cognition 64. 1–37.
Graumann, C.F. (1989). Perspective setting and taking in verbal interaction. In R. Dietrich & C.F. Graumann (Eds.). Language processing in social context. Amsterdam: North Holland. 95–122.
Graumann, C.F. & T. Herrmann (1989). Speaker: The role of the listener. Clevedon: Multilingual Matters.
Herrmann, T. (1989). Sprachpsychologische Beiträge zur Partnerbezogenheit des Sprechens. In H. Scherer (Ed.) Sprache in Situation. Eine Zwischenbilanz. Bonn: Romanistischer Verlag. 179–204.
Herrmann, T. & Grabowski, J. (1994). Sprechen. Psychologie der Sprachproduktion. Heidelberg: Spektrum Akademischer Verlag.

Hopper, P. (1979). Aspect and foregrounding in discourse. In T. Givón (Ed.). Discourse and Syntax (Syntax and Semantics 12). London: Academic Press. 213–241.

Klein, W. (1982). Local deixis in route directions. In R.J. Jarvella & W. Klein (Eds.). Speech, Place and Action. Chichester: Wiley. 161–182.

Klein, W. (1994). Time in Language. London: Routledge.

Klein, W. & v. Stutterheim, C. (1992). Textstruktur und referentielle Bewegung. Zeitschrift für Literaturwissenschaft und Linguistik 86. 67–92.

Kohlmann, U. (1997). Objektreferenzen im Kontext. Eine Untersuchung zum Zusammenhang von kommunikativer Aufgabe, Textstruktur und Objektreferenzen. Frankfurt/M.: Lang.

Levelt, W.J.M. (1982). Cognitve styles in the use of spatial direction terms. In R.J. Jarvella & W. Klein (Eds.). Speech, Place and Action. Chichester: Wiley. 251–270.

Levelt, W.J.M. (1989). Speaking. From intention to articulation. Cambridge: MIT Press.

Levinson, S. (1997). From outer to inner space: linguistic categories and non-linguistic thinking. In J. Nuyts & E. Pederson (Eds.). Language and conceptualisation. Cambridge: Cambridge University Press. 13–45.

Mikame, H. (1996). Markierte Perspektive, perspektivische Annäherung des Sprechers an das Objekt und direkte Wahrnehmung. Sprachwissenschaft 21. 367–420.

Sandig, B. (1996). Sprachliche Perspektivierung und perspektivierende Stile. Zeitschrift für Literaturwissenschaft und Linguistik 26/102. 36–63.

Slobin, D.I. (1991). Learning to think for speaking. Native language, cognition and rhetorical style. Pragmatics 1. 7–26.

v. Stutterheim, C. (1997). Einige Prinzipien des Textaufbaus. Empirische Untersuchungen zur Produktion mündlicher Texte. (Reihe Germanistische Linguistik 184). Tübingen: Niemeyer.

v. Stutterheim, C. & Klein, W. (1989). Textstructure and referential movement. In R. Dietrich & C.F. Graumann (Eds.). Language processing in social context. Amsterdam: North Holland. 39–76.

v. Stutterheim, C. & Kohlmann, U. (1998). Selective hearer-adaptation. Linguistics 36/3. 517–549.

v. Stutterheim, C. & Lambert, M. (2005). Cross-linguistic analysis of temporal perspectives in text production. In H. Hendriks (Ed.). The Structure of learner varieties. Berlin: De Gruyter. 203–230.

Talmy, L. (1988). The relation of grammar to cognition. In B. Rudska-Ostyn (Ed.). Topics in Cognitive Linguistics. Amsterdam: Benjamins. 165–205.

Tversky, B., Taylor, H.A. & Mainwaring, S. (1997). Language et perspective spatiale. In M. Denis (Ed.). Langage et cognition spatiale. Paris: Masson. 25–50.

Finiteness, universal grammar and the language faculty[1]

> This is excellent research, but it's so terribly boring.
> *Dan Slobin*, p.c.

1 Kantian questions

Die menschliche Vernunft hat das besondere Schicksal in einer Gattung ihrer Erkenntnisse: daß sie durch Fragen belästigt wird, die sie nicht abweisen kann, denn sie sind ihr durch die Natur der Vernunft selbst aufgegeben, die sie aber auch nicht beantworten kann, denn sie übersteigen alles Vermögen der menschlichen Vernunft. (Immanuel Kant, 1781).[2]

If it is indeed the fate of the human mind to be haunted by questions which, by its very nature, it is not able to answer, then the study of human language has to offer some good candidates for such questions, for instance

– *What is the origin of language?*

Our species is the only one which nature, or God, has endowed with this remarkable gift. How and when did it come into existence?

– *Is there a 'Universal Grammar'?*

Do the many linguistic systems that mankind has developed over the millenia share some properties above and beyond the obvious ones, for example that they have a lexicon and a grammar?

– *What is the relationship between language and the mind?*

---

[1] This paper was written for Dan Slobin. The editors of his Festschrift asked us to begin with a short paragraph, briefly stating our relationship with Dan and the way in which this work is influenced by him or related to his work and interest. How can one explain 30 years of friendship and continuous discussion in a short paragraph? So, I thought I would simply try to write something in which the traces of this are found everywhere – and which Dan enjoys. – I wish to thank Christine Dimroth and Clive Perdue for helpful discussions. Thanks also to Leah Roberts who checked my English.
[2] 'Human reason, in one sphere of its cognition, is called upon to consider questions, which it cannot decline, as they are presented by its own nature, but which it cannot answer, as they transcend every faculty of the mind.' (Kritik der reinen Vernunft, first sentence, translated by J. M. D. Meiklejohn).

Note: This article originally appeared as Klein, W. (2009). Finiteness, universal grammar, and the language faculty. In J. Guo, E. Lieven, N. Budwig, S. Ervin-Tripp, K. Nakamura and S. Ozcaliskan (eds.). Crosslinguistic Approaches to the Psychology of Language: Research in the Tradition of Dan Isaac Slobin. New York: Psychology Press. 333–344.

https://doi.org/10.1515/9783110549119-015

We are the only 'speaking animal' – but we are also the only one who is able to divide by 17, to compose a symphony, or to put together a *Festschrift*. How is the gift of language related to these other talents?

These questions have been with us since the days of the Greek philosophers, they have been and still are the object of vivid discussion. But we are still very far from a generally accepted answer. Are they indeed of the Kantian type – that is, questions whose answer is beyond our intellectual capacities, just as algebraic topology is beyond the intellectual capacities of the average cow? This may well be. But there may be less dramatic reasons, for example the lack of reliable empirical evidence. This holds obviously for the first question, the origin of language; the evidentiality marker that could mark the weakness of the evidence on this issue must still be invented. Maybe just this fact renders the question so popular. When the Societé de Linguistique de Paris was founded in 1866, it stated in its constitution:

> **Article 2.** La Société n'admet aucune communication concernant, soit l'origine du langage, soit la création d'une langue universelle. [The society does not admit any discussion on the origin of language or on the creation of a universal language]

But more than a century later, discussions are as vivid as ever, and the evidence is almost as thin as ever.

It is less obvious but no less true that our empirical knowledge about most of the world's about 6000 existing languages is quite limited. For how many of these do we have reliable descriptions? Let us assume that three grammars and three dictionaries suffice for a reliable description. Over the years, I have asked numerous colleagues how many languages meet this criterion. Estimates vary, but they go hardly beyond 100. This means that at most, three percent of the world's languages are well-described, 97 percent are not. Therefore claims about universal traits of human languages must be considered with caution.

But the main problem with the linguistic 'Kantian questions' are fundamental conceptual unclarities. What is 'language', whose origin, whose universal properties, whose relation to the mind are at issue? Saussure once made a threefold distinction, which is found in a great deal of later linguistic work. There is, first, 'la faculté de langage' – the language faculty, with which, pathological cases aside, we are all born. Second, there is 'la langue', that is, the individual linguistic system such as Tzeltal or Chinese. And finally, there is 'la parole' – the product of linguistic knowledge in actual communication. Obviously, the question of the origin of language varies considerably with the notion of language at stake. It may well be that the necessary changes in our brain and other parts of our physiology occurred many thousand years before the first linguistic systems were created in some complex social activity. Similarly, very different components of the mind come into play, depending on whether we relate the mind to the 'language faculty', to a particular linguistic system or to actual communication.

In fact, the situation is more complicated. Consider the 'language faculty' whose study is considered by many to be the core task of linguistics. Under this view, it is not the structural or functional properties of specific linguistic systems, which are at the heart of our endeavours, but the language faculty behind those properties. But does it really make sense to speak of the language faculty? It appears to me that here, too, at least a three-fold distinction must be made. There is, first, THE CAPACITY TO CONSTRUCT A LINGUISTIC SYSTEM – and that's what our ancestors had to do in the first place, as soon as their brain and other parts of their body, eyes, ears, larynx, hands, were ready for it. This capacity is not the same as THE CAPACITY TO COPY A LINGUISTIC SYSTEM – and that's what we have to do in first or second language acquisition.[3] These two capacities are related but surely not identical. The types of social activities, which they operate, are partly different, and so are probably the parts of our brain that are involved in them. It is one thing to learn that [rir] means 'to give audible expression to an emotion (as mirth, joy, derision, embarrassment, or fright) by the expulsion of air from the lungs resulting in sounds ranging from an explosive guffaw to a muffled titter and usually accompanied by movements of the mouth or facial muscles and a lighting up of the eyes' (according to Websters' Third), and another thing to invent a sound sequence or a gesture which among a group of people evokes a certain idea, a certain concept. There is, third, THE CAPACITY TO USE A LINGUISTIC SYSTEM, once stored in the head, for communicative and other purposes. Note that we speak here of the CAPACITY to use a linguistic system, not the actual use itself – 'parole' or 'performance'. This capacity involves, for example, the integration of information encoded by the system and information that comes from context.

In other words, it is misleading to say 'There is a language faculty'. There are several such faculties – at least what we might call the Construction Faculty, the Copying Faculty, and the Communication Faculty. They share many characteristics, but they also differ in essential respects. They may well have different origins in the history of our species; and they may well bear different relations to what we consider to be the mind.

They also give rise to different interpretations of the notion 'Universal Grammar'. It may have taken the Construction Faculty a long time to develop particular structural devices, for example subordination or, at a still later stage, extractions from subordinate structures. Should we understand by 'Universal

---

3 Note that this is not the capacity to copy 'the input' but the regularities of the linguistic system which underlies the input.

Grammar' the set of structures which is shared by all linguistic systems developed up to a certain time; or should we rather see it as the set of features which are, so to speak, in the reach of the Construction Faculty, even if they are not found in all linguistic systems – perhaps not in a single linguistic system existing right now? In the words of the Scholars, does Universal Grammar consist of 'universalia actu' [operative universals] or of 'universalia potentia'[potential universals]?

How can all of this be related to the mind? The heated debates about the modularity of mind some years ago often give the impression that people know what they speak about when they argue that the mind is modular or not. But what, then, is the mind? The Encyclopaedia Britannica characterizes the human mind as 'the complex of faculties involved in perceiving, remembering, considering, evaluating, and deciding'. If it is correct, then 'the mind' is surely not something specifically human: cats and mice, too, perceive, remember, consider, evaluate, and decide.

It appears to me that any attempt to determine the relationship between 'language' and 'the mind' is a hopeless enterprise. What we can do, perhaps, is to look at characteristic properties of linguistic systems, in particular, properties which are shared by all known linguistic systems, and ask how these are related to other capacities that appear to be unique to our species.

In this paper I will have a look at such a property – finiteness, in the sense of 'finite' vs. 'non-finite' verb forms. This is a perhaps an unexpected choice. Finiteness is not among the foremost candidates for a linguistic universal; in fact, a number of languages are generally considered to have no finite verbs, and hence no finiteness, at all. But this reasoning may be premature. There are four reasons why I have chosen finiteness, rather than, for example, the distinction between nouns and verbs or recursive devices:

- First, finiteness is not what one might call a 'trivial universal', such as the fact that all linguistic systems (a) couple sounds or gestures with meaning in (b) either elementary expressions ('words') or complex expressions (brought forth by grammatical rules). These are indeed observed in all human languages; but they are also found in programming languages or flag codes.
- Second, all attempts to define non-trivial syntactic universals, for example universal constraints on transformations, have not turned out to be very successful so far.
- Third, it is not trivial how finiteness could be related to other 'parts of our mind'. All known languages can express temporal and spatial relations, and all known languages have devices to relate the meaning of many expressions to the here-and-now of the speech situation. But temporality, spatiality or deictic anchoring are also found in other domains of our cognition. It is also clear that compound linguistic expressions exhibit a 'hierarchical' structure, as described in terms of

parts of speech, constituent structure etc; but other areas of human cognition and action exhibit hierarchical structures, as well, for example composing a string trio or preparing a seven-course dinner. This is not true for finiteness, and therefore, it might indeed be a purely linguistic universal.
- Fourth, recent work in language acquisition has shown that the finiteness distinction plays an important role in the structure of early utterances in first as well as in second language acquisition (e.g., Dimroth & Lasser, 2002).

2 Finiteness

2.1 Finiteness as an inflectional category

The notion of finiteness goes back to Priscianus' *Institutiones grammaticae*. He distinguished between expressions (verbs as well as nouns) which only specify general properties of objects or actions – bare lexical items, as it were -, and expressions which apply to a concrete case. The meaning of these latter expressions is somehow 'delimited', whence the term *finitum*. The original distinction is not particularly clear, and 1500 years of research has not really changed this, except that the term is no longer used for nouns. Finiteness is one of those notions that is used by everybody and understood by nobody. David Crystal (in Bright 1992, IV, 299), for example, characterizes it as follows:

> **finite** Characteristic of a verb or construction that can occur on its own in an independent clause, permitting formal contrasts of tense and mood; contrasts with a **non-finite** verb or construction, which occurs in its own only in a dependent clause, and which lacks tense and mood contrasts; examples are infinitives and participles

This definition mirrors the common understanding that finiteness is an inflectional category of the verb. Typically, it is not defined but introduced by means of some characteristic examples: *amor, amabis, amavisti* are finite, whereas *amare, amata, amavisse* are non-finite; and then, the intelligent student is supposed to generalize. And the intelligent student concludes that finiteness is an inflectional category of the verb.

This idea faces at least two substantial problems. First, the distinction between finite and non-finite is also made for languages in which it is hardly ever marked on the verb. English, the drosophila of linguistics, is a good example. With very few exceptions, such as *has* or *swam*, all finite forms can also be non-finite; and similarly, with the exception of the present participle and some irregular forms, such as *swum*, all non-finite forms can also be finite. Nevertheless, everybody considers *left* in *He left* as finite, and as non-finite in *He has left*. Some modal verb forms, such as *ought* or *can*, are unfailingly considered as finite, although they are not inflected all. Hence, FINITENESS CANNOT JUST BE AN INFLECTIONAL CATEGORY OF THE VERB. Verb morphology is just one way to encode it.

Second, there are numerous syntactic, semantic and pragmatic phenomena which go with finiteness. The most obvious of those is the 'Finiteness restriction':

(1) Finiteness restriction
A syntactically complex verb form can contain several non-finite forms but maximally one finite form.

In German, for example, it is possible to say *Er muss tanzen können*, whereas the English counterpart *He must can dance* is strictly forbidden. The restriction is not semantic: *He must be able to dance* is easily possible. But *can* is finite, and *must* is finite, and hence, the combination *He must can dance* is impossible. What is the reason for this restriction?

There are many other 'finiteness phenomena', and in what follows, I will go through some of them. Examples are mostly from German because it has a relatively clear and consistent marking of finiteness.

2.2 Syntactic properties of finiteness

There is a long-standing discussion about the basic word order in German – is it SOV or SVO? The facts are relatively clear and can, minor complications aside, be described by three rules:

(2) Basic word order
 a. In declarative clauses, the finite verb is in second position.
 b. In subordinate clauses, the finite verb is in final position.
 c. In yes/no questions and in imperatives, the finite verb is in initial position.

Since the basic word order is usually determined with respect to declaratives, immediate observation speaks for SVO. But note that all three rules in 2 are only correct with reference to the finite verb: a sentence can have many verbs, but only one finite verb, and this one is decisive. Now, a finite verb such as *kam* [came] or *schlief* [slept], merges a finite component, abbreviated fin, and a lexical component, abbreviated V (the latter specifying its argument structure and its descriptive properties). When fin and V are separated, then it is easy to see that fin is relevant for word order:

(3) a. *Gestern ist Isolde zum ersten Mal nicht gekommen.*
 Yesterday has Isolde for the first time not come.
 b. *…, obwohl Isolde gestern zum ersten Mal nicht gekommen ist.*
 …, although Isolde yesterday for the first time not come has.
 c. *Ist Isolde gestern zum ersten Mal nicht gekommen? Sei nicht traurig!*
 Has Isolde yesterday for the first time not come? Be not sad!

Hence, German is neither SOV nor SVO – it is 'fin-second'; the verb as a carrier of lexical information is irrelevant in this regard. Similarly, subordinate clauses are 'fin-last', yes-no-questions and imperatives are 'fin-first'.[4] This points to another important fact: there appears to be a close connection between finiteness and the illocutionary role of the clause: A SENTENCE CAN ONLY EXPRESS AN ASSERTION WHEN FIN IS IN SECOND POSITION.[5]

A second syntactic property that goes with finiteness is 'licensing', i.e., the fact that some element can only show up if some other element is present. In German, finiteness functions as a licensor for the grammatical subject as well as for expletive elements.[6]

(4) Licensing
 a. No explicit grammatical subject without finiteness.
 b. No expletive element without finiteness.

There are a few exceptions to 4a, for example:

---

4 Note that this entire reasoning applies analogously under the assumption that, on some deeper level of description, the word order is SOV, and then V is 'moved' into its various positions. In this case, what is moved is fin, and if it so happens that fin and the lexical component of the verb are realised in one morphological form, then both components are 'moved'.
5 This does not mean that sentences with fin in second position are necessarily assertions. First, there may be other markers (such as a wh-word) that lead to a different illocutionary role, and second, the position of fin must be accompanied by an intonational fall at the end.
6 Neither the term 'subject' nor the term 'expletive' are clearly defined across languages (in fact, not even within languages); therefore, the following two constraints should be read with some caution: there may well be items called 'expletive' which need no such licensing (Nigel Duffield pointed out this problem to me). – This, incidentally, is a very general problem of cross-linguistic claims. Consider, for example, the 'Binding principles' of generative grammar, which, subject to parameterized variation of the notion 'governing category', are supposed to be universals. Thus, binding principle A states that anaphors are bound by their governing category. In English, anaphors are words such as *himself* or *each other*. But I am not aware of a language-independent definition of 'anaphor' – except that it is an element which is bound by its governing category – which would render the principle circular.

(5) *Ich eine Krawatte tragen – niemals!*
   I wear a necktie – never!

Sentences like (5) have a peculiar flavour. They describe a state of affairs without either taking a stand on its truth, as in an assertion, or challenging someone else to do this, as in a question, or instructing someone to do something which would make it true, as in an imperative: They raise a topic but lack an illocutionary role.

How could finiteness be related to the presence of an expletive element or a grammatical subject? It could be a matter of the argument structure, i.e., finiteness introduces a new argument variable that is required for the subject or for the expletive; or it could have to do with the informational status of expletives and grammatical subjects. At least in the case of the subject, the first hypothesis is not plausible: the grammatical subject clearly fills an argument variable provided by the non-finite component of the verb, for example the agent, if the lexical verb is agentive. But typically, the grammatical subject not only matches one of the verb's argument slots: it also has *topic status* in the utterance. Similarly, expletive elements typically lead to a particular information structure. Thus, the two licensing constraints appear to be connected to what counts as 'topic information' in the utterance: there is no 'topic slot' without finiteness.

We may sum up these observations in two points:
1. Finiteness is not just an issue of verb inflection; it is deeply rooted in the way in which utterances are structured. We must distinguish between the 'finiteness' and the way in which it is encoded in a particular language, e.g., by verb inflection.
2. Finiteness is connected to the 'illocutionary status' of the sentence and the 'topic-status' of constituents.

2.3 Semantic properties of finiteness

2.3.1 Specific and non-specific interpretation of noun phrases

Indefinite noun phrases such as *a castle, three castles* can have both a specific and a non-specific reading. Some verbs enforce a specific reading, when the noun phrase is in object position; other verbs do not resolve the ambiguity regarding specificity:

(6) a. *Marke kaufte ein Schloss.*
       Marke bought a castle.

b. *Marke suchte ein Schloss.*
   Marke looked for a castle.

In 6b, Marke may have tried to find a particular castle, for example one in which he suspects Tristan and Isolde are hidden; or he may have tried to find something which meets the properties of being a castle. In 6a, only the first reading is available. Since the two utterances only differ in the lexical meaning of the verbs *kaufen* 'buy' and *suchen* 'search', the difference in the NP interpretation is usually related to the difference between these two lexical verbs. Quine, who first studied this phenomenon, dubbed verbs of the type *kaufen* as transparent, and verbs of the type *suchen* as opaque. Note now that *kaufte* and *suchte* in 6 are finite, hence, they include V, the carrier of lexical content, as well as fin. When the verb is not finite, the difference disappears:

(7) a. *Es ist teuer, ein Schloss zu kaufen.*
       It is expensive to buy a castle.
    b. *Ein Schloss zu kaufen passiert einem ja nicht selten.*
       To buy a castle, does not happen very often to someone.

Here, the direct object has a specific as well as a non-specific reading, although the verb is transparent. The difference shows up again, if the indefinite noun phrase is in the scope of some 'higher' transparent or opaque finite verb (note that the lexical character of the non-finite verb, here *kaufen*, is irrelevant):

(8) a. *Marke gelang es, ein Schloss zu kaufen.*
       Marke succeeded to buy a castle.
    b. *Marke wünschte, ein Schloss zu kaufen.*
       Marke wished to buy a castle.

In other words, finiteness is somehow crucial for specific interpretation of indefinite noun-phrases. Consider now 9:

(9) a. *Dreimal hat Marke ein Schloss gekauft.*
       Three times has Marke a castle bought.'
    b. *Marke hat ein Schloss dreimal gekauft.*
       Marke has three times a castle bought.'

In 9a, three different times in the past are talked about. About each of them, it is said that Marke bought a castle at that time. There is a t_1-castle, a t_2-castle, and a t_3-castle bought by Marke. It could be the same castle, but it need not. This means that 'specificity' is relative to the times about which something is said – it is relative to 'topic times', in other words. We may state this as a restriction on the interpretation of indefinite noun phrases:

(10) Indefinite specificity reading
'Specific' means 'unique with respect to a topic time'.

In 9b, the adverbial is in a different position. The assertion relates to a – possibly very long – time in the past, which is assumed to include three castle-buying situations. But there is only one topic-time, and therefore, the castle is normally understood to be the same: Since 'specific' means 'unique with respect to the topic time', there is only one entity since there is only one topic time.

How is this connected to finiteness? Non-finite constructions, such as *to buy a castle,* selectively describe a buying situation (omitting the buyer). But they do not link this situation to some topic time, and no assertion is made that such a buying situation obtains at such a time. Hence, the term *a castle* is not confined to a specific reading: it is not 'topic time unique'. In brief: No finiteness – no topic time, and no topic time – no specificity. Somehow, finiteness links the descriptive content of the entire sentence to the topic time.

2.3.2 Tense

Traditionally, tense is often connected to finiteness. But what is tense? Under its received definition, it is a deictic time-relational category of the verb, whose function is to locate the situation described by the clause to the time of utterance. Thus, in *The Pope was ill*, his being ill is placed into the past; in *The Pope is ill*, it is said to encompass the time of utterance; and in *The Pope will be ill*, it is in the future. This seems so obvious that one is almost embarrassed to mention it. But in fact, it cannot be correct in general. Consider 11:

(11) *(Why didn't the Pope give an audience yesterday?)* – *He was ill.*

This does not assert that his illness precedes the time of utterance; it could as well include it, that is, he could still be ill. And in *The Pope was dead*, it is almost certain, even for the Pope, that he is still dead at the moment of speech – a function which is normally assigned to the present tense.

The function of the preterite is rather to assert (or to ask) something about some particular time span in the past, and about this 'topic time'-, it is said that he was ill. The 'time of the situation' – the time at which the state of affairs described by the non-finite component obtains – can be much longer; but nothing is said about that. In other words, tense serves to mark whether the topic time precedes, contains, or follows the time of utterance. The time of the situation in turn may precede, contain, or follow the topic time. I think it is this relation between topic time and situation time that underlies the traditional notion of (grammatical) 'aspect'.

If finiteness introduces a topic-time, and if tense imposes a temporal restriction on how the topic time is situated relative to the here-and-now, it should not be surprising that tense and finiteness can be clustered in one form, and this is indeed what happens in many languages.

2.4 Prosodic properties of finiteness

If we want to describe what some expression contributes to the meaning of the entire construction in which it appears, then it often helps to contrast this expression to some other expression by intonation. What happens when the highlighted expression is a finite verb, which merges V with fin:

(12) *Tristan LAG auf dem Sofa.*
 Tristan was lying on the sofa'

Intuitively, the contrast can go in three directions:

(13) a. *(Er saß nicht auf dem Sofa). – Er lag auf dem Sofa.*
  (He was not sitting on the sofa). – He was lying on the sofa.
 b. *(Er liegt nicht auf dem Sofa). – Er lag auf dem Sofa.*
  (He is not lying on the sofa). He was lying on the sofa.
 c. *(Er lag nicht auf dem Sofa). – Doch, er lag auf dem Sofa.*
  (He was not lying on the sofa). – Oh yes, he was lying on the sofa.

In 13a, the highlighting targets the lexical meaning of the bare verb *lieg* ' lay'-, in contrast to *sitz-* 'sit'. In 13b, the highlighting targets the tense component of *lag*; the topic time is in the past, rather than right now. The most interesting case, though, is 13c: the contrast is between 'his lying on the sofa is not asserted – is asserted'. Thus, fin is the carrier of tense and of assertion: it relates the descriptive content of the sentence, as described by its non-finite part ('Tristan lay on the sofa') to a topic time, and it asserts that this descriptive content – the mere proposition, so to speak – obtains at that time.

Not all sentences with a finite verb express an assertion. Other illocutionary roles may come into play, for example questions or imperatives, in which, as we have seen, fin has a different position and perhaps a different intonation. Or else the assertion is somehow overruled by higher functional elements, which give the clause a different status, for example in temporal clauses or in relative clauses. These important issues will not be pursued here. Instead I will try to put the core notion of topic time into a somewhat wider perspective. So far, it has been assumed that fin relates the 'bare proposition' to the topic time: is it just the topic time, or are there other topic components which play a role in connection with fin?

2.5 The topic situation

Is the following assertion, uttered here and now, true or false?

(14) *Es gab keinen Wein mehr.*
       There was no more wine.

Even if you know German perfectly well, and even if you know what the world is, was and will be like – maybe even what all possible worlds are like -, you are not able to answer this question. To achieve this, you must know about which situation the person who utters 14 is talking. Depending on this information, the answer is 'yes' or 'no'. Every assertion is relative to a topic situation. The topic time is but one of the parameters which fix this topic situation; others are the place talked about, the entity talked about (often encoded as grammatical subject), or even the world talked about (real world *vs.* some fictitious world). The necessary information about the topic situation may come from context, but also from the utterance itself; in this case, the 'topic-hood' is often marked, for example by position, by special particles or perhaps by other devices.

2.6 Finite utterance organisation

Our observations so far lead to an incipient picture of the role of finiteness. For an utterance to fulfil an illocutionary function, such as making an assertion, it must encode three meaning components:
1. A topic component. It minimally includes a 'topic time'; it is plausible that it also contains a 'topic world' and a 'topic place'. Optionally, other elements can be added, for example a 'topic entity', typically realised by the grammatical subject.
2. A (non-finite) sentence base. Minimally, this is a (non-finite) lexical verb, whose argument slots are filled appropriately. Other elements, such as adverbials, particles can be added.

3. A linking Component. It relates the sentence base to the topic component, for example by indicating that the former holds at the latter. This is the function of 'finiteness'. The exact type of linking requires additional means, for example the choice of a particular position or intonational cues.

These components can be encoded in different ways. In many languages, finiteness and topic time are jointly expressed by verb inflections. Similarly, finiteness and the 'topic world' can be brought together by verb inflection – resulting in the category of mood (cf. Crystal's definition from section 1). But languages may have very different devices, grammatical as well as lexical, in which they encode this overall structure.

If this picture is essentially correct, then it suggests explanations of a number of facts which initially seem unrelated and which otherwise are completely mysterious, such as the reason why subjects and expletives typically must be licensed by finiteness, or why specific readings of noun phrases depend on finiteness. It is also completely in line with the 'one-finite-element constraint' stated in 1: there is only one such linking between topic component and descriptive content in a sentence. It also raises a number of problems, for example about the role of finiteness in subordinate clauses. I will not follow up these problems here but return to the Kantian questions from section 1.

3 Finiteness and Universal Grammar

Finiteness is a not a peripheral property of some inflectional systems; it is a fundamental organizational principle of human languages with numerous important consequences in syntax, semantics and pragmatics. This principle can be 'language-specific' in one of two ways: it is either
(a) specific to linguistic systems, in contrast to other manifestations of the human mind, or
(b) specific to particular languages or universal.

As was pointed out in the first section, there is limited agreement on what the human mind is and what its various manifestations are. But we can look at some other activities, which we feel are uniquely human, and ask whether they involve a similar organizational principle. In all cases I can think of, the answer is negative. Consider, for example, the ability to divide by seven, the ability to cook pea soup, the ability to design a tuxedo, the ability to play straw poker (whatever that is); and so on. I see no evidence that organisational principles similar to finiteness are found in these activities. There is one potential exception – pointing, in the sense of intentionally directing another person's attention to some object or action in the environment and thus somehow introducing a 'topic'. But pointing alone does not have the organisational power of finiteness. As an organisational principle, finiteness is specific to linguistic systems.

Is it found in all human languages? Most structural universals are fairly trivial: linguistic systems consist of expressions, which combine sounds, gestures or some other 'carrier' with meaning that can be simple or compound. There are other, less trivial candidates like recursion and, as a consequence, the possibility of constructing infinitely many sentences. I think that this possibility may be a bit overrated: after all, each apple tree is 'recursive', because each branch can in principle have another branch. But recursion is often considered to be a highlight of human language, in contrast to other communicative systems. Imagine now a language English*, which is exactly like English except that it lacks subordination and other recursive devices. Would we say that English* is not a human language? I think not: it is still a product of the human language faculty, although its structural and communicative potential is reduced. In fact, it may have taken many millenia in the history of mankind before the first devices that make recursion possible were created. Thus, recursion, finiteness and perhaps other principles are something like 'universalia potentia' – organisational principles which the human language faculty is able to construct, copy, and process.

The notion of Universal Grammar can be construed in at least two ways. It can be a set of structural or functional properties that are found in all linguistic systems; or it is a set of constraints that state which properties are excluded from such systems, that is, which are beyond the range of what our language faculties can construct, copy, or use. Both notions of Universal Grammar lead into serious problems as soon as we go beyond the trivial. I think we should therefore stop the quest for Universal Grammar and be happy to look for non-trivial and 'interesting' principles which underlie the design of linguistic systems – interesting in the sense that they are not marginal properties of a particular language but have numerous consequences for the syntax, semantics and pragmatics of many linguistic systems. Finiteness is such a principle.

We may call such principles elements of 'Universal Grammar', because they are somehow fundamental to the structure of human languages. Or we may simply call them 'important principles of linguistic systems'.[7] In any case, this is only a matter of terminology.

---

[7] Other 'important principles' are, as we have argued in Klein and Perdue (1997), for example 'Focus last' or 'Agent first'. In contrast to finiteness, they are already found in very elementary learner systems.

4 'Universal Grammar' and the human language faculty, or: the properties of the bread are not the properties of the baker

Suppose that there are indeed principles of Universal Grammar beyond the obvious, of which finiteness may be one. What does this mean for our understanding of the human language faculty? The answer, I believe, is: close to nothing. There are two reasons. First, there is not one language faculty – there are several, and the question of how universal, language-specific principles are related to the 'language faculty' is a different one, depending on whether we mean the Construction Faculty, the Copying Faculty or the Communication Faculty.

The second reason why non-trivial universal principles do not tell us very much about the human language faculties is very different. In linguistics, it has become common to set 'Universal Grammar' and the 'language faculty' in parallel. In Chomsky's words:

> 'the language organ is the faculty of language (FL); the theory of the initial state of FL, an expression of the genes, is universal grammar (UG); theories of states attained are particular grammars; the states themselves are internal languages, 'languages' for short', (Chomsky 2002, 64).

This is what one might call the 'Structural Analogy Fallacy'. Universal properties of linguistic systems, just like specific properties of linguistic systems, are a product of our linguistic faculties, and we must not confuse the properties of a product with the properties of its producer. Here, as elsewhere, the relation between product and producer is one of causation, rather than of structural similarities. This also applies when the product itself is a capacity that can be used to bring forth other products. Thus, the capacity to process linguistic knowledge and to use it for communicative and other purposes – the Communication Faculty – is a product of the Construction Faculty and the Copying Faculty, and at the same time, it allows these faculties to do more of their job.

My mother's apple-pie, an old-fashioned wig, and Michelangelo's 'David' have something in common – they all are hand-made. No analysis of all of these and similar objects tells us much about the shape of the hands, or the neural mechanism that controls them. In this case, the products are artefacts. But the same considerations apply to 'natural' products. Chlorophyll is green, but the genetic information which leads to its production in plants is not green. Linguistic systems share properties of artefacts and natural products, and opinions are at variance as to how the relation between both sides should be seen; but in any case, they are products. Finiteness is a property of these products. It is neither in the mind nor in the brain, although the human brain brings about linguistic systems, which, in turn, make finite constructions possible. It is a property of utterances, brought about by the ability to integrate the expressions into the flow of discourse and to invent or copy grammatical and lexical devices which encode this integration.

5 Conclusions

When we say that our species is the only one born with the 'language faculty', then this means that there are several components in the human brain, whose joint effort allows us
- to construct systems of linguistic knowledge,
- to copy linguistic knowledge from others, including its storage in the brain, and
- to integrate this knowledge into the flow of ongoing information.

Each of these capacities involves many subcomponents, such as memory access and motor control, and each of these may be affected, with specific results for the interaction.[8] They also may change in different ways over the life span. Adult second language learners maintain the ability to pair sounds or gestures with meanings, and they maintain the ability to form complex expressions – at least for a long time. But their ability – and perhaps their willingness – to do this in exactly the same way as is done in the input diminishes over time. Adults do it, but like Frank Sinatra, they can say 'I did it my way'. Age appears to affect the Copying Faculty much more than the Construction Faculty. This suggests that to some extent, different parts of the brain are involved in both faculties. It is even more obvious that the Communication Faculty requires different neural activities, for example all of those that are needed to monitor and integrate contextual information.

All three language faculties are products of our brain – products, which in turn, bring forth other products, namely linguistic systems or, in the case of the Communicative Faculty, utterances that are integrated into the flow of discourse. Many of the brain components, which produce these three capacities, are also involved in other tasks which our species is able to achieve, such as playing dominoes, creating religions, and frying eggs. Each of these non-linguistic abilities is a product of the human brain. It appears to me that it is not only an ill-defined,

---

[8] Thus, if a subcomponents drops out, for example due to a genetic deficit, then this does not say very much about the three language faculties in their entirety. If a spark-plug does not work, then the car does not work, or does not work properly. But the spark-plug is but a little component in a complex machine.

but also a relatively fruitless task to compare these products of the human brain with one of its other products – linguistic knowledge.[9]

These considerations have a number of substantial consequences. First, it should be clear that principles of Universal Grammar tell us practically nothing about the human language faculties, just as little as the in-depth and comparative study of bread and cake tells us little about the brain and the hand of the baker. Even if it could be shown that all breads have a crust, this does not mean that the baker has a crust.

Second, just as the study of the baker's hand and brain tells us little about the bread and the cake, physiological research, in particular brain research, tells us little about the structure of human languages. It is interesting in its own right, but it sheds no light on the way in which finiteness, or whichever important organizational principle, helps to structure utterances, let alone on questions such as how Chinese argument structure or Inuktitut verb inflection is organized. This does not mean that research on the 'language side' of the brain is irrelevant. It is just a different issue. It can tell us where certain types of linguistic knowledge are stored and how they are activated under specific conditions. But it cannot tell us anything about this linguistic knowledge itself. Religious systems are also stored somewhere in the brain, and they are accessed under specific conditions; but studies on location and processing of religious beliefs in the left temporal lobe, or wherever else, do not really inform us about these beliefs. It is one thing to believe whether Virgin Mary went straight to heaven, the only infallibility decision of a Pope so far, and another to know where this belief is stored in the cells and how it is processed as need arises.

Third, if we want to understand the various human language faculties, the 'producers' rather than their products, then we should investigate them 'on the job' – that is, when they create linguistic knowledge, a case that is rarely observed in our times; when they copy linguistic knowledge, a case that is regularly observed in language acquisition; and when they integrate linguistic knowledge into the flow of information, and that's what we do every day when we speak and listen.

In the first place, however, the linguist should be pleased to study the many structural and functional properties of linguistic systems, what they have in

---

9 I believe, incidentally, that 'real' languages such as Latin or Yiddish are only a special case of the many manifestations of the human language faculties. The normal case are 'learner varieties', i.e., much less elaborate systems. Most people all over the world develop several such systems, and the fact that they are not counted as 'languages' because they are imperfect replications of what is spoken in their environment is no reason to exclude them from the linguistic systems which the human language faculties are able to bring about.

common and what they do not share, how they are processed, and how they are acquired. And in view of the little we really know about all of these issues, studying any of them should be enough of a challenge.

References

Blom, E. (2001). From root infinitive to finite sentence. Phil. Diss: Utrecht: Utrecht University Repository.
Bright, W. (Ed.) (1992). International Encyclopedia of Linguistics. Oxford: Oxford University Press.
Chomsky, N. (2002). On Nature and Language. Cambridge: Cambridge University Press.
Dimroth, C. & Lasser, I. (Eds.) (2002). Finite options. How L1 and L2 learners cope with the Acquisition of Finiteness. Berlin, New York: Mouton de Gruyter [Special issue of Linguistics, 40–44].
Klein, W. & Perdue, C. (1997). The Basic Variety, or: Couldn't natural languages be much simpler?. Second Language Research 13, 301–347.
Lasser, I. (1997). Finiteness in adult and in child language. MPI Series in Psycholinguistics 8. Nijmegen: Max Planck Institute for Psycholinguistics.

The basic variety (or: couldn't natural languages be much simpler?)[1]

1 Introduction

Natural languages, such as English, Chinese, Latin, are extremely complex systems. It takes the child about ten years to master them "perfectly", that is, as well as its social environment, and the second language learner hardly ever reaches this level of proficiency. Couldn't languages be much simpler? Linguists normally do not think about this question, and when urged to do so, they would probably take a Hegelian position – what is real, is reasonable, and what is reasonable, is real – and support a negative answer along one of two possible lines of argument: The complexity is due to inherent properties of the human language processor, hence necessary, or else it is needed for functional reasons, because otherwise, language would not be as powerful an instrument as it is.

Both arguments are weak. The processing argument suffers from the obvious fact that we are able to process simple language. In fact, one might even say that the simpler the structure, the easier it is to produce and understand. There may be exceptions, but this is surely the rule. Therefore, the human language capacity provides us with the POTENTIAL to process very complex structures but does not FORCE us to do so. If the potential to become complex is exploited, then this must have different reasons, which have to do with what language is for: the simpler the language, the poorer its expressive power, and if complex thoughts are to be expressed, then the means to express them have to be complex, as well. This argument has a high degree of plausibility for the richness of the lexicon. If you want to talk about love and hate, about the good and the bad, then this is perhaps not impossible if you have not, but much easier if you have words such as *love* and *hate*, *good* and *bad*. But is it really necessary to have a dozen different noun paradigms, as in Latin? There are much simpler ways to mark case – if obligatory case marking is necessary at all. German distinguishes three genders (*der Löffel, die Gabel, das Messer*), and most Germans take it for granted that such a distinction is a natural if not necessary

---

[1] Many thanks are due to Mary Carroll, Maya Hickmann, Ray Jackendoff and Anna Ramat for commenting on earlier versions of the paper, and to all the members of the European Science Foundation's project on adult language acquisition for discussions over the years. Last but not least, we wish to thank our many informants for their co-operation and their patience.

Note: This article was written in cooperation with Clive Perdue and originally appeared as Klein, W. and Perdue, C. (1997). The basic variety (or: Couldn't natural languages be much simpler?). Second Language Research 13. 301–347.

https://doi.org/10.1515/9783110549119-016

thing to have. But speakers of English do not necessarily share this view. English, by contrast, systematically distinguishes two aspectual forms of the verb (*he left, he was leaving*) and this distinction has a clear functional value. It is a very natural if not indispensable thing to have. But German gets along very well without such morphological complexities, and its speakers are somewhat reluctant to adopt them whenever they try to speak English. In French, the direct object follows the finite verb when it is lexical, and it precedes the verb when it is a pronoun (*Charlie voit la jeune fille – Charlie la voit*). Couldn't one think of a simpler solution? French grammarians, before and after Hegel, would probably deny this; but other views are imaginable.

In this paper, we shall not try to give a general answer to the question raised above – any such attempt would be totally speculative – but report some findings from second language acquisition which might shed some light on it, and thus on the question as to what are necessary and what are more accidental properties of the human language capacity. We shall describe a language which indeed is simple and still extremely functional.

In the course of a large cross-linguistic, longitudinal project on adult second language acquisition outside the classroom,[2] we noted that after some time, all 40 learners investigated developed a relatively stable system to express themselves which
- seemed to be determined by the interaction of a small number of organisational principles
- was largely (though not totally) independent of the specifics of source and target language organisation
- was simple, versatile, and highly efficient for most communicative purposes.

This system we call the BASIC VARIETY. For about one third of the learners investigated,[3] acquisition ended on this structural level; some minor variation aside, they only increased their lexical repertoire and learned to make more fluent use of the basic variety.

---

[2] This project – 'Second Language Acquisition by Adult Immigrants' – took place from 1981–1988 in five European countries (France, Germany, Great Britain, The Netherlands and Sweden). It was co-ordinated from the Max-Planck-Institute for Psycholinguistics in Nijmegen, under the auspices of the European Science Foundation. For a comprehensive account, see Perdue (1993).
[3] It should be kept in mind that we are talking here about second language acquisition outside the classroom. No such system has ever been observed in second language acquisition in a classroom setting. The reason is simply that classroom acquisition not only reflects natural principles of the human language capacity – which lead to the basic variety – but also the effect of a particular teaching method, which, for example, may devote considerable time and effort to very specific features (say verb inflection). However, classroom learners of different language backgrounds have been observed to create and use outside the classroom – in the playground – a language of functional communication whose characteristics do seem to correspond to the basic variety (Bouton 1969:148).

We believe that the basic variety not only plays a particular role in the process of second language acquisition but also that it represents a particularly natural and transparent interplay between function and form in human language. In a way, fully-fledged natural languages are but elaborations of this basic variety. They add some specific devices, such as inflectional morphology or focus constructions; they also add some decoration, pleasant to the ear, hard to learn, but faithfully handed down from one generation to the next. But essentially, they build on the same organisational principles.

If this assumption is correct, then three questions must be answered:
1. What are the structural properties of the basic variety?
2. Why is it as it is?
3. Why are "fully-fledged" languages more complex than the basic variety

In this paper, we shall mainly deal with the first of these questions. In section 4, we will try to characterise the basic variety in four respects: its lexical repertoire, the principles according to which utterances are structured, the expression of temporality and the expression of spatiality. In section 5, we will illustrate how the basic variety is put to use. These two sections sum up the results of a whole series of empirical studies. As is normally the case with empirical projects of this size, there is some variation, there are exceptions, and there are additional – supporting as well as disturbing – observations. In what follows, we shall try to carve out the main lines; for a full account, the reader is referred to the original studies (see below).

We have no answer to the second question, except the very general – and very strong – speculation that the basic variety simply and directly reflects the necessary, rather than the more accidental, properties of the human language capacity. This will be discussed in section 6.2, in the broader context of what place the Basic Variety occupies within the human language capacity and how it relates to particular theories of this capacity, notably generative grammar.

As to the third question, we again have no full answer – but some empirically based ideas about what such an answer could look like. It has to do with the way in which speakers of the basic variety try to overcome conflicting organisational principles in particular communicative constellations. This will be discussed in section 5.2.

The idea of something like a "basic variety" is not new. In one way or the other, it surfaces in earlier work on second language acquisition (Schumann 1978, Klein & Dittmar 1979, von Stutterheim 1986). It is also found in the notion of a "Basic Child Grammar" (Slobin 1985), or in the idea that there might be a specific 'pragmatic mode', in contrast to a 'syntactic mode' (Givón 1979), or even a 'protolanguage' (Bickerton 1990). There are also obvious relations to pidgins and other forms of simplified or reduced languages. These issues will be briefly discussed in section 6.3.

The basic variety is a type of language which, as far as we know, regularly develops during second language acquisition (outside the classroom). Our findings, and the way in which we interpret them, reflects a particular perspective on second language acquisition research which is somewhat at variance with the dominant view.[4] A brief discussion of these two perspectives will be useful to explain why we feel that a concept such as the basic variety helps us to understand not only second language acquisition but the human language capacity in general.[5]

2 Two perspectives on SLA research

The study of language acquisition, and of second language acquisition in particular, is often led by the tacit but firm assumption that the learner's productions at any time of the acquisitional process are more or less successful attempts to reproduce the structural properties of target language utterances. The learner tries to do what the mature speaker does, but does it less well. Consequently, the learner's utterances are not analysed in their own right, according to their inherent structural characteristics, whatever these are, but in relation to the target language (TL). More precisely, they are analysed not in relation to the TL itself, but to some alleged structural characterisation of TL which the researcher believes to be correct and appropriate. For example, the following four utterances are perceived

---

[4] A recent, comprehensive and balanced survey of the field of second language acquisition is Ellis (1994).

[5] We will not discuss, however, particular theories of SLA, for example 'parameter-setting' accounts of second language acquisition, as developed during the Eighties by a number of authors (see, for example, White 1989, and for a more recent survey, Ellis 1994, chapter 7). This does not mean that we believe parameter-setting approaches are uninteresting; in fact, as shall be discussed in section 6.2, an essential part of the BV can be characterised as a specifically parameterised form of language (or, more precisely, I-language). But first, present SLA accounts in the generative framework are based on versions of generative grammar which operate with principles and parameters that have largely become obsolete. Parameterized constraints on movement, such as Subjacency, for example, play no role in the feature theory of raising (cf. section 6.2). Second, with very few exceptions (cf. footnote 33), this work deals with SLA in the classroom, in which, for example, considerable attention is paid to the teaching of complex inflectional morphology. As we shall see below, the BV has no inflectional morphology, a point with considerable theoretical impact. Thus, whereas there are surely commonalities between SLA within and outside the classroom, there are also divergencies in crucial respects, which render an immediate comparison highly problematic.

not as constructions in their own right but as 'attempts to speak English', successful to the extent that they are understandable, but just 'bad English':

(1) Steal girl bread.
(2) The girl stealed the bread.
(3) Later, the girl has stolen the bread.
(4) Which girl did John deny that has stolen the bread?

The "deviations" from the TL standard may be massive or subtle: in (1), the 'underlying English syntax' is hardly recognisable, whereas in (2), it is 'almost correct', and (3) merely sounds a bit odd. 'Deviations' can vary with the linguistic background of the learner: the 'illegal extraction' in (4) is more likely if the speaker's mother tongue allows him to use such a construction. 'Deviations' are observed on all levels of linguistic competence – pronunciation, morphology, syntax, choice of lexical items, all aspects of communicative behaviour. Accordingly, they are classified, counted, and subjected to statistical analysis. Attempts are made to relate their occurrence (and sometimes non-occurrence) and their distribution to various causal factors. The course and success of the acquisitional process are described in terms of decreasing divergencies between TL utterances and the learner's attempts to reproduce them. The language of the learner at some given time is not so very much a language but rather an imperfect, deficient imitation of a language, and it is the latter which serves as the base of description. The 'learner variety' is not perceived and studied in terms of what it is but in terms of what it is not.

This TARGET DEVIATION PERSPECTIVE on language acquisition has found its most straightforward expression in classical 'error analysis', where, in its most elementary form, simply the hits and misses under varying conditions are counted, and a dichotomy created between 'error' and 'non- error'. But it is also taken by many other approaches, however much these differ in the methods by which the deviations are determined and in the causal considerations which are offered to explain them. This is not accidental. There are two important reasons which render the target deviation perspective very attractive. First, it provides the researcher with a straightforward design for empirical work. There is a yardstick against which the actual data can be measured. The target language, or rather the description of some of its aspects, is the base of reference, and what is measured are the differences between what the learner does and what this base of reference asks for. Second, it is the perspective of the teacher. Second language teaching is a normative process, and it is the teacher's responsibility to bring the learner as close to the norm as possible. From its very beginnings, second language acquisition research was inspired by the needs of foreign language teaching; it had, and still has, its focus in classroom learning: subjects are typically students of a foreign language. Thus, it is natural to take some norm as a stable base of reference and to investigate how and why the learner misses it. For example, the English learner of German must learn not to diphthongise long vowels, and to place the subject behind the verb if the object is fronted or if the sentence begins with an adverb. There are many reasons why it is important to do so. Exams in school may be failed, and in any contact outside the classroom, there is the much more rigorous examination of the social environment which decides on the question: 'Is this person one of us?' Therefore, these and all other features of the TL must be precisely copied. Consequently, research on language teaching must try to understand to which extent and for which reasons learners have problems with perfect imitation. Hence, the target deviation perspective is perfectly natural in teaching research. But this does not mean that it is equally natural and rewarding when we want to know something about how the human language capacity functions and which principles determine the acquisitional process.[6]

In this paper, we will advocate a different perspective for language acquisition research.[7] It can be characterised by four key assumptions:

A. During the acquisitional process, the learner passes through a series of LEARNER VARIETIES. Both the internal organisation of each variety at a given time as well as the transition from one variety to the next are essentially systematic in nature.

B. There is a limited set of organisational principles of different kinds which are present in ALL learner varieties. The actual structure of an utterance in a learner variety is determined by a particular interaction of these principles. The kind of interaction may vary, depending on various factors, such as the learner's source language. With successive input analysis, the interaction changes over time. For example, picking up some component of noun morphology from the input may cause the learner to modify the weight of other factors to mark argument status. From this perspective, learning a new feature is not adding a new piece to a puzzle which the learner has to put together. Rather, it entails a sometimes minimal, sometimes substantial reorganisation of the whole variety, where the balance of the various factors successively approaches the balance characteristic of the target language.

---

[6] It is no surprise, therefore, that in first language acquisition, the target deviation perspective is rather the exception than the rule.

[7] This perspective has its historical roots in the late sixties, when notions such as 'interlanguage' (Selinker 1972) were first forged. Historically close notions are also Corder's (1967) 'simple code' and Clyne's (1968) 'Gastarbeiterdeutsch'.

C. Under this perspective, learner varieties are not imperfect imitations of a "real language" – the target language – but systems in their own right, error-free by definition, and characterised by a particular lexical repertoire and by a particular interaction of organisational principles. Fully developed languages, such as English, German, French, are simply borderline cases of learner varieties. They represent a relatively stable state of language acquisition – that state where the learner stops learning because there is no difference between his variety and the input – the variety of his social environment.[8]
D. If all learner varieties, including the final one, are manifestations of the human language capacity, then the study of this capacity should NOT start with the most complex of these manifestations, and go from there to the simpler ones. Rather, it is advisable FIRST to study the various organisational principles of human language and their interplay in relatively simple cases, those where the various form-function relations are more elementary, and more transparent (if seen in their own right, and not as an imperfect imitation of the target).

The study of learner varieties and the way in which they evolve should therefore shed light on how linguistic systems function in general, including the most complex case of 'fully-fledged' languages. Rather than taking the latter as a point of departure and working back in trying to understand how acquisition works, the study of language acquisition should help us to understand how the human language capacity functions – in its elementary manifestations no less than in the most complex cases it normally attains.

3 Empirical background

In this section, we will briefly sketch the project on which our empirical findings are based. The presentation concentrates on what seems indispensable for an understanding of the following sections. For details, the reader is referred to Perdue (1993, Vol. I).[9]

---

[8] This does not mean, of course, that the process cannot come to a halt at a much earlier phase. First language acquisition normally stops when there is no salient difference between the learner's language and the language of the social environment; second language acquisition typically fossilises much before – for example at the level of the 'basic variety'.

[9] See also Trévise & Porquier (1986) for methodological issues, and especially Feldweg (1993) for a detailed description of the transcribed and computerised data bank emanating from this project, whose results are based on the analysis of approximately 15,000 pages of transcription.

The project was longitudinal, cross-linguistic, and it only dealt with second language acquisition OUTSIDE THE CLASSROOM. All our results are based on the productions of 40 adult learners of Dutch, English, French, German and Swedish (or a sub-set of these). All were recently arrived immigrants with legal status, and in daily contact with the language of their new social environment.[10] Languages were organised as shown in Figure 1, see (5), in order to control systematically for source language and target language effects.

This comparison makes us all the more sanguine in reporting regularities which are independent of individual language pairings.

All learners were observed and recorded over a period of about 30 months. Various techniques of data collection were used; they were ordered into three data-collection cycles, such that all learners performed each task at least three times. The present data base consists of four 'complex verbal tasks' – film retellings, personal narratives, instructions ('stage-directions') and picture descriptions – supplemented by selected passages of spontaneous conversation. In the 'stage directions' task, the learner instructs a naive interlocutor to move about, and to move objects from one place to another (as a director would instruct an actor), following a silently enacted scene which the learner has just observed. In the picture description task, the learner tries to make an interlocutor under-

(5)

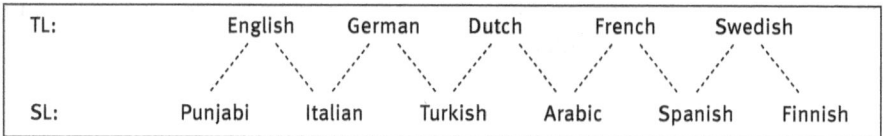

Figure 1: The source language – target language combination.

---

[10] For the criteria for informant selection, see Chapter 3 of Perdue (1993, Vol. 1). The research design of the project allowed us to discern (through the inevitable variability encountered while studying real-life learners who acquire at their own pace) the shared structural characteristics of their progress from a noun-based utterance organisation (Klein & Perdue 1992, Dorriots 1986, Perdue 1987, Dietrich 1989a, Perdue 1995), right up to a finite-verb-based organisation (Klein & Perdue 1992, Perdue & Klein 1992, Perdue 1995, 1996). Not all learners attained this last stage. The 'plateau' referred to here as the basic variety represents a potential fossilisation point. For the learners who indeed developed no further, this point was reached more than a year before the end of the observation period. Although, by definition, we know nothing of their development after the end of the observation period, it is as striking that this plateau is so similar, for so many learners, for such a long period of time (for a detailed discussion, see Perdue & Klein 1992), as it is striking that the 'better' learners also pass through a stage where their learner variety is similarly structured.

stand what is depicted on a picture which the interlocutor cannot see. In a personal narrative, the learner relates events in which he was involved at a specific moment in the past. In the film retelling task, the learner recounts the second half of an edited Charlie Chaplin film ('Modern Times'), the first half of which has been viewed by learner and interlocutor together. These tasks were run because piloting had shown that they provide ample linguistic material relevant to the research areas from which the present results are taken: temporal and spatial reference, and utterance structure. Thus the stage directions and description tasks consist in locating entities in relation one to another under various conditions, and the film-retelling requires introduction of referents, and maintaining reference to them, under a wide range of semantic functions. Personal narratives have a clearly defined temporal structure. Accordingly, different types of data were used for different aspects of learners' production. The analysis of utterance structure is mainly based on film retellings, the expression of temporality was primarily studied in personal narratives, and the expression of spatiality used picture descriptions and the 'stage-directions' task. In all cases, the data sets were cross-checked in relation to the other research areas, and extra data, in particular extracts from free conversations, were used wherever necessary (again, the reader is referred to Perdue 1993 for details).

In the more guided tasks, the aim was both to obtain stretches of connected texts of different types, and also to have at least some control over what the learner was trying to communicate – the film clip, video-recording and picture provide a degree of extra-linguistic correlational evidence of his communicative intentions. This is particularly important, if for one reason or the other, learner utterances DEVIATE from the patterns commonly found. For example, Madan's:[11]

(6) stealing bread girl   (MPE)

'means' in context, the GIRL stole the bread, and not, e.g., that some unspecified agent stole the bread-girl; here, we have a particular constellation of case roles ('thematic roles') and focussing, which leads to a very specific structure; we shall return to this example in 5.2. The systematic comparison with an external 'reality check' helped at least to a certain extent to resolve interpretation problems.

---

11 Identification of examples is as follows: 1st letter is the informant's initial, 2nd letter is his/her SL, 3rd letter is the TL. Thus MPE means 'Madan, source language Punjabi, target language English'. The languages are to be found in example (5). All names of informants are pseudonyms. Some examples are glossed. These glosses, marked by < >, are only meant to help understanding; they are never intended as a grammatical analysis of the example. + indicates a silent pause, * * enclose borrowings from the source language, and [ ] enclose broad phonetic transcription.

In-depth contextual interpretation is therefore necessary in order reliably to establish regular form-function correspondences. Once an interpretation has been established, the surest way of MISSING learner-language regularities is to imagine a 'corresponding' utterance in another language – the target language or the source language -, then attribute its organisation back to the learner's utterance (cf the 'closeness fallacy', Klein & Perdue 1989). One cannot rely on TL sentence-internal functions such as 'subject', 'object', as this would amount to analysing the learner's language AS IF IT WERE (IMPERFECT) TARGET LANGUAGE. Nor could we call on phenomena such as agreement and case which are conspicuous by their absence from the basic variety, as we shall see. Thus the fact that 'the girl' is grammatical subject of the 'corresponding' TL utterance to Madan's (6), does not a priori warrant *girl* being given the status of 'subject' in Madan's own utterance.

4 The structure of the basic variety

4.1 The lexical repertoire

There is no inflection in the basic variety, hence no marking of case, number, gender, tense, aspect, agreement by morphology. Thus, lexical items typically occur in one invariant form. It corresponds to the stem, the infinitive or the nominative in the target language; but it can also be a form which would be an inflected form in the target language. Occasionally, a word shows up in more than one form, but this (rare) variation does not seem to have any functional value: the learners simply try different phonological variants.[12]

The lexicon in the basic variety varies in two respects – in size and origin. Normally, it increases steadily during the acquisition process, but this increase varies considerably from learner to learner (see Broeder, Extra & van Hout 1993). The main source is normally the target language, of course. But there are also many borrowings from the source language; again, this varies from learner to learner, and generalisations are difficult.

Three types of regular interaction between source and target language systems are however worth mentioning. The first concerns the phonological form of the lexical item, which is often strongly influenced by the learner's mother tongue. This influence is very salient but not particularly interesting in the present context.

---

[12] Broeder, Extra & van Hout (1993) note random variation in the lemmatised basic variety lexicon, whatever the word class of the lemma, whereas in more advanced stages, variation becomes confined to verb lemmas (in particular), as some learners develop a functional morphology.

The second is at the borderline between lexical repertoire and structural principles – in word formation, more precisely in the relative order in hierarchical compounds of head and complement. Generally speaking, this order in the basic variety reflects that of the corresponding TL. In a well-documented study, Broeder et al. (1993) observe that the basic variety favours noun-noun compound constructions over derivational word formation (as do pidgins, cf. Mühlhäusler 1986), and that the interplay of SL-T L particularities gives the following picture: noun-noun composition is determined by TL organisation where this organisation is unambiguous, but the more ambiguous the TL organisation is, the stronger the impact of SL organisation. Take the following attempts to refer to a baker in the film retelling. Lerners of French coin compounds that are systematically head-initial *(un monsieur la boulanger)*, as is TL – French. TL-Dutch allows both head-initial and head-final compounds; speakers of Moroccan (head-initial) tend to transfer their pattern *(de baas van brood)*, whereas speakers of Turkish (head-final) coin head-final compounds *(brood-baas)*.

The third example of a SL-T L interaction concerns the type of item used to express spatial relations. Again, this is determined by TL organisation, as the French and German examples of section 4.4.3. below make clear. However, source language preferences emerge where the TL system offers a choice: Schenning and van Hout (1994) note, for example, that Moroccan learners of Dutch use prepositional phrases to express location and direction, whereas Turkish learners prefer TL adverbials to express these relations.

What does NOT vary is the composition of the lexicon. Essentially, it consists of a repertoire of noun-like and verb-like words, with some adjectives and adverbs (Dietrich 1989a, b).[13] The pronoun system consists of minimal means to refer to speaker, hearer, and a third person (functioning deictically and anaphorically). Anaphoric pronominal reference to inanimates is not observed. There are a few quantifiers, a word for negation, a few prepositions with overgeneralised lexical meanings, but no complementisers and, as has already been mentioned, no inflexional morphology, hence no markers of agreement, tense, aspect, or case. In other words, the repertoire consists mainly of 'open class', and a small list of 'closed class' items with lexical meaning. There are some determiners (in particular demonstratives) but hardly ever a determiner system (Carroll & Dietrich 1985), and there are no expletive elements, such as

---

[13] The longitudinal studies described in section 4. systematically investigated how each learner's linguistic repertoire was put to use at different points along the acquisition process. These repertoires may be consulted in Klein & Perdue (1992), Dietrich, Klein & Noyau (1995), Becker and Carroll (1997) and, for a quantitative study, Broeder, Extra & van Hout (1993).

English existential *there*. Broeder, Extra and van Hout (1993) determine the relative share of each grammatical category in the learners' lexicon, and note that the share of articles, conjunctions and pronouns increases only after the basic variety stage. Parallel to this increase, there is a decrease in the share of nouns, adjectives, and adverbs.

As usual in linguistic theory, lexical items should be seen as sets of feature complexes – phonological, semantical, grammatical, perhaps others. Grammatical features include categorial properties (being a noun, a verb etc), but also case role features (or 'theta-features'), such as 'requires an agentive argument and a theme argument', etc. In what follows, we shall not systematically discuss these and other features. But it should be clear that whenever we speak of a lexical item such as *bread* or *steal*, this is just an abbreviation of set of feature complexes.

4.2 Utterance organisation

Given the lexical repertoire, how do speakers of the basic variety put its items together, when they produce an utterance? We found that their utterance structure is determined by the interaction of three types of constraints (or, as we often say, organisational principles):

1. There are absolute constraints on the form and relative order of constituents: PHRASAL CONSTRAINTS.[14]
2. There are constraints which have to do with the case role properties of arguments: SEMANTIC CONSTRAINTS.
3. There are, finally, constraints which have to do with the organisation of information in connected text (introduction and maintenance of reference, topic-focus-structure): PRAGMATIC CONSTRAINTS.

The phrasal constraints observed in the basic variety admit three basic phrasal patterns with some subvariants (the subscripts of NP1 and NP2 correspond to differences in their possible internal structures, set out below):

---

[14] It is these constraints which correspond to what is commonly called 'syntax' in the narrower sense of this word – that is, constraints that narrow down the ways in which larger units can be made of more elementary units and which are stated without reference to semantic or pragmatic factors. But since one also might have a broader understanding of what 'syntax' is, we prefer the label 'phrasal constraints' (see also section 6.2).

PH1a $NP_1 - V$
PH1b $NP_1 - V - NP_2$
PH1c. $NP_1 - V - NP_2 - NP_2$[14]
PH2. $NP_1 - COP - \begin{Bmatrix} ADJ \\ NP_2 \\ PP \end{Bmatrix}$

PH3. $\begin{Bmatrix} V \\ COP \end{Bmatrix} - NP_2$

All patterns may be preceded or followed by an adverbial, normally an adverbial of time or space. They may also be preceded by the conjunction *and* (or its counterpart in other languages). Note that there is only one v-final construction used by all learners: PH1a.[15]

The basic variety shows a "non-finite utterance organisation": utterances contain verbs, and are structured according to the valency of this verb (where arguments may be left implicit under conditions specified below). But there is no trace of finite verbs, in whatever function.

The phrasal constraints impose strong restrictions on possible sentence structures. Note, however, that a pattern such as NP – V – NP does not mean that the first NP is the 'subject' and the second NP is the 'object'; in fact, it is not easy to define these notions within the basic variety – except by their alleged parallelism to target (or source) language utterances. Hence, the question arises which argument takes which position. We found that the assignment primarily follows a simple (semantic) principle which is based on the CONTROL ASYMMETRY between referents of noun phrases: one can rank each argument of a verb by the greater or lesser degree of control that its referent exerts, or intends to exert, over the referents of the other argument(s). Strength of control is a continuum (Comrie 1981, but see note 18), depends on the semantics of the verb and is reflected in its case role properties (or theta-features).[16] Strength ranges from clear agent-patient relations at one extreme (with verbs such as *hit, break*) to weak asymmetries (with

---

15 Some learners, though, also use the pattern NP – NP – V. It is only attested in the English of Punjabi, but not Italian learners, and in the German and Dutch of Turkish, but not Moroccan or Italian learners. It is the case that Punjabi and Turkish, but not Moroccan and Italian, are predominantly verb-final, although alternative word orders are not uncommon. While this pattern thus clearly reflects SL influence, such influence is rare overall. From a longitudinal perspective, use of this particular pattern is restricted, and these learners also acquire PH1b.

16 It is perhaps arguable whether features such as 'is an agent' (in the case of an NP) or 'requires an agent as argument' (in the case of a verb) should be called 'semantical' or not. We have done so, because in one way or the other, they have something to do with the meaning of the verb – with the type of action, process or event that it describes. But nothing hinges on this terminology.

verbs such as *kiss, meet*) and finally to complete absence at the other extreme (as in copular constructions). Where control obtains, the following constraint can be observed:

SEM1. THE NP-REFERENT WITH HIGHEST CONTROL COMES FIRST

Hence the NP with the more agentive referent appears in initial position. The NP1-referent is therefore most often human (agentive referents tend to be animate, Silverstein 1976), but human referents may also appear in NP2-position: semantic role properties, rather than intrinsic features of NPs, are crucial in assigning position.

Some verbs, notably verbs of saying and of giving take three arguments (four arguments are never observed in the basic variety). These verbs are regularly of the 'telic' type, that is, their lexical meaning involves two distinct states as a part of their lexical meaning (cf. Klein 1994, chapter 5). What is crucial is the fact that the control relation between the various arguments is not the same in both states. This is best illustrated by an example such as Santo's:

(7) Charlie give present for young children   (SIE)

There is a first state, the 'source state', in which Charlie is in control of the present, and is active in bringing about a distinct state, the 'target state'. In the target state, 'young children' are in control of (i.e., have) the present. The control status of the NP which refers to the present is low in both states. Therefore, the principle 'Controller first' requires that this argument not come first (its exact position in the utterance will be specified below in section 4.4.2). It does not say, however, which controller – the one of the source state or the one of the target state – comes first. Therefore, 'Controller first' has to be supplemented by an additional constraint, which defines the relative weight of source and target state in determining word order. It is:

SEM2. CONTROLLER OF SOURCE STATE OUTWEIGHS CONTROLLER OF
        TARGET STATE

These considerations apply analogously to verbs of saying if we assume that what changes in both states is 'the control of information'. There is one referent who is in control of the information in both states, and another referent who does not control the information in the source state but only in the target state. Thus, the 'sayer' comes first, the hearer comes second, and the 'said' comes last. (Speech is directly quoted in the basic variety.)

The two control constraints impose additional restrictions on the way utterances can be put together. But they are not always operative, either because there is no asymmetry between the NP-referents, or because the verb has only one argument.[17] In the following examples from Ramon, there is no control asymmetry. Nevertheless, the constituent order variation is not random:

(8) a. il [setruv] avec la fille (RSF)
      <he (=Chaplin) finds himself with the girl>
    b. il [setruv] avec Chaplin (RSF)
      <'he' (=the girl) finds herself with Chaplin>
    c. il arrive (RSF)
      <he arrive>
    d. arrive *otra* personne (RSF)
      <arrive other person>

Some examples from the acquisition of Dutch illustrate the same point:

(9) a. hier is die cafe (MMD)
      <here is that cafe>
    b. dann auto is hier (MMD)
      <then car is here>
    c. die meneer valt van water (FMD)
      <that mister fall from water, i.e. Charlie fell into the water>
    d. met valt drie (FMD)
      <with fall three, i.e., there were three of them fell>

In copula constructions, and for verbs which take only one argument, NP position depends on the way in which information is distributed over an utterance in context, that is, by pragmatic factors.

The pragmatic constraints which we found in the basic variety are of two types. They may have to do with information status, i.e., which information in the utterance is NEW and which is MAINTAINED from the preceding utterance(s), on the one hand, or with the TOPIC-FOCUS-STRUCTURE, on the other. These two factors must be carefully kept apart, although in practice, they often go hand in hand. The topic-focus-structure reflects the fact that a part of the utterance

---

17 This argument is certainly in a semantic relation to the verb – it has a case role (or theta-role) -, and can be 'in control' in the sense that Comrie (1981) uses this term, but (i) there is no control ASYMMETRY, and (ii) the semantic relation remains constant whether the argument is pre-verbal or post-verbal (pattern PH1: 'Charlie arrive' or pattern PH3: 'arrive Charlie').

defines a set of alternatives to be decided (the 'topic') and then selects one of those which is claimed to hold (the 'focus'). This idea, which goes back to authors such as Weil, von der Gabelentz and Paul in the last century, can be made more precise in various ways. This has been done in recent work on focus in formal semantics (see, for example, von Stechow 1991, Rooth, 1992). The details are complicated and not relevant for our purpose; therefore, we shall only explain the basic idea by a simple example. The utterance *The girl stole the bread* can be used as an answer to (at least) three different questions:

(10) a. Who stole the bread?
 b. What did the girl steal?
 c. What did the girl do?

In (10a), the alternatives are the persons that could have stolen the bread – this is the topic, repeated in the answer by *stole the bread* – and the focus is the person specified by the NP *the girl*. In (10b), the topic is the set of things that the girl could have stolen, and the focus constituent *the bread* specifies one of them – the focus. In (10c), the set of alternatives are all the events involving the girl that could have happened on that occasion, and the verb phrase specifies the one selected from this set – the focus.[18]

The particular status of an expression as focus expression or topic expression can be marked by specific devices such as intonation, clefting, or sometimes (as in Japanese) special particles. In the basic variety, it is mainly by word order. The relevant constraint is very simple:

PR1. FOCUS EXPRESSION LAST

---

18 Both pragmatic factors – introduction and maintenance of information and topic-focus-structure – can be brought together if we assume that not just individual utterances but the entire text to which they belong constitutes an answer to a QUAESTIO – an explicit or implicit question (Klein and von Stutterheim 1987). Thus, a question such as *What does your flat look like?* can be answered by a single utterance *(It looks like a pigsty)* but also by an organised sequence of utterances. Not all of these are direct answers to the initial quaestio, i.e., give (partial) descriptions; there may be all sorts of supportive information, commentaries, etc. Accordingly, the text may be partitioned into a MAIN STRUCTURE (the 'foreground' in narratives) and various SIDE STRUCTURES. Different quaestiones lead to different text types, e.g., personal narratives ('What happened to you yesterday?'), argumentations ('Why should one marry? Are there several gods?'), directions ('How do I get to the station from here?'), etc. The quaestio determines the structure of the text which answers it in different ways: It defines the partitioning into main structure and side structures, the way in which the information flows from one utterance to the next ('referential movement'), the topic-focus structure of all main structure utterances, etc.

The argument of one argument verbs has a semantic role, but there is no semantic role ASYMMETRY, and hence, the controller constraints cannot apply. Thus, only PR1. and phrasal constraints interact: if the referent of the NP is topical, then pattern PH1. is used; if it is in focus then pattern PH3. is used. This is the difference between (8c) and (8d) above. The same constraint stipulates the NPs' position in symmetrical (and therefore copular) constructions, as in examples (8a) and (8b): in the former, the girl is in focus, in the latter, it is Chaplin. Note that this interaction determines word order without reference to ill-defined notions such as 'subject' or 'object', but it explains the topic ingredience often found in the subject (cf. Keenan 1976, Reis 1982).

The pragmatic constraint PR1. also governs other aspects of utterance structure, in particular the place of adverbials. We only give the main lines here. Time adverbials may occur in utterance- initial position, most clearly in narratives. An utterance in the main of a narrative answers a 'quaestio' such as *what happened at time tx?*. Thus, the topic of a foreground utterance contains a time span tx, and the focus is the event that happened at that time. Therefore, a time adverbial specifying the time span of the 'quaestio' occurs naturally with pattern PH3, giving ADV – V – NP. A background clause, by contrast, may answer an implicit question such as *When did this happen?* In this case, it is the specification of the time span which is in focus, and hence, an adverbial which specifies this time span comes in final position. Similar considerations apply for spatial adverbials, for example in descriptive texts (see section 5.1). Time and space adverbs are, then, not 'preposed' (from where?), but occur where their topic or focus status dictates.[19] Indeed, BV utterances can contain two adverbs of the same type, one in topic position, one in focus position; Starren (1996) examines pairs such as *altijd ik wakker om acht uur* (<always I wake-up at eight o'clock>, MTD). to which we shall return in section 4.3 below.

The other pragmatic factor which influences the structure of the utterance is the 'given-new distinction': Is whatever some expression refers to maintained from a preceding utterance, or is it new? In fact, this distinction interacts with the topic-focus status and results in different types of NPs. These, in turn, are restricted to certain positions, as indicated by the numbers in the phrasal rules PH1 – PH3 above. Here, we find some (limited!) variation within the basic variety. In particular, we find some numerals and – though rarely – a definiteness marker,

---

19 The topic-focus-structure also plays an important role in some other respects, not discussed here in detail. Thus, negation and (other) scope particles occur at the topic-focus boundary. This position can be marked: Santo and Ravinder use [iz(a)] (Huebner 1989), Ergün (TD) uses '*is* + V' (Klein & Perdue 1992), Abdelmalek (MF) uses *li* (Véronique 1983). See also Huebner (1983).

mostly a demonstrative; we have marked this in the following diagram by optional DET.[20] As a rule, however, nouns are bare. Thus, the main lines are as follows:

NP₁ NOP₂
proper name proper name
(DET) noun (DET) noun
pronoun
0

Choices among these forms depend on whether a referent is introduced or maintained, and whether the referring expression is in topic or focus. The most general opposition lies between use of a lexical noun (or proper name), on the one hand, and 0 (or pronoun), on the other. The latter is exclusively used to maintain reference in the context of movement of a controller from topic to topic in successive utterances. For some learners, the conditions under which zero anaphor occurs are even more highly constrained: the antecedent has to be the ONLY potential controller, i.e., if the preceding utterance contains two human referents, then reference to the controller is maintained by a full noun in topic. Zero anaphor is not possible in place of *de mädch* in the second utterance of Angelina's:

(11)   de mädch gucke de mann mit brot
       <the girl look the man with bread>
       und DE MÄDCH wolle essen   (AIG)
       <and the girl want to eat>

Maintenance of semantic role and position (controller first) is thus not in itself sufficient to licence zero where there are two potential controllers in the previous utterance (and is a further indication that 'subject of' is not a basic variety function). With names and lexical nouns, the topic/focus status of the referent is indicated solely by position. It follows from the observed distribution that reference maintenance in focus cannot be achieved by pronominal means. So, there are clear constraints on how things can be expressed in the basic variety, and where, consequently, its speakers might get into problems. These problems we believe, are a major source of structural complexification, a point to which we shall return in section 5.2.

---

[20] We also occasionally find an adjective before or after N and a PP following the initial head in a compound.

4.3 The expression of temporality[21]

Time and space are probably the two most fundamental categories of human cognition, and accordingly, all human languages have developed rich means to express them. In most languages – for example in all source and target languages of the present project – the finite verb has to mark tense, aspect, or both; hence, with each normal sentence, the speaker has to refer to time, whether he wants to or not – it is an obligatory category. This is normally not the case for spatial information, but its structural and communicative importance is beyond doubt. In this section, we will discuss how temporality is expressed with the means of the basic variety; the next section will be devoted to space.

The main data source for the investigation of temporality were personal narratives, embedded in conversations. They were completed by other conversational passages where informants speak about their future plans. Just as in other domains, the acquisitional process turns out to be continuous and gradual, without sharp boundaries between the various learner varieties. Here, we only consider the basic variety. Some minor variation aside, it can be characterised by four features:

1. As was set out in section 4.1, utterances typically consist of uninflected verbs, their arguments and, optionally, adverbials. THIS MEANS THAT THE BASIC VARIETY LACKS THE USUAL GRAMMATICAL MEANS TO EXPRESS TENSE AND ASPECT.
2. Lexical verbs show up in a 'base form', and there is often no copula. Most learners of English use the bare stem as their base form, but V-*ing* also occurs. Learners of other languages may use the infinitive (German, French) or even a generalised inflected form (as often in Swedish). Turkish learners of Dutch, for example, use the infinitive, Moroccan learners of Dutch use the bare stem.
3. There is a fairly rich repertoire of temporal adverbials. Minimally, this repertoire includes: (a) the calendaric type adverbials (*Sunday, in the evening*); (b) anaphoric adverbials expressing the relation AFTER (*then, after*), and also typically an adverbial which expresses the relation BEFORE; (c) some deictic adverbials such as *yesterday, now*; (d) a few frequency adverbials, notably *always, often, two time*, etc; (e) a few durational adverbials, normally as bare nouns, such as *two hour*, etc. Temporal adverbials involving two reference points such as *again, still, already* do not belong to the standard repertoire of the basic variety.

---

[21] The empirical findings reported in this section are based on joint work by Rainer Dietrich, Colette Noyau and Wolfgang Klein. A detailed analysis is found in Dietrich, Klein & Noyau (1995). See also Noyau (1990).

4. There are some boundary markers, which allow the learner to express the beginning and the end of some situation, as in constructions like *work finish*, 'after work is/was/will be over'.

Compared to the rich expressive tools for temporality in fully-fledged languages, this seems to impose strong restrictions on what can be said. This impression, however, is premature. At this stage, learners are often extremely good story tellers, and telling a story requires the expression of all sorts of temporal information. Their guitar, so to speak, has only one string, but they play it with masterly skill. How is this possible?

What the basic variety allows, is the specification of temporal relations such as BEFORE, AFTER, SIMULTANEOUS, etc. In particular, it allows the specification of some time span t (in relation to some other time span s, for example the time of utterance). It can also express duration and frequency of time spans. Suppose that some time span t, about which the speaker wants to say something, is introduced. Such a time span will be called 'topic time' (abbreviated TT). The topic time is simply the time about which the speaker wants to make an assertion – in contrast to the "time of the situation" (abbreviated TSit) – that is, the time at which the event, process or state to be situated in time obtains. All the speaker has to do is to introduce and, if there is need, to shift, TT, and to relate TSit to it.[22] More systematically, the functioning of the basic variety is described by the following three principles:

I. At the beginning of the discourse, a time span TT_1 is fixed. This can be done in one of three ways:
   (a) by explicit introduction on the informant's part; this is usually done by a temporal adverbial in initial position, in topic;
   (b) by explicit introduction on the interviewer's part (e.g., *what happened last sunday?*);
   (c) by implicitly taking the "default topic time" – the time of utterance; in this case, nothing is explicitly marked.

---

[22] We assume that the notional category of TENSE expresses the relation of TT to the time at which the utterance is made – the deictically given time of utterance. The notional category of ASPECT expresses the relation between TT and TSit (Klein 1994). Note that this definition of aspect is not at variance with other, more metaphorical characterisations of aspect, as often found in published work: it only makes them more precise. Take, for example, the case that the time about which an assertion is made is fully included in the time of the situation (TT IN TSit) this gives the feeling that the situation is 'viewed from the interior', 'as ongoing, in its development – it is imperfective. If, by contrast, TSit is fully included in TT, then this gives the impression that the event, state, process, is 'presented as a whole, as completed, as seen from the exterior' – it represents perfective aspect.

TT1 is not only the assertion time of the first utterance. It also serves as a point of departure for all subsequent assertion times in the text.

II. If TT_I is given, then TT_{I+1} is either maintained or changed. If it is maintained, nothing is marked. If it is changed, there are two possibilities:
   (a) the shifted assertion time is explicitly marked by an adverbial in initial position;
   (b) the new assertion time follows from a principle of text organisation. For narratives, this is the classical principle of chronological order "unless marked otherwise, the order of mention corresponds to the order of events".[23] In other words, TT_{I+1} is some interval more or less right-adjacent to TT_I.

This principle does not obtain in all text types. It is only characteristic of narratives and other texts with a similar overall temporal organisation – texts which answer a question like *What next?* Even in these texts, it only applies to foreground sequences. In other text types, such as descriptions or arguments, the principle of chronological order does not apply, nor does it hold for side structures in narratives, i.e., those sequences which give background information, evaluations, comments etc. For those cases, change of TT must be marked by adverbials.

Principles I and II provide the temporal scaffold of a sequence of utterances – the time spans about which something is said. The "time of situation" TSit is then given by a third principle:

III. The relation of TSit to TT in the basic variety is always 'more or less simultaneous'. TT can be contained in TSit, or TSit can be contained in TT or TT and TSit contained in each other.

Thus, the various aspectual distinctions often observed in fully-fledged languages are collapsed in the basic variety. However, within this simultaneity, cleverly managed combinations of adverbs and Aktionsarten of verbs allow learners to distinguish habituality from iterativity:

(12) a. altijd ik les om half twee   (MTD)
        <always I lesson at half past-one>
     b. vandaag ik altijd weg met auto   (FMD)
        <today I always away with car>

---

[23] See, for example, Clark 1971, Labov 1972, von Stutterheim 1986.

For habituality (12a), one TSit is linked to a series of TTs, whereas for iterativity (12b), a complex TSit is linked to one TT (Starren 1996).

This system is very simple (compared to what we find in all source and target languages) but extremely versatile. It allows an easy expression of when what happens, or is the case – provided that (a) there are enough adverbials, and (b) it is cleverly managed. Therefore, one way the learner has of improving his expressive power is simply to enrich his vocabulary, especially by adding temporal adverbials, and to perfect his technique on this instrument. And about one third of the 40 learners whose acquisition was investigated do exactly this: they do not go beyond the basic variety, but they steadily improve it in these two respects – more words, better practice, no unnecessary complications. The speaker of the basic variety can say what he wants to say about temporal relations – not what the structure of the language forces him to say.

4.4 The expression of spatiality[24]

4.4.1 Theme, relatum and spatial relation

In fully-fledged languages, the expression of space is no less complex and varied than the expression of time: there are adverbs, prepositions, case marking, verbs of posture and of movement, and other devices available to express such complex messages as *The second suspect from the left pulled this little gun out from under the chair behind the table over there*. In the basic variety, the expression of spatial relations is reduced to its basic ingredients. These are:
- the entity which is located, the THEME;
- the entity in relation to which it is located, the RELATUM;
- the SPATIAL RELATION which obtains between theme and relation, for example those expressed by *at, behind, under, to the left of*, etc.

It is useful to distinguish between static locations and changes of location, where the latter involve two positions (SOURCE POSITION and TARGET POSITION) of the theme. Thus, *The book is on the table* is static: the book is the theme, the

---

[24] We have drawn on the work of Mary Carroll and Angelika Becker in writing this section, and refer the reader to Carroll 1990, Carroll & Becker 1993, and Becker and Carroll 1997 for a full analysis of the expression of spatial relations by these learners. Further details on TL Dutch comes from Schenning & van Hout 1994, and on TL French, from Giacobbe 1993.

table is the relatum, and the spatial relation is described by *on*. The utterance *The book was put on the table* is a dynamic event, with the source state characterised by 'book not on table' and the target state characterised by 'book on table'. The THEME can be an object, a person, but also some event (a case normally not observed in the basic variety). The RELATUM is some entity which is assumed to be known to speaker and listener, or else must be explicitly mentioned; it can be deictically given, or lexically specified.

Many spatial relations between theme and relatum are possible, and languages differ as to which ones they encode (Haviland & Levinson 1994, Klein 1991). Which ones of these can be expressed, is essentially a matter of the lexicon, hence subject to considerable variation. Since the lexicon of the basic variety largely stems from the language to be learned, there is some variation in this respect. Nevertheless, learners share some clear preferences for which relations they express. What is (quite) constant across learners is the STRUCTURE of (dynamic and static) spatial expressions – a fact which brings us back to the constraints on utterance structure of section 4.1. We first discuss the structure and then the lexicon.

4.4.2 The structure of spatial expressions

In the expression of space, the basic variety operates exactly with the constraints discussed in section 4.1. But the concrete results depend on whether one or two spatial constellations are to be expressed. In the static case, the phrasal pattern is PH1b, for verbs of posture, and otherwise PH2 (copula constructions). The situation is more complex for change of location. Here, speakers distinguish whether only the theme's change of place is described ("locomotion", PH1b), or whether a potential controller, who causes the change of location, is mentioned as well ("causative motion", PH1c). We illustrate the latter case by returning below to the discussion (section 4.1) of verbs of giving. Major constituents of these patterns may be left implicit where the context allows recoverability of information, and these contexts will be examined in more detail in the following section.

We saw in 4.1 that for verbs of saying, learners observe a strict division between reported speech and its frame: reported speech comes after mention of speaker and addressee. For verbs of giving, a different constraint is at work. These verbs are a sub-class of the verbs of causative motion (there is a parallel between *John gave the book to Mary*, and *John put the book on the table*), where a theme undergoes a movement from a source (the controller) to a target position. The constraint:

SEM3. THEME BEFORE RELATUM IN TARGET POSITION

operates for all verbs of causative motion, in all text-types, as we shall see below in section 5, and reflects the absence of indirect object cliticisation in French, or dative movement in English from the basic variety. Note that SEM3 regularly maps the relatum onto NP2 of patterns PH1, which implies that for causative motion, the relatum is always in focus, even if mutually known.

4.4.3 Spatial relations

What are the spatial relations that are normally encoded in these patterns of the basic variety? In general, perceptual space is characterised by DIMENSIONAL and by TOPOLOGICAL relations.[25] The former are given by the speaker's co-ordinate axes: VERTICAL (up-down), LATERAL (left-right), SAGITTAL (front-back). These normally vary with the speaker's perspective on the relatum, including the case where the speaker himself is taken to be the relatum (as in the case in spatial deixis). The topological structure has to do with the inclusion of (the place of) the theme in the place of the relatum (or the neigbourhood of the relatum). It is based on spatial relations which are invariant: use of such relations is therefore not dependent on entities or places with specific features (assymetrical sides), nor on a particular perspective. The most neutral topological relation may be termed AT-PLACE : the theme is somehow 'with' the relatum, for example there where the relatum is, or is at its 'canonical position' in relation to the relatum. (In English, for example, people canonically sit 'at tables', but 'in cars'). Some languages of the sample specifically encode this relation, others do not, but for the everyday world such canonical relations are often visually perceptible and understood, thus obviating the communicative need for explicit encoding. The AT-PLACE of a theme-relatum relation may be more finely divided into a set of topological sub-spaces, among which the following are often encoded:
- the INNER space,
- the EXTERIOR space,
- the BOUNDARY space, comprising a boundary (typically coinciding with the outer surface of the relatum),
- the NEIGHBOURING space.

---

[25] This is a very simplified picture of spatial relations, but it suffices for an analysis of what is normally expressed in the basic variety. For a more detailed discussion, see Klein 1991, Giacobbe 1993.

A region of space may be delimited in terms of two relata, defining a relation of INTERPOSITION, but (just as with temporal adverbs involving two reference points) such an expression involving two relata is absent from the basic variety. Dynamic spatial configurations additionally require the notion of the PATH of an entity in motion, whose trajectory determines three subspaces: the SOURCE (from), INTERMEDIATE (along), and GOAL (to): a specification of these (sub)-relata functions to indicate the DIRECTION of a moving theme.

In the basic variety, all speakers – with minor exceptions – denote the same set of spatial relations in the same contexts: the basic variety contains more highly differentiated means to express dynamic as opposed to static constellations, and to express topological as opposed to dimensional relations. We will take each opposition in turn:

1. Static descriptions in the basic variety are mainly confined to the opposition between AT-PLACE and NEIGHBOURING, with a subset of learners expressing a finer distinction than AT-PLACE, namely: IN. The neutral relation AT-PLACE may be expressed by the fixed order theme-relatum – if nothing is made explicit, the neutral spatial relation is intended -, or by an overgeneralised preposition: *en, avec* (Fr), *met* (Du), and the exact (canonical) relation is inferred. NEIGHBOURING is rendered by a transparent form, namely 'side' (*côté, seite, kant*) in all basic varieties, independently of the grammatical status of this usage in the TLs. That subset of learners who express IN restrict its use to relata which can be conceptualised as containers, and use the AT relation in other contexts (see example 18). There is no expression of the relation EXTERIOR, presumably as it is communicatively more economical to relate the theme to another relatum.

   All learners use a lexical item which corresponds to English *there*, i.e., a lexical item which merges the topological relation AT with a deictically or anaphorically given relatum, to be interpreted as "not here". It is interesting that the positive counterpart – the word which would correspond to English *here* is only found in the lexical repertoire of some speakers of the basic variety. We have no clear explanation for this asymmetry. It may be that *here* is communicatively less important to express, as it is the 'default' relation to the speaker's origo. The lexical repertoire for dimensional relations is much more restricted. A subset of learners expresses vertical (*top/bottom; en haut/ en bas; oben/unten, boven/beneden*) and lateral (*left/right; gauche/droite; links/rechts*), and less so sagittal relations (*front/back; face; voor/achter*) in static contexts.

2. Changes of location are expressed explicitly by a variety of terms simultaneously encoding a topological or dimensional component. We give some examples from French and German:

(13) French
away from source: *[sorti], [part]*
to goal: *[ariv], [vjẽ]*
from inner to outer/outer to inner space: *[ãtr], [sorti]*
upward/downward/leftward/rightward: *[mõt], [desãd], à gauche, à droite*
straight ahead: *en face*
along unbounded path: *[pas]*

(14) German
away from source: *raus, weg*
to goal: *bis, nach, zu*
back: *zurück*
from inner to outer/outer to inner space: *raus, zurück*
upwards: *auf*

These examples clearly show the influence of the TL system on learners' analysis: the French items are mainly derived from TL verbs, whereas the German items are derived from TL prepositions or particles. (The only motion verb systematically used by learners of Dutch or German is 'come': *kommen/komen.*) The relative richness of lexical items for dynamic cases, in relation to that of static ones, is not an artefact of the data analysed, since learners were faced with a task requiring static relations to be expressed – the description task. However, many chose to acquit themselves by expressing direction, and turned a description into a guided tour.

5 The basic variety in use

5.1 Its functioning...

How is this basic variety put to use in complex verbal tasks? We have already seen how a personal narrative is organised, and give here two further illustrations of how learners proceed: in the retelling, and in the stage directions task.

In the film retelling, learners narrate a complex overall event whose foreground comprises singular events, each of which answers the quaestio: *What happens (with p) at Ti+1?,* where Ti expresses one of a series of time intervals, and p a protagonist (in this particular elicitation task, Charlie Chaplin, and other characters). Learners construct this foreground obeying the principle of chronological order (recount the events in the order they occur), and by using pattern PH1a-c in contexts of referential 'flow': inter-utterance cohesion is observed in the use of anaphoric forms (pronouns or 0) in NP1. Pattern PH 3 is used to signal that there is a break. The NP is never a pronoun in this pattern: its referent is in focus, and 'answers' a question of the form 'What happens at ti+1? ', where no protagonist is presupposed (compare Labov's 'Then what happened?', 1972:370). This is why a time adverbial associates naturally with this pattern, in topic: it functions either to indicate a major temporal break ('after ten days'), or to indicate, redundantly, that the upcoming utterance expresses a break in the event chain and/or the protagonists involved. An utterance such as Andrea's:

(15) after + comeback the brigade fire   (AIE)
     <=then the fire brigade arrived>

is characteristic of this use of the adverbial – here, introducing an 'arrival on the scene' – in a context where the temporal structure of the retelling does not really require one.

In the stage directions task, the spatial configuration "theme-relation-relatum" maps on to the three argument (causative motion) variant of pattern PH1, as we saw above, with optional V and NP1. The speaker must draw the hearer's attention to the entity to be moved (thus making it identifiable for the hearer), convey the type of action required in the transition, and the new location of the entity at goal. Reference is therefore first made to the entity to be moved before the entity designating its position at goal. The performer (controller) need not be referred to

(16) [ame] le chapeau avec le tabouret   (ZMF)
     <(put?) the hat with the stool>

If expressed, the verb of causative motion normally precedes the theme, but such motion can also be left unexpressed, as in this example of Jarnail's:

(17) bag in the table   (JPE)
     <= put the bag on the table> (Carroll 1990:1027)

or the theme may precede the (explicit) verb in the contexts discussed immediately below. If the theme has to be identified, because invisible to the performer, or one of a set, then it is simply mentioned, as in the following example of Jarnail's (even if the source relatum is mutually known, it cannot be mentioned before the theme):

(18) book
    <the performer looks for and finds a book>
    ++ book in the table (JPE)
    <=put the book on the table> (Carroll 1990:1027)[26]

It is in such a context that the theme may precede the verb, as in the second mention of *livre* in Abdelmalek's:

(19) avec un livre + livre [don] le sac   (AMF)
    <with a book + book give (=put) the bag>

We said in section 4.4.2 above that the relatum is confined to the focus expression. This strong constraint is the consequence of the use of verbs of causative motion in this task. The presentational order 'relatum – theme' (*next to Chaplin (is) policeman*) is confined to static locations, with the copula variant of pattern PH3 with an initial adverbial, and is rare because in the absence of a functional determiner system for most speakers of the basic variety, word order constitutes the most functional means for distinguishing theme from relatum (Carroll 1990, Carroll & Dietrich 1985).

These examples show clearly how simple phrasal patterns are adapted to task and context. The constituents left implicit in example (17) can be explained by the fact that adult learners know that a 'manipulative activity scene' (Slobin 1985) links through the notion of causative motion to a theme-relatum configuration at goal. The controller is unambiguously derivable from the context, and the specification of the spatial configuration at goal allows causative motion to be left unexpressed.

The basic variety thus shows regular form-function correspondences: constituent order is semantically and pragmatically constrained, is not an 'imperfect reflection' of SL or TL constraints, and is in no way random. Adult learners have communicational needs that require sequences of utterances performing a range of discourse functions, and the basic variety is developed, in which lexemes are combined into patterns to express a definable range of semantic and pragmatic functions. In sum, the basic variety is a complex of interrelations between lexical expressions, order constraints and the discourse structure of different communicative tasks.

---

[26] These English examples nicely show a flat surface conceptualised as a container ('in', in the absence of 'on' from Jarnail's basic variety).

5.2 ... And where it fails

The basic variety provides an efficient means of communication just so long as its organising principles coalesce, where, for example, the first NP of PH1 is both controller and topic. Discourse contexts occur, however, where its constraints come into conflict: the controller may be in the focus component, or else the NP-referent in topic may not be the controller (as typically the subject of an English passive sentence). This fact has two distinct consequences: (a) learners override one of the constraints, or (b) they develop specific means to accomodate the 'competition' (Bates & MacWhinney 1987).

We will illustrate the first case with reference to example (10) of section 4. When *The girl stole the bread* answers the question *Who stole the bread?* the focus is the person specified by the NP *the girl*, but this person is also the controller of the utterance. By SEM1, the NP should come first, but by PR1, it should come last. Two things are observed in such a conflict situation.

A. The competition is regularly resolved as a function of the weight of the corresponding constraint in the learner's source language. Thus to return to example (6):

(6)   stealing bread girl   (MPE)

discourse-pragmatic factors play an important role in constraining Punjabi word-order, and the Punjabi learner Madan relaxes the semantic constraint and places the controller-thief in focus.[27] Italian's pragmatic word order possibilities act together with its rich verbal morphology. But, lacking any functional morphology, Italian learners of German and English rely rather on the semantic ordering constraint (for the importance of this 'cue' in comprehension studies of Italian, see e.g. Bates & MacWhinney 1987): sacrificing the focus constraint keeps the controller in NP1:

(20)   mädchen nehme brot   (VIG)
       <girl take bread>

Transfer of this rather subtle type accounts for much inter-group (SL-TL pairing) variation among speakers of the basic variety.

---

[27] We have no explanation why he doesn't simply flip around the other argument, thus keeping the non-finite verb form in the middle. A possible explanation might be that he follows a more complicated variant of PR1, with a full ranking of focus values throughout the sentence, according to which the verb has the lowest focus value in this particular context, and the girl has the highest value.

B. It is communicatively important to be able to mark the focus boundary in such contexts, and this motivates some learners to develop beyond the basic variety. The focus marker (see note 14) is maintained by some learners in order to resolve the "controller in focus" conflict: it functions as an embryonic cleft construction, as in this example of Ravinder's, corresponding to Madan's (6):

(21) IS the girl pinching the bread   (RPE)

Such embryonic marking further develops in some learners towards recognisable cleft constructions. The Spanish learners in particular use, with the focus marker [se], a multifunctional particle *qué*,[28] further analysed by the most successful learner – Gloria – into oblique *que* versus nominative *qui*:

(22) [se] la dame QUI a volé le pain   (GFS)
       <is the woman who has stolen the bread>

This example of Gloria's – an advanced learner – shows correct TL verbal morphology: she uses the *passé composé*. It can clearly be shown (Perdue, 1990), that in texts with an overall temporal organisation, morphological oppositions appear on the verb in contexts where the learner attempts to break the basic variety constraint that events be proposed and interpreted according to the principle of chronological order. Overriding this chronological constraint motivates here the development of morphology.[29]

The second case of competition we mentioned will be illustrated by a scene from the film- retelling where the protagonist in topic loses control: it could be expressed in English as 'Chaplin opens the door and gets hit over the head by a falling beam'. The problem for the learner is thus to signal both a continuity in personal reference and a discontinuity of control: it is the beam which has more "control" over the situation than the protagonist. In English, such a constellation can be solved by 'is hit' or 'gets hit', hence some variant of the passive, a possibility not available in the Basic Variety, This is the discourse context where the first approximations to a TL oblique pronominal form are attested, in initial position of structure PH3:

---

28 The Spanish-speaking learners of our sample acquiring French are quick to use the formal similarity between markers of subordination in both languages, so that their learner varieties show precocious subordination with *por* and *(parce) qué* (Chevalier 1986).
29 Anna Ramat points out that where TLs have a richer and more regular verb morphology than the ones of our sample – Italian and Spanish, for example – then this development is facilitated, and tends to be precocious (Ramat 1992).

(23) a. [hiz] drop-on the timber   (RPE)
    b. [le] tombe un bois sur la tête   (PSF)
       <to him falls a beam on the head>

In both cases, the controller is placed into last position, where it belongs according to its focus status but where it violates SEM1. The first NP is somehow marked by incipient case marking of the pronoun. Thus, these structures are a first idiosyncratic attempt to overcome the competition.

Such contexts of competition provide the language acquisition researcher's contribution to question 3 of the introduction – why are fully-fledged languages so complex? – as they are the seedbed for the development of TL-specific morpho-syntax. In other words, TL-specific morpho-syntax allows the learner to elaborate a more cohesive organisation of information in identifiable discourse contexts (Véronique 1989, Trévise, Perdue & Deulofeu 1991, Perdue & Klein 1992).

6 Basic variety and the human language capacity

6.1 A short summary

In this section, we will put the basic variety into the somewhat broader context of how human language in general is organised. It will be helpful to start with a brief recapitulation of our findings, as presented in the preceding sections. They can be summed up in four points.

    I. Adult second language learners (outside the classroom) regularly develop a particular form of language, the Basic Variety. Some of them fossilise at this level, that is, they keep its structural properties and only enrich the lexical repertoire, whereas others complexify the variety to a greater or lesser extent.

    II. The lexicon of the basic variety is essentially taken from the target language (with some borrowings from other sources). It mainly consists of (uninflected and often phonologically distorted) open class items; closed class items appear but are rare. Formation of new words is limited to noun-noun compounds.

    III. Structurally, the basic variety is characterised by a small set of organisational principles. It is the interaction of these principles which determines, for example, the concrete form of utterances or the way in which time and space are encoded. these principles seem to be the same for all learners, irrespective of source and target language. What varies to some

extent, is their interaction, and in particular which constraints are abandoned in contexts where they come into conflict.
IV. Strikingly absent from the basic variety are (a) free or bound morphemes with purely grammatical function, and (b) complex hierarchical structures, in particular subordination.

Before turning to the question as to what these empirical findings may tell us about the human language capacity, some caveats are in order. First, there are some exceptions. We do not think that this is a particular problem. We are talking here about learners who acquire and use their language for social survival, and if they can't make themselves understood with what the basic variety provides them, a word or even a construction from their mother tongue – or even a third language – might easily slip in. In any event, these exceptions are rare. Second, there are some aspects of the basic variety which have not been investigated so far. The most important of these concern scope phenomena. Among the few closed class items of the basic variety, we normally find some element to express negation, some quantifiers and some focus particles (such as *also, only* and their equivalents). Preliminary studies (Giacomi et al. 1994, Dimroth and Klein 1995) indicate that they tend to precede the part of the utterance over which they have scope. But these are very first observations, and the problem awaits further investigation.

6.2 Basic variety, theory of grammar and second language acquisition

Is the BV a 'real language', or is it just a kind of more or less rudimentary protoform? Stated in this way, the question is hardly answerable, because the notion of 'real language' is anything but clearly defined. The BV is a highly efficient system of communication, and in this sense, it is surely a real language; at the same time, it lacks some of the structural characteristics which we typically find in fully-fledged languages. Are these characteristics constitutive of the language capacity which is specific to our species, or are they rather a sort of stunted growth of this capacity? Such a question only makes sense with respect to a particular theory of human language. The best-known of these theories is generative grammar, as developed by Noam Chomsky and others since the early Fifties. In what follows, we shall discuss this question with respect to this theory. This is not easily done because, while the basic tenets of generative grammar have remained the same over the years, its concrete form has undergone many substantial changes. We shall base our discussion on its most recent version, as outlined in Chomsky (1995, chapter 4). It will turn out that our findings about the

BV and the key ideas of the 'Minimalist Program' are not only compatible but also naturally lead to a very simple theory of second language acquisition – or, more precisely, of the grammatical side of second language acquisition.

Many assumptions of the Minimalist Program are very much in flux, but for present purposes, it will suffice to consider some of its key ideas, no matter which concrete form these will eventually take. As in all variants of generative grammar, the human language faculty is seen to consist of a number of different components, among which 'I-language' plays a central role.[30]

Any I-language is an instantiation of Universal Grammar (UG), a particular way in which UG stabilises after having been exposed to linguistic input from the social environment of a learner. An I-language allows its speaker to construct an infinite set of formal objects – linguistic expressions -, whose structural properties can be described on various linguistic levels. Minimally, these are Phonetic Form (PF) and Logical Form (LF), and in contrast to earlier versions of generative grammar, it is assumed that there are no more than these two levels. Thus, a full structural description is a pair (φ, λ), where φ is a PF representation, and λ is a LF representation, respectively; each level functions as an interface to other components of the human language faculty: φ is somehow interpreted by the articulatory-perceptual system, λ is interpreted by the conceptual-intentional system, and a fundamental requirement for φ and λ to be legitimate objects is that they must be 'interpretable' by the respective system.[31]

An I-language consists of a lexicon and a computational system. An element of the lexicon (lexical entry) is a complex sets of features. Usually, three types of features are distinguished – semantical, phonological, 'formal' (such as the categorial feature 'is a noun', or the case feature 'accusative' etc). A lexical entry need not necessarily have all three types of features; it can be phonologically empty, or void

---

30 I-language is reminiscent of 'internal, individual, intensionel language, in contrast to E-language (see Chomsky 1986). Within the generative school, it is quite common to speak of "language" in the sense of I-language. This is somewhat unfortunate, since the term 'language' is most often used in a much broader sense. Since this has led to endless misunderstandings and fruitless discussion, we shall strictly speak of I-language. It should be clear that I-language is but one of the many components of what constitutes the individual's linguistic knowledge in general (and which the learner has to know at the end of the acquisitional process).

31 It should be stressed that notions such as 'grammatical' or 'well-formed' play no role in this approach, quite in contrast to much of the work in SLA inspired by generative grammar; see, for example, Flynn (1987) or White (1989). This may well be a misunderstanding of what generative grammar is about; in this theory, it does not matter whether a particular structure is grammatical or not according to some informants but whether it can be interpreted by the relevant components of the human language faculty, cf. Chomsky (1995: 213): 'The concepts 'well-formed' or 'grammatical' remain without characterization or known empirical justification; they played virtually no role in early work on generative grammar except in informal exposition, or since.'

of semantical content. It is also common to distinguish between substantive categories, such as nouns, verbs, adjectives, and non-substantive or functional categories, such as T(ense), D(eterminer), Agr(eement). The computational system selects entries from the lexicon and constructs more complex units from them (phrases, sentences) by successive application of some operations. These are more or less standard assumptions of all explicit linguistic theories, from Aristotle to Hjelmsev and to Montague: basically, it says that I- language is an algebra. What is particular about the Minimalist Program is the radical reduction of the computational component. It is assumed that it contains only two very simple operations, MERGE and MOVE F, where F stands for 'feature'. Essentially, MERGE has taken the place of the phrase structure component or of X-bar theory in earlier versions of generative grammar, whereas MOVE F has taken the place of the transformational component or of 'move alpha' (as constrained by principles such as "subjacency" etc). We informally sketch these two operations. MERGE takes two elements (elementary elements or else the result of an earlier application of MERGE), forms a new element and labels it as being of the same category as one of its constituents (the head, the other being its complement). MERGE says nothing about relative order of its constituents. Thus, there is no X-bar structure, let alone a phrase structure in the traditional sense of the word (although conventional 'trees' and labels such as VP or N continue to be used for informal presentation). MERGE is the same for all I-languages.

In a 'perfect' I-language, merge should suffice to generate all legitimate linguistic expressions. But for some reason – a point to which we shall return at the end of this section -, elements of such an expression are often not in the position in which they are interpreted: they are 'displaced'. MOVE F is a radically simplified way to describe the displacement possibilities of I-language. What is moved, is not a full expression, say a maximal projection in the sense of X- bar theory, but a feature F (from the set of "formal" features), and it is left to special (largely phonological) conditions whether other features of the element which contains F are "carried along". The basic mechanism which drives MOVE F is 'feature checking'. Formal features of a lexical entry, such as 'accusative', 'plural', 'past tense' can be 'weak' or 'strong'. Typically, though not necessarily, this distinction corresponds to the richness of morphology; in Latin, for example, accusative is strong, whereas it is weak in English or in Chinese. Movement is driven by the necessary match between a (strong) feature in a functional category, say Agr(ement), and a corresponding form, for example an inflected verb; the latter, or actually the relevant feature of the latter, has to be moved into a 'checking position', and when checked appropriately, the resulting structure passed on to LF. The details of this mechanism need not concern us here; what matters, is the general idea that there is a strong interrelation between (rich) morphology and movement. MOVE F is parameterized, depending on which features are strong in a particular I- language.

After this very brief sketch, let us now return to the BV and its status. Is it an I-language? Clearly, it has a lexicon, and the entries of this lexicon are complexes of semantic, phonological and formal features; it is not clear, though, whether the BV also has purely functional categories, a point to which we shall return. Consider first the computational component. We have described the organisation of the BV in terms of three constraints – phrasal, semantic, pragmatic. Ignoring the latter two for the moment, it is clear that the phrasal constraints from section 4.2 above can easily described by MERGE (if we assume, that NP is simply a convenient label for the simple or compound structures discussed in section 4.2 above). There is apparently no counterpart to the other operation MOVE F. This seems to leave us with two clear discrepancies, (a) no functional categories, and (b) no MOVE F. There is, thirdly, no morphology, at least at the surface, but this is also basically true for I-languages such as Chinese.

It is easy to see that these three facts are somehow interrelated. Let us now examine this connection, starting with the possible lack of functional categories.[32] There is not full agreement on what the functional categories of I-language are; Chomsky (1995) discusses T(ense), D(eterminer), C(omplement), Agr(eement), and it is shown that the latter is not necessary; other proposals include, for example, ASP(ect) and NEG(ation). Functional categories can, but need not, have phonological features; it is a standard assumption, for example, that in English, C is overtly present in subordinate clauses (for example *that*) but not in main clauses. Therefore, it is not easy to decide which functional categories, if any, are present in the BV; we must look for other non-phonological cues, for example the reflex of semantic or formal features typically associated with functional categories. D, for example, is semantically related to different types of referentiality, which are found and to some extent marked in the BV (see section 4.2 above). Thus, it is plausible that D is there, although its marking is optional. The case is less clear for T; as was said in section 4.3, the BV has no inflectional marking of past, present,

---

[32] This is a problem that has recently begun to exercise SLA researchers working in the generative tradition, who formulate it the following terms: "are functional categories available in the adult learner's 'initial state'"? (Schwarz & Sprouse, 1996:65) answer in the affirmative: the learner has available "all the properties of the L1 computational system", and they appeal to the knowledge/performance distinction in explaining that: "early Interlanguage utterances are often fragmentary, as well as deviant in inflectional morphology (from the perspective of the TL)" Vainikka & Young-Scholten (1996, which sums up previous work) suggest on the other hand that all that is available to the adult beginner is knowledge of lexical categories and their linear order (VP): functional projections have to be re-acquired. This hypothesis would explain the absence from early learner varieties of: "verb raising, auxiliaries and modals, an agreement paradigm, complementizers, WH-movement" (p.16). As we will show below, the Minimalist Program allows for a much simpler and more natural explanation of these facts.

or future. But under other theories of what tense is (see, for example, Klein 1995), there may be good reasons to assume that T is also present in the BV. The functional category ASP is usually related to lexical aspect, i.e., the distinction between telic and atelic, resultative and non-resultative etc. (rather than to perfective and imperfective), and aspect in this sense plays an eminent role in the BV (see SEM2. in section 4.2 and the discussion related to this constraint); hence, ASP seems to be there. By contrast, there is no obvious reflex of C; but again, whether it is really there or not depends on which features one assumes to be constitutive of C.

Summing up this brief discussion, the evidence for functional categories in the Basic Varieties is quite mixed: there is evidence for semantic features of the sort typically linked to functional categories, there is no evidence for phonological features (with the possible exception of D), and there is no clear evidence for formal features and their various structural consequences. Thus, the picture is quite inconsistent. But there is a natural way to account for precisely this picture: feature strength. Remember that formal features necessitate MOVE F only if the relevant feature is strong. Feature strength is parameterized: in a normal I-language, some features are strong, others are weak, with the relevant structural consequences for MOVE F. The BV is a radical case of parametrization:

(24) In the Basic Variety, all features are weak.

This naturally accounts for all of the structural particularities of the BV: no inflectional morphology, no complex structures which would require some kind of movement. The BV is not only an I-language, it is a 'perfect' I-language in the sense of Chomsky (1995:9, 317s). But of course, it does not exploit what is possible in an I-language, and what is normally used in I- languages. To this end, the learner has to strengthen some of the features. Thus, second I- language acquisition BEYOND the B V is esssentially a process of selecting the appropriate features to be made strong – those which happen to be strong in the target language.

What allows the learner to make this choice? A strong feature can be identified in two ways: (a) by its structural consequences, as brought about by MOVE F, (b) by the "rich" morphology which is typically linked to it. The first kind of evidence is clear in principle but often difficult to detect (it is surely not easy for a learner to unveil the structure of *Who did John claim to have been told to be the friend of* in the input). The second kind of evidence is much more obvious; everybody can see, or rather hear, that French varies its verbs more than English. But there are two problems. First, it is not unambiguous: rich morphology typically goes with strong features, but this is not necessarily the case; second, whilst it is easy to note that French has a rich verb morphology, it may be anything but easy to sort it out; in fact, the richer it is, the more difficult it may be to learn (see the discussion of the acquisition of French in Dietrich, Klein & Noyau 1995). Therefore, many learners, at least adult learners, may be unwilling or unable to attack this task. Children do, they have to, if they want to became a member of their social environment.[33]

Note that we are talking here about the acquisition of I-language, not of 'language at large', that is, about all of the other components which belong to the capacity to understand and make oneself understood in English, German or whatever language. Among the organising principles of the BV, we also noted semantic constraints such as 'Controller first' and pragmatic constraints, such as 'Focus last' (cf. SEM1. and PR1. from section 4.2 above). These have no place in I-language, as it is defined in the Minimalist Program and in generative grammar in general. But this does not mean that they do not exist or are irrelevant. Within the minimalist program, they would have to find their place in other components of the language faculty, for example in the pragmatic system or in the conceptual-intensional system which interprets the interface level λ. Not very much is said about these systems in the Minimalist Program, nor in other older versions of generative grammar. But it would appear natural to restate them in terms of "principles of interpretation", for example:

(25) The referent of first noun phrase is interpreted to have the highest degree of control over the entire situation (= SEM1.)
(26) The last constituent has the highest focus value (= PR1.).

Thus, constraints as 'Controller first' or 'Focus last' – whatever their precise form might be – are not at variance with the general idea of generative grammar or the Minimalist Program in particular; but they have a different locus within the various knowledge components which in their entirety constitute the human language faculty. However, the syntax-semantics-pragmatics correspondences of the BV are so tight that these constraints appear to be central to its functioning. This brings us to the next question: Are semantic and pragmatic constraints of this type a part of Universal Grammar?

There is no reason why these constraints, whatever their precise form may be, cannot belong to the genetical endowment of our species. Otherwise, we

---

[33] Incidentally, it may well be that the apparent ease with which children master rich morphology and relatively complex structures at a relatively early age is quite fallacious. The mere fact that they produce complex sentences with perfect morphology does not prove at all that they have the appropriate parameterized association between feature strength and its various structural consequences; it could well be that they are just better in imitating structures, without a real understanding of the underlying principles. This could be only decided by systematical tests, but such tests have hardly ever been done.

would be forced to assume that they are inductively learned from the input, and although this is not logically excluded, it is hard to imagine how it should be possible. If this is correct, however, then the innate, universal component of our language faculty goes substantially beyond I-language. Consequently, Universal Grammar is much more than the initial state of I-language. This possibility is not necessarily at variance with the general idea of generative grammar (see, for example, Bierwisch 1992 for such a wider perspective), but it goes far beyond what is commonly assumed to belong to UG.

This leaves us with a final question: if the BV is a 'real language', why do most (though not all) learners go beyond it? The first answer is obvious: in principle, they want to adapt to the language of their social environment, and therefore, they have to find out what its strong features are. But this answer immediately needs to a more general question: Why do normal I-languages go beyond such a simple parametrisation? Couldn't they be much simpler in this regard? Chomsky (1995) devotes a short section (4.7.1) to the question 'Why move?', and he says:

> [This] question – why do natural languages have such devices? – arose in the early days of generative grammar. Speculations about it invoked considerations about language use: facilitation of parsing on certain assumptions, the separation of theme-rheme structures from base-determined semantic (theta) relations, and so on. [Footnote with references omitted] Such speculations involve [...] conditions imposed on CHL [the computational system] by the way it interacts with external systems. That is where we would hope the source of 'imperfections' would lie, on minimalist assumptions. (p.317)

We have nothing to say here about facilitation of parsing, except that the complex structures produced by MOVE F do not always seem particularly easy to parse. But what we have found in our investigation of the BV (cf. section 5.2 above) exactly confirms the second speculation – a I-language fails when case role constraints and focus constraints – thus constraints which belong to external systems – lead to conflicts which cannot be overcome by the structural means of a 'perfect' I-language.

6.3 Language before language

If all of this is correct, then there is no need to stipulate two essentially distinct modes of language, both provided for by the human language capacity. Such claims have been made by various authors, in particular by Givón (1979) and by Bickerton (1981, 1984, 1990). Before turning to these, we will briefly address another question which naturally rises in this context: how is the BV related to pidgins?

Pidgins are normally seen as the product of some rudimentary SLA process; therefore, they should bear some similarity to the BV. In fact, it is often reported that they lack inflectional morphology, tend to an SVO word order and hardly ever have complex constructions – properties which we also find in the BV. A precise comparison, however, is quite problematic, for at least three reasons. First, there is anything but agreement on what should count as a pidgin; Hancock, for example, gives very different lists in (1971) and (1977). Second, there is apparently considerable variation between pidgins based on the same language, say English, hence no uniform structure but at best similarities (for a discussion of this and the previous problem, see Romaine 1988, chapter 2). Third, pidgins have hardly ever been systematically investigated with respect to organising principles of the type discussed in section 4.2 – 4.4 above. Therefore, all we can say at this point is that there are certainly similarities, but it is quite unclear how deep-reaching these are.

Let us now come back to our earlier question. Givón (1979) postulates two extreme modes of communication: the 'pragmatic mode' and the 'syntactic mode', with the former characterising early child language, second language and, indeed, pidgins. A speaker gradually acquires the syntactic mode, while retaining the capacity of the other mode: 'The type of communication used by adults acquiring a second language is essentially the pragmatic mode' (1979: 102). Givón suggests extra-linguistic pressures from the communicative situation, and psycholinguistic pressures of efficient, automated language processing, to explain grammaticalisation processes leading from the pragmatic to the syntactic mode. He sees the pragmatic mode as being poorly structured: there is no stable syntax, the one clear principle governing word order, for example, is 'go from given to new'. If this is correct, then the 'pragmatic mode' is something quite different from the BV. As was shown above, the BV is very highly structured. There is a very tight interplay of constraints of different types, and an appeal to just one type – Givón's pragmatic organisation – does not suffice. This does not preclude, however, that the pragmatic mode characterises some form of communication which, in second language acquisition, precedes the BV, and which is also found in some forms of language called pidgin.

Similar considerations apply to Bickerton's notion of a protolanguage. He writes (1990: 122): "The evidence just surveyed gives grounds for supposing that there is a mode of linguistic expression that is quite separate from normal human language and is shared by four classes of speakers: trained apes, children under two, adults who have been deprived of language in early years, and speakers of pidgin. If there is such a protolanguage, it is not surprising, therefore, that its functional and structural characterisations are quite different from what we found for the BV.[34]

---

34 There are some doubts, incidentally, that early child language is indeed fully comparable to the other variants of one and the same mode, be it the 'protolanguage' or Givón's 'pragmatic

The pragmatic mode as well as the protolanguage are manifestations of some innate language capacity, but they are characteristically distinct from human languages. Givón's two modes, despite the processes linking them, have different structural properties and function differently. Bickerton explicitly postulates a discontinuity between protolanguage and language: 'There is evidence, from at least two areas, that protolanguage can change into language without any intervening stage, as well as evidence ... that there can be no plausible intermediate stage between the two.' (1990:165). In considering the basic variety from an acquisitional perspective, one cannot but notice the CONTINUITY of its organising principles upstream and downstream. The weight of each type of principle varies over time, but not the nature of the principles interacting in successive learner varieties, of which fully-fledged languages are but the final, borderline case.[35]

---

mode'. Adults – be it early second language speakers or of pidgins, use simple means to construct temporally and spatially contextualised utterances in connected discourse, with complex inter-utterance relations. Children produce utterances embedded in the here-and-now. These two cases cannot be subsumed under one single mode of communication.

35 Another type of simple language discussed in the literature is Slobin's 'Basic child grammar'. A comparison with the basic variety clearly illustrates the different preoccupations of the child and adult learner. The adult's task is first and foremost linguistic, whereas the child has also to identify and understand the notions relevant for grammatical construction. The basic variety is thus a linguistic object, and the cross-linguistic generalisations we have made are first and foremost linguistic. Basic child grammar on the other hand is a linguistic-conceptual object, and the cross-linguistic generalisations reflect this interplay – an available concept is encoded by different linguistic means (including morphology) across languages. A relevant example of this is Slobin's 'manipulative activity scene', where an agent directly affects (or affects with an instrument he directly controls) the place or nature of an object. The child conceptualises this scene as a Gestalt-like prototype, and seeks some salient (initially uninterpreted) linguistic means to mark the Gestalt. Slobin cites work on the acquisition of Russian (Gvozdev 1949) and Kaluli (Schieffelin 1985) which shows that in the first case the TL's accusative marker on objects, and in the second case the TL's ergative marker on agents are used early to mark the same, highly transitive (Hopper & Thompson 1982) predicates such as *break*, *hit*. The markers are used only later for less transitive predicates such as *see*, *meet*. Slobin comments "we should expect to find particles and affixes in early child speech if they are perceptually salient and expressive of basic notions" (1985, note 9) – basic for the child, who, in this example, is not yet using the morphology as the TL's accusative or ergative, but as a means to mark the scene. Slobin adverts to Schlesinger's (1982) process of semantic assimilation by similarity and metaphor to account for the spread of this morphology to less prototypical cases of transitivity, hence the parallel analysis of the notion which is grammaticalised in the TL. The contrast is striking with the adult speaker of the basic variety, who has no difficulty in assimilating prototypical and less prototypical instances of transitivity under the control constraint (SEM1), but who cross-linguistically relies on word order alone as the expressive device.

6.4 Second language acquisition and second I-language acquisition

This paper is not primarily about the study of second language acquisition, but about some findings from this field and what they might tell us about the human language faculty in general. But if these findings and what we conclude from them are basically correct, then this should also have some consequences for a theory of second language acquisition. In section 6.2 above, it was argued that the BV can be naturally interpreted as an I-language with a particular feature parametrisation; further acquisition beyond the BV is basically a process of "feature strengthening": the learner has to find out by input analysis which features are strong in the target language. This leads to a very simple picture of the acquisition process, and it assigns the BV a natural locus in this process.

It should be very clear, however, that we are talking here about the acquisition of I-language. I-language is only a small fraction of the knowledge which is required to be a fluent speaker of a language. Perfect replication of pronunciation, correct choice of noun declension paradigm, appropriate usage of present perfect vs. simple past, correct identification of word meaning, appropriate usage of deictic terms, of discourse rules, of specific ways of focus marking and so on, in short, almost everything someone has to learn, when he or she wants to become a speaker of the target language, is irrelevant for this subpart of language acquisition. It is arguable, and perhaps simply a matter of personal preference, which importance one should attribute to these various components of linguistic competence. But it should be clear that there is a difference between a theory of second language acquisition and of second I-language acquisition: the latter is a very small – and perhaps not particularly interesting – part of the former.

7 Concluding remarks

We started with the question: 'Couldn't languages be much simpler?' The answer is 'Yes, but perhaps not very much.' We have seen that adult language learners who, unlike children, do not end up by faithfully reproducing all the idiosyncrasies and oddities presented to them by their social environment but organise their utterances and texts according to elementary principles of their innate human language capacity regularly develop a type of language which is perfectly well-structured, highly efficient – and very simple. It has definable short-comings, though, and we assume that the attempts which the human language capacity makes to overcome these are largely responsible for all of this fabric which makes natural languages so opaque and so complex. The universal core is simple. But when it is transgressed, the complications begin.

We do not believe that our characterisation of the basic variety, in particular the way in which the various organisational principles are stated, is the last word on this issue; nor do we believe that there are no other sources of complexity; there might be a reason to have case morphology, but his does not justify ten different paradigms of noun inflection. But we do believe that the general perspective on the human language capacity and its achievements suggested here is correct.

References

Bates, E. & MacWhinney, B. (1987). Competition, variation and language learning. In B. MacWhinney (ed.). Mechanisms of language learning. Hillsdale, NJ: Lawrence Erlbaum. 157–194.
Becker, A. & Carroll, M. (1997). The Expression of Spatial Relations in a Second Language. Amsterdam: Benjamins.
Bickerton, D. (1981). The roots of language. Ann Arbor: Karoma.
Bickerton, D. (1984) The language bioprogram hypothesis. Behavioral and Brain Sciences 7. 173–221.
Bickerton, D. (1990). Language and Species. Chicago: University of Chicago Press.
Bierwisch, M. (1992). Probleme der biologischen Erklärung natürlicher Sprache. In P. Suchslang (ed.). Biologische und soziale Grundlagen der Sprache. Tübingen: Niemeyer. 7–45.
Bouton, C. (1969). Les Méchanismes d'Acquisition du Français Langue Etrangère chez l'Adulte. Paris: Klincksieck.
Broeder, P. (1991). Talking about People. A Multiple Case Study on Adult Language Acquisition. Amsterdam: Swets & Zeitlinger.
Broeder, P., Coenen, J., Extra, G., Hout, R. van & Zerrouk, R. (1984). Spatial reference by Turkish and Moroccan Learners of Dutch: the initial stages. In G.Extra and M. Mittner (eds.). Studies in Second Language by Adult Immigrants. Tilburg: Tilburg University Press. 147–184.
Broeder, P., Extra, G. & Hout, R. van (1986). Acquiring the linguistic devices for pronominal reference to persons: A crosslinguistic perspective on complex tasks with small words. In F. Beukema & A. Hulk (eds.). Linguistics in The Netherlands. Amsterdam: Foris. 27–40.
Broeder, P., Extra, G. & Hout, R. van (1993). Richness and variety in the developing lexicon. In C. Perdue (ed.). Adult language acquisition: Cross-linguistic perspectives, Vol. 1: Field methods. Cambridge: Cambridge University Press. 145–163.
Broeder, P., Extra, G., Hout, R. van & Voionmaa, K. (1993). Word formation processes in talking about entities. In C. Perdue (ed.). Adult language acquisition: Cross-linguistic perspectives, Vol. 2: The results. Cambridge: Cambridge University Press. 41–72.
Carroll, M. (1990). Word order in instructions in learner languages of English and German. Linguistics 28(5). 1011–1037.
Carroll, M. & Becker, A. (1993). Reference to space in learner varieties. In C.Perdue (ed.). Adult language acquisition: Cross-linguistic perspectives, Vol. 2: The results. Cambridge: Cambridge University Press. 119–149.
Carroll, M. & Dietrich, R. (1985). Observations on object reference in learner languages. Linguistische Berichte 98: 310–337.

Chevalier, J.-Cl. (1986). Structuration d'un discours français par un migrant, apprenant en milieu naturel. Langue Française 71. 17–31.
Chomsky, N. (1981). Lectures on Government and Binding. Amsterdam: Foris.
Chomsky, N. (1982). Some Concepts and Consequences of the Theory of Government and Binding. Cambridge, Mass.: MIT Press.
Chomsky, N. (1986). Knowledge of Language: Its Nature, Origin and Use. New York: Praeger.
Chomsky, N. (1995). The Minimalist Program. Cambridge, Mass.: MIT Press.
Clark, E. (1971). On the acquisition of the meaning of 'before' and 'after'. Journal of Verbal Learning and Verbal Behaviour 10. 266–275.
Clyne, M. (1968). Zum Pidgin-Deutsch der Gastarbeiter. Zeitschrift für Mundartforschung 35. 130–139.
Comrie, B. (1981). Language universals and linguistic typology. Chicago: University of Chicago Press.
Corder, S.P. (1967). The significance of learners' errors. International Review of Applied Linguistics 5. 161–170.
Dietrich, R. (1989a). Communicating with few words. An empirical account of the second language speaker's lexicon. In R. Dietrich & C. Graumann (eds.). Language Processing in Social Context. Amsterdam: North Holland. 233–276.
Dietrich, R. (1989b). Nouns and verbs in the learner's lexicon. In H. Dechert (ed.). Current Trends in European Second Language Acquisition Research. Clevedon: Multilingual Matters. 13–23.
Dietrich, R., Klein, W. & Noyau, C. (eds.) (1995). The acquisition of temporality in a second language acquisition. Amsterdam: John Benjamins.
Dimroth, C. & Klein, W. (1995). Fokuspartikeln in Lernervarietäten. Zeitschrift für Literaturwissenschaft und Linguistik 104. 73–114.
Dorriots, B. (1986). How to succeed with only fifty words—analysis of a role play in the frame of adult language acquisition. Göteborg Papers in Theoretical Linguistics. 52–80.
Ellis, R. (1994). The Study of Second Language Acquisition. Oxford: Oxford University Press.
Feldweg, H. (1993). Transcription, storage and retrieval of data. In C. Perdue (ed.). Adult language acquisition: Cross-linguistic perspectives, Vol. 1: Field methods. Cambridge: Cambridge University Press. 108–130.
Flynn, S. (1987). A parameter setting model of L2 acquisition. Dordrecht: Reidel.
Giacalone Ramat, A. (1992). The grammaticalization of temporal and modal relations. Studies in Second Language Acquisition 14. 297–322.
Giacobbe, J. (1992). A cognitive view of the L1 in the L2 acquisition process. Second Language Research 8. 232–250.
Giacobbe, J. (1993) Acquisition d'une Langue Etrangère: Cognition et Interaction. Paris: CNRS Editions.
Giacomi, A., Stoffel, H. & Véronique, D. (1994). "Acquisition de la portée de quelques particules en français L2.". 4th EUROSLA Conference, Aix-en-Provence, September.
Givón, T. (1979). From discourse to syntax: grammar as a processing strategy. In T. Givón (ed.). Syntax and Semantics 12. Discourse and Syntax. New York: Academic Press. 81–111.
Gvozdev, A.N. (1949). Formirowanie u rebenka grammaticeskogo stroja russkogo jazyka. Moskva: Izdatelsvo Akad. ped. nauk RSFSR.
Hancock, I.F. (1971). A survey of the pidgins and creoles of the world. In D. Hymes (ed.). Pidginization and Creolization of Languages. Cambridge: Cambridge University Press. 509–525.

Hancock, I.F. (1977). Repertory of Pidgin and Creole Languages. In A. Valdman (ed.). Pidgin and Creole Linguistics. Bloomington: Indiana University Press. 277–294.
Haviland, J. & Levinson, S. (eds) (1994). Spatial Conceptualization in Mayan Languages. [Special Issue]. Linguistics 32 (4/5).
Huebner, T. (1983). The Acquisition of English. Ann Arbor: Karoma.
Huebner, T. (1989). Establishing point of view: the development of coding mechanisms in a second language for the expression of cognitive and perceptual organization. Linguistics 27. 111–143.
Hopper, P. & Thompson, S. (eds.) (1982). Studies in transitivity. New York: Academic Press.
Keenan, E. (1976). Towards a universal definition of "subject". In C. Li (ed.). Subject and Topic. New York: Academic Press. 303–333.
Klein, W. (1991). Raumausdrücke. Linguistische Berichte 132. 77–114.
Klein, W. (1994). Time in language. London: Routledge & Kegan.
Klein, W. (1995). A time-relational theory of Russian aspect. Language 71. 669–694.
Klein, W. & Dittmar, N. (1979). Developing Grammars. Heidelberg: Springer Verlag.
Klein, W. & Perdue, C. (1989). The learner's problem of arranging words. In B. MacWhinney and E. Bates (eds.). The cross- linguistic study of sentence processing. Cambridge: Cambridge University Press. 292–327.
Klein, W. & Perdue, C. (eds.) (1992). Utterance structure. Developing grammars again. Amsterdam: John Benjamins.
Klein, W. & von Stutterheim, C. (1987). Quaestio und referentielle Bewegung in Erzählungen. Linguistische Berichte 109. 163–183.
Labov, W. (1972). Language in the inner city. Philadelphia: University of Pennsylvania Press.
Mühlhäusler, P. (1986). Pidgin and creole linguistics. Oxford: Blackwell.
Noyau, C. (1989). The development of means for temporality in the unguided acquisition of L2: cross-linguistic perspectives. In H. Dechert (ed.). Current Trends in European Second Language Acquisition Research. Clevedon: Multilingual Matters. 143–170.
Noyau, C. (1990). Structure conceptuelle, mise en texte et acquisition d'une langue étrangère. Langages 100. 101–114.
Perdue, C. (1987) Real beginners, real questions. In H. Blanc, M. Le Douaron & D. Véronique (eds.). S'Approprier une Langue Etrangère. Paris: Didier-Erudition. 196–210.
Perdue, C. (1990). Complexification of the simple clause in the narrative discourse of adult language learners. Linguistics 28. 983–1009.
Perdue, C. (1995). L'acquisition du français et de l'anglais par des adultes: former des énoncés. Paris: CNRS Editions.
Perdue, C. (1996): Pre-basic varieties: the first stages of second language acquisition. Toegepaste Taalwetenschap in Artikelen 55. 135–150.
Perdue, C. (ed.) (1993). Adult language acquisition: Cross-linguistic perspectives. Volume 1: Field methods. Cambridge: Cambridge University Press.
Perdue, C. (ed.) (1993). Adult language acquisition: Cross-linguistic perspectives. Volume 2: The results. Cambridge: Cambridge University Press.
Perdue, C. & Klein, W. (1992). Why does the production of some learners not grammaticalize? Studies in Second Language Acquisition 14. 259–272.
Perdue, C. & Deulofeu, J. (1986). La structuration de l'énoncé: étude longitudinale. Langages 84. 43–64.

Perdue, C. & Schenning, S. (1996). The expression of spatial relations in a second language: two longitudinal studies. Zeitschrift für Literaturwissenschaft und Linguistik 104. 6–34.
Reis, M. (1982). Zum Subjektbegriff im Deutschen. In W. Abraham (ed.). Satzglieder im Deutschen. Tübingen: Narr. 171–211.
Romaine, S. (1988). Pidgin & Creole Languages. London: Longman.
Rooth, M. (1992). A Theory of Focus Interpretation. Natural language semantics 1. 75–116.
Schenning, S. & van Hout, R. (1994). Dimensional spatial relations in adult language acquisition. In R. Bok-Bennema & C. Cremers (eds.). Linguistics in the Netherlands. Amsterdam: John Benjamins. 235–246.
Schieffelin, B. (1985). The acquisition of Kaluli. In D. Slobin (ed.) The cross-linguistic study of language acquisition, Vol. 1. Hillsdale, N.J.: Lawrence Erlbaum. 525–593.
Schlesinger, I. (1982). Steps to language. toward a theory of native language acquisition. Hillsdale, N.J.: Lawrence Erlbaum.
Schumann, J. (1978). The pidginization process: a model for second language acquisition. Rowley: Newbury House.
Schwartz, B. & Sprouse, P. (1996). L2 Cognitive States and Full Transfer/Full Access Model. Second Language Research 12(1). 40–72.
Selinker, L. (1972). Interlanguage. International Review of Applied Linguistics 10. 209–231.
Silverstein, M. (1976). Hierarchy of features and ergativity. In R. Dixon (ed.). Grammatical Categories in Australian Languages. New Jersey: Humanities Press. 112–171.
Slobin, D. I. (1985). Cross-linguistic evidence for the language-making capacity. In D. Slobin (ed.). The cross- linguistic study of language acquisition, Vol. 2. Hillsdale, N.J.: Lawrence Erlbaum. 1157–1256.
Stechow, A. von (1991). Current issues in the theory of focus. In A. von Stechow & D. Wunderlich (eds.). Semantics: An International Handbook of Current Research. Berlin: De Gruyter. 804–825.
Starren, M. (1996). Temporal adverbials in adult second language acquisition. Ms. Nijmegen: MPI for Psycholinguistics.
Stutterheim, C. von (1986).Temporalität in der Zweitsprache: Eine Untersuchung zum Erwerb des Deutschen durch Türkische Gastarbeiter. Berlin: De Gruyter.
Trévise, A. (1987). Toward an analysis of the (inter)language activity of referring to time in narratives. In C. Pfaff (ed.). First and Second Language Acquisition Processes. Rowley: Newbury House. 225–251.
Trévise, A. & Porquier, R. (1986). Second language acquisition by adult immigrants: exemplified methodology. Studies in Second Language Acquisition 8. 265–275.
Trévise, A., Perdue, C. & Deulofeu, J. (1991). Word order and discursive coherence in L2. In G. Appel & H. Dechert (eds.). A Case for Psycholinguistic Cases. Amsterdam: John Benjamins. 163–176.
Vainikka, A. & Young-Scholten, M. (1996). Gradual Development of L2 Phrase Structure. Second Language Research 12 (1). 7–39.
Véronique, D. (1983). Observations préliminaires sur "li" dans l'interlangue d'Abdelmalek. GRAL, Papiers de travail 1. Aix-en-Provence: Université de Provence. 155–180.
Véronique, D. (1987). Reference to past events and actions in narratives in L2: insights from North African learners' French. In C. Pfaff (ed.). First and Second Language Acquisition Processes. Rowley: Newbury House. 252–272.

Véronique, D. (1989). Reference and discourse structure in the learning of French by adult Moroccans. In H. Dechert (ed.). Current Trends in European Second Language Acquisition Research. Clevedon: Multilingual Matters. 171–201.

Véronique, D. & Porquier, R. (1986). Acquisition de la référence spatiale en français par des adultes arabophones et hispanophones. Langages 84. 79–103.

White, L. (1989): Universal Grammar and second language acquisition. Amsterdam: John Benjamins.

The contribution of second language acquisition research

> I've discovered that it is not difficult at all to learn French; where we say "cup", they say "tasse"; and so is it with the other words, too.
>
> *Unknown learner*

1 Introduction

As one looks back into the development of our field in the last 25 years, one cannot but be impressed how much progress has been made in many important respects. Perhaps the clearest case is second language acquisition by everyday interaction, a subarea about which hardly anything beyond anecdotical evidence was known in the early seventies. In classroom acquisition, research could build on a certain stock of knowledge; but in the course of these years, this stock was enormously enlarged in almost all domains of language, from phonology to syntax, from the lexicon to communicative behaviour. On the more theoretical side, many insights from general linguistics have made their way into our field, and although not everyone may share in this line of thought, there is no doubt that it has considerably changed and sharpened our perception. Methodologically, we normally meet, and sometimes – for example in clean statistical analysis – surpass, the standards of empirical research in other fields devoted to the investigation of language. It is not accidental that there are more and more good textbooks, and these are more and more comprehensive. It may be an exaggeration, but if so, it is only a mild one, if we say that a new discipline has been established. There is reason to be proud.

This is a good feeling. But since, as Immanuel Kant put it, the human mind suffers from the peculiar fate of being permanently haunted by questions which it cannot answer properly, it might, once in a while, also be haunted by questions such as, for example, the following ones:
1. Has, as a result of all of these achievements, our work provided a solid basis to foreign language teaching?
2. How close have we come to a general theory of second language acquisition?
3. What is the status of SLA research within the various linguistic disciplines?

Our endeavour is research: we want to discover the principles according to which people who already master a language acquire another language; this is a the-

---

Note: This article originally appeared as Klein, W. (1998). The contribution of second language acquisition research. Language Learning 48. 527–550.

https://doi.org/10.1515/9783110549119-017

oretical, not a practical aim. But concerns of foreign language teaching were at the very beginning of our field, and therefore, the first question appears to be a very legitimate one. I am afraid, there is little doubt about the answer. Alerted by this insight, one might ask whether we at least made substantial progress in this direction. This depends on what is understood by "substantial"; but on the whole, I am not convinced that the answer is positive, either. In general, foreign language teachers are very interested in SLA research; in fact, a great deal of SLA work is carried out by researchers who have or had practical teaching experience. But does this fact have more than occasional and declamatory repercussions in the everyday practice of instruction? Among the many theories propagated in our field over the last 25 years, Monitor Theory is probably closest to concrete application, and in fact, it has found considerable resonance in the world of education. To which extent did Monitor Theory really change the preparation of course material, or the way in which this material is presented and processed in the classroom? I suspect the answer is not very flattering to our discipline.

But as was already said, our aim is not primarily a practical one: we want to discover the underlying principles of SLA; what we are aiming for is a theory of SLA, based on solid empirical findings. Is there any such theory in sight? I am sure that some might now get up and raise their finger and say "Yes, MY theory". They should sit down again and think for a moment about the many acquisitional phenomena that must be accounted for – from vocabulary learning to pronunciation, from syntax to interactive behaviour. The truth is simply that, while many theories have been advocated, not one of those has even remotely been accepted by the scientific community, and for good reasons. At best some specific phenomena within the wide field of SLA, for example some selected syntactical or morphological constructions, have found a general and reliable explanation, and even this is highly arguable.

Turning now to the third question, I am afraid we must simply face the fact that among the various disciplines that investigate the manifold manifestations of the human language capacity, the study of how people acquire a second language does not rank very high. This is hardly ever explicitly stated; there is some politeness in academia. But the facts leave little doubt. Second language researchers often cite work from theoretical linguistics or from psycholinguistics; the opposite is hardly ever the case. We like to invite people from other linguistic disciplines to our conferences; this is normally not matched by invitations in the other direction. Our findings, our theoretical considerations are normally not considered to be crucial arguments in other domains of language studies; in that regard, the impact of first language acquisition research is different. There are exceptions, of course, and they are gratefully noted; but they are rare; on the whole, second language researchers are bottom dwellers in the language sciences.

These considerations evoke a gloomy picture. But this picture is as one-sided as the glorious picture which one gets when looking over the undeniable achievements over the last 25 years. The truth is simply that considerable progress has been made; it is just not enough. In the next three sections, I will have a closer look at the present situation and why it is as it is.

2 What can SLA research contribute to the understanding of the human language faculty?

> I see another language as distorted English, and then, I try to work it out.
> *Well-known linguist*

2.1 Our status within the linguistic sciences

Why are we at the bottom end? It could be, of course, that this simply results from irrational but firm caste prejudices against the newcomer. To the extent to which this is the case, there is little hope to fight against them. But although prejudices are not completely absent from the academic world, it is perhaps too easy an excuse as to assign our present status to the irrationality of the other inhabitants of this world. If we really want to climb up some steps on the ladder, we better look for more realistic explanations. There is one obvious candidate. It may well be that the empirical and theoretical standards in SLA research do not meet the established criteria of serious scientific work. This is surely false for the empirical side, at least in comparison to what is found in other language sciences. To a native speaker of German, for example, recent work in theoretical linguistics, whatever its theoretical standard may be, is a reliable source of surprise and amusement: it is full of strong and unwarranted statements about the grammaticality or non-grammaticality of specific constructions. And given that German is one of the best-studied languages in the world, with abundant descriptive grammars, dictionaries and people around to consult, one wonders whether this is much better for what is said about Warlbiri or Mohawk. No second language researcher would normally dare to make such strong claims with so little evidence. Now, theoretical linguistics is perhaps not the most serious competitor in terms of empirical reliability. But first, its low standards in this regard do not seem to have been harmful to its reputation. And second, does our empirical work score much worse when compared to, for example, typological linguistics, a field with relatively strong empirical ambitions? There are excellent typological studies, no doubt, and just as with theoretical linguistics, we can only benefit from taking them into account. But how well-founded are claims about typological universals of language? Take, for example word order universals, perhaps the best-known case. It is most impressive to see that an author is able to say something about 500 languages – but this is still a little share of the world's languages, about 10% perhaps. It could be, of course, that these 10% are representative of the world's languages; but who would dare to say so without having had a more than casual look at the other 90%? How much time must such an author have spent on each of the 500 languages – one day, two days? It could be, of course, that there are excellent descriptions of these 500 languages, and it suffices to look up what the word order of some particular language is, just as one might look up whether this language has unaspirated stops or a word for *hell*. But how many languages are really well-described? Even in the case of Latin, English, French or German – languages that have really been extensively studied -, it is extremely difficult to say what "the basic word order" is. How reliable are the available grammars of Dyirbal, Twi or Mopan in this regard? Or take a notion such as "aspect", which underlies, for example, the distinction between English *he worked* and *he was working*. This is a notorious problem for the linguist as well as for the learner; German, though historically closely related, has no progressive form, and hence, a German learner of English has normally a hard time to understand its precise meaning. So do linguists: there are endless studies, but no generally accepted analysis. If this is true for one of the most salient constructions in the best-investigated study of the world – what should one think of statements on "imperfective, progressive, non-completive aspect" in, say, Estonian or Gorontalo? One cannot but have the impression that any claim on typological universals must be based on very superficial evidence, and hence should be looked at with appropriate suspicion. This is not to belittle this kind of research, quite to the opposite: how else should one proceed in these difficult issues? But I do believe that, when compared to typological linguistics, SLA research need not hide as concerns its empirical respect standards. This does not mean that the empirical basis of our field is flawless, and every effort should be made to broaden and solidify it. But on the average, we do not fare worse in this regard than other fields of linguistics; in fact, if it comes to quantitative analysis, SLA research ranks relatively high; hence, inadequate empirical standards cannot be the reason for the low ranking of SLA research.

The situation is more ambivalent on the theoretical side, in particular since there is less agreement on what "high theoretical standards" are. I cannot see, however, that the concepts and theories that underlie present-day SLA research are less well defined, less clear, less consistent than those of normal descriptive linguistics. In fact, the key concepts are more or less the same. There are good reasons to argue that notions such as "passive", "tense", "case role" are not particularly well defined; but this is in no way specific to SLA research. In typological linguistics, it is often not very clear what, for example, "accusative" or "subjunctive" means in a particular language, say in Guugu Yimidhirr as compared to Eipo. But this has never been detrimental to the reputation of these linguistic disciplines, and therefore, it should not be detrimental to SLA research. So, as compared to the vast majority of work done on language and languages, there is no reason to hide because of low theoretical standards. But can we live up to the scientific level of, for example, Montagovian formal semantics or Chomskyan generative grammar? Opinions may be greatly at variance here. Personally, I believe that our work, on the average, is indeed considerably beneath the level of logical semantics, with its rigidly defined concepts and systems; but in this regard, logical semantics is quite exceptional within linguistics, only comparable to the mathematical study of formal languages and maybe some areas of computational linguistics. The immediate comparison should perhaps be to research in the tradition of generative grammar, especially since ideas from this field have also played a considerable role in recent SLA research. Many feel that work in this tradition is theoretically way ahead of what we are doing. I am inclined to share in this view, although the case is perhaps less clear than it might be. In its initial phases, generative grammars were relatively rigidly defined, their formal properties were clear, and it was comparatively ease to test the consequences of particular theoretical assumptions. Over the years, and in particular with the increasing move from specific rules to more general principles, on the one hand, and from language-specific description towards universal properties of grammar, on the other, theoretical as well as empirical statements have become increasingly fuzzy. It is not at all clear what notions such as "subject, small pro, theta role, weak feature", to mention but a few, really mean, and whether they are used in a consistent way by different authors, or by the same author in different publications. But for the sake of the argument, let us assume that generative grammar in its most recent, minimalist version is theoretically far ahead of SLA research. Would it help us climbing up some steps in the rank order, if we rigidly adopt this, or some other, theoretically more advanced, framework?

No one really knows; but I do not believe it. First, numerous attempts in the past ten years have been made in this direction; but one cannot say that they have found strong repercussions in other areas of linguistics; no theoretical linguist has ever changed his or her views because of some findings from SLA research; at best, he or she would say that such findings corroborate these views; but even this is hardly ever found. Second, development in theoretical linguistics is fast, and as soon as some version has found its way into empirical work on language acquisition, it is outdated in its own field; work on "parameter-setting" is a good example. Third, it is hard to apply this framework to some of the central acquisitional phenomena, say vocabulary learning or problems with the use of tense forms. Theoretical linguistics in this sense is confined to some highly selective morphological and syntactical properties. But the fourth and main reason is this: I do not believe that our low ranking is fundamentally connected to our empirical or theoretical standards. As was said above, these could surely be improved, but on the average, they are not worse than in other fields of language studies. The main reason is that we have nothing interesting to say to people in these fields.

Why should the analysis of the odd productions of the second language learner, this distorted, flawed, ridiculous, chaotic mimicking of "real language", be able to tell us something new, something principled, something fundamental about function and structure of a particular language, about the human languages in general, about the very nature of the human language faculty? No matter how much we improve on our theories and our empirical work – it will not change very much, so long as we do not demonstrate that we are able to make an independent, a genuine, a substantial contribution to the study of the human language faculty.

There is no real reason why the investigation of an activity as common as the acquisition of a second language should not be able to make such a contribution. The fact that it hasn't, or at least that it is not seen this way in the academic world, results to my mind from a particular way of looking at language acquisition. This view, to be discussed in the next section, is a consequence, first, of the fact that our field has its primary origin in practical problems of language teaching and, second, of a particular perspective on the object of linguistic investigation in general. These two points are closely interconnected to each other.

2.2 Two views on SLA research

As so many other disciplines, in fact, as any scientific endeavour, the study of second language acquisition has its origin in practical concerns – in problems of second language teaching. This origin has naturally led to a particular view on SLA. Two assumptions are constitutive of this view:

A. There is a well-defined target of the acquisition process – the language to be learned. This "target language", as any "real language", is a clearly fixed entity, a structurally and functionally balanced system, mastered by those who have learned it in childhood, and more or less correctly described in grammars and dictionaries.
B. Learners miss this target at varying degrees and in varying respects – they make errors in production as well as in comprehension, because they lack the appropriate knowledge or skills.

I shall call this view the TARGET DEVIATION PERSPECTIVE. It is the teacher's task to erase or at least to minimise the deviations; it is the researcher's task to investigate which "errors" occur when and for which reasons. As a consequence, the learner's performance in production or comprehension is not so very much studied in its own right, as a manifestation of his or her learner capacity, but in relation to a set norm; not in terms of what the learner does but in terms of what he or she fails to do. The learner's utterances at some time during the process of acquisition are considered to be more or less successful attempts to reproduce the structural properties of target language utterances. The learner tries to do what the mature speaker does, but does it less well.

There are three reasons which make the target deviation perspective so natural and attractive, in fact, almost self-evident. The first of those was already mentioned: it is the natural perspective of the language teacher: language teaching is a normative process, and the teacher is responsible for moving the student as closely to some norm as possible. And if the student misses this norm in one or the other way, this must be changed. Nothing could be more sensible.

Second, it is also the natural perspective of all of those who had to learn a second language in the classroom – and that means, of practically every language researcher. It is very difficult to get rid of the perspective which the teacher's red ink burned into our mind: there is language to be learned, it is very well defined, and you missed it. I believe that this normative experience has also deeply shaped the way in which linguists usually perceive the object of their efforts – a point to which I will return in the next section.

Third, the target deviation perspective provides the researcher with a simple and clear design for empirical work. There is a yardstick against which the learner's production and comprehension can be measured: the target language, or actually what grammar books and dictionaries say about it. What IS measured are the differences between what the learner does and what the set norm demands. As a rule, therefore, the research design is a – much subtler and often highly refined – elaboration of the 'red ink method': errors are marked, counted, and statistically analysed. One may count, for example, how often Spanish and French learners of English omit the subject pronoun in classroom tests, and if there is a significant difference, then – everything else being equal -, this may be attributed to the influence of the first language. Alternatively, one might also look at the individual error and try to analyse how it came about, that is, quantitative analysis and hypothesis testing can be replaced or complemented by more qualitative approaches. All of these methods are well-established in the sciences, there are certain standards in their application, and when these standards are met – and usually, they are met in SLA research -, there is not the least methodological objection. But this analysis, no matter how well it is done, does not inform us about what the human language faculty does; it tells us to which extent and perhaps why it differs sometimes from a certain norm. At the very best, it tells us where and why our species-specific capacity to learn and to process languages does not work under particular circumstances; but it does not tell us much about its structural and functional properties.

And therefore, people who want to understand this faculty and its specific manifestations do not find these results relevant to their concern.

The alternative to the target deviation perspective is to understand the learner's performance at a given time as an immediate manifestation of his or her capacity to speak and to understand: form and function of these utterances are governed by principles, and these principles are those characteristic of the human language faculty. Early attempts in this direction are reflected in notions such as "interlanguage" (Selinker), "approximate systems" (Nemser), and related ones. But these notions are still based on the assumption that there is "the real thing" – the target language and, similarly, the source language -, and there are systems in-between, or systems that only miss the "real thing" just a bit. The view which I have in mind – THE LEARNER VARIETY PERSPECTIVE – is somewhat more radical. It goes back to early attempts to analyse the language of adult foreign workers in Germany (Klein and Dittmar 1979); much the same idea is found in Bley-Vroman (1983). The learner variety perspective can be characterised by three key assumptions (Klein and Perdue 1997: 307s):

A. During the acquisitional process, the learner passes through a series of LEARNER VARIETIES. Both the internal organisation of each variety at a given time as well as the transition from one variety to the next are essentially systematic in nature.

B. There is a limited set of organisational principles of different kinds which are present in ALL learner varieties. The actual structure of an utterance in a learner variety is determined by a particular interaction of these principles. The kind of interaction may vary, depending on various factors, such as the learner's source language. With successive input analysis, the interaction changes over time. For example, picking up some component of noun morphology from the input may cause the learner to modify the weight of other factors to mark argument status. From this perspective, learning a new feature is not adding a new piece to a puzzle which the learner has to put together. Rather, it entails a sometimes minimal, sometimes substantial reorganisation of the whole variety, where the balance of the various factors successively approaches the balance characteristic of the target language.

C. Under this perspective, learner varieties are not imperfect imitations of a "real language" – the target language – but systems in their own right, error-free by definition, and characterised by a particular lexical repertoire and by a particular interaction of organisational principles. Fully developed languages, such as English, German, French, are special cases of learner varieties. They represent a relatively stable state of language acquisition – that state where the learner stops learning because there is no difference between his variety and the input – the variety of his social environment.

In other words, the process of language acquisition and of SLA in particular is not to be characterised in terms of errors and deviations, but in terms of the two-fold systematicity which it exhibits: the inherent systematicity of a learner variety at a given time, and the way in which such a learner variety evolves into another one. If we want to understand the acquisitional process, we must try to uncover this two-fold systematicity, rather than look at how and why a learner misses the target.

I do not believe that it is uninteresting or unimportant to investigate errors and deviations, quite to the opposite. Such an investigation tells us a lot about the problems of the learner, their causes and how they can possibly be avoided. No reasonable person can take this to be irrelevant. But it will never lead us to a real understanding of how the human faculty works when exposed to new input – that is, it will never lead us to a real understanding how language acquisition, and second language acquisition in particular, functions. This is the reason why the answer to the second question from section 1 is negative. Nor will it tell us something substantial about the nature of the human language faculty itself. This, I believe, is the reason why our work ranks low within the linguistic sciences. Maybe we do find out something, maybe our findings are even reliable and of practical importance – but they contribute little to the general aim of linguistics.

But are we able to make such a contribution without leaving our field proper? After all, we are concerned with learners and what they do with their language faculty – that is, we are concerned with learner varieties, very elementary ones and very advanced ones; as soon as the target language is reached, our job is done. But can the investigation of learner varieties constitute a substantial, a fundamental contribution to the investigation of the human language faculty? I believe the answer is yes, in fact, I believe that learner varieties are the normal manifestation of this capacity, and "real languages" are just a special case, defined only on social and normative rather than on structural grounds. This is surely not the common way in which language researchers or the person on the street would see this; therefore, it needs some explanation.

2.3 The "real language hoax", or: Learner varieties are the normal case

There are many ways to look at language, and linguistic thought in the 20th century in particular is anything but uniform. Thus, the two dominant currents in this century, classical structuralism and generative grammar, have defined the primary object of their efforts in somewhat different ways. The following two famous passages, though somewhat simplifying the position of their authors, illustrate the point:

> La linguistique a pour unique et véritable object la langue envisagée en elle- même et pour elle-même. (Saussure 1916: 317)

> Linguistic theory is concerned primarily with an ideal speaker-listener, in a completely homogeneous speech-community, who knows its language perfectly and is unaffected by such grammatically irrelevant conditions as memory limitations, distractions, shift of attention and interest, and errors (randomly or characteristic) in applying his knowledge of the language in actual performance. (Chomsky 1965: 3)

In Saussure's view, the object to be investigated is a social entity, a "fait social" – a system which is defined by inherent structural relations between its elements; there is nothing specific to the individual speaker in this system. In Chomsky's view, the object of investigation is an individual entity – the knowledge which the ideal speaker has of his or her language; there is also a social dimension, but it is not felt to be of primary importance. In actual fact, however, the difference is much smaller than it looks like. Under both views, the object of investigation is an ideal entity. Neither Saussure nor Chomsky would deny that there is social variation, that is, that speakers speak in different ways; but they abstract away from this variation. Saussure would surely not say that "la langue" exists anywhere and anyhow except by virtue of the fact that its speakers know it; where should it exist? Any "fait social", religious convictions, values, norms, they all are nothing but belief systems in the head of people. Similarly, the knowledge of the ideal speaker must be knowledge of something – the language of some community, "une langue", and this knowledge must not be incomplete, or imperfect, or false. It must be the perfect reproduction of some external language.

Saussure, Chomsky, all of us are used to take perfect mastery of a language to be the crucial case, and the linguistic knowledge of a perfect speaker – a speaker who masters a "real language" up to perfection – to be the primary object of the linguist's efforts. But what does it mean that a speaker masters a language perfectly well, what must his or her knowledge be like in order to qualify as native? Our common *façon de parler* in these matters somehow implies that there are such entities as "real, fully-fledged languages", such as English, Latin or Kilivila, and speakers 'know' them to a higher or lesser degree. But this is a myth. Neither is there a structurally well-defined "external language", a point that has been repeatedly made by sociolinguists as well as by theoretical linguists. Nor is, a fortiori, the perfect internal representation of such a structurally well-defined and stable entity the normal case. The fact that it is a myth is clear to everybody who ever tried to answer the most frequent question posed to the linguist ('How many languages do you speak?') or the second-most frequent question ('How many languages are there on earth?'). I always say 'five thousand' (to the second question), and I have found that the only person who is not happy with this answer is myself – because I know that there is no clearly-shaped and well-defined entity such as 'a language', let alone five thousand. The honest scholar feels obliged to explain that there are no clear borderlines, that there are many dialects, registers, that it is arbitrary whether we count Frisian and Dutch, Dutch and Standard German, Standard German and Swiss German dialects as variants of one and the same language or not, that a language is a dialect with an army and a navy, etc etc. No layman wants to hear this, and understandably so. Most linguists don't want to hear it, either, and this is not understandable.

There are at least five thousend languages on earth. There are 193 countries on earth. This means that there are – on the average – 26 languages per country, with a range between 1 and several hundred. Two semesters of statistical training inform the linguist that this does not necessarily mean that every inhabitant of a country speaks 26 languages (on the average). Multilingualism of a country does transfer to the multilingualism of its inhabitants. But it would be equally silly to conclude that monolingualism is the normal case. THE NORMAL CASE IS THAT A PERSON HAS VARYING KNOWLEDGE OF DIFFERENT LANGUAGES. That is a good way to state the facts for the layman who believes that there are well-defined entities called languages. But there aren't. A "real language" is a normative fiction. What really happens is that human beings, equipped with this species-specific mental capacity called human language faculty, manage to copy, with varying degrees of success, the ways in which other people speak. They develop learner varieties – one, two, many. In some cases, they push this process to a degree where their own competence to speak and to understand does not saliently differ from that of their social environment (or, perhaps, a special group within their social environment, like school teachers). Then, we speak of "perfect mastery". But this perfect mastery is just mastery of a special case of a learner variety. It reflects that case in which neither the learner nor his neighbours notice any difference, or at least no difference they would consider to be of particular social importance. It is not the cognitive representation of something – "a real language" – that is fundamentally different from the representation of other learner varieties.

Normally, the speaker's language faculty also allows him or her to develop and to store many different learner varieties at the same time. All of those are manifestations of the human language faculty; their investigation can not only inform us about the nature of the acquisition process but also about the nature of the human language faculty itself. They do not enjoy the same social and normative reputation as a "real language". But this does not mean that "a real language" is more important for an understanding of the human language capacity than other learner varieties that are "less perfect". Since this perspective is surely not the received one, I will consider it in some more detail.

2.4 Can learner varieties really tell us something about the human language capacity?

> Der Sinese hat sich durch seine steife Einsilbigkeit den Weg zu aller weitern Kultur verschlossen; aber die Sprache des Huronen oder Grönländers hat alles in sich, sich zu der Sprache eines Plato oder Voltaire zu erheben. [The Chinese, by his stiff monosyllabicity, has precluded himself from any further culture; but the language of the Greenlander and the Huron has any chance to rise to the language of a Plato or Voltaire]
>
> *(Adelung, 1806: XXV)*

We laugh at Adelung's odd idea that a language should have a rich morphological structure in order to qualify as a serious language. But one wonders whether the common view to look at "real languages" is so far from a perspective, which sees the learner's way to express him- or herself as a highly imperfect manifestation of the our innate capacity to learn and to use "a language", a manifestation that is restricted, flawed, poor in its structural and lexical possibilities, and hence, simply not of particular interest to anyone who wants to understand the nature of the human language capacity. I believe this view is understandable but wrong, and this for at least two reasons. First, even if learner varieties are taken to be imperfect manifestations, then this still does not mean that their study cannot be highly instructive for an understanding of the underlying capacity. To deny this fact would be as ridiculous as the idea, biology should not deal with more elementary forms of life, such as bacteria, molluscs, or the humble drosophila melanogaster, and only devote its attention to life in its most advanced, in its most complex manifestations, for example the gentle tiger or the human being. In fact, it is just the study of elementary forms which has advanced biology to its present rank within the sciences; these forms do not show everything that is possible in the evolution of living organisms; but they are more transparent in what their structural properties are.

Second, learner varieties vary considerably; after all, they reflect a transition of simple to very complex forms; hence, they also differ in what in particular they can tell us about the human language faculty. There is no reason to assume that the variety of a very advanced learner who speaks German with a strong accent, distinct traces of English word order, wrong choice of prepositions and without any case marking on nouns is less perfect a manifestation of the human language capacity as Standard German, as spoken by the native speakers of Standard German, or the more educated among them. This learner's variety of German is just not as the German grammar books want to have it, and as the indigenous population speaks if it speaks as the grammar wants to have it. It is "imperfect" because it deviates from a norm; this norm can be set by a descriptive grammar, or by the habits of some social group. The fact that this variety is "imperfect" has nothing to do with the nature of the human language capacity; after all, German could be like this learner variety (maybe it should).

The case is different for very elementary learner varieties – say the variety of a learner who has just arrived in a country and knows nothing but a few nouns, a verb or two, and some rote forms. The investigation of such a learner's production may be not very telling; most of the potential with which the human language capacity has endowed us cannot apply. Still – some of its properties may be visible even at this elementary level. One might ask, for example, what happens if the learner tries to put two words together – is this done completely at random, does he or she follow the principles of the first language, or are there some universal constraints? And it becomes more and more instructive, the more complex and richer the learner variety gets. One such case will now be discussed in some more detail.

In a large crosslinguistic and longitudinal research project, we examined how 40 adult learners picked up the language of their social environment by everyday communication (Perdue 1993). Their production was regularly registered and analysed over about 30 months. This production, and the way in which evolves, varies in many respects; but it also shows a number of striking similarities. One of the core findings is the existence of a special language form which we called the "Basic Variety". It was developed and used by all learners, independent of source language and target language; about one third of our learners also fossilised at this level, i.e., they learned more words, but they did not complexity their utterances in other respects, in particular in morphology or syntax. As any form of human language, the Basic Variety has a lexicon, i.e., a repertoire of minimal meaningful expressions, and compositional rules, i.e., rules which allow the speaker to construct more complex expressions from simpler ones. In the Basic Variety, the lexical items mostly stem from the target language. They are uninflected, and although there is occasional variation in form, this variation is not accompanied by functional variation; in other words, there is no functional morphology. By far most lexical items correspond to nouns, verbs and adverbs; closed class items, in particular determiners, subordinating elements, prepositions, are rare, if present at all.

We noted three types of rules according to which these lexical items are combined into larger units:

A. Phrasal; they have to do with the lexical category (noun, verb, etc); if a verb – i.e., the uninflected verb stem – governs two arguments, then it is normally placed between these arguments.
B. Semantical: they relate to semantic properties of the arguments; thus, the argument which exerts the strongest control over the situation, is normally placed first.

C. Pragmatical: they relate to specific pragmatic functions, such as topic-focus structure, the introduction and maintenance of informations etc; in the basic variety, the element which is in focus is regularly in last position.

In the production of a concrete utterance, these organisational principles interact; normally, they go hand in hand; but sometimes, they also get into conflict, and these conflicts turn out to be germs of further elaboration. I shall not work out this here (see Klein and Perdue 1997 for a detailed presentation, and the papers by Bierwisch, Comrie, Schwartz and Meisel in the same issue of "Second Language Research" for a critical discussion).

In the present context, two facts about the Basic Variety are particularly remarkable. First, ALL speakers in our sample use it at some time – in fact, many stop at this level. If this is correct in principle, then the properties of the Basic Variety cannot be derived from the particular languages involved, except for the choice of lexical items – it must somehow reflect principles dictated by the human language faculty. Second, it is highly efficient for communicative purposes. If there is a communicative problem, then it is usually due to a lexical gap, rather than to the absence of a particular morphosyntactical feature. Now, note that there is no functional inflection whatsoever. This means that there is no tense, no aspect, no mood, no agreement, no case marking, no gender assignment; nor are there, for example, any expletive elements. Still, people tell, for example, very complex stories, just by clever use of some adverbials, some particles with temporal meaning, and pragmatical principles. In other words, a great deal of what we, with Adelung, feel so constitutive for "a real language", and what constitutes a great deal of classroom acquisition, is simply absent – but it does not seem to matter so much. And after all, there are languages such as Mandarin Chinese which, same traces aside, also lack functional inflection, and it does not seem to harm its speakers.

Two lessons are to be drawn from this. First, it may well be that we totally overrate the role of particular structural properties of "real languages". Sure, German has this complex system of noun inflection ("I rather decline two beers than a single German noun", Mark Twain), and Spanish has a complex system of verb forms, and Sanskrit has a complex system of everything. But the existence of such features is in no way a constitutive trait of the human language faculty. Second, one wonders why some manifestations of the human language capacity have these, and other, complexifications, whereas others don't. Where and why are they necessary, where are they just decorum, faithfully traded down from one generation to the next without any deeper reason, highly esteemed by linguists, utterly detested by second language learners? It is the study of learner varieties, of their internal systematicity and of their systematical development over time which allows us to address and to eventually to answer these questions. It is second language acquisition research which allows us to get a more realistic picture of what is essential and of what is peripheral in the human language capacity.

3 Conclusion

> This is just a theory. But I need facts.
> From a detective novel

In the introduction, three questions concerning the present state of SLA research were raised: what have we achieved for language teaching, how close are we to a theory of second language acquisition, what is our status within the chorus of disciplines that deal with language? To all of these, the answer was quite sceptical. In section 2, I tried to explain why our work had so little impact on linguistics in general. The reason, I argued, is simply that so far, we have nothing of real interest to contribute to a deeper understanding of human language. We must consider learner varieties as primary manifestations of our innate language faculty, no less important than so-called "real languages". They are not just bad copies of some target, from which they deviate to varying extent, but as objects in their own right; real languages are just a special case – that case in which a learner variety does not perceivably differ from the way in which the learner's social environment speaks; as a research object, it is not privileged in any way. In this concluding section, I will briefly return to the two other questions.

No scientific endeavour can be pleased with the mere discovery of some facts, interesting as these may be: what we eventually are aiming for is a set of general principles, from which the individual observations can be deduced. What we want is "a theory". Now, this term can be understood in various ways, and more often than not, it is just a label for a collection of more or less well motivated speculations. In this sense, there are many theories of second language acquisition. If the term is meant to be more than "just a theory", it is fair to say that we do not have a theory of second language acquisition. Is the learner variety perspective, defended in the preceding section, such a theory, or is it at least close to such a theory? The answer is "no", for two reasons. First, it is just a way of looking at a range of linguistic phenomena. It is an approach which eventually leads us to a deeper understanding of the acquisition process and of the human language faculty. But as such, it does not state strong general principles which cover all known evidence and correctly predict new findings, as a serious theory, say the theory of gravity or quantum mechanics, does. Second, it seems a wrong ambition to look for a comprehensive theory of second language acquisition.

The phenomena to be covered are simply too divergent. It would be like the quest for "a theory of nature". Someone who sets out to learn a new language has to acquire all sorts of new knowledge and skills. Suppose you are in a German pub, you just had a beer and you want another beer, then the most straightforward and therefore the best way to express this is *Noch ein Bier, bitte!* You may learn this as a rote form, a particular useful one in this case. But if you want it to be part of your productive competence, if you want to do this in the same way in which a native speaker does it, then you must learn a wealth of things; you must learn

- the sound-meaning coupling of these four words
- you must learn that *noch* does not mean "still" in this case, but something like "another one"
- you must learn to pronounce the long vowel in *Bier* without any diphtongisation, as normally done by speakers with English as a source language
- you must learn to omit some parts of the underlying full expression (it is an elliptical construction)
- you must learn to mark the accusative – something that is simple in this case, because it is identical with the nominative, but more difficult if you happen to order a wine (where you have to say *einen Wein* rather than *ein Wein* in this context)
- you must learn to use *bitte* appropriately (in German, it is used as a first turn, but also as a third turn, in response to "thank you")

and so on and so on. A great deal of this knowledge concerns entirely peripheral properties of German. There is no deeper reason why [iː] is not slightly diphthongised in German (except in some northern dialects), or why the final [r] in *Bier* is usually vocalised, rather than, for example, flapped or retroflex. These are just things you have to learn piece for piece. Such a piecemeal learning may also obey some general rules; but if this should be the case, the underlying principles are surely not the same as those which tell you what the precise range of usages of some lexical item is, or which elements you can omit in an elliptical utterance, or when you should say *bitte* and when you better don't. If one really wants to understand what happens, and what ought to happen, when people learn a language, all of this must be investigated. But I do not believe that there can be a universal, meaningful theory of the entire processes that happen when someone learns a language. Hence, it seems pointless to strive for "a theory of second language acquisition". No such theory is possible if it is not to become void of content and hence uninteresting. This does not mean, however, that the aim of our efforts should be just a listing of facts. What is needed, therefore, are PARTIAL THEORIES, that is, theories which state the principles behind what happens in particular areas of knowledge acquisition; and we may hope that one day, some of these partial theories converge without losing their empirical content.

When I said that a great deal, if not most, of what has to be learned concerns "peripheral properties", this does not mean that these properties are unimportant; they are just not essential to the understanding of the human language capacity. Whether the German word *Getränk* covers alcoholic as well as non-alcoholic beverages, whether the voiceless stops in this word are aspirated or not, whether it is *der Getränk, das Getränk, die Getränk* – all of this does not matter when we want to understand the principles which underlie function and structure of human language. But it is utterly important if you want to speak German like a native speaker, or as some norm wants to have it. Then, you must precisely copy these features, funny and idiosyncratic as they may be, because deviation is punished. It should make us think that is just these features which seem most difficult for adult learners, in contrast to children; the age effect in language learning is essentially observed for peripheral properties. In any event – this is the point where the TARGET DEVIATION PERSPECTIVE has its legitimate place. Therefore, I do not believe that the two perspectives contrasted in section 2.1 are mutually exclusive. No perfect replication is possible without taking something for the norm; and if we want to understand why some learners miss this norm in certain ways, then we must study their errors; and the better we have understood the reasons of their errors, the better we can systematically intervene in the learning process. But this perspective tells us little about the nature of the human language capacity, and it tells us little about the principles of acquisition. To this end, the learner's production and comprehension must be analysed in their own right: learner varieties must be seen as independent, as normal manifestations of the human language faculty, and we are the ones that study them and uncover the principles that determine their structure and their function.

References

Adelung, Johann Christoph (1806). Mithridates. Berlin: Reimer.
Bley-Vroman, Richard (1983). The comparative fallacy in interlanguage studies: the case of systematicity. Language Learning 33, 1. 1–17.
Chomsky, Noam (1965). Aspects of the Theory of Syntax. Cambridge, Mass.: MIT Press.
Klein, Wolfgang, and Dittmar, Norbert (1979). Developing Grammars. Heidelberg, Berlin, New York: Springer.
Klein, Wolfgang, and Perdue, Clive (1997): The Basic Variety, or Couldn't languages be much simpler? Second Language Research 13. 301–347.
Perdue, Clive (ed.) (1993). Adult language acquisition; crosslinguistic perspectives. Cambridge: Cambridge University Press.
Saussure, Ferdinand de (1916). Cours de Linguistique Génerale. Paris: Payot.

Why case marking?[1]

> En vieillissant on devient plus fou, et plus sage.
> *La Rochefoucault*

1 Introduction

In the memorable year of '68, on a hot summer day, Dieter Wunderlich and I were lying at the beach of Laboe, north of Kiel, and wondered about why languages can be so different. In those days, I tried to learn Chinese and Basque at the same time, two languages which are structurally as different as one can imagine. In both cases, the success was somewhat limited. But there was one thing I gained from this experience: this is the deep conviction that inflectional morphology is largely superfluous, because unlike the Basque, the Chinese easily do without it. Dieter did not quite share in this view, but the sun was hot, and the sea was cool, and we did not settle the issue on the spot. Some 33 years and an endless number of morphology papers later, he finally took the bull by the horns: 'Why is there morphology?' was the title of his talk at the 23rd Annual Meeting of the German Linguistic Society – that society whose co-founder and first president he was. The following remarks are a variation on this theme, and again, as in Laboe, they are from the perspective of the second language learner. Their gist is this: If we want to understand the nature of the human language faculty and the nature of linguistic systems, we should see what this capacity does when it brings about such a system, and not just look at the final result. The normal manifestation of the human language faculty are learner varieties, and 'fully-fledged languages' are only a special case of learner varieties. This view is strongly at variance with the traditional perspective in linguistics; but I believe it might help us to get a fresh view on old phenomena. In the first part of this paper, I will elaborate on this perspective, and in its second part, I will illustrate what it might help us to understand the function in case marking.

---

1 This one was written for Dieter Wunderlich. I wish to thank Ingrid Kaufmann and Barbara Stiebels for most helpful comments on an earlier version of this paper.

Note: This article originally appeared as Klein, W. (2002). Why case marking? In I. Kaufmann and B. Stiebels (eds.). More than words: Festschrift for Dieter Wunderlich. Berlin: Akademie Verlag. 251–273.

https://doi.org/10.1515/9783110549119-018

2 Learner varieties are the normal case

Within the various disciplines that investigate the manifold manifestations of the human language faculty, research on how people learn a second language does not rank very high. Does this fact only reflect irrational but rock-solid caste prejudices on the part of those who want to protect their privileges? Or has it anything to do with second language acquisition (SLA) research itself – its object, its methods, its theoretical or empirical standards, its potential benefit for mankind?

To begin with the latter, it appears that among the various linguistic disciplines, SLA research is probably the only one that is, or at least can be, of any substantial practical use. This should be a solid base of self-confidence, and a good reason to be held in some esteem by others. In fact, when linguists find themselves in a situation where they are urged to justify their existence in the eye of the common beholder, this is one of their arguments (together with aphasia, machine translation and automatic speech recognition).

As to the second explanation, I do not think that the field of SLA in general scores so badly as regards the standards of cogent argumentation, of conceptual clarity, of clean data collection and of empirical validation. This is not to mean that it could not improve considerably in many ways, and any effort in this direction should be made. But there is little reason to assume that the empirical basis of typological comparison is on the average more solid than what is normally done in SLA research. If, for example, a study of word order typology is based on 400 languages, then this means that the author cannot have spent much time on understanding what the word order regularities of each language are. Nor is there a good reason to believe that notions commonly used in theoretical linguistics are of necessity clearer and better defined than those used in the study of second language acquisition; we shall discuss this for ubiquitous notions such as 'subject' or 'object' below.

The problem seems to be rather that no one sees how the analysis of the odd productions of the second language learner, this distorted, flawed, ridiculous, chaotic mimicking of 'real language', could tell us something substantial, something principled, something fundamental about the nature of the human mind. It is this perception that must be changed in the first place. Learner varieties are a genuine manifestation of the human language faculty, and the careful and systematic investigation of how they are internally structured and how they develop over time is a genuine contribution to the understanding of this faculty. In fact, I believe that learner varieties are its core manifestations, and 'real languages' – or a speaker's perfect knowledge of a 'real language' – are just borderline cases. They are particularly interesting for social and cultural reasons, they are also interesting because they often exploit the structural potential of the human language faculty to a particularly high extent. But to the linguist, they should be no more privileged than is the noble lion over the humble *drosophila melanogaster* to the biologist.

We are used to take perfect mastery of a language to be the normal case, and the linguistic knowledge of a perfect speaker – a speaker who masters a 'real language' up to perfection – to be the primary object of the linguist's efforts. But what does it mean that a speaker masters a language perfectly well, what must his or her knowledge be like in order to qualify as native? Our common *façon de parler* in these matters somehow implies that there are such entities as 'real, fully-fledged languages', such as German, Greek or Yukatec, and speakers 'know' them to a higher or lesser degree. But this is simply a myth.

There are five thousand languages on earth. There are about 200 countries on earth. This means that there are – on the average – 25 languages per country, with a range between 1 and several hundred. As a consequence, the normal case is simply that a person has varying knowledge of different languages. That would be the good way to state the facts for the layman who believes that there are well-defined entities called 'languages'. But there aren't. What really happens is this: HUMAN BEINGS, EQUIPPED WITH THIS SPECIES-SPECIFIC MENTAL CAPACITY CALLED HUMAN LANGUAGE FACULTY, MANAGE TO COPY, WITH VARYING DEGREES OF SUCCESS, THE WAYS IN WHICH OTHER PEOPLE SPEAK. They develop LEARNER VARIETIES. Under specific conditions, they push this process to a degree where their own competence to speak and to understand does not perceivably differ from that of their social environment (or, perhaps, a special group within their social environment, like school teachers). Then, we speak of 'perfect mastery'. But this perfect mastery is just a special case of a learner variety – that case in which neither the learner nor his neighbours notice any difference, or at least no difference they would consider to be of particular social importance. Normally, the speaker's language faculty also allows him or her to develop more than just one such learner variety; the degree to which these come close to 'perfection' varies considerably. But all of them are manifestations of the human language faculty. Many learner varieties do not exploit the full potential of this faculty, for example in terms of syntactic or morphological structure or of lexical repertoire. But even my Russian learner variety, which is very elementary indeed, uses more of the human language faculty's morphological potential than the 'fully-fledged language' with most native speakers on earth, Chinese.

If we really want to understand the nature of the human language faculty, we must investigate how its manifold manifestations are organised and how they develop over time. This includes the study of fully-fledged languages – or more precisely, the speaker's knowledge of a fully-fledged language – as a special case. This case is perhaps particular interesting for cultural and sometimes even for structural reasons. After all, the ways in which Friedrich Schiller, Thomas Bernhard and the average inhabitant of Niederkassel put their words together are more complex, more refined, more multifarious and therefore perhaps more instructive to an understanding of the human language capacity than the learner variety of Keiko Watanabe, Ergün Üzlemir or Giuseppe Tonfoni after five years in Oberbilk. But we should keep in mind that the learner varieties of the latter are the normal case, nowadays as well as in the history of mankind; and here as everywhere in science, the investigation of the normal case should not be something peripheral, left to those at the bottom end, who are graciously, and with occasional friendly applause, allowed to borrow from those working higher up on the ladder. The systematical and careful study of how people process linguistic input in communicative situations, of how they use their innate capacities in order to turn this input into learner varieties and of how they abandon these for other, more complex or just differently organised learner varieties until this process eventually comes to a halt, in short: the study of second language acquisition is not a minor, a derived branch within the various disciplines that set out to investigate the human language faculty. It is central to an understanding of that remarkable capacity with which a friendly nature has endowed us.

Whilst I believe that this argument is perfectly logical, I realise that it would be more convincing to demonstrate how work on learner systems can lead to new insights about the structure and the functioning of language. In the remainder of this paper, I will try to do this for an area which has always been in the focus of research from the days of the Greek grammarians to the days of SFB 282 – inflectional morphology.

3 Two questions

> Fortwährend schiebt sich die Tradition zwischen die Tatsache und den Betrachter.
> *Jellinek* 1913: 21

There is considerable research on how second language learners acquire the inflectional morphology of the target language. Numerous studies document the learners' struggles with the oddities of German noun declension, Spanish irregular verbs or agreement marking in French. By far most of this work deals with SLA in the classroom, where – as especially those among us who had to learn Latin or Greek in school will remember (*forsan et haec olim meminisse iuvabit*, Aeneis I) – the memorization of morphology[2] plays an eminent role. Implicitly or explicitly, this research is strongly norm-oriented: there are clearly defined rules of how words should change their form, these rules are made explicit to the learner, and

---

2 Throughout this paper, the term 'morphology' *tout court* relates to inflectional morphology only.

acquisition research measures the learner's successes and failures to apply them. This work does not require any deep understanding of why certain morphological regularities are as they are. What counts is the mere fact that it is not *die Flücher* but *die Flüche*, whereas it is not *die Tüche* but *die Tücher*; or that it is *j'ai fait la communication* and not *j'ai faite la communication*, but *la communication que j'ai faite* rather than *la communication que j'ai fait*. Therefore, this research is of only moderate interest to the linguist.

There is much less research on how learners approach inflectional morphology outside the classroom. It is this research that might help to answer the question of how learners construct inflectional morphology out of the material with which they are confronted. This material takes the form of a more or less continuous sound stream uttered in a communicative context, and by processing and interpreting this input, the learner must somehow derive how certain lexical entries change their form under certain conditions – in other words, how words are inflected and what this inflection is good for. Other than in the classroom, this process is not determined by the particular way in which the rules to be learned are presented to the learner. It is entirely governed by the inherent properties of the learner's innate language faculty, on the one hand, and by whatever he knows about other languages, in particular about his first language, on the other. Hence, the investigation of this process should inform us about the natural principles of second language acquisition. But it can also help us to answer a second question which goes beyond the immediate concerns of the acquisition researcher. This is the question of what these findings can tell us about the nature of inflectional morphology and hence, as our tradition has it, about a core part of the human language faculty.

In the Western tradition of linguistics, the notion of 'grammar' was for two millenia almost equivalent to 'inflectional morphology'. Most of Donatus or Priscianus deals with the rules according to which words change their form, rather than with the rules according to which they are put together. Even phenomena which we now tend to view as syntactic or semantic, such as argument structure, were mainly seen from the perspective of case marking: *uti* requires the genitive, *persuadere* requires the dative, *videre* requires the accusative. The study of how time is expressed in language was, and still is, mostly concerned with what some morphological changes on the verb contribute to this task. The first grammars of modern languages, such as English, German or French, readily adopted this morphology bias, and the fact that the inflectional systems of these languages were less elaborate than in Latin or Greek was generally seen as a sign of erosion and decay (see Jellinek 1913 for a most instructive documentation of this tradition).

This view was hardly ever challenged before the end of the 19th century. How is it at the beginning of the 21st century? The answer to this question is more difficult as might appear. First, the fact that some languages, such as Chinese or

Vietnamese have virtually no inflectional morphology renders the classical view obsolete. In the design of human language, inflectional morphology is a common but by no means indispensable part. Second, there is good reason to assume that the way in which we investigate firmly established grammatical categories such as Tense, Mood or Case is still strongly determined by this traditional perspective and, as a consequence, is often led the garden path. Third, odd as the notion of a grammatical decay may seem to us – it is simply a fact that to the extent to which we have clear historical records, languages tend to reduce or to give up inflectional morphology rather than to elaborate it. There are some exceptions, such as the formation of future marking in Romance languages (*aimerai* from *amare habeo* and similar ones). These are often referred to in the linguistic literature, but all in all, they are rare and do not affect the overall picture.[3] English, Dutch, and even German show very reduced inflectional systems when compared to their common Westgermanic origin, let alone when compared to older stages of Indoeuropean. Chinese, the paradigmatic example of a language without inflection is assumed by some scholars to once have had it, but alas, it is gone and has only left some traces in form of lexical tones. So, some exceptions aside, the entire historical development seems to go away from morphology, or to vary on a theme by Dr. Samuel Johnson: 'Inflectional morphology has, like governments, a natural tendency to degenerate'. These observations face the general linguist with two questions:

– Why do we have this asymmetry?, and
– Why do languages have inflectional morphology in the first place?

This now is the point where the study of other manifestations of the human language capacity than 'fully-fledged languages' with all their oddities inherited from the past can help us. We should have a look at how this capacity constructs learner varieties when exposed to some input. I do not want to argue that this broader perspective provides the final answer; but it can give us some evidence on how and why inflectional morphology is born. In earlier work on untutored second language acquisition (see Perdue 1993; Klein and Perdue 1997), it could be shown that after some time, learners regularly develop a special type of linguistic system – the 'basic variety' (BV). The BV is a relatively stable and well-structured

---

[3] In their comments to the first version of this paper, Ingrid Kaufmann and Barbara Stiebels give some more examples of morphology creation. These examples are correct – but still, the asymmetry between formation and loss of morphology in historical time is overwhelming. I do not think, therefore, that there is strong evidence in favour of a 'morphological cycle', as discussed by Wunderlich (2001). It is correct, however, that we can only oversee – at the very most – the last ten percent in the evolution of human language, and in the dark ages, there could have been some such cycles.

form of language not found in first language acquisition and tutored second language acquisition; its structure seems to be independent of source and target language, i.e., it seems to reflect universal properties of the human language faculty. About one third of the learners we have investigated fossilise at the level of the BV, i.e., they stick to its structural characteristics and only enlarge their vocabulary; others go more or less beyond that stage, but hardly anyone comes close to the language of the learning environment.

As any other language, the BV has a lexical repertoire, i.e., a set of elementary expressions, and a grammar, i.e., rules which turn these elementary expressions into more complex ones. But there is no functional inflection of words. Still, the BV is a well-organised and a highly efficient linguistic system. As a rule, the absence of inflectional morphology does not seriously harm the speakers' communicative potential – in contrast to the absence of appropriate lexical items. Nevertheless, many of them go beyond the BV level – not only in lexical but also in structural respects. They develop morphology. Why?

First observations show that this is a very complicated and tedious process. Do they start this long march just because their social environment exhibits this kind of linguistic behaviour? Or are there inherent reasons – communicative and structural deficits in the form of language they use? To the extent to which the latter is the case, that is, to which the acquisition of morphology is more than mimicking the input, we might have some evidence on the question why and how inflectional morphology develops at all. At this point, this is only a possibility and a reason to rethink the role of inflectional morphology.

4 Learner varieties and 'real' languages

The study of second language acquisition has its origin in practical concerns – in problems of second language teaching. This background has naturally led to a particular view on SLA, for which two assumptions are constitutive:
- There is a well-defined target of the acquisition process, and only this is a 'real language', and
- learners miss this target at varying degrees and in varying respects – they make 'errors' in production as well as in comprehension.

We may this view the 'target deviation perspective', and it is this view which dominates the teacher's as well as the linguist's unreflected attitude towards SLA.

The alternative to the target deviation perspective is to understand the learner's performance at a given time as an immediate manifestation of his or her capacity to speak and to understand: form and function of these utterances

are governed by principles, and these principles are those characteristic of the human language faculty. This LEARNER VARIETY PERSPECTIVE can be characterised by three key assumptions (Klein and Perdue 1997: 307s):
- During the acquisitional process, the learner passes through a series of LEARNER VARIETIES. Both the internal organisation of each variety at a given time as well as the transition from one variety to the next are essentially systematic in nature.
- There is a limited set of organisational principles of different kinds which are present in ALL learner varieties. The actual structure of an utterance in a learner variety is determined by a particular interaction of these principles.
- Learner varieties are not imperfect imitations of a 'real language' but systems in their own right and characterised by a particular lexical repertoire and by a particular interaction of organisational principles. Fully developed languages, such as Japanese, Chinese or Kpelle are special cases of learner varieties. They represent a relatively stable state of language acquisition – that state where the learner stops learning because there is no difference between his variety and the input – the variety of his social environment.

In other words, the process of language acquisition is not to be characterised in terms of errors and deviations, but in terms of the two-fold systematicity which it exhibits: the inherent systematicity of a learner variety at a given time, and the way in which such a learner variety evolves into another one. If we want to understand the acquisitional process, we must try to uncover this two-fold systematicity. And if we want to understand fully fledged language, we should try to understand how our innate language faculty constructs them, when exposed to a certain input. This applies to all parts of a language – including inflectional morphology.

5 Lexical repertoire and rules of composition

In whichever way views vary on the nature of human language, two points seem uncontroversial: There must be a set of elementary expressions (lexemes), and there must be 'rules of composition' which describe how complex expressions are formed from simpler ones. This holds for all manifestations of the human language faculty, ranging from very elementary learner varieties to fully fledged languages.

A lexeme is a cluster of minimally three types of features
- semantic, i.e., those which describe the lexical meaning (or lexical content) of an expression

- phonological, i.e., those which describe its phonological shape
- categorial, i.e., those which characterise its behaviour with respect to rules of composition.

Other properties may be linked to a word, such as graphematical features; but what seems crucial are the three types mentioned above. This does not preclude, however, that in some specific cases, semantic features are absent or phonological features are absent. What seems indispensable are categorial features; but this is perhaps a matter of dispute. Grammatical rules are traditionally divided into morphological and syntactic, depending on whether they operate within the shape of a word or go beyond the individual word; there are some borderline cases, just as there are borderline cases between lexicon and grammar.

So far, I have more or less re-stated the obvious. The next point is much less uncontroversial. I would want to make a rigid distinction between two types of rules of composition – those which operate on lexical information, on the one hand, and those which serve to integrate the complex expression into the context, on the other. I will call the former LC-rules (for lexical content) and the latter CI-rules (for context integration), respectively. LC-rules serve to form complex lexical contents from simple ones; in doing so, they also affect categorial and phonological features of the times on which they operate. Typical examples are

- the constituent which expresses agent comes first (based on semantic features)
- the plural of German nouns of class 17 is formed by attaching -n (based on categorial information)
- a lexeme of type 'article' and a lexeme of type 'noun' form an expression of type 'noun phrase' (again based on categorial information)

and so on. Note that rules of this type are not purely 'syntactic' or 'morphological' in the traditional sense; they may also exclusively operate on semantic information provided by lexemes. There are also rules (Sandhi) which only have to do with phonological information. All that matters is that they are stated in terms of the information provided by the lexemes involved. Typical CI-rules are, for example

- focus constituents come last
- lexemes which preserve information from the preceding sentence come first
- lexemes which preserve information from the preceding sentence are deaccented, i.e., deprived of their suprasegmental information
- lexemes which preserve information from the preceding sentence can be deprived of their segmental phonological features (ellipsis)

and so on. They also include rules which concern the illocutionary status of a sentence, when made in some communicative context, such as
- a question is marked by a final rise
- an assertion is marked by having finite component of the verb in second position
- an imperative is marked by bare stem in initial position

and the like. Clearly, these rules are not based on merely lexical information. After all, nothing in the meaning of the lexeme *schweig-* says that it should be used as a question, an assertion or an imperative, just as nothing in the lexical information of this lexeme tells us whether, in a given utterance, this information is new or maintained from a preceding utterance.

The distinction between LC-rules and CI-rules is a principled one. It does not preclude that in a given language, bits and pieces of both types are clustered together to one complex rule. In fact, I believe that the apparent opacity of fully fledged languages is very often due to such a clustering, whereas the separation is relatively neat in more elementary manifestations of the human language capacity. In the Basic Variety, we seem to have very simple rules such as 'Controller [agent] first' or 'Focus last'; the problem there is that under specific communicative circumstances, the two types of rules are in conflict and hence, when applied simultaneously, do not allow the formation of a complex expression. Such cases call for additional devices, and this, we believe, is one potential source of morphological marking, a point to which I will return in section 7.1 below.

If we take grammar to be the overarching term (in contrast to opposing it to lexicon), then a grammar is organised as follows:

(1) grammar

lexicon	rules of composition	
clusters of features	LC-rules	CI-rules
– semantic – categorial – phonological – perhaps others	relate only to lexical information	relate to contextual information

Where does inflectional morphology fit into this picture? It belongs to the rules of composition, but to which sort? This will be discussed in the next section.

6 What is inflection good for?

Inflection is not just a change in the shape of a word. As a rule, it operates on all three types of lexical information – phonological, semantic and categorial. Take, for example, the rule which turns the German verb stem *schweig-* into the 'past participle' *geschwiegen*. It changes the phonological properties in various ways: it adds the prefix *ge-*, the suffix *-en*, and it turns the diphthong [aɪ] into the long vowel [iː]. Next, it somehow modifies the meaning, an effect which is much harder to describe – maybe it indicates a 'posttime'; we shall turn to this point in section 7.2 below. Finally, it also affects the categorial properties; thus, the resulting form cannot be made finite, as is the case with the bare stem; but it can, for example, be combined with an auxiliary to form a present perfect.

The role of temporal marking and of finiteness in acquisition beyond the Basic Variety has repeatedly been addressed in the literature on SLA outside the classroom (see, e.g., Starren and van Hout 1996, Giacalone Ramat 1997). Therefore, I will not elaborate on these two inflectional categories here but turn to another no less fundamental such category – case marking. The more specific question to be addressed in the remainder is thus: What is case marking good for?

Hard to tell. In the BV, it is strikingly absent. What do its speakers loose apart from the fact that their language does not sound like the language of their social environment? Could it be that the wisdom of the adult language learner, when not under the teacher's whip, simply chooses to ignore something because there is no reason to learn it? The idea sounds blasphemous; but then, we should come up with a clear idea what case marking is good for.

Traditionally, case marking on a noun phrase may be 'absolute' or 'governed'. Examples of the first type include the 'ablativus absolutus' (*his rebus gestis, Caesar pontem fecit*) and 'adverbial noun-phrases', for example *Roma* 'in Rome' vs. *Romam* 'towards Rome'. The latter type also exists in German, but it is restricted to some isolated adverbials such as *den ganzen Tag* 'all day'. In any event, it seems a very different phenomenon than 'governed case marking', where a noun-phrase must be inflected in a particular way because some other element with which it is combined requires such a case marking. In German, as in most other languages, these 'case-requiring' elements are primarily prepositions and verb stems; others, such as adjectives, are marginal.

Consider, first, prepositions. With one remarkable exception, case marking in prepositional phrases is just decorum; neither to the BV speaker nor to the linguist is it transparent why *ohne* governs the accusative, *mit* governs the dative and *wegen* governs the genitive. In fact, native speakers were well-advised if they adopted the learner's way in this regard – no case marking at all.

The only exception is variable case marking with prepositions such as *in, auf, vor*: with the dative, they denote a location, and with the accusative, they mark in addition that this location is the target of some change of location. Thus, *auf dem Tisch* indicates a place which is higher than and in contact with the table; *auf den Tisch* indicates in addition that this place is the endpoint of some movement.

Whereas there are only a few prepositions, there are thousands of verb stems which require a particular case on their arguments; what is this marking good for? In what follows, I will discuss this question first for the 'Basic Variety' and then for 'Standard German', a language which is notorious for its complex noun declension in general and its case marking in particular ('I rather decline two beers than a single German noun', Mark Twain).

7 Case marking and the 'Argument-Time Structure' of verbs

7.1 Where the BV fails

Elementary utterances in the BV usually consist of an uninflected verb and one or two nominal arguments. There are three types of organisational principles; in Klein and Perdue (1997), these were called phrasal, semantic and pragmatical; the most important ones are:[4]

(2)   Structural constraints in the BV

   PH1. NP_1 – V
   PH2. NP_1 – V – NP_2
   PH3. V – NP_2
   SEM. The NP-referent with highest control comes first[5]
   PR.   Focus expression comes last

---

[4] The following exposition is confined to what is essential in the present context; copula constructions, for example, or constructions with three arguments – rare anyway – are not discussed here. For a more comprehensive account, see Klein and Perdue (1997) and the literature quoted there.

[5] The 'control asymmetry' is based on the idea that the arguments of a verb can be ranked by the greater or lesser degree of control that their referents exert, or intend to exert, over the referents of the other argument(s). Strength of control is a continuum, including the possibility that two arguments rank equally high (in which case, of course, the 'control principle' cannot be decisive in what comes first).

Phrasal rules exclusively operate with categorial features; hence, they are LC-rules in the terminology used above. Semantic rules operate with semantic features. Note, however, that these features do not come from the NP itself but from the verb; it is not inherent to the referent of an NP to be an agent ('high control') or a patient ('low control'). The pragmatic constraint, finally, is a clear example of a CI-rule. The fact that some constituent is focussed is not a property of its lexical information. Hence, we have a clean separation of these rule types.

This is a very elegant and versatile system. But problems arise when these neat principles get into conflict. The clearest case we noted is a scene in the re-telling of Chaplin's 'Modern Times', in which one of the protagonists – the girl – is accused to have stolen a (loaf of) bread, a situation which can be easily described by (3):

(3) Mädchen stehle Brot
     Girl   steal bread

There are two nominal arguments, the first one is the 'controller', the second one is focussed (probably together with the verb, a point which does not matter here). These three rules take together result in an utterance such as (3). But as the story goes on, the speaker has to express that (allegedly) it was not the girl who stole the bread but Charlie. Now, the speaker must either violate PR, as in (4a), since *Charlie* is focussed and hence should be in final position, or SEM, as in (4b), since Charlie is the controller and hence should be in first position:

(4) a. Charlie stehle Brot
         Charlie steal bread
     b. Brot stehle Charlie
         Bread steal Charlie

Here, the BV system is structurally too simple: it cannot handle these conflicting requirements.

There are two ways to deal with this problem. The first one consists in a *ranking* of the two principles, for example as in (5):

(5) Semantic constraints outweigh pragmatic constraints.

I suspect that native speakers of English indeed have such a ranking. They would always consider the first argument to be the controller. Therefore, sentence (4b) intuitively sounds very bizarre to a native speaker of English – but much less so to a native speaker of German, where the controller might easily be in final position;

hence, in cases of ambiguity, they tend to follow the opposite ranking. Whichever ranking is chosen – the fact remains that one of the constraints is violated. If we adopt the English strategy, for example, it is not clear which argument is in focus; if we adopt the German strategy, it is not clear which element is the controller (except that, in this particular example, it is unlikely that the bread is the controller).[6]

The other way, and in fact the only principled way, to solve the problem is the invention of another device which allows the speaker to mark either what is focus or what is controller. In the case of a BV speaker, this 'invention' is not free – it is directed by what is the case in the target language, maybe also by what is the case in the source language. By contrast, the first *homines sapientes*, whilst in principle in the same situation, had no model to lean on: they had to create something freely. It appears that natural languages have used two options for the additional device – they either use suprasegmental means, or they create a specific segmental expression, a morpheme. This morpheme may be free, or it may be attached to one of the relevant words. In the present context, I will not go into suprasegmental devices. Let me just note, first, that they are widely used to this end, and second, that to the best of my knowledge, they only mark an expression as focussed or non-focussed but never as agent, patient or the like. They serve CI-functions, not LC-functions.

The other choice, the formation of a specific morpheme, has both options. It is possible to invent/adopt a morphological focus marker (or non-focus marker), and it is possible to invent/adopt a morphological controller marker, a patient marker and so on. In SLA, the first possibility is exemplified by some learners of French who use a particle [se] to mark an element in initial position as focussed – a precursor of the cleft construction *c'est ... que* (see Klein and Perdue 1997: 330s). The other possibility is tantamount to case marking, either by inflection or by some free morpheme. Various options to achieve this are possible, for example
- controller is marked by a special suffix, and non-controller is marked by another suffix
- only controller is marked
- only non-controller is marked
- non-focus is marked by a special suffix (thus indicating something like topic-hood)

and so on. It may also be that the relevant marking only occurs when (at least) two arguments are present (otherwise, confusion can arise), but it is also possi-

---

[6] Languages differ in their ranking, and as we argued in Klein and Perdue 1989, there is some evidence to assume that learners transfer the priorities of their source language into their learner varieties.

ble that the 'case role' is marked in all occurrences, no matter whether there is a second argument with which it can be confused.

In the case of language acquisition, the learner is not free to choose between these various options and to build his or her own system. Eventually, the learner has to copy what the social environment does, irrespective of whether he really understands it or not. Adult learners may be somewhat reluctant to do this, if it is difficult for them and if they do not see what it is good for. This may be one of the reasons why they often get stuck at one point. Children normally don't; this may be either due to the fact that they are simply better in imitating things which they do not understand, or that they are more willing to do it. No one understands why *ohne* has an accusative and *mit* has a dative; but some people simply learn it without asking, and others don't.

Our ancestors, who first invented inflectional morphology including case marking, were not under the influence of an already existing system. But we have no direct evidence of what they did: all we have is the result of a long process of transformation, elaboration, reduction. A fully-fledged language, and its inflectional morphology in particular, resembles an old city on which many generations have left their traces, to the better or to the worse. This explains many oddities, such as the quaint case assignment of some verbs or prepositions; but it does not preclude a very systematic basis – a set of default principles. In the next section, I will discuss what this set of default principles could look like in the case of Standard German.

7.2 Case marking and the 'argument-time structure' of German verbs

Conventional wisdom has it that verbs, in contrast to nouns, refer to 'events' or, more generally speaking, to 'situations'. This is a very misleading notion. To which situation does *schlaf-* refer? It is the entire sentence which refers to a situation, and the verb makes a – substantial – contribution to the description of this situation. Consider, for example, the situation referred to by following sentence, when uttered on some occasion:

(6) Tessi öffnete das Pförtchen.
    Tessi opened the little door.

The verb stem *öffn-* indicates some properties which the two NP-referents have at some time intervals. The little door must first be not open and then open, Tessi must do something, for example turn a knob and push the door into a certain direction, or push a button, or say 'Sesame, open!' – whatever; more generally speaking, she must somehow be 'in control of' the situation, in contrast to the referents of the other arguments.[7]

If all of this is essentially correct, then THE FUNCTION OF THE VERB IS TO INDICATE PROPERTIES OF ARGUMENT-TIME PAIRS. These pairs themselves are not expressed by the verb but by noun phrases, by adverbials, by morphological variation of the stem and perhaps by other means. Sometimes, they are to be derived by context. What the verb itself provides are open slots to be filled appropriately, i.e. pairs of argument-time variables. In what follows, I shall use A, B, C, ... as variables for arguments and $t_1, t_2, t_3, ...$ as variables for time spans; an argument-time pair (briefly AT-pair) is denoted by $<A, t_i>$. It will be helpful to consider some examples.

In (7), there is only one argument variable and one time variable, and the descriptive property is 'open'. The argument variable is specified by *das Pförtchen*, the time variable is only vaguely restricted by the morphological tense marking on the copula:

(7) Das Pförtchen war offen.
    The little door was open.

In (8), there is only one argument variable, as well; but properties are assigned to it at two times, which I will call FT ('first time') and ST, respectively:

(7) Das Pförtchen öffnete sich.
    The little door opened (itself).

The FT-property of the single argument is 'not open', the ST-property is 'open'. In this case, the argument-variable is filled twice, by an NPN and by *sich*.[8] The two time-variables are not specified (but they are restricted by the past tense marking, i.e., they must be before the utterance time).

Let us now return to (6). Here, the verb assigns varying properties to two entities at different times. The entity which specifies the first argument variable is said to do something, whatever this may be, and the entity which specifies the second argument variable is first said to be not open and then, to be open. Hence, we have three AT-pairs which are assigned descriptive properties by the

---
[7] Exactly this is the origin of the 'control asymmetry' in the Basic Variety.
[8] Here and in what follows, NP_N is a noun phrase marked as nominative, NP_D is a noun phrase marked as dative, and NP_A is a noun phrase marked as accusative.

verb stem. The lexical meaning of the verb can then be described as a Boolean cluster of elementary predications over AT-pairs (leaving aside for the moment whether the descriptive properties are adequately described by terms such as 'active', etc.):

(9) offensei-   open <A, ti >
    öffn-   not-open <A, ti > & open <A, tj >
    öffn-   not-open <A, ti > & open <A, tj > & 'active' <B, tk >

This does not exhaust the lexical content of verb stems. If there is more than one AT-specification, as in (9b) and (9c), then the relationship between these must be indicated, too. In the first place, this includes the temporal relation between the time spans. Thus, tj must be AFTER ti; this is what we covered above by the labels first time FT and second time ST. If there is a third time span, as in (9c), the relation between tk (the time of B's being active) and ti as well as tj must be indicated, as well. For sentence (6) to be true, Tessi may still push the button of her automatic door opener, although the door is already open. But the sentence is not true if the door opened but he started his activity only when it was already open. Thus, tk must overlap with ti; it may but need not overlap with tj.[9]

As any lexical entry, a verb is a cluster of phonological, categorial and semantic features, the latter being called here lexical content (cf. section 6 above). The lexical content of a verb has a STRUCTURAL COMPONENT and a DESCRIPTIVE COMPONENT. The structural component is the AT-structure, which consists of the various AT-pairs together with a specification of the temporal and non-temporal relations between these. The descriptive component consists of the various qualitative or spatial properties assigned to an AT-pair. These two components can be coupled in different ways. They may be conflated into a single morpheme, for example, as is the case with *öffn-* (in both variants). In *offensei-*, the descriptive property is contributed by *offen*, whereas the verb *sei-* does not specify a qualitative or spatial property; it only has an AT-structure, and it can be made finite (in contrast to the other component *offen*). Other cases are possible, but I will not go into these details here. Before now turning to what all of this has to do with case marking, it will be useful to sum up in which way the present view differs from the traditional perspective.

---

9 There are other than merely temporal relations between different AT-specifications. In (6), for example, it does not suffice that Tessi did something and the door made a transition from not open to open. For this sentence to be true, this temporal coincidence must not be accidental: we assume that the latter were not the case if the former were not the case. Hence, a sort of counter-

Traditionally, lexical verbs are assumed to have an 'argument structure'. It is also assumed that verbs (and more complex expressions such as full VPs) can be classified according to their inherent temporal properties into 'event types', 'Aktionsarten' etc. They have an ARGUMENT STRUCTURE as well as an EVENT STRUCTURE. The present view takes these two notions together: verbs have an ARGUMENT-TIME STRUCTURE. This has a number of consequences. One of these[10] relates to the way in which semantic and formal 'government' is analysed, i.e., the semantic and formal restrictions which the verb imposes on the 'filling' of its argument variables. By semantic government, I mean 'case roles' or 'thematic roles' such as agent, theme, experiences, benefactive, patient etc. I believe that these notions, whose fuzziness has often been lamented, are nothing but a gross classification of the descriptive properties which Vs may assign to an AT-pair. I see little use in such a classification beyond an initial orientation of the 'descriptive component' – except it can be shown that such an assignment has clear structural consequences. But this already relates to the other side of government, i.e., to constraints on morphological properties such as accusative, dative or to syntactic properties such as 'subject' or 'direct object'. These constraints are traditionally seen as a part of the verb's categorial features. It would be much more elegant, however, if they could be derived from the AT-structure or from the Descriptive Component. Thus, one might look for principles such as 'If an argument is described at two times, then it is realised as NPA' or 'An argument which is assigned the property "active" is always encoded as an NPN'. It is unlikely that this is possible for the entire verb lexicon of a language; but it should be possible for the default case. Languages are the product of a complex historical development, and just as there are idiosyncrasies in other parts of the lexical information, we should expect them here, as well.[11]

---

factual relation may obtain between various AT-specifications; this, I believe, is the background of the predicate CAUSE found in many decompositional analyses of verbs. As is usually the case for lexical entries, such a relation, where it exists, may be individually marked for each entry or covered by a lexical default rule; this is an empirical issue which we will not follow up here.
10 Another one concerns the notion of 'event time'. If, for example, the verb in itself contains several temporal variables, a notion such as 'event time' turns out to be a gross oversimplification: what, for example, is the 'event time' in (6): is it t_i, t_j or t_k? Or is it some interval which contains all or some of these? Similarly, notions such as 'anteriority' or 'posteriority' or even 'simultaneous' turn out to be highly problematic. What, for example, is the 'posttime' in (6)? Is it the time where the little door is open, or is it the time after Tessi's activity?
11 Under this view, there is not so very much a distinction between 'structural case' and 'lexical case' but between 'assignment by default' and 'assignment by exception'.

With this caveat in mind, it appears that German has a number of very simple default principles for case assignment by the verb, and a rule which determines their relative weight in cases of conflict.[12] These are:

(10) DP A: One argument variable is filled by an NP_N.
　　　DP B: Two-times argument variables are filled with NP_A.
　　　DP C: One-time argument variables are filled with NP_D.
　　　DP D: If the verb assigns the property 'active' to an argument, then this argument is realised as NP_N.[13]
　　　DP E: If the verb is lexically empty, then the argument which expresses the descriptive property is realised as NP_A.[14]

In cases of conflict, DP A is strongest.

This means that an NP_A can encode one-time arguments as well as two-times arguments; it also encodes a 'controller', if there is such an argument. Other NPs are much more restricted in what they can encode.

The rules in 10 are extremely simple, and if we are to believe the Scholars that *simplicitas est sigillum veritatis*, then there is good reason to assume that they are true. But there are also various problems, one of which I will discuss now.

Under the analysis suggested here, an NP_A is always a 'two-times argument'. This is plausible in cases such as *Dieter opened the door*, where the door is first not open and then open. But it is not plausible for other cases, such as *Dieter hated his uncle*, where the second argument is NP_A. This fact is nicely reflected in Dowty's idea that the 'prototypical' patient is a 'change-of-state' argument (Dowty 1991). It appears to me, however, that the notion of 'change-of-state' in general confounds two interrelated but in principle independent features of verb meaning, which are clearly kept apart in the notion of AT-structure. These are its DESCRIPTIVE PROPERTIES, such as being open or being in Heringsdorf, and its TEMPORAL STRUCTURE i.e., the intervals and subintervals at which some argu-

---

[12] I believe that very similar principles also apply to other languages – but I am very hesitant to make any claim for universals in general, and for a universal hierarchy in particular. Therefore, I will confine this discussion to what I believe is the case in German. One reason for this hesitation is the fact that I do not believe in a universal notion of, for example, 'accusative case'. At best, there is some family resemblance between accusative in, for instance, English and Basque. It would make sense, however, to replace these traditional notions by notions such as 'two-times case', i.e., case of an argument which is specified for two time variables. But his would lead us far beyond the scope of this paper.
[13] It is this default principle which gives rise to the controller asymmetry discussed in section 7.1.
[14] This principle primarily concerns the descriptively empty 'two-place copula' *haben*, as in *Karl hat Angst/rote Haare*.

ment is assigned these descriptive properties. Compare, for example, the two sentences *Dieter slept* and *Dieter woke up*. In the first case, a descriptive property ('asleep') is assigned to Dieter at some time ti; morphological marking indicates that this time is (normally) in the past. In the second case, two distinct properties are assigned to Dieter; first, say at tj, he must be asleep, and then, say at tk, he is not asleep. Hence, the lexical content of the verb *to wake up* comprises two temporal variables, tj and tk, which are sequentially ordered and which are associated with different descriptive properties. In this case, the properties are mutually exclusive, a constellation which is perfectly well covered by the notion of a 'change-operator' (such as the familiar BECOME). But it is also imaginable that the lexical content of a verb lexeme has two time variables with less divergent properties. Take, for example, *The temperature fell* and *The temperature rose*. For the first sentence to be true, it is necessary that at some interval tk, the temperature is 'lower' on some scale than at some earlier interval tj; for the second sentence to be true, the temperature must be 'lower' at the first interval tj than at the second interval tk. Verbs of this sort are not 'telic' or 'resultative'. The Vendler tests identify them as activities, rather than as accomplishments or achievements. I am not sure whether they should be described by a change-operator.

Is it possible that the lexical content of a verb provides two time variables with identical descriptive properties? At first, this idea sounds bizarre: why should this be the case? But compare the two sentences *Dieter was in Heringsdorf* and *Dieter remained in Heringsdorf*. They both assign a 'static' spatial property to Dieter. But somehow, the second sentence gives the impression that Dieter was there at some time tj and then, at some time tk, could have gone but hasn't. The difference is brought out more clearly if we add a modal verb, such as in *Dieter was allowed to be in Heringsdorf* and *Dieter was allowed to remain in Heringsdorf*. In the first case, the permission concerns his entire stay, whereas in the second case, it only concerns the second subinterval. In order to describe the semantic effect of this morphosyntactic operation appropriately, we must assume that it has SELECTIVE access to the verb content – to a subinterval which is descriptively not different from the first interval. The addition of a modal verb is not the only morphosyntactic process which demonstrates this. Negation is another case. In *Dieter was not in Heringsdorf*, his entire stay there is denied; in *Dieter did not stay in Heringsdorf*, it is only denied that he was not there at a second subinterval during which he could have been there. The possibility to have two temporal intervals with the same descriptive properties is not confined to verbs with only one argument. It is also found with 'transitive verbs' such as *to leave* in sentences like *Could you please leave the door open*. Here, the idea is that the door is open at a first time and should also be open at a second time, in contrast to the possibility that, due to the addressee's action, it is closed at this second time.

The conclusion is therefore, that we must carefully distinguish whether a verb content has one, two or even more temporal variables and whether the descriptive properties assigned to these variables are identical, slightly different or 'radically' different. An operator such as BECOME conflates these notions. There is no change in a verb such as *to remain* or *to stay*, and similarly in German *bleiben*; still, there are two subintervals which are selectively accessible to morphosyntactic operations.[15] The linguist's decision of whether a verb stem involves one or more temporal variables can therefore not be based on mere semantic intuition; it must explore how the content of this verb stem can be modified by all sorts of morphosyntactic operations.

Such an operation is the formation of the 'past participle', briefly mentioned in section 6.1 above.[16] I will call this operation GE-; V is the lexeme to which it applies. The way in which the attachment of GE- affects the phonological information of V is complex but well studied; it brings about the forms of the past participle. The change in categorial information is somewhat less clear; some operations applicable to the verb are now blocked, for example, the past participle can no longer be made finite (unless some other verb is attached). How does GE- affect the semantic features provided by V? Under the present approach, it changes its AT-structure and possibly adds further descriptive properties. I assume that the latter is not the case but that GE- only operates on the AT-structure as follows:

(11) The past participle denotes ST-properties of V.

Remember that under the present approach, ST-properties are relative to an argument, typically the NP_A. If the verb does not provide any ST-properties, because there is no appropriate AT-pair specified for two times, then the past participle can still be formed; but when attached to an argument, the resulting construction is not interpretable: there is no appropriate argument slot. This is the case for verb stems such as *schweig-* or *gehör-*; therefore, *das geschwiegene Kind* or *der (mir) gehörte Apfelsaft* should not make sense, and so it is. A stem such as *einschlaf-*, by contrast, does have two time slots for its single argument, and therefore, *das eingeschlafene Kind* should be possible, and so it is. The stem *öffn-* has two time slots only for one

---

[15] There are also exceptions in the opposite direction. The situation described by *Dieter worked in a shoe factory* includes many quite heterogenous subintervals, hence many 'changes'. None of these subintervals, however, is selectively accessible to any morphosyntactic operation, such as negation, adverbial modification or addition of another verb stem.
[16] For a detailed discussion of how its various usages can be captured under the present treatment, see Klein 2000.

of its arguments, and therefore, *das geöffnete Tor* assigns the SL-properties (being open after having been not open) to this argument, i.e., to the door.

In conclusion, the assumption that an accusative indicates, in the default case, that an argument has two time variables makes perfect sense, so long as we do not confuse the existence of two time variables with a 'change of state'.[17] On the other hand, the AT-analysis suggested here explains a number of additional facts of German. Only transitive objects 'passivise' – that is, only these objects provide the two time slots that are necessary for a past participle to apply. As just stated, it explains why *das geschwiegene Kind* is odd, whereas *das eingeschlafene Kind* or *das gestillte Kind* are fine. It naturally accounts for the ambiguity between 'unergative' and 'unaccusative' verbs with one argument. The argument of an 'unergative verb' is specified at one temporal interval, and thus, it behaves like the 'subject' of a transitive verb. The argument of an 'unaccusative verb' is specified at two time intervals, that is, it behaves like the 'direct object' of a transitive verb. Finally, the analysis also makes plausible why *auf dem Tisch*, i.e., with dative, is 'static', whereas *auf den Tisch*, with its accusative, is 'dynamic' – the latter involves two temporal variables.

8 What is a subject, what is an object?

> Right after I had joined the project, I began to study linguistics, and very soon, I was deeply bewildered by the fact that there is not the faintest unanimity in this apparently so precise, this allegedly so mathematiced and physicalised branch of science. In this discipline, the authorities don't even concur on most elementary, quasi introductory issues such as what's a morpheme or a phoneme.
>
> Stanislaw Lem, The master's voice

It has often been noted (see, e.g., Reis 1982) that what is called 'subject' is actually a cluster of heterogenous features – morphological features such as case marking, syntactic features such as position, semantic features such as agentivity, and pragmatical features such as topic status; these may but need not be present. In other words – this notion is a cloud. This is in no way different for 'direct object'. How is it defined? In school grammar, no definition is given at all; normally, these notions are illustrated by examples, and the relevant generalisations are left to the reader. Modern approaches, lest they simply continue this tradition, define

---

[17] I do think, however, that there are accusatives which encode a 'single-state argument', for example measure phrases such as 'The colossus of Rhodes weighed one hundred tons'. Characteristically, these cannot form a 'passive'.

them either in terms of case roles, such as 'theme, benefactive, patient', etc., or in terms of tree geometry.

The first way is unsatisfactory because these notions themselves are most unclear – a fact that has often been deplored (see the extensive discussion in Helbig 1973). Moreover, they do not make sense in many cases. It may be justified to call the NP_D a 'benefactive' in *Er half ihr*, but surely not in *Errötend folgt er ihren Spuren*. The tree geometry approach, generally used in Generative Grammar and in some other branches of structural linguistics, looks much clearer – in fact, so much clearer that it is most often taken as self-evident. One might say, for example: 'The direct object is the first NP immediately dominated by V on D-structure' (this is the definition in Chomsky's 'Aspects', where this idea was first worked out, the argument is analogous for other variants of generative grammar). But this clarity is only apparent. Such an account only shifts the problem to the question why a particular tree structure is assumed in a specific case. It is neither the Lord nor the Pope who places *einen Apfel* immediately under VP in *Adam aß einen Apfel*. It is the linguist who draws pictures. Trees, as this term is used in linguistics, are abstract structures based on two types of structural relations between its elements – dominance and precedence. These, and only these, relations are available to represent the structural relationship between simple or complex expressions. It is the linguist's task to decide why certain elements are connected to each other by a vertical stroke, i.e., by a dominance relation, and why a certain element is placed in the tree such that it precedes some other element. Very often, the two relations available turn out to be insufficient, and the linguist's way out is usually to stipulate several trees, together with some mechanism to relate these to each other ('transformations', 'reanalysis', and other ones). In any case, it is not the tree which says why something is connected to something else in a particular way – why, for example, an NP is in the 'direct object relation' to a V. It is the linguist who constructs the tree in a given case, and this decision must be based on clear and reasonable criteria. Mere reference to the position in the tree is no solution.

Recently, a number of linguists, in particular Manfred Bierwisch, Paul Kiparsky and Dieter Wunderlich, developed an analysis of this problem which potentially overcomes these difficulties, although it operates with trees, as well. Details vary; the most elaborate version is found the 'Lexical Decomposition Grammar' of Wunderlich and his group (1996, see also Wunderlich 1997, 2000). In this approach, the asymmetry of argument variables is defined by the features 'higher role available (in the same clause)' – 'lower role available'. Consider, for example, the sentence *Tessi gab ihm den Schlüssel*. The variable filled by *den Schlüssel* is assigned the feature complex 'higher role available, no lower role available', the variable which is filled by *Tessi* gets assigned the feature complex 'no higher role available, lower role available', and finally, the third variable, which corresponds to *ihm* gets assigned 'higher role available, lower role available.' Morphological case marking is then easily defined on the basis of such a feature complex, such as, for example, 'no higher role available, lower role available' is marked by nominative in German.

This is a very elegant approach, indeed. But it raises two basic problems. First, which independent criteria are crucial to decide why some element is 'higher' than some other element? They cannot be based on morphological marking, because this would render the analysis circular. Are they based on case roles – say 'benefactive' is lower than 'agent' but higher than 'theme'? Then, we are back to the familiar problems with these notions. The other way – and this is the main criterion taken in Lexical Decomposition Grammar – is to exploit the depth of embedding in lexical decomposition. But it does not work for verbs which, under this approach, are not lexically decomposable, that is, to those which do not involve a BECOME operator or a CAUSE; in other words, it is essentially confined to telic verbs. – Second, I do not see how this analysis works for Vs with NP_N and NP_D alone, such as *helf-, gebühr-* or *ähnel-*? In Wunderlich (1997), this case is analysed as a lexically marked deviation from the case assignment dictated by the 'role hierarchy'. This is surely not false; we must always be prepared that there are exceptions, and they must be individually marked in the lexical entry. But this should always be the last resort. In these cases, however, there seems to be more involved than a lexical idiosyncray. After all, there should be a reason why it is possible to say *die von uns unterstützten Flüchtlinge*, but not *die von uns geholfenen Flüchtlinge*. The lexical content must contain some feature which predicts that this fact is on a par with the peculiar case marking; precisely this is done by the 'argument-time'-analysis suggested above: In the case of *unterstütz-*, one of the two arguments is specified for two times; therefore, this argument is marked as accusative, and its past participle can directly combine with an argument, such as in attributive use. By contrast, *help-* has no argument specified for two times; hence, of them is marked for dative, and the past participle cannot directly combine with an argument.

9 Conclusion

> Was soll der Scheiss?
> Unknown linguist, repeatedly

I surely do not believe that the analysis sketched in the preceding sections is the final answers to the problem of why there is case marking. There is hardly an area in linguistics in which this is so manifest as inflectional morphology with which linguists have now been struggling for more than two thousand years. Here as elsewhere, being the inheritor of a long tradition is both beneficial and burdensome. But I firmly believe that looking with an open eye to the way in which second language learners try to make sense of the sounds that hit their ears may help us to get a fresh understanding of the principles that rule all manifestations of the human language faculty.

References

Dowty, David (1991). Thematic proto-roles and argument selection. Language 67. 547–619.
Giacalone Ramat, Anna (1997). Progressive periphrases, markedness, and second language data. In S. Eliasson & E.H. Jahr (eds.) Language and its Ecology. Essays in Memory of Einar Haugen. Berlin: Mouton de Gruyter. 261–285.
Gould, Stephen Jay (1989). Wonderful Life. The Burgess shale and the nature of history. New York: Norton.
Helbig, Gerhard (1973). Die Funktionen der substantivischen Kasus in der deutschen Gegenwartssprache. Halle: Niemeyer.
Jellinek, Max Hermann (1913). Geschichte der neuhochdeutschen Grammatik. Erster Halbband. Heidelberg: Carl Winters Universitätsbuchhandlung.
Klein, Wolfgang (1998). Assertion and Finiteness. In Norbert Dittmar and Zvi Penner (eds.). Issues in the Theory of Language Acquisition. Frankfurt/M.: Lang. 225–245.
Klein, Wolfgang (2000). An analysis of the German Perfekt. Language 76/2. 358–382.
Klein, Wolfgang (2000). The argument-time structure of recipient constructions in German. To appear in Werner Abraham & Jan-Wouter Zwart (eds.). Typological Studies on West Germanic. Amsterdam: Benjamins.
Klein, Wolfgang; and Perdue, Clive (1989). The learner's problem of arranging words. In B. MacWhinney & E. Bates (eds.). The crosslinguistic study of sentence processing. Cambridge: Cambridge University Press. 292–327.
Klein, Wolfgang; and Perdue, Clive (1997). The basic variety, or Couldn't natural languages be much simpler. Second Language Research 13. 301–347.
Perdue, Clive (ed.) (1993). Adult language acquisition: Cross-linguistic perspectives. Cambridge: Cambridge University Press.
Reis, Marga (1982). Zum Subjektbegriff im Deutschen. In Werner Abraham (ed.). Satzglieder im Deutschen. Tübingen: Niemeyer. 171–211.
Starren, Marianne; and van Hout, Roeland (1996). The expression of temporality in a second language. Zeitschrift für Literaturwissenschaft und Linguistik 104. 35–50.
Wunderlich, Dieter (1996). Dem Freund die Hand auf die Schulter legen. In Gisela Harras and Manfred Bierwisch (eds.). Wenn die Semantik arbeitet. Klaus Baumgärtner zum 65. Geburtstag. Tübingen: Niemeyer. 331–360.
Wunderlich, Dieter (1997). CAUSE and the structure of verbs. Linguistic Inquiry 28. 27–68.
Wunderlich, Dieter (2000). The force of lexical case: German and Icelandic compared. [to appear in a Festschrift]
Wunderlich, Dieter (2001). Why is there morphology? Paper presented at the 23rd Annual Meeting of the Deutsche Gesellschaft für Sprachwissenschaft, Leipzig, March 2001. [References relate to the handout].

The grammar of varieties

1 Linguistic variability and its analysis

Natural languages such as Greek, Russian or Tagalog are not very well-defined entities; they include numerous varieties – dialects, registers, sociolects, historical variants –, which share a number or regularities while differing in others. A speaker's linguistic knowledge reflects this heterogeneity in varying degrees. In childhood, he (or she) normally learns to replicate one such variety, the speech habits of his social environment, 'up to perfection', i.e., such that other members of this social group accept the speaker as a 'native', as one of theirs. In the course of life, he is regularly faced with many other varieties of 'his' language and gathers knowledge about these. This knowledge may be less perfect, it may also be asymmetric with respect to comprehension and production (many speakers understand other dialects perfectly well but cannot reproduce them perfectly well); but it may also be felt to be more perfect than his original knowledge, for example if dialectal pronunciation and grammar are improved in school. This variability of languages and in linguistic knowledge faces the linguist who takes reality seriously with three descriptive tasks:

A. The characteristic properties of the individual varieties must be described. These properties include phonological, morphological, syntactical regularities, the specific lexical repertoire, but also pecularities in communicative behaviour (for example the choice of appropriate address forms or the rules of turn taking).
B. The relationship between the individual varieties must be accounted for. This task is difficult for at least three reasons. First, the descriptive tools of modern linguistics are usually designed for homogeneous, idealised forms of language; hence, additional devices must be created to adapt these tools to the comparison of various varieties. Second, the range of properties in which varieties may agree or differ precludes the application of a uniform method; phonological variation can normally not be described with the same instruments as differences in forms of address. Third, the differences between two varieties are often not categorial but gradual, i.e., varieties do not differ in the presence or absence of a particular rule but in its weight, as reflected, for example, in the more or less of its application.
C. It must be described how linguistic variation correlates with extralinguistic factors. These include, for example, social class, geographical distribution, the specific communicative situation, the medium (written or spoken), or

Note: This article originally appeared as Klein, W. (2005). The grammar of varieties. In U. Ammon, N. Dittmar, K. J. Mattheier and P. Trudgill (eds.). Sociolinguistics: An international handbook of the Science of Language and Society. Berlin: Walter de Gruyter. 1163–1171.

https://doi.org/10.1515/9783110549119-019

development over time, be it of an individual ('language acquisitition') or a speech community ('historical change').

One way to deal with these tasks is *variety grammar*. It is easy to apply, and if appropriate empirical evidence is available, it allows a precise modelling of virtually all types of grammatical variation. It is less appropriate for lexical variation and not apt for pragmatic aspects of variability. In what follows, we will only be concerned with syntax; but it should be clear that this analysis can easily be extended to other parts of grammar, for which precise rules are available. Modern linguistics has provided the researcher with several types of grammars which allow a precise description of syntactical rules. They include, for example, phrase structure grammar (context-free or context-sensitive), transformational grammar, dependency grammar, categorial grammar. Irrespective of their respective advantages and disadvantages, about which opinions are strongly at variance and which will not to be discussed here, they have two features in common. First, they are explicit and precise; this is in remarkable contrast to most of traditional school grammar, which still dominates empirical research on languages. Second, they were developed for homogeneous languages, hence they are not fit for the tasks A-C mentioned above. Variety grammars try to overcome this inadequacy while keeping the explicitness and precision of a formal grammar. The core idea is to take such a formal grammar, say a phrase structure grammar or transformational grammar, as a constant, stable base of comparison and to restrict it in such a way that the specific properties of individual varieties are precisely captured; this is done by assigning probabilistic values to the rules of the underlying common grammar. Thus, the rules of all varieties are the same; what differs from variety to variety is the 'weight' of these rules; this weight is described by the probability with which a rule is applied in a particular variety, including the borderline cases that the probability is 1 (i.e., the rule is obligatory) and 0 (i.e., the rule does not show up at all). This procedure is sufficiently flexible to account for categorial distinctions between varieties as well as for very fine-grained differences. In section 2, this idea will be explained in more detail; sections 3–4 are devoted to various types of probabilistic weighing. These parts are fairly theoretical; but variety grammar is in first place a versatile instrument for empirical analysis; in the concluding section 5, we will therefore briefly discuss some aspects of its practical application.

2 Variety space, overall grammar and probabilistic weighing

A VARIETY SPACE is an ordered set of varieties under investigation. Suppose someone wants to study the syntactical properties of

- love letters as compared to business letters (factor 'register' with values r_1 for love letters and r_2 for business letters);
- around 1900, 1950 and 2000 (factor 'time' with values t_1, t_2 and t_3);
- in Boston and in Oxford (factor 'space' with values s_1 and s_2).

This yields a three-dimensional variety space with 2 x 3 x 2 = 12 varieties; for instance, (r_1, t_2, s_1) is the variety of love letters of Bostonians around 1950. This may not be a particularly interesting variety space; but this is a matter of the researcher's individual preferences, on the one hand, and of what looks scientifically meaningful and rewarding, on the other.

An OVERALL GRAMMAR is a formal grammar of whichever type, which covers all syntactic rules that show up in at least one of the varieties in the variety space. Thus, it does not yet discriminate between varieties and is therefore not very meaningful in itself; it says what is possible in the variety space but not what is the case in individual varieties. To this end, its rules must be appropriately restricted; this is done by probabilistic weighing. The idea is best explained with (context-free) phrase structure grammars. In such a grammar, certain rules can be applied alternatively, namely those rules which rewrite the same symbol. Thus, a context-free grammar may contain, for example, the following rules for noun phrases:

(1) 1. NP → N
     2. NP → DET   N
     3. NP → DET   ADJ   N

i.e., an NP can be expanded as a bare noun (*books*), as a noun preceded by a determiner (*the books, some books*) or as a noun preceded by an adjective and a determiner (*the old books*). One of those rules must be applied in a derivation. All alternative rules form a sort of rule block, often indicated by brackets:

(2)

$$NP \rightarrow \begin{Bmatrix} N \\ DET\ N \\ DET\ ADJ\ N \end{Bmatrix}$$

Note that (2) is not a rule but a conventional abbreviation for three rules. Rule blocks may contain an arbitrary but finite number of rules; it is useful to include rule blocks with just one rule (which, since there is no alternative, is then obligatory).

Whenever the lefthand symbol, here NP, shows up in the course of a derivation, then one of the rules of the rule block must be applied. But the individual rules may vary in their likelihood: there are rules which are are very likely in a particular variety, whereas others are rare, and this may vary from one variety to the other. This fact can be covered by assigning probabilities to the rules of a block. The probability of some event, here the application of a rule, is normally expressed by a real number between 0 and 1, where 0 stands for 'happen never'and 1 stands for 'happens in all possible cases'; values in between refer to intermediate stages between these extremes. The rules within a block can thus have different probabilities; but they inevitably must add up to 1. In other words, the entire block has the probability 1 ('obligatory'), which can be distributed in various ways over its rules, including the borderline case that it contains only one rule (which then gets the probability 1). Consider, for instance, the NP-example in (1). In some variety A, rule NP → N may have the probability 0.2, rule NP → DET N may have the probability 0.3, and rule NP → DET ADJ NP may have the probability 0.5, whereas in variety B, the values may be 0.7, 0.1 and 0.2, respectively. In other words, noun phrases are of the same type in A and B, but in B, simple NPs are preferred: more than two third NPs are just bare nouns. In some variety C, the values might be 0.8, 0.2 and 0.0, respectively; that means that in this variety, NPs tend to be even simpler, and the most complex possible pattern DET ADJ N does not exist at all – it has probability zero.

We can use this technique to model the NP acquisition of a second language learner who passes through a series of 'learning stages' say the six stages V_1–V_6. They constitute a very simple, one-dimensional variety space. The overall grammar is a fragment of a context-free grammar which includes all NP rules observed in these six varieties. Let us assume that it contains the three rules mentioned above and two more rules:

(1')   ...
   4. NP → DET N ADJ
   5. NP → DET N ADV

Rule 4 generates NPs such as *the books old*, which is not possible in Standard English but might well appear in the language of a learner; rule 5 generates structures such as *the books there*. A variety grammar – or more precisely, a fragment of a variety grammar – could then look as follows:

(3)	V_1	V_2	V_3	V_4	V_5	V_6
NP → N	0.9	0.6	0.3	0.2	0.2	0.2
NP → DET N	0.1	0.3	0.3	0.3	0.3	0.3
NP → DET ADJ N	0	0	0	0	0.4	0.4
NP → DET N ADJ	0	0.1	0.3	0.4	0	0
NP → DET N ADV	0	0	0.1	0.1	0.1	0.1
Whole rule block	1	1	1	1	1	1

This is a precise account of a whole bundle of developmental processes. In the first learning stage, V_1, bare nouns are predominant, with a small share of NPs such as *the book*; more complex NPs are still absent. In V_2, we note the first NPs with an adjective; but this adjective is placed after the noun; moreover, determiners become more frequent. This development continues in V_3: bare nouns are increasingly rare, adjectives are found more often (though still in 'wrong' position), and we note the first occurrences of a new pattern. There is hardly any change from V_3 to V_4. From V_4 to V_5, there is only one development – but a very salient one: the learner all of a sudden got the 'right' position of adjectives within an NP. There is no change from V_5 to V_6, i.e., the learner may have reached the endpoint of this acquisitional process. Note that this final variety may still be very different from the 'target variety', i.e., the language to be learned. The example is very simple: there is only one dimension of variation with a limited number of varieties, and only a few NP structures are considered; but it should be clear that variety space as well as overall grammar can easily be made much richer. It should also be clear that continuous as well as abrupt changes (e.g., complete dropping of a rule) can be modelled with a degree of precision that is only restricted by the available data.

2 Probabilistic weighing I: phrase structure grammars

2.1 Probabilities

In what follows, we shall informally sketch some basic ideas of probability theory (for a thorough introduction, see e.g., Milton and Arnold 1990). Probabilities, as the term is used here, are numbers associated with the possible outcomes of repeatable incidents. Such an incident is, for instance, the toss of a die: it has six possible outcomes, which are mutually exclusive and one of which MUST happen: 'one' or 'two' or 'three' or 'four' or 'five' or 'six'. Usually, one is not only interested in the likelihood of these 'elementary events' but also in combinations, such as the likelihood of having 'one or two' or 'not five', and so on. The set of elementary events is called SAMPLE SPACE O; in the case of tossing a die, $O = \{o_1, o_2, o_3, o_4, o_5, o_6\}$, where o_1 is the event that the die falls on 1, and so on. The set of all elementary and complex events is called *event space* F. F is usually considered to be the power set of O; thus, the subset $\{o_1, o_3, o_5\}$ is the event that the die falls on an odd number.

The probability of an event is expressed by a real number p between 0 and 1, where 1 is 'the certain event'. The event $\{o_1, o_2, o_3, o_4, o_5, o_6\}$, that is, the sample space itself, includes all possible outcomes; hence, the sample space gets the probability 1. This entire probability of 1 may distributed in different ways over the elementary events. If the die is not somehow loaded, there is no reason to assume that one outcome should be preferred over another; hence, a priori considerations lead to the assumption that each elementary event has the probability of 1/6. How do we get from there to the likelihood of a complex event such as $\{o_1, o_3, o_5\}$, i.e., the chance that the die falls on an odd number? It is apparently the same probability as getting an even number, i.e. 1/2, and this value is reached by adding the probability of the elementary events: $p(o_1) + p(o_3) + p(o_5) = 1/2$. The probability of getting a five is 1/6, the probability of getting *no* five, i.e. of the event $\{o_1, o_2, o_3, o_4, o_5, o_6\}$ is $1 - 1/6 = 5/6$.

Suppose now the die is loaded, such that some outcomes are more likely than others. Then, a priori considerations are no longer helpful. But by tossing the die many times, we can empirically determine how often the six possible elementary events occur. If, for example, o_5 occurs n times in m trials, then n/m is called the relative frequency f of o_5, in brief $f(o_5)$. This value stabilises with the number of trials, and we can INTERPRET it as the probability p of o_5. Under this statistical interpretation, the probability of an event is the limit of its relative frequency, which is empirically determined in some finite experiment. Suppose, for instance, that many tosses of a loaded die have lead to the following relative frequencies:

(4)	Event	o_1	o_2	o_3	o_4	o_5	o_6	O
	relative frequency	1/18	1/9	1/9	1/9	1/9	1/2	$\Sigma = 1$

Note that these values, as resulting from empirical observation, are not probabilities but relative frequencies: they are interpreted as probabilities. This statistical interpretation of probability underlies virtually all empirical investigations, including those of variety grammar. It is not without mathematical problems, but we shall not enter this discussion here (see, e.g., Stegmüller 1973).

In variety grammar, the events are not tosses of a die but applications of rules. In order to assign them probabilities, two questions must be answered: (1) What is the sample space? (2) How can we empirically determine the probabilities of a given sample space? The second question will be addressed in section 6. The answer to the first question depends on the type of grammar; we begin with context-free grammars.

2.2 Suppes-type weighing

Context-free phrase structure grammars are an attempt to formalize the traditional notion of constituent structure grammar. They consider a language to be a (normally infinite) set of sentences, and they describe these sentences as well as their structures by 'generating' them, i.e., by deriving them systematically from a start symbol, usually called S. S is replaced by some string of symbols, these symbols in turn are replaced by other strings of symbols, until this process cannot be further continued. Replacement possibilities are explicitly defined by a set of rules. These rules must be formulated such that the symbol strings which are eventually derivable from the start symbol correspond precisely to the possible sentences of the language to be described. A more precise definition is as follows:

---

(5) A context-free grammar G is a quadruple <V_T, V_N, S, R>, where

- V_T is a finite set of symbols, the *terminal vocabulary* (roughly speaking, the 'words' of the language);
- V_N is a finite set of symbols, the *nonterminal vocabulary* (roughly speaking, the 'syntactic categories');
- S is a distinguished element from V_N, the 'start symbol' or 'axiom';
- R is a finite set of sequences of the form A → x, where A ∈ V_N, x ∈ ($V_T \cup V_N$)+, where ($V_T \cup V_N$)+ = ($V_T \cup V_N$)* − {0} (R includes the 'replacement rules'; A is some syntactic category and x an a non-empty string of symbols of whatever sort).

This is best illustrated by a simple example of a context-free grammar which produces correct sentences of English – not all sentences, of course, but infinitely many:

(6) V_T = {the, some, lions, pigs, mice, love, see, dance, dangerous, tiny, there, here, and, or}

   V_N = {S, NP, VP, CON, DET, N, ADJ, VI, VT, ADV}

   R = {r_1, ..., r_{22}}, where

r_1:	S	→	S CON S
r_2:	S	→	NP VP
r_3:	S	→	NP VP ADV
r_4:	VP	→	VT NP
r_5:	VP	→	VI
r_6:	NP	→	DET N
r_7:	NP	→	DET ADJ N
r_8:	NP	→	DET N ADV
r_9:	DET	→	the
r_{10}:	DET	→	some
r_{11}:	CON	→	and

r_{12}:	CON	→	or
r_{13}:	N	→	lions
r_{14}:	N	→	pigs
r_{15}:	N	→	mice
r_{16}:	VT	→	love
r_{17}:	VT	→	see
r_{18}:	VI	→	dance
r_{19}:	ADJ	→	dangerous
r_{20}:	ADJ	→	tiny
r_{21}:	ADV	→	here
r_{22}:	ADV	→	there

These rules allow, for example, the following derivation:

(7) S   (start symbol)
　　　NP VP ADV   (by rule r_3)
　　　NP VT NP ADV   (by rule r_4)
　　　DET N VT NP ADV   (by rule r_6)
　　　DET N VT DET ADJ N ADV   (by rule r_7)
　　　some mice VT DET ADJ N ADV   (by rule r_{15})
　　　some mice love DET ADJ N ADV   (by rule r_{16})
　　　some mice love the DET ADJ N ADV   (by rule r_9)
　　　some mice love the dangerous N ADV   (by rule r_{19})
　　　some mice love the dangerous lions ADV   (by rule r_{13})
　　　some mice love the dangerous lions there   (by rule r_{22})

After the application of r_{22}, no further rule is applicable, and the derivation is terminated. In many but not in all cases, another rule could have been applied, resulting in somewhat a different structure. It is these alternatives which are probabilistically weighed. Our sample grammar can be broken down into ten rule blocks with alternative rules, one for each of the ten non-terminal symbols. Each of these blocks is considered to be a sample space, hence it gets the entire probability 1. Empirical investigation of corpora which are representative for some variety must show how this probability is distributed over the individual rules which constitute the entire block. This simple way of probabilistic weighing was independently developed by several mathematicians. It was Patrick Suppes who first applied it to the study of natural language. Therefore, it is called here 'Suppes type weighing'. We give a precise definition:

(8) A probabilistic grammar GS of type Suppes is a quintupel $<V_T, V_N, S, R, p>$, where

$<V_T, V_N, S, R>$ is a context-free grammar, and p is a function on R into the real number such that
- (a) for all $r \in R$, $p(r) \geq 0$
- (b) for all $A_i \in V_N$: if there are m many sequences $x_j \in (V_T \cup V_N)+$ such that $A_i \text{ à } x_j \in R$, then

$$\sum_{j=1}^{m} p(A_i \to x_j) = 1.$$

Thus, the function p assigns a value equal or larger than 0 to each rule (condition (a)); condition (b) guarantees that the probabilities of all rules within a block (i.e., those which expand the same symbol) adds up to 1; m is the number of rules within a block. A VARIETY GRAMMAR, type Suppes, is a set of Suppes type grammars with the same underlying context-free grammar (the 'overall grammar') and varying probabilistic weighings, one for each variety.

In a Suppes type grammar, the probabilistic value of a rule does not 'look beyond its block', i.e., it is the same, independent on what happens in other blocks. This makes probabilistic weighing simple, but may be empirically inadequate. According to our sample grammar (6), an NP can be introduced in 'subject position', i.e., by rule r_2, or in 'object position', i.e., by rule r_4. It may now be that the further expansion of such an NP by rules $r_6 - r_8$ is sensitive to this distinction, because, for instance, NPs in subject position might on the average be much simpler than NPs in object position. There are some ad hoc measures to solve this problem within this type of probabilistic weighing, for example by assuming different rules for 'object NPs' and 'subject NPs'. But this is not very intuitive, it leads to an inflation of syntactical categories, and it does not work for recursive rules, such as r_1. A better way are probabilistic weighings which take into account potential dependencies between rule applications. This will be shown in section 3.3. First, however, we will briefly discuss two potential misunderstandings.

The probabilistic weighings considered here relate to *rules*, not to *sentences* (or to the full derivations which generate these sentences). The probability of a sentence is always close to zero and hence completely uninteresting. A somewhat more realistic grammar than (5) may contain, for example, 200 rules in 50 blocks. Then, the average probability of a rule within block is 0.25. Suppose now that 40 rules altogether are applied in a derivation (not every block must be represented since its 'lefthand symbol' may never be introduced and hence need not be expanded). Then, the probability of the resulting sentence is 1 divided by 0.25^{40}, a ridiculously small number, in contrast to the probabilistic weight of each rule, which is substantial. The second misunderstanding is somewhat hilarious but still occasionally found in the literature. It is the argument that the speaker has no 'counter' in his or her head that could tell him how often to apply a rule. This is a curious misunderstanding of the notion of probability; a die does not count, either, how often it has fallen, or has to fall, on 5. The circumstance that certain rules are applied by certain speakers with a certain probability is simply a descriptive fact, just as the fact that the probability to marry someone from the same town is, say, 0.31, or the probability to die before age 90 is, say, 0.84; here, too, no one calculates whether he or she is within the marriage quota or whether the time has come to kick the bucket.

2.3 Derivation weighing grammars

If the probability with which a rule is applied depends on whether some other rule has been applied before, then there must be a device to keep track of what is applied when in a derivation. This can be done by a CONTROL WORD. Each rule in the grammar is supposed to have a label, say $r_1,..., r_{22}$ in our sample grammar. A control word is a string of such labels, in the order in which the rules are applied. There are two small complications. The first line in the derivation is not brought about by a rule; for the sake of generality, it is useful to assume an 'empty rule', called r_0, which is responsible for the first line and hence is the first symbol in the control word. Moreover, it must be determined in which order the symbols in a given string are replaced, because otherwise, several control words could lead to the same result. A simple way to achieve this is to adopt the principle 'from left to right', as we have tacitly done in derivation (6). The control word of (6) is then: $r_0r_3r_4r_6r_7r_{15}r_{16}r_9r_{19}r_{13}r_{23}$. The set of all control words of a given grammar is called its control language, and probabilistic restrictions (and, incidentally, other restrictions, as well) can now be defined for this control language, rather than for individual rules. Such an approach provides the linguist with a very mighty instrument which makes it possible to account for all sorts of dependencies between rules. For most practical purposes, however, it rapidly gets to complicated; therefore, we do not go into details here (see Klein and Dittmar 1979, 48–56). A reasonable compromise is to look only at effects 'neighbouring rule effects', for example at the influence of a rule in the immediately preceding step in a derivation. This is done by considering all 'digrams', i.e., all strings such as r_1r_1, r_1r_2, r_1r_3 etc, that can occur in the control language. Many such digrams are automatically excluded; in our sample grammar, r_1r_1 and r_1r_3 are possible, whereas r_2r_2 is not. Impossible digrams get the value zero; the probabilities of possible digrams must be empirically determined by corpus analysis. Whether such an approach is useful for the study of variability or not, is an empirical issue.

2.4 Context-sensitive grammars

In context-free grammars, a symbol A in some string can replaced by x, if there is a rule A → x; it does not matter what precedes or follows this symbol A. This is different for context-sensitive grammars, whose rules have the general form u A v → u x v, where, as before, A is a symbol from the nonterminal vocabulary and x is a nonempty string of symbols; u and v are strings of symbols, too; but they can be empty (alternatively, the notation A → x/u_v is used for 'A is replaced by x in context u_v'). It is easy to see that context-free grammars are simply a special case of context-sensitive grammars, namely those in which u and v are always empty. Context-sensitive grammars can be probabilistically weighted in much the same ways as described in section 3, the only difference being that not all rules which expand the same symbol form the sample space but all rules which expand the same symbol in the same context. Otherwise, everything remains the same; in particular, they can also be used as an overall grammar in a variety grammar. An advantage of context-sensitive rules is the fact that with them, even Suppes type weighings can account for some kinds of rule dependencies. Consider, for example, the potential asymmetry between subject-NP and object-NP discussed in section 3.2. Since subject-NPs only appear in context__VP, whereas object-NPs only appear in context VT__, it is easily possible to assign different probabilities to their expansion in these positions. This cannot be generalized, however; recursive rules such as r_1, for example, cannot be treated in this way, although their application probability normally diminishes with each application in some derivation.

3 Probabilistic weighing II: transformational grammars

Phrase structure grammars generate structures – trees whose end nodes, the 'leaves' of the tree, correspond to a sentence of the language to be described. Transformational rules turn such a tree into another tree. We shall here not review here the linguistic merits of these rules but only discuss how they can be integrated into a variety grammar.

A transformational rule has two components. The first of these, the 'structural description' (SD) specifies to which trees the rule applies; the second component, the 'structural change' (SC) specifies how a tree which matches the SD is modified. We may think of the SD as a sort of cut through the nodes of a tree. The sample grammar (5) can generate, for instance, the tree shown in (9). This tree matches the SD_1: NP – VT – DET – N, as indicated by the broken line, but it does not match the SD_2: NP – VT – DET – ADJ – N:

(9)

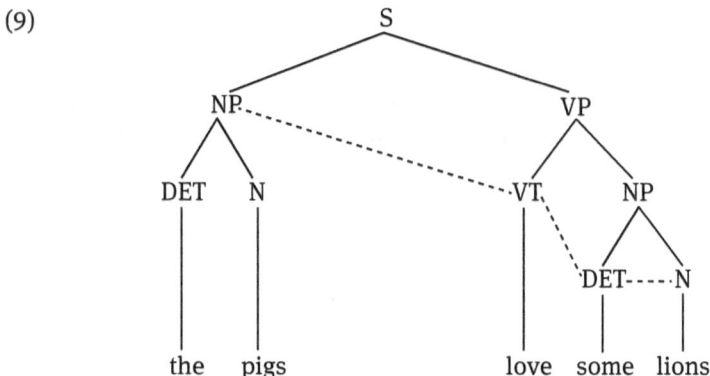

A SD may be more complex; for example, it may indicate that a 'subtree' is identical to another 'subtree', or it may state that the tree must contain a specific nonterminal element; these refinements are not relevant to our present concern, however; all that matters is that the SB precisely indicates what the transformation applies to.

The SC indicates what happens with the various subtrees thus cut off. In (9), these are the subtrees dominated by the first NP, by VT, by the second DET and by the second N. They may be moved to a different position, replaced by another subtree or even omitted. A full transformational rule could then look as follows:

(10) SD: NP – VT – DET – N
      SC: 1 2 3 4 → 2 1 0 4

This means: the first subtree is moved into the position of the second subtree, the second subtree is moved into the position of the first subtree, the third subtree is omitted (i.e., replaced by the empty subtree 0), and the fourth subtree is left as is. When applied to (9), the result is as follows:

(11)

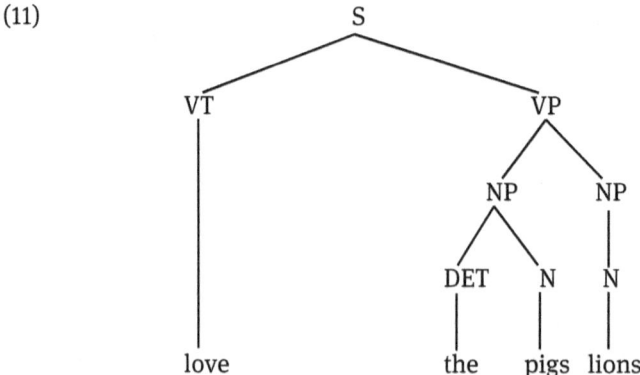

Clearly, rule (10) is not a top candidate for a meaningful transformation; in reality, all of these rules must be linguistically well-motivated; but here, we are only interested in the principle. A precise formalisation of transformational rules is extremely difficult, and we will skip it here. It is usually assumed, that transformational rules can be optional or obligatory; in the latter case, it must be applied whenever a given tree fits the SD.

The probabilistic weighing of transformational rules is straightforward; we only sketch the basic ideas (for details, see Klein and Dittmar 1979: 57–63). Much in parallel to the 'rule blocks' of a phrase structure grammar, all rules with the same SD are taken together as a 'T-block'. Each such T-block is considered as a sample space. The entire probability of 1 associated with such a T-block is then distributed over the various possible SC, which a tree falling under the SD may undergo. This leads into a problem when there is only one SC for a given SD. Then, this SC automatically gets the probability value 1. This means that the rule is obligatory, although this may not desirable for linguistic reasons. This problem can be avoided if each T-block also includes, as one possible SC, an 'identical transformation'. i.e., a transformation which does not change anything. The alternative is then 'change' or 'don't change', and this alternative can then be probabilistically weighed as any other alternative.

4 Variety grammars in empirical research

Probabilistic weighing of grammars has not been invented by linguists but by mathematicians who were interested in certain formal properties of these grammars (Habel 1979 gives an excellent account of this background). Their first and still very elementary application to problems of linguistic variability is due to Suppes (1972). The notion of 'variety grammar' with various types of weighing was elaborated in Klein (1974) and subsequently applied in a number of comprehensive empirical investigations, such as Klein and Dittmar 1979, Senft 1982, Tropf 1983 or Carroll 1984). There are no comparable studies of variability afterwards. But more recently, probabilistic grammars started to play an important role in other fields of linguistics, in particular in automatic parsing (see, e.g., Manning and Schütze 1999).

Variety grammars are a very precise and flexible instrument which allow the modelling of virtually any kind of grammatical variability. Their application in empirical research faces the linguist with a number of tasks that have to be solved in a certain order:
1. *Choice of variety space.* It must be decided which kind of extralinguistically defined variation is to be covered. This decision is not arbitrary; it depends on a number of heuristic considerations on what the relevant factors of variation are.

2. *Selection of linguistic structures.* The linguistic variables to be investigated must be selected. Normally, it is not meaningful to consider full grammars; this would be by far too complex. Instead, specific structural phenomena in which the relevant varieties differ must be selected – phonological change, variation in inflectional morphology, differences in word order, in the structure of noun phrases, whatever. Again, the precise way in which these 'dependent variables' are defined is based on heuristic considerations, on the one hand, and the specific interests of the researcher, on the other.
3. *Data collection.* The next crucial step is to find or to collect appropriate corpora which are representative for the varieties and the linguistic variables under investigation.
4. *Corpus analysis.* The relative frequency of the relevant linguistic structures in these corpora must be determined.
5. *Definition of overall grammar.* The fragment of a grammar which covers all rules represented in the various corpora must be worked out. This concerns the choice of an appropriate type of grammar, the formulation of the rules and they way in which they are combined into rule blocks.
6. *Probabilistic weighing.* This weighing depends on the type of grammar, the type of weighing and, of course, the relative frequencies found in corpora.

Just as with any other way to account for linguistic variability, these tasks raise a number of empirical as well as theoretical problems, which we will not discuss here. There are three main advantages of this particular approach:
(a) It can be used for practically any grammatical phenomenon, and it is not restricted to a particular type of grammar – provided is can be precisely defined.
(b) It allows a precise modelling of arbitrary many extralinguistic factors of variation, such as development of linguistic knowledge in the individual, in a speech community, dialectal differences, in register, communicative intention and so on – again provided these factors can be given a precise definition.
(c) It can model continuous as well as categorial differences between varieties.

In all three respects, its application is only delimited by the data available. On the other hand, it should be clear that variety grammar is not a theory of variation or even of the human language faculty. It is a clear and precise descriptive instrument, no more, no less.

References

Carroll, Mary (1984). Cyclic learning processes in second language production. Frankfurt, M.: Lang.
Habel, Christopher (1979). Aspekte bewertender Grammatiken. Berlin: Einhorn Verlag.
Klein, Wolfgang (1974). Variation in der Sprache. Kronberg, Ts.: Scriptor.
Klein, Wolfgang, and Dittmar, Norbert (1979). Developing grammars. Berlin, Heidelberg, NewYork: Springer.
Manning, Christopher, and Schütze, Hinrich (1999). Statistical Natural Language Processing. Cambridge, Mass: MIT Press.
Milton, J.S., and Arnold, Jesse (1990). Introduction to Probability and Statistics. New York: McGraw Hill.
Senft, Gunter (1984). Sprachliche Varietät und Variation im Sprachverhalten Kaiserslauterer Metallarbeiter. Bern, Frankfurt, M.: Lang.
Stegmüller, Wolfgang (1973). Statistische und personelle Wahrscheinlichkeit. Berlin, Heidelberg, New York: Springer.
Suppes, Patrick (1972). Probabilistic grammars for natural language. In: Donald Davidson and Gilbert Harman (eds.). Semantics of natural language. Dordrecht: Reidel. 741–762.
Tropf, Herbert (1983). Variation in der Phonologie des ungesteuerten Spracherwerbs. Phil. Diss., Heidelberg: Universität Heidelberg.

Index

aboutness 335, 336
Abraham, Werner 81, 284, 285, 316
accessible argument 170, 171
accessible pair 165, 169
addition 9, 36, 49, 51, 52, 55, 71, 78, 114, 118, 119, 123, 125, 164, 187, 191, 246, 247, 266, 288, 289, 294, 297, 298, 305, 306, 307, 310, 312, 313, 318, 319, 332, 340, 348, 350, 361, 362, 477, 485, 486
Adelung, Johann Christoph 460, 462
adverbials 5, 16, 22, 24, 25, 29, 35, 43, 49, 51, 63, 69, 70, 74, 79, 87, 88, 110, 127, 132, 137, 142, 151, 155, 216, 233, 234–236, 251, 263, 301, 314, 343, 370–371, 376, 396, 413, 419, 421, 423, 424, 462, 476, 481
Aktionsart 16, 36, 37, 55, 76, 114, 148, 155, 160, 179, 184, 423, 483
ALIUD 302–304, 306, 307, 309–313, 315, 317–321
alternative semantics 297, 336, 339–340, 345
anaphoric 29, 31–32, 124, 197, 200, 222, 248, 250, 259, 356, 413, 421, 427, 429
anaphoric relatum 31–32
apple tree 398
argument 9, 12, 35, 46, 74, 79, 80–84, 89–100, 125, 139, 148–180, 186, 187, 192, 197, 219, 224–226, 231, 251, 264, 265, 269, 271, 285, 298, 316, 327, 338, 342–344, 349, 351, 357, 361, 372, 390, 392, 396, 401, 403, 408, 414–419, 421, 423, 429, 431, 450, 453, 456, 461, 467, 469, 470, 499
argument structure 80, 158, 179, 390, 392, 401, 470, 483
argument-time 81, 90, 97, 100, 148, 153, 155, 163, 165, 179, 251, 489
argument-time structure 80–82, 90, 148, 153, 155, 163–165, 179, 477–487
Aristotle 1, 2, 3, 7, 12, 19, 22, 123, 149, 184, 185, 187–188, 191, 254, 436
Aristotle's entailment 184, 185, 187–188, 191
aspect 1, 2, 14, 16, 34–66, 73, 76–78, 103–128, 129–146, 148, 160, 179–180, 183, 184, 187, 189, 203, 290, 291, 315, 342, 343, 356–357, 359, 363, 376, 377, 382, 395, 412, 413, 421, 422, 438, 452, 462
assertion 3, 48, 55, 56–66, 76, 77, 86, 87, 89, 99, 100, 103–146, 173, 174, 177, 178, 180, 241, 253, 257–259, 264–269, 273, 278, 280, 285–287, 298, 299, 300, 302–308, 310–314, 318, 319, 335, 339, 344, 351, 376, 379, 391, 392, 394–396, 422, 423, 475
assertion time 55, 57, 60, 62–66, 137, 140, 423
association with focus 275, 319–321
atelic 2, 47, 94, 104, 134, 158, 160, 184, 187, 236, 310, 438
Augustine, St. 5, 7, 9, 12, 20–21, 22

background 9, 60, 71, 76–82, 106, 141, 144–145, 250, 278, 286, 293, 298, 319, 336, 341, 344, 345, 351, 357, 362, 365, 367, 380, 382, 404, 407, 409–412, 419, 423, 472, 483, 503
baker 399–402, 413
basic time structure 6, 23, 24–28, 29, 32
basic variety 403–444, 461, 462, 471, 475–477, 481
Becker, A. 413, 424
BECOME 154, 155, 244–247, 485, 489
Bickerton, D. 405, 440–442
Bierwisch, Manfred 34, 68, 92, 148, 216, 253, 283, 363, 440, 462, 488
binding principles 391
Bondarko, Alexandr V. 39, 43, 44
boundary 37, 38, 43–47, 49, 50, 53, 54, 63, 64, 104, 109–111, 124, 137, 312, 315, 377, 419, 422, 426, 432
Breu, Walter 45
Bühler, K. 194, 196, 373, 374, 377
Bybee, Joan L. 40, 106

calendaric relata 29
Carroll, M. 375, 378, 403, 413, 424, 429, 430, 503
case marking 158, 216, 221, 327, 403, 424, 433, 460, 462, 466–489

CAUSE 152, 154, 244, 245, 483, 489
change 11, 12, 15, 16–19, 26, 30, 39, 52, 55, 78, 92, 96, 99, 126, 127, 134, 142, 155, 158, 160, 163, 166, 168, 169, 179, 188, 191, 197, 198, 211, 224, 225, 236, 237, 245, 246, 285, 289, 292, 293, 346, 360, 374, 375, 378, 380–382, 400, 423, 425, 442, 450, 454, 469, 470, 476, 477, 484–486, 492, 495, 501, 503, 504
Chao, Yuan R. 103–105, 108, 128, 137–140, 454, 467
Chomsky, Noam 256, 399, 434, 435, 437, 438, 440, 453, 458, 488
Chu, Chauncey C. 112, 113, 132, 136
cleft 331–333, 339, 341, 349, 350, 369, 432, 479
clitic 334, 351, 356
closeness fallacy 412
cognitive maps 203, 204, 208
communication faculty 387, 399, 400
completed 2, 38, 42–44, 63, 64, 73, 76, 78, 87, 104, 105, 131, 133, 134, 136, 137, 166, 174, 180, 207, 210, 354, 363, 421, 422
complex verbal tasks 241, 410, 428
Comrie, B. 34, 39, 40, 44, 106, 109, 134, 170, 291–292, 356, 415, 417, 462
conative use 64
constituent negation 269
construction faculty 387, 388, 399, 400
context-dependency 221–223
context-free grammar 493, 494, 496, 497, 499, 501
context-sensitive grammars 501
control asymmetry 415, 417, 477, 481
controller 416, 419, 420, 425, 429–433, 439, 475, 478, 479, 484
control word 500
copying faculty 387, 399, 400
cyclic time 19

Dahl, Östen 44, 110, 148, 253, 264
d-definite 191, 192
de Cat, Cécile 324, 327, 335, 336, 414
Declerck, Renaat 159
deictic 25, 26, 29–31, 58, 76, 120, 149, 194–202, 207–210, 259, 356, 359, 363, 374, 375, 377, 388, 394, 421, 443

deictic relatum 29–31
deictic space 195–197, 199, 200, 201, 208, 210
deixis 194–211, 222, 374, 426
Dietrich, R. 16, 68, 354, 410, 413, 421, 430, 439
discourse representation 360–363, 366, 373
dislocations 330, 332, 333–339, 346, 350
distinguished phase 129, 130, 132, 133, 135, 137, 138, 140, 142
distinguished state 54, 55, 58, 60, 61
Donatus, Aelius 1, 470
Dowty, David 94, 119, 154, 160, 184, 189, 231, 245, 484
duration 4, 8, 9, 10–16, 20, 25–27, 48, 50, 78, 124, 132, 141, 142, 151, 155, 162, 178, 187, 188, 191, 193, 234, 421, 422

egg 11, 95, 169
Ehrich, Veronika 75, 88, 149, 194, 216, 222, 263, 316
Einstein, Albert 9, 10, 21, 48, 49, 50, 69, 85, 86
Elsness, Johan 170
error analysis 407
event 4, 7, 9, 13, 15, 20, 23, 25, 26, 29, 31, 39, 45–47, 56, 57, 69, 75, 76, 78, 79, 81, 88, 90, 98, 101, 103–107, 111–113, 115, 118–120, 124, 133, 135–138, 142–145, 148, 149–154, 157, 158, 161, 162–163, 165–167, 173, 176, 178–180, 185, 187–192, 227, 238, 241, 242, 245, 249, 251, 253, 292, 312, 314, 354, 355, 357, 359, 362, 367, 368, 369, 371, 376, 377, 415, 419, 422, 425, 428, 429, 434, 465, 476, 483, 494–496
event time 46, 56, 75, 76, 81, 88, 105, 118, 119, 148–154, 162–163, 176, 178, 179, 238, 251, 314, 376, 377, 483
expletive 83, 272, 273, 391, 392, 397, 413, 462
external time 150, 161, 162, 164, 171, 173, 174, 176–179

Fabricius-Hansen, Cathrine 68, 74, 158, 176, 231, 232, 233–234, 236, 237, 253, 265, 354
Fery, Caroline 332

finite 4, 53, 56, 61–63, 68, 71–73, 77, 79, 82, 87, 90, 91, 99, 100, 131, 132, 143, 152–154, 162, 165–168, 172–176, 216, 236, 250, 254, 255, 261, 264, 265, 267, 271, 273, 284, 285, 299, 301, 303, 308, 309, 338, 339, 342, 343, 388–390, 393, 395, 396–397, 400, 404, 410, 415, 421, 475, 476, 482, 486, 493, 496, 497
finite component 71, 72, 73, 79, 82, 152, 250, 255, 271, 301, 308, 390, 392, 475
finiteness 3, 62, 72, 132, 165, 166, 172–174, 264–266, 332, 342, 343, 385–402, 476
fin-linkable 72, 73, 79, 83, 91, 95, 96, 99, 154, 166–168, 170–173
focus 1, 255, 262, 275–278, 283, 289–291, 293, 295–299, 302, 313, 319–321, 332–333, 335, 337, 339–341, 344–345, 347, 354, 362, 366–369, 376, 379–381, 398, 405, 408, 414, 418–420, 426, 429–434, 439–440, 443, 462, 469, 474–475, 478–479
focus particles 255, 266, 275, 283, 290, 297, 301, 302, 321, 340, 434
foreground 250, 365, 367, 380, 418, 419, 423, 428
Forsyth, James 36, 37, 39, 55, 60, 64, 65, 114

Gast, Volker 333
granularity 361, 362, 374, 381, 382
Graumann, C. 359, 373

Hajicova, Eva 275
Haviland, J. 425
H-connected 82, 90, 95
head-final 327, 413
Heidegger, Martin 7, 8
Herrmann, T. 358, 373
hidden parameters 186, 189, 191
Horn, Lawrence R. 254, 278–279
Hume, David 82, 152

Iatriou, Sabine 170
I-language 406, 435–440, 443
illocutionary status 143, 392, 475
imperfective 2, 34, 36, 37, 39, 40, 41, 43–46, 54, 56, 60, 61, 77, 103, 105, 106, 107, 109, 110, 114, 116, 117, 120, 123, 130, 135, 140–142, 144, 145, 174, 176, 177, 180, 183–193, 290, 291, 292, 314, 377, 422, 438, 452
imperfective paradox 183–193
implicature 53, 54, 64, 65, 124, 127, 305, 311
inchoative 36, 54, 117, 133, 134, 137, 377
inclusion 24, 58, 426
indefinite noun phrases 392, 393
inflection 1, 83, 325, 326–328, 338, 351, 392, 401, 404, 412, 444, 462, 470, 471, 472, 475–477, 479
inflectional morphology 1, 103, 326, 405, 406, 437, 441, 466, 469–473, 475, 480, 489, 504
information structure 3, 255, 278, 283, 299, 301, 319, 321, 324–352, 382, 392
intake 359–360, 365, 371
intonation 208, 230–231, 238, 240–241, 248, 250, 264–266, 272, 273, 275–278, 285, 295, 299, 302, 308–309, 313, 320–321, 325, 331–333, 334–337, 341, 343, 350, 363, 368–369, 376, 391, 395, 397, 418
irreversibility 11, 18
Isačenko, Alexander V. 35–40, 42, 44, 55

Jacobs, Joachim 254, 272, 275, 278, 297, 301
Jespersen, Otto 268–270

Kamp, Hans 66, 231, 266
Kant, Immanuel 7, 21, 226–228, 385, 449
König, Ekkehard 161, 255, 283, 284, 290, 297
Kratzer, A. 150, 194
Krifka, Manfred 290, 297–299, 318

Labov, W. 202, 316, 317, 423, 429
Lahousse, Karen 348
Lambrecht, Knud 299, 324, 332, 333, 335, 345
Lang, Ewald 275, 278–279
language acquisition 387, 389, 401, 403–410, 433, 434–440, 441, 443, 449–489
language capacity 403, 404–406, 408, 409, 433–444, 450, 459–463, 465, 469, 471, 475
language faculty 385–402, 435, 439, 440, 443, 451–463, 465–473, 490, 504
language production 342, 356, 358, 376

learner variety perspective 456, 463, 473
Leibniz, Gottfried Wilhelm 9
Levelt, W.J.M. 194, 358, 361, 373
Levinson, S. 216, 217, 305, 359, 425
lexical content 44, 47–56, 58, 59, 64, 70, 76, 78–82, 84, 86, 89, 90, 92–96, 98–100, 123–128, 129, 131, 132, 136, 144, 148, 152, 154, 157, 160, 162, 177, 183, 189, 190–193, 216, 245–248, 250, 251, 264, 271, 302, 344, 347, 393, 473, 474, 482, 485, 489
licensing 391, 392
Li, Charles N. 103–106, 108, 110–112, 128, 137, 138, 145
Li, Dingxuan 105, 108, 114, 118, 119–120, 121, 138, 145
linearisation 242, 361, 362, 375, 381
linear time 15, 19
Löbner, Sebastian 285, 290–294, 297–298

main structure 365, 366, 369, 372, 381, 418
Mangione, L. 105, 108, 114, 118–120, 121, 138, 145
McTaggart, John 7, 12
Meertens, Piet 335
MERGE 436, 437
metalinguistic negation 260, 280
metaphorical 11, 40, 42, 63, 77, 87, 109, 130, 137, 145, 180, 195, 220, 356, 360, 363, 379, 382, 422
minimalist program 435–437, 439
monitor theory 40
MOVE F 436–438, 440
Musan, Renate 68, 88, 89, 96, 153, 176, 324, 354

negation 65, 118, 186, 246, 247, 253–280, 285, 298, 301, 343, 413, 419, 434, 485, 486
Newton, Isaac 8, 9, 10, 20, 23, 25
now 12, 21–23, 25, 30
Noyau, C. 413, 421, 439

1-phase 108, 125–133, 135, 137, 140, 145
1-state 40, 48, 50–55, 58–61, 64, 65, 81, 125
1-state contents 50–55, 58, 64, 65, 125
opaque 343, 393, 444
order of events 13, 141, 202, 216, 231, 240–243, 249, 251, 317, 423

order of mention 216, 240–243, 249, 251, 317, 423
origo 25–27, 29–31, 195–201, 208, 211, 363, 374, 377, 378, 427

parameter-setting 406, 453
Partee, Barbara 34, 63, 188, 274
passiv 91, 98, 100
passive 1, 73, 91, 92, 94, 95–97, 148–149, 168, 169–170, 176–178, 354, 357, 362, 431, 432, 452, 487
path 127, 218, 225, 226, 228, 427, 428, 471
Paul, Hermann 12, 149, 331, 333, 418
Payne, John R. 253, 254
p-definite 191, 235
Perdue, C. 34, 385, 398, 403, 404, 409–413, 419, 432, 433, 456, 461, 462, 465, 471, 473, 477, 479
perfect 40, 51, 55, 59, 60, 68, 69, 70, 71, 74, 75, 85–87, 93, 95, 100, 103–105, 112, 122, 123, 126, 130, 131, 137, 138, 142, 148, 149, 163, 168, 170–172, 176, 179, 180, 185, 234, 246, 271, 314, 315, 354, 408, 424, 436, 438–440, 443, 458–460, 465, 467, 468, 476, 487, 491
perfective 2, 34, 36, 39–41, 44–47, 60, 73, 103, 104, 107, 109, 110, 112, 114, 116, 117, 120, 122–124, 130, 131, 133, 134–136, 144, 174, 177, 180, 291, 292, 377, 422, 438
Perfekt 68–101, 148
peripheral properties 397, 464, 465
phrase-initial 327, 330
Piaget, Jean 14
pidgins 405, 413, 440–442
POST 83–89, 98
poststate 80
posttime 59, 80, 83, 84, 86–88, 92, 97, 98, 99, 126, 129, 130, 137, 154, 155, 164, 171, 172, 174, 175, 177, 476, 483
Präteritum 69, 70, 73, 74, 75, 82, 86, 87, 100, 101
presentationals 331, 333, 430
presupposition 82, 266, 290–296, 335
pretime 126, 129, 132, 135, 136, 154, 164, 169–170, 174
Priscianus 389, 470
probabilistic weighing 492–502, 503, 504

probability 492, 494–496, 498, 499–501, 503
progressive 2, 46, 55, 58–61, 65, 68–70, 86, 103, 106, 107, 109, 114, 117, 130, 131, 142, 148, 149, 160, 166, 168, 171–172, 174, 176–178, 179, 184, 187, 189, 315, 452
proximity 25, 26

q-definite 191
quaestio 354–383, 418, 419, 428
question 5–6, 11, 14, 16, 17, 21, 23–24, 34, 43, 57, 62, 64, 66, 71, 75, 83, 115, 117, 121, 125, 129, 141–142, 151, 155, 163–164, 178, 185, 188, 190, 197, 203, 205–206, 208–210, 217, 220, 224, 227, 241–242, 244, 250, 253, 264–265, 267, 285–286, 293, 296, 298–300, 306, 308, 312, 331–332, 335, 339–340, 343–345, 347–348, 350–351, 354, 358, 360–361, 364–369, 371–374, 376, 380, 385–387, 390–392, 395–397, 399, 401, 403–405, 408, 415, 418, 419, 423, 429, 431, 433–434, 439–441, 443, 449–450, 457–458, 463, 469–472, 475–477, 488, 496

realization 46, 112–114, 163, 187, 261
real language 401, 409, 434, 440, 454, 456–460, 462, 463, 467, 472–473
recursion 398
referential movement 243, 244, 250, 366, 371–372, 418
region 26–28, 427
Reichenbach, Hans 11, 46, 74, 75, 120, 149–150, 174
relatum 28–32, 424–427, 429, 430
replacement 348–350, 497
replacive negation 279
resultative verb construction 104, 111, 127, 141
Rossdeutscher, Antje 231
route direction 194, 196, 198, 202–211, 242, 316, 358, 374, 380, 381

Saussure, Ferdinand de 39, 386, 458
scale 19, 246, 293, 295–296, 298, 318–319, 485

scheduled time 178
scope 55–56, 57, 59, 61–62, 85, 87–88, 121, 133, 135–136, 144, 157, 186, 231–236, 243–245, 247, 249–251, 253–256, 258, 260–264, 268–278, 280, 283–284, 287, 289–290, 296, 298, 301–302, 307–312, 322, 393, 419, 434
scope sensitivity 262–264
secondary assertion 264–266, 268, 302–303, 311
secondary imperfectivisation 54, 55
segment 24, 204, 331, 377–378, 474, 479
selection 361, 362, 373, 504
self-referential 259
sentence base 79, 82–85, 87, 91, 307, 396, 397
Shannon, Thomas 72, 170
side structures 365–367, 369, 371, 372, 383, 418, 423
simplex verbs 36, 38, 43, 54, 55, 63, 65
simultaneity 10, 15, 16, 20, 23, 24, 423
situation type aspect 114
Slobin, D.I. 375, 378, 385, 405, 430, 442
Smith, Carlota 44, 104–109, 111, 114–118, 120, 125, 129, 134–140, 142, 144, 145
source place 224–226, 228
source state 51–55, 58–61, 64, 66, 81, 84, 89, 90, 94, 416, 425
space 3, 7, 9, 20, 195–197, 199–201, 208–211, 216, 218, 219–221, 222, 224, 226–228, 328, 333, 366, 370, 371, 415, 419, 421, 424–428, 433, 492–496, 498, 501, 503
spatial relations 216, 220, 222, 223, 226, 227, 388, 413, 424–427
stage level 153, 309, 310
subinterval entailment 184, 188–189, 191
subject 1, 3, 47, 68, 79, 83, 86, 96, 97, 98, 100, 153, 160, 163–166, 168, 172, 174–176, 184, 222, 233–234, 239, 247, 254, 268, 271, 273, 274, 283, 285, 300, 303, 310, 327, 329, 338, 344–348, 350, 359, 362, 373–375, 379–380, 382, 391, 392, 396, 397, 408, 412, 415, 419, 420, 425, 431, 453, 455, 467, 483, 487, 499, 501
subordination 264, 376, 378–382, 387, 398, 432, 434
succession 7, 8, 10, 13, 15, 16, 20, 23, 24, 39

Tai, James 113, 141
target deviation perspective 407, 408, 454–456, 465, 472
target place 128, 136, 224–226, 228
target state 52, 53, 54, 56, 58–61, 64, 65, 66, 81, 84, 89, 90, 93, 94, 95, 225, 228, 248, 416, 425
telic 2, 47, 91, 94, 104, 134, 158, 160, 184, 230, 236, 245–247, 310, 416, 438, 485, 489
tense 1, 2, 4, 6, 16, 22, 25, 29, 31, 35, 37, 40, 46, 56–59, 62, 63, 65, 66, 69, 71, 72, 74, 76–78, 82, 83, 103, 104, 108, 120–122, 124, 130, 132, 137, 138, 143, 148, 149, 161, 174, 178, 179, 183, 184, 216, 256, 264, 267, 273, 300, 303, 308, 326, 338, 363, 370, 373, 394–395, 412, 413, 421, 422, 436, 438, 452, 453, 462, 471, 481
thematic role 89, 411, 483
theme 6, 7, 17–22, 28, 29, 348, 414, 424, 425, 426, 427, 429, 430, 466, 471, 483, 488, 489
theory 1, 3, 5, 7, 9, 10, 14, 16, 100, 111, 114, 117, 118, 194, 271, 301, 359, 399, 406, 414, 434–436, 443, 449, 450, 463, 464, 495, 504
thetic sentences 298
Thieroff, Rolf 71, 75, 176
Thompson, Sandra A. 103–106, 108, 110–112, 128, 137, 138
Timberlake, Alan 34, 44, 46, 64
topic 1, 3, 241, 256–257, 265, 267, 272, 273, 274, 300, 308, 333, 335, 337, 350–351, 362–363, 366–369, 379, 381–382, 392, 396–397, 487
topic consistency 256–259, 261, 265, 269, 280
topic situations 243, 257–258, 260, 265–268, 273, 277, 280, 299–300, 303–304, 306, 311, 314, 317, 345, 347, 351, 396
topic time 57, 77, 82, 100, 120–121, 129–131, 133, 137, 174–180, 238, 239, 244, 251, 256, 273, 300, 303, 304, 306, 308, 314–317, 344, 360, 369, 376–378, 394–397, 422
tradition 2, 3, 6, 16, 25, 35, 36, 73, 148, 217, 219, 290, 325, 338, 352, 367, 374, 437, 453, 470, 487, 489
transformational grammars 492, 501–503
transparent 127, 255, 393, 405, 409, 427, 460, 476
Trévise, A. 328, 409, 433
truth reversal function 254, 256–257, 268–269, 280
2-phase expression 126, 127, 129, 130, 131, 133, 135–137, 142, 144
2-state contents 50–55, 58, 64
2-state verbs 40, 50–55, 56, 59, 60, 81

unergative-unaccusative 163, 487
universal grammar 385–402, 435, 439, 440
update 277, 335, 345, 360, 361

variety grammar 492, 494, 496, 499, 501, 503–504
variety space 492–495, 503
Vendler, Zeno 36, 44, 80, 123, 158, 160, 184, 187, 236, 246, 485
view-point aspect 114
von Stechow, Arnim 68, 81, 119, 176, 194, 230, 231, 234, 245, 253, 263, 265, 297, 301, 354, 418
von Stutterheim, Christiane 68, 227, 243, 250, 336, 354, 363, 366, 371, 375, 378, 379, 405, 418, 423

Weinrich, Harald 74, 87
word-order 327–329
Wunderlich, Dieter 74, 75, 91, 154, 161, 176, 194, 197, 216, 217, 219, 466, 471, 488, 489
Wundt, Wilhelm 216

Zeijlstra, Hedde 261
0-phase 125, 126
0-state 50–54, 125, 192
0-state contents 51, 125
Zustandspassiv 91, 96, 100

www.ingramcontent.com/pod-product-compliance
Lightning Source LLC
Chambersburg PA
CBHW051156300426
44116CB00006B/327